THE RSV HANDY CONCORDANCE

D0066883

ZONDERVAN PUBLISHING HOUSE

OF THE ZONDERVAN CORPORATION
GRAND RAPIDS, MICHIGAN 49506

INTRODUCTION

This concordance is the result of an extensive investigation of ways in which such helps to Bible study can be made truly reflective of Scripture content and fully useful to the average reader. In the preparation of this concordance, the first step was to examine carefully five different short concordances in order to determine the extent of agreement, the proportionate treatment of various books of the Bible, and the manner in which important biblical themes are handled. The short concordances were then compared with two exhaustive concordances in order to evaluate the objectivity and balance of content. This examination indicated that in order to avoid rather mechanical quotas for words and lines, and at the same time to guard against arbitrary selections or the accidental omission of certain important elements of the biblical message, several detailed procedures were necessary as a means of best guaranteeing relevance, balance, and objectivity. First, about three hundred key theological terms, for example, *grace, salvation, redemption, sin, justify, holy, love, faith,* and *hope,* were chosen in order that they might be given proportionately heavier treatment since they represent such significant themes in the biblical message. Second, lists of favorite passages and golden texts (including the last twenty-five years of the International Sunday School Lesson Series) were gleaned for important verses which people would most likely want to find. Third, in the selection of context lines, careful attention was paid to the location of a word within the passage. If the same word occurred more than once, special care was exercised to select that occurrence which was best known and the one with which there would be the most obvious associations. Fourth, since in the treatment of proper names it was obviously impossible to cite all the passages in which certain prominent individuals are mentioned in the Scriptures, short biographical summaries were prepared so as to provide a brief outline of the most important references to the events of these persons' lives. Fifth, in order that the words selected for any one passage might be those which the reader would most likely remember, attention was given to the "picturable quality" of the word in question. For example, in 1 Corinthians 13.1, words such as *speak, noisy,* and *clanging* are not as picturable as words such as *tongues, angels,* and *cymbal,* though of course the abstract word *love* is also listed in this verse, for it is the theme of the entire chapter.

Certain features of this concordance should be carefully noted in order that the reader may use it with the greatest facility and understanding:

1. Various grammatical forms of the same word (for example, the singular and plural of nouns and the various tense forms of the verbs) are included under the same key word, normally listed as such forms would be in a standard dictionary. When related forms of the same word differ radically, separate entries are employed.
2. In some instances, context lines are taken from material which is in a footnote to the text. Whenever this occurs, the letter *n* is placed immediately after the reference in order to indicate that this passage is to be found in the note and not in the text itself.
3. Wherever certain words have been omitted from the context line in order to include other words or phrases which are more meaningful, the omission is indicated by two dots.
4. The key word in any context line is represented by the first letter of the word in an italic font.
5. The punctuation of the context line is given exactly as in the text, including any initial or final marks of punctuation, since these signs often provide useful clues to the significance of the line in question.

The principal and immediate purpose of this concordance is not to provide a study guide for various biblical subjects, but rather to help the reader locate passages with which he is somewhat familiar. Nevertheless, because of the fact that many key theological themes, as reflected in a number of important words, are given proportionately heavier treatment, this concordance does have certain significant advantages over many others. A number of these words may be studied with at least some degree of completeness, not of course in the number of passages cited, but in the range of meaning which the selection of these passages reflects.

A limited concordance with multiple and practical purposes, designed to serve many different kinds of users, cannot be expected to meet all the needs of every reader. Nevertheless, in the extent of coverage, relevance of inclusion, and objectivity of selection, this concordance should prove to be a valuable tool for Bible reading, study, and comprehension.

—Eugene A. Nida, Ph.D.

THE RSV HANDY CONCORDANCE

Twelfth printing November 1981
ISBN 0-310-32391-6

CONCORDANCE

TO THE REVISED STANDARD VERSION

OF THE HOLY BIBLE

A

AARON
Brother of Moses, Ex 4.14; 7.1; commended for his eloquence, Ex 4.14; chosen to assist Moses, Ex 4.16, 27–28; co-leader with Moses, Ex 5.1; 8.25; supported Moses' arms, Ex 17.12; set apart as priest, Ex 28; Heb 5.4; made a golden calf, Ex 32; Acts 7.40–41; found fault with Moses, Num 12; his rod budded, Num 17; Heb 9.4; with Moses disobedient at Meribah, Num 20.10–13; died on Mount Hor, Num 20.26–29.

ABANDON — ED
The LORD will not *a* him	Ps 37.33
thou wilt not *a* my soul to	Acts 2.27
you have *a* the love you	Rev 2.4

ABASE
look on..proud and *a* him.	Job 40.11
a that which is high.	Ezek 21.26
walk in pride he is able to *a*.	Dan 4.37

ABEL
Now *A* was a keeper of sheep,	Gen 4.2
Cain said to *A* his brother,	4.8
another child instead of *A*,	4.25
from the blood of innocent *A*	Mt 23.35
By faith *A* offered to God	Heb 11.4
graciously than the blood of *A*.	12.24

ABHOR — RED
my intimate friends *a* me,	Job 19.19
They *a* me, they keep aloof	30.10
utterly *a* by his people	1Sam 27.12

ABIATHAR
A, escaped and fled after	1Sam 22.20
When *A*..fled to David	23.6
David said to *A* the priest,	30.7
Zadok and *A* carried the ark	2Sam 15.29
Zadok and *A* were priests;	20.25
when *A* was high priest,	Mk 2.26

ABIDE — S
spirit shall not *a*..for ever,	Gen 6.3
presence of the LORD, and *a*	1Sam 1.22
A in me, that I in you.	Jn 15.4
So faith, hope, love *a*,	1Cor 13.13
then you will *a* in the Son	1Jn 2.24
who *a* in..shadow of..Almighty,	Ps 91.1
My Spirit *a* among you; fear not.	Hag 2.5
No one who *a* in him sins;	1Jn 3.6
if we love one another, God *a*	4.12
because of the truth which *a*	2Jn 2

ABILITY
with *a* and intelligence,	Ex 31.3
according to the *a* of him	Lev 27.8
according to their *a* they	Ezra 2.69
to each according to his *a*.	Mt 25.15

ABIMELECH
And *A*..sent and took Sarah.	Gen 20.2

ABISHAI
Sought to kill Saul, 1Sam 26.5–9; pursued Abner, 2Sam 2.19,24; desired to kill Shime-i, 2Sam 16.9–11; 19.21; one of David's key warriors, 2Sam 23.18–19; slew the Edomites, 1Chr 18.12.

ABLE
well *a* to overcome it."	Num 13.30
the LORD was not *a* to bring	14.16
no man..*a* to withstand you	Josh 23.9
"Who is *a* to stand before	1Sam 6.20
"The LORD is *a* to give you	2Chr 25.9
whom we serve is *a* to deliver	Dan 3.17
has your God,..been *a* to deliver	6.20
for I tell you, God is *a* from	Mt 3.9
"Do you believe that I am *a*	9.28
Are you *a* to drink the cup	20.22
not *a* to do as small a thing	Lk 12.26
no one is *a* to snatch them	Jn 10.29
God is *a* to provide you with	2Cor 9.8
is *a* to do far more abundantly	Eph 3.20
he is *a* to help those..tempted.	Heb 2.18

ABLUTIONS
with instruction about *a*,	Heb 6.2
deal only with food..various *a*,	9.10

ABNER
Captain of Saul's host, 1Sam 14.50; made Ish-bosheth king, 2Sam 2.8–11; fought David's forces, 2Sam 2.12–32; made a league with David, 2Sam 3.6–21; slain by Joab, 2Sam 3.22–30; mourned by David, 2Sam 3.31–39.

ABODE
mount..God desired for his *a*,	Ps. 68.16
blesses..*a* of the righteous.	Prov 3.33

ABOLISH — ED
I will *a*..war from the land;	Hos 2.18
Jesus,..*a* death..brought life	2Tim 1.10

ABOMINABLE
for every *a* thing which	Deut 12.31
corrupt, they do *a* deeds,	Ps 14.1

ABOMINATION — S
has not fins and scales,..an *a*	Lev 11.10
an *a* to the LORD your God.	Deut 17.1
seven which are an *a* to him:	Prov 6.16
A false balance is an *a* to	11.1
both alike an *a* to the LORD.	17.15
Diverse weights are an *a*	20.23
even his prayer is an *a*.	28.9
incense is an *a* to me.	Isa 1.13
the *a* that makes desolate.	Dan 11.31
a has been committed in Israel	Mal 2.11
"Go in, and see the vile *a*	Ezek 8.9
they will remove..all its *a*.	11.18
make known to Jerusalem her *a*,	16.2
upon the wing of *a* shall come	Dan 9.27
a golden cup full of *a* and	Rev 17.4

ABOUND — S — ED
and peace *a*, till the moon	Ps 72.7
faithful..*a* with blessings,	Prov 28.20
God's truthfulness *a* to his	Rom 3.7
where sin increased, grace *a*	5.20

ABRAHAM — 'S
Born, Gen 11.26; married Sarai, Gen

ABRAHAM — 'S (cont.)
*11.29; migrated from Ur to Haran, Gen
11.31; called by God, Gen 12.1–5; Heb
11.8; went to Egypt, Gen 12.10–20; separated from Lot, Gen 13.7–11; rescued
Lot, Gen 14.13–16; God's covenant with
him, Gen 15.18; 17.1–21; Ishmael is born
to him, Gen 16.15–16; entertained angels,
Gen 18.1–21; interceded for Sodom, Gen
18.22–33; banished Hagar and Ishmael, Gen
21.9–21; offered up Isaac, Gen 22.1–14;
buried Sarah, Gen 23; married Keturah,
Gen 25.1; death and burial, Gen 25.8–10.*

your name shall be *A;*   Gen 17.5
A journeyed toward..the Negeb,   20.1
God tested *A*, and said   22.1
'We have *A* as our father';   Mt 3.9
to you, before *A* was, I am."   Jn 8.58
By faith *A* obeyed when..called Heb 11.8
carried by..angels to *A* bosom. Lk 16.22

ABSALOM
*Third son of David, 2Sam 3.3; avenged
Tamar and fled, 2Sam 13.20–39; returned
to Jerusalem, 2Sam 14.23–33; conspired
against David, 2Sam 15.1–12; slain by
Joab, 2Sam 18.9–17; mourned by David,
2Sam 18.33.*

ABSENT
a in body..present in spirit,   1Cor 5.3
a in body..with you in spirit,   Col 2.5

ABSTAIN
write to them to *a* from   Acts 15.20
a from every form of evil.   1Thess 5.22

ABUNDANCE
than the *a* of many wicked.   Ps 37.16
gave..bread from heaven in *a*,   105.40
from the *a* of her glory."   Isa 66.11
out of the *a* of the heart   Mt 12.34
life does not consist in..*a*   Lk 12.15
their *a*, but she out of..poverty   21.4
their *a* of joy and..poverty   2Cor 8.2
with every blessing in *a*,   9.8

ABUNDANTLY
it has increased *a;*   Gen 30.30
may have life, and have it *a*.   Jn 10.10

ACCEPT — ED
a the work of his hands;   Deut 33.11
Was it a time to *a* money and 2Ki 5.26
I will *a* his prayer not to   Job 42.8
offering, I will not *a* them;   Jer 14.12
offerings; and I will *a* you, Ezek 43.27
a that which is good and we   Hos 14.2
your..offerings, I will not *a* Amos 5.22
will not *a* your testimony   Acts 22.18
will you not be *a*?   Gen 4.7

ACCEPTABLE
offering..*a* in the sight of   Lev 10.19
it will not be *a* for you.   22.20
proclaim..*a* year of the Lord." Lk 4.19
no prophet is *a* in his own   4.24
"At the *a* time I have listened 2Cor 6.2

ACCESS
Through him we have obtained *a* Rom 5.2
we both have *a* in one Spirit Eph 2.18
confidence of *a* through..faith   3.12

ACCOMPLISH — ED
works..Father..granted me to *a*, Jn 5.36

if only I may *a* my course   Acts 20.24
narrative of..things..*a* among us, Lk 1.1
having *a* the work which thou   Jn 17.4

ACCORD
and serve him with one *a*.   Zeph 3.9
one *a* gave heed to..Philip,   Acts 8.6
What *a* has Christ with Belial? 2Cor 6.15

ACCOUNT (v)
a for every careless word   Mt 12.36
I do not *a* my life of any   Acts 20.24

ACCOUNT — S (n)
Turn in..*a* of your stewardship, Lk 16.2
give *a* of himself to God.   Rom 14.12
anything, charge that to my *a*. Philem 18
king who wished to settle *a*   Mt 18.23

ACCURSED
a hanged man is *a* by God;   Deut 21.23
sinner a hundred years..be *a*. Isa 65.20
wish that I myself were *a*   Rom 9.3
no love..let him be *a*.   1Cor 16.22
gospel contrary..let him be *a*.   Gal 1.8

ACCUSATION
"What *a* do you bring against   Jn 18.29

ACCUSE — D
Yet let no one contend, and..*a*, Hos 4.4
at his right hand to *a* him.   Zech 3.1
so that they might *a* him.   Mt 12.10
has *a* his brother falsely,   Deut 19.18
Chaldeans..maliciously *a*..Jews. Dan 3.8
when he was *a* by the chief   Mt 27.12
the chief priests *a* him of   Mk 15.3
charge on which they *a* him, Acts 23.28

ACCUSER
Make friends with..your *a*,   Mt 5.25
As you go with your *a* before Lk 12.58

ACHAIA
Gallio was proconsul of *A*,   Acts 18.12
pass through Macedonia and *A*   19.21
Macedonia and *A* have been Rom 15.26
saying that *A* has been ready 2Cor 9.2
to all the believers..in *A*.   1Thess 1.7

ACKNOWLEDGE — S — D
turn again to thee, and *a* thy 1Ki 8.33
Then will I also *a* to you,   Job 40.14
In all your ways *a* him, and he Prov 3.6
Only *a* your guilt, that you   Jer 3.13
We *a* our wickedness, O Lord,   14.20
those who *a*..he shall magnify Dan 11.39
until they *a* their guilt   Hos 5.15
every one who *a* me before men, Mt 10.32
who *a* me before men, the Son Lk 12.8
I *a* my sin to thee, and I did Ps 32.5
having *a*..they were strangers Heb 11.13

ACQUIRE — D
The simple *a* folly, but the   Prov 14.18
a great wisdom, surpassing all Ecc 1.16

ACQUIT — TED
who *a* the guilty for a bribe, Isa 5.23
but I am not thereby *a*.   1Cor 4.4

ACQUITTAL
may they have no *a* from thee. Ps 69.27
righteousness leads to *a* and Rom 5.18

ACT — S — ED — ING (v)
is time for the Lord to *a*,   Ps 119.126
so *a* as those..to be judged   Jas 2.12
prudent man *a* with knowledge Prov 13.16

ACT — S — ED — ING (v) (cont.)
I *a* for the sake of my name, Ezek 20.14
suspect us of *a* in worldly 2Cor 10.2

ACTION — S
God shall stand firm..take *a*. Dan 11.32
and by him *a* are weighed. 1Sam 2.3

ACTS (n)
made known..his *a* to..Israel Ps 103.7
a child..known by his *a*, Prov 20.11

ADAM
God made for *A*..garments Gen 3.21
book of the generations of *A*. 5.1
When *A* had lived a hundred 5.3
the son of *A*, the son of God. Lk 3.38
death reigned from *A* to Moses, Rom 5.14
as in *A* all die, so also 1Cor 15.22
first man *A* became a living 15.45
For *A* was formed first, then 1Tim 2.13

ADD — S
LORD *a* to me another son!" Gen 30.24
You shall not *a* to the word Deut 4.2
you shall not *a* to it 12.32
Do not *a* to his words, lest Prov 30.6
this book: if any one *a* to Rev 22.18

ADMONISH
to *a* every one with tears. Acts 20.31
but to *a* you as my beloved 1Cor 4.14
brethren, *a* the idle, 1Thess 5.14

ADMONITION
whose ear heeds wholesome *a* Prov 15.31

ADOPTION
as we wait for *a* as sons, Rom 8.23
we might receive *a* as sons. Gal 4.5

ADORN — ED
may *a* the doctrine of God Tit 2.10
as a bride *a* for her husband; Rev 21.2

ADULTERERS
They are all *a;* they are like Hos 7.4
the sorcerers, against the *a*, Mal 3.5

ADULTERESS
love a woman,who..is an *a;* Hos 3.1
a if she lives with another man Rom 7.3

ADULTERY — IES
"You shall not commit *a*. Ex 20.14
"If a man commits *a* Lev 20.10
"'Neither..commit *a*. Deut 5.18
who commits *a* has no sense; Prov 6.32
I fed them..they committed *a* Jer 5.7
'You shall not commit *a*.' Mt 5.27
already committed *a* with her 5.28
marries another, commits *a*." 19.9
heart of men, come..murder, *a*, Mk 7.21
marries another, commits *a* 10.11
and marries another commits *a*, Lk 16.18
woman..had been caught in *a*, Jn 8.3n
They have eyes full of *a*, 2Pet 2.14
for all the *a* of..Israel, I had sent Jer 3.8
your abominations, your *a* 13.27

ADVANCE — D
served to *a* the gospel, Phil 1.12
and *a* her and her maids to Est 2.9

ADVANTAGE
you ask, 'What *a* have I? Job 35.3
man has no *a* over the beasts; Ecc 3.19
a king is an *a* to a land with 5.9
an *a* to those who see the sun. 7.11

Then what *a* has the Jew? Rom 3.1
not seeking my own *a*, but 1Cor 10.33
keep Satan from gaining the *a* 2Cor 2.11
Christ will be of no *a* to you. Gal 5.2

ADVERSARY — IES
a shall surround the land Amos 3.1
when the *a* of Judah and Ezra 4.1
Give me not up to..my *a;* Ps 27.12

ADVERSITY
He thinks..I shall not meet *a*." Ps 10.6
If you faint in..day of *a*, Prov 24.10

ADVICE
Listen to *a* and accept Prov 19.20
king, who..no longer take *a*, Ecc 4.13
in this matter I give my *a;* 2Cor 8.10

ADVOCATE
we have an *a* with the Father, 1Jn 2.1

AFFLICT — ED (v)
not *a* any widow or orphan. Ex 22.22
O LORD, and *a* thy heritage. Ps 94.5
you, I will *a* you no more. Nah 1.12
when the LORD has *a* me and Ruth 1.21
Before I was *a* I went astray; Ps 119.67
in faithfulness thou hast *a* 119.75
a,..he opened not his mouth; Isa 53.7
and gather..those whom I have *a;* Mic 4.6
If we are *a*, it is for your 2Cor 1.6
We are *a* in every way, but not 4.8

AFFLICTED (n)
he heard the cry of the *a*— Job 34.28
but gives the *a* their right. 36.6
not forget the cry of the *a*. Ps 9.12
The *a* shall eat and be satisfied; 22.26
let the *a* hear and be glad. 34.2
satisfy the desire of the *a*, Isa 58.10
bring good tidings to the *a;* 61.1

AFFLICTION — S
LORD..given heed to your *a*. Gen 16.11
LORD has looked upon my *a;* 29.32
God saw my *a* and the labor 31.42
"I have seen the *a* of my people Ex 3.7
the bread of *a*—for you came Deut 16.3
LORD will look upon my *a*, 2Sam 16.12
LORD saw that the *a* of Israel 2Ki 14.26
see the *a* of our fathers in Neh 9.9
days of *a* have taken hold Job 30.16
For he has not despised..the *a* Ps 22.24
thou didst lay *a* on our loins; 66.11
adversity and the water of *a* Isa 30.20
tried you in..furnace of *a*. 48.10
In..their *a* he was afflicted, 63.9
I am the man who has seen *a* Lam 3.1
to comfort those..in any *a*, 2Cor 1.4
I wrote you out of much *a* 2.4
With all our *a*, I am overjoyed. 7.4
that we were to suffer *a;* 1Thess 3.4
LORD will bring on you..*a*, Deut 28.59
Many..the *a* of the righteous; Ps 34.19
great endurance, in *a*, 2Cor 6.4
what is lacking in Christ's *a* Col 1.24

AFRAID
I was *a*, because I was naked; Gen 3.10
Then Jacob was greatly *a* 32.7
And the men were *a* 43.18
Then Moses was *a*, and thought, Ex 2.14
Moses..was *a* to look at God. 3.6
were you not *a* to speak Num 12.8
Saul was *a* of David, because 1Sam 18.12

AFRAID (cont.)
not *a* to put forth your hand 2Sam 1.14
not be *a*..of the Chaldean 2Ki 25.24
David was *a* of God that day 1Chr 13.12
and made them *a* to build, Ezra 4.4
I am not *a* of ten thousands of Ps 3.6
my life; of whom shall I be *a*? 27.1
am *a*, I put my trust in thee. 56.3
I am *a* of thy judgments. 119.120
be not *a* of the Assyrians Isa 10.24
trust, and will not be *a*; 12.2
a, nor..rend their garments. Jer 36.24
and none shall make them *a*." Zeph 3.13
the crowds saw it, they were *a*, Mt 9.8
the angel said.."Do not be *a*; 28.5
a as they entered the cloud. Lk 9.34
for I was *a* of you, because 19.21
neither let them be *a*. Jn 14.27
Pilate..was the more *a*; 19.8
disciples;..were all *a* of him, Acts 9.26
'Do not be *a*, Paul; you 27.24
not *a* of the king's edict. Heb 11.23

AGE — S
be at the close of the *a*. Mt 13.40
was about thirty years of *a*, Lk 3.23
A ago I was set up, at the Prov 8.23

AGED
Wisdom is with the *a*, Job 12.12
and the *a* are among us, 15.10
and the *a* rose and stood; 29.8

AGONY
Pangs and *a* will seize them; Isa 13.8
in..*a* he prayed more earnestly; Lk 22.44

AGREE — D
if two of you *a* on earth Mt 18.19
not *a* with me for a denarius? 20.13
and their witness did not *a*. Mk 14.56
I *a* that the law is good. Rom 7.16
I entreat Syntyche to *a* in Phil 4.2
Abraham *a* with Ephron; Gen 23.16
So he *a*,..to betray him to them Lk 22.6
you have *a* together to tempt Acts 5.9

AGREEMENT
with Sheol we have an *a*; Isa 28.15
What *a* has the temple of God 2Cor 6.16

AGRIPPA
A the king and Bernice Acts 25.13
A said to Paul, "You have 26.1
King *A*, do you believe the 26.27

AHAB
and *A* his son reigned in 1Ki 16.28
Elijah..said to *A*, "As the LORD 17.1
When *A* saw Elijah, *A* said 18.17
after this *A* said to Naboth, 21.2
how *A* has humbled himself 21.29
make you like Zedekiah and *A*, Jer 29.22

AI
Bethel on the west and *A* Gen 12.8
between Bethel and *A*, 13.3
sent men from Jericho to *A*, Josh 7.2
and arise, go up to *A*; see, 8.1

AID
thou my help, hasten to my *a*! Ps 22.19
to Jerusalem with *a* for the Rom 15.25

AIM (v)
we *a* at what is honorable 2Cor 8.21
a at righteousness,..faith, 1Tim 6.11

AIM (n)
Make love your *a*, and 1Cor 14.1
my conduct, my *a* in life, 2Tim 3.10

ALARM (n)
When you blow an *a*, Num 10.5
said in my *a*, "I am driven Ps 31.22

ALARMED (v)
the visions of my head *a* me. Dan 4.5
rumors of wars, do not be *a*; Mk 13.7

ALEXANDRIA
Apollos, a native of *A*, Acts 18.24
ship of *A* sailing for Italy, 27.6
a ship of *A*, with the Twin 28.11

ALIENS
desolate, as overthrown by *a*. Isa 1.7
a have come into..holy places Jer 51.51
Beloved, I beseech you as *a* 1Pet 2.11

ALIVE
you who held fast..are all *a* Deut 4.4
my son was dead, and is *a* Lk 15.24
whom Paul asserted to be *a*. Acts 25.19
and *a* to God in Christ Jesus. Rom 6.11
your spirits are *a* because 8.10
in Christ..all be made *a*. 1Cor 15.22
he made *a*, when you were dead Eph 2.1
made us *a* together with Christ 2.5

ALL
For *a* things come from thee, 1Chr 29.14
If I give away *a* I have, 1Cor 13.3
able for *a* time to save those Heb 7.25

ALLEGORY — IES
riddle, and speak an *a* to Ezek 17.2
an *a* to the rebellious house 24.3
women are two covenants. Gal 4.24
'Is he not a maker of *a*?'" Ezek 20.49

ALMIGHTY
"I am God *A*; walk before me, Gen 17.1
"God *A* appeared to me 48.3
as destruction from the *A* it Isa 13.6
Lord our God the *A* reigns. Rev 19.6

ALMOND — S
the *a* tree blossoms, the Ecc 12.5
I said, "I see a rod of *a*." Jer 1.11
and it bore ripe *a*. Num 17.8

ALMS
when..give *a*, sound no trumpet Mt 6.2
give for *a* those things which Lk 11.41
a..ascended as a memorial Acts 10.4

ALONE
not good that the man..*a*; Gen 2.18
nor let me *a* till I swallow Job 7.19
No one is good but God *a*. Lk 18.19
I am not *a*, for the Father Jn 16.32
by works and not by faith *a*. Jas 2.24

ALTAR — S
Then Noah built an *a* Gen 8.20
Abram..built there an *a* 12.7
Abram..built an *a* to..LORD. 13.18
Abraham built an *a* there, 22.9
So he built an *a* there 26.25
There he erected an *a* 33.20
make there an *a* to the God 35.1
And Moses built an *a* Ex 17.15
make the *a* of acacia wood, 27.1
make an *a* to burn incense 30.1
He made the *a* of burnt offering 38.1
and the blood, on the *a* Deut 12.27

ALTAR — S (cont.)

build an *a* to the LORD your	Deut 27.5
built an *a* in Mount Ebal	Josh 8.30
built an *a* at the frontier	22.11
building an *a* to turn away	22.23
Saul built an *a* to the LORD;	1Sam 14.35
caught..horns of the *a*.	1Ki 1.50
repaired the *a* of the LORD	18.30
the *a* that was at Damascus.	2Ki 16.10
He made an *a* of bronze,	2Chr 4.1
I will go to the *a* of God,	Ps 43.4
coal..taken with tongs from..*a*.	Isa 6.6
an *a*..in the midst of..Egypt,	19.19
dimensions of..*a* by cubits	Ezek 43.13
LORD standing beside the *a*,	Amos 9.1
at the *a*, and there remember	Mt 5.23
an *a* with this inscription,	Acts 17.23
We have an *a* from which those	Heb 13.10
shall break down their *a*,	Deut 7.5
shall tear down their *a*,	12.3
he erected *a* for Baal, and	2Ki 21.3

AMALEK

Joshua mowed down *A* and his	Ex 17.13
"*A* was the first of the	Num 24.20
'I will punish what *A* did	1Sam 15.2

AMALEKITES

Agag the king of the *A*."	1Sam 15.32
destroyed the remnant of..*A*	1Chr 4.43

AMAZED

And they were *a* at him.	Mk 12.17
all were *a* and perplexed,	Acts 2.12
miracles performed, he was *a*.	8.13

AMAZEMENT

looked at one another in *a*.	Gen 43.33
And they were overcome with *a*.	Mk 5.42

AMBASSADOR — S

I am an *a* in chains; that I	Eph 6.20
which sends *a* by the Nile,	Isa 18.2
by sending *a* to Egypt,	Ezek 17.15
So we are *a* for Christ, God	2Cor 5.20

AMBUSH

they went to the place of *a*,	Josh 8.9
the LORD set an *a* against	2Chr 20.22

AMEN

everlasting to everlasting! *A*	Ps 41.13
can..outsider say the "*A*"	1Cor 14.16
'The words of the *A*, the	Rev 3.14

AMEND — S

A your ways and your doings,	Jer 7.3
Now therefore *a* your ways	26.13
deference..*a* for..offenses.	Ecc 10.4

AMMON

frontier of the sons of *A*,	Deut 2.19

AMMONITES

Ben-ammi..father of the *A*	Gen 19.38
cut down the *A* until the	1Sam 11.11
A paid tribute to Uzziah,	2Chr 26.8
and the *A* shall obey them.	Isa 11.14

AMOS

The words of *A*, who was	Amos 1.1
"*A* has conspired against you	7.10
A answered.."I am no prophet,	7.14
said, "*A*, what do you see?"	8.2

ANATHOTH

A with its pasture lands,	Josh 21.18
"Go to *A*, to your estate;	1Ki 2.26

Cry aloud,..Answer her, O *A*!	Isa 10.30
of the priests who were in *A*	Jer 1.1
why..not rebuked Jeremiah of *A*	29.27
'Buy my field which is at *A*,	32.7

ANDREW

Simon..Peter and *A* his brother,	Mt 4.18
Peter, and *A* his brother;	10.2
James and John and *A* asked him	Mk 13.3
One..who..followed him, was *A*,	Jn 1.40
A, Simon Peter's brother, said	6.8
Philip went and told *A*; *A* went	12.22
and John and James and *A*,	Acts 1.13

ANGEL — S

the *a* of God called to Hagar	Gen 21.17
he will send his *a* before you,	24.7
I send an *a* before you,	Ex 23.20
I will send an *a* before you,	33.2
sent an *a* and brought us	Num 20.16
my sight as an *a* of God;	1Sam 29.9
the king is like the *a*	2Sam 14.17
king is like the *a* of God;	19.27
an *a* spoke to me by the word	1Ki 13.18
an *a* touched him, and said	19.5
sent his *a* and delivered his	Dan 3.28
his *a*..shut the lions' mouths,	6.22
He strove with the *a* and	Hos 12.4
The *a* who talked with me said	Zech 1.9
the *a* said to her, "Do not be	Lk 1.30
appeared to him..*a* from heaven,	22.43
"An *a* has spoken to him."	Jn 12.29
was like the face of an *a*.	Acts 6.15
an *a* appeared in..Mount Sinai,	7.30
he saw..in a vision an *a* of God	10.3
no resurrection, nor *a*, nor spirit;	23.8
stood by me an *a* of the God	27.23
Satan disguises..as an *a*	2Cor 11.14
if we, or an *a* from heaven,	Gal 1.8
a of the church in Philadelphia	Rev 3.7
another mighty *a* coming down	10.1
a mighty *a* took up a stone	18.21
I saw an *a* standing in the sun,	19.17
"I Jesus have sent my *a* to you	22.16
The two *a* came to Sodom	Gen 19.1
the *a* urged Lot, saying,	19.15
the *a* of God were ascending	28.12
the *a* of God met him;	32.1
Man ate of the bread of the *a*;	Ps 78.25
will give his *a* charge of you	91.11
Bless the LORD, O you his *a*,	103.20
Praise him, all his *a*, praise	148.2
'He will give his *a* charge of you,'	Mt 4.6
devil left him, and behold, *a*	4.11
and the reapers are *a*.	13.39
a..behold..face of the Father	18.10
he will send out his *a* with	24.31
and the *a* ministered to him.	Mk 1.13
'He will give his *a* charge	Lk 4.10
comes in his glory and..holy *a*.	9.26
will be denied before the *a*	12.9
joy before..*a*..over one sinner	15.10
and the *a* of God ascending	Jn 1.51
and she saw two *a* in white,	20.12
law..by *a* and did not keep it."	Acts 7.53
death, nor life, nor *a*, nor	Rom 8.38
spectacle to the world, to *a*	1Cor 4.9
know that we are to judge *a*?	6.3
veil..because of the *a*.	11.10
the tongues of men and of *a*,	13.1
insisting on..worship of *a*,	2.18
little while lower than the *a*,	Heb 2.7
into which *a* long to look.	1Pet 1.12

ANGEL — S (cont.)

if God did not spare the *a*	2Pet 2.4
the *a* that did not keep their	Jude 6
I saw four *a* standing at the	Rev 7.1
"Release the four *a* who are	9.14

ANGEL OF THE LORD

The *a*..found her by a spring	Gen 16.7
the *a*..called to him,.."Abraham,	22.11
a..appeared to him in a flame	Ex 3.2
ass saw..*a*..standing in the	Num 22.23
he saw the *a*..standing in..way,	22.31
a..came and sat..under..oak	Judg 6.11
the *a*..appeared to the woman	13.3
But the *a*..said to Elijah	2Ki 1.3
that night the *a*..went forth,	19.35
David..saw the *a*..standing	1Chr 21.16
The *a*..encamps around those	Ps 34.7
the *a*..went forth, and slew	Isa 37.36
a..appeared to him in a dream,	Mt 1.20
for an *a*..descended from heaven	28.2
there appeared to him an *a*..	Lk 1.11
And an *a*..appeared to them,	2.9
an *a*..went down..into the pool,	Jn 5.4*n*
an *a*..opened the prison doors	Acts 5.19
an *a*..said to Philip, "Rise	8.26
a..struck Peter on the side	12.7

ANGER — ED (v)

merciful..gracious, slow to *a*	Ps 103.8
He who is slow to *a* has	Prov 14.29
slow to *a* quiets contention.	15.18
who is slow to *a* is better	16.32
Be not quick to *a*, for *a* lodges	Ecc 7.9
The LORD is slow to *a* and	Nah 1.3
our fathers had *a* the God	Ezra 5.12
a him at..waters of Meribah,	Ps 106.32

ANGER (n)

until your brother's *a* turns	Gen 27.45
Jacob's *a* was kindled	30.2
let not your *a* burn against	44.18
the *a* of the LORD was kindled	Ex 4.14
dancing, Moses' *a* burned	32.19
when the LORD heard it, his *a*	Num 11.1
the *a* of the LORD was kindled	12.9
But God's *a* was kindled	22.22
the fierce *a* of the LORD	25.4
a of the LORD against Israel!	32.14
their *a* against him was abated	Judg 8.3
the *a* of the LORD was kindled	10.7
Then Saul's *a* was kindled	1Sam 20.30
the *a* of the LORD..kindled	2Sam 24.1
because of the *a* to which	1Ki 15.30
a of the LORD was kindled	1Chr 13.10
God will send his fierce *a*	Job 20.23
thy burning *a* overtake them.	Ps 69.24
the *a* of God rose against them	78.31
A gift in secret averts *a*;	Prov 21.14
the *a* of the LORD was kindled	Isa 5.25
his *a* is not turned away and	9.21
Ah, Assyria, the rod of my *a*,	10.5
upon him the heat of his *a*	42.25
for the fierce *a* of the LORD	Jer 4.8
a of the LORD will not turn	23.20
How the Lord in his *a* has set	Lam 2.1
the day of the *a* of the LORD	2.22
let my *a* and thy wrath turn	Dan 9.16
Samaria. My *a* burns against	Hos 8.5
I will not execute my fierce *a*,	11.9
endure the heat of his *a*?	Nah 1.6
a,..at their hardness of heart,	Mk 3.5

ANGRY

And he was *a* with Eleazar	Lev 10.16
The LORD was *a* with me also	Deut 1.37
Why then are you *a* over	2Sam 19.42
Naaman was *a*, and went away,	2Ki 5.11
Asa was *a* with the seer,	2Chr 16.10
LORD was *a* with Amaziah	25.15
Be *a*, but sin not; commune with	Ps 4.4
thou hast been *a*; oh, restore	60.1
wicked man sees it and is *a*;	112.10
he with whom the LORD is *a*	Prov 22.14
backbiting tongue, *a* looks.	25.23
mother's sons were *a* with me,	Sol 1.6
will he be *a* for ever, will	Jer 3.5
"Do you do well to be *a*?"	Jonah 4.4
LORD was..*a* with your fathers.	Zech 1.2
one who is *a* with his brother	Mt 5.22
he was *a* and refused to go	Lk 15.28
nation I will make you *a*."	Rom 10.19
Be *a* but do not sin; do not	Eph 4.26

ANGUISH

and *a* have come upon me, but	Ps 119.143
a day of distress and *a*,	Zeph 1.15

ANNUL

not *a* a covenant previously	Gal 3.17

ANOINT — EST — ED (v)

shall *a* them and ordain them	Ex 28.41
you shall *a* with it the tent	30.26
shall *a* Aaron and his sons,	30.30
Wash..and *a* yourself, and put	Ruth 3.3
you shall *a* him to be prince	1Sam 9.16
you shall *a* for me him whom	16.3
"Arise, *a* him; for this is	16.12
I *a* you king over Israel.'	2Ki 9.3
and to *a* a most holy place.	Dan 9.24
that they might go and *a* him.	Mk 16.1
Jesus, whom thou didst *a*,	Acts 4.27
and salve to *a* your eyes,	Rev 3.18
thou *a* my head with oil, my	Ps 23.5
Bethel, where you *a* a pillar	Gen 31.13
on Aaron's head, and *a* him,	Lev 8.12
the LORD *a* you to be prince	1Sam 10.1
a Solomon..blew the trumpet;	1Ki 1.39
proclaimed him king, and *a*	2Ki 11.12
heard that David had been *a*	1Chr 14.8
"Touch not my *a* ones, do my	16.22
they *a* him as prince for the LORD,	29.22
your God, has *a* you with the	Ps 45.7
with my holy oil I have *a*	89.20
saying, "Touch not my *a* ones,	105.15
a me to bring good tidings	Isa 61.1
With an *a* guardian cherub	Ezek 28.14
to the coming of an *a* one,	Dan 9.25
a with oil many that were sick	Mk 6.13
she has *a* my body..for burying.	14.8
because he has *a* me to preach	Lk 4.18
and *a* them with the ointment.	7.38
It was Mary who *a* the Lord	Jn 11.2
and *a* the feet of Jesus and	12.3
how God *a* Jesus of Nazareth	Acts 10.38
have been *a* by the Holy One,	1Jn 2.20

ANOINTED (n)

go in and out before my *a*	1Sam 2.35
LORD's *a* is before him.'	16.6
for he is the LORD's *a*.'	24.10
hand against the LORD's *a*,	26.9
your lord, the LORD's *a*.	26.16
to destroy the LORD's *a*?	2Sam 1.14
steadfast love to his *a*,	22.51
against the LORD and his *a*,	Ps 2.2

ANOINTED (n) (cont.)

shows steadfast love to his *a*,	Ps 18.50
the saving refuge of his *a*.	28.8
look upon the face of thine *a*!	84.9
not turn away. .face of thy *a*	132.10
the LORD to his *a*, to Cyrus,	Isa 45.1
for the salvation of thy *a*.	Hab 3.13
the. .*a* who stand by the LORD	Zech 4.14

ANOINTING (n)

a which you received from him	1Jn 2.27

ANSWER — S — ED (v)

the LORD did not *a* him,	1Sam 28.6
king's command was, "Do not *a*	2Ki 18.36
How then can I *a* him, choosing	Job 9.14
let the Almighty *a* me!)	31.35
'He will *a* none of my words'?	33.13
A me when I call, O God of my	Ps 4.1
The LORD *a* you in. .trouble!	20.1
be gracious to me and *a* me!	27.7
When he calls to me, I will *a*	91.15
call upon me,. .I will not *a*;	Prov 1.28
A not a fool according to	26.4
when he hears it, he will *a*	Isa 30.19
Before they call I will *a*,	65.24
I called you, you did not *a*,	Jer 7.13
Call to me and I will *a* you,	33.3
I will *a* the heavens and they	Hos 2.21
what have I wearied you? *A* me!	Mic 6.3
how or what you are to *a*	Lk 12.11
who *a* by fire, he is God."	1Ki 18.24
an altar to the God who *a*	Gen 35.3
Then the LORD *a* Job out of	Job 38.1
Then Job *a* the LORD: "I know	42.1,2
I *a* you in the secret place of	Ps 81.7

ANSWER (n)

give Pharaoh a favorable *a*."	Gen 41.16
angry. .they had found no *a*,	Job 32.3
an *a* for those who taunt me,	Ps 119.42
A soft *a* turns away wrath,	Prov 15.1
a of. .tongue is from the LORD.	16.1
If one gives *a* before he hears,	18.13
I called him, but he gave no *a*.	Sol 5.6
questioned. .but he made no *a*.	Lk 23.9

ANTICHRIST

have heard that *a* is coming,	1Jn 2.18
This is the *a*, he who denies	2.22
This is the spirit of *a*, of	4.3
is the deceiver and the *a*.	2Jn 7

ANTIOCH

Phoenicia and Cyprus and *A*,	Acts 11.19
in *A* the disciples were. .called	11.26
at *A* there were prophets	13.1
and came to *A* of Pisidia.	13.14
Jews came there from *A* and	14.19
from there they sailed to *A*,	14.26
Paul and Barnabas remained in *A*,	15.35
and then went down to *A*.	18.22
But when Cephas came to *A* I	Gal 2.11
what befell me at *A*, at	2Tim 3.11

ANXIETY — IES

A in a man's heart weighs	Prov 12.25
my *a* for all the churches.	2Cor 11.28
Have no *a* about anything,	Phil 4.6
Cast all your *a* on him, for	1Pet 5.7

ANXIOUS

my spirit within me was *a*,	Dan 7.15
do not be *a* about your life,	Mt 6.25
do not be *a* how. .to speak	10.19
Martha, you are *a* and troubled	Lk 10.41

do not be *a* how. .to answer	12.11
The unmarried man is *a* about	1Cor 7.32
genuinely *a* for your welfare.	Phil 2.20

APOLLOS

a Jew named *A*, a native of	Acts 18.24
While *A* was at Corinth, Paul	19.1
Paul," or "I belong to *A*,"	1Cor 1.12
another, "I belong to *A*,"	3.4
As for our brother *A*, I. .urged him	16.12
the lawyer and *A* on their way;	Tit 3.13

APOSTASY

and your *a* will reprove you.	Jer 2.19
if they then commit *a*,	Heb 6.6

APOSTLE — S

I am an *a* to the Gentiles,	Rom 11.13
called. .to be an *a* of Christ	1Cor 1.1
Am I not free? Am I not an *a*?	9.1
Paul an *a*—not from men nor	Gal 1.1
Paul, an *a* of Christ Jesus	1Tim 1.1
appointed a preacher and *a*	2Tim 1.11
a returned to Jesus, and told	Mk 6.30
the *a* told. .what they had done.	Lk 9.10
at table, and the *a* with him.	22.14
through the Holy Spirit to. .*a*	Acts 1.2
the *a* and. .brethren. .in Judea	11.1
appointed in the church. .*a*,	1Cor 12.28
inferior to these superlative *a*.	2Cor 11.5
been revealed to his holy *a*	Eph 3.5
that some should be *a*, some	4.11
commandment. .through your *a*.	2Pet 3.2
the predictions of the *a* of	Jude 17
call themselves *a* but are not,	Rev 2.2
names of the twelve *a* of the Lamb.	21.14

APOSTLESHIP

and *a* from which Judas turned	Acts 1.25
grace and *a* to bring about	Rom 1.5

APPALLED

and pulled hair. .and sat *a*.	Ezra 9.3
Upright men are *a* at this,	Job 17.8
be *a* because of their shame	Ps 40.15
I was *a*,. .no one to uphold;	Isa 63.5
but I was *a* by the vision	Dan 8.27

APPEAL (v)

that I cannot *a* to my Father,	Mt 26.53
to them. I *a* to Caesar."	Acts 25.11
I *a* to you therefore, brethren,	Rom 12.1
I *a* to you for my child,	Philem 10

APPEAL (n)

God making his *a* through us.	2Cor 5.20
Mend your ways, heed my *a*,	13.11
as an *a* to God for a clear	1Pet 3.21

APPEAR — ED — ING

your males *a* before the LORD	Ex 23.17
"When you come to *a* before me,	Isa 1.12
outwardly *a* righteous to men,	Mt 23.28
then will *a* the sign of the Son	24.30
kingdom. .was to *a* immediately.	Lk 19.11
all *a* before the judgment	2Cor 5.10
you. .will *a* with him in glory.	Col 3.4
to *a* in the presence of God	Heb 9.24
Christ,. .will *a* a second time	9.28
not yet *a* what we shall be,	1Jn 3.2
the LORD *a* to him by. .Mamre,	Gen 18.1
the LORD *a* to him, and said,	26.2
"God Almighty *a* to me	48.3
angel of the LORD *a* to him	Ex 3.2
the LORD *a* in the cloud.	16.10
glory of the LORD *a* to all	Num 16.19

APPEAR — ED — ING (cont.)

And the LORD a in the tent   Deut 31.15
angel of the LORD a to him   Judg 6.12
God a to Solomon, and said   2Chr 1.7
LORD a to Solomon in the night   7.12
the LORD a to him from afar.   Jer 31.3
he a first to Mary Magdalene,   Mk 16.9n
who a in glory and spoke of   Lk 9.31
God of glory a to our father   Acts 7.2
vision a to Paul in the night: 16.9
he has a once for all at the   Heb 9.26
until the a of our Lord   1Tim 6.14
to all who have loved his a.   2Tim 4.8

APPLE — S

kept. .as the a of his eye.   Deut 32.10
Keep me as the a of the eye;   Ps 17.8
keep my teachings as the a of   Prov 7.2
As an a tree among the trees   Sol 2.3
touches the a of his eye: Zech 2.8
word fitly spoken is like a   Prov 25.11

APPLY

A your mind to instruction   Prov 23.12
careful to a themselves to good   Tit 3.8

APPOINT — ED

shall a Aaron. .to. .priesthood; Num 3.10
I will a a place for my people   2Sam 7.10
he a his own priests for   2Chr 11.15
I was a to be their governor   Neh 5.14
to the house a for all   Job 30.23
my God; thou hast a a judgment.   Ps 7.6
the LORD a a great fish to   Jonah 1.17
LORD God a a plant, and made   4.6
God a a worm which attacked   4.7
he a twelve, to be with him,   Mk 3.14
After this the Lord a seventy   Lk 10.1
as my Father a a kingdom for me,   22.29
I chose you and a you that   Jn 15.16
the Christ a for you, Jesus,   Acts 3.20
God of our fathers a you   22.14
For this gospel I was a a   2Tim 1.11
Son, whom he a the heir of all   Heb 1.2

APPROACH

for who would dare. .to a me?   Jer 30.21
the priests who a the LORD   Ezek 42.13

APPROVAL

you will receive his a,   Rom 13.3
men of old received divine a.   Heb 11.2

APPROVE — D — ING

but a those who practice them. Rom 1.32
and a what is excellent,   2.18
you may a what is excellent,   Phil 1.10
God has already a what you do.   Ecc 9.7
yourself to God as one a,   2Tim 2.15
also was standing by and a,   Acts 22.20

AQUILA

And he found a Jew named A,   Acts 18.2
with him Priscilla and A.   18.18
when Priscilla and A heard   18.26
Greet Prisca and A, my fellow   Rom 16.3
A and Prisca, together with   1Cor 16.19
Greet Prisca and A, and the   2Tim 4.19

ARABIA

and from all the kings of A   1Ki 10.15
thickets in A you will lodge,   Isa 21.13
but I went away into A; and   Gal 1.17
Hagar is Mount Sinai in A;   4.25

ARARAT

ark came. .the mountains of A.   Gen 8.4

ARCHANGEL — 'S

when the a Michael, contending   Jude 9
with the a call, and with   1Thess 4.16

ARGUE — S — D

desire to a my case with God.   Job 13.3
A your case with. .neighbor   Prov 25.9
who a with God,. .answer it."   Job 40.2
And they a with one another,   Mk 11.31
for three weeks he a with them   Acts 17.2
he a in the synagogue with. .Jews 17.17
he a in the synagogue every   18.4

ARGUMENT — S

If. .wise man has an a with   Prov 29.9
We destroy a and every proud   2Cor 10.5

ARIMATHEA

rich man from A, named Joseph, Mt 27.57
After this Joseph of A, who   Jn 19.38

ARISE

A, walk through the length   Gen 13.17
Moses said, "A, O LORD,   Num 10.35
a, go over this Jordan,   Josh 1.2
A, O LORD! Let not man prevail; Ps 9.19
A, O LORD! confront them,   17.13
Let God a, let his enemies be   68.1
a, O captive Jerusalem; loose   Isa 52.2
A, shine; for. .light has come,   60.1
trouble they say, 'A and save   Jer 2.27
"Little girl, I say to you, a."   Mk 5.41
"Young man, I say to you, a."   Lk 7.14
called, saying, "Child, a."   8.54
sleeper, and a from the dead,   Eph 5.14

ARK

Make yourself an a   Gen 6.14
the a came to rest upon. .Ararat.   8.4
"They shall make an a   Ex 25.10
Bezalel made the a of acacia   37.1
the a of the covenant   Num 10.33
"When you see the a of the   Josh 3.3
a of the LORD to compass   6.11
(for the a of the covenant   Judg 20.27
Let us bring the a of the   1Sam 4.3
the a of God was captured;   4.11
Philistines took the a of God   5.2
saw the a, they rejoiced   6.13
looked into the a of the LORD;   6.19
"Bring hither the a of God."   14.18
up from there the a of God,   2Sam 6.2
Levites, bearing the a   15.24
let us bring again the a of   1Chr 13.3
they brought in the a of God,   16.1
to bring up the a of the   2Chr 5.2
no more say, "The a of the   Jer 3.16
and the a of the covenant   Heb 9.4
a of his covenant was seen   Rev 11.19

ARM — S

With him is an a of flesh;   2Chr 32.8
Have you an a like God,   Job 40.9
nor did their own a give them   Ps 44.3
His right hand and his holy a,   98.1
and his a rules for him;   Isa 40.10
to whom has the a of the Lord   Jn 12.38
are the everlasting a.   Deut 33.27
taking him in his a, he said   Mk 9.36
took them in his a and blessed   10.16

ARMAGEDDON

which is called in Hebrew A.   Rev 16.16

ARMOR

clothed David with his a;   1Sam 17.38
Put on the whole a of God,   Eph 6.11

ARMY — IES
as commander of the *a* of the Josh 5.14
But the *a* of the Chaldeans 2Ki 25.5
great *a*, like an *a* of God. 1Chr 12.22
my great *a*, which I sent Joel 2.25
hast not gone out with our *a*. Ps 44.9

AROMA
we are the *a* of Christ to God 2Cor 2.15

AROUSE — D
to *a* you by way of reminder, 2Pet 1.13
This city has *a* my anger Jer 32.31

ARRAY (n)
worship the LORD in holy *a*. Ps 29.2
Worship the LORD in holy *a*; 96.9

ARRAYED (v)
was not *a* like one of these. Mt 6.29
was not *a* like one of these. Lk 12.27

ARRESTED
he heard that John had been a, Mt 4.12
after John was *a*, Jesus came Mk 1.14

ARROGANCE
Let not the foot of *a* come Ps 36.11
you boast in your *a*. Jas 4.16

ARROGANT
who is *a* is an abomination Prov 16.5
we deem the *a* blessed; Mal 3.15
Some are *a*, as though I 1Cor 4.18
And you are a! Ought you not 5.2

ARROW — S
"The LORD's *a* of victory, 2Ki 13.17
till an *a* pierces its entrails; Prov 7.23
And I will shoot three *a* 1Sam 20.20
the *a* of the Almighty are in me. Job 6.4
making his *a* fiery shafts. Ps 7.13
he sent..*a*, and scattered 18.14
thy *a* have sunk into me, and 38.2
Your *a* are sharp in the heart 45.5
a are sharp,..their bows bent, Isa 5.28
loose..my deadly *a* of famine, Ezek 5.16

ASCEND — ED — ING
Who..shall *a*..hill of the LORD? Ps 24.3
Thou didst *a* the high mount, 68.18
I *a* to heaven, thou art there! 139.8
a to heaven; above the stars Isa 14.13
"Who will *a* into heaven?" Rom 10.6
angel..*a* in the flame of the Judg 13.20
Who has *a* to heaven and come Prov 30.4
No one has *a* into heaven but Jn 3.13
I have not yet *a* to the Father; 20.17
"He *a*," what does it mean Eph 4.9
were to see the Son of man *a* Jn 6.62

ASHAMED
naked, and were not *a*. Gen 2.25
"O my God, I am *a* and blush Ezra 9.6
be *a* who are..treacherous. Ps 25.3
so your faces shall never be *a*. 34.5
were..*a* when they committed Jer 6.15
Were they *a* when they committed 8.12
shall be *a* of their harvests 12.13
whoever is *a* of me and of my Mk 8.38
whoever is *a* of me and of my Lk 9.26
I am not *a* of the gospel: Rom 1.16
not write this to make you *a*, 1Cor 4.14
Do not be *a* then of testifying 2Tim 1.8
But I am not *a*, for I know 1.12

ASHER
Leah..called his name *A*." Gen 30.13

from *A*, Pagiel..son of Ochran; Num 1.13
And of *A* he said, "Blessed Deut 33.24
A sat still at the coast Judg 5.17

ASHES
I who am but dust and *a*. Gen 18.27
maxims are proverbs of *a*. Job 13.12
I have become like dust and *a*. 30.19

ASIA
Cappadocia, Pontus and *A*, Acts 2.9
those from Cilicia and *A*, arose 6.9
forbidden..to speak..in *A*. 16.6
all the residents of *A* heard 19.10
she whom all *A*..worship." 19.27
first convert in *A* for Christ. Rom 16.5
The churches of *A* send 1Cor 16.19
Cappadocia, *A*, and Bithynia, 1Pet 1.1
seven churches that are in *A*: Rev 1.4

ASK — ED
that they *a*, every man of his Ex 11.2
"*A* what I shall give you." 1Ki 3.5
"*A* what I shall give you." 2Chr 1.7
A of me, and I will make the Ps 2.8
Two things I *a* of thee; deny Prov 30.7
"*A* a sign of the LORD your Isa 7.11
by those who did not *a* for me; 65.1
They shall *a* the way to Zion, Jer 50.5
A rain from the LORD in the Zech 10.1
knows what you need before you *a* Mt 6.8
"*A*, and it will be given you; 7.7
And whatever you *a* in prayer 21.22
king said to the girl, "*A* me Mk 6.22
do for us whatever you *a* of you." 10.35
I tell you, *A*, and it will be Lk 11.9
give..Holy Spirit to those who *a* 11.13
Whatever you *a* in my name, Jn 14.13
and my words abide in you, *a* 15.7
a, and you will receive, 16.24
than all that we *a* or think, Eph 3.20
lacks wisdom, let him *a* God, Jas 1.5
not have, because you do not *a*. 4.2
from him whatever we *a*, 1Jn 3.22
if we *a* anything according 5.14
not a mortal sin, he will *a*, 5.16
a of the Egyptians jewelry Ex 12.35
"I have *a* him of the LORD." 1Sam 1.20
One thing have I *a* of the LORD, Ps 27.4
he gave them what they *a*, but 106.15
and *a* for the body of Jesus. Mt 27.58
and *a* for the body of Jesus. Lk 23.52

ASLEEP
or perhaps he is *a* and must 1Ki 18.27
by the waves; but he was *a*. Mt 8.24
in the stern, *a* on the cushion; Mk 4.38
come suddenly and find you *a*. 13.36
as they sailed he fell *a*. Lk 8.23
when he..said this, he fell *a*. Acts 7.60
though some have fallen *a*. 1Cor 15.6
concerning those who are *a*, 1Thess 4.13

ASS — 'S
And the *a* saw the angel Num 22.23
the *a*..said to Balaam, 22.28
humble, and mounted on an *a*, Mt 21.5
dumb *a* spoke with human voice 2Pet 2.16
coming, sitting on an *a* colt!" Jn 12.15

ASSEMBLE — D
A and hear, O sons of Jacob, Gen 49.2
a..the congregation at the door Lev 8.3
"*A* yourselves and come, draw Isa 45.20
cry aloud..'*A*, and let us go Jer 4.5

ASSEMBLE — D (cont.)

a you out of the countries	Ezek 11.17
all beasts of the field, '*A*	39.17
they *a* the whole congregation	Num 1.18
Solomon *a* the elders of Israel	1Ki 8.1
Solomon *a* the elders of Israel	2Chr 5.2
people of Israel were *a* with	Neh 9.1
When you are *a*, and my spirit	1Cor 5.4

ASSEMBLY

to. . LORD; it is a solemn *a*;	Lev 23.36
David said to all the *a*,	1Chr 29.20
the *a* made a covenant with	2Chr 23.3
Let the *a*. . be gathered about	Ps 7.7
praise in. . *a* of the faithful!	149.1
a fast; call a solemn *a*;	Joel 2.15
settled in the regular *a*.	Acts 19.39
to the *a* of the first-born	Heb 12.23
if a man. . comes into your *a*,	Jas 2.2

ASSURANCE

he has given *a* to all men	Acts 17.31
realizing the full *a* of hope	Heb 6.11
faith. . the *a* of things hoped for,	11.1

ASSYRIA

Hiddekel,. . east of *A*.	Gen 2.14
king of *A* came and captured	2Ki 15.29
king of *A* I have heard.	19.20
bee which is in the land of *A*.	Isa 7.18
calling to Egypt, going to *A*.	Hos 7.11
A shall not save us, we will	14.3

ASTONISHED

every one passing. . will be *a*,	2Chr 7.21
King Nebuchadnezzar was *a*	Dan 3.24
crowds were *a* at his teaching,	Mt 7.28
multitude. . *a* at his teaching.	Mk 11.18
they were *a* at his teaching,	Lk 4.32

ASTRAY

The wicked go *a* from the womb,	Ps 58.3
Before. . afflicted I went *a*;	119.67
those who lead this people. . *a*,	Isa 9.16
spirit of harlotry. . led. . *a*,	Hos 4.12
and they will lead many *a*	Mt 24.5
heed that no one leads you *a*.	Mk 13.5
heed that you are not led *a*;	Lk 21.8
he is leading the people *a*."	Jn 7.12
"Are you led *a*, you also?	7.47

ASUNDER

"Let us burst their bonds *a*,	Ps 2.3
together, let no man put *a*."	Mt 19.6

ATE

Saul *a* with Samuel that day.	1Sam 9.24
a them with the blood.	14.32
Thy words were found, and I *a*	Jer 15.16
and *a* grass like an ox, and	Dan 4.33
Those who *a* were four thousand	Mt 15.38
They *a*, they drank, they married	Lk 17.27
he took it and *a* before them.	24.43

ATHENS

brought him as far as *A*;	Acts 17.15
"Men of *A*, I perceive that	17.22
After this he left *A* and went	18.1
willing to be left. . at *A*	1Thess 3.1

ATONE — D

evil. . for which you cannot *a*;	Isa 47.11
to *a* for iniquity, to bring in	Dan 9.24
iniquity is *a* for, and	Prov 16.6

ATONEMENT

as a sin offering for *a*.	Ex 29.36

perhaps I can make *a* for. . sin."	32.30
accepted for him to make *a*	Lev 1.4
consecrated. . to make *a* for it.	8.15
people, and make *a* for them;	9.7
priest shall make *a* for him	14.18
that *a*. . made for the people	16.34
it is the blood that makes *a*,	17.11
tenth day. . is the day of *a*;	23.27
and make *a* for them;	Num 16.46
make *a* for ourselves before	31.50
to make *a* for all Israel.	2Chr 29.24
shall make *a* for the temple.	Ezek 45.20

ATTENTION

Gallio paid no *a* to this.	Acts 18.17
centurion paid more *a* to. . captain	27.11
we must pay the closer *a* to	Heb 2.1

ATTENTIVE

Lord, let thy ear be *a* to	Neh 1.11
My son, be *a* to my words;	Prov 4.20
My son, be *a* to my wisdom,	5.1

ATTESTED

Jesus. . *a* to you by God with	Acts 2.22
was *a* as having pleased God.	Heb 11.5

AUTHORITY — IES

commit your *a* to his hand;	Isa 22.21
he taught. . as one who had *a*,	Mt 7.29
a man under *a*, with soldiers	8.9
the Son of man has *a*. . to forgive	9.6
great men exercise *a* over them.	20.25
"By what *a* are you doing these	21.23
"All *a* in heaven and on earth	28.18
he taught. . as one who had *a*,	Mk 1.22
Son of man has *a* on earth to	2.10
and have *a* to cast out demons:	3.15
their great men exercise *a*	10.42
"By what *a* are you doing these	11.28
"To you I will give all this *a*	Lk 4.6
with *a* and power he commands	4.36
the Son of man has *a* on earth	5.24
given. . *a* to tread upon serpents	10.19
by what *a* you do these things,	20.2
given him *a* to execute judgment,	Jn 5.27
has *a* from the chief priests	Acts 9.14
there is no *a* except from God,	Rom 13.1
a little too much of our *a*,	2Cor 10.8
and the *a* of his Christ have	Rev 12.10
the dragon gave. . great *a*.	13.2
be submissive to rulers and *a*,	Tit 3.1

AVENGE — D

that I may *a* on Jezebel the	2Ki 9.7
Jews were to be ready. . to *a*	Est 8.13
I will. . *a* myself on my foes.	Isa 1.24
I will *a* their blood, and I	Joel 3.21
never *a* yourselves, but leave	Rom 12.19
I swear I will be *a* upon you,	Judg 15.7
be *a* upon the Philistines	16.28
he has *a* on her the blood	Rev 19.2

AVENGER

refuge from the *a*, that	Num 35.12
the Lord is an *a* in all	1Thess 4.6

AVOID

path of the wicked,. . *A* it;	Prov 4.15
may *a* the snares of death.	14.27
A such godless chatter, for	2Tim 2.16
to *a* quarreling, to be gentle,	Tit 3.2

AWAIT — ING

from it we *a* a Savior,	Phil 3.20
a our blessed hope, the	Tit 2.13

AWAKE — S — N

A, my soul! A, O harp and	Ps 57.8
a, put on your strength, O	Isa 52.1
master finds a when he comes;	Lk 12.37
I go to a him out of sleep."	Jn 11.11
Blessed is he who is a,	Rev 16.15
are like a dream when one a,	Ps 73.20
nor a love until it please.	Sol 8.4

AWE

held in a above all gods.	1Chr 16.25
the world stand in a of him!	Ps 33.8
stands in a of thy words.	119.161
they were filled with a,	Mt 27.54

AXE — S

his a head fell into the water;	2Ki 6.5
Shall the a vaunt itself over	Isa 10.15
now the a is laid to the root	Mt 3.10
the a is laid to the root of	Lk 3.9
labor with saws and..a;	1Chr 20.3
hacked..wooden trellis with a.	Ps 74.5

AZAZEL

LORD and the other lot for A.	Lev 16.8

B

BAAL — S

"Will you contend for B?	Judg 6.31
served B, and worshiped him.	1Ki 16.31
host of heaven, and served B.	2Ki 17.16
the prophets prophesied by B,	Jer 2.8
and gold which they used for B.	Hos 2.8
served the B and..Ashtaroth.	Judg 2.13

BABE — S

the b leaped in her womb;	Lk 1.41
by the mouth of b and infants,	Ps 8.2
and b shall rule over them.	Isa 3.4
hidden..revealed them to b;	Mt 11.25
'Out of the mouth of b and	21.16
and revealed them to b; yea,	Lk 10.21
men of..flesh, as b in Christ.	1Cor 3.1

BABEL

its name was called B,	Gen 11.9

BABYLON

king..brought people from B,	2Ki 17.24
Judah was taken into..B	1Chr 9.1
By the waters of B,..wept,	Ps 137.1
Go forth from B, flee from	Isa 48.20
time of the deportation to B.	Mt 1.11
She who is at B, who is	1Pet 5.13
fallen is B the great, she	Rev 14.8

BABYLONIA

up from B to Jerusalem.	Ezra 1.11

BACK — S

cast..my sins behind thy b.	Isa 38.17
are these wounds on your b?'	Zech 13.6
make my enemies turn their b	Ps 18.40

BACKSLIDING — S

turned away in perpetual b?	Jer 8.5
b are many, we have sinned	14.7

BALAAM

sent messengers to B	Num 22.5
And B said to Balak, "Build	23.1
When B saw that it pleased	24.1
also slew B the son of Beor	31.8
what B the son of Beor answered	Mic 6.5
have followed the way of B,	2Pet 2.15
who hold the teaching of B,	Rev 2.14

BALANCE — S

A false b is an abomination	Prov 11.1
scales and the hills in a b?	Isa 40.12
rider had a b in his hand;	Rev 6.5
my calamity laid in the b!	Job 6.2
take b..and divide the hair.	Ezek 5.1
TEKEL, you..weighed in the b	Dan 5.27
in whose hands are false b,	Hos 12.7

BALDHEAD

saying, "Go up, you b! Go	2Ki 2.23

BANQUET — ING

a great b, and invited many;	Lk 14.16
He brought me to the b house,	Sol 2.4
queen,..came into the b hall;	Dan 5.10

BAPTISM

The b of John, whence was it?	Mt 21.25
b with which I am baptized?"	Mk 10.38
Was the b of John from heaven	11.30
preaching a b of repentance	Lk 3.3
I have a b to be baptized	12.50
Was the b of John from heaven	20.4
one Lord, one faith, one b,	Eph 4.5
you were buried with him in b,	Col 2.12
B, which corresponds to this,	1Pet 3.21

BAPTIZE — D — ING

"I b..with water for repentance,	Mt 3.11
"I b you with water; but he	Lk 3.16
"I b with water; but among you	Jn 1.26
Christ did not send me to b	1Cor 1.17
were b by him in the river	Mt 3.6
who believes and is b will	Mk 16.16n
justified God, having been b	Lk 7.29
shall be b with the..Spirit."	Acts 1.5
were b, both men and women.	8.12
the eunuch, and he b him.	8.38
Then he rose and was b,	9.18
she was b, with her household,	16.15
Rise and be b, and wash away	22.16
who have been b into Christ	Rom 6.3
you b in the name of Paul?	1Cor 1.13
fathers..were b into Moses	10.2
were all b into one body—	12.13
b on behalf of the dead?	15.29
For as many of you as were b	Gal 3.27
disciples of all nations, b	Mt 28.19
John also was b at Aenon	Jn 3.23
Jesus was making and b more	4.1

BAPTIZER

John the b appeared in the	Mk 1.4
"John the b..raised from..dead;	6.14

BARABBAS

for you?" And they said, "B."	Mt 27.21
there was a man called B.	Mk 15.7
release for them B instead.	15.11
released..B; and..scourged Jesus,	15.15
cried.."Not this man, but B!"	Jn 18.40

BAREFOOT

David..b and with his head	2Sam 15.30
Isaiah has walked naked and b	Isa 20.3

BAR-JONA

"Blessed are you, Simon B!	Mt 16.17

BARNABAS

Benevolent Acts 4.36–37; introduced Paul to the apostles, Acts 9.26–27; preached at Antioch, Acts 11.22–24; ministered with Paul at Antioch, Acts 11.25–26; took relief offerings to Judea, Acts 11.29–30; accompanied Paul on his first missionary journey,

BARNABAS (cont.)
Acts 13.1–14.28; attended the Council of Jerusalem, Acts 15.1–31; separated from Paul, Acts 15.36–41.

BARNS
then your *b* will be filled	Prov 3.10
sow nor reap nor gather into *b*,	Mt 6.26
my *b*, and build larger ones;	Lk 12.18

BARREN
Sarai was *b*; she had no child.	Gen 11.30
but Rachel was *b*.	29.31
Manoah; and his wife was *b*	Judg 13.2
He gives the *b* woman a home,	Ps 113.9
"Sing, O *b* one, who did not	Isa 54.1
had no child. . Elizabeth was *b*,	Lk 1.7
"Rejoice, O *b* one that dost	Gal 4.27

BARTHOLOMEW
Philip and *B*; Thomas and	Mt 10.3
and John, and Philip, and *B*,	Lk 6.14
and Thomas, *B* and Matthew,	Acts 1.13

BARUCH
the deed of purchase to *B*	Jer 32.12
and *B* wrote upon a scroll	36.4
B answered them, "He dictated	36.18
but *B*. . has set you against us,	43.3
Jeremiah the prophet spoke to *B*	45.1

BASKET — S
took. . a *b* made of bulrushes,	Ex 2.3
behold, a *b* of summer fruit.	Amos 8.1
wall, lowering him in a *b*.	Acts 9.25
but I was let down in a *b*	2Cor 11.33
two *b* of figs placed before	Jer 24.1
they took up twelve *b* full	Mt 14.20
they took up seven *b* full of	15.37
how many *b*. . of broken pieces	Mk 8.19

BATHE — D — ING
he shall *b* himself in water,	Deut 23.11
Then I *b* you with water and	Ezek 16.9
from the roof a woman *b*;	2Sam 11.2

BATHSHEBA
Taken by David, 2Sam 11.1–5; became the mother of Solomon, 2Sam 12.24; interceded for Solomon's succession on the throne, 1Ki 1.15–31; petitioned for Adonijah, 1Ki 2.12–25.

BATTLE
has come from the *b*; I fled	1Sam 4.16
"If thy people go out to *b*	1Ki 8.44
b is not yours but God's.	2Chr 20.15
who will get ready for *b*?	1Cor 14.8
to assemble them for *b* on	Rev 16.14

BEAR — S — ING (v)
greater than I can *b*.	Gen 4.13
then let me *b* the blame	43.9
then I shall *b* the blame	44.32
Aaron shall *b* their names	Ex 28.12
Aaron shall *b* the judgment	28.30
b iniquity. . with the sanctuary	Num 18.1
not an enemy. . then I could *b*	Ps 55.12
he shall *b* their iniquities.	Isa 53.11
LORD could no longer *b*. . evil	Jer 44.22
does not *b* his own cross	Lk 14.27
b it if a man makes slaves	2Cor 11.20
as a man *b* his son, in all	Deut 1.31
the Lord, who daily *b* us up;	Ps 68.19
went out, *b* his own cross,	Jn 19.17
be saved through *b* children,	1Tim 2.15

BEAR (n)
there came a lion, or a *b*,	1Sam 17.34
beast, a second one, like a *b*.	Dan 7.5

BEAST — S
"Whoever lies with a *b*	Ex 22.19
Then I saw another *b* which	Rev 13.11
b that you saw was, and is not,	17.8
creeping things and *b*	Gen 1.24
you may eat among all the *b*	Lev 11.2
wild *b* grow too numerous	Deut 7.22
the *b*. . at peace with you.	Job 5.23
ask the *b*, and they will teach	12.7
he is like the *b* that perish.	Ps 49.12
when all the *b*. . creep forth.	104.20
show them. . they are but *b*.	Ecc 3.18
dwelling shall be with the *b*	Dan 4.25
I fought with *b* at Ephesus?	1Cor 15.32

BEAUTIFUL
you are a woman *b* to behold;	Gen 12.11
and the woman was very *b*.	2Sam 11.2
the maiden was *b* and lovely,	Est 2.7
holy mountain, *b* in elevation,	Ps 48.2
He has made everything *b* in	Ecc 3.11
You are *b* as Tirzah, my love,	Sol 6.4
branch of the LORD shall be *b*	Isa 4.2
was given you, your *b* flock?	Jer 13.20
You grew exceedingly *b*, and	Ezek 16.13

BEAUTIFY
to *b* the house of the LORD	Ezra 7.27
In vain you *b* yourself	Jer 4.30

BEAUTY
to behold the *b* of the LORD,	Ps 27.4
the king will desire your *b*.	45.11
Do not desire her *b* in your	Prov 6.25
Charm is deceitful, . . *b* is vain,	31.30
said, 'I am perfect in *b*.'	Ezek 27.3
proud because of your *b*;	28.17

BED — S
When I say, 'My *b* will comfort	Job 7.13
the *b* is too short to stretch	Isa 28.20
"Rise, take up your *b* and go	Mt 9.6
with his *b* through the tiles	Lk 5.19
Woe to those. . upon *b* of ivory,	Amos 6.4

BEE — S
for the *b* which is in the land	Isa 7.18
Amorites. . chased you as *b* do	Deut 1.44
b in the body of the lion,	Judg 14.8

BEELZEBUL
"It is only by *B*, the prince	Mt 12.24
"He is possessed by *B*, and	Mk 3.22

BEER-SHEBA
in the wilderness of *B*.	Gen 21.14
they made a covenant at *B*.	21.32
went together to *B*;	22.19
came to *B*, and offered	46.1
to *B* knew that Samuel was	1Sam 3.20
number Israel, from *B* to	1Chr 21.2
not enter. . or cross over to *B*;	Amos 5.5

BEFITS
Rejoice. . Praise *b* the upright.	Ps 33.1
teach what *b* sound doctrine.	Tit 2.1

BEGGAR
Bartimaeus, a blind *b*,	Mk 10.46
who had seen him before as a *b*,	Jn 9.8

BEGINNING
In the *b* God created	Gen 1.1
for you the *b* of months;	Ex 12.2

BEGINNING (cont.)

fear of the LORD is the *b* of   Ps 111.10
fear of..LORD..*b* of knowledge; Prov 1.7
The *b* of wisdom..Get wisdom,   4.7
but the *b* of the sufferings.   Mt 24.8
The *b* of the gospel of Jesus   Mk 1.1
In the *b* was the Word, and   Jn 1.1

BEGUILED

"The serpent *b* me,   Gen 3.13

BEGUILING

no one..delude..with *b* speech Col 2.4
teaching and *b* my servants   Rev 2.20

BEHAVE — D — ING

know how one ought to *b* in 1Tim 3.15
we have *b* in the world, and 2Cor 1.12
and *b* like ordinary men?   1Cor 3.3
he is not *b* properly toward his   7.36

BEHAVIOR

changed his *b* before them, 1Sam 21.13
revile your good *b* in Christ 1Pet 3.16

BEHEADED

and had John *b* in the prison, Mt 14.10
"John, whom I *b*, has been Mk 6.16

BEHEMOTH

"Behold, *B*, which I made as Job 40.15

BEHOLD — ING

I..*b* thy face in righteousness Ps 17.15
Come, *b* the works of the LORD,   46.8
all the peoples *b* his glory.   97.6
pleasant for..eyes to *b*..sun. Ecc 11.7
cities of Judah, "*B* your God!"   40.9
where I am, to *b* my glory Jn 17.24
with unveiled face, *b* the glory 2Cor 3.18

BELIEVE — S — D

for he did not *b* them.   Gen 45.26
"that they may *b* that the LORD, Ex 4.5
"Because you did not *b* in me, Num 20.12
you did not *b* the LORD   Deut 1.32
you..did not *b* him or obey   9.23
b his prophets, and you will 2Chr 20.20
not *b* that he was listening Job 9.16
I *b*..I shall see the goodness Ps 27.13
for I *b* in thy commandments. 119.66
speaks graciously, *b*..not, Prov 26.25
If you will not *b*, surely you Isa 7.9
that you may know and *b* me   43.10
b them not, though they speak Jer 12.6
a work..that you would not *b* Hab 1.5
"Do you *b*..I am able to do Mt 9.28
'Why then did you not *b* him?' 21.25
come down..and we will *b* in him. 27.42
repent, and *b* in the gospel." Mk 1.15
said.."Do not fear, only *b*."   5.36
ask in prayer, *b* that you receive it, 11.24
there he is!' do not *b* it.   13.21
seen by her, they would not *b* 16.11n
because you did not *b* my words, Lk 1.20
no root, they *b* for a while   8.13
only *b*, and she shall be well." 8.50
'Why did you not *b* him?'   20.5
"If I tell you, you will not *b*; 22.67
to *b* all that the prophets   24.25
that all might *b* through him. Jn 1.7
he who does not *b* is condemned 3.18
we *b*, for we have heard..ourselves 4.42
If you *b* Moses, you would *b* me, 5.46
his brothers did not *b* in him.   7.5
"Do you *b* in the Son of man?" 9.35

but you do not *b*, because   10.26
even though you do not *b* me, 10.38
I was not there, so..you may *b*. 11.15
yet they did not *b* in him;   12.37
b in God, *b* also in me.   14.1
also pray..for those who *b* 17.20
truth—that you also may *b*. 19.35
hand in his side, I will not *b*." 20.25
have not seen and yet *b*."   20.29
Philip said, "If you *b* with Acts 8.37n
we *b* that we shall be saved 15.11
"*B* in the Lord Jesus, and 16.31
Agrippa, do you *b* the prophets? 26.27
faith in..Christ for all who *b*. Rom 3.22
and *b* in your heart that God 10.9
preach to save those who *b*. 1Cor 1.21
not only *b*..but also suffer Phil 1.29
would draw near to God must *b* Heb 11.6
The simple *b* everything, but Prov 14.15
who *b* will not be in haste.' Isa 28.16
All..possible to him who *b*." Mk 9.23
who *b* and is baptized will 16.16n
whoever *b*..may have eternal Jn 3.15
who hears my word and *b* him 5.24
one who *b* in him receives Acts 10.43
he who *b*..not..put to shame." Rom 9.33
"No one who *b* in him will be put 10.11
Love bears all things, *b* all 1Cor 13.7
who *b* that Jesus is the Christ 1Jn 5.1
He who *b* in the Son of God has 5.10
And he *b* the LORD;   Gen 15.6
And the people *b*; and when they Ex 4.31
they *b* in the LORD and   14.31
Then they *b* his words; they Ps 106.12
Who has *b* what we have heard? Isa 53.1
done for you as you have *b*." Mt 8.13
blessed is she who *b* that Lk 1.45
they *b* the scripture and the Jn 2.22
Samaritans from that city *b* 4.39
The man *b* the word..Jesus spoke 4.50
will live"; and he himself *b*, 4.53
we have *b*, and have come to know 6.69
Yet many of the people *b* in him; 7.31
Jews..had seen what he did, *b* 11.45
also went in, and he saw and *b*; 20.8
many who heard the word *b*; Acts 4.4
throughout all Joppa, and many *b* 9.42
great number that *b* turned 11.21
Then the proconsul *b*, when 13.12
that a great company *b*, both 14.1
Many of them therefore *b*, 17.12
and *b*, among them Dionysius 17.34
ruler of the synagogue, *b* 18.8
Abraham "*b* God, and it was Gal 3.6
so that those who have *b* in God Tit 3.8

BELIEVER — S

son of a Jewish woman..a *b*; Acts 16.1
more than ever *b* were added 5.14
word of God..at work in..*b*. 1Thess 2.13

BELLY

upon your *b* you shall go, Gen 3.14
out of..*b* of Sheol I cried, Jonah 2.2

BELONG — ED

for to thee *b* all the nations! Ps 82.8
b to..him who has been raised Rom 7.4
you live as if you still *b* to Col 2.20

BELOVED

"The *b* of the LORD,..dwells Deut 33.12
he was *b* by his God, and Neh 13.26
That thy *b* may be delivered, Ps 60.5

BELOVED (cont.)

he gives to his *b* in sleep. Ps 127.2
My *b* is to me a cluster of Sol 1.14
My *b* is mine and I am his, 2.16
What is your *b* more than another 5.9
I am my beloved's. . my *b* is mine; 6.3
coming up. . leaning upon her *b*? 8.5
Daniel, . . greatly *b*, give heed Dan 10.11
"This is my *b* Son, with whom Mt 3.17
"This is my *b* Son, with whom 17.5
"Thou art my *b* Son; with thee Mk 1.11
"This is my *b* Son; listen to him." 9.7
a *b* son; finally he sent him 12.6
"Thou art my *b* Son; with thee Lk 3.22
not *b* I will call 'my *b*.' " Rom 9.25
b for. . sake of. . forefathers. 11.28
Greet Ampliatus, my *b* in the 16.8
freely bestowed on us in the *B*. Eph 1.6
who benefit. . believers and *b*. 1Tim 6.2
"This is my *b* Son, with whom 2Pet 1.17
you, *b*, build yourselves up Jude 20

BELT — S

looses the *b* of the strong. Job 12.21
no bag, no money in their *b*; Mk 6.8

BENEFIT — S

I say this for your own *b*, 1Cor 7.35
and forget not all his *b*, Ps 103.2

BEN-HADAD I

King of Syria, 1Ki 15.18; made alliance with Asa, 1Ki 15.19; ravaged cities in northern Israel, 1Ki 15.20–21 (see also 2Chr 16.1–6).

BEN-HADAD II

King of Syria, 1Ki 20.1; besieged Samaria, 1Ki 20.1; defeated twice by Ahab, 1Ki 20.2–30; granted conditions of peace, 1Ki 20.31–34.

BEN-HADAD III

King of Syria, 2Ki 13.3,24; oppressed cities of Israel, 2Ki 13.3–13; defeated by Jehoahaz, king of Israel, 2Ki 13.22–25.

BENJAMIN (Son of Jacob)

*Born, Gen 35.16–18; brought to Egypt, Gen 43; accused of theft but interceded for by Judah, Gen 44; blessed by Jacob, Gen 49.27.
Tribe of Benjamin: blessed by Moses, Deut 33.12; allotted its territory, Josh 18.11–28; decimated almost to extinction, Judg 20; rebuilt through new wives and families, Judg 21; Saul, the first king of Israel, and Paul, the apostle, from this tribe, 1Sam 9.1; Phil 3.5.*

BEREAVE — D

b them till none is left. Hos 9.12
"You have *b* me of. . children: Gen 42.36
have *b* them, I have destroyed Jer 15.7

BESEECH

"Remember now, O Lord, I *b* 2Ki 20.3
"We *b* thee, O Lord, let us Jonah 1.14
We *b* you on behalf of Christ, 2Cor 5.20
Brethren, I *b* you, become as Gal 4.12

BESET

They *b* me with words of hate, Ps 109.3
Thou dost *b* me behind and 139.5

BESIDE

He leads me *b* still waters; Ps 23.2
they said, "He is *b* himself." Mk 3.21

BESIEGE — D

then you shall *b* it; Deut 20.12
b you in all your towns, 28.52
if their enemies *b* them 2Chr 6.28
a great king came. . and *b* it, Ecc 9.14
cucumber field, like a *b* city. Isa 1.8
city. . *b* till the eleventh year Jer 52.5

BESTIR

B thyself, and awake for my Ps 35.23
Let. . nations *b* themselves, Joel 3.12

BESTOWED

understand the gifts *b* on us 1Cor 2.12
grace which he freely *b* on us Eph 1.6

BETHANY

went. . to *B* and lodged there. Mt 21.17
at *B* in. . house of Simon the leper, 26.6
and *B*, at the mount. . Olivet, Lk 19.29
led them out as far as *B*, 24.50
a. . man was ill, Lazarus of *B*, Jn 11.1
Jesus came to *B*, where Lazarus 12.1

BETHEL

mountain on the east of *B*, Gen 12.8
I am the God of *B*, 31.13
and lay between *B* and Ai, Josh 8.9
circuit year by year to *B*, 1Sam 7.16
And he set one in *B*, and 1Ki 12.29
dwelt an old prophet in *B*. 13.11
The men of *B* and Ai, two Ezra 2.28
"Come to *B*, and transgress; Amos 4.4
Amaziah the priest of *B* sent 7.10
never again prophesy at *B*, 7.13

BETHLEHEM

way to Ephrath (that is, *B*), Gen 35.19
on until they came to *B*. Ruth 1.19
commanded, and came to *B*. 1Sam 16.4
his father's sheep at *B*. 17.15
water out of the well of *B* 2Sam 23.16
But you, O *B* Ephrathah, who Mic 5.2
Now when Jesus was born in *B* of Mt 2.1
you, O *B*, in the land of Judah, 2.6
city of David, . . called *B*, Lk 2.4
from David, and comes from *B*, Jn 7.42

BETH-SAIDA

woe to you, *B*! for if the Mt 11.21
disciples. . go before him. . to *B*, Mk 6.45
And they came to *B*. And some 8.22
withdrew. . to a city called *B*. Lk 9.10

BETRAY — ED — ING

sought. . opportunity to *b* him. Mt 26.16
he sought an opportunity to *b* Mk 14.11
"Truly. . one of you will *b* me, 14.18
how he might *b* him to them. Lk 22.4
he knew who was to *b* him; Jn 13.11
by whom the Son of man is *b*! Mt 26.24
Son of man is *b* into the hands 26.45
Judas Iscariot, who *b* him. Mk 3.19
the Son of man is *b* into 14.41
Judas, who *b* him, also knew Jn 18.2
when he was *b* took bread, 1Cor 11.23
"I have sinned in *b* innocent Mt 27.4

BETROTH — ED

I will *b* you to me for ever; Hos 2.19
seduces a virgin who is not *b*, Ex 22.16
b a wife and has not taken Deut 20.7
Mary had been *b* to Joseph, Mt 1.18
to a virgin *b* to a man whose Lk 1.27
to be enrolled with Mary, his *b*, 2.5
I *b* you to Christ to present 2Cor 11.2

BETTER
am I *b* off than if I..sinned?　Job 35.3
nothing *b*..than to be happy　Ecc 3.12
but in humility count others *b*　Phil 2.3
the covenant he mediates is *b*,　Heb 8.6
with *b* sacrifices than these.　9.23

BEWAILING
all were weeping and *b* her;　Lk 8.52

BEWARE
My son, *b* of anything beyond　Ecc 12.12
"*B* of false prophets, who come　Mt 7.15
b of the leaven of..Pharisees　16.6
"Take heed, *b* of the leaven of　Mk 8.15
"*B* of the scribes, who like　12.38

BID
do you want us to *b* fire come　Lk 9.54
I now *b* you take heart;　Acts 27.22

BIND — S
B them upon your heart　Prov 6.21
I will *b* up the crippled,　Ezek 34.16
whatever you *b* on earth shall　Mt 16.19
whatever you *b* on earth　18.18
He *b* up the waters in..clouds,　Job 26.8
He heals..*b* up their wounds.　Ps 147.3

BIRD — S — 'S
how can you say.."Flee like a *b*　Ps 11.1
I am like a lonely *b* on the　102.7
escaped as a *b* from the snare　124.7
a net..in the sight of any *b*;　Prov 1.17
like a speckled *b* of prey?　Jer 12.9
Does a *b* fall in a snare　Amos 3.5
let *b* fly above the earth　Gen 1.20
Like *b* hovering, so the LORD　Isa 31.5
and *b* of the air have nests;　Mt 8.20
b of the air come and make nests　13.32
so..*b* of the air can make nests　Mk 4.32
and *b* of the air have nests;　Lk 9.58
the *b* of the air made nests in　13.19
you..come upon a *b* nest,　Deut 22.6

BIRTH
forgot..God who gave you *b*.　Deut 32.18
Your origin and your *b* are of　Ezek 16.3
the *b* of Jesus..took place in　Mt 1.18

BIRTHRIGHT
"First sell me your *b*."　Gen 25.31
He took away my *b*;　27.36
according to his *b*　43.33

BISHOP — S
aspires to the office of *b*,　1Tim 3.1
a *b*, as God's steward, must　Tit 1.7
at Philippi, with the *b* and　Phil 1.1

BIT
will put my *b* in your mouth,　2Ki 19.28
and my *b* in your mouth,　Isa 37.29

BITTER
made life *b* for Isaac　Gen 26.35
is your doom, and it is *b*;　Jer 4.18
it will be *b* to your stomach,　Rev 10.9

BITTERNESS
shall have the water of *b*　Num 5.18
speak in the *b* of my soul.　Job 10.1
Another dies in *b* of soul,　21.25
The heart knows its own *b*,　Prov 14.10

BLADE
first the *b*, then the ear,　Mk 4.28

BLAME
then let me bear the *b*　Gen 43.9
then I shall bear the *b*　44.32
that no one should *b* us　2Cor 8.20

BLAMELESS
b in his generation; Noah　Gen 6.9
walk before me, and be *b*.　17.1
rest of you shall be *b*."　44.10
be *b* before the LORD　Deut 18.13
the heart of Asa was *b* all　2Chr 15.17
whose heart is *b* toward him.　16.9
Job..was *b* and upright,　Job 1.1
God will not reject a *b* man,　8.20
though I am *b*, he would prove　9.20
With the *b*..thou dost show..*b*;　Ps 18.25
Mark the *b* man, and behold the　37.37
Blessed are those whose way is *b*,　119.1
May my heart be *b* in thy　119.80
You were *b* in your ways　Ezek 28.15
in..ordinances of the Lord *b*.　Lk 1.6
righteousness under..law *b*.　Phil 3.6

BLASPHEME — S — D — ING
and tried to make them *b*;　Acts 26.11
whoever *b* against the..Spirit　Mk 3.29
Israelite woman's son *b*　Lev 24.11
again your fathers *b* me,　Ezek 20.27
"The name of God is *b* among　Rom 2.24
I formerly *b* and persecuted　1Tim 1.13
to themselves, "This man is *b*."　Mt 9.3
b his name and his dwelling,　Rev 13.6

BLASPHEMOUS
b words against Moses and　Acts 6.11
and a *b* name upon its heads.　Rev 13.1

BLASPHEMY — IES
sin and *b* will be forgiven　Mt 12.31
"He has uttered *b*. Why do we　26.65
You have heard his *b*. What　Mk 14.64
for no good work but for *b*;　Jn 10.33
"Who is this that speaks *b*?　Lk 5.21

BLEMISH
None..who has a *b* may　Lev 21.17
in which there is no *b*,　Num 19.2
lambs a year old without *b*,　28.3
there was no *b* in him.　2Sam 14.25
youths without *b*, handsome　Dan 1.4

BLESS — ES — ED — ING (v)
and I will *b* you,　Gen 12.2
nations..shall *b* themselves by him?　18.18
I will indeed *b* you,　22.17
all..nations of the earth *b*　22.18
I may *b* you before I die."　27.4
not..go, unless you *b* me."　32.26
by God Almighty who will *b* you　49.25
The LORD *b* you and keep you: Num 6.24
will love you, *b* you,　Deut 7.13
stand upon Mount Gerizim to *b*　27.12
willingly, *b* the LORD!　Judg 5.2
answered, "The LORD *b* you."　Ruth 2.4
thou wouldst *b* me and enlarge 1Chr 4.10
please thee to *b* the house　17.27
"Stand up and *b* the LORD　Neh 9.5
LORD *b* his people with peace!　Ps 29.11
I will *b* the LORD at all times;　34.1
B our God, O peoples, let the　66.8
B the LORD, O my soul; and　103.1
From this day on I will *b* you." Hag 2.19
B those who persecute you;　Rom 12.14
When reviled, we *b*; when　1Cor 4.12
"Surely I will *b* you and　Heb 6.14

BLESS — ES — ED — ING (v) (cont.)
he who *b* himself in the land Isa 65.16
And God *b* them, saying, Gen 1.22
God *b* Noah and his sons, 9.1
LORD had *b* Abraham in all things. 24.1
said, "*B* be the LORD, 24.27
b be every one who blesses you!" 27.29
LORD *b* the Egyptian's house 39.5
and Jacob *b* Pharaoh. 47.7
the people, for they are *b*." Num 22.12
b, and I cannot revoke it. 23.20
B be every one who blesses 24.9
Moses the man of God *b* the Deut 33.1
since. .the LORD has *b* me?" Josh 17.14
tent-dwelling women most *b*. Judg 5.24
boy grew, and the LORD *b* him. 13.24
B be the man who took notice Ruth 2.19
the LORD *b* Obededom and all 2Sam 6.11
"*B* be the LORD who has given 1Ki 8.56
b the household of Obededom 1Chr 13.14
B be the LORD, the God of 16.36
for there they *b* the LORD; 2Chr 20.26
b be the name of the LORD." Job 1.21
LORD *b* the latter days of Job 42.12
B is the man who walks not in Ps 1.1
B is he whose transgression is 32.1
B is he who considers the poor! 41.1
B is the man who fears. .LORD Prov 28.14
children rise up and call her *b*; 31.28
b are all. .who wait for him. Isa 30.18
people whom the LORD has *b*. 61.9
"*B* is the man who trusts in Jer 17.7
Daniel *b* the God of heaven. Dan 2.19
we deem the arrogant *b*; Mal 3.15
"*B* are the poor in spirit, Mt 5.3
b are your eyes, for they see, 13.16
he. .*b*, and broke. .the loaves 14.19
B is he who comes in the name 21.9
B is that servant whom his 24.46
and *b* them, laying his hands Mk 10.16
"Hosanna! *B* is he who comes 11.9
"*B* are you among women, and *b* Lk 1.42
"*B* be the Lord God of Israel, 1.68
him up in his arms and *b* God 2.28
"*B* are you poor, for yours is 6.20
"*B* are the eyes which see 10.23
"*B* is the womb that bore you, 11.27
awake. .*b* are those servants! 12.38
'*B* is he who comes in the name 13.35
"*B* is the King who comes in 19.38
lifting up his hands. .*b* them. 24.50
b are you if you do them. Jn 13.17
B are those who have not seen 20.29
more *b* to give than to Acts 20.35
God who is over all be *b* for Rom 9.5
shall all the nations be *b*." Gal 3.8
who has *b* us in Christ with Eph 1.3
if you suffer. .you will be *b*. 1Pet 3.14
"Write this: *B* are the dead Rev 14.13
B is he who keeps the words 22.7
B are those who wash their robes, 22.14
loosed, and he spoke, *b* God. Lk 1.64
continually in the temple *b* 24.53
same mouth come *b* and cursing. Jas 3.10

BLESSED (n)
'Come, O *b* of my Father, inherit Mt 25.34
Christ, the Son of the *B*?" Mk 14.61

BLESSING — S (n)
I will command my *b* upon you Lev 25.21
before you this day a *b* Deut 11.26
turned the curse into a *b* 23.5

words of the law, the *b* Josh 8.34
b of the LORD makes rich, Prov 10.22
By the *b* of the upright a 11.11
b in the midst of the earth, Isa 19.24
they shall be showers of *b*. Ezek 34.26
a *b* may rest on your house. 44.30
pour down. .an overflowing *b*. Mal 3.10
fulness of the *b* of Christ. Rom 15.29
The cup of *b* which we bless, 1Cor 10.16
all these *b* shall come Deut 28.2
dost meet him with goodly *b*; Ps 21.3
holy and sure *b* of David.' Acts 13.34

BLIND — S — ED (v)
bribe to *b* my eyes with it? 1Sam 12.3
for a bribe *b* the eyes Deut 16.19
god of this world has *b* the 2Cor 4.4
the darkness has *b* his eyes. 1Jn 2.11

BLIND (n)
as the *b* grope in darkness, Deut 28.29
lame and the *b*, who are hated 2Sam 5.8
I was eyes to the *b*, and Job 29.15
LORD opens the eyes of the *b*. Ps 146.8
the eyes of the *b* shall see. Isa 29.18
eyes of the *b* shall be opened, 35.5
I will lead the *b* in a way 42.16
grope for. .wall like the *b*, 59.10
the *b* receive their sight Mt 11.5
the lame, the maimed, the *b*, 15.30
recovering of sight to the *b*, Lk 4.18
invite the poor,. .the *b*, 14.13
demon open the eyes of the *b*?" Jn 10.21
a guide to the *b*, a light Rom 2.19

BLIND (adj)
to open the eyes that are *b*, Isa 42.7
or *b* as the servant of the LORD? 42.19
people who are *b*, yet have eyes, 43.8
His watchmen are *b*, they 56.10
wandered, *b*, through. .streets, Lam 4.14
offer *b* animals in sacrifice, Mal 1.8
two *b* men followed him, crying Mt 9.27
b and dumb demoniac. .brought 12.22
Let them alone; they are *b* 15.14
two *b* men. .by the roadside, 20.30
"Woe to you, *b* guides, who 23.16
people brought to him a *b* man, Mk 8.22
And the *b* man said to him, 10.51
"Can a *b* man lead a *b* man? Lk 6.39
on many. .*b* he bestowed sight. 7.21
b man. .sitting by the roadside 18.35
he saw a man *b* from his birth. Jn 9.1
this. .our son. .was born *b*; 9.20
though I was *b*, now I see." 9.25
those who see may become *b*." 9.39
lacks these things is *b* and 2Pet 1.9
pitiable, poor, *b*, and naked. Rev 3.17

BLINDNESS
struck with *b* the men Gen 19.11
"Strike this people. .with *b*." 2Ki 6.18
strike every horse. .with *b*. Zech 12.4

BLOOD
your brother's *b* is crying Gen 4.10
not eat flesh with. .its *b*. 9.4
Whoever sheds the *b* of man, 9.6
a reckoning for his *b*." 42.22
Nile. .shall be turned to *b*, Ex 7.17
took the *b* of the covenant 24.8
part of the *b* of the bull 29.12
some of the *b* of the bull, Lev 16.14
the *b* that makes atonement, 17.11
you shall not eat the *b*; Deut 12.16

BLOOD (cont.)

people ate them with the *b.*	1Sam 14.32
turned their waters into *b,*	Ps 105.29
his *b* I..require at your hand.	Ezek 3.18
shedding..*b* of the prophets.'	Mt 23.30
from the *b* of innocent Abel to	23.35
this is my *b* of the covenant,	26.28
"I am innocent of this man's *b*;	27.24
a flow of *b* for twelve years,	Mk 5.25
"This is my *b* of the covenant,	14.24
from the *b* of Abel to the *b* of	Lk 11.51
the new covenant in my *b*	22.20n
Son of man and drink his *b,*	Jn 6.53
was called..Field of *B.*)	Acts 1.19
"Your *b* be upon your heads!	18.6
we are now justified by his *b,*	Rom 5.9
flesh and *b* cannot inherit	1Cor 15.50
have redemption through his *b,*	Eph 1.7
brought near in the *b* of Christ.	2.13
and not without taking *b*	Heb 9.7
but his own *b,* thus securing	9.12
enter..sanctuary by..*b* of Jesus	10.19
profaned the *b* of the covenant	10.29
with..precious *b* of Christ,	1Pet 1.19
the *b* of Jesus his Son cleanses	1Jn 1.7
but with the water and the *b.*	5.6
white in the *b* of the Lamb.	Rev 7.14
waters to turn them into *b,*	11.6
conquered..by the *b* of the Lamb	12.11
avenged on her the *b* of his	19.2

BLOODSHED

for justice, but behold, *b*;	Isa 5.7
keeps back his sword from *b.*	Jer 48.10

BLOT — S — TED

if not, *b* me,..out of thy book	Ex 32.32
and *b* out their name from	Deut 9.14
b out the remembrance	25.19
LORD would *b* out his name	29.20
he would *b* out the name of	2Ki 14.27
mercy *b* out my transgressions.	Ps 51.1
b out their sin from..sight.	Jer 18.23
who *b* out your transgressions	Isa 43.25
not..sin of..mother be *b* out!	Ps 109.14
that your sins may be *b* out,	Acts 3.19

BLOW

When you *b* an alarm,	Num 10.5
south wind! *B* upon my garden,	Sol 4.16

BOAST — S — ED (v)

we *b* of the name of the LORD	Ps 20.7
not rejoice over me, who *b*	38.16
Do not *b* about tomorrow,	Prov 27.1
and *b* of your relation to God	Rom 2.17
You who *b* in the law, do you	2.23
do not *b* over the branches.	11.18
So let no one *b* of men.	1Cor 3.21
I also dare to *b* of that.	2Cor 11.21
works, lest any man should *b.*	Eph 2.9
Let the lowly brother *b* in	Jas 1.9
the wicked *b* of the desires	Ps 10.3
buyer..goes away, then he *b.*	Prov 20.14
b of a gift he does not give.	25.14
"Let him who *b, b* of..Lord."	1Cor 1.31
"Let him who *b, b* of..Lord."	2Cor 10.17
In God we have *b* continually,	Ps 44.8

BOAST — ING (n)

My soul makes its *b* in..LORD;	Ps 34.2
this *b* of mine shall not	2Cor 11.10
Then what becomes of our *b*?	Rom 3.27
b before Titus..proved true.	2Cor 7.14
proof..of your love and of our *b*	8.24

BOAT

left the *b* and their father,	Mt 4.22
told his disciples to have a *b*	Mk 3.9
into a *b* with his disciples,	Lk 8.22
immediately the *b* was at..land	Jn 6.21

BODILY

Spirit descended..in *b* form,	Lk 3.22
it was because of a *b* ailment	Gal 4.13
fulness of deity dwells *b,*	Col 2.9

BODY — IES

took the *b* of Saul and the	1Sam 31.12
kill..*b* but cannot kill..soul;	Mt 10.28
Wherever the *b* is, there the eagles	24.28
"Take, eat; this is my *b.*"	26.26
asked for the *b* of Jesus.	27.58
they came and took his *b,*	Mk 6.29
said, "Take; this is my *b.*"	14.22
asked for the *b* of Jesus.	15.43
them, saying, "This is my *b.*	Lk 22.19
spoke of the temple of his *b.*	Jn 2.21
in one *b* we have many members,	Rom 12.4
b is not meant for immorality,	1Cor 6.13
your *b* is a temple of the..Spirit	6.19
For just as the *b* is one	12.12
God has so adjusted the *b,*	12.24
Now you are the *b* of Christ	12.27
With what..*b* do they come?"	15.35
on my *b* the marks of Jesus.	Gal 6.17
the church, which is his *b,*	Eph 1.23
There is one *b* and one Spirit,	4.4
the whole *b,* joined and knit	4.16
we are members of his *b.*	5.30
change our lowly *b* to be like	Phil 3.21
He is the head of the *b,*	Col 1.18
Head, from whom the whole *b,*	2.19
a *b* hast thou prepared for me;	Heb 10.5
the putting off of my *b.*.soon,	2Pet 1.14
disputed about the *b* of Moses,	Jude 9
nothing left..but our *b* and	Gen 47.18
these were all dead *b.*	Isa 37.36
your *b* are members of Christ?	1Cor 6.15
dead *b* will lie in the street	Rev 11.8

BOG

He drew me..out of the miry *b,*	Ps 40.2

BOIL — ED (v)

not *b* a kid in its mother's	Deut 14.21
we *b* my son, and ate him.	2Ki 6.29

BOILS (n)

dust..become *b* breaking out	Ex 9.9
smite you with..*b* of Egypt,	Deut 28.27

BOLD — NESS

wicked man puts on a *b* face,	Prov 21.29
such a hope, we are very *b,*	2Cor 3.12
are much more *b* to speak	Phil 1.14
saw the *b* of Peter and John,	Acts 4.13
speak thy word with all *b,*	4.29
Lord, in whom we have *b* and	Eph 3.12

BOND — S

the Spirit in the *b* of peace.	Eph 4.3
not despise his own..in *b.*	Ps 69.33
loose the *b* of wickedness,	Isa 58.6

BONDAGE

out of the house of *b.*	Ex 20.2
out of the house of *b.*	Deut 5.6
were subject to lifelong *b.*	Heb 2.15

BONE — S

nor break a *b* of it;	Num 9.12
we are your *b* and flesh.	1Chr 11.1

BONE — S (cont.)

"Not a *b* of him..be broken."   Jn 19.36
you shall carry up my *b*   Gen 50.25
Moses took the *b* of Joseph   Ex 13.19
The *b* of Joseph which the   Josh 24.32
man touched the *b* of Elisha,   2Ki 13.21
I can count all my *b*—they   Ps 22.17
He keeps all his *b*; not one   34.20
the *b* of the kings of Judah,   Jer 8.1
b came together, *b* to its *b*.   Ezek 37.7

BOOK — S

took the *b* of the covenant,   Ex 24.7
the *B* of the Wars of the Lord   Num 21.14
write for himself in a *b*   Deut 17.18
"Take this *b* of the law,   31.26
This *b* of the law shall not   Josh 1.8
the *b* of the law of Moses,   8.31
found the *b* of the law in the   2Ki 22.8
words of the *b* of the covenant   23.2
brought the *b* to the king,   2Chr 34.16
I found the *b* of the genealogy   Neh 7.5
bring the *b* of the law of Moses   8.1
were inscribed in a *b*!   Job 19.23
in thy *b* were written,..days   Ps 139.16
words of a *b* that is sealed.   Isa 29.11
inscribe it in a *b*, that it   30.8
read from the *b* of the LORD: 34.16
everything written in this *b*,   Jer 25.13
Jeremiah wrote in a *b* all   51.60
inscribed in the *b* of truth: Dan 10.21
whose name..written in the *b*.   12.1
a *b* of remembrance was written   Mal 3.16
The *b* of the genealogy of Jesus   Mt 1.1
The *b* of the prophet Isaiah.   Lk 4.17
signs..not written in this *b*;   Jn 20.30
names are in the *b* of life.   Phil 4.3
sprinkled both the *b* itself   Heb 9.19
"Write what you see in a *b*   Rev 1.11
not blot his name out of the *b*   3.5
in the *b* of life of the Lamb   13.8
Also another *b* was opened,   20.12
in the Lamb's *b* of life.   21.27
Of making many *b*..is no end,   Ecc 12.12
in judgment,..*b* were opened.   Dan 7.10
in the *b* the number of years   9.2
could not contain the *b* that   Jn 21.25
brought their *b*..and burned   Acts 19.19
also the *b*, and above all   2Tim 4.13

BOOTH — S

I will raise..the *b* of David   Amos 9.11
made a *b* for himself there.   Jonah 4.5
Jacob..made *b* for his cattle   Gen 33.17
the feast of *b* to the LORD.   Lev 23.34
dwell in *b* for seven days;   23.42
feast of *b* seven days,   Deut 16.13
Israel should dwell in *b*   Neh 8.14
I will make three *b* here, one   Mt 17.4
let us make three *b*, one for you   Mk 9.5
"Master,..let us make three *b*,   Lk 9.33

BOOTY

b remaining of the spoil   Num 31.32
men of war had taken *b*,   31.53

BORE

many *b* false witness against   Mk 14.56
God also *b* witness by signs   Heb 2.4
He himself *b* our sins in   1Pet 2.24

BORN

be *b* to the house of David,   1Ki 13.2
Man..*b* of woman..of few days,   Job 14.1
who is *b* of woman be clean?   25.4

time to be *b*,..a time to die;   Ecc 3.2
For to us a child is *b*, to us   Isa 9.6
before..*b* I consecrated you;   Jer 1.5
Mary, of whom Jesus was *b*,   Mt 1.16
when Jesus was *b* in Bethlehem   2.1
among those *b* of women..no one   11.11
child..*b* will be called holy,   Lk 1.35
who were *b*, not of blood nor   Jn 1.13
unless one is *b* anew, he cannot   3.3
"You were *b* in utter sin,   9.34
for joy that a child is *b*   16.21
You have been *b* anew, not of   1Pet 1.23
No one *b* of God commits sin;   1Jn 3.9
one *b* of God does not sin,   5.18

BORROW — S

"Go outside, *b* vessels of all   2Ki 4.3
do not refuse him who would *b*   Mt 5.42
The wicked *b*, and cannot pay   Ps 37.21

BORROWER

b is..slave of the lender.   Prov 22.7
the lender, so with the *b*;   Isa 24.2

BOSOM

Can a man carry fire in his *b*   Prov 6.27
he will carry them in his *b*,   Isa 40.11
Son..in the *b* of the Father,   Jn 1.18

BOTHER — S

'Do not *b* me; the door is now   Lk 11.7
because this widow *b* me, I   18.5

BOTTLE

gathered..waters of the sea in..*b*;   Ps 3.7
put thou my tears in thy *b*!   56.8

BOUGH — S

Joseph is a fruitful *b*,   Gen 49.22
its *b* will be broken in   Ezek 31.12

BOUGHT

have *b* from the hand of Naomi   Ruth 4.9
I have *b* to be my wife,   4.10
have *b* back our Jewish brethren   Neh 5.8
I *b* her for fifteen shekels   Hos 3.2
you were *b* with a price.   1Cor 6.20
You were *b* with a price;   7.23
denying the Master who *b* them,   2Pet 2.1

BOUND (v)

his life is *b* up in the lad's   Gen 44.30
Are you *b* to a wife? Do not   1Cor 7.27
is *b* to keep the whole law.   Gal 5.3

BOUNDS (n)

he fixed the *b* of the peoples   Deut 32.8
fixed all the *b* of the earth.   Ps 74.17

BOUNTY

crownest the year with thy *b*;   Ps 65.11
LORD for all his *b* to me?   116.12

BOW — ED — ING (v)

father's sons shall *b*   Gen 49.8
not *b* down to their gods,   Ex 23.24
not *b* down to them or serve   Deut 5.9
not *b* down to a foreign god.   Ps 81.9
All the nations..shall..*b* down   86.9
b..to the host of the heavens;   Zeph 1.5
of Jesus every knee should *b*,   Phil 2.10
and *b* down before your feet,   Rev 3.9
maids..their children..*b* down;   Gen 33.6
Joseph's brothers came,..*b*   42.6
And they *b* their heads   43.28
that have not *b* to Baal,   1Ki 19.18
who is *b* down shall speedily   Isa 51.14
he *b* his head and gave up his   Jn 19.30
fell at his feet, *b* to the ground;   2Ki 4.37

BOW (n)

I set my *b* in the cloud,	Gen 9.13
an expert with the *b*.	21.20
For not in my *b* do I trust,	Ps 44.6
he breaks the *b*, and shatters	46.9
I will break the *b* of Israel	Hos 1.5

BOWL — S

new *b*, and put salt in it."	2Ki 2.20
seven *b* of the wrath of God."	Rev 16.1

BOY — S

Josiah..was yet a *b*, he began	2Chr 34.3
I will make *b* their princes,	Isa 3.4
city..of *b* and girls playing	Zech 8.5

BRANCH — ES

In that day the *b* of the LORD	Isa 4.2
a *b* shall grow..of his roots.	11.1
raise..for David a righteous *B*,	Jer 23.5
cause a righteous *B* to spring	33.15
I will bring my servant the *B*.	Zech 3.8
Every *b* of mine that bears no	Jn 15.2
and others spread leafy *b*	Mk 11.8
they took *b* of palm trees	Jn 12.13
do not boast over the *b*.	Rom 11.18

BREACH

"For every *b* of trust,	Ex 22.9
there was no *b* left in it	Neh 6.1
Moses,..stood in the *b*	Ps 106.23
stand in the *b* before me	Ezek 22.30

BREAD

I will rain *b* from heaven	Ex 16.4
man does not live by *b* alone,	Deut 8.3
but the *b* of the Presence,	1Sam 21.6
they eat the *b* of wickedness	Prov 4.17
blessed, for he shares his *b*	22.9
Cast your *b* upon the waters,	Ecc 11.1
taking away..whole stay of *b*,	Isa 3.1
loaf of *b* was given him daily	Jer 37.21
they may lack *b* and water,	Ezek 4.17
stones to become loaves of *b*."	Mt 4.3
he..ate the *b* of the Presence,	12.4
not fair to take..children's *b*	15.26
"Where are we to get *b* enough	15.33
Jesus took *b*, and blessed,	26.26
not right to take..children's *b*	Mk 7.27
can one feed these men with *b*	8.4
he took *b*, and blessed, and	14.22
command this stone to become *b*."	Lk 4.3
he took *b*, and when he had	22.19
he took the *b* and blessed,	24.30
not Moses who gave you the *b*	Jn 6.32
"I am the *b* of life; he who	6.35
Jesus came and took the *b*	21.13
when we..gathered..to break *b*,	Acts 20.7
The *b* which we break, is	1Cor 10.16
he was betrayed took *b*,	11.23

BREAK — ING

nor *b* a bone of it;	Num 9.12
shall *b* down their altars,	Deut 7.5
shall we *b* thy commandments	Ezra 9.14
So will I *b* this people and	Jer 19.11
If you can *b* my covenant	33.20
they did not *b* his legs.	Jn 19.33
have..code..but *b* the law.	Rom 2.27
weeping and *b* my heart?	Acts 21.13

BREASTPLATE

put on righteousness as a *b*,	Isa 59.17
put on the *b* of righteousness,	Eph 6.14
put on the *b* of faith and	1Thess 5.8

BREASTS

Your two *b* are like two fawns,	Sol 4.5
Beat upon your *b* for the	Isa 32.12

BREATH

the *b* of the Almighty, that	Job 32.8
LORD, at the blast of the *b* of	Ps 18.15
made,..by the *b* of his mouth.	33.6
Men of low estate are but a *b*,	62.9
thoughts of man,..are but a *b*.	94.11
Man is like a *b*, his days	144.4
b departs he returns to his earth;	146.4
They all have the same *b*,	Ecc 3.19
the *b* of his lips..shall slay	Isa 11.4
fades, when the *b* of the LORD	40.7
bones:..I..cause *b* to enter	Ezek 37.5
prophesy,..and say to the *b*,	37.9
b to the image of the beast	Rev 13.15

BREATHE — S — D — ING

and they *b* out violence.	Ps 27.12
Let everything that *b* praise	150.6
and *b* into his nostrils..life;	Gen 2.7
Saul, still *b* threats and	Acts 9.1

BRETHREN

my *b* who went up with me	Josh 14.8
to battle against our *b*	Judg 20.23
let us send abroad to our *b*	1Chr 13.2
or fight against your *b*.	2Chr 11.4
but you even sell your *b*	Neh 5.8
My *b* are treacherous as a	Job 6.15
put my *b* far from me,	19.13
will tell of thy name to my *b*;	Ps 22.22
become a stranger to my *b*,	69.8
one teacher, and you are all *b*.	Mt 23.8
these my *b*, you did to me.'	25.40
tell my *b* to go to Galilee,	28.10
The saying spread..among the *b*	Jn 21.23
you are *b*, why do you wrong	Acts 7.26
when..*b* knew..they sent him	9.30
send relief to..*b* in Judea;	11.29
gave great joy to all the *b*.	15.3
needs were supplied by the *b*	2Cor 11.9
not ashamed to call them *b*,	Heb 2.11
life, because we love the *b*.	1Jn 3.14

BRIBE — S

trustworthy and who hate a *b*;	Ex 18.21
a *b* blinds the officials,	23.8
you shall not take a *b*,	Deut 16.19
whose hand have I taken a *b*	1Sam 12.3
A *b* is like a magic stone	Prov 17.8
who take a *b*, and turn aside	Amos 5.12
give judgment for a *b*,	Mic 3.11
prince and..judge ask for a *b*,	7.3
took *b* and perverted justice.	1Sam 8.3
right hands are full of *b*.	Ps 26.10
he who hates *b* will live.	Prov 15.27

BRIBERY

fire consumes the tents of *b*.	Job 15.34

BRICK — S

a *b*..portray upon it a city,	Ezek 4.1
"Come, let us make *b*,	Gen 11.3
no longer give..straw to make *b*,	Ex 5.7
"The *b* have fallen, but we	Isa 9.10

BRIDE

You..ravished my heart,..my *b*,	Sol 4.9
a *b* adorns..with her jewels.	Isa 61.10
forget..a *b* her attire?	Jer 2.32
make to cease..voice of the *b*;	7.34
present you as a pure *b* to her	2Cor 11.2

BRIDE (cont.)

prepared as a *b* adorned for — Rev 21.2
I will show you the *B*, the wife — 21.9

BRIDEGROOM

"You are a *b* of blood," — Ex 4.26
which comes forth like a *b* — Ps 19.5
mourn as long as the *b* is with — Mt 9.15
wedding guests fast while the *b* — Mk 2.19
fast while the *b* is with them? — Lk 5.34
the friend of the *b*, who stands — Jn 3.29

BRIDLE (v)

I will *b* my mouth, so long as — Ps 39.1
and does not *b* his tongue — Jas 1.26
he is..able to *b* the whole body — 3.2

BRIDLE (n)

must be curbed with bit and *b*, — Ps 32.9

BRIGHT — ER

I am..the *b* morning star." — Rev 22.16
your life will be *b* then — Job 11.17
from heaven, *b* than the sun, — Acts 26.13

BRIMSTONE

the LORD reigned on Sodom..*b* — Gen 19.24
fire and *b* rained from heaven — Lk 17.29
tormented with fire and *b* — Rev 14.10
lake of fire..burns with *b*. — 19.20

BRING — S

I..will *b* you back — Gen 28.15
b your father, and come. — 45.19
to *b*..his soul from the Pit, — Job 33.30
b your sons in their bosom, — Isa 49.22
anointed me to *b* good tidings — 61.1
b them together into the midst — Jer 21.4
"Did you *b* to me sacrifices — Amos 5.25
B..tithes into the storehouse, — Mal 3.10
not..come to *b* peace on earth; — Mt 10.34
I *b* you good news of a great — Lk 2.10
when the LORD *b* you into — Ex 13.11
God *b* him out of Egypt; — Num 24.8
feet of him who *b* good tidings, — Isa 52.7
him who *b* good tidings, — Nah 1.15
and some one *b* him back, — Jas 5.19

BROKE — N

at ease, and he *b* me asunder; — Job 16.12
he has *b* my covenant." — Gen 17.14
my plans are *b* off, the — Job 17.11
bones; not one of them is *b*. — Ps 34.20
He has *b* my strength in — 102.23
act, for thy law has been *b*. — 119.126
a *b* spirit who can bear? — Prov 18.14
b my covenant, and transgressed — Hos 8.1
(and scripture cannot be *b*), — Jn 10.35

BROKENHEARTED

The LORD is near to the *b*, — Ps 34.18
sent me to bind up the *b*, — Isa 61.1

BRONZE

instruments of *b* and iron. — Gen 4.22
Moses made a *b* serpent, — Num 21.9
you..a fortified wall of *b*; — Jer 15.20
its belly and thighs of *b*, — Dan 2.32

BROOD

as a hen gathers her *b* under — Mt 23.37
"You *b* of vipers! Who warned you — Lk 3.7

BROOKS

I will make them walk by *b* — Jer 31.9
the water *b* are dried up, — Joel 1.20

BROTHER — S — 'S

Cain rose up against his *b* — Gen 4.8

given your *b* a thousand pieces — 20.16
he is our *b*, our own flesh." — 37.27
"I am your *b*, Joseph, — 45.4
"If your *b* becomes poor, — Lev 25.25
"Thus says your *b* Israel: — Num 20.14
between a man and his *b* — Deut 1.16
his neighbor, his *b*, because — 15.2
Edomite, for he is your *b*; — 23.7
her husband's *b* shall go in — 25.5
saying, "Alas, my *b*!" — 1Ki 13.30
still live? He is my *b*." — 20.32
a *b* is born for adversity. — Prov 17.17
A *b* helped is like a strong city — 18.19
who sticks closer than a *b*. — 18.24
near than a *b* who is far — 27.10
and put no trust in any *b*; — Jer 9.4
say,..every one to his *b*, — 23.35
devise evil against his *b* — Zech 7.10
"Is not Esau Jacob's *b*?" — Mal 1.2
every one..angry with his *b* — Mt 5.22
B will deliver up *b* to death, — 10.21
my *b*, and sister, and mother." — 12.50
"If your *b* sins against you, — 18.15
how often shall my *b* sin — 18.21
does the will of God is my *b*, — Mk 3.35
raise up children for his *b*. — 12.19
And *b* will deliver up *b* to death, — 13.12
if your *b* sins, rebuke him, — Lk 17.3
hands on him he said, "*B* Saul, — Acts 9.17
Why..pass judgment on your *b*? — Rom 14.10
that makes your *b* stumble. — 14.21
who bears the name of *b* if — 1Cor 5.11
b goes to law against *b*, — 6.6
sending the *b* who is famous — 2Cor 8.18
except James the Lord's *b*. — Gal 1.19
wrong his *b* in this matter, — 1Thess 4.6
enemy, but warn him as a *b*. — 2Thess 3.15
a beloved *b*, especially to me — Philem 16
he who hates his *b* is in the — 1Jn 2.11
sees his *b* in need, yet closes — 3.17
"I love God," and hates his *b*, — 4.20
his *b* were jealous of him, — Gen 37.11
Judah, your *b* shall praise you; — 49.8
at Ophrah, and slew his *b* — Judg 9.5
went and greeted his *b*. — 1Sam 17.22
Judah became strong among..*b* — 1Chr 5.2
pledges of your *b* for nothing, — Job 22.6
man who sows discord among *b*. — Prov 6.19
his mother and his *b* stood — Mt 12.46
are not his *b* James and Joseph — 13.55
were indignant at the two *b* — 20.24
mother and..*b* are..outside, — Lk 8.20
his *b* did not believe in him. — Jn 7.5
made himself known to his *b*, — Acts 7.13
until your *b* anger turns — Gen 27.45
kingdom has..become my *b*, — 1Ki 2.15
speck that is in your *b* eye, — Lk 6.41

BROUGHT

Moses *b* their case before — Num 27.5
Andrew..*b* him to Jesus..Simon — Jn 1.42

BRUISE — D

he shall *b* your head, — Gen 3.15
a *b* reed he will not break, — Isa 42.3

BUCKET

nations are..drop from a *b*, — Isa 40.15

BUILD — S — ING (v)

to *b* the house of the LORD. — 1Ki 6.1
He shall *b* a house for me, — 1Chr 17.12
Arise and *b* the sanctuary — 22.19
who is able to *b* him a house, — 2Chr 2.6

BUILD — S — ING (v) (cont.)

"Let us rise up and *b*." Neh 2.18
shall *b* up the ancient ruins, Isa 61.4
B houses and live in them; Jer 29.5
bring wood and *b* the house, Hag 1.8
"They may *b*,..I will tear down, Mal 1.4
on this rock I..*b* my church, Mt 16.18
began to *b*, and was not able Lk 14.30
which is able to *b* you up Acts 20.32
but not all things *b* up. 1Cor 10.23
b one another up, just 1Thess 5.11
beloved, *b* yourselves up on Jude 20
Unless the LORD *b* the house, Ps 127.1
Wisdom *b* her house, but folly Prov 14.1
Woe..who *b* a town with blood, Hab 2.12
like a man *b* a house, who dug Lk 6.48
excel in *b* up the church. 1Cor 14.12
the Lord gave for *b* you up 2Cor 10.8

BUILDERS

stone which the *b* rejected Ps 118.22
stone which the *b* rejected Lk 20.17

BUILDING — S (n)

you are God's field, God's *b*. 1Cor 3.9
stones and what wonderful *b*!" Mk 13.1

BUILT

So we *b* the wall; and all Neh 4.6
Wisdom has *b* her house, she Prov 9.1
By wisdom a house is *b*, and 24.3
b houses and planted vineyards Ecc 2.4
great Babylon, which I have *b* Dan 4.30
b upon the foundation of the Eph 2.20

BULRUSHES

she took..a basket made of *b*, Ex 2.3

BULWARK — S

thou hast founded a *b* because Ps 8.2
salvation as walls and *b*. Isa 26.1
her *b* have fallen, her walls Jer 50.15

BURDEN — ED — ING (v)

I myself did not *b* you? 2Cor 12.13
we might not *b* any of you. 2Thess 3.8
you have *b* me with your sins, Isa 43.24
not..others..eased and you *b*, 2Cor 8.13
I..will refrain from *b* you 11.9

BURDEN — S (n)

thou dost lay the *b* of all Num 11.11
the *b* is too heavy for me. 11.14
they weigh like a *b* too heavy Ps 38.4
Cast your *b* on the LORD, and 55.22
the yoke of his *b* and the staff Isa 9.4
in that day his *b* will depart 10.27
not bear a *b* on the sabbath Jer 17.21
'What is the *b* of the LORD?' 23.33
the *b* is..man's own word, 23.36
yoke is easy,..my *b* is light." Mt 11.30
equal to us who have..the *b* 20.12
no greater *b* than these Acts15.28
not lay upon you any other *b*; Rev 2.24
and looked on their *b*; Ex 2.11
They bind heavy *b*, hard to bear, Mt 23.4
load men with *b* hard to bear, Lk 11.46
Bear one another's *b*, Gal 6.2

BURN — ED — ING

urged..king not to *b*..scroll, Jer 36.25
"Did not our hearts *b* within Lk 24.32
the mountain *b* with fire Deut 4.11
and he *b* Hazor with fire. Josh 11.11
He even *b* his son as an 2Ki 16.3
mused, the fire *b*; then I spoke Ps 39.3

Chaldeans *b* the king's house Jer 39.8
he *b* the house of the LORD, 52.13
he has *b* like a flaming fire Lam 2.3
Gather the weeds..to be *b*, Mt 13.30
If any man's work is *b* up, 1Cor 3.15
deliver my body to be *b*, 13.3
books together and *b* them Acts 19.19
a *b* fire shut up in my bones, Jer 20.9
my loins are filled with *b*, Ps 38.7

BURNT OFFERING — S

where is the lamb for a *b*..?" Gen 22.7
it is a *b*..to the LORD; Ex 29.18
"If his offering is a *b*..from Lev 1.3
is on the fire; it is a *b*.., 1.17
This is the law of the *b*... 6.9
but if you make ready a *b*.., Judg 13.16
offered..whole *b*..to the LORD; 1Sam 7.9
myself, and offered the *b*..." 13.12
him for a *b*..upon the wall. 2Ki 3.27
B..and sin offering thou hast Ps 40.6
were I to give a *b*.., thou 51.16
the prince provides..a *b*..or Ezek 46.12
continual *b*..was taken away Dan 8.11
Noah..offered *b*..on the altar. Gen 8.20
LORD as great delight in *b*.. 1Sam 15.22
I will not offer *b*..to 2Sam 24.24
to offer *b*..to the LORD upon 1Chr 16.40
and presented *b*..and peace 21.26
offered the daily *b*..by number Ezra 3.4
your *b*..are continually before Ps 50.8
I have had enough..*b*..of rams Isa 1.11
"Add..*b*..to your sacrifices, Jer 7.21
Shall I come..with *b*.., with Mic 6.6

BURY — ING — IED

Do not *b* me in Egypt, Gen 47.29
"Lord, let me first go and *b* Mt 8.21
let me first go..*b* my father." Lk 9.59
she..anointed my body..for *b*. Mk 14.8
Abraham *b* Sarah his wife Gen 23.19
Esau and Jacob *b* him. 35.29
and he *b* him in the valley Deut 34.6
We were *b* therefore with him Rom 6.4
he was *b*,..he was raised 1Cor 15.4
you were *b* with him in baptism, Col 2.12

BUSH

out of the midst of a *b*; Ex 3.2
in the passage about the *b*, Lk 20.37
in a flame of fire in a *b*. Acts 7.30

BUSHEL

lamp and put it under a *b*, Mt 5.15
"Is a lamp..put under a *b*, Mk 4.21
a lamp..under a *b*, but Lk 11.33

BUSY

as your servant was *b* here 1Ki 20.40
to *b* myself with wicked deeds Ps 141.4

BUSYBODIES

mere *b*, not doing any work. 2Thess 3.11
but gossips and *b*, saying 1Tim 5.13

BUTLER

b told his dream to Joseph, Gen 40.9

BUY

When you *b* a Hebrew slave, Ex 21.2
but no man will *b* you." Deut 28.68
"No, but I will *b* it of you 2Sam 24.24
"No, but I will *b* it for 1Chr 21.24

BYWORD

a *b*, among all the peoples Deut 28.37
a proverb and a *b* among all 2Chr 7.20

BYWORD (cont.)

made me a *b* of the peoples,   Job 17.6
made us a *b* among the nations,   Ps 44.14

C

CAESAR — 'S

"Render therefore to *C* the   Mt 22.21
a king sets himself against *C*."   Jn 19.12
standing before *C* tribunal,   Acts 25.10
the saints..of *C* household.   Phil 4.22

CAESAREA

into..district of *C* Philippi,   Mt 16.13
to the villages of *C* Philippi;   Mk 8.27
preached..till he came to *C*.   Acts 8.40
At *C* there was..Cornelius,   10.1
three men arrived..from *C*.   11.11
When he had landed at *C*,   18.22
came to *C* and delivered the   23.33
Paul was being kept at *C*,   25.4

CAIAPHAS

High priest, Mt 26.3, 57; Lk 3.2; Jn 18.13; "prophesied that Jesus should die," Jn 11.49–53; 18.14; took part in the trial of Jesus, Mt 26.62–66 (Mk 14.60–64; Jn 18.19–24,28); present at examination of Peter and John, Acts 4.6–21.

CAIN

Eve..conceived and bore *C*,   Gen 4.1
C brought..the LORD an offering   4.3
C rose up against his brother   4.8
C went away from..the LORD,   4.16
Abel, for *C* slew him."   4.25
more acceptable..than *C*,   Heb 11.4
like *C* who was of the evil one   1Jn 3.12
they walk in the way of *C*,   Jude 11

CAKE — S

"Let them take a *c* of figs,   Isa 38.21
Ephraim is a *c* not turned.   Hos 7.8
knead it, and make *c*."   Gen 18.6

CALAMITY

Cannot my taste discern *c*?   Job 6.30
They came upon me in..my *c*;   Ps 18.18
I also will laugh at your *c*;   Prov 1.26
c of Moab is near at hand   Jer 48.16
the LORD has kept ready the *c*   Dan 9.14
gloated..in the day of his *c*;   Obad 1.13

CALEB

Sent with the spies, Num 13.1–6; exhorted the people, Num 13.30; 14.6–10; was promised entrance into Canaan, Num 14.22–38 (32.10–12; Deut 1.34–36); Num 26.65; received Hebron as an inheritance, Josh 14.6–15; 15.13–19; Judg 1.20.

CALF — VES

took a *c*, tender and good,   Gen 18.7
and made a molten *c*;   Ex 32.4
there came out this *c*."   32.24
They made a *c* in Horeb and   Ps 106.19
bring the fatted *c*..kill it.   Lk 15.23
they made a *c* in those days,   Acts 7.41
and made two *c* of gold.   1Ki 12.28
Sacrifice..Men kiss *c*!   Hos 13.2

CALL — S — ED — ING (v)

c upon the name of the LORD.   Gen 4.26
Then *c*, and I will answer;   Job 13.22
Thou wouldest *c*, and I would   14.15
bread, and do not *c* upon God?   Ps 53.4
But I *c* upon God; and the LORD   55.16
and we will *c* on thy name!   80.18

answer me..in the day..I *c*!   102.2
give thanks..*c* on his name,   105.1
c on him as long as I live.   116.2
the LORD is near to all who *c*   145.18
Does not wisdom *c*, does not   Prov 8.1
and he shall *c* on my name;   Isa 41.25
I *c* you by..name, I surname   45.4
c upon him while he is near;   55.6
Before they *c* I will answer,   65.24
I thought you would *c* me, My   Jer 3.19
C to me and I will answer you,   33.3
a fast; *c* a solemn assembly;   Joel 2.15
all who *c* upon the name of   2.32
bestows riches upon all who *c*   Rom 10.12
how are men to *c* upon him   10.14
c upon the Lord from a pure   2Tim 2.22
He *c* to the heavens above and   Ps 50.4
When he *c* to me, I will answer   91.15
no one that *c* upon thy name,   Isa 64.7
he *c* together his friends   Lk 15.6
where he *c* the Lord the God   20.37
he *c* his own sheep by name   Jn 10.3
whoever *c* on..name of the Lord Acts 2.21
Abram..*c* on..name of the   Gen 12.8
Abram *c* on..name of the LORD   13.4
Abraham *c* the name of..place   22.14
God *c* to him out of the bush,   Ex 3.4
LORD *c* Moses to the top   19.20
Then Samson *c* to the LORD   Judg 16.28
LORD *c*, "Samuel! Samuel!"   1Sam 3.4
c and you refused to listen,   Prov 1.24
I *c* him, but he gave no answer.   Sol 5.6
c from its farthest corners,   Isa 41.9
I have *c* you in righteousness,   42.6
The LORD *c* me from the womb,   49.1
c..they have not answered."   Jer 35.17
son; and he *c* his name Jesus.   Mt 1.25
"Out of Egypt have I *c* my son."   2.15
And he *c*..his twelve disciples   10.1
went up into the hills, and *c*   Mk 3.13
And he *c* to him the twelve,   6.7
be *c* the Son of the Most High;   Lk 1.32
he *c* the twelve together and   9.1
first time *c* Christians.   Acts 11.26
he *c* together the..leaders   28.17
who are *c* to belong to Jesus   Rom 1.6
whom he predestined he also *c*;   8.30
who are *c*, both Jews and   1Cor 1.24
For God has *c* us to peace.   7.15
quickly deserting him who *c* you   Gal 1.6
For you were *c* to freedom,   5.13
he is *c* by God, just as Aaron   Heb 5.4
Abraham obeyed when he was *c*   11.8
he was *c* the friend of God.   Jas 2.23
To those who are *c*, beloved in   Jude 1
"Take heart; rise, he is *c*   Mk 10.49
"Behold, he is *c* Elijah."   15.35

CALL (n)

the *c* of God are irrevocable.   Rom 11.29
consider your *c*, brethren;   1Cor 1.26
confirm your *c* and election,   2Pet 1.10

CALM

sea; and there was a great *c*.   Mt 8.26
and there was a great *c*.   Mk 4.39
ceased, and there was a *c*.   Lk 8.24

CAME

king *c* back to the Jordan;   2Sam 19.15
these presidents and satraps *c*   Dan 6.6
he desired; and they *c* to him.   Mk 3.13
Son of man..*c* not to be served   10.45
Lord *c* with his holy myriads,   Jude 14

CAMEL — S — 'S
easier for a *c* to go through Mt 19.24
out a gnat and swallowing a *c*! 23.24
easier for a *c* to go through Mk 10.25
easier for a *c* to go through Lk 18.25
took ten of his master's *c* Gen 24.10
John wore a garment of *c* hair, Mt 3.4

CAMP
When the *c* is to set out, Aaron Num 4.5
put out of the *c* every leper, 5.2

CANA
a marriage at *C* in Galilee, Jn 2.1
came again to *C* in Galilee, 4.46
Nathanael of *C* in Galilee, 21.2

CANAAN — ITE
Ham, the father of *C*, saw Gen 9.22
"Cursed be *C*; a slave 9.25
to go into the land of *C*; 11.31
to go to the land of *C*. 12.5
famine. .in the land of *C*. 42.5
give them the land of *C*, Ex 6.4
view the land of *C*, which Deut 32.49
sacrificed to the idols of *C*; Ps 106.38
a *C* woman from that region Mt 15.22

CAPERNAUM
he went and dwelt in *C* by the Mt 4.13
As he entered *C*,. .centurion came 8.5
you *C*, will you be exalted 11.23
they came to *C*, the collectors 17.24
he returned to *C* after some days, Mk 2.1
of the people he entered *C*. Lk 7.1
you *C*, will you be exalted 10.15
at *C* there was an official Jn 4.46
synagogue, as he taught at *C*. 6.59

CAPTIVE — S
kinsmen had been taken *c*, Gen 14.14
loose. .bonds. .O *c* daughter of Isa 52.2
LORD's flock has been taken *c*. Jer 13.17
shall carry them *c* to Babylon, 20.4
carried away *c* of the Jews 52.30
be led *c* among all nations; Lk 21.24
making me *c* to the law of sin Rom 7.23
take every thought *c* to obey 2Cor 10.5
If any one is to be taken *c*, Rev 13.10
among the *c* a beautiful Deut 21.11
mount, leading *c* in thy train, Ps 68.18
Assyria lead. .the Egyptians as Isa 20.4
on high he led a host of *c*, Eph 4.8

CAPTIVITY
who came up out of the *c* Ezra 2.1
their idols. .go into *c*. Isa 46.2
those who are for *c*, to *c*." ' Jer 15.2
your lovers shall go into *c*; 22.22
Israel went into *c* for their Ezek 39.23

CAPTORS
our *c* required of us songs, Ps 137.3
will take captive. .their *c*, Isa 14.2

CARE — S — ST — D (v)
the son of man that thou dost *c* Ps 8.4
shepherds over them who will *c* Jer 23.4
do you not *c* if we perish?" Mk 4.38
land. .LORD your God *c* for; Deut 11.12
no refuge. .no man *c* for me. Ps 142.4
Zion, for whom no one *c*!' Jer 30.17
son of man, that thou *c* for him? Heb 2.6
he *c* for him, he kept him Deut 32.10

CARE — S (n)
to an inn, and took *c* of him. Lk 10.34

take *c* how he builds upon it. 1Cor 3.10
members may have the same *c* 12.25
puts the same earnest *c* for 2Cor 8.16
c of the world, and. .delight Mk 4.19
choked by the *c* and riches Lk 8.14
drunkenness and *c* of this life, 21.34

CAREFUL
You shall be *c* to do Deut 5.32
if you will be *c* to do 11.22
"If you are not *c* to do 28.58
Jehu was not *c* to walk in 2Ki 10.31

CARELESS
a fool. .restraint and is *c*. Prov 14.16
account for every *c* word Mt 12.36

CARMEL
king of Jokneam in *C*, one; Josh 12.22
"Saul came to *C*, and. .set 1Sam 15.12
"Go up to *C*, and go to Nabal, 25.5
Israel to me at Mount *C*, 1Ki 18.19
Your head crowns you like *C*, Sol 7.5
the majesty of *C* and Sharon. Isa 35.2

CARNAL
but I am *c*, sold under sin. Rom 7.14

CARPENTER — 'S
The *c* stretches a line, he Isa 44.13
Is not this the *c*, the son of Mk 6.3
Is not this the *c* son? Is not Mt 13.55

CARRY — ING — IED
you shall *c* up my bones Gen 50.25
when he, dies he will *c* nothing Ps 49.17
take nothing. .he may *c* away Ecc 5.15
to gray hairs I will *c* you. Isa 46.4
seize. .*c* them to Babylon. Jer 20.5
Simon. .to *c* his cross. Mk 15.21
to *c* out his purpose by being Rev 17.17
always *c* in the body the 2Cor 4.10
He *c* away all Jerusalem, and 2Ki 24.14
also *c* part of the vessels 2Chr 36.7
he lifted them up and *c* them Isa 63.9
and was *c* up into heaven Lk 24.51*n*

CASE
Moses brought their *c* before Num 27.5
"If any *c* arises requiring Deut 17.8
I have prepared my *c*; I know Job 13.18
I would lay my *c* before him 23.4
He who states his *c* first Prov 18.17
Argue your *c* with. .neighbor 25.9
Set forth your *c*, says. .LORD; Isa 41.21
Festus laid Paul's *c* before Acts 25.14

CAST — S — ING
"*C* out this slave woman Gen 21.10
I will *c* off the remnant 2Ki 21.14
Why are you *c* down, O my soul, Ps 42.5
Why are you *c* down, O my soul, 43.5
C your burden on the LORD, 55.22
wicked are *c* down to ruin. Prov 21.12
C your bread upon the waters, Ecc 11.1
I will *c* you out of my sight, Jer 7.15
have authority to *c* out demons: Mk 3.15
"Why could we not *c* it out?" 9.28
they *c* him out of the vineyard Lk 20.15
teach us?" And they *c* him out. Jn 9.34
"*C* the net on the right side 21.6
by the prince of demons he *c* Mk 3.22
"He *c* out demons by Beelzebul, Lk 11.15
we saw a man *c* out demons in 9.49

CATCH — ES — ING
They set a trap; they *c* men. Jer 5.26

CATCH — ES — ING (cont.)

"He c the wise in their	1Cor 3.19
henceforth you will be c men."	Lk 5.10

CATTLE

c according to their kinds,	Gen 1.25
Why are we counted as c?	Job 18.3

CAUGHT

c up to the third heaven—	2Cor 12.2
be c up together with them	1Thess 4.17

CAUSE

to God would I commit my c;	Job 5.8
without c they hid their net	Ps 35.7
those who hate me without c;	69.4
Plead my c and redeem me;	119.154
maintains. .c of the afflicted,	140.12
plead their c against you.	Prov 23.11
pleads the c of his people:	Isa 51.22
judge not with justice the c	Jer 5.28
'They hated me without a c.'	Jn 15.25

CAVE — S

Lot. .dwelt in a c with his	Gen 19.30
buried Sarah his wife in the c	23.19
buried him in the c of Mach-pelah	,25.9
with my fathers in the c	49.29
buried. .in the c. .Mach-pelah,	50.13
escaped to the c of Adullam;	1Sam 22.1
hid them by fifties in a c,	1Ki 18.4
he came to a c, and lodged	19.9
people hid themselves in c	1Sam 13.6
men shall enter. .c of. .rocks	Isa 2.19

CEASE — S — D — ING

"Do not c to cry to the LORD	1Sam 7.8
force and power made them c.	Ezra 4.23
the wicked c from troubling,	Job 3.17
He makes wars c to the end	Ps 46.9
quarreling and abuse will c.	Prov 22.10
c to do evil, learn. .good;	Isa 1.16
sacrifice and offering to c;	Dan 9.27
and night they never c to sing,	Rev 4.8
The. .love of the LORD never c,	Lam 3.22
the sea c from its raging.	Jonah 1.15
boat with them and the wind c.	Mk 6.51
whoever. .suffered. .c from sin,	1Pet 4.1
sin. .by c to pray for you;	1Sam 12.23

CEDAR — S

the beams of our house are c,	Sol 1.17
liken you to a c in Lebanon,	Ezek 31.3
devour the c of Lebanon.'	Judg 9.15
voice of the LORD breaks. .c,	Ps 29.5
against all the c of Lebanon,	Isa 2.13
we will put c in their place."	9.10

CENSUS

a c of all the congregation	Num 26.2
Judas. .arose in. .days of the c	Acts 5.37

CENTURION

he entered Capernaum, a c came	Mt 8.5
When the c. .saw the earthquake	27.54
when the c, who stood facing	Mk 15.39
a c had a slave who was dear	Lk 7.2
when the c saw what had taken	23.47

CEPHAS

that he appeared to C, then	1Cor 15.5

CEREAL OFFERING

"When any one brings a c. .as an	Lev 2.1
"And this is the law of the c. . .	6.14

CHAFF

like c that the storm carries	Job 21.18
wicked. .like c which the wind	Ps 1.4
them be like c before the wind,	35.5
like c on the mountains	Isa 17.13
the ruthless like passing c.	29.5
conceive c,. .bring forth stubble;	33.11
shall make the hills like c;	41.15
like the c of the. .threshing	Dan 2.35
like the c that swirls from	Hos 13.3
the c he will burn with. .fire."	Mt 3.12
the c he will burn with. .fire."	Lk 3.17

CHAIN — S

no one could bind him. .with a c;	Mt 5.3
I am bound with this c."	Acts 28.20
I am—except for these c."	26.29
he was not ashamed of my c,	2Tim 1.16

CHANGE — ST — D

purify yourselves, and c	Gen 35.2
his own hurt and does not c;	Ps 15.4
Can the Ethiopian c his skin	Jer 13.23
I will c their glory into shame.	Hos 4.7
"For I the LORD do not c;	Mal 3.6
c our lowly body to be like	Phil 3.21
"The Lord. .will not c his mind,	Heb 7.21
Thou c them like raiment,	Ps 102.26
you. .c my wages ten times.	Gen 31.41
which had been c to a day	Est 9.1
my people have c their glory	Jer 2.11
his mind be c from a man's,	Dan 4.16
but we shall all be c,	1Cor 15.51
being c into his likeness	2Cor 3.18

CHANNELS

He cuts out c in the rocks,	Job 28.10
the c of the sea were seen,	Ps 18.15

CHARACTER

endurance produces c, and c	Rom 5.4
unchangeable c of his purpose,	Heb 6.17

CHARGE — D (v)

But c Joshua, and encourage	Deut 3.28
c certain persons not to teach	1Tim 1.3
c them not to be haughty,	6.17
Isaac called Jacob and. .c him	Gen 28.1
he c Solomon his son, saying,	1Ki 2.1
he has c me to build. .a house	Ezra 1.2
he sternly c him, and sent him	Mk 1.43
he strictly c them that no one	5.43
he c them to tell no one what	9.9
he c them to tell no one what	Lk 8.56
strictly c you not to teach	Acts 5.28
for I have already c that all	Rom 3.9

CHARGE — S (n)

will give his angels c of you	Ps 91.11
will give his angels c of you,'	Mt 4.6
over his head they put the c	27.37
puts his servants in c, each	Mk 13.34
will give his angels c of you,	Lk 4.10
brought no c in his case of	Acts 25.18
any c against God's elect?	Rom 8.33
To the married I give c,	1Cor 7.10
I brought c against the nobles	Neh 5.7
against him many serious c	Acts 25.7
not to indicate the c	25.27

CHARIOT — S

a c of fire and horses of	2Ki 2.11
horses, upon thy c of victory?	Hab 3.8
Canaanites. .have c of iron,	Josh 17.16
and c of fire round. .Elisha.	2Ki 6.17
Some boast of c, and some of	Ps 20.7
trust. .c because they are many	Isa 31.1
As with the rumbling of c,	Joel 2.5

CHARIOT — S (cont.)
The *c* rage in the streets,   Nah 2.4
four *c* came out from between   Zech 6.1

CHARMER — S
there is no advantage in a *c.*   Ecc 10.11
it does not hear..voice of *c*   Ps 58.5

CHASE — D
you shall *c* your enemies,   Lev 26.7
Amorites..*c* you as bees do   Deut 1.44
therefore I *c* him from me.   Neh 13.28

CHASTE
your reverant and *c* behavior.   1Pet 3.2
with women, for they are *c*;   Rev 14.4

CHASTEN — S — ED (v)
anger, nor *c* me in thy wrath.   Ps 6.1
anger, nor *c* me in thy wrath!   38.1
When thou dost *c* man with   39.11
Blessed..whom thou dost *c*,   94.12
will *c* you in just measure,   Jer 30.11
I will *c* you in just measure,   46.28
whom I love, I reprove and *c*;   Rev 3.19
He who *c* the nations, does he   Ps 94.10
'Thou hast *c* me, and I was *c*,   Jer 31.18
we are *c* so that we may not   1Cor 11.32

CHASTENING (n)
despise not the *c* of the   Job 5.17
prayer when thy *c* was upon   Isa 26.16

CHASTISE — D
I will *c* you again sevenfold   Lev 26.18
and *c* you myself sevenfold   26.28
c them for their wicked deeds.   Hos 7.12
wayward people to *c* them;   10.10
therefore *c* him and release   Lk 23.16
My father *c* you with whips,   1Ki 12.11

CHASTISEMENT
upon him was the *c* that made   Isa 53.5
LORD..established them for *c*.   Hab 1.12

CHED-OR-LAOMER
the days of..*C* king of Elam,   Gen 14.1

CHEEK — S
struck Micaiah on the *c*,   1Ki 22.24
struck Micaiah on the *c*,   2Chr 18.23
give his *c* to the smiter,   Lam 3.30
strikes you on the right *c*,   Mt 5.39
Your *c*..comely with ornaments,   Sol 1.10
my *c* to those who pulled out   Isa 50.6

CHEER
I will..be of good *c*,'   Job 9.27
be of good *c*, I have overcome   Jn 16.33

CHEERFUL — NESS
A glad heart makes a *c*   Prov 15.13
A *c* heart is a good medicine,   17.22
for God loves a *c* giver.   2Cor 9.7
does acts of mercy, with *c*.   Rom 12.8

CHERISHED
If I had *c* iniquity in my   Ps 66.18
you *c* perpetual enmity,   Ezek 35.5

CHERUB
He rode on a *c*, and flew;   2Sam 22.11
With an anointed guardian *c*   Ezek 28.14

CHERUBIM
east..he placed the *c*,   Gen 3.24
you shall make two *c* of gold;   Ex 25.18
with *c* skilfully worked   26.1
he made two *c* of olivewood,   1Ki 6.23
art enthroned above the *c*,   Isa 37.16
glory..had gone up from the *c*   Ezek 9.3

c were standing on the south   10.3
above it were the *c* of glory   Heb 9.5

CHEW — S
does not *c*..cud is unclean   Lev 11.26
c the cud, among the animals,   Deut 14.6

CHILD — HOOD — LESS
and hurt a woman with *c*,   Ex 21.22
Naomi took the *c* and laid   Ruth 4.16
I am but a little *c*; I do not   1Ki 3.7
like the flesh of a little *c*,   2Ki 5.14
a *c* quieted at its mother's   Ps 131.2
a *c* makes himself known by   Prov 20.11
Train up a *c* in the way he   22.6
Folly..in the heart of a *c*,   22.15
a *c* left to himself brings   29.15
For to us a *c* is born, to us   Isa 9.6
a little *c* shall lead them.   11.6
c..die a hundred years old,   65.20
Israel was a *c*, I loved him,   Hos 11.1
with *c* of the Holy Spirit;   Mt 1.18
and search diligently for the *c*,   2.8
And calling to him a *c*, he put   18.2
alas for those who are with *c*   24.19
he took a *c*, and put him in   Mk 9.36
death, and the father his *c*,   13.12
"What then will this *c* be?"   Lk 1.66
you, *c*, will be called..prophet   1.76
the *c* grew and became strong   1.80
the *c* grew and became strong,   2.40
called, saying, "*C*, arise."   8.54
he took a *c* and put him by   9.47
I was a *c*, I spoke like a *c*,   1Cor 13.11
Timothy, my true *c* in..faith: 1Tim 1.2
To Timothy, my beloved *c*:   2Tim 1.2
who lives on milk..is a *c*.   Heb 5.13
who believes..is a *c* of God,   1Jn 5.1
she was with *c* and she cried   Rev 12.2
that he might devour her *c*   12.4
how from *c* you have been   2Tim 3.15
give me, for I continue *c*,   Gen 15.2

CHILDREN — 'S
he may charge his *c*   Gen 18.19
c..God has graciously given   33.5
when your *c* say to you,   Ex 12.26
iniquity of fathers upon *c*,   Num 14.18
your *c*, who this day have   Deut 1.39
they may teach their *c* so.'   4.10
with your *c* after you,   4.40
teach..diligently to your *c*,   6.7
not speaking to your *c*   11.2
with your *c* after you,   12.25
command them to your *c*,   32.46
you or your *c*, and do not keep   1Ki 9.6
c..death for the fathers;   2Ki 14.6
or the *c* be put to death for   2Chr 25.4
If your *c* have sinned against   Job 8.4
If his *c* forsake my law and   Ps 89.30
and his righteousness to..*c*,   103.17
your *c*..like olive shoots   128.3
Her *c*..call her blessed;   Prov 31.28
the *c* whom the LORD has given   Isa 8.18
c born in..your bereavement   49.20
c in sacrifice to..idols,   Ezek 23.39
Tell your *c* of it, and let   Joel 1.3
hearts of fathers to their *c*   Mal 4.6
sent and killed all the male *c*   Mt 2.16
able..to raise up *c* to Abraham.   3.9
give good gifts to your *c*,   7.11
Then *c* were brought to him   19.13
"Let the *c* come to me, and   19.14
c crying out in the temple,   21.15

CHILDREN — 'S (cont.)
said.."Let the c first be fed,	Mk 7.27
"Let the c come to me, do not	10.14
hearts of..fathers to the c,	Lk 1.17
from these stones to raise up c	3.8
like c sitting in the market	7.32
"Let the c come to me, and	18.16
gave power to become c of God;	Jn 1.12
"If you were Abraham's c,	8.39
Little c, yet a little while	13.33
promise is to you and..your c	Acts 2.39
witness..that we are c of God,	Rom 8.16
c of the promise are reckoned	9.8
your c would be unclean,	1Cor 7.14
do not be c in your thinking;	14.20
for c ought not to lay up	2Cor 12.14
like Isaac, are c of promise.	Gal 4.28
we were by nature c of wrath,	Eph 2.3
that we may no longer be c,	4.14
C, obey your parents in the Lord,	6.1
c of God without blemish	Phil 2.15
C, obey your parents in the	Col 3.20
As obedient c, do not be	1Pet 1.14
C, it is the last hour; and	1Jn 2.18
we should be called c of God;	3.1
your c following the truth,	2Jn 4
May you see your c children!	Ps 128.6
good man leaves..to his c	Prov 13.22
the c teeth are set on edge.'	Jer 31.29
the c teeth are set on edge'?	Ezek 18.2

CHOKE — D
delight in riches c the word,	Mt 13.22
cares..enter in and c the word,	Mk 4.19
the thorns grew up and c it,	4.7
thorns grew with it and c it.	Lk 8.7
they are c by the cares and riches	8.14

CHOOSE — S — ING
rod of the man whom I c	Num 17.5
c out of all your tribes	Deut 12.4
the LORD your God will c.	17.15
therefore c life, that you	30.19
c this day whom you will	Josh 24.15
C a man for yourselves, and	1Sam 17.8
Three things I offer you; c	2Sam 24.12
Three things I offer you; c	1Chr 21.10
who c another god multiply	Ps 16.4
instruct in the way..should c.	25.12
Blessed is he whom thou dost c	65.4
did not c..fear of the LORD,	Prov 1.29
refuse..evil and c the good.	Isa 7.15
Is such the fast that I c,	58.5
Zion and again c Jerusalem.' "	Zech 1.17
do what I c with what belongs	Mt 20.15
You did not c me, but I c you	Jn 15.16
to c men and send them to you	Acts 15.25
which I shall c I cannot tell.	Phil 1.22
man whom the LORD c shall	Num 16.7
c, to set his name there,	Deut 14.24
c..to share ill-treatment	Heb 11.25

CHORAZIN
"Woe to you, C! woe to you,	Mt 11.21
"Woe to you, C! woe to you,	Lk 10.13

CHOSE — N (v)
Lot c..the Jordan valley,	Gen 13.11
Moses c able men out of	Ex 18.25
and c their descendants	Deut 4.37
set his love upon you and c you,	7.7
I c him out of all the tribes	1Sam 2.28
He c our heritage for us, the	Ps 47.4
but he c the tribe of Judah,	78.68

the two families which he c'?	Jer 33.24
and c from them twelve, whom	Lk 6.13
how they c the places of honor,	14.7
they c Stephen, a man full of	Acts 6.5
God c what is foolish in	1Cor 1.27
arranged the organs..as he c.	12.18
he c us..before the foundation	Eph 1.4
God c you from..beginning	2Thess 2.13
No, for I have c him,	Gen 18.19
ones c from the congregation,	Num 1.16
your God has c him out	Deut 18.5
him whom the LORD has c?	1Sam 10.24
thy people whom thou hast c,	1Ki 3.8
Jerusalem which I have c."	11.13
which I have c, Jerusalem,	2Ki 23.27
sons of Jacob, his c ones!	1Chr 16.13
LORD has c you to build	28.10
for the LORD has c you to	2Chr 29.11
made a covenant with my c one,	Ps 89.3
led..his c ones with singing.	105.43
had not Moses, his c one,	106.23
c the way of faithfulness,	119.30
for I have c thy precepts.	119.173
good name is to be c rather	Prov 22.1
servant, Jacob, whom I have c,	Isa 41.8
my servant whom I have c,	43.10
because..the LORD,..has c you."	48.7
These have c their own ways,	66.3
signet ring; for I have c you,	Hag 2.23
my servant whom I have c,	Mt 12.18
many are called, but few..c."	22.14
I know whom I have c; it is	Jn 13.18
he is a c instrument of mine	Acts 9.15
Put on then, as God's c ones,	Col 3.12
by God, that he has c you;	1Thess 1.4
c and destined by God the	1Pet 1.2
you are a c race, a royal	2.9

CHOSEN (n)
my c, in whom..soul delights;	Isa 42.1
For the sake of..Israel my c,	45.4
my c shall inherit it, and my	65.9
my c shall long enjoy the work	65.22
"This is my Son, my C; listen	Lk 9.35

CHRIST
Jesus was born, who is called C.	Mt 1.16
"You are the C, the Son of..God."	16.16
God judges..secrets of men by C	Rom 2.16
the supernatural Rock..was C.	1Cor 10.4

CHRISTIAN — S
you think to make me a C!"	Acts 26.28
yet if one suffers as a C,	1Pet 4.16
the first time called C.	Acts 11.26

CHURCH — ES
on this rock I will build my c,	Mt 16.18
he refuses..tell it to the c;	18.17
the c throughout all Judea	Acts 9.31
came to the ears of the c	11.22
some who belonged to the c.	12.1
prayer..to God by the c.	12.5
to feed the c of the Lord	20.28
greet..the c in their house.	Rom 16.5
no offense..to the c of God,	1Cor 10.32
God has appointed in the c	12.28
he who prophesies edifies the c.	14.4
because I persecuted the c	15.9
head over all things for the c,	Eph 1.22
to him be glory in the c	3.21
As the c is subject to Christ,	5.24
how can he care for God's c?	1Tim 3.5
let the c not be burdened,	5.16

CHURCH — ES (cont.)

and the c in your house:	Philem 2
and puts them out of the c.	3Jn 10
c were strengthened in..faith,	Acts 16.5
shown in the c of Macedonia,	2Cor 8.1
John to the seven c..in Asia:	Rev 1.4
all the c shall know that I	2.23

CIRCLE

he drew a c on the face of	Prov 8.27
above the c of the earth,	Isa 40.22

CIRCUMCISE — D

C therefore the foreskin	Deut 10.16
God will c your heart	30.6
C yourselves to the LORD,	Jer 4.4
you c a man upon the sabbath.	Jn 7.22
Every male..shall be c.	Gen 17.10
and every male was c,	34.24
and c the people of Israel	Josh 5.3
"Unless you are c according	Acts 15.1
was not compelled to be c,	Gal 2.3
In him also you were c with	Col 2.11

CIRCUMCISION

of blood," because of the c.	Ex 4.26
the c party criticized him,	Acts 11.2
his uncircumcision be..as c?	Rom 2.26
He received c as a sign or seal	4.11
neither c counts for anything	1Cor 7.19
in Christ Jesus neither c nor	Gal 5.6
by what is called the c,	Eph 2.11

CISTERN — S

Drink water from your own c,	Prov 5.15
and cast him into the c of	Jer 38.6
hewed out c for themselves,	2.13

CITY — IES

You shall march around the c,	Josh 6.3
a breach was made in the c;	2Ki 25.4
streams make glad the c of God,	Ps 46.4
praised in the c of our God!	48.1
wealth is his strong c;	Prov 10.15
righteous, the c rejoices;	11.10
a little c with few men in it;	Ecc 9.14
called the c of righteousness,	Isa 1.26
a breach was made in the c.	Jer 39.2
How lonely sits the c that	Lam 1.1
said, "The c has fallen."	Ezek 33.21
because thy c and thy people	Dan 9.19
Jerusalem..the faithful c,	Zech 8.3
c set on..hill cannot be hid.	Mt 5.14
whole c was gathered together	Mk 1.33
the c was full of idols.	Acts 17.16
he looked forward to the c	Heb 11.10
the name of the c of my God,	Rev 3.12
the holy c, new Jerusalem,	21.2
to measure the c and its gates	21.15
shall be the six c of refuge,	Num 35.6
set apart three c for you	Deut 19.2
'Appoint the c of refuge,	Josh 20.2
you are to be over five c.'	Lk 19.19

CLAY

thou hast made me of c; and	Job 10.9
your defenses are..of c.	13.12
was formed from a piece of c.	33.6
potter be regarded as the c;	Isa 29.16
Does the c say to him who	45.9
we are the c,..thou..our potter;	64.8
like..c in the potter's hand,	Jer 18.6
made c of the spittle and	Jn 9.6

CLEAN — NESS

seven pairs of all c animals,	Gen 7.2
"You may eat all c birds.	Deut 14.11
flesh was restored..he was c.	2Ki 5.14
Who can bring a c thing out	Job 14.4
man, that he can be c? Or	15.14
he who is born of woman be c?	25.4
You say, 'I am c, without	33.9
the fear of the LORD is c,	Ps 19.9
He who has c hands and a pure	24.4
in vain have I kept my heart c	73.13
Who can say,..my heart c;	Prov 20.9
Wash..make yourselves c;	Isa 1.16
How long..before you are..c?"	Jer 13.27
if you will, you can make me c."	Mt 8.2
you will, you can make me c."	Mk 1.40
you will, you can make me c."	Lk 5.12
everything is c for you.	11.41
You are..made c by the word	Jn 15.3
Everything is indeed c, but	Rom 14.20
according to the c of my hands	Ps 18.20

CLEANSE — S — D

people of Israel, and c them.	Num 8.6
and does not c himself,	19.13
house of the LORD to c it,	2Chr 29.16
and c my hands with lye,	Job 9.30
iniquity, and c me from my sin!	Ps 51.2
Blows that wound c away	Prov 20.30
will c them from all the guilt	Jer 33.8
from all your idols I will c	Ezek 36.25
I will save..and..c them;	37.23
fall, to refine and to c them	Dan 11.35
raise the dead, c lepers,	Mt 10.8
you c the outside of the cup	23.25
let us c ourselves from every	2Cor 7.1
C your hands, you sinners,	Jas 4.8
And the priest who c him	Lev 14.11
c the bloodstains of Jerusalem	Isa 4.4
a land that is not c, or	Ezek 22.24
none of them was c, but..Naaman	Lk 4.27
as they went they were c.	17.14
"What God has c, you must	Acts 10.15
'What God has c you must not	11.9
having c her by the washing	Eph 5.26

CLEAR

how can we c ourselves?	Gen 44.16
C thou me from hidden faults.	Ps 19.12
Thou didst c the ground for it;	80.9
to c his threshing floor, and	Lk 3.17

CLEAVE — S — ING

shall c to the inheritance	Num 36.7
to c to him, and to serve	Josh 22.5
but c to the LORD your God	23.8
My bones c to my skin and	Job 19.20
I c to thy testimonies, O LORD;	Ps 119.31
a man..c to his wife,	Gen 2.24
My soul c to the dust; revive	Ps 119.25
obeying his voice, and c	Deut 30.20

CLEVER — NESS

cleverness of the c I will	1Cor 1.19
c of the clever I will thwart."	1.19

CLOAK

let him have your c as well;	Mt 5.40
bring the c that I left with	2Tim 4.13

CLOSE

sign..of the c of the age?"	Mt 24.3
with you..to the c of the age."	28.20

CLOTH — S

unshrunk c on an old garment,	Mt 9.16
wrapped him in swaddling c,	Lk 2.7

CLOTHE — S — D (v)

will c him with your robe,	Isa 22.21
if God so c..grass of the field,	Mt 6.30
if God so c the grass which	Lk 12.28
God made for Adam..and c	Gen 3.21
with the spoil they c all	2Chr 28.15
righteousness, and it c me;	Job 29.14
clean turban on his head and c	Zech 3.5
demoniac sitting there, c and	Mk 5.15
they c him in a purple cloak,	15.17
c and in his right mind;	Lk 8.35

CLOTHING (n)

Your c did not wear out upon	Deut 8.4
if I have seen..lack of c,	Job 31.19
lambs will provide your c,	Prov 27.26
and the body more than c?	Mt 6.25
false prophets,..in sheep's c	7.15
for my c they cast lots."	Jn 19.24

CLOUD

I set my bow in the c,	Gen 9.13
in a pillar of c to lead them	Ex 13.21
Then the c covered the tent	40.34
the c covered the tabernacle,	Num 9.15
LORD came down in a pillar of c,	12.5
the pillar of c stood by the	Deut 31.15
over her assemblies a c by day,	Isa 4.5
a bright c overshadowed them,	Mt 17.5
And a c overshadowed them,	Mk 9.7
c took him out of their sight.	Acts 1.9
baptized into Moses in the c	1Cor 10.2

CLOVEN-FOOTED

and is c and chews the cud,	Lev 11.3

COAL — S

having in his hand a burning c	Isa 6.6
c flamed forth from him.	Ps 18.8
Let burning c fall upon them!	140.10
heap c of fire on his head,	Prov 25.22
heap burning c upon his head."	Rom12.20

COAT — S

sue you and take your c, let	Mt 5.40
cloak do not withhold your c	Lk 6.29
two c, let him share with him	3.11

COCK

immediately the c crowed.	Mt 26.74
before the c crows twice,	Mk 14.30
gateway and the c crowed.	14.68n
Peter, the c will not crow	Lk 22.34
still speaking, the c crowed.	22.60
the c will not crow, till you	Jn 13.38

COIN — S

Bring me a c, and let me look	Mk 12.15
"Show me a c. Whose likeness	Lk 20.24
widow..put in two copper c,	Mk 12.42
poor widow put in two copper c.	Lk 21.2

COLD

most men's love will grow c.	Mt 24.12
you are..neither c nor hot,	Rev 3.16

COLLECTOR — S

a Pharisee and..a tax c.	Lk 18.10
Zacchaeus..was a chief tax c,	19.2
tax c and the harlots go into	Mt 21.31
tax c and sinners were sitting	Mk 2.15
Tax c also came to be baptized,	Lk 3.12
drink with tax c and sinners?"	5.30
and the tax c justified God,	7.29
friend of tax c and sinners!'	7.34

COLT

humble and riding..on a c	Zech 9.9
you will find a c tied, on	Mk 11.2
where..you will find a c tied,	Lk 19.30

COME — S — ING (v)

"C in, O blessed of the LORD;	Gen 24.31
c with us, and we will	Num 10.29
"Lo, I c;..it is written of me;	Ps 40.7
C and hear,...you who fear God,	66.16
C into his presence with singing!	100.2
none who go to her c back	Prov 2.19
better to be told, "C..here,"	25.7
C, my beloved, let us go forth	Sol 7.11
"C..let us reason together,	Isa 1.18
"C, let us go up to the mountain	2.3
c, let us walk in the light	2.5
C, my people, enter your	26.20
God. He will c and save you."	35.4
who thirsts, c to the waters;	55.1
"C, let us return to the LORD;	Hos 6.1
"C, let us go to the mountain	Mic 4.2
will suddenly c to his temple;	Mal 3.1
Thy kingdom c, Thy will be done,	Mt 6.10
I say..to another, 'C,' and he c,	8.9
"Are you he who is to c, or	11.3
C to me, all who labor and	11.28
"If any man would c after me,	16.24
For many will c in my name,	24.5
"C away by yourselves..and rest	Mk 6.31
"If any man would c after me,	8.34
Many will c in my name, saying,	13.6
He said to them, "C and see."	Jn 1.39
"C, see a man who told me all	4.29
"You know me,..where I c from?	7.28
let him c to me and drink.	7.37
loud voice, "Lazarus, c out."	11.43
not..desolate; I will c to you.	14.18
Jesus,..will c in the same	Acts 1.11
"C over to Macedonia and help	16.9
longed for many years to c	Rom 15.23
be accursed. Our Lord, c!	1Cor 16.22
Do your best to c to me soon.	2Tim 4.9
But you have c to Mount Zion	Heb 12.22
"C out of her, my people,	Rev 18.4
Spirit and the Bride say, "C."	22.17
God c, he does not keep silence,	Ps 50.3
LORD..c to judge the earth.	96.13
Who is this that c from Edom,	Isa 63.1
day c, burning like an oven,	Mal 4.1
terrible day of the LORD c.	4.5
Blessed is he who c in the name	Mt 21.9
'Blessed be he who c in the name	23.39
"When the Son of man c in his	25.31
ashamed, when he c in the glory	Mk 8.38
who c in..name of the Lord!' "	Lk 13.35
who c to me shall not hunger,	Jn 6.35
who c to me I will not cast out.	6.37
Blessed..he who c in the name	12.13
Lord's death until he c.	1Cor 11.26
a god c up out of..earth."	1Sam 28.13
on what day your Lord is c.	Mt 24.42
c on the clouds of heaven."	26.64
the Son of man c in clouds	Mk 13.26
c with the clouds of heaven."	14.62
Son of man is c at an hour	Lk 12.40
Son of man c in a cloud with	21.27
third time I am c to you.	2Cor 13.1
the c one shall..not tarry;	Heb 10.37
Behold, he is c with the clouds,	Rev 1.7
I am c soon; hold fast what	3.11
I am c soon, bringing my	22.12
says, "Surely I am c soon."	22.20

COMELY

I am..dark, but c, O daughters	Sol 1.5
my love, c as Jerusalem, terrible	6.4

COMFORT — S — ED (v)

to condole with him and c	Job 2.11
you c me with empty nothings?	21.34
rod and thy staff, they c me.	Ps 23.4
thou wast angry..thou didst c	Isa 12.1
C, c my people, says your God.	40.1
For the LORD will c Zion;	51.3
he will c..her waste places,	51.3
our God; to c all who mourn;	61.2
his mother c, so I will c you;	66.13
she has none to c her; all	Lam 1.2
Therefore c one another	1Thess 4.18
I am he that c you; who are	Isa 51.12
So Isaac was c after	Gen 24.67
he refused to be c,	37.35
my soul refuses to be c.	Ps 77.2
LORD, hast helped me and c me.	86.17
the LORD has c his people,	Isa 49.13
for the LORD has c his people,	52.9
he is c..you are in anguish.	Lk 16.25
c us by the coming of Titus,	2Cor 7.6
Therefore we are c. And besides	7.13

COMFORT (n)

This is my c in my affliction	Ps 119.50
of mercies and God of all c,	2Cor 1.3
God..who..gave us eternal c	2Thess 2.16

COMFORTERS

miserable c are you all.	Job 16.2
and for c, but I found none.	Ps 69.20
whence shall I seek c for her?	Nah 3.7

COMING (n)

what will be the sign of your c	Mt 24.3
so will be the c of the Son	24.27
so..the c of the Son of man.	24.37
'My master is delayed in c.'	Lk 12.45
at his c those who belong	1Cor 15.23
before our Lord..at his c?	1Thess 2.19
at the c of our Lord Jesus	3.13
left until the c of the Lord,	4.15
blameless at the c of our Lord	5.23
concerning the c of our Lord	2Thess 2.1
patient,..until..c of the Lord.	Jas 5.7
the power and c of our Lord	2Pet 1.16
"Where is the promise of his c?	3.4
shrink..in shame at his c.	1Jn 2.28

COMMAND — S — ED (v)

speak all that I c you;	Ex 7.2
I will c my blessing upon you	Lev 25.21
LORD will c the blessing	Deut 28.8
whatever I c..you shall speak.	Jer 1.7
do all that I c you. So shall you	11.4
I c you to speak to them;	26.2
friends if you do what I c	Jn 15.14
he c even wind and water,	Lk 8.25
God c the man, saying,	Gen 2.16
Noah..did all that God c	6.22
all that the LORD had c Moses;	Ex 39.32
did all..the LORD c by Moses.	Lev 8.36
his covenant, which he c	Deut 4.13
Moses c us a law, as a possession	33.4
Have I not c you? Be strong	Josh 1.9
so Moses c..and so Joshua did;	11.15
he c, and it stood forth.	Ps 33.9
he c and they were created.	148.5
Jesus c them, "Tell no one	Mt 17.9
to observe all..I have c you;	28.20
Lord c..those who proclaim	1Cor 9.14

COMMAND (n)

At the c of the LORD	Num 9.18
you rebelled against my c	20.24
beyond the c of the LORD	22.18
The Lord gives the c; great is	Ps 68.11
Keep the king's c, and because	Ecc 8.2
what I am writing..is a c	1Cor 14.37

COMMANDER — S — 'S

Phicol the c of his army	Gen 21.22
as c of the army of the LORD	Josh 5.14
then c shall be appointed at	Deut 20.9
a c portion was reserved;	33.21

COMMANDMENT — S

who respects the c will be	Prov 13.13
A new c I give to you, that	Jn 13.34
and the c is holy and just	Rom 7.12
no new c, but an old c which	1Jn 2.7
not..writing you a new c, but	2Jn 5
the covenant, the ten c.	Ex 34.28
the c which..LORD commanded	Lev 27.34
keeping his statutes, his c	1Ki 2.3
break thy c..and intermarry	Ezra 9.14
and all thy c are true.	Ps 119.151
my words; keep my c, and live;	Prov 4.4
Fear God, and keep his c;	Ecc 12.13
enter life, keep the c."	Mt 19.17
love of God,..keep his c.	1Jn 5.3

COMMEND — S — ED

I c enjoyment, for man has no	Ecc 8.15
now I c you to God and to	Acts 20.32
I c to you our sister Phoebe,	Rom 16.1
beginning to c ourselves	2Cor 3.1
of those who c themselves,	10.12
the man whom the Lord c.	10.18
man is c according to his	Prov 12.8
master c the dishonest steward	Lk 16.8

COMMISSION (n)

According to the c of God given	1Cor 3.10
I am entrusted with a c.	9.17

COMMISSIONED (v)

in Christ, and has c us;	2Cor 1.21
as c by God, in the sight of God	2.17

COMMIT — TED

to God would I c my cause;	Job 5.8
Into thy hand I c my spirit;	Ps 31.5
C your way to the LORD; trust	37.5
C your work to the LORD,	Prov 16.3
into thy hands I c my spirit!"	Lk 23.46
have not c this treachery	Josh 22.31
to thee have I c my cause.	Jer 20.12
for the treason he has c	Ezek 17.20
the treachery..c against thee.	Dan 9.7

COMMON

and had all things in c;	Acts 2.44
they had everything in c.	4.32
cleansed,..you must not call c."	10.15
no temptation..not c to man.	1Cor 10.13
write..of our c salvation,	Jude 3

COMMONWEALTH

alienated from..c of Israel,	Eph 2.12
But our c is in heaven,	Phil 3.20

COMMUNE

c with your own hearts on your	Ps 4.4
I c with my heart in the night;	77.6

COMPANION — S

wife was given to his c,	Judg 14.20
a c of all who fear thee,	Ps 119.63
the c of fools will suffer	Prov 13.20

COMPANION — S (cont.)
c of gluttons shames his father. Prov 28.7
though she is your *c* and..wife Mal 2.14
c..listening for your voice; Sol 8.13

COMPANY — IES
you keep *c* with adulterers. Ps 50.18
in the *c* of the upright, in 111.1
adulterers, a *c* of treacherous Jer 9.2
sit in the *c* of merrymakers, 15.17
"Bad *c* ruins good morals." 1Cor 15.33
sit down by *c* upon the..grass. Mk 6.39

COMPARE — D
none can *c* with thee! Were I Ps 40.5
c me, that we may be alike? Isa 46.5
shall I *c* this generation? Mt 11.16
Not..to class or *c* ourselves 2Cor 10.12
who in the skies can be *c* to Ps 89.6

COMPASSION
c on you, and multiply you, Deut 13.17
Israel had *c* for Benjamin Judg 21.6
people had *c* on Benjamin 21.15
gracious to them and had *c* 2Ki 13.23
your children will find *c* 2Chr 30.9
he had *c* on his people 36.15
LORD..have *c* on his servants. Ps 135.14
The LORD will have *c* on Jacob Isa 14.1
with great *c* I will gather you. 54.7
I will again have *c* on them, Jer 12.15
God gave Daniel favor and *c* Dan 1.9
He will again have *c* upon us, Mic 7.19
pour out..a spirit of *c* Zech 12.10
When he saw..crowds, he had *c* Mt 9.36
he had *c* on them, and healed 14.14
said, "I have *c* on the crowd, 15.32
saw a great throng, and..had *c* Mk 6.34
"I have *c* on the crowd, because 8.2
he had *c* on her and said to Lk 7.13
when he saw him, he had *c*, 10.33
father saw him and had *c*, 15.20
you had *c* on the prisoners, Heb 10.34

COMPASSIONATE
I will hear, for I am *c*. Ex 22.27
he, being *c*, forgave their Ps 78.38
the Lord is *c* and merciful. Jas 5.11

COMPEL — LED
and *c* people to come in, Lk 14.23
how can you *c* the Gentiles Gal 2.14
they *c* to carry his cross. Mt 27.32
was not *c* to be circumcised, Gal 2.3

COMPETE
how will you *c* with horses? Jer 12.5
in a race all..runners *c*, 1Cor 9.24

COMPLAIN — ED
I will *c* in the bitterness Job 7.11
Abraham *c* to Abimelech Gen 21.25
people *c* in the hearing Num 11.1

COMPLAINT
"Today also my *c* is bitter, Job 23.2
and at noon I utter my *c* and Ps 55.17
I pour out my *c* before him, 142.2
ground for *c* against Daniel Dan 6.4
I will answer concerning my *c*. Hab 2.1

COMPLETE — D — ING
iniquity..not yet *c*." Gen 15.16
that you may be perfect and *c*, Jas 1.4
When therefore I have *c* this, Rom 15.28
and faith was *c* by works, Jas 2.22
matched by your *c* it out of 2Cor 8.11

COMPREHEND
things which we cannot *c*. Job 37.5
may have power to *c* with all Eph 3.18

CONCEAL — S — ED
glory of God to *c* things, Prov 25.2
prudent man *c* his knowledge, 12.23
He who *c* his transgressions 28.13
if I have *c* my transgressions Job 31.33

CONCEIT
any..wise in their own *c*." Job 37.24
he is puffed up with *c*, he 1Tim 6.4

CONCEIVE — D
they *c* words of deceit. Ps 35.20
Eve..*c* and bore Cain, Gen 4.1

CONCUBINE — S
his *c* became angry with him, Judg 19.2
Absalom..to his father's *c* 2Sam 16.22

CONDEMN — S — ED
When he is quiet, who can *c*? Job 34.29
c me that you may be justified? 40.8
and *c* the innocent to death. Ps 94.21
save him from those who *c* 109.31
and they will *c* him to death, Mt 20.18
they will *c* him to death, Mk 10.33
this generation and *c* it; Lk 11.32
not to *c* the world, but that Jn 3.17
who is to *c*? Is it Christ Rom 8.34
if our hearts do not *c* us, 1Jn 3.21
a man of evil devices he *c*. Prov 12.2
none..who take refuge..be *c*. Ps 34.22
let him be *c* when..to trial. 37.33
are they? Has no one *c* you?" Jn 8.10*n*
Cephas..because he stood *c*. Gal 2.11

CONDEMNATION
trespass led to *c* for all men, Rom 5.18
now no *c* for those..in Christ 8.1

CONDUCT — S (v)
let us *c* ourselves becomingly Rom 13.13
C yourselves wisely toward Col 4.5
who *c*..affairs with justice. Ps 112.5

CONDUCT (n)
wise *c* is a pleasure to a man Prov 10.23
good *c* among the Gentiles, 1Pet 2.12

CONDUIT
by the *c* of the upper pool, 2Ki 18.17
he made the pool and the *c* 20.20
he stood by the *c* of the..pool Isa 36.2

CONFESS — ES — ED — ING
c the sin he has committed, Lev 5.5
"But if they *c* their iniquity 26.40
c his sin..he has committed; Num 5.7
"I will *c* my transgressions Ps 32.5
one should *c* him to be Christ, Jn 9.22
if you *c* with your lips that Rom 10.9
every tongue *c*..Jesus..Lord, Phil 2.11
c your sins to one another, Jas 5.16
we *c* our sins, he is faithful 1Jn 1.9
I will *c* his name before my Rev 3.5
he who *c* and forsakes them Prov 28.13
c with his lips and..is saved. Rom 10.10
Whoever *c* that Jesus is the 1Jn 4.15
He *c*, he did not deny, but *c*, Jn 1.20
baptized by him..*c* their sins. Mt 3.6
baptized by him..*c* their sins. Mk 1.5
now believers came, *c* and Acts 19.18

CONFESSION
Ezra prayed and made *c*, Ezra 10.1

CONFESSION (cont.)

then make ⸴c to the LORD	Ezra 10.11
made c, saying, "O Lord, the	Dan 9.4
Jesus who..made the good c,	1Tim 6.13
let us hold fast our c.	Heb 4.14

CONFIDENCE

On what do you rest this c	2Ki 18.19
people took c from the words	2Chr 32.8
for the LORD will be your c	Prov 3.26
On what do you rest this c	Isa 36.4
have no c in a friend; guard	Mic 7.5
I have great c in you;	2Cor 7.4
I have c in the Lord that	Gal 5.10
reason for c in the flesh,	Phil 3.4
we have c in the Lord about	2Thess 3.4
Through him you have c in God,	1Pet 1.21
c for the day of judgment,	1Jn 4.17
the c which we have in him,	5.14

CONFIDENT

though war..yet I will be c.	Ps 27.3
is c that he is Christ's,	2Cor 10.7

CONFIRM — S — ED

c the word which the LORD	Deut 9.5
c the word of his servant,	Isa 44.26
sworn an oath and c it, to	Ps 119.106
every word..c by the evidence	Mt 18.16
c the message by the signs	Mk 16.20n

CONFORMED

Do not be c to this world	Rom 12.2
do not be c to the passions	1Pet 1.14

CONFRONT

this song shall c them	Deut 31.21
Arise, O LORD! c them,	Ps 17.13

CONFUSION

and will throw into c	Ex 23.27
all Jerusalem was in c.	Acts 21.31
God is not a God of c but	1Cor 14.33

CONFUTE — D — ING

to c those who contradict it.	Tit 1.9
there was none that c Job,	Job 32.12
powerfully c the Jews in	Acts 18.28

CONGREGATION

"If the whole c of Israel	Lev 4.13
"Take a census of all the c	Num 1.2
the c shall judge between	35.24
in the..c I will praise thee:	Ps 22.22
in the great c I will bless	26.12
concealed..from the great c.	40.10
Let them extol him in the c	107.32
in the c in the wilderness	Acts 7.38
midst of the c I will praise	Heb 2.12

CONQUER — S — ED — ING

the Lamb will c them, for	Rev 17.14
To him who c I will give..manna	2.17
He who c shall be clad thus	3.5
who c, I will grant him to sit	3.21
who c shall have this heritage,	21.7
through faith c kingdoms,	Heb 11.33
Judah,..Root of David, has c,	Rev 5.5
have c him by the blood of	12.11
those who had c the beast	15.2
he went out c and to conquer.	6.2

CONQUERORS

more than c through him who	Rom 8.37

CONSCIENCE

before God in all good c	Acts 23.1
take pains to have a clear c	24.16

their c also bears witness	Rom 2.15
not lying; my c bears me witness	9.1
but also for the sake of c.	13.5
encouraged if his c is weak,	1Cor 8.10
I mean his c, not yours—	10.29
holding faith and a good c.	1Tim 1.19
whom I serve with a clear c,	2Tim 1.3
perfect the c of the worshiper,	Heb 9.9
keep your c clear, so that,	1Pet 3.16
appeal to God for a clear c,	3.21

CONSECRATE — D — ING

"C to me all the first-born;	Ex 13.2
"Go to the people and c them	19.10
ordain them and c them,	28.41
you shall do to them to c them,	29.1
C yourselves therefore,	Lev 20.7
You shall c him, for he offers	21.8
you shall c to the LORD	Deut 15.19
anointed the tabernacle..c	Lev 8.10
I c them for myself,	Num 8.17
before you were born I c you;	Jer 1.5
the unbelieving husband is c	1Cor 7.14
willingly, c himself today	1Chr 29.5

CONSENT — S — ING

if sinners entice..do not c.	Prov 1.10
and she c to live with him,	1Cor 7.12
And Saul was c to his death.	Acts 8.1

CONSIDER — S — ED

c it, take counsel, and	Judg 19.30
for c what great things	1Sam 12.24
Job;..c the wondrous works	Job 37.14
but I c thy testimonies.	Ps 119.95
Go to the ant, O sluggard; c	Prov 6.6
C how you have fared.	Hag 1.5
Pray now, c what will come	2.15
C the lilies of the field,	Mt 6.28
C the ravens: they neither sow	Lk 12.24
must c yourselves dead to sin	Rom 6.11
c Jesus, the apostle and high	Heb 3.1
let us c how to stir up one	10.24
C him who endured from sinners	12.3
Blessed is he who c the poor!	Ps 41.1
Who c the power of thy anger,	90.11
No one c, nor is..knowledge	Isa 44.19
"Have you c my servant Job,	Job 1.8
Then I saw and c it; I looked	Prov 24.32
since she c him faithful	Heb 11.11
He c that God was able to raise	11.19

CONSIGNED

I am c to the gates of Sheol	Isa 38.10
c all men to disobedience,	Rom 11.32

CONSOLATION — S

and let this be your c.	Job 21.2
nor..give him the cup of c	Jer 16.7
done, becoming a c to them.	Ezek 16.54
the dreamers..give empty c.	Zech 10.2
looking for the c of Israel,	Lk 2.25
Are the c of God too small	Job 15.11

CONSOLE — D

come to Martha and Mary to c	Jn 11.19
you will be c for the evil	Ezek 14.22

CONSPIRACY

And the c grew strong,	2Sam 15.12
"Do not call c all that this	Isa 8.12
than forty who made this c.	Acts 23.13

CONSPIRE — D

Why do the nations c, and the	Ps 2.1
they c against him to kill	Gen 37.18

CONSPIRE — D (cont.)
his servant..*c* against him.   1Ki 16.9
"Amos has *c* against you in   Amos 7.10

CONSTRAINED
but they *c* him, saying, "Stay   Lk 24.29

CONSTRAINS
the spirit within me *c* me.   Job 32.18

CONSULT — S — ED
when they say.."*C* the mediums Isa 8.19
do not look to..or *c* the LORD!   31.1
he *c* the teraphim, he looks   Ezek 21.21
David *c* with the commanders 1Chr 13.1

CONSUME — S — D — ING
I may *c* them in a moment."   Num 16.21
c them in wrath, *c* them till   Ps 59.13
where neither moth nor rust *c*   Mt 6.20
and the servants, and *c* them;   Job 1.16
what is left in his tent will be *c*.   20.26
For we are *c* by thy anger;   Ps 90.7
for our God is a *c* fire.   Heb 12.29

CONTAIN
highest heaven cannot *c* thee;   1Ki 8.27
world..could not *c* the books   Jn 21.25

CONTEMPT
looked with *c* on her mistress.   Gen 16.4
with *c* upon their husbands,   Est 1.17
there is *c* for misfortune;   Job 12.5
into *c* the land of Zebulun   Isa 9.1

CONTEND — ING
do not *c* with them; for I   Deut 2.5
"Will you *c* for Baal? Or will   Judg 6.31
why thou dost *c* against me.   Job 10.2
Who..will *c* with me?   13.19
C, O LORD, with those who *c*   Ps 35.1
LORD has taken his place to *c*,   Isa 3.13
I will *c* with those who *c*   49.25
with your..children I will *c*.   Jer 2.9
Yet let no one *c*, and..accuse,   Hos 4.4
you to *c* for the faith which   Jude 3
we are not *c* against flesh   Eph 6.12

CONTENT
that we had been *c* to dwell   Josh 7.7
and be *c* with your wages."   Lk 3.14
I am *c* with weaknesses,   2Cor 12.10
whatever state I am, to be *c*.   Phil 4.11
with these we shall be *c*.   1Tim 6.8

CONTENTIOUS
with a *c* and fretful woman.   Prov 21.19
dripping..and a *c* woman are   27.15

CONTINUAL — LY
the *c* burnt offering was taken   Dan 8.11
praise shall *c* be in my mouth.   Ps 34.1

CONTINUE — D
O *c* thy steadfast love to   Ps 36.10
"If you *c* in my word, you   Jn 8.31
urged them to *c* in the grace   Acts 13.43
c in sin that grace may abound? Rom 6.1
I shall remain and *c* with you   Phil 1.25
c in what you have learned   2Tim 3.14
have *c* my faithfulness to you.   Jer 31.3
they would have *c* with us;   1Jn 2.19

CONTRIBUTION — S
make some *c* for the poor   Rom 15.26
concerning..*c* for the saints: 1Cor 16.1
by the generosity of your *c*   2Cor 9.13
faithfully brought in the *c*,   2Chr 31.12

CONTRITE
sacrifice acceptable..*c* heart,   Ps 51.17
he..is humble and *c* in spirit   Isa 66.2

CONTROL — S (v)
Joseph could not *c* himself   Gen 45.1
the love of Christ *c* us,   2Cor 5.14

CONTROL (n)
having his desire under *c*,   1Cor 7.37
left nothing outside his *c*.   Heb 2.8

CONTROVERSY
c with..inhabitants of the land. Hos 4.1
Hear, you mountains, the *c* of   Mic 6.2

CONVERT — S
the first *c* in Asia for Christ.   Rom 16.5
He must not be a recent *c*,   1Tim 3.6
the first *c* in Achaia, and   1Cor 16.15

CONVICT — S — ED
to *c* all the ungodly for   Jude 15
Which of you *c* me of sin?   Jn 8.46
outsider enters, he is *c*   1Cor 14.24

CONVINCE — D
he will *c* the world of sin   Jn 16.8
And *c* some, who doubt;   Jude 22
fully *c* that God was able   Rom 4.21
Let every one be fully *c* in   14.5

CONVOCATION
sabbath of..rest, a holy *c*;   Lev 23.3
you shall have a holy *c*;   Num 28.26

COOL
God walking..in the *c*..day   Gen 3.8
c spirit is..understanding.   Prov 17.27

COPY
upon the stones a *c* of the law   Josh 8.32
Mordecai also gave him a *c*   Est 4.8
They serve a *c* and shadow of   Heb 8.5

CORBAN
C' (that is, given to God)—   Mk 7.11

CORD — S
A threefold *c* is not quickly   Ecc 4.12
before..silver *c* is snapped,   12.6
The *c* of death encompassed me, Ps 18.4
LORD..cut the *c* of the wicked.   129.4
led them with *c* of compassion, Hos 11.4

CORINTH
left Athens and went to *C*.   Acts 18.1
While Apollos was at *C*, Paul   19.1
church of God which is at *C*,   1Cor 1.2

CORNELIUS
man named *C*, a centurion   Acts 10.1
an angel..saying to him, "*C*."   10.3
C was expecting them and   10.24
'*C*, your prayer has been heard   10.31

CORNER
this was not done in a *c*.   Acts 26.26
become the head of the *c*,"   1Pet 2.7

CORNERSTONE
Jesus himself being the *c*,   Eph 2.20
in Zion a..*c* chosen..precious,   1Pet 2.6

CORRECT
seek justice, *c* oppression;   Isa 1.17
C me,..but in just measure;   Jer 10.24

CORRECTION
your children, they took no *c*;   Jer 2.30
but they refused to take *c*.   5.3

CORRECTION (cont.)
to no voice, she accepts no *c*. Zeph 3.2
fear me, she will accept *c*; 3.7

CORRUPT (adj)
earth was *c* in God's sight, Gen 6.11
astray, they are all alike *c*; Ps 14.3

CORRUPTED (v)
your people,..*c* themselves; Ex 32.7
They have deeply *c* themselves Hos 9.9
have *c* the covenant of Levi, Mal 2.8

CORRUPTION
nor let thy Holy One see *c*. Acts 2.27
not let thy Holy One see *c*.' 13.35

CORRUPTLY
c by making a graven image Deut 4.16
They have dealt *c* with him, 32.5

COST (v)
offerings..*c* me nothing." 2Sam 24.24
offerings..*c* me nothing." 1Chr 21.24

COST (n)
let the *c* be paid from the Ezra 6.4
sit down and count the *c*, Lk 14.28
gospel without *c* to you? 2Cor 11.7

COUNCIL — S
you listened in the *c* of God? Job 15.8
God has..place in the divine *c*; Ps 82.1
feared in the *c* of the holy ones, 89.7
stood in the *c* of the LORD Jer 23.18
He was a member of the *c* Lk 23.50
they will deliver you..to *c*, Mt 10.17

COUNSEL — S
I will give you *c*, Ex 18.19
by the *c* of Balaam, to act Num 31.16
the *c* which Ahithophel has 2Sam 17.7
But he forsook the *c* which 1Ki 12.8
forsook the *c* which the old 2Chr 10.8
The *c* of the wicked is far Job 21.16
"Who is this that darkens *c* 38.2
walks not in the *c* of..wicked, Ps 1.1
rulers take *c* together, against 2.2
c of the nations to nought; 33.10
c of the LORD stands for ever, 33.11
Thou dost guide me with thy *c*, 73.24
they did not wait for his *c*. 106.13
I have *c* and sound wisdom, Prov 8.14
Without *c* plans go wrong, 15.22
the spirit of *c* and might, Isa 11.2
LORD..he is wonderful in *c*, 28.29
performs..*c* of his messengers; 44.26
nor *c* from the wise, nor the Jer 18.18
great in *c* and mighty in deed; 32.19
O king, let my *c* be acceptable Dan 4.27
the Pharisees went and took *c* Mt 22.15
elders of the people took *c* 27.1
declaring to you the whole *c* Acts 20.27
according to..*c* of his will, Eph 1.11
c of..wicked are treacherous. Prov 12.5
but walked in their own *c* and Jer 7.24

COUNSELOR — S
his *c* in doing wickedly. 2Chr 22.3
you a royal *c*? Stop! Why 25.16
the *c* and the skilful magician Isa 3.3
name will be called "Wonderful *C*, 9.6
as his *c* has instructed him? 40.13
among these there is no *c* 41.28
Has your *c* perished, that pangs Mic 4.9
he will give you another *C*, Jn 14.16
when the *C* comes, whom I shall 15.26

the *C* will not come to you; 16.7
Thy testimonies..are my *c*. Ps 119.24
your *c* as at the beginning. Isa 1.26

COUNT — ED — ING
Who can *c* the dust of Jacob, Num 23.10
c them,..more than the sand. Ps 139.18
Indeed I *c* everything as loss Phil 3.8
C it all joy, my brethren, Jas 1.2
sin is not *c* where..no law. Rom 5.13
not *c* their trespasses 2Cor 5.19

COUNTENANCE
Cain was..angry,..his *c* fell. Gen 4.5
my *c* they did not cast down. Job 29.24
Lift up the light of thy *c* upon Ps 4.6
A glad heart..a cheerful *c*, Prov 15.13

COUNTRY
and came to his own *c*; and his Mk 6.1
they desire a better *c*, Heb 11.16

COURAGE
Be strong and of good *c*; Josh 1.6
Be strong and of good *c*; 1.9
be strong and of good *c*; 10.25
Take *c*, and acquit yourselves 1Sam 4.9
Be of good *c*, and let us 2Sam 10.12
Be of good *c*, and let us 1Chr 19.13
"Be strong and of good *c*, 28.20
Asa..took *c*, and put away 2Chr 15.8
and let your heart take *c*; Ps 27.14
and let your heart take *c*, 31.24
Can your *c* endure, or can Ezek 22.14
"Take *c*, for as you have Acts 23.11
Paul thanked God and took *c*. 28.15
So we are always of good *c*; 2Cor 5.6

COURAGEOUS — LY
in your faith, be *c*, be strong. 1Cor 16.13
Deal *c*, and may the LORD be 2Chr 19.11

COURSE
strong man runs its *c* with joy. Ps 19.5
only I may accomplish my *c* Acts 20.24

COURT
make the *c* of the tabernacle. Ex 27.9
judged by..any human *c*. 1Cor 4.3

COVENANT — S
I will establish my *c* Gen 6.18
I establish my *c* with you 9.9
I will make my *c* between me and you, 17.2
and the two men made a *c*. 21.27
let us make a *c* with you, 26.28
Come now, let us make a *c*, 31.44
God remembered his *c* with Ex 2.24
established my *c* with them, 6.4
make no *c* with them or..their 23.32
"Behold the blood of the *c* 24.8
the *c*, the ten commandments. 34.28
will confirm my *c* with you. Lev 26.9
execute vengeance for the *c*; 26.25
remember..my *c* with Abraham, 26.42
give to him my *c* of peace; Num 25.12
he will not..forget the *c* Deut 4.31
did the LORD make this *c*, 5.3
you shall make no *c* with them, 7.2
faithful God who keeps *c* 7.9
God will keep with you the *c* 7.12
does..evil..in transgressing his *c*, 17.2
These are the words of the *c* 29.1
that you may enter into the sworn *c* 29.12
they forsook the *c* of the LORD, 29.25
thy word, and kept thy *c*. 33.9
so now make a *c* with us." Josh 9.6

COVENANT — S (cont.)

So Joshua made a c..people   Josh 24.25
never break my c with you,   Judg 2.1
you shall make no c with the   2.2
Jonathan made..c with David, 1Sam 18.3
brought your servant into a sacred c   20.8
they may make a c with you,   2Sam 3.21
King David made a c with them   5.3
made with me an everlasting c,   23.5
keeping c and showing..love   1Ki 8.23
Israel have forsaken thy c,   19.10
Jehoiada..made a c with them   2Ki 11.4
Jehoiada made a c between the LORD 11.17
book of the c..had been found   23.2
the people joined in the c.   23.3
mindful of his c for ever,   1Chr 16.15
no God like thee,..keeping c   2Chr 6.14
a c to seek the LORD, the   15.12
of David, because of the c   21.7
made a c before the LORD,   34.31
let us make a c with our God   Ezra 10.3
for those who keep his c and   Ps 25.10
he makes known to them his c.   25.14
thee, or been false to thy c.   44.17
faithful ones, who made a c   50.5
against..friends, he violated his c.   55.20
Have regard for thy c; for   74.20
they were not true to his c.   78.37
against thee they make a c—   83.5
made a c with my chosen one,   89.3
to those who keep his c and   103.18
to Israel as an everlasting c,   105.10
remembered..his c,..and relented 106.45
If your sons keep my c and my   132.12
and forgets the c of her God;   Prov 2.17
your c with death..annulled,   Isa 28.18
given you as a c to the people,   42.6
this is my c with them, says   59.21
an everlasting c with them.   61.8
Israel..Judah have broken my c Jer 11.10
do not break thy c with us.   14.21
"Because they forsook the c   22.9
I will make a new c with..Israel   31.31
with them an everlasting c,   32.40
then also my c with David   33.21
join..LORD in an everlasting c   50.5
yet I will remember my c   Ezek 16.60
with you an everlasting c.   16.60
by keeping his c it might stand.)   17.14
I will make a c of peace   37.26
he shall make a strong c with   Dan 9.27
heart..set against..holy c.   11.28
at Adam they transgressed the c; Hos 6.7
that my c with Levi may hold,   Mal 2.4
companion and your wife by c.   2.14
this is my blood of the c,   Mt 26.28
"This is my blood of the c,   Mk 14.24
and to remember his holy c,   Lk 1.72
sons of..prophets and of..c   Acts 3.25
gave him..c of circumcision.   7.8
this will be my c with them   Rom 11.27
"This cup is the new c in   1Cor 11.25
to be ministers of a new c,   2Cor 3.6
when they read the old c,   3.14
annul a c previously ratified   Gal 3.17
Jesus the surety of a better c.   Heb 7.22
when I will establish a new c   8.8
he is the mediator of a new c,   9.15
"This is the c that I will make   10.16
the ark of his c was seen   Rev 11.19
C are broken, witnesses are   Isa 33.8

with empty oaths they make c;   Hos 10.4
strangers to the c of promise,   Eph 2.12

COVER — S — ED — ING (v)

I will c you with my hand   Ex 33.22
thou dost c him with favor as   Ps 5.12
will c you with his pinions,   91.4
as the waters c the sea.   Isa 11.9
say to the mountains, C us,   Hos 10.8
say..to the hills, 'C us.'   Lk 23.30
but love c all offenses.   Prov 10.12
took her veil and c herself.   Gen 24.65
cloud c the tabernacle,   Num 9.15
behold, the cloud c it,   16.42
and with two he c his feet,   Isa 6.2
nothing is c that will not be   Mt 10.26
Nothing is c up that will not   Lk 12.2
prophesies with his head c   1Cor 11.4
waters..c them fifteen cubits   Gen 7.20

COVERING (n)

He made darkness his c around Ps 18.11
the c too narrow to wrap   Isa 28.20

COVERT

In the c of thy presence thou   Ps 31.20

COVET — ED — ING

"You shall not c your   Ex 20.17
"Neither shall you c   Deut 5.21
They c fields, and seize them;   Mic 2.2
law..said, "You shall not c."   Rom 7.7
You shall not steal, You shall not c," 13.9
fifty shekels, then I c them,   Josh 7.21
I c no one's silver or gold   Acts 20.33
c, wickedness, deceit,..envy,   Mk 7.22

COVETOUS — NESS

who is c (that is, an idolater),   Eph 5.5
Because of..iniquity of his c   Isa 57.17
Take heed,..beware of all c;   Lk 12.15
wickedness, evil, c, malice.   Rom 1.29
wrought in me all kinds of c.   7.8

CRAFT — INESS

against all the beautiful c.   Isa 2.16
takes the wise in their..c;   Job 5.13
catches the wise in their c,"   1Cor 3.19
by their c in deceitful wiles.   Eph 4.14

CRAFTSMAN — MEN

c encourages the goldsmith,   Isa 41.7
and the c are but men;   44.11

CRAFTY

frustrates..devices of the c,   Job 5.15
choose the tongue of the c.   15.5

CREATE — S — D

C in me a clean heart, O God,   Ps 51.10
LORD will c over..Mount Zion   Isa 4.5
I make weal and c woe, I am   45.7
I c new heavens and..earth;   65.17
for thou didst c all things,   Rev 4.11
and c the wind, and declares   Amos 4.13
God c the heavens..earth.   Gen 1.1
God c..sea monsters   1.21
God c man in his own image,   1.27
your father, who c you,   Deut 32.6
thy Spirit, they are c;   Ps 104.30
he commanded and they were c.   148.5
LORD c me at the beginning   Prov 8.22
high and see: who c these?   Isa 40.26
Holy One of Israel has c it.   41.20
the LORD, who c the heavens   42.5
whom I c for my glory, whom   43.7
the LORD, who c the heavens   45.18

CREATE — S — D (cont.)
the LORD has c a new thing   Jer 31.22
c in Christ Jesus for good   Eph 2.10
in him all things were c,   Col 1.16
everything c by God is good,   1Tim 4.4
who c heaven and what is in it,   Rev 10.6

CREATION
from the beginning of the c   Mk 13.19
the c itself will be set free   Rom 8.21
the whole c has been groaning   8.22
if..in Christ, he is a new c;   2Cor 5.17
uncircumcision, but a new c.   Gal 6.15
from the beginning of c."   2Pet 3.4

CREATOR
Remember..your C in the days   Ecc 12.1
C of the ends of the earth.   Isa 40.28
the C of Israel, your King."   43.15
creature rather than the C,   Rom 1.25

CREATURES
swarms of living c,   Gen 1.20
the spirit of the living c   Ezek 10.17
four living c, full of eyes   Rev 4.6

CREDITOR — S
"A certain c had two debtors;   Lk 7.41
which of my c is it to whom   Isa 50.1

CREEPING
cattle and c things and beasts   Gen 1.24

CRETE
Phoenix, a harbor of C,   Acts 27.12
This is why I left you in C,   Tit 1.5

CRIME — S
requited the c of Abimelech,   Judg 9.56
"I find no c in this man."   Lk 23.4
in him no c deserving death;   23.22
told them, "I find no c in him.   Jn 18.38
that I find no c in him."   19.4
for I find no c in him."   19.6
the land is full of bloody c   Ezek 7.23

CRINGE — ING
thy enemies c before thee.   Ps 66.3
obeyed me; foreigners came c   18.44

CRIPPLE — D
he was a c from birth, who   Acts 14.8
son of Jonathan; he is c   2Sam 9.3
had a son who was c in his feet.   4.4
I will bind up the c,   Ezek 34.16

CROOKED
men whose paths are c, and   Prov 2.15
c cannot be made straight,   Ecc 1.15
make straight what he..made c?   7.13
they have made their roads c,   Isa 59.8

CROPS
have nowhere to store my c?'   Lk 12.17
the first share of the c.   2Tim 2.6

CROSS
he who does not take his c and   Mt 10.38
take up his c and follow me..   16.24
man..compelled to carry his c.   27.32
deny himself and take up his c   Mk 8.34
compelled..Simon..to carry his c.   15.21
and come down from the c!"   15.30
take up his c daily and follow   Lk 9.23
does not bear his own c and   14.27
laid on him the c, to carry   23.26
went out, bearing his own c,   Jn 19.17
lest..c of Christ be emptied   1Cor 1.17
the stumbling block of the c   Gal 5.11

not be persecuted for the c   6.12
to glory except in the c of..Christ.   6.14
unto death, even death on a c.   Phil 2.8
enemies of the c of Christ.   3.18
aside, nailing it to the c.   Col 2.14
endured the c, despising the   Heb 12.2

CROWD — S
"I have compassion on the c,   Mk 8.2
And great c followed him   Mt 4.25

CROWN — EST (v)
dost c him with glory and honor.   Ps 8.5
Thou c the year with thy bounty;   65.11

CROWN (n)
king's son, and put the c   2Chr 23.11
thou dost set a c of fine gold   Ps 21.3
bestow on you a beautiful c."   Prov 4.9
wife is the c of her husband,   12.4
hoary head is a c of glory;   16.31
Woe to the proud c of the   Isa 28.1
LORD..will be a c of glory,   28.5
You shall be a c of beauty   62.3
c has fallen from our head;   Lam 5.16
beautiful c upon your head.   Ezek 16.12
make a c, and set it upon   Zech 6.11
for me the c of righteousness,   2Tim 4.8
that no one may seize your c.   Rev 3.11
son of man, with a golden c   14.14

CROWS
before the cock c twice,   Mk 14.30

CRUCIBLE
The c is for silver, and   Prov 17.3

CRUCIFY — IED
men..whom you will kill and c,   Mt 23.34
they cried out again, "C him."   Mk 15.13
they led him out to c him.   15.20
they shouted out, "C, c, him!"   Lk 23.21
they cried out, "C him, c him!"   Jn 19.6
power to release..and..c you?"   19.10
mocked and scourged and c,   Mt 20.19
They all said, "Let him be c."   27.22
And when they had c him,   27.35
I know..you seek Jesus who was c.   28.5
Jesus of Nazareth, who was c.   Mk 16.6
The Skull, there they c him,   Lk 23.33
There they c him, and with him   Jn 19.18
c and killed by..lawless men.   Acts 2.23
our old self was c with him   Rom 6.6
divided? Was Paul c for you?   1Cor 1.13
except Jesus Christ and him c.   2.2
they would not have c the Lord   2.8
For he was c in weakness,   2Cor 13.4
I have been c with Christ;   Gal 2.20
was publicly portrayed as c?   3.1
the world has been c to me,   6.14
Egypt, where their Lord was c.   Rev 11.8

CRUEL — LY
Thou hast turned c to me;   Job 30.21
but a c man hurts himself.   Prov 11.17
jealousy is c as the grave.   Sol 8.6
She deals c with her young,   Job 39.16

CRUMBS
yet even the dogs eat the c   Mt 15.27
dogs..eat the children's c."   Mk 7.28

CRUSE
the c of oil shall not fail,   1Ki 17.14

CRUSH — ED
by thee I can c a troop; and   Ps 18.29
assembly..to c my young men;   Lam 1.15

CRUSH — ED (cont.)
crowd, lest they should *c* him; Mk 3.9
on any one it will *c* him." Lk 20.18
God..will soon *c* Satan under Rom 16.20
has *c* and abandoned the poor, Job 20.19

CRY — ING — IED
I will surely hear their *c*; Ex 22.23
and *c*, 'Unclean, unclean.' Lev 13.45
I *c* out, 'Violence!' but Job 19.7
Hearken to the sound of my *c*, Ps 5.2
I *c* out in the night before thee. 88.1
LORD; let my *c* come to thee! 102.1
With my whole heart I *c*; 119.145
In my distress I *c* to the LORD, 120.1
Out of the depths I *c* to thee, 130.1
will not *c* or lift up his voice, Isa 42.2
great city, and *c* against it; Jonah 1.2
will not wrangle or *c* aloud, Mt 12.19
very stones would *c* out." Lk 19.40
your brother's blood is *c* Gen 4.10
and lo, the babe was *c*. Ex 2.6
words of his father, he *c* out Gen 27.34
Samuel *c* to the LORD for 1Sam 7.9
Samuel was angry; and he *c* 15.11
to my God I *c* for help. From Ps 18.6
They *c* to..LORD,..he answered 99.6
c to the LORD in their trouble, 107.28
blind men..*c* out, "Have mercy Mt 20.30

CUNNING
we refuse to practice *c* or 2Cor 4.2
carried about..by..*c* of men Eph 4.14

CUP
and put my *c*, the silver *c*, Gen 44.2
be the portion of their *c*. Ps 11.6
LORD..chosen portion and my *c*; 16.5
head with oil, my *c* overflows. 23.5
hand of the LORD there is a *c*, 75.8
will lift up the *c* of salvation 116.13
drunk..the *c* of his wrath, Isa 51.17
they refuse to accept the *c* Jer 25.28
The *c* in the LORD's right hand Hab 2.16
a *c* of cold water because he Mt 10.42
able to drink the *c* that I am 20.22
cleanse the outside of the *c* 23.25
he took a *c*, and when he had 26.27
Father,..let this *c* pass from me; 26.39
a *c* of water to drink because Mk 9.41
able to drink the *c*..I drink, 10.38
he took a *c*, and when he had 14.23
remove this *c* from me; yet 14.36
cleanse the outside of the *c* Lk 11.39
he took a *c*, and when he had 22.17
willing, remove this *c* from me; 22.42
shall I not drink the *c* which Jn 18.11
The *c* of blessing which we 1Cor 10.16
"This *c* is the new covenant 11.25
c of the fury of his wrath. Rev 16.19

CURDS
he took *c*, and milk, Gen 18.8
He shall eat *c* and honey when Isa 7.15

CURED
In that hour he *c* many..diseases Lk 7.21
the rest..came and were *c*. Acts 28.9

CURSE — S — D (v)
who curses you I will *c*; Gen 12.3
Come..*c* this people for me, Num 22.6
How can I *c* whom God has not 23.8
he will *c* thee to thy face." Job 1.11
hold fast your integrity? *C* God, 2.9
loved to *c*; let curses come Ps 109.17

Even in..thought, do not *c* Ecc 10.20
bless those who *c* you, pray Lk 6.28
"Whoever *c* his father or his Ex 21.17
c his father or his mother, Prov 20.20
c are you above all cattle, Gen 3.14
you are *c* from the ground 4.11
C be their anger, for it is fierce; 49.7
"*C* before the LORD be the man Josh 6.26
"*C* be the man who eats 1Sam 14.24
as he came he *c* continually. 2Sam 16.5
"Naboth *c* God and the king." 1Ki 21.13
he *c* them in the name of the 2Ki 2.24
and *c* the day of his birth Job 3.1
"*C* is..man who trusts in man Jer 17.5
C be the day..I was born! 20.14
"*C* is..work..with slackness; 48.10
fig tree..you *c* has withered." Mk 11.21
ever says "Jesus be *c*!" 1Cor 12.3
"*C* be every one who hangs Gal 3.13
they *c* the name of God who Rev 16.9

CURSE — S — ING (n)
a blessing and a *c*: Deut 11.26
stand upon Mount Ebal for the *c*: 27.13
law, the blessing and the *c*, Josh 8.34
The LORD's *c* is on the house Prov 3.33
make them..a hissing and a *c*, Jer 25.18
c that goes out over the..land; Zech 5.3
then I will send the *c* upon you Mal 2.2
of the law are under a *c*; Gal 3.10
"Their mouth is full of *c* Rom 3.14
you have been a byword of *c* Zech 8.13
mouth come blessing and *c*. Jas 3.10

CURTAIN — S
the *c* of the temple was torn Mt 27.51
the *c* of the temple was torn Mk 15.38
the *c* of the temple was torn Lk 23.45
Behind..second *c* stood a tent Heb 9.3
opened for us through the *c*, 10.20
the tabernacle with ten *c* Ex 26.1

CUSH
flows around..land of *C*. Gen 2.13

CUSTODIAN
law was our *c* until Christ Gal 3.24
we are no longer under a *c*; 3.25

CUSTOM — S
impose tribute, *c*, or toll Ezra 7.24
to the synagogue, as his *c* was, Lk 4.16
any of these abominable *c* Lev 18.30
c of the peoples are false. Jer 10.3

CUT
you shall not *c* yourselves Deut 14.1
cried aloud, and *c* themselves 1Ki 18.28
c off..name and remnant, Isa 14.22
anointed one shall be *c* off, Dan 9.26
hand causes you to sin, *c* it off; Mk 9.43
they were *c* to the heart, Acts 2.37

CYMBAL — S
noisy gong or a clanging *c*. 1Cor 13.1
Praise him with sounding *c*; Ps 150.5

CYPRUS
Barnabas..a native of *C*, Acts 4.36
as far as Phoenicia and *C* 11.19
from there they sailed to *C*. 13.4
Barnabas took Mark..to *C*, 15.39
sailed under the lee of *C*, 27.4

CYRUS
first year..*C* king of Persia, Ezra 1.1
as King *C*..has commanded 4.3

CYRUS (cont.)

first year of *C* king of Babylon, Ezra 5.13
of *C*, 'He is my shepherd, Isa 44.28
LORD to his anointed, to *C*, 45.1
the first year of King *C*. Dan 1.21

D

DAILY

take up his cross *d* and follow Lk 9.23
Give us each day our *d* bread; 11.3

DAMASCUS

to Hobah, north of *D*. Gen 14.15
put garrisons in Aram of *D*; 2Sam 8.6
For the head of Syria is *D*, Isa 7.8
The word of the LORD..upon *D*. Zech 9.1
letters to..synagogues at *D*, Acts 9.2
'Rise, and go into *D*, and 22.10
At *D*, the governor under 2Cor 11.32
and again I returned to *D*. Gal 1.17

DAN (Son of Jacob)

Born, Gen 30.6; blessed by Jacob, Gen 49.16–17.
Tribe of Dan: blessed by Moses, Deut 33.22; allotted territory, Josh 19.40–48; migrated north, judg 18; became center of idolatry, 1Ki 12.28–30.

DAN (the City)

in pursuit as far as *D*. Gen 14.14
And they named the city *D*, Judg 9.29
Israel came out, from *D* to 20.1
from *D* to Beersheba knew 1Sam 3.20

DANCE — D (v)

daughters of Shiloh..to *d* Judg 21.21
'We piped..and you did not *d*; Mt 11.17
'We piped..and you did not *d*; Lk 7.32
David *d* before the LORD 2Sam 6.14
the daughter of Herodias *d* Mt 14.6
Herodias' daughter came..and *d*, Mk 6.22

DANCING (n)

saw..*d*, Moses' anger burned Ex 32.19
turned..my mourning into *d*; Ps 30.11
our *d*..turned to mourning. Lam 5.15

DANIEL (BELTESHAZZAR)

Trained in the king's palace, Dan 1.1–7; abstained from the king's food, Dan 1.8–16; interpreted Nebuchadnezzar's dreams, Dan 2; 4; interpreted the handwriting on the wall, Dan 5.10–30; delivered from the lion's den, Dan 6; visions and dreams, Dan 7—8; 10—12; prayed for his people, Dan 9.

DARE

good man will *d* even to die. Rom 5.7
brother, does he *d* go to law 1Cor 6.1

DARIUS

until the reign of *D* king Ezra 4.5
Then *D*..made a decree, and 6.1
D the Mede received..kingdom, Dan 5.31
prospered during..reign of *D* 6.28
In..second year of *D* the king, Hag 1.1
in the second year of *D*, Zech 1.1

DARK

In the *d* they dig through Job 24.16
I am very *d*, but comely, Sol 1.5
What I tell you in the *d*, utter Mt 10.27
a lamp shining in a *d* place, 2Pet 1.19

DARKEN — S — ED

d the earth in broad daylight. Amos 8.9
"Who is this that *d* counsel Job 38.2
stars..*d* and the clouds return Ecc 12.2
sun will be *d*, and the moon Mk 13.24

DARKNESS

great *d* fell upon him. Gen 15.12
d over the land of Egypt, Ex 10.21
land of gloom and deep *d*, Job 10.21
with the terrors of deep *d*. 24.17
and covered us with deep *d*. Ps 44.19
the *d* is not dark to thee, 139.12
but behold, distress and *d*, Isa 8.22
your God before he brings *d*, Jer 13.16
d and gloom, a day of clouds Joel 2.2
If..the light in you is *d*, Mt 6.23
cast him into the outer *d*; 22.13
cast..servant into the outer *d*; 25.30
there was *d* over all the land 27.45
there was *d* over the..land Mk 15.33
was *d* over the whole land Lk 23.44
out of *d* into his marvelous 1Pet 2.9

DAUGHTER — S

sister, the *d* of my father Gen 20.12
adopted her as his own *d*. Est 2.7
Shout aloud, O *d* of Jerusalem! Zech 9.9
"My *d* has just died; but come Mt 9.18
"Tell the *d* of Zion, Behold, 21.5
"My..*d* is at..point of death. Mk 5.23
the demon has left your *d*." 7.29
he had an only *d*, about twelve Lk 8.42
Pharaoh's *d* adopted him and Acts 7.21
the son of Pharaoh's *d*, Heb 11.24
Turn back, my *d*, go your way, Ruth 1.12
our *d* like corner pillars Ps 144.12
the heads of the *d* of Zion, Isa 3.17

DAVID

Anointed by Samuel, 1Sam 16.1–13; played the harp for Saul, 1Sam 16.14–23; killed Goliath, 1Sam 17; won Jonathan's friendship, 1Sam 18.1–4; incurred Saul's jealousy, 1Sam 18.5–9; married Michal, 1Sam 18.20–29; fled from Saul, 1Sam 19—22; fought the Philistines, 1Sam 23; spared Saul at En-gedi, 1Sam 24; David and Abigail, 1Sam 25; spared Saul at Ziph, 1Sam 26; lived among the Philistines, 1Sam 27.1—28.2; 29; defeated the Amalekites, 1Sam 30; made king over Judah, 2Sam 2.1–7; made king over Israel, 2Sam 5.1–16; brought the ark to Jerusalem, 2Sam 6; God's covenant with David, 2Sam 7; extended his kingdom, 2Sam 8; David and Bath-sheba, 2Sam 11.1—12.25; fled Absalom's revolt, 2Sam 15—16; returned to Jerusalem, 2Sam 19; David's song, 2Sam 22.1—23.7; numbered Israel and Judah, 2Sam 24; charged Solomon, 1Ki 2.1–9; died, 1Ki 2.10–12. (See also 1Chr 11—29.)

He chose *D* his servant, and Ps 78.70
raise up for *D* a righteous Jer 23.5
one shepherd, my servant *D*, Ezek 34.23
"Have you not read what *D* did, Mt 12.3
"Have..never read what *D* did, Mk 2.25
the throne of his father *D*, Lk 1.32
For *D* says concerning him, Acts 2.25
descended from *D* according to Rom 1.3
the Root of *D*, has conquered, Rev 5.5

DAWN

rise before d..cry for help;   Ps 119.147
light break forth like the d,   Isa 58.8
toward the d of the first day   Mt 28.1
when the day shall d upon us   Lk 1.78

DAY — S

God called the light D,   Gen 1.5
God blessed the seventh d   2.3
There has been no d like it   Josh 10.14
This d is a d of good news;   2Ki 7.9
knows that a d of darkness   Job 15.23
D to d pours forth speech, and   Ps 19.2
By d the LORD commands..love;   42.8
Thine is the d, thine also   74.16
This is the d..LORD has made;   118.24
Every d I will bless thee,   145.2
LORD of hosts has a d against   Isa 2.12
In that d the root of Jesse   11.10
You will say in that d: "I will   12.1
Wail, for the d of the LORD   13.6
the LORD has a d of vengeance,   34.8
'This d is a d of distress,   37.3
d of the Lord GOD of hosts,   Jer 45.10
the d of the LORD is near;   Ezek 30.3
the d of the LORD is near,   Joel 1.15
the d of the LORD is great   2.11
Why..have the d of the LORD? Amos 5.18
great d of the LORD is near,   Zeph 1.14
a d of the LORD is coming,   Zech 14.1
endure the d of his coming,   Mal 3.2
the d comes, burning like an oven,   4.1
trouble be sufficient for the d.   Mt 6.34
that d or..hour no one knows,   Mk 13.32
when the d shall dawn upon us   Lk 1.78
rejoiced..he was to see my d;   Jn 8.56
every d in the temple and at   Acts 5.42
becomingly as in the d, not   Rom 13.13
our Lord, I die every d!   1Cor 15.31
On the first d of every week,   16.2
on the d of the Lord Jesus.   2Cor 1.14
helped you on..d of salvation."   6.2
completion at the d of Jesus   Phil 1.6
the d of the Lord will come   1Thess 5.2
you see the D drawing near.   Heb 10.25
the d of the Lord will come   2Pet 3.10
as your d, so shall your   Deut 33.25
So teach us to number our d   Ps 90.12
My d..like an evening shadow;   102.11

DEACONS

with the bishops and d: Phil 1.1
D likewise must be serious,   1Tim 3.8

DEAD

your d bodies shall fall   Num 14.29
between the d and..living;   16.48
behold, these were all d   2Ki 19.35
after that they go to the d.   Ecc 9.3
leave..d to bury their own d."   Mt 8.22
girl is not d but sleeping."   9.24
deaf hear, and the d are raised   11.5
He is not God of the d, but   22.32
child is not d but sleeping."   Mk 5.39
wondered if he were already d;   15.44
"Your daughter is d; do not   Lk 8.49
"Leave the d to bury their..d;   9.60
my son was d, and is alive   15.24
Paul..supposing..he was d.   Acts 14.19
fell down from the third story..d.   20.9
although your bodies are d   Rom 8.10
If the d are not raised   1Cor 15.29
you were d through..trespasses   Eph 2.1
trees in late autumn, twice d,   Jude 12

name of being alive, and..are d.   Rev 3.1
Blessed are the d who die in   14.13
I saw the d, great and small,   20.12

DEAF

You shall not curse the d   Lev 19.14
In that day the d shall hear   Isa 29.18
brought to him a man who was d Mk 7.32
the d hear and the dumb speak."   7.37

DEAL — T

not d..according to our sins, Ps 103.10
he d well with Abram;   Gen 12.16
d thus with any other nation;   Ps 147.20

DEALINGS

Jews have no d with Samaritans. Jn 4.9

DEAR

consume like a moth what is d   Ps 39.11
servants hold her stones d,   102.14
centurion had a slave who was d Lk 7.2

DEATH

die the d of the righteous,   Num 23.10
life and good, d and evil.   Deut 30.15
whether for d or for life,   2Sam 15.21
snares of d confronted me.   22.6
the gates of d been revealed   Job 38.17
the valley of the shadow of d,   Ps 23.4
snares of d encompassed me;   116.3
Precious is..d of his saints.   116.15
its end is the way to d.   Prov 14.12
He will swallow up d for ever,   Isa 25.8
way of life and the way of d.   Jer 21.8
no pleasure in..d of any one, Ezek 18.32
O D, where are your plagues? Hos 13.14
powers of d shall not prevail   Mt 16.18
daughter is at the point of d.   Mk 5.23
against Jesus to put him to d;   14.55
those who sit..in..shadow of d, Lk 1.79
some here who will not taste d   9.27
seeking how to put him to d: 22.2
show by what d he was to die. Jn 12.33
to show by what d he was to   21.19
d reigned from Adam to Moses, Rom 5.14
by the Spirit you put to d   8.13
I am sure that neither d,   8.38
"D..swallowed up in victory." 1Cor 15.54
"O d, where is thy victory?   15.55
a fragrance from d to d,   2Cor 2.16
Put to d..what is earthly   Col 3.5
Jesus, who abolished d and   2Tim 1.10
not be hurt by the second d.'   Rev 2.11

DEBORAH

Now D, a prophetess, the wife   Judg 4.4
And D said to Barak, "Up!   4.14
Then sang D and Barak the son   5.1

DEBT — S

and every one who was in d,   1Sam 22.2
and the exaction of every d.   Neh 10.31
him and forgave him the d.   Mt 18.27
sell the oil and pay your d,   2Ki 4.7

DEBTORS

"A certain creditor had two d; Lk 7.41
summoning his master's d one   16.5
we are d, not to the flesh,   Rom 8.12

DECEIT

and their heart prepares d."   Job 15.35
my tongue will not utter d.   27.4
cursing and d and oppression;   Ps 10.7
my prayer from lips free of d!   17.1
in whose spirit there is no d.   32.2

DECEIT (cont.)
and your lips from speaking d. Ps 34.13
and your tongue frames d.   50.19
D is in the heart of those   Prov 12.20
there was no d in his mouth.   Isa 53.9
and the d of their own minds.   Jer 14.14
wickedness, d, licentiousness,   Mk 7.22
murder, strife, d, malignity,   Rom 1.29

DECEITFUL — LY — NESS
LORD abhors bloodthirsty and d   Ps 5.6
words that devour, O d tongue.   52.4
Charm is d,..beauty is vain,   Prov 31.30
heart is d above all things,   Jer 17.9
false apostles, d workmen,   2Cor 11.13
their craftiness in d wiles.   Eph 4.14
deal d with false balances,   Amos 8.5
hardened by the d of sin.   Heb 3.13

DECEIVE — S — D — ING
"Why did you d us, saying,   Josh 9.22
Did I not say, Do not d me?''   2Ki 4.28
'Do not let Hezekiah d you,   18.29
Do not d yourselves, saying,   Jer 37.9
and flattering words they d   Rom 16.18
Let no one d you with empty   Eph 5.6
Let no one d you in any way;   2Thess 2.3
deceive him, as one d a man?   Job 13.9
who d his neighbor and says,   Prov 26.19
Every one d his neighbor,   Jer 9.5
Why then have you d me?''   Gen 29.25
"Why have you d me thus,   1Sam 19.17
d and the deceiver are his.   Job 12.16
GOD,..thou hast utterly d   Jer 4.10
O LORD, thou hast d me, and   20.7
called to my lovers but they d   Lam 1.19
Do not be d; neither..immoral,   1Cor 6.9
Do not be d: "Bad company   15.33
serpent d Eve by his cunning,   2Cor 11.3
Do not be d; God is not mocked, Gal 6.7
Adam was not d, but the woman 1Tim 2.14
nations were d by thy sorcery. Rev 18.23
against the LORD by d his   Lev 6.2

DECEIVER — S
is the d and the antichrist.   2Jn 7
Satan,..d of the whole world—   Rev 12.9
men, empty talkers and d,   Tit 1.10

DECENTLY
all things should be done d   1Cor 14.40

DECIDE — D
Now d what answer I shall   1Chr 21.12
and d with equity for the meek   Isa 11.4
He..shall d for strong nations   Mic 4.3
I d to know nothing among you 1Cor 2.2

DECISION — S
shall declare to you the d.   Deut 17.9
multitudes, in..valley of d!   Joel 3.14
Inspired d are on the lips   Prov 16.10
d..reached by the apostles   Acts 16.4

DECLARE — D
D his glory among..nations   1Chr 16.24
D his glory among the nations,   Ps 96.3
and I will d thy greatness.   145.6
d my glory among the nations,   Isa 66.19
And then will I d to them,   Mt 7.23
d to you the things..to come.   Jn 16.13
When I d not my sin, my body   Ps 32.3
"The former things I d of old,   Isa 48.3

DECREE — D (v)
Woe to those who d iniquitous   Isa 10.1
which God d before the ages   1Cor 2.7

heritage d for him by God.''   Job 20.29
"Seventy weeks of years are d   Dan 9.24

DECREE — S (n)
I make a d regarding what   Ezra 6.8
I will tell of the d of the LORD: Ps 2.7
It is a d of the Most High,   Dan 4.24
a d, that in all my..dominion   6.26
d went out from Caesar Augustus Lk 2.1
Thy d are very sure; holiness   Ps 93.5
against the d of Caesar,   Acts 17.7

DEDICATE — S — D
my God and d it to him for   2Chr 2.4
a man d his house to be holy   Lev 27.14
King David d to the LORD,   2Sam 8.11
which David his father had d,   1Ki 7.51
Israel d the house of the LORD.   8.63
From spoil won..they d gifts   1Chr 26.27

DEDICATION
the d of the altar on the day   Num 7.10
offered at the d of..house   Ezra 6.17
at the d of the wall of   Neh 12.27
come to the d of the image   Dan 3.2
feast of the D at Jerusalem;   Jn 10.22

DEED — S
bring every d into judgment,   Ecc 12.14
but in d and in truth.   1Jn 3.18
where are..his wonderful d   Judg 6.13
Praise him for his mighty d;   Ps 150.2
recompense..according to..d   Jer 25.14
they have made their d evil.   Mic 3.4
the due reward of our d; but   Lk 23.41
because their d were evil.   Jn 3.19
put to death the d of the body   Rom 8.13
to be rich in good d, liberal   1Tim 6.18
saved us, not because of d   Tit 3.5
for their d follow them!''   Rev 14.13

DEEP
find out the d things of God?   Job 11.7
D calls to d at the thunder   Ps 42.7
LORD! Thy thoughts are very d!   92.5
Thou didst cover it with the d   104.6
when..the fountains of the d,   Prov 8.28
he reveals d and mysterious   Dan 2.22
to Simon, "Put out into the d   Lk 5.4
call the d things of Satan,   Rev 2.24

DEFEAT
To have lawsuits..is d for you. 1Cor 6.7

DEFEND
I will d this city to save   2Ki 19.34
will d this city for my own   20.6
cause of truth and to d the   Ps 45.4
I will d this city to save   Isa 37.35

DEFENSE
his..d will be the fortresses   Isa 33.16
hear the d which I now make   Acts 22.1
my imprisonment and in the d   Phil 1.7

DEFENSELESS
I seek refuge; leave me not d!   Ps 141.8

DEFER — RED
"For my name's sake..d..anger, Isa 48.9
Hope d makes the heart sick,   Prov 13.12

DEFILE — S — D — ING
"Do not d yourselves by   Lev 18.24
You shall not d the land   Num 35.34
you d yourselves with..idols   Ezek 20.31
They shall not d themselves   37.23
not d himself with the king's   Dan 1.8

DEFILE — S — D — ING (cont.)
which come out of a man..*d* Mk 7.15
does not cleanse himself, *d* Num 19.13
from the heart,..this *d* a man. Mt 15.18
comes out of a man is what *d* Mk 7.20
since he has *d* the priesthood Num 19.20
they have *d* the priesthood Neh 13.29
they have *d* thy holy temple; Ps 79.1
when you came in you *d* my land, Jer 2.7
you have *d* my sanctuary with Ezek 5.11
they have *d* my sanctuary 23.38
They have *d* my holy name 43.8
played the harlot, Israel is *d*. Hos 5.3
conscience, being weak, is *d*. 1Cor 8.7
uncleanness..*d* my tabernacle Lev 15.31

DEFRAUDED
if I have *d* any one of anything Lk 19.8
wrong? Why not rather be *d*? 1Cor 6.7

DEFY
"I *d* the ranks of Israel 1Sam 17.10
men who maliciously *d* thee, Ps 139.20

DELIGHT — S — ED (v)
would the king *d* to honor Est 6.6
you will *d*..in the Almighty, Job 22.26
I *d* to do thy will, O my God; Ps 40.8
for thou didst *d* in them. 44.3
then..*d* in right sacrifices, 51.19
How long will scoffers *d* in Prov 1.22
I do not *d* in..blood of bulls, Isa 1.11
and *d* yourselves in fatness. 55.2
seek..and *d* to know my ways, 58.2
the messenger..in whom you *d*, Mal 3.1
I *d* in the law of God, in my Rom 7.22
If the LORD *d* in us, he will Num 14.8
whom the king *d* to honor." Est 6.11
not a God who *d* in wickedness; Ps 5.4
establishes..whose way he *d*. 37.23
greatly *d* in his commandments! 112.1
reproves..son in whom he *d*. Prov 3.12
for the LORD *d* in you, and Isa 62.4
because he *d* in steadfast love. Mic 7.18
Saul's son, *d* much in David. 1Sam 19.1
delivered me, because he *d* 2Sam 22.20
your God, who has *d* in you 1Ki 10.9

DELIGHT — S (n)
the tree was..a *d* to the eyes, Gen 3.6
as the LORD took *d* in..good Deut 28.63
again take *d* in prospering 30.9
"Has the LORD as great *d* 1Sam 15.22
he take *d* in the Almighty? Job 27.10
that he should take *d* in God.' 34.9
his *d* is in the law of the LORD, Ps 1.2
Take *d* in the LORD, and he will 37.4
thou hast no *d* in sacrifice; 51.16
live; for thy law is my *d*. 119.77
I was daily his *d*, rejoicing Prov 8.30
of blameless ways are his *d*. 11.20
prayer of..upright is his *d*. 15.8
Righteous takes are the *d* of 16.13
With..*d* I sat in his shadow, Sol 2.3
to take the *d* of your eyes Ezek 24.16
cares..and the *d* in riches, Mk 4.19
drink from the river of thy *d*. Ps 36.8

DELIVER — S — ED — ING
D me, I pray thee, from Gen 32.11
I have come down to *d* them Ex 3.8
d our lives from death." Josh 2.13
men that lapped I will *d* you, Judg 7.7
Say also: "*D* us, O God of 1Chr 16.35

Arise, O LORD! *D* me, O my God! Ps 3.7
O LORD, save my life; *d* me 6.4
that he may deliver their soul 33.19
D us for the sake of..love! 44.26
D me from my enemies, O my God, 59.1
nor will wickedness *d* those Ecc 8.8
saying, "The LORD will *d* us." Isa 36.18
none who can *d* from my hand; 43.13
"*D* me, for thou art my god!" 44.17
Or have I no power to *d*? 50.2
for I am with you to *d* you, Jer 1.8
I will *d* you on that day, 39.17
and gold are not able to *d* Ezek 7.19
able to *d* us from the burning Dan 3.17
Daniel, "May your God,..*d* you!" 6.16
and *d* him to the Gentiles; Mk 10.33
they will *d* you up to councils; 13.9
brother will *d* up brother 13.12
Who will *d* me from this body Rom 7.24
you are to *d* this man to Satan 1Cor 5.5
to *d* us from the present evil Gal 1.4
d..those..subject to..bondage. Heb 2.15
LORD helps them and *d* them; Ps 37.40
and thy right hand *d* me. 138.7
righteousness *d* from death. Prov 11.4
God..who has *d* your enemies Gen 14.20
"An Egyptian *d* us out of Ex 2.19
thou·hast not *d* thy people 5.23
he had *d* them out of the hand 18.9
I *d* you from the hand of Judg 6.9
'My own hand has *d* me.' 7.2
LORD *d* Israel that day; 1Sam 14.23
"The king *d* us from the 2Sam 19.9
He *d* me from my strong enemy, 22.18
d me, because he delighted 22.20
because I *d* the poor who Job 29.12
He *d* me from my strong enemy, Ps 18.17
warrior is not *d* by..strength. 33.16
and *d* me from all my fears. 34.4
hast *d* me from every trouble, 54.7
and *d* them from the..enemy. 106.10
he *d* them from their distress; 107.6
he *d* them from their distress; 107.19
thou hast *d* my soul from death, 116.8
righteous is *d* from trouble, Prov 11.8
by his wisdom *d* the city. Yet Ecc 9.15
time your people shall be *d*, Dan 12.1
All things have been *d* to me Mt 11.27
Son of man is to be *d* into 17.22
the Son of man will be *d* to 20.18
Son of man will be *d* up to be 26.2
d him to Pilate the governor. 27.2
led him away..*d* him to Pilate. Mk 15.1
will be *d* to the Gentiles, Lk 18.32
will be *d* up even by parents 21.16
d them to what has been raised, Rom 15.28
d us from so deadly a peril, 2Cor 1.10
has *d* us from the dominion of Col 1.13
d you from the way of evil, Prov 2.12

DELIVERANCE
is hot, you shall have *d*.' " 1Sam 11.9
LORD has wrought *d* in Israel." 11.13
D belongs to the LORD; thy Ps 3.8
that..I may rejoice in thy *d*. 9.14
his *d* to a people yet unborn, 22.31
thou dost encompass me with *d*. 32.7
Say to my soul, "I am your *d*!" 35.3
d for Israel..come from Zion! 53.6
I bring near my *d*, it is not Isa 46.13
My *d* draws near speedily, 51.5
D belongs to the LORD!" Jonah 2.9
light; I shall behold his *d*. Mic 7.9

DELIVERANCE (cont.)
God was giving them *d* by his — Acts 7.25
this will turn out for my *d*, — Phil 1.19

DELIVERER
LORD raised up a *d* for the — Judg 3.9
and my fortress, and my *d*. — 2Sam 22.2
my fortress, and my *d*, my God, — Ps 18.2
my strong *d*, thou hast covered — 140.7

DELUDE — D
d you with beguiling speech. — Col 2.4
a *d* mind has led him astray, — Isa 44.20

DELUSION
Behold, they are all a *d*; — Isa 41.29
God sends..a strong *d*, to — 2Thess 2.11

DEMON — S
daughter..possessed by a *d*." — Mt 15.22
and you say, 'He has a *d*.' — Lk 7.33
casting out a *d* that was dumb; — 11.14
people answered, "You have a *d*! — Jn 7.20
diseases, and cast out many *d*; — Mk 1.34
by..prince of *d* he casts out..*d*." — 3.22
casting out *d* in your name, — 9.38
pagans sacrifice..to *d* and — 1Cor 10.20
spirits and doctrines of *d*, — 1Tim 4.1
the *d* believe—and shudder. — Jas 2.19
nor give up worshiping *d* — Rev 9.20
Babylon..dwelling place of *d*, — 18.2

DEMONSTRATION
in *d* of the Spirit and power, — 1Cor 2.4

DEN
a *d* of robbers in your eyes? — Jer 7.11
you make it a *d* of robbers." — Mt 21.13

DENY — ING — IES — IED
I also will *d* before my Father — Mt 10.33
let him *d* himself and take up — 16.24
you will *d* me three times." — 26.34
let him *d* himself and take up — Mk 8.34
you will *d* me three times." — 14.30
three times *d* that you know — Lk 22.34
if we *d* him, he also will *d* — 2Tim 2.12
they *d* him by their deeds; — Tit 1.16
you did not *d* my faith even — Rev 2.13
heresies, even of the Master — 2Pet 2.1
who *d* me before men will be *d* — Lk 12.9
antichrist,..who *d* the Father — 1Jn 2.22
Peter..*d* it before them all, — Mt 26.70
he *d* it, saying, "I neither know — Mk 14.68
But he *d* it, saying, "Woman, — Lk 22.57
one of his disciples?" He *d* it — Jn 18.25

DEPART — ED
said to God, 'D from us,' — Job 22.17
D from evil, and do good; — Ps 34.14
d, go out thence, touch no — Isa 52.11
at his left hand, 'D from me, — Mt 25.41
asked him to *d* from them; — Lk 8.37
Israel *d* to their tents. — 1Ki 12.16
not wickedly *d* from my God. — Ps 18.21

DEPARTURE
in glory and spoke of his *d*, — Lk 9.31
after my *d* you may..recall — 2Pet 1.15

DEPRAVED
They are all alike *d*; there — Ps 53.3
men who are *d* in mind and — 1Tim 6.5

DEPRIVE
d the innocent of his right! — Isa 5.23
d..of my ground for boasting. — 1Cor 9.15

DEPTHS
Out of the *d* I cry to thee, — Ps 130.1
Spirit searches..*d* of God. — 1Cor 2.10

DERBE
fled to Lystra and *D*, cities — Acts 14.6
he came..to *D* and to Lystra. — 16.1
Gaius of *D*, and Timothy; — 20.4

DERIDED
who passed by *d* him, wagging — Mt 27.39
those who passed by *d* him, — Mk 15.29

DESCEND — ED
Lord himself will *d* from — 1Thess 4.16
And the LORD *d* in the cloud — Ex 34.5
the Holy Spirit *d* upon him — Lk 3.22
our Lord was *d* from Judah, — Heb 7.14

DESCENDANTS
d I will give this land." — Gen 12.7
your *d* after you, the land — 17.8
through Isaac shall your *d* — 21.12
will give to your *d*..lands; — 26.4
establish your *d* for ever, — Ps 89.4
told, "So shall your *d* be." — Rom 4.18
"Through Isaac shall your *d* — 9.7

DESECRATED
they *d* the dwelling place of — Ps 74.7

DESERT (n)
Some wandered in *d* wastes, — Ps 107.4
break forth..streams in the *d*; — Isa 35.6
I will set in the *d* the cyprus, — 41.19
d..cities lift up their voice, — 42.11
d like the garden of the LORD; — 51.3

DESERTED (v)
Demas,..has *d* me and gone — 2Tim 4.10

DESERTING (v)
quickly *d* him who called you — Gal 1.6

DESERVE — S — ING
the man did not *d* to die, — Deut 19.6
for the laborer *d* his food. — Mt 10.10
They answered, "He *d* death." — 26.66
"The laborer *d* his wages." — 1Tim 5.18
condemned him as *d* death. — Mk 14.64

DESIGNATED
and *d* Son of God in power — Rom 1.4
being *d* by God a high priest — Heb 5.10

DESIGNS
favor the *d* of the wicked? — Job 10.3
we are not ignorant of his *d*. — 2Cor 2.11

DESIRABLE
for whom is all that is *d* in — 1Sam 9.20

DESIRE — S — ST — D (v)
We do not *d* the knowledge — Job 21.14
and offering thou dost not *d*; — Ps 40.6
the king will *d* your beauty. — 45.11
nothing..I *d* besides thee. — 73.25
Do not *d* her beauty in your — Prov 6.25
no beauty that we should *d* — Isa 53.2
days..coming when you will *d* — Lk 17.22
earnestly *d*..higher gifts. — 1Cor 12.31
earnestly *d* to prophesy, — 14.39
you who *d* to be under law, — Gal 4.21
soul of the wicked *d* evil; — Prov 21.10
thou *d* truth in..inward being; — Ps 51.6
of Sheba all that she *d*, — 2Chr 9.12
orders..to do as every man *d*. — Est 1.8
More to be *d*..than gold, even — Ps 19.10
kings *d* to see what you see — Lk 10.24

DESIRE — S — ST — D (v) (cont.)
earnestly *d* to eat..passover   Lk 22.15
Herod..had long *d* to see him,   23.8

DESIRE — S (n)
your *d*..for your husband,   Gen 3.16
prosper all my help and..*d*?   2Sam 23.5
wilt hear the *d* of the meek;   Ps 10.17
thou satisfiest the *d* of every   145.16
fulfils the *d* of all who fear   145.19
d of..righteous..be granted.   Prov 10.24
The *d* of the righteous ends   11.23
d fulfilled is a tree of life.   13.12
d fulfilled is sweet to the soul;   13.19
The *d* of the sluggard kills   21.25
eyes than the wandering of *d*;   Ecc 6.9
and *d* fails; because man goes   12.5
my beloved's,..*d* is for me.   Sol 7.10
thy memorial name is the *d*   Isa 26.8
Brethren, my heart's *d* and   Rom 10.1
broken off,..*d* of my heart.   Job 17.11
give you the *d* of your heart.   Ps 37.4
Grant not, O LORD, the *d* of   140.8
the *d* of the flesh are against   Gal 5.17
following the *d* of body and   Eph 2.3

DESOLATE
God gives the *d* a home to dwell   Ps 68.6
country lies *d*, your cities   Isa 1.7
the LORD will..make it *d*,   24.1
your house is forsaken and *d*.   Mt 23.38

DESOLATION
"The whole land shall be a *d*;   Jer 4.27
know..its *d* has come near.   Lk 21.20

DESPISE — S — D — ING
will this people *d* me?   Num 14.11
therefore *d* not the chastening   Job 5.17
Even young children *d* me;   19.18
therefore I *d* myself, and   42.6
fools *d* wisdom..instruction.   Prov 1.7
do not *d* the LORD's discipline   3.11
"Because you *d* this word,   Isa 30.12
Your lovers *d* you; they seek   Jer 4.30
"I hate, I *d* your feasts,   Amos 5.21
devoted to..one and *d* the other.   Mt 6.24
do not *d* one of these little ones;   18.10
devoted to..one..*d* the other.   Lk 16.13
Or do you *d* the church of   1Cor 11.22
let no one *d* him. Speed him   16.11
you did not scorn or *d* me,   Gal 4.14
defiling passion..*d* authority.   2Pet 2.10
He who *d* the word brings   Prov 13.13
Esau *d* his birthright.   Gen 25.34
he..*d* the word of the LORD,   Num 15.31
these men have *d* the LORD."   16.30
she *d* him in her heart.   2Sam 6.16
They *d* his statutes, and   2Ki 17.15
we are *d*; turn back their taunt   Neh 4.4
scorned by men, and *d* by the   Ps 22.6
they *d* the pleasant land,   106.24
I am small and *d*, yet I do   119.141
they have *d* the Holy One of   Isa 1.4
d the word of the Holy One   5.24
deeply *d*, abhorred by..nations,   49.7
all the day my name is *d*.   52.5
He was *d* and rejected by men;   53.3
I will make you..*d* among men.   Jer 49.15
has *d* the day of small things   Zech 4.10
were righteous and *d* others?   Lk 18.9
God chose what is low and *d*   1Cor 1.28
of God, *d* his words, and   2Chr 36.16

DESPOIL — ED
you shall *d* the Egyptians."   Ex 3.22
Thus they *d* the Egyptians.   12.36
"Because the poor are *d*,   Ps 12.5

DESTINE — D
I will *d* you to the sword,   Isa 65.12
He *d* us in love to be his sons   Eph 1.5
God has not *d* us for wrath,   1Thess 5.9
was *d* before the foundation   1Pet 1.20

DESTITUTE
he will regard..prayer of..*d*,   Ps 102.17
d, afflicted, ill-treated—   Heb 11.37

DESTROY — S — ED
d all their figured stones,   Num 33.52
d them from the camp,   Deut 2.15
you must utterly *d* them;   7.2
you shall utterly *d* them,   20.17
Amalek, and utterly *d* all   1Sam 15.3
the LORD would not *d* Judah,   2Ki 8.19
d all the wicked in the land,   Ps 101.8
they shall *d* with the sword."   Jer 5.17
wilt thou *d* all that remains   Ezek 9.8
'I am able to *d* the temple   Mt 26.61
He will come and *d* the tenants,   Mk 12.9
heard him say, 'I will *d* this   14.58
the people sought to *d* him;   Lk 19.47
"*D* this temple, and in three   Jn 2.19
through death he might *d* him   Heb 2.14
complacence of fools *d* them;   Prov 1.32
approaches and no moth *d*.   Lk 12.33
If any one *d* God's temple,   1Cor 3.17
they should be utterly *d*,   Josh 11.20
house of..wicked will be *d*,   Prov 14.11
The Lord has *d* without mercy   Lam 2.2
are *d* for lack of knowledge;   Hos 4.6

DESTROYERS
I will prepare *d* against you,   Jer 22.7
destroying..*d* of the earth."   Rev 11.18

DESTRUCTION
end he shall come to *d*."   Num 24.20
till the storms of *d* pass by.   Ps 57.1
Pride goes before *d*, and a   Prov 16.18
decree of *d* from the Lord   Isa 28.22
grief because of the *d* of the   Lam 2.11
for the *d* of the flesh,   1Cor 5.5
in the same *d* with them,   2Pet 2.12

DETERMINED
know that evil is *d* by him.   1Sam 20.7
God has *d* to destroy you,   2Chr 25.16
Haman..saw that evil was *d*   Est 7.7
Since his days are *d*, and   Job 14.5
for what is *d* shall be done.   Dan 11.36
Son..goes as it has been *d*;   Lk 22.22
having *d* allotted periods   Acts 17.26
and has *d* this in his heart,   1Cor 7.37

DETESTABLE
Cast away the *d* things   Ezek 20.7
d like the thing they loved.   Hos 9.10

DEVIL
wilderness to be tempted by..*d*.   Mt 4.1
enemy who sowed them is the *d*;   13.39
the *d* comes and takes away   Lk 8.12
You are of your father the *d*,   Jn 8.44
d..put it into the heart of Judas   13.2
give no opportunity to the *d*.   Eph 4.27
Resist the *d* and he will flee   Jas 4.7
Your adversary the *d* prowls   1Pet 5.8
d..sinned from the beginning.   1Jn 3.8

DEVIL (cont.)
the *d* is about to throw some	Rev 2.10
the *d* has come down to you	12.12
the *d* who had deceived them	20.10

DEVISE — D
for their minds *d* violence,	Prov 24.2
these are..men who *d* iniquity	Ezek 11.2
Woe to those who *d* wickedness	Mic 2.1
son of Remaliah, has *d* evil	Isa 7.5

DEVOTE — D
d their gain to the LORD,	Mic 4.13
every *d* thing is most holy	Lev 27.28
Every *d* thing in Israel	Num 18.14
take any of the *d* things	Josh 6.18
in regard to the *d* things;	7.1
every *d* thing in Israel	Ezek 44.29

DEVOTION
because of my *d* to the house	1Chr 29.3
sincere..pure *d* to Christ.	2Cor 11.3

DEVOUR — S — ED
"Shall the sword *d* for ever?	2Sam 2.26
all who *d* you shall be *d*,	Jer 30.16
and they *d* their rulers. All	Hos 7.7
for you *d* widows' houses and	Mt 23.14*n*
but a foolish man *d* it.	Prov 21.20
each *d* his neighbor's flesh,	Isa 9.20
you shall be *d* by the sword;	1.20

DEVOUT
Simeon,..was righteous and *d*,	Lk 2.25
Jews, *d* men from every nation	Acts 2.5
a *d* man who feared God with	10.2
Ananias, a *d* man according	22.12

DEW
if there is *d* on the fleece	Judg 6.37
It is like the *d* of Hermon,	Ps 133.3
the clouds drop down the *d*.	Prov 3.20
but his favor is like *d*	19.12
like the *d* that goes early away,	Hos 6.4
the *d* that goes early away,	13.3
I will be as the *d* to Israel;	14.5

DIE — S — D
eat of it you shall *d*."	Gen 2.17
men *d* the common death	Num 16.29
shall *d* in the wilderness."	26.65
I must *d* in this land,	Deut 4.22
d on the mountain which	32.50
me *d* with the Philistines."	Judg 16.30
"Why did I not *d* at birth,	Job 3.11
and wisdom will *d* with you.	12.2
enemies say.."When will he *d*,	Ps 41.5
I shall not *d*, but..live,	118.17
fools *d* for lack of sense.	Prov 10.21
who despises the word will *d*.	19.16
why will you *d*, O house of	Ezek 33.11
"If I must *d* with you, I will	Mk 14.31
you will *d* in your sins unless	Jn 8.24
go, that we may *d* with him."	11.16
this disciple was not to *d*;	21.23
being raised..never *d* again;	Rom 6.9
if we *d*, we *d* to the Lord;	14.8
our Lord, I *d* every day!	1Cor 15.31
is Christ, and to *d* is gain.	Phil 1.21
man *d*, and is laid low;	Job 14.10
One *d* in full prosperity,	21.23
wise man *d* just like the fool!	Ecc 2.16
if it *d*, it bears much fruit.	Jn 12.24
all flesh *d* that moved	Gen 7.21
Abraham..*d* in a good old age,	25.8
Isaac..*d* and was gathered	35.29

the king of Egypt *d*.	Ex 2.23
Moses..servant of the LORD *d*	Deut 34.5
d, being a hundred and ten	Josh 24.29
Saul *d*, and his three sons,	1Sam 31.6
I had *d* instead of you, O	2Sam 18.33
So the king *d*, and was	1Ki 22.37
lap till noon, and then he *d*.	2Ki 4.20
Saul *d* for..unfaithfulness;	1Chr 10.13
and at evening my wife *d*.	Ezek 24.18
a man who had *d* was being	Lk 7.12
Christ *d* for the ungodly.	Rom 5.6
who *d* to sin still live in it?	6.2
d to the law through..Christ,	7.4
came, sin revived and I *d*;	7.9
brother for whom Christ *d*.	1Cor 8.11
and ill, and some have *d*.	11.30
that Christ *d* for our sins	15.3
convinced that one..*d* for all;	2Cor 5.14
I through the law *d* to the law,	Gal 2.19
Christ also *d* for sins once	1Pet 3.18
every living thing *d*..in..sea.	Rev 16.3

DIFFERENCE
d between..unclean and	Ezek 22.26
d between..holy and..common,	44.23

DIFFERENT
who sees anything *d* in you?	1Cor 4.7
and turning to a *d* gospel—	Gal 1.6

DIG — S
I am not strong enough to *d*,	Lk 16.3
who *d* a pit will fall into it;	Prov 26.27
who *d* a pit will fall into it;	Ecc 10.8

DILIGENT
The hand of the *d* will rule,	Prov 12.24
the soul of the *d* is richly	13.4
plans of..*d* lead..to abundance,	21.5

DIM
his eye was not *d*, nor his	Deut 34.7
My eyes grow *d* with waiting for	Ps 69.3

DINE
the men are to *d* with me	Gen 43.16
a Pharisee asked him to *d*	Lk 11.37

DINNER
a *d* of herbs where love is	Prov 15.17
I have made ready my *d*, my oxen	Mt 22.4
"When you give a *d* or..banquet,	Lk 14.12

DIPPED
"He who has *d* his hand in	Mt 26.23
when he had *d* the morsel,	Jn 13.26

DIRECT — S — ED
d your heart to the LORD,	1Sam 7.3
and *d* their hearts toward	1Chr 29.18
d my steps by..thy precepts;	Ps 119.128
but the LORD *d* his steps.	Prov 16.9
Who has *d* the Spirit of the	Isa 40.13
mountain to which Jesus had *d*	Mt 28.16
d by a holy angel to send	Acts 10.22

DIRECTION
did not ask *d* from the LORD.	Josh 9.14

DISAPPOINTED
the hope of man is *d*;	Job 41.9
they trusted, and were not *d*.	Ps 22.5

DISASTER
for *d*..will rise suddenly,	Prov 24.22
nor..desired the day of *d*,	Jer 17.16

DISCERN — EST — ED — ING
that I may *d* between good and	1Ki 3.9

DISCERN — EST — ED — ING (cont.)

thou *d* my thoughts from afar.   Ps 139.2
they are spiritually *d*.   1Cor 2.14
drinks without *d* the body   11.29

DISCHARGED

husband dies she is *d* from..law Rom 7.2
But now we are *d* from the law,   7.6

DISCIPLE — S

"A *d* is not above his teacher,   Mt 10.24
A *d* is not above his teacher,   Lk 6.40
does not renounce..cannot be..*d*. 14.33
his *d*, but we are *d* of Moses.   Jn 9.28
saw his mother, and the *d*   19.26
Joseph of Arimathea, who was a *d* 19.38
to Simon Peter and the other *d*,   20.2
d at Damascus named Ananias. Acts 9.10
seal the teaching among my *d*.   Isa 8.16
he called to him his twelve *d*   Mt 10.1
the *d* gave them to the crowds.   14.19
your *d* transgress the tradition   15.2
your *d*,..could not heal him."   17.16
Olives, then Jesus sent two *d*,   21.1
tell his *d* that he has risen   28.7
Go..and make *d* of all nations,   28.19
withdrew with his *d* to the sea,   Mk 3.7
he made his *d* get into the boat   6.45
to his *d* to set before the people; 8.6
teaching his *d*, saying to them,   9.31
and the *d* rebuked them.   10.13
John, calling..two of his *d*,   Lk 7.19
broke..and gave them to the *d*   9.16
Olivet, he sent two of the *d*,   19.29
Olives; and the *d* followed   22.39
and his *d* believed in him.   Jn 2.11
between John's *d* and a Jew   3.25
many of his *d* drew back and   6.66
my word, you are truly my *d*,   8.31
know that you are my *d*, if   13.35
fruit, and so prove to be my *d*.   15.8
doors..shut where the *d* were   20.19
d did not know..it was Jesus.   21.4

DISCIPLINE — S (v)

hear..that he might *d* you;   Deut 4.36
D your son while there is   Prov 19.18
D your son, and he will give   29.17
had earthly fathers to *d* us   Heb 12.9
that, as a man *d* his son,   Deut 8.5

DISCIPLINE (n)

hate *d*, and you cast my words Ps 50.17
do not despise the LORD's *d*   Prov 3.11
severe *d* for him who forsakes   15.10
Do not withhold *d* from a child;   23.13
do not regard lightly the *d*   Heb 12.5
all *d* seems painful rather   12.11

DISCORD

who sows *d* among brothers.   Prov 6.19
may be no *d* in the body,   1Cor 12.25

DISCOURAGE — D

Why will you *d* the heart   Num 32.7
He will not fail or be *d*   Isa 42.4

DISCOVER

would not God *d* this? For he   Ps 44.21

DISCRETION

Blessed be your *d*, and   1Sam 25.33
may the LORD grant you *d*   1Chr 22.12
keep *d*, and..guard knowledge. Prov 5.2

DISCUSS — ING

why..*d* among yourselves the   Mt 16.8
"What were you *d* on the way?" Mk 9.33

DISEASE — S — D

even in his *d*..did not seek   2Chr 16.12
smote..with an incurable *d*.   21.18
sent a wasting *d* among them.   Ps 106.15
healing every *d* and..infirmity Mt 4.23
felt..she was healed of her *d*. Mk 5.29
I will put none of the *d* upon Ex 15.26
none of the evil *d* of Egypt,   Deut 7.15
infirmities and bore our *d*."   Mt 8.17
all who had *d* pressed upon him Mk 3.10
and to be healed of their *d*;   Lk 6.17
age he was *d* in his feet.   1Ki 15.23

DISGRACE — FUL

a day of..rebuke, and of *d*;   2Ki 19.3
I am filled with *d* and look   Job 10.15
day long my *d* is before me,   Ps 44.15
wise..honor, but fools get *d*. Prov 3.35
and with dishonor comes *d*.   18.3
I bore the *d* of my youth.'   Jer 31.19
is *d* for a woman to be shorn 1Cor 11.6
We have renounced *d*,..ways;   2Cor 4.2

DISGUISE — D — ING

to his wife, "Arise, and *d*   1Ki 14.2
d myself and go into battle.   2Chr 18.29
Josiah..*d* himself..to fight   35.22
d himself with a bandage   1Ki 20.38
d themselves as apostles   2Cor 11.13

DISH

his hand in the *d* with me,   Mt 26.23
cleanse the outside of the..*d*, Lk 11.39

DISHONEST

eyes and heart..for..*d* gain,   Jer 22.17
the *d* gain which you..made,   Ezek 22.13
master commended the *d* steward Lk 16.8

DISHONOR (v)

d all the honored of..earth,   Isa 23.9
do not *d* thy glorious throne; Jer 14.21

DISHONOR — ING (n)

accusers be clothed with *d*;   Ps 109.29
and let our *d* cover us; for   Jer 3.25
to the *d* of their bodies   Rom 1.24

DISINHERIT

I will..*d* them, and I will   Num 14.12

DISMAYED

When I think of it I am *d*,   Job 21.6
be not *d*, for I am your God;   Isa 41.10
Daniel,..was *d* for a moment,   Dan 4.19
your mighty men shall be *d*,   Obad 1.9

DISOBEDIENCE

by one man's *d* many were   Rom 5.19
now at work in the sons of *d*.   Eph 2.2

DISOBEDIENT

the *d* to..wisdom of the just, Lk 1.17
King Agrippa, I was not *d* to   Acts 26.19
held out my hands to a *d*   Rom 10.21
For we..were once foolish, *d*,   Tit 3.3
but to those who were *d*?   Heb 3.18

DISOBEY — ED

do not *d* either of them;   Prov 24.21
'Because you have *d* the word   1Ki 13.21
"It is the man of God, who *d*   13.26
and I never *d* your command;   Lk 15.29

DISOWNED

he *d* his brothers, and   Deut 33.9
he has *d* the faith and is   1Tim 5.8

DISPERSE — D
d you through the countries,	Ezek 22.15
and gather the *d* of Judah	Isa 11.12
d through the countries;	Ezek 36.19

DISPERSION
to the *D* among the Greeks	Jn 7.35
To the exiles of the *D* in	1Pet 1.1

DISPLEASE — D — ING
d God and oppose all men	1Thess 2.15
head of Ephraim, it *d* him;	Gen 48.17
But the thing *d* Samuel when	1Sam 8.6
David had done *d* the LORD.	2Sam 11.27
had never.. *d* him by asking,	1Ki 1.6
God was *d* with this thing,	1Chr 21.7
lest the LORD see..and be *d*,	Prov 24.18
The LORD saw it, and it *d* him	Isa 59.15
But it *d* Jonah exceedingly,	Jonah 4.1
was very *d* to Abraham	Gen 21.11
d in the sight of the LORD,	Gen 38.10

DISPLEASURE
and you shall know my *d*.'	Num 14.34
hot *d* which the LORD bore	Deut 9.19

DISPOSSESS — ED
go in to *d* nations greater and	Deut 9.1
with Joshua when they *d* the	Acts 7.45

DISPUTE — D (v)
not able to *d* with..stronger	Ecc 6.10
he.. *d* against the Hellenists;	Acts 9.29

DISPUTE (n)
then both parties to the *d*	Deut 19.17
A *d* also arose among them,	Lk 22.24

DISQUALIFY — IED
Let no one *d* you, insisting	Col 2.18
lest..I myself should be *d*.	1Cor 9.27

DISREPUTE
this trade..may come into *d*	Acts 19.27
You..in honor, but we in *d*.	1Cor 4.10

DISSENSIONS
note of those who create *d*	Rom 16.17
there be no *d* among you,	1Cor 1.10
genealogies, *d*, and quarrels	Tit 3.9

DISSOLVED
elements will be *d* with fire,	2Pet 3.10
these things are thus to be *d*,	3.11

DISTANCE
while he was yet at a *d*,	Lk 15.20
Peter followed at a *d*;	22.54

DISTINCT
we are *d*, I and thy people,	Ex 33.16

DISTINCTION — S
the LORD makes a *d* between the	Ex 11.7
make a *d* between the unclean	Lev 11.47
make a *d* between the clean	20.25
he made no *d* between us	Acts 15.9
believe. For there is no *d*;	Rom 3.22
no *d* between Jew and Greek;	10.12
made *d* among yourselves, and	Jas 2.4

DISTINGUISH — ED
d between..holy and..common,	Lev 10.10
d..the unclean and..clean.	Ezek 44.23
d..the righteous and..wicked,	Mal 3.18
practice to *d* good from evil.	Heb 5.14
beloved.. *d* among ten thousand.	Sol 5.10
Daniel became *d* above all the	Dan 6.3

DISTRESS (n)
therefore is this *d* come	Gen 42.21
in the time of your *d*."	Judg 10.14
And every one who was in *d*,	1Sam 22.2
when in their *d* they turned	2Chr 15.4
In.. *d* he became..more faithless	28.22
in *d* he entreated the favor	33.12
Thou hast given me room..in *d*.	Ps 4.1
delivered them from their *d*;	107.6
I suffered *d* and anguish.	116.3
In my *d* I cry to the LORD,	120.1
d and anguish come upon you.	Prov 1.27
but behold, *d* and darkness,	Isa 8.22
LORD, in *d* they sought thee,	26.16
it is a time of *d* for Jacob;	Jer 30.7
to the LORD, out of my *d*,	Jonah 2.2
great *d* shall be upon..earth	Lk 21.23
in view of the impending *d*	1Cor 7.26

DISTRESSED (adj)
And now do not be *d*, or angry	Gen 45.5
She was deeply *d* and prayed	1Sam 1.10
Then the king,..was much *d*,	Dan 6.14
And they were greatly *d*.	Mt 17.23
Lot, greatly *d* by..wicked	2Pet 2.7

DISTRIBUTED
which Moses *d* in the plains	Josh 13.32
gifts of the Holy Spirit *d*	Heb 2.4

DISTURBED
"Why have you *d* me by	1Sam 28.15
authorities.. *d* when they heard	Acts 17.8

DIVIDE — D — ING
d the booty into two parts,	Num 31.27
"*D* the living child in two,	1Ki 3.25
thou didst *d* the sea before	Neh 9.11
d the spoil with the strong;	Isa 53.12
"Teacher, bid my brother *d* the	Lk 12.13
"Take this, and *d* it among	22.17
and the waters were *d*.	Ex 14.21
in death they were not *d*;	2Sam 1.23
and no longer *d* into two	Ezek 37.22
kingdom *d* against itself is	Mt 12.25
kingdom is *d* against itself,	Mk 3.24
and *d* his garments among them.	15.24
every kingdom *d* against itself	Lk 11.17
will be *d*, father against son	12.53
Christ *d*? Was Paul crucified	1Cor 1.13
they finished *d* the land.	Josh 19.51

DIVINATION
learned by *d* that the LORD	Gen 30.27
fees for *d* in their hand;	Num 22.7
no more any..flattering *d*	Ezek 12.24
girl who had a spirit of *d*	Acts 16.16

DIVINE
according to the *d* office	Col 1.25
partakers of the *d* nature.	2Pet 1.4

DIVISION — S
d between my people and	Ex 8.23
No, I tell you, but rather *d*;	Lk 12.51
again a *d* among the Jews	Jn 10.19
piercing to the *d* of soul	Heb 4.12
The *d* of the sons of Aaron	1Chr 24.1
I hear that there are *d*	1Cor 11.18

DIVORCE (v)
"Moses allowed a man to.. *d*,	Mk 10.4
her, she should not *d* him.	1Cor 7.13

DIVORCE (n)
he writes her a bill of *d*	Deut 24.1
Israel,..with a decree of *d*;	Jer 3.8
to give a certificate of *d*,	Mt 19.7

DO — DOES — DONE
God has..approved what you *d.* Ecc 9.7
Thus says the LORD: *D* justice Jer 22.3
humble..who *d* his commands; Zeph 2.3
wish that men would *d* to you, Mt 7.12
all that Jesus began to *d* Acts 1.1
hears my words and *d* them, Lk 6.47
which he had *d* in creation. Gen 2.3
God had *d* for the people; 2Chr 29.36
repay..man for what he has *d.* Mt 16.27
God had *d* among the Gentiles Acts 21.19
judged..by what they had *d.* Rev 20.12

DOCTRINE — S
you say, 'My *d* is pure, Job 11.4
carried..with every wind of *d,* Eph 4.14
not to teach any different *d,* 1Tim 1.3
give instruction in sound *d* Tit 1.9
adorn the *d* of God our Savior. 2.10
not abide in the *d* of Christ 2Jn 9
as *d* the precepts of men.' Mk 7.7

DOERS
the *d* of the law..justified. Rom 2.13
But be *d* of the word, and Jas 1.22

DOG — S
with his tongue, as a *d* laps, Judg 7.5
look upon a dead *d* such as 2Sam 9.8
your servant, who is but a *d,* 2Ki 8.13
takes a passing *d* by..ears. Prov 26.17
living *d* is better than a dead Ecc 9.4
The *d* turns back to his own 2Pet 2.22
shall *d* lick your..blood, 1Ki 21.19
they come back, howling like *d* Ps 59.6
they are all dumb *d,* they Isa 56.10
"Do not give *d* what is holy; Mt 7.6
bread and throw it to the *d.* 15.26
even the *d* under the table eat Mk 7.28
d came and licked his sores. Lk 16.21
Look out for the *d,* look out Phil 3.2

DOMINION
For *d* belongs to the LORD, Ps 22.28
May he have *d* from sea to sea, 72.8
Bless..in all places of his *d.* 103.22
break there the *d* of Egypt, Ezek 30.18
for his *d* is an everlasting *d,* Dan 4.34
his *d* shall be to the end. 6.26
his *d* shall be a great. 11.5
his *d* shall be from sea to sea, Zech 9.10
death no longer has *d* over him. Rom 6.9

DOOR — S
Valley of Achor a *d* of hope. Hos 2.15
"Strive to enter..narrow *d;* Lk 13.24
knock at the *d,* saying, 'Lord, 13.25
I am the *d* of the sheep. Jn 10.7
I am the *d;* if any one enters 10.9
he had opened a *d* of faith Acts 14.27
a wide *d* for effective work 1Cor 16.9
open to us a *d* for the word, Col 4.3
have set before you an open *d,* Rev 3.8
I stand at the *d* and knock; 3.20
and lo, in heaven an open *d!* 4.1
and be lifted up, O ancient *d!* Ps 24.7
I will break in pieces the *d* Isa 45.2

DOORKEEPER
rather be a *d* in the house of Ps 84.10

DOORPOSTS
blood, and put it on..*d* and Ex 12.7

DORCAS
Tabitha, which means *D* or Acts 9.36
garments which *D* made while 9.39

DOT
not a *d,* will pass from the law Mt 5.18
one of *d*..law to become void. Lk 16.17

DOUBLE
they took *d* the money Gen 43.15
a *d* share of your spirit." 2Ki 2.9
flattering lips and a *d* heart Ps 12.2
received..*d* for all her sins. Isa 40.2
I will restore to you *d.* Zech 9.12

DOUBT (v)
if you have faith and never *d,* Mt 21.21
and does not *d* in his heart, Mk 11.23

DOUBT (n)
your life shall hang in *d* Deut 28.66
he who has *d* is condemned, Rom 14.23

DOVE — S
he sent forth a *d* from him, Gen 8.8
"O that I had wings like a *d!* Ps 55.6
Ephraim is like a *d,* silly and Hos 7.11
Spirit..descending like a *d,* Mt 3.16
Spirit..in bodily form, as a *d,* Lk 3.22
saw the Spirit descend as a *d* Jn 1.32
His eyes are like *d* beside Sol 5.12

DOWNFALL
righteous will look upon..*d.* Prov 29.16
tremble..on..day of your *d.* Ezek 32.10

DOWNTRODDEN
Let not the *d* be put to shame; Ps 74.21
The LORD lifts up the *d,* he 147.6

DRAGON
you are like a *d* in the seas; Ezek 32.2
behold, a great red *d,* with Rev 12.3

DRANK
to them, and they all *d* of it. Mk 14.23
d from the supernatural Rock 1Cor 10.4

DRAW — N
women go out to *d* water. Gen 24.11
"I will *d* for your camels 24.19
D near..me, redeem me, set me Ps 69.18
D me after you,..make haste. Sol 1.4
D near, O nations, to hear, Isa 34.1
d near with a true heart Heb 10.22
D near..God and he will *d* near Jas 4.8
O LORD, for thou hast *d* me up, Ps 30.1

DRAWERS
and *d* of water for all the Josh 9.21

DREAD
land..whose two kings you..*d* Isa 7.16
and do not fear..nor be in *d.* 8.12

DREAM — S — ED (v)
your old men shall *d* dreams, Acts 2.17
a hungry man *d* he is eating Isa 29.8
d that there was a ladder Gen 28.12
both *d*—the butler and..baker 40.5
I *d* a dream; and lo, a cake Judg 7.13

DREAM — S (n)
God came to Laban..in a *d* Gen 31.24
Joseph had a *d,* and..told 37.5
Pharaoh told them his *d,* 41.8
speak with him in a *d.* Num 12.6
appeared to Solomon in a *d* 1Ki 3.5
Let..prophet who has a *d* tell Jer 23.28
angel..appeared to him in a *d,* Mt 1.20
suffered..over him in a *d.*" 27.19
Joseph remembered the *d* Gen 42.9
d increase, empty words grow Ecc 5.7

DREAM — S (n) (cont.)
Nebuchadnezzar had *d*; and his   Dan 2.1
your old men shall dream *d*,   Joel 2.28

DREAMER
"Here comes this *d*.   Gen 37.19
"If..arises..a *d* of dreams,   Deut 13.1

DRENCH
I *d* my couch with my weeping.   Ps 6.6
d the land..with your..blood; Ezek 32.6

DREW
he *d* me out of many waters.   Ps 18.16
time of the promise *d* near,   Acts 7.17

DRINK — S — ING (v)
make our father *d* wine,   Gen 19.32
'*D*, and I will water your camels'   24.14
"*D* no wine nor strong drink,   Lev 10.8
would give me water to *d*   2Sam 23.15
thou hast given us wine to *d*   Ps 60.3
He will *d* from the brook by   110.7
D water from your..cistern.   Prov 5.15
thirsty, give him water to *d*;   25.21
and *d*: *d* deeply, O lovers!   Sol 5.1
made all the nations..*d* it: Jer 25.17
answered, "We will *d* no wine,   35.6
neighbors *d*..cup of his wrath, Hab 2.15
tasted it, he would not *d* it.   Mt 27.34
do not seek what..to eat..*d*,   Lk 12.29
So, whether you eat or *d*,   1Cor 10.31
and *d* the cup, you proclaim   11.26
made to *d* of one Spirit,   12.13
No longer *d* only water, but   1Tim 5.23
whoever *d* of the water that I   Jn 4.14
John..neither eating nor *d*,   Mt 11.18
before the flood..eating and *d*,   24.38
eating no bread and *d* no wine;   Lk 7.33

DRINK (n)
givest them *d* from the river   Ps 36.8
strong *d* to him..perishing,   Prov 31.6
drink no wine nor strong *d*,   Lk 1.15
said to her, "Give me a *d*."   Jn 4.7
not to be..slaves to *d*; they   Tit 2.3

DRIVE — S — ING
Manasseh did not *d* out the   Judg 1.27
thou with thy own hand didst *d*   Ps 44.2
Jehu..for he *d* furiously."   2Ki 9.20
which the wind of the LORD *d*.   Isa 59.19
angel of the LORD *d* them on!   Ps 35.5

DROSS
the wicked..dost count as *d*; Ps 119.119
Take away the *d* from..silver, Prov 25.4
Your silver has become *d*,   Isa 1.22
and will smelt away your *d*   1.25

DROUGHT
a *d* upon the land and..hills, Hag 1.11

DROVE
and he *d* away all his cattle,   Gen 31.18
the LORD *d* the sea back   Ex 14.21
Jesus..*d* out all who sold and   Mt 21.12

DROWNED
better..to be *d* in the depth   Mt 18.6
the herd,..were *d* in the sea.   Mk 5.13
down..into the lake..were *d*.   Lk 8.33

DRUNK
Noah..became *d*,..lay uncovered Gen 9.21
so that he made him *d*;   2Sam 11.13
Be *d*, but not with wine;   Isa 29.9

have *d* to the dregs the bowl   51.17
For these men are not *d*,   Acts 2.15

DRUNKARD — S
a glutton and a *d*, a friend   Mt 11.19
'Behold, a glutton and a *d*,   Lk 7.34
an idolater, reviler, *d*, or   1Cor 5.11
the *d* make songs about me.   Ps 69.12
crown of the *d* of Ephraim,   Isa 28.1

DRUNKEN — NESS
made Egypt stagger..as a *d*   Isa 19.14
eats and drinks with the *d*,   Mt 24.49
for strength, and not for *d*!   Ecc 10.17
you will be filled with *d*   Ezek 23.33

DRY — IED (v)
I will *d* up your rivers';   Isa 44.27
the LORD *d* up the..Red Sea   Josh 2.10

DRY (adj)
face of the ground was *d*.   Gen 8.13
priests..stood on *d* ground   Josh 3.17

DUE
not..a gift but as his *d*.   Rom 4.4
blood to drink..is their *d*!"   Rev 16.6

DUG
he moved..and *d* another well, Gen 26.22
one talent went and *d* in   Mt 25.18

DULL
people's heart has grown *d*,   Acts 28.27
you have become *d* of hearing. Heb 5.11

DUMB
But I am like..a *d* man who   Ps 38.13
I was *d* and silent, I held my   39.2
d and unable to reprove them; Ezek 3.26
toward the ground and was *d*.   Dan 10.15
d demoniac was brought to him. Mt 9.32
that the *d* man spoke and saw.   12.22
the maimed, the blind, the *d*,   15.30
deaf hear and the *d* speak."   Mk 7.37
signs to them and remained *d*.   Lk 1.22
d man spoke..people marveled.   11.14

DUST
God formed man of *d*   Gen 2.7
and *d* you shall eat   3.14
you are *d*, and to *d*..return."   3.19
descendants as the *d*   13.16
I who am but *d* and ashes.   18.27
and man would return to *d*.   Job 34.15
when the *d* runs into a mass   38.38
turnest man back to the *d*,   Ps 90.3
he remembers that we are *d*.   103.14
die and return to their *d*.   104.29
from the *d*, and all turn to *d*   Ecc 3.20
and the *d* returns to..earth   12.7
shake off the *d* from your feet Mt 10.14
d of your town..we wipe off   Lk 10.11

DUTY
the *d* of a husband's brother   Deut 25.5
first learn their religious *d*   1Tim 5.4

DWELL — S — T
they could not *d* together,   Gen 13.6
And Moses was content to *d*   Ex 2.21
I will *d* among the people   29.45
that you may *d* in the land   Deut 30.20
Jebusites *d* with the people   Josh 15.63
I *d* in a house of cedar,   2Sam 7.2
I will *d* among the children   1Ki 6.13
God indeed *d* on the earth?   8.27
will God *d* indeed with man   2Chr 6.18
let not wickedness *d* in your   Job 11.14

DWELL — S — T (cont.)

shall *d* in..house of the LORD	Ps 23.6
I may *d* in the house of..LORD	27.4
Blessed..who *d* in thy house,	84.4
No..deceit shall *d* in my house;	101.7
there he lets the hungry *d*,	107.36
good..when brothers *d* in unity!	133.1
can *d* with..devouring fire?	Isa 33.14
Israel shall *d*..without king	Hos 3.4
return..*d* beneath my shadow,	14.7
again make you *d* in tents,	12.9
Christ may *d* in your hearts	Eph 3.17
spirit which he has made to *d*	Jas 4.5
He will *d* with them, and	Rev 21.3
d in..shelter of the Most High,	Ps 91.1
exalted, for he *d* on high;	Isa 33.5
the Father who *d* in me does	Jn 14.10
but sin which *d* within me.	Rom 7.17
that God's Spirit *d* in you?	1Cor 3.16
Abram *d* in..land of Canaan,	Gen 13.12
Lot..who *d* in Sodom,	14.12
Lot..*d* in a cave with his	19.30
Word became flesh and *d* among	Jn 1.14

DWELLING — S

d between his shoulders."	Deut 33.12
thy holy hill and to thy *d*!	Ps 43.3
He forsook his *d* at Shiloh,	78.60
in his own hired *d*	Acts 28.30n
the *d* of God is with men.	Rev 21.3
and his *d* shall be glorious.	Isa 11.10

DWELLING PLACE

The eternal God is your *d*..	Deut 33.27
How lovely is thy *d*.., O LORD	Ps 84.1
LORD, thou hast been our *d*..	90.1
a *d*..for the Mighty One	132.5
"Let us go to his *d*..; let us	132.7
d..shall be with them;	Ezek 37.27

DYING

as *d*, and behold we live;	2Cor 6.9

E

EAGER

I am *e* to preach the gospel	Rom 1.15

EAGLE — S

are an abomination: the *e*,	Lev 11.13
your command..the *e* mounts	Job 39.27
the way of an *e* in the sky,	Prov 30.19
the fourth the face of an *e*.	Ezek 10.14
A great *e* with great wings	17.2
mount up with wings like *e*,	Isa 40.31
"Where..body is, there the *e*	Lk 17.37

EAR — S

his master shall bore his *e*	Ex 21.6
heard of thee by..the *e*,	Job 42.5
thou hast given me an open *e*.	Ps 40.6
planted the *e*, does he not hear?	94.9
your *e* attentive to wisdom	Prov 2.2
the slave..and cut off his *e*.	Mt 26.51
the slave..and cut off his *e*.	Mk 14.47
and cut off his right *e*.	Lk 22.50
slave and cut off his right *e*.	Jn 18.10
no eye has seen, nor *e* heard,	1Cor 2.9
And if the *e* should say,	12.16
He who has an *e*, let him hear	Rev 2.29
and his *e* toward their cry.	Ps 34.15
have *e*, but they hear not,	135.17
people,..have *e*, but hear not.	Jer 5.21
have *e* to hear, but hear not;	Ezek 12.2
He who has *e*, let him hear."	Mt 13.9

"He who has *e* to hear, let him	Mk 4.9
If any man has *e* to hear,	4.23
He who has *e* to hear, let him	Lk 14.35

EARTH

God created the heavens..*e*.	Gen 1.1
God called the dry land *E*,	1.10
Lord of all the *e* is to pass	Josh 3.11
hangs the *e* upon nothing.	Job 26.7
The *e* is the LORD's and the	Ps 24.1
the *e* is full of the steadfast love	33.5
visitest the *e* and waterest it,	65.9
whole *e* is full of his glory."	Isa 6.3
e shall yield its increase,	Ezek 34.27
let all the *e* keep silence	Hab 2.20
didst bestride the *e* in fury,	3.12
all the *e* shall be consumed.	Zeph 3.8
the *e* shook, and the rocks	Mt 27.51
The *e* produces of itself,	Mk 4.28
For "the *e* is the Lord's,	1Cor 10.26
first man was from the *e*,	15.47
new *e* in which righteousness	2Pet 3.13
to take peace from the *e*,	Rev 6.4

EARTHLY

not by *e* wisdom but by..grace	2Cor 1.12
if..*e* tent we live in is destroyed,	5.1

EARTHQUAKE — S

and after the wind an *e*,	1Ki 19.11
thunder..*e* and great noise,	Isa 29.6
two years before the *e*.	Amos 1.1
great *e*; for..angel..descended	Mt 28.2
suddenly there was a great *e*,	Acts 16.26
e such as had never been	Rev 16.18
there will be *e* in various	Mk 13.8
there will be great *e*, and	Lk 21.11

EASE

I am not at *e*, nor am I quiet;	Job 3.26
are the wicked; always at *e*,	Ps 73.12
"Woe to those who are at *e*	Amos 6.1
take your *e*, eat, drink, be	Lk 12.19

EAST

we have seen his star in the *E*,	Mt 2.2
many will come from *e* and west	8.11
men will come from *e* and west,	Lk 13.29

EASY — IER

the way is *e*,..to destruction,	Mt 7.13
yoke is *e*,..burden is light."	11.30
which is *e*, to say, 'Your sins	9.5

EAT — S — EN — ING

tree of knowledge..not *e*,	Gen 2.17
the Egyptians might not *e*	43.32
shall *e* unleavened bread;	Ex 12.15
sat down to *e* and drink,	32.6
Moreover you shall *e* no blood	Lev 7.26
not *e*..flesh with the blood	19.26
you shall *e* before the LORD	Deut 12.7
evildoers who *e* up my people	Ps 14.4
When you..*e* with a ruler,	Prov 23.1
you shall *e*..good of the land;	Isa 1.19
"Let us *e* and drink, for	22.13
open..mouth, and *e* what I give	Ezek 2.8
e this scroll, and go, speak	3.1
"Why does your teacher *e* with	Mt 9.11
"Take, *e*; this is my body."	26.26
where I am to *e* the passover	Mk 14.14
"Why do you *e* and drink with	Lk 5.30
take your ease, *e*, drink, be	12.19
besought him.."Rabbi, *e*."	Jn 4.31
"Rise, Peter; kill and *e*."	Acts 10.13
'Rise, Peter; kill and *e*.'	11.7

EAT — S — EN — ING (cont.)

e whatever is set before you	1Cor 10.27
So, whether you e or drink,	10.31
"Let us e and drink, for	15.32
will not work, let..not e.	2Thess 3.10
come in to him and e with him,	Rev 3.20
Let not him who e despise him	Rom 14.3
when they had e enough,	Acts 27.38
before the flood they were e	Mt 24.38

EBENEZER

Samuel took a stone..name E;	1Sam 7.12

EDEN

God planted a garden in E,	Gen 2.8
make her wilderness like E,	Isa 51.3
You were in E, the garden	Ezek 28.13
land is like the garden of E	Joel 2.3

EDIFICATION

Let all things be done for e.	1Cor 14.26

EDOM — ITES

his name was called E.)	Gen 25.30
E refused to give Israel	Num 20.21
And he put garrisons in E;	2Sam 8.14
upon E I cast my shoe; over	Ps 108.9
Who is this that comes from E,	Isa 63.1
may possess the remnant of E	Amos 9.12
Esau the father of the E	Gen 36.9

EGYPT

Abram went down to E	Gen 12.10
they took Joseph to E.	37.28
set him over the land of E.	41.33
all my splendor in E,	45.13
I will lay my hand upon E	Ex 7.4
LORD brought us out of E,	13.14
alliance with Pharaoh..of E;	1Ki 3.1
and out of E I called my son.	Hos 11.1
flee to E, and remain there	Mt 2.13
"Out of E have I called my son."	2.15
greater wealth than..of E,	Heb 11.26

ELDER — S

e shall serve the younger."	Gen 25.23
e will serve the younger."	Rom 9.12
The e to the elect lady and	2Jn 1
The e to the beloved Gaius,	3Jn 1
the e of the congregation	Lev 4.15
seventy men..the e of Israel	Num 11.16
ten men of the e of the city,	Ruth 4.2
Her husband..sits among..e	Prov 31.23
suffer many things from the e	Mt 16.21
sent to him e of the Jews,	Lk 7.3
called..the e of the church.	Acts 20.17
when the e laid their hands	1Tim 4.14
Let the e who rule well be	5.17
appoint e in every town as	Tit 1.5
sick? Let him call for the e	Jas 5.14
I exhort the e among you,	1Pet 5.1
on..thrones were twenty-four e,	Rev 4.4
the twenty-four e and the four	19.4

ELECT

but for the sake of the e	Mt 24.22
gather his e from..four winds,	24.31
but for the sake of the e,	Mk 13.20
gather his e from the four winds,	13.27
any charge against God's e?	Rom 8.33
The e obtained it, but the rest	11.7
endure..for the sake of the e,	2Tim 2.10

ELECTION

God's purpose of e..continue,	Rom 9.11
as regards e they are beloved	11.28
confirm your call and e,	2Pet 1.10

ELEMENTS

the e will be dissolved	2Pet 3.10
the e will melt with fire!	3.12

ELEVEN

Afterward he appeared to the e	Mk 16.14n
found the e gathered together	Lk 24.33

ELI

two sons of E,..were priets	1Sam 1.3
Hannah rose. Now E the priest	1.9
they brought the child to E.	1.25
presence of E the priest.	2.11
ministering to..LORD under E.	3.1
two sons of E,..were slain.	4.11
E was ninety-eight years old	4.15

ELIJAH

Predicted the drought, 1Ki 17.1; fed by ravens, 1Ki 17.2–7; fed by the widow of Zarephath, 1 Ki 17.8–16; revived the son of the widow, 1Ki 17.17–24; met Ahab, 1Ki 18.1–19; triumphed over the prophets of Baal, 1Ki 18.20–40; prayed for rain, 1Ki 18.41–46; fled to Mount Horeb, 1Ki 19.1–8; heard the still small voice, 1Ki 19.9–18; chose Elisha, 1Ki 19.19–21; reproved Ahab, 1Ki 21.17–29; called fire from heaven, 2Ki 1.3–16; taken up into heaven, 2Ki 2.1–11.

I will send you E the prophet	Mal 4.5
he is E who is to come.	Mt 11.14
appeared to them Moses and E,	17.3
I tell you that E has come,	Mk 9.13
"Behold, he is calling E."	15.35
in the spirit and power of E,	Lk 1.17
to bid fire come..as E did?"	9.54n
"What then? Are you E?" He said	Jn 1.21
E was a man of like nature	Jas 5.17

ELISHA

Called, 1Ki 19.19–21; succeeded Elijah, 2Ki 2.1–15; purified the water, 2Ki 2.19–22; cursed the children, 2Ki 2.23–25; prophesied victory over the Moabites, 2Ki 3; increased the widow's oil, 2Ki 4.1–7; restored the life of the Shunammite's son, 2Ki 4.8–37; purified the pottage, 2Ki 4.38–41; fed a multitude, 2Ki 4.42–44; healed Naaman's leprosy, 2Ki 5; caused Syrians' blindness, 2Ki 6.8–23; promised food in time of famine 2Ki 6.24—7.2; prophesied Hazael's cruelty, 2Ki 8.7–15; anointed Jehu, 2Ki 9.1–10; prophesied victory over Syria, 2Ki 13.14–19; death and burial, 2Ki 13.20; bones of Elisha, 2Ki 13.21.

ELIZABETH

a wife..and her name was E.	Lk 1.5
wife E will bear you a son,	1.13
of Zechariah and greeted E.	1.40

ELOQUENT

my Lord, I am not e,	Ex 4.10
preach..not with e wisdom,	1Cor 1.17

EMBRACED

Joseph..kissed..and e them.	Gen 48.10
and that his right hand e me!	Sol 2.6

EMMANU-EL

and his name shall be called E"	Mt 1.23

EMMAUS

going to a village named E,	Lk 24.13

EMPTY
God does not hear an *e* cry, Job 35.13
praying do not heap up *e* phrases Mt 6.7

ENCAMP — S
"The people of Israel shall *e* Num 2.2
and *e* round about my tent. Job 19.12
Though a host *e* against me, Ps 27.3
I will *e* against you round Isa 29.3
The angel of the LORD *e* around Ps 34.7

ENCOURAGE — D
e him, for he shall cause Deut 1.38
charge Joshua, and *e* and 3.28
that he may *e* your hearts. Eph 6.22
and you have *e* the wicked, Ezek 13.22
that their hearts may be *e* as Col 2.2

ENCOURAGEMENT
(which means, Son of *e*), Acts 4.36
if there is any *e* in Christ, Phil 2.1

END — S (v)
thy years will never *e*." Heb 1.12
Love never *e*; as for 1Cor 13.8

END — S (n)
make an *e* of all flesh; Gen 6.13
their words to the *e* of. .world. Ps 19.4
"LORD, let me know my *e*, and 39.4
years come to an *e* like a sigh. 90.9
yet there is no *e* to. .his toil, Ecc 4.8
The *e* of the matter; all has 12.13
our *e* drew near; our days Lam 4.18
The *e* has come upon the four Ezek 7.2
come to his *e*,. .none to help Dan 11.45
"The *e* has come upon my people Amos 8.2
the vision. .hastens to the *e*— Hab 2.3
and then the *e* will come. Mt 24.14
with the guards to see the *e*. 26.58
he loved them to the *e*. Jn 13.1
and to the *e* of the earth." Acts 1.8
Christ is the *e* of the law, Rom 10.4
e of all things is at hand, 1Pet 4.7
what will be the *e* of those 4.17
e of the earth your possession. Ps 2.8

ENDOWMENT
Every good *e* and every perfect Jas 1.17

ENDURANCE
By. .*e* you will gain your lives. Lk 21.19
and *e* produces character, Rom 5.4
great *e*, in afflictions, 2Cor 6.4
For you have need of *e*, so Heb 10.36
call for the *e* of the saints, Rev 14.12

ENDURE — S — D
can I *e* to see the calamity Est 8.6
hold of it, but it does not *e*. Job 8.15
May his name *e* for ever, his Ps 72.17
They will perish,. .thou. .*e*; 102.26
Can your courage *e*, or can Ezek 22.14
Who can *e*. .heat of his anger? Nah 1.6
who can *e* the day of his coming, Mal 3.2
have no root. .but *e* for a while; Mk 4.17
that you may be able to *e* 1Cor 10.13
if we *e*, we shall also reign 2Tim 2.12
people will not *e* sound teaching, 4.3
his righteousness *e* for ever. Ps 111.3
"His steadfast love *e* for ever." 118.2
his steadfast love *e* for ever. 136.2
who *e* to. .end will be saved. Mt 10.22
he who *e* to the end will be saved. 24.13
who *e* to the end will be saved. Mk 13.13
food which *e* to eternal life, Jn 6.27
Love. .hopes all things, *e* all 1Cor 13.7

Blessed is the man who *e* trial, Jas 1.12
for he *e* as seeing him who Heb 11.27
e the cross, despising the shame, 12.2

ENEMY — IES
"Have you found me, O my *e*?" 1Ki 21.20
and count me as thy *e*? Job 13.24
not rejoice when. .*e* falls, Prov 24.17
If your *e* is hungry, give him bread 25.21
neighbor and hate your *e*.' Mt 5.43
"if your *e* is hungry, feed Rom 12.20
last *e*. .destroyed is death. 1Cor 15.26
become your *e* by telling you Gal 4.16
your *e* who settle in it Lev 26.32
be defeated before your *e*; Deut 28.25
perish all thine *e*, O LORD! Judg 5.31
Jews got relief from their *e*, Est 9.22
him, and his *e* lick the dust! Ps 72.9
thy *e*, O LORD,. .shall perish; 92.9
makes. .his *e* to be at peace. Prov 16.7
I put thy *e* under thy feet'? Mt 22.44
Love your *e*, do good to those Lk 6.27
many. .live as *e* of the cross Phil 3.18

ENGRAVE
you *e* the two stones with Ex 28.11
I will *e* its inscription, Zech 3.9

ENJOY
my chosen. .long *e* the work Isa 65.22
than to *e*. .fleeting pleasures Heb 11.25

ENJOYMENT
and find *e* in his toil. Ecc 2.24
fitting is to eat and. .find *e* 5.18

ENLARGE — ST — D
E the place of your tent, Isa 54.2
when thou *e* my understanding! Ps 119.32
among you may be greatly *e*, 2Cor 10.15

ENLIGHTENED
a zeal. .but it is not *e*. Rom 10.2
after you were *e*, you endured Heb 10.32

ENLIGHTENING
commandment. .pure, *e* the eyes; Ps 19.8

ENOCH
To *E* was born Irad; Gen 4.18
Jared. .became. .father of *E*. 5.18
E walked with God after 5.22
E walked with God;. .God took 5.24
son of *E*, the son of Jared, Lk 3.37
By faith *E* was taken up so Heb 11.5
It was of these also that *E* Jude 14

ENRAGED
be *e* and will curse their king Isa 8.21
LORD is *e* against all the nations, 34.2

ENRICH — ED
kills him, the king will *e* 1Sam 17.25
e in him with all speech 1Cor 1.5
You will be *e* in every way 2Cor 9.11

ENROLLED
all the world should be *e*. Lk 2.1
the first-born. .*e* in heaven, Heb 12.23

ENSIGN — S
the root of Jesse. .as an *e* Isa 11.10
the *e* of their fathers' houses; Num 2.2

ENSLAVED
might no longer be *e* to sin. Rom 6.6
I will not be *e* by anything. 1Cor 6.12

ENTANGLED
the cords of Sheol *e* me, 2Sam 22.6
the cords of Sheol *e* me, Ps 18.5

ENTER — S — ED

Moses..not able to e the tent   Ex 40.35
for he shall not e the land   Num 20.24
shall not e the assembly   Deut 23.1
may e into the sworn covenant   29.12
they should not e my rest.   Ps 95.11
E his gates with thanksgiving,   100.4
my people, e your chambers,   Isa 26.20
you will never e the kingdom   Mt 5.20
"E by the narrow gate; for   7.13
says.."Lord, Lord,' shall e   7.21
than for a rich man to e   19.24
no one can e a strong man's   Mk 3.27
who have riches to e the kingdom   10.23
you did not e yourselves,   Lk 11.52
he cannot e the kingdom of God.   Jn 3.5
Blessed..who e in the name of   Ps 118.26
Noah and his sons..e the ark,   Gen 7.13

ENTHRONED

But the LORD sits e for ever,   Ps 9.7
who art e upon the cherubim,   80.1
O thou who art e in..heavens!   123.1

ENTICE — S — D

said to Samson's wife, "E   Judg 14.15
"E him, and see wherein his   16.5
LORD said, 'Who will e Ahab,   1Ki 22.20
he said, 'You are to e him,   2Chr 18.21
My son, if sinners e you,   Prov 1.10
man of violence e his neighbor   16.29
"If my heart has been e to   Job 31.9

ENTREAT — ED

"E the LORD to take away   Ex 8.8
"E me not to leave you or to   Ruth 1.16
to e the favor of the LORD,   Zech 7.2
we e you not to accept the   2Cor 6.1
I, Paul, myself e you, by   10.1
Then Manoah e the LORD, and   Judg 13.8
not e thee for their good,   Jer 15.11
father came out and e him,   Lk 15.28

ENTREATY

how God received his e,   2Chr 33.19
and he listened to our e.   Ezra 8.23

ENTRUST — ED — ING

who will e to you..true riches?   Lk 16.11
e to faithful men who will   2Tim 2.2
do right and e their souls   1Pet 4.19
he is e with all my house.   Num 12.7
the Jews are e with the oracles   Rom 3.2
I am e with a commission.   1Cor 9.17
guard what has been e to you.   1Tim 6.20
guard..what has been e to me.   2Tim 1.12
and e to us the message of   2Cor 5.19

ENVIOUS

be not e of wrongdoers!   Ps 37.1
For I was e of the arrogant,   73.3
Be not e of evil men, nor   Prov 24.1

ENVOY — S

a faithful e brings healing.   Prov 13.17
e of the princes of Babylon,   2Chr 32.31
the e of peace weep bitterly.   Isa 33.7

ENVY — IED (v)

Do not e a man of violence   Prov 3.31
Let not your heart e sinners,   23.17
the Philistines e him.   Gen 26.14
no children, she e her sister;   30.1

ENVY (n)

out of e..they..delivered him   Mt 27.18
out of e..the chief priests   Mk 15.10

EPHESUS

came to E, and he left them   Acts 18.19
Paul..came to E. There he found   19.1
decided to sail past E, so   20.16
I fought with beasts at E?   1Cor 15.32
remain at E that you may   1Tim 1.3
the angel of the church in E   Rev 2.1

EPHRAIM

the second he called E,   Gen 41.52
two sons, Manasseh and E.   48.1
the leader of the men of E: Num 7.48
And E did not drive out the   Judg 1.29
did not choose the tribe of E;   Ps 78.67
E is joined to idols, let him   Hos 4.17
E mixes himself with the peoples;   7.8
How can I give you up, O E!   11.8

EPILEPTIC — S

have mercy on my son,..an e   Mt 17.15
demoniacs, e, and paralytics,   4.24

EQUAL

making himself e with God.   Jn 5.18
faith of e standing with ours   2Pet 1.1

EQUITY

He will judge..peoples with e.   Ps 98.9
thou hast established e; thou   99.4

ERECT — ED

e no graven image or pillar,   Lev 26.1
There he e an altar   Gen 33.20

ERR — ED

"But if you e, and do not   Num 15.22
are a people who e in heart,   Ps 95.10
they not e that devise evil?   Prov. 14.22
me understand how I have e.   Job 6.24

ERROR — S

atonement for him for the e   Lev 5.18
because it was an e,   Num 15.25
my e remains with myself.   Job 19.4
e proceeding from the ruler: Ecc 10.5
the due penalty for their e.   Rom 1.27
our appeal..not..from e or   1Thess 2.3
But who can discern his e?   Ps 19.12
offers..for the e of the people.   Heb 9.7

ESAU

Born, Gen 25.24–26; sold his birthright, Gen 25.29–34; married Hittite women, Gen 26.34; lost Isaac's blessing, Gen 27.30–40; hated Jacob, Gen 27.41; married Mahalath, Gen 28.9; reconciled with Jacob, Gen 33.1–15.

ESCAPE — S — D (v)

palace you will e any more   Est 4.13
none..come to..Egypt shall e   Jer 44.14
there shall be those that e,   Obad 1.17
how shall we e if we neglect   Heb 2.3
he who pleases God e her, but   Ecc 7.26
e and fled after David.   1Sam 22.20
e as a bird from the snare   Ps 124.7
man who e from Jerusalem   Ezek 33.21
they have e the defilements   2Pet 2.20

ESCAPE (n)

also provide the way of e,   1Cor 10.13
and there will be no e.   1Thess 5.3

ESTABLISH — ED

I will e my covenant   Gen 17.7
e my covenant with Isaac,   17.21
LORD..e you as a people holy   Deut 28.9
that he may e you this day   29.13

ESTABLISH — ED (cont.)

I will *e* his kingdom. 2Sam 7.12
I will *e* your royal throne 1Ki 9.5
e..work of our hands upon us, Ps 90.17
and over his kingdom, to *e* it, Isa 9.7
to *e* in your faith and 1Thess 3.2
that he may *e* your hearts 3.13
God..will himself restore, *e*, 1Pet 5.10
who made you and *e* you? Deut 32.6
LORD had *e* him king over 2Sam 5.12
his kingdom was firmly *e*. 1Ki 2.12
his throne shall be *e* for ever. 1Chr 17.14
and the stars which thou hast *e*; Ps 8.3
thou hast *e* the luminaries 74.16
justice, thou hast *e* equity; 99.4
by understanding he *e* the Prov 3.19
e as the highest of..mountains, Isa 2.2
will not believe,..shall not be *e*.' " 7.9
throne..*e* in steadfast love 16.5
e the world by his wisdom, Jer 10.12
who..*e* the world by his wisdom, 51.15
it is God who *e* us with you 2Cor 1.21

ESTEEM — S — ED

e them very highly in love 1Thess 5.13
another man *e* all days alike. Rom 14.5
before those who are least *e* 1Cor 6.4

ESTHER

is *E*, the daughter of his uncle, Est 2.7
The command of Queen *E* fixed 9.32

ETERNAL

to be thrown into the *e* fire. Mt 18.8
what..must I do, to have *e* life?" 19.16
receive..and inherit *e* life. 19.29
e fire prepared for the devil 25.41
but is guilty of an *e* sin"— Mk 3.29
must I do to inherit *e* life?" 10.17
shall I do to inherit *e* life?" Lk 10.25
receive you into..*e* habitations. 16.9
not perish but have *e* life. Jn 3.16
will keep it for *e* life. 12.25
his commandment is *e* life. 12.50
to give *e* life to all whom thou 17.2
unworthy of *e* life, behold, Acts 13.46
ordained to *e* life believed. 13.48
to those..he will give *e* life; Rom 2.7
through righteousness to *e* life 5.21
things that are unseen are *e*. 2Cor 4.18
in hope of *e* life which God, Tit 1.2
he has promised us, *e* life. 1Jn 2.25
know that you have *e* life. 5.13
This is the true God and *e* life. 5.20

ETERNITY

has put *e* into man's mind, Ecc 3.11
lofty One who inhabits *e*, Isa 57.15

ETHIOPIA — N

let *E*..stretch out her hands Ps 68.31
E and Seba in exchange for Isa 43.3
an *E*, a eunuch, a minister Acts 8.27

EUNUCH — S

chief *e*, to bring some..people Dan 1.3
an Ethiopian, a *e*, a minister Acts 8.27
e who have been so from birth, Mt 19.12

EUPHRATES

fourth river is the *E*. Gen 2.14
Egypt to..the river *E*, 15.18
as far as the great river,..*E*, Josh 1.4
lived of old beyond the *E*, 24.2
arise, go to the *E*, and hide Jer 13.4
bowl on the great river *E*, Rev 16.12

EVANGELIST — S

the house of Philip the *e*, Acts 21.8
do the work of an *e*, fulfil 2Tim 4.5
some prophets, some *e*, some Eph 4.11

EVE

called his wife's name *E*, Gen 3.20
Adam knew *E* his wife, 4.1
as the serpent deceived *E* 2Cor 11.3
Adam..formed first, then *E*; 1Tim 2.13

EVENING

That *e* they brought to him many Mt 8.16
That *e*,..they brought to him Mk 1.32
e he came with the twelve. 14.17

EVERLASTING

remember the *e* covenant Gen 9.16
an *e* covenant, to be God to you 17.7
name of the LORD, the *E* God. 21.33
and lead me in the way *e*! Ps 139.24
Thy kingdom is an *e* kingdom, 145.13
Mighty God, *E* Father, Prince Isa 9.6
the LORD GOD is an *e* rock. 26.4
LORD will be your *e* light, 60.19
with you an *e* covenant. Ezek 16.60
shall awake, some to *e* life, Dan 12.2
Art thou not from *e*, O LORD Hab 1.12

EVIL — S

if it is *e* in thy sight, Num 22.34
So you shall purge the *e* Deut 13.5
Israel again did what was *e* Judg 4.1
Israel again did what was *e* 10.6
that *e* is determined by him. 1Sam 20.7
Solomon did what was *e* in 1Ki 11.6
Omri did what was *e* in the 16.25
He did much *e* in the sight 2Chr 33.6
did more *e* than the nations 33.9
they did *e* again before thee, Neh 9.28
he saw that *e* was determined Est 7.7
the wicked man conceives *e*, Ps 7.14
according to the *e* of their deeds; 28.4
Let them..who devise *e* against me! 35.4
no *e* shall befall you, no 91.10
let *e* hunt down the violent 140.11
do not walk in..way of *e* men. Prov 4.14
feet that..haste to run to *e*, 6.18
preserve you from the *e* woman, 6.24
heart..is fully set to do *e*. Ecc 8.11
Woe to those who call *e* good Isa 5.20
for they proceed from *e* to *e*, Jer 9.3
'Why..this great *e* against us? 16.10
bring upon them the day of *e*; 17.18
set my face against you for *e*, 44.11
turn back from your *e* ways; Ezek 33.11
Does *e* befall a city, unless Amos 3.6
plotted *e* against the LORD, Nah 1.11
you shall fear *e* no more. Zeph 3.15
If you..who are *e*,..give good Mt 7.11
seven other spirits more *e* 12.45
separate the *e* from the righteous, 13.49
out of the heart come *e* thoughts, 15.19
"Why, what *e* has he done?" 27.23
"Why, what *e* has he done?" Mk 15.14
who are *e*, know how to give Lk 11.13
seven other spirits more *e* 11.26
I testify..that its works are *e*. Jn 7.7
keep them from the *e* one. 17.15
'You shall not speak *e* of a ruler Acts 23.5
distress for..human..who does *e*, Rom 2.9
why not do *e* that good may come? 3.8
but the *e* I do not want..I do. 7.19
not..leaven of malice and *e*, 1Cor 5.8
Let no *e* talk come out of your Eph 4.29

EVIL — S (cont.)

none of you repays e for e, 1Thess 5.15
to speak e of no one, to avoid Tit 3.2
you have overcome the e one. 1Jn 2.13
money is the root of all e; 1Tim 6.10

EVILDOER — S

Let the e still do evil, Rev 22.11
depart from me, you e.' Mt 7.23

EXALT — S — ED — ING

I will begin to e you in the Josh 3.7
Prize her..she will e you; Prov 4.8
e that which is low, and Ezek 21.26
Righteousness e a nation, Prov 14.34
he e himself to show mercy Isa 30.18
who e himself will be humbled, Lk 14.11
LORD e Joshua in the sight Josh 4.14
the son of Haggith e himself, 1Ki 1.5
God is e in his power; who Job 36.22
e be the God of my salvation, Ps 18.46
God..I am e in the earth!'' 46.10
Be e, O God, above the heavens! 57.5
Be e, O God, above..heavens! 108.5
e above everything thy name 138.2
for his name alone is e; his 148.13
the LORD alone..e in that day. Isa 2.11
and e those of low degree; Lk 1.52
God e him at his right hand Acts 5.31
Therefore God has highly e him Phil 2.9
e yourself against my people, Ex 9.17

EXAMINE — D — ING

sat down to e the matter; Ezra 10.16
Let us test and e our ways, Lam 3.40
defense to those who would e 1Cor 9.3
Let a man e himself, and so 11.28
E yourselves, to see whether 2Cor 13.5
find him, he e the sentries Acts 12.19
ordered him..e by scourging, 22.24
and after e him before you, Lk 23.14
eagerness, e the scriptures Acts 17.11

EXAMPLE — S

I have given you an e, that Jn 13.15
you..an e to all..believers 1Thess 1.7
our conduct an e to imitate. 2Thess 3.9
his perfect patience for an e 1Tim 1.16
set..believers an e in speech and 4.12
an e,..follow in his steps. 1Pet 2.21
but being e to the flock. 5.3

EXCEED — S

latter works e the first. Rev 2.19
unless your righteousness e Mt 5.20

EXCELLENT

in counsel, and e in wisdom. Isa 28.29
an e spirit, knowledge, and Dan 5.12
show you a still more e way. 1Cor 12.31
you may approve what is e, Phil 1.10

EXCHANGED

They e..glory of God for Ps 106.20
women e natural relations for Rom 1.26

EXCUSE — S

made. So they are without e; Rom 1.20
they have no e for their sin; Jn 15.22
all alike began to make e. Lk 14.18

EXECUTE

by fire will..LORD e judgment, Isa 66.16
e vengeance upon the nations Mic 5.15

EXHORTATION

they rejoiced at the e. Acts 15.31

he who exhorts, in his e; Rom 12.8
bear with my word of e, for Heb 13.22

EXILE (n)

into e for want of knowledge; Isa 5.13
as men do who must go into e. Ezek 12.4

EXILED (v)

Israel was e from their..land 2Ki 17.23
captives..being e to Babylon. Jer 40.1

EXPECTATION

e of the wicked in wrath. Prov 11.23
"Gone is..my e from LORD." Lam 3.18
were in e,..concerning John, Lk 3.15

EXPERIENCE

you e so many things in vain?— Gal 3.4
same e of suffering is required 1Pet 5.9

EXPIATION

and makes e for the land Deut 32.43
how shall I make e, that 2Sam 21.3
whom God put forward as an e Rom 3.25
to make e for the sins..people. Heb 2.17
he is the e for our sins, 1Jn 2.2
Son to be the e for our sins. 4.10

EXPLAIN — ED

no one who could e it to me." Gen 41.24
Moses undertook to e this law, Deut 1.5
to..disciples he e everything. Mk 4.34

EXPOSE — D

works of darkness,..e them. Eph 5.11
lest his deeds should be e. Jn 3.20

EXPOUNDED

and e to him the way of God Acts 18.26
he e the matter to them 28.23

EXTEND — S

the Lord will e his hand Isa ·1.11
as grace e to more..people 2Cor 4.15

EXTERNAL

nor is true circumcision..e Rom 2.28

EXTOL — LED

E the LORD our God; worship Ps 99.5
e your love more than wine; Sol 1.4
name of..Lord Jesus was e. Acts 19.17

EXULT

name is the LORD, e before him! Ps 68.4
how long shall the wicked e? 94.3
your doom? Can you then e? Jer 11.15
and e with all your heart, Zeph 3.14
hearts shall e in the LORD. Zech 10.7

EYE — S

e for e, tooth for tooth, Ex 21.24
e for e, tooth for tooth; Lev 24.20
e for e, tooth for tooth, Deut 19.21
his e sees every precious Job 28.10
but now my e sees thee; 42.5
My e wastes away..of grief, Ps 6.7
counsel you with my e upon you. 32.8
e of the LORD is on..who fear 33.18
no e has seen a God besides Isa 64.4
If..sight e causes you to sin, Mt 5.29
'An e for an e and a tooth 5.38
if your e is sound, your whole 6.22
the speck..in your brother's e, 7.3
if your e causes you to sin, 18.9
if your e causes you to sin, Mk 9.47
e is the lamp of your body; Lk 11.34
no e has seen, nor ear heard, 1Cor 2.9
Noah found favor in the e Gen 6.8
you will serve as e for us. Num 10.31

EYE — S (cont.)

the *e* of the LORD your God Deut 11.12
is right in his own *e*; 12.8
or *e* to see, or ears to hear. 29.4
what was right in his own *e*. Judg 17.6
was right in his own *e*. 21.25
the *e* of all Israel are upon you, 1Ki 1.20
that thy *e* may be open night 8.29
Asa did..right in the *e* of 15.11
LORD opened the *e* of the 2Ki 6.17
that thy *e* may be open day 2Chr 6.20
the *e* of the LORD run to and fro 16.9
but our *e* are upon thee." 20.12
was righteous in his own *e*. Job 32.1
his *e* behold, his eyelids Ps 11.4
not speak; *e*, but do not see. 115.5
Open my *e* that I may behold 119.18
My *e* shed streams of tears, 119.136
I lift up my *e* to the hills. 121.1
To thee I lift up my *e*, O thou 123.1
have *e*, but they see not, 135.16
e beheld my unformed substance; 139.16
The *e* of all look to thee, 145.15
your *e* look directly forward, Prov 4.25
fool is right in his own *e*, 12.15
The *e* of the LORD are in every 15.3
The *e* of the LORD keep watch 22.12
who are pure in their own *e* 30.12
lest they see with their *e*, Isa 6.10
the LORD..has closed your *e*, 29.10
then the *e*..will not be closed, 32.3
Your *e* will see the king in 33.17
open thy *e*, O LORD, and see; 37.17
Lift up your *e* round about 49.18
forgotten..hid from my *e*. 65.16
people,..have *e*, but see not, Jer 5.21
and my *e* a fountain of tears, 9.1
set my *e* upon them for good, 24.6
e of the LORD..upon the sinful Amos 9.8
of purer *e* than to behold evil Hab 1.13
the *e* which see what you see! Lk 10.23
their *e* were opened and they 24.31
e that should not see and Rom 11.8
Look..what is before your *e*. 2Cor 10.7
would have plucked out your *e* Gal 4.15
laid bare to the *e* of him Heb 4.13
the *e* of the Lord are upon 1Pet 3.12
and salve to anoint your *e*, Rev 3.18

EYESERVICE

not..*e*, as men-pleasers, but Eph 6.6
Slaves, obey..not with *e*, Col 3.22

EYEWITNESSES

from the beginning were *e* and Lk 1.2
we were *e* of his majesty. 2Pet 1.16

EZEKIEL

*Call: Ezek 2—3. Visions: cherubim, Ezek
1; 10; abominations in Jerusalem, Ezek
8—9; valley of dry bones, Ezek 37; the
temple, Ezek 40.1—47.12; division of land,
47.13—48.35. Prophecies: against Israel,
Ezek 4—7; 11—12; 14—24; 33; against
false prophets, Ezek 13; 34; against other
nations, Ezek 25—32; 35; 38—39; of
restoration, Ezek 11.14—20; 34; 36;
39.23—29.*

EZRA

E went up from Babylonia. Ezra 7.6
For *E* had set his heart 7.10
While *E* prayed and made 10.1
told *E* the scribe to bring Neh 8.1

F

FACE — S

LORD,..speak to Moses *f* to *f*, Ex 33.11
but my *f* shall not be seen." 33.23
the skin of his *f* shone 34.29
make his *f* to shine upon you, Num 6.25
LORD spoke with you *f* to *f* Deut 5.4
whom the LORD knew *f* to *f*, 34.10
look one another in the *f*." 2Ki 14.8
seek the *f* of the God of Jacob. Ps 24.6
"Thy *f*, LORD, do I seek." 27.8
Let thy *f* shine on thy servant; 31.16
The *f* of the LORD is against 34.16
make his *f* to shine upon us, 67.1
Make thy *f* shine upon thy 119.135
see your *f*,..hear your voice, Sol 2.14
could not look at Moses' *f* 2Cor 3.7
hypocrites,..disfigure their *f* Mt 6.16

FACTIONS

there must be *f* among you 1Cor 11.19

FAIL — ED

he will not *f* you or destroy Deut 4.31
"Let no man's heart *f* 1Sam 17.32
not *f* you a man on the throne 1Ki 2.4
will not *f* or be discouraged Isa 42.4
not one of them has *f*. Josh 23.14
my close friends have *f* me; Job 19.14

FAINT

and do not let your heart be *f* Isa 7.4
He gives power to the *f*, and 40.29
he has left me..*f* all the day Lam 1.13
send..away hungry, lest they *f* Mt 15.32
the crowd..will *f* on the way; Mk 8.3

FAIR — EST

a *f* garland for your head, Prov 1.9
You are the *f* of the sons of men; Ps 45.2
If you..O *f* among women, Sol 1.8

FAITH

because you broke *f* with me Deut 32.51
Israel broke *f* in regard to Josh 7.1
because they had no *f* in God, Ps 78.22
righteous shall live by his *f*. Hab 2.4
not even in Israel..such *f*. Mt 8.10
afraid, O men of little *f*?" 8.26
"O woman, great is your *f*! 15.28
"Because of your little *f*. 17.20
if you have *f* and never doubt, 21.21
when Jesus saw their *f*, he said Mk 2.5
are you afraid? Have you no *f*?" 4.40
your *f* has made you well; 5.34
Jesus answered them, "Have *f* 11.22
when he saw their *f* he said, Lk 5.20
not even in Israel..such *f*." 7.9
"Daughter, your *f*..made you well; 8.48
clothe you, O men of little *f*? 12.28
to the Lord, "Increase our *f*!" 17.5
your *f* has made you well." 17.19
will he find *f* on earth?" 18.8
your *f* has made you well." 18.42
prayed for you that your *f* 22.32
he had *f* to be made well, Acts 14.9
he had opened a door of *f* 14.27
and of *f* in our Lord Jesus 20.21
are sanctified by *f* in me.' 26.18
for I have *f* in God that 27.25
because your *f* is proclaimed Rom 1.8
to every one who has *f*, to 1.16
overthrow the law by this *f*? 3.31
That is why it depends on *f*, 4.16

FAITH (cont.)

He did not weaken in f when   Rom 4.19
since we are justified by f,   5.1
according to the measure of f   12.3
the man who is weak in f,   14.1
not proceed from f is sin.   14.23
to another f by. .same Spirit,   1Cor 12.9
we have the same spirit of f   2Cor 4.13
now preaching the f he once   Gal 1.23
justified by f in Christ,   2.16
but f working through love.   5.6
who are of the household of f.   6.10
I have heard of your f in the   Eph 1.15
you have been saved through f;   2.8
taking the shield of f, with   6.16
we have heard of your f in   Col 1.4
work of f and labor of love   1Thess 1.3
comforted. .through your f;   3.7
great confidence in the f   1Tim 3.13
he has disowned the f and is   5.8
Fight the good fight of the f;   6.12
reminded of your sincere f,   2Tim 1.5
sharing of your f may promote   Philem 6
it did not meet with f in   Heb 4.2
my righteous one shall live by f,   10.38
Now f is the assurance of things   11.1
through f conquered kingdoms,   11.33
life, and imitate their f.   13.7
my works will show you my f.   Jas 2.18
You see that f was active   2.22
the genuineness of your f,   1Pet 1.7
you to contend for the f   Jude 3
who. .keep. .the f of Jesus.   Rev 14.12

FAITHFUL

raise up for myself a f priest,   1Sam 2.35
who. .is so f as David,   22.14
and f before the LORD his   2Chr 31.20
more f and God-fearing man   Neh 7.2
thou didst find his heart f   9.8
The LORD preserves the f,   Ps 31.23
"Gather to me my f ones, who   50.5
whose spirit was not f to God.   78.8
will look with favor on the f   101.6
but a f man who can find?   Prov 20.6
F are the wounds of a friend;   27.6
f city has become a harlot,   Isa 1.21
formed of old, f and sure.   25.1
he was f, and no error or fault   Dan 6.4
Judah. .is f to the Holy One.   Hos 11.12
"Who then is the f and wise   Mt 24.45
'Well done, good and f servant;   25.21
is the f and wise steward,   Lk 12.42
who is f in a very little is   16.10
you have been f in a very little,   19.17
to remain f to the Lord   Acts 11.23
God is f, by whom you were   1Cor 1.9
God is f, and he will not   10.13
Epaphras. .a f minister of   Col 1.7
He who calls you is f,   1Thess 5.24
But the Lord is f; he will   2Thess 3.3
entrust to f men who will   2Tim 2.2
since she considered him f   Heb 11.11
Be f unto death, and I will   Rev 2.10
He. .is called F and True,   19.11

FAITHFULNESS

heavens, thy f to the clouds.   Ps 36.5
I have spoken of thy f and   40.10
thy f to the clouds.   57.10
F will spring up from. .ground,   85.11
declared. .thy f in Abaddon?   88.11
thy f is firm as the heavens.   89.2

I will not. .be false to my f.   89.33
to declare. .thy f by night,   92.2
the f of the LORD endures   117.2
Thy f endures. .generations;   119.90
thy testimonies. .in all f.   119.138
In thy f answer me, in thy   143.1
I have continued my f to you.   Jer 31.3
every morning; great is thy f.   Lam 3.23
There is no f or kindness,   Hos 4.1

FAITHLESS — LY

way of the f is their ruin,   Prov 13.15
she did, that f one, Israel,   Jer 3.6
"O f and perverse generation,   Mt 17.17
"O f and perverse generation,   Lk 9.41
do not be f, but believing."   Jn 20.27
as for the cowardly, the f,   Rev 21.8
because they have acted f,   Ezek 15.8

FAITHLESSNESS

in this f the hand of the   Ezra 9.2
I will heal their f; I will   Hos 14.4
Does. .f nullify. .faithfulness   Rom 3.3

FALL — S — EN (v)

let none of his words f to   1Sam 3.19
he f,. .not be cast headlong,   Ps 37.24
make them f in the wilderness,   106.26
Let the wicked. .f into. .nets,   141.10
say. .to the hills, F upon us.   Hos 10.8
when I f, I shall rise; when   Mic 7.8
And then many will f away,   Mt 24.10
"You will all f away because   26.31
immediately they f away.   Mk 4.17
"You will all f away; for   14.27
they stumbled so as to f?   Rom 11.11
that no one f by. .disobedience.   Heb 4.11
rock that will make them f";   1Pet 2.8
not rejoice when. .enemy f,   Prov 24.17
"How are the mighty f   2Sam 1.25
"How you are f from heaven,   Isa 14.12
"F, f is Babylon; and all   Isa 21.9
Suddenly Babylon has f and   Jer 51.8
you have f away from grace.   Gal 5.4
"F, f is Babylon the great,   Rev 14.8

FALL — ING (n)

this child is set for the f   Lk 2.34
a cause of my brother's f,   1Cor 8.13

FALSE — LY

he was f to the LORD his   2Chr 26.16
I should have been f to God   Job 31.28
Put f ways.far from me; and   Ps 119.29
therefore I hate every f way.   119.104
for his images are f, and   Jer 51.17
Their heart is f; now they   Hos 10.2
"Beware of f prophets, who come   Mt 7.15
For f Christs and f prophets   24.24
God. .true though. .man be f,   Rom 3.4
make them believe what is f,   2Thess 2.11
you will not deal f with me   Gen 21.23

FALSEHOOD

left of your answers but f."   Job 21.34
They take pleasure in f. They   Ps 62.4
abhor f, but I love thy law.   119.163
Remove. .from me f and lying;   Prov 30.8
draw iniquity with cords of f,   Isa 5.18
spoken f and divined a lie;   Ezek 13.6
putting away f, let every one   Eph 4.25

FAME

who. .heard thy f will say,   Num 14.15
Herod. .heard about. .f of Jesus;   Mt 14.1
And at once his f spread   Mk 1.28

FAMILY — IES

taken away from his *f*,	Num 27.4
the *f* of the earth shall bless	Gen 12.3
makes their *f* like flocks.	Ps 107.41
God of all the *f* of Israel,	Jer 31.1
of all the *f* of the earth;	Amos 3.2

FAMINE

there was a *f* in the land.	Gen 12.10
arise seven years of *f*,	41.30
f was severe upon them.	47.20
judges ruled there was a	Ruth 1.1
a *f* in the days of David	2Sam 21.1
the *f* was severe in Samaria.	1Ki 18.2
was a great *f* in Samaria,	2Ki 6.25
the *f* was so severe in the	25.3
either three years of *f*;	1Chr 21.12
In *f* he will redeem you	Job 5.20
he summoned a *f* on the land,	Ps 105.16
'Sword and *f* shall not come	Jer 14.15
I will send sword, *f*, and	24.10
with the burning heat of *f*.	Lam 5.10
not a *f* of bread, nor. .thirst	Amos 8.11
a great *f* over all the world;	Acts 11.28

FAST — ED — ING (v)

but your disciples do not *f*?"	Mt 9.14
but your disciples do not *f*?"	Mk 2.18
"The disciples of John *f* often	Lk 5.33
before the LORD, and *f*	1Sam 7.6
we *f*, and thou seest it not?	Isa 58.3
was it for me that you *f*?	Zech 7.5
he *f* forty days and forty nights,	Mt 4.2
I continued *f* and praying	Neh 1.4

FAST — ING (n)

proclaimed a *f*. .all Judah.	2Chr 20.3
I proclaimed a *f* there,	Ezra 8.21
hold a *f* on my behalf, and	Est 4.16
Nineveh. .proclaimed a *f*,	Jon 3.5
and the *f* of the seventh,	Zech 8.19
Israel were assembled with *f*	Neh 9.1
mourning among the Jews, with *f*	Est 4.3
My knees are weak through *f*;	Ps 109.24
"return. .with *f*, with weeping,	Joel 2.12
that their *f* may be seen by men.	Mt 6.16
out except by prayer and *f*"	17.21*n*
driven out by. .prayer and *f*	Mk 9.29*n*

FATE

the *f* of the. .men and. .beasts	Ecc 3.19
since one *f* comes to all, to	9.2

FATHER — S — 'S

a man leaves his *f*	Gen 2.24
Adam. .became the *f* of. .Seth.	5.3
f of a multitude of nations.	17.5
go. .and bury my *f*; then I	50.5
Is not he your *f*, who	Deut 32.6
to the voice of their *f*;	1Sam 2.25
"Pray let my *f* and my mother	22.3
I will be his *f*, and he	2Sam 7.14
His *f* had never at any time	1Ki 1.6
I will be his *f*, and he	1Chr 17.13
I was *f* to the poor, and	Job 29.16
"Has the rain a *f*, or who	38.28
f and my mother have forsaken	Ps 27.10
F of the fatherless and. .is God	68.5
As a *f* pities his children,	103.13
A wise son makes a glad *f*,	Prov 10.1
the *f* of a fool has no joy.	17.21
Hearken to. .*f* who begot you.	23.22
who robs his *f* or his mother	28.24
Yet, O LORD, thou art our *F*;	Isa 64.8
nor the *f* suffer for. .son;	Ezek 18.20

Have we not all one *f*? Has	Mal 2.10
that you may be sons of your *F*	Mt 5.45
as your heavenly *F* is perfect.	5.48
Pray. .Our *F* who art in heaven,	6.9
he who does the will of my *F*	7.21
I. .will acknowledge before my *F*	10.32
loves *f* or mother more than me	10.37
a man shall leave his *f* and mother	19.5
call no man your *f* on earth,	23.9
'If a man tells his *f* or his	Mk 7.11
man shall leave. .*f* and mother	10.7
let me first go and bury my *f*."	Lk 9.59
heavenly *F* give the Holy Spirit	11.13
be divided, *f* against son	12.53
and does not hate his own *f*	14.26
F who sent me has. .given me	Jn 12.49
Abraham. .*f* of all who believe	Rom 4.11
I became your *f* in Christ	1Cor 4.15
and I will be a *f* to you,	2Cor 6.18
He is without *f* or mother	Heb 7.3
coming down from the F of	Jas 1.17
put to death for the *f*;	Deut 24.16
the inheritance of my *f*."	1Ki 21.3
f. .not be put to death for	2Ki 14.6
against the God of their *f*,	1Chr 5.25
our *f* have told us, what deeds	Ps 44.1
hearts of children to their *f*,	Mal 4.6
turn. .the *f* to the children,	Lk 1.17
F, do not provoke your children	Eph 6.4
F, do not provoke. .children,	Col 3.21
I am writing to you, *f*,	1Jn 2.13
Hear,. .your *f* instruction,	Prov 1.8
I must be in my F house?"	Lk 2.49

FATHERLESS

executes justice for the *f*	Deut 10.18
the sojourner, the *f*, and	14.29
even cast lots over the *f*,	Job 6.27
arms of the *f* were crushed.	22.9
those who snatch the *f* child	24.9
the *f* who had none to help	29.12
hast been the helper of the *f*.	Ps 10.14
your *f* children, I will keep	Jer 49.11

FAULT

I have found no *f* in him	1Sam 29.3
no ground for complaint or. .*f*,	Dan 6.4
"Why does he still find *f*?	Rom 9.19
so that no *f* may be found	2Cor 6.3
For he finds *f* with them when	Heb 8.8

FAVOR — ED

Noah found *f* in the eyes	Gen 6.8
if I have found *f* in your sight,	18.3
may find *f* in your sight.' "	32.5
find *f* in the sight of my lord."	33.8
And I will give this people *f*	Ex 3.21
LORD gave the people *f* in the	11.3
LORD had given the people *f*	12.36
also found *f* in my sight.'	33.12
if I find *f* in thy sight,	Num 11.15
I have found *f* with thee,	Judg 6.17
"Why have I found *f* in your	Ruth 2.10
I. .found *f* in your sight,	2Sam 14.22
If I find *f* in the eyes of the LORD,	15.25
for a brief moment *f* has	Ezra 9.8
Esther found *f* in. .eyes of all	Est 2.15
If I have found *f* in the	5.8
His children will seek the *f*	Job 20.10
Tyre will sue your *f* with	Ps 45.12
LORD God. .bestow *f* and honor.	84.11
the *f* of the Lord. .be upon us,	90.17
So you will find *f* and good	Prov 3.4
to the humble he shows *f*.	3.34

FAVOR — ED (cont.)

He who. .seeks good seeks *f*,	Prov 11.27
his *f* is like the clouds	16.15
and obtains *f* from the LORD.	18.22
words of a wise. .win him *f*,	Ecc 10.12
in my *f* I. .had mercy on you.	Isa 60.10
for I will show you no *f*.	Jer 16.13
you have found *f* with God.	Lk 1.30
the *f* of God was upon him.	2.40
and in *f* with God and man.	2.52
found *f* in the sight of God	Acts 7.46
to do the Jews a *f*, Felix left Paul	24.27
O *f* one, the Lord is with you!"	Lk 1.28

FAVORABLE

words of the prophets. .are *f*	1Ki 22.13
LORD, thou wast *f* to thy land;	Ps 85.1

FEAR — S — ED (v)

and you will live, for I *f* God:	Gen 42.18
"F not, stand firm,	Ex 14.13
people, such as *f* God,	18.21
LORD is with us; do not *f*.	Num 14.9
do not *f* or be dismayed.'	Deut 1.21
to *f* me and to keep all my	5.29
you may *f* the LORD your God,	6.2
Israel shall hear, and *f*,	13.11
people shall hear, and *f*,	17.13
do not *f* or be dismayed."	31.8
said to Joshua, "Do not *f*	Josh 8.1
therefore *f* the LORD,	24.14
says the LORD. ."F not,	2Chr 20.15
friendship. .for those who *f*	Ps 25.14
not *f* though the earth. .change,	46.2
nations. .*f* the name of the LORD,	102.15
food for those who *f* him;	111.5
thy promise,. .for those who *f*	119.38
f the LORD,. .turn. .from evil.	Prov 3.7
son, *f* the LORD and the king,	24.21
dreams increase,. .do you *f* God.	Ecc 5.7
be well with those who *f* God,	8.12
F God,. .keep. .commandments;	12.13
f not, for I am with you,	Isa 41.10
not say. .'Let us *f* the LORD	Jer 5.24
who shall hear. .*f* and tremble	33.9
f not, O Jacob my servant,	46.27
f before the God of Daniel,	Dan 6.26
F not. .let. .hands be strong."	Zech 8.13
do not *f* to take Mary your wife	Mt 1.20
F not,. .you are of more value	10.31
his mercy is on those who *f*	Lk 1.50
f him who. .has power to cast	12.5
"F not, daughter of Zion;	Jn 12.15
Who shall not *f* and glorify	Rev 15.4
woman who *f* the LORD is	Prov 31.30
Who among you *f* the LORD and	Isa 50.10
But the midwives *f* God,	Ex 1.17
he who *f* the word of the LORD	9.20
I *f* the people and obeyed	1Sam 15.24
they *f* the LORD but also	2Ki 17.33
Then Jehoshaphat *f*, and	2Chr 20.3
those who *f* the LORD spoke	Mal 3.16
Herod. .*f* the people, because	Mt 14.5
Herod *f* John, knowing he was	Mk 6.20
destroy him; for they *f* him,	11.18
this because they *f* the Jews,	Jn 9.22
a devout man who *f* God with	Acts 10.2

FEAR (n)

they were in great *f*.	Ex 14.10
f of you upon the peoples	Deut 2.25
f of God came on. .kingdoms	2Chr 20.29
instructed him in the *f* of God;	26.5
the *f* of the Jews had fallen	Est 8.17

f of the Lord,. .is wisdom;	Job 28.28
Serve the LORD with *f*, with	Ps 2.11
the *f* of the LORD is clean,	19.9
no *f* of God before his eyes.	36.1
f of the LORD. .the beginning	Prov 1.7
f of the LORD is the beginning	9.10
f of the LORD is a fountain	14.27
f of the LORD leads to life;	19.23
The *f* of man lays a snare,	29.25
let him be your *f*, and. .dread.	Isa 8.13
And they cried out for *f*.	Mt 14.26
heart, it is I; have no *f*."	Mk 6.50
doors. .shut. .for *f* of. .Jews,	Jn 20.19
"There is no *f* of God before	Rom 3.18
Would you have no *f* of him	13.3
and in much *f* and trembling;	1Cor 2.3
knowing the *f* of the Lord,	2Cor 5.11
fighting without and *f* within.	7.5
f. .with which you received him.	7.15
he was heard for his godly *f*.	Heb 5.7
There is no *f* in love, but	1Jn 4.18

FEAST — ED (v)

They *f* on the abundance of thy	Ps 36.8
My soul is *f* as with marrow	63.5
Those who *f* on dainties perish	Lam 4.5

FEAST — S — ING (n)

you shall keep a *f* to me.	Ex 23.14
a *f* to the LORD seven days	Lev 23.41
Solomon held the *f* at that	1Ki 8.65
for all peoples a *f* of fat	Isa 25.6
King Belshazzar made a great *f*	Dan 5.1
"Not during the *f*, lest there	Mt 26.5
Now at the *f* the governor was	27.15
at the *f* he used to release	Mk 15.6
every year at. .*f* of. .Passover.	Lk 2.41
Levi made him. .*f* in his house;	5.29
the *f* of Unleavened Bread	22.1
appointed *f* of the LORD	Lev 23.2
LORD at your appointed *f*,	Num 29.39
turn your *f* into mourning,	Amos 8.10
and made that a day of *f*	Est 9.17

FED

the bread with which I *f* you	Ex 16.32
who *f* you in the wilderness	Deut 8.16

FEEBLE

"What are these *f* Jews doing?	Neh 4.2
Therefore all hands will be *f*,	Isa 13.7

FEED

commanded a widow there to *f*	1Ki 17.9
The lips of the righteous *f*	Prov 10.21
He will *f* his flock like a	Isa 40.11
will *f* you with the heritage	58.14
Aliens. .stand and *f* your flocks,	61.5
and he shall *f* on Carmel	Jer 50.19
Should not shepherds *f* the	Ezek 34.2
he shall stand and *f* his flock	Mic 5.4
"How can one *f* these men with	Mk 8.4
Jesus said to him, "F my sheep.	Jn 21.17
to *f* the church of the Lord	Acts 20.28

FEET

kiss his *f*, lest he be angry,	Ps 2.12
hast put all things under his *f*,	8.6
turn my *f* to thy testimonies;	119.59
Thy word is a lamp to my *f*	119.105
How graceful are. .*f* in sandals,	Sol 7.1
the *f* of him who brings good	Nah 1.15
put thy enemies under thy *f*'?	Mt 22.44
hold of his *f* and worshiped	28.9
put thy enemies under thy *f*.'	Mk 12.36

FEET (cont.)

to wet his *f* with her tears,	Lk 7.38
Mary, who sat at the Lord's *f*	10.39
See my hands and my *f*, that	24.39
and anointed the *f* of Jesus	Jn 12.3
began to wash the disciples' *f*,	13.5
f are swift to shed blood,	Rom 3.15
all his enemies under his *f*.	1Cor 15.25

FELL

Moses and Aaron *f* on their	Num 14.5
Moses heard it, he *f* on his face;	16.4
And they *f* on their faces,	16.22
they *f* on their faces.	16.45
Abigail..*f* before David on	1Sam 25.23
I *f* at his feet as though dead.	Rev 1.17

FELLOW

"This *f* came to sojourn,	Gen 19.9
"Why do you strike your *f*?"	Ex 2.13
fall, one will lift up his *f*;	Ecc 4.10
"Away with such a *f* from	Acts 22.22
how the Gentiles are *f* heirs,	Eph 3.6
my brother and *f* worker	Phil 2.25
f workers for..kingdom of God,	Col 4.11
be *f* workers in the truth.	3Jn 8

FELLOWSHIP

the apostles' teaching and *f*,	Acts 2.42
called into the *f* of his Son,	1Cor 1.9
and the *f* of the Holy Spirit	2Cor 13.14
Barnabas the right hand of *f*,	Gal 2.9
that you may have *f* with us;	1Jn 1.3

FEVER

Simon's mother-in-law..with *f*,	Mk 1.30
Simon's mother-in-law..high *f*,	Lk 4.38
seventh hour the *f* left him."	Jn 4.52
father of Publius lay..with *f*	Acts 28.8

FEW

therefore let your words be *f*.	Ecc 5.2
and those who find it are *f*.	Mt 7.14
will those who are saved be *f*?"	Lk 13.23

FIELD

who add *f* to *f*, until there	Isa 5.8
'Buy my *f*..at Anathoth, for	Jer 32.7
like treasure hidden in a *f*,	Mt 13.44
f was called..F of Blood.)	Acts 1.19
you are God's *f*, God's	1Cor 3.9

FIGHT — ING

The LORD will *f* for you,	Ex 14.14
God..will himself *f* for you,	Deut 1.30
the LORD..goes.. to *f* for you	20.4
shall not go up or *f* against	2Chr 11.4
come down to *f* upon Mount Zion	Isa 31.4
fast only to quarrel and to *f*	58.4
They will *f* against you; but	Jer 1.19
I myself will *f* against you	21.5
Judah will *f*..Jerusalem.	Zech 14.14
my servants would *f*, that I	Jn 18.36
F the good *f* of the faith;	1Tim 6.12
f without and fear within.	2Cor 7.5

FIGS

nor *f* on the fig tree; even	Jer 8.13
two baskets of *f* placed before	24.1

FIG TREE — S

f..puts forth its figs,	Sol 2.13
like leaves falling from the *f*..	Isa 34.4
sit every man..under his *f*..,	Mic 4.4
Though the *f*..not blossom,	Hab 3.17
the *f*..withered at once.	Mt 21.19
And seeing..a *f*..in leaf,	Mk 11.13

"From the *f*..learn its lesson:	13.28
man had a *f*..planted..vineyard;	Lk 13.6
parable: "Look at the *f*..,	21.29
under the *f*.., I saw you."	Jn 1.48
Can a *f*.., yield olives,	Jas 3.12
It has..and splintered my *f*..;	Joel 1.7

FILL — ED (v)

and *f* the waters in the seas,	Gen 1.22
f the earth and subdue it;	1.28
f the whole world with fruit.	Isa 27.6
said.."F the jars with water."	Jn 2.7
the glory of the LORD *f* the	Ex 40.35
be *f* with the glory of the	Num 14.21
come and eat and be *f*;	Deut 14.29
glory of the LORD *f* the house	1Ki 8.11
he *f* Jerusalem with innocent	2Ki 24.4
glory of the LORD *f*. the	2Chr 5.14
glory of the LORD *f*..temple.	Ezek 43.5
glory of the LORD *f* the temple	44.4
earth..*f* with the knowledge	Hab 2.14
he has *f* the hungry with good	Lk 1.53
Every valley shall be *f*, and	3.5
all *f* with the Holy Spirit	Acts 2.4
you have *f* Jerusalem with	5.28
Already you are *f*! Already	1Cor 4.8
but be *f* with the Spirit,	Eph 5.18

FILL (n)

let us take our *f* of love	Prov 7.18
ate your *f* of the loaves.	Jn 6.26

FINAL

time of your *f* punishment,	Ezek 21.25
oath is *f* for confirmation.	Heb 6.16

FIND — S

your sin will *f* you out.	Num 32.23
seek the LORD..will *f* him,	Deut 4.29
where I might *f* him, that I	Job 23.3
understanding..*f* him out.	Prov 28.11
For he who *f* me *f* life and	8.35
who *f* a wife *f* a good thing,	18.22

FINGER

"This is the *f* of God."	Ex 8.19
written with the *f* of God.	31.18
written with the *f* of God;	Deut 9.10
not move them with their *f*.	Mt 23.4
if it is by the *f* of God	Lk 11.20
thy heavens, the work of thy *f*,	Ps 8.3
the *f* of a man's hand appeared	Dan 5.5
burdens with one of your *f*.	Lk 11.46

FINISH — ED

to *f* the transgression, to	Dan 9.24
the third day I *f* my course.	Lk 13.32
heavens..earth were *f*,	Gen 2.1
built the house, and *f* it.	1Ki 6.14
house of the LORD is *f*.	1Chr 28.20
and this house was *f* on	Ezra 6.15
So the wall was *f* on the	Neh 6.15
he said, "It is *f*"; and..bowed	Jn 19.30
I have *f* the race, I have kept	2Tim 4.7

FIRE

Gomorrah brimstone and *f*	Gen 19.24
And *f* came forth from before	Lev 9.24
f came forth from..the LORD	10.2
out of the midst of the *f*;	Deut 4.12
your God is a devouring *f*,	4.24
LORD spoke..out of the *f*,	5.4
haste to set the city on *f*.	Josh 8.19
smote..and set the city on *f*.	Judg 1.8
Then the *f* of the LORD fell,	1Ki 18.38
the LORD was not in the *f*;	19.12

FIRE (cont.)

and horses of *f* separated   2Ki 2.11
ended his prayer, *f* came   2Chr 7.1
we went through *f* and..water;   Ps 66.12
As *f* consumes the forest, as   83.14
For lack of wood the *f* goes   Prov 26.20
when you walk through *f* you   Isa 43.2
their *f* shall not be quenched,   66.24
burning *f* shut up in my bones,   Jer 20.9
Is not my word like *f*, says   23.29
scroll was consumed in the *f*   36.23
"From on high he sent *f*; into   Lam 1.13
four men..walking in the..*f*,   Dan 3.25
cut down and thrown into the *f*.   Mt 3.10
the Holy Spirit and with *f*.   3.11
eternal *f* prepared for the devil   25.41
the Holy Spirit and with *f*.   Lk 3.16
do you want us to bid *f* come   9.54
"I came to cast *f* upon..earth;   12.49
they saw a charcoal *f* there,   Jn 21.9
shook..creature into the *f*   Acts 28.5
the *f* will test what sort   1Cor 3.13
saved, but only as through *f*.   3.15
mighty angels in flaming *f*,   2Thess 1.7
for our God is a consuming *f*.   Heb 12.29
And the tongue is a *f*. The   Jas 3.6
a punishment of eternal *f*.   Jude 7
snatching them out of the *f*;   23
the lake that burns with *f*   Rev 21.8

FIRMAMENT

"Let there be a *f* in the midst   Gen 1.6
the *f* proclaims his handiwork.   Ps 19.1

FIRST

LORD, the, *f*, and..the last;   Isa 41.4
But seek *f* his kingdom and   Mt 6.33
many that are *f* will be last,   19.30
"If any one would be *f*, he   Mk 9.35
let me *f* go..bury my father."   Lk 9.59
f convert in Asia for Christ.   Rom 16.5
The *f* man was from..earth,   1Cor 15.47
the *f* converts in Achaia,   16.15
but *f* they gave themselves   2Cor 8.5
Diotrephes,..to put himself *f*,   3Jn 9
"Fear not, I am the *f* and the   Rev 1.17
This is the *f* resurrection.   20.5

FIRST-BORN

all the *f* in the land of Egypt   Ex 11.5
Levites instead of all the *f*   Num 3.45
For all the *f* among the people   8.17
He smote all the *f* in Egypt,   Ps 78.51
make him the *f*, the highest   89.27
He is..the *f* of all creation;   Col 1.15

FIRSTLING

as a *f* belongs to the LORD,   Lev 27.26

FISH

dominion over the   Gen 1.26
the *f* in the Nile died;   Ex 7.21
LORD appointed a great *f*   Jonah 1.17
the LORD spoke to the *f*,   2.10
for a *f*, will give..a serpent?   Mt 7.10
five loaves here and two *f*."   14.17
"Seven, and a few small *f*."   15.34
take the first *f* that comes   17.27
they said, "Five, and two *f*."   Mk 6.38
And they had a few small *f*;   8.7
if his son asks for a *f*, will   Lk 11.11
five barley loaves and two *f*;   Jn 6.9
haul..in..the quantity of *f*.   21.6

FISHERMEN

The *f* will mourn and lament,   Isa 19.8
in the sea; for they were *f*.   Mk 1.16

FISHERS

I am sending for many *f*,   Jer 16.16
I will make you..*f* of men."   Mk 1.17

FIVE

Do you..remember the *f* loaves   Mt 16.9
they said, "F, and two fish."   Mk 6.38
ate the loaves were *f* thousand   6.44
"We have no more than *f* loaves   Lk 9.13
for you have had *f* husbands,   Jn 4.18

FIXED

eyes of all..were *f* on him.   Lk 4.20
because he has *f* a day on   Acts 17.31

FLAME

fire, and his Holy One a *f*;   Isa 10.17
the *f* shall not consume you.   43.2

FLASHES

jealousy..Its *f* are *f* of fire,   Sol 8.6
from the throne..*f* of lightning,   Rev 4.5

FLATTER — S — ING

For I do not know how to *f*,   Job 32.22
he *f* himself in his own eyes   Ps 36.2
he who *f* with his tongue.   Prov 28.23
who *f* his neighbor spreads   29.5
with *f* lips and a double heart   Ps 12.2
and a *f* mouth works ruin.   Prov 26.28

FLED

and she *f* from her.   Gen 16.6
But Moses *f* from Pharaoh,   Ex 2.15
"Joab has *f* to the tent of   1Ki 2.29
I have *f* to thee for refuge!   Ps 143.9
as you *f* from the earthquake   Zech 14.5

FLEE

f to one of these cities   Deut 19.5
"Should such a man as I *f*?   Neh 6.11
how can you say to me, "F   Ps 11.1
wicked *f* when no one pursues,   Prov 28.1
F for safety, O people of   Jer 6.1
Jonah rose to *f* to Tarshish   Jonah 1.3
child and his mother, and *f* to   Mt 2.13
persecute you in one town, *f*   10.23
warned you to *f* from the wrath   Lk 3.7
let those who are in Judea *f*   21.21

FLEECE

I am laying a *f* of wool   Judg 6.37

FLEET (n)

King Solomon built a *f* of   1Ki 9.26
Moreover the *f* of Hiram, which   10.11

FLEETING (adj)

let me know how *f* my life is!   Ps 39.4
enjoy the *f* pleasures of sin.   Heb 11.25

FLESH

we are your bone and *f*.   1Chr 11.1
With him is an arm of *f*;   2Chr 32.8
without my *f* I shall see God,   Job 19.26
let all *f* bless his holy name   Ps 145.21
all *f* shall see it together,   Isa 40.5
All *f* is grass, and all its beauty   40.6
willing, but the *f* is weak."   Mt 26.41
willing, but the *f* is weak."   Mk 14.38
all *f* shall see the salvation   Lk 3.6
the Word became *f* and dwelt   Jn 1.14
life of the world is my *f*."   6.51
life, the *f* is of no avail;   6.63
nothing good dwells..in my *f*.   Rom 7.18

FLESH (cont.)

Son in the likeness of sinful *f*   Rom 8.3
To set..mind on the *f* is death,   8.6
But you are not in the *f*,   8.9
their race, according to the *f*,   9.5
but as men of the *f*, as babes   1Cor 3.1
for the destruction of the *f*,   5.5
For not all *f* is alike, but   15.39
f and blood cannot inherit   15.50
thorn was given me in the *f*,   2Cor 12.7
the Spirit are against the *f*;   Gal 5.17
reason for confidence in the *f*,   Phil 3.4

FLESHPOTS

when we sat by the *f* and ate   Ex 16.3

FLOAT — ED

a stick,..made the iron *f*.   2Ki 6.6
the ark *f* on..face of the waters.   Gen 7.18

FLOCK

stronger of the *f* were breeding   Gen 30.41
thy *f* found a dwelling in it;   Ps 68.10
lead thy people like a *f* by the hand   77.20
thy people, the *f*..give thanks   79.13
He will feed his *f* like a   Isa 40.11
like the *f* at Jerusalem   Ezek 36.38
"Fear not little *f*, for it   Lk 12.32
Tend the *f* of God that is   1Pet 5.2

FLOOD — S

I will bring a *f* of waters   Gen 6.17
never again..*f* to destroy   9.11
LORD sits enthroned over..*f*;   Ps 29.10
the *f* came and destroyed them   Lk 17.27
the rain fell, and the *f* came,   Mt 7.27

FLOW — ING (v)

all the nations shall *f* to it,   Isa 2.2
f from the throne of God   Rev 22.1

FLOW (n)

a *f* of blood for twelve years.   Mk 5.25
a *f* of blood for twelve years   Lk 8.43

FLOWER — S

He comes forth like a *f*,   Job 14.2
grass withers, the *f* fades,   Isa 40.7
The *f* appear on the earth,   Sol 2.12

FLY — IES

LORD will whistle for the *f*   Isa 7.18
I will send swarms of *f*   Ex 8.21
Dead *f* make the perfumer's   Ecc 10.1

FOES

three months before your *f*   2Sam 24.13
O LORD, how many are my *f*!   Ps 3.1
God..will tread down our *f*.   108.13
man's *f* will be those of his   Mt 10.36

FOLD

they have forgotten their *f*.   Jer 50.6
other sheep,..not of this *f*;   Jn 10.16

FOLLOW — ED — ING

If the LORD is God, *f* him;   1Ki 18.21
adversaries because I *f*..good.   Ps 38.20
They shall *f* my ordinances   Ezek 37.24
"*F* me, and I will make you   Mt 4.19
"Teacher, I will *f* you wherever   8.19
"*F* me, and leave the dead to   8.22
Jesus..said to him, "*F* me."   9.9
and he said to him, "*F* me."   Mk 2.14
allowed no one to *f* him except   5.37
and he said to him, "*F* me."   Lk 5.27
take up his cross daily and *f*   9.23
because he does not *f* with us."   9.49

"I will *f* you wherever you go."   9.57
in heaven; and come, *f* me."   18.22
Philip and said to him, "*F* me."   Jn 1.43
sheep *f* him, for they know his   10.4
I know them, and they *f* me;   10.27
If any one serves me, he must *f*   12.26
"Lord, why cannot I *f* you   13.37
After this he said.."*F* me."   21.19
also *f*..example of the faith   Rom 4.12
they..wholly *f* the LORD.'   Num 32.12
yet I wholly *f* the LORD   Josh 14.8
they *f* the nations that were   2Ki 17.15
stubbornly *f* their own hearts   Jer 9.14
Peter *f* him at a distance,   Mt 26.58
they left their nets and *f* him.   Mk 1.18
we have left everything and *f*   10.28
Peter had *f* him at a distance,   14.54
women..*f* him and ministered   15.41
left our homes and *f* you."   Lk 18.28
Peter *f* at a distance;   22.54
heard John speak, and *f* him,   Jn 1.40
Simon Peter *f* Jesus, and so   18.15
your children *f* the truth,   2Jn 4

FOLLY — IES

she has wrought *f* in Israel   Deut 22.21
Nabal is his name, and *f*   1Sam 25.25
do not do this wanton *f*.   2Sam 13.12
The devising of *f* is sin,   Prov 24.9
a fool that repeats his *f*.   26.11
through..*f* of what we preach   1Cor 1.21
gifts of..Spirit..are *f* to him.   2.14
their hearts overflow with *f*.   Ps 73.7

FOOD — S

you shall have them for *f*.   Gen 1.29
tree was good for *f*,   3.6
there is no *f* and no water,   Num 21.5
children beg for *f*, but no one   Lam 4.4
For life is more than *f*,   Lk 12.23
"I have *f* to eat of which   Jn 4.32
"*F* is meant for the stomach   1 Cor 6.13
the right to our *f* and drink?   9.4
but if we have *f* and clothing,   1Tim 6.8
enjoin abstinence from *f*   4.3

FOOL — S

I have played the *f*, and   1Sam 26.21
Abner die as a *f* dies?   2Sam 3.33
Surely vexation kills the *f*,   Job 5.2
The *f* says.."There is no God."   Ps 14.1
f and the stupid alike must perish   49.10
The *f* says.."There is no God."   53.1
prating *f* will come to ruin.   Prov 10.8
but a *f* flaunts his folly.   13.16
Leave the presence of a *f*,   14.7
rather than a *f* in his folly.   17.12
Wisdom is too high for a *f*;   24.7
honor is not fitting for a *f*.   26.1
Answer a *f* according to his folly,   26.5
"What befalls the *f* will..me   Ecc 2.15
The *f* folds his hands, and eats   4.5
Be not wicked..neither..a *f*;   7.17
whoever says, 'You *f*!' shall   Mt 5.22
'*F*! This night your soul is   Lk 12.20
folly is the chastisement of *f*.   Prov 16.22
and *f* shall not err therein.   Isa 35.8
You *f*!..who made the outside   Lk 11.40
they became *f*, and exchanged   Rom 1.22
We are *f* for Christ's sake,   1Cor 4.10

FOOLISH

and makes their knowledge *f*;   Isa 44.25
"For my people are *f*, they   Jer 4.22

FOOLISH (cont.)
a *f* man who built his house — Mt 7.26
"O *f* men, and slow of heart — Lk 24.25

FOOT
He will not let your *f* be moved, — Ps 121.3
you have raced with men on *f*, — Jer 12.5
if your *f* causes you to sin, — Mk 9.45
If the *f* should say, — 1Cor 12.15

FOOTSTOOL
till I make..enemies your *f*." — Ps 110.1
and the earth is my *f*; — Isa 66.1

FORBADE
in your name, and we *f* him, — Mk 9.38
in your name, and we *f* him, — Lk 9.49

FORBEARANCE
because in his divine *f* he — Rom 3.25
count the *f* of our Lord as — 2Pet 3.15

FORBID — DEN
"My lord Moses, *f* them." — Num 11.28
not *f* speaking in tongues; — 1Cor 14.39
f by the Holy Spirit to speak — Acts 16.6

FORCE (n)
men of violence take it by *f*. — Mt 11.12
take him by *f* to make him king, — Jn 6.15

FORCED (v)
I *f* myself, and offered — 1Sam 13.12
slothful..be put to *f* labor. — Prov 12.24
I have been a fool! You *f* me — 2Cor 12.11

FOREHEAD — S
a hard *f* and..stubborn heart. — Ezek 3.8
marked on the right hand or..*f*, — Rev 13.16
a mark upon the *f* of the men — Ezek 9.4

FOREIGN
and from the *f* wives." — Ezra 10.11
the LORD's song in a *f* land? — Ps 137.4

FOREIGNER — S
To a *f* you may lend upon — Deut 23.20
"Likewise when a *f*,..comes — 1Ki 8.41
praise to God except this *f*?" — Lk 17.18
be a *f* to the speaker — 1Cor 14.11
admitting *f*, uncircumcised — Ezek 44.7

FOREKNEW
whom he *f* he also predestined — Rom 8.29
God has not rejected..whom he *f*. — 11.2

FOREKNOWLEDGE
definite plan and *f* of God, — Acts 2.23

FORFEIT — ED
gain..world and *f* his life? — Mk 8.36
yield be *f* to the sanctuary, — Deut 22.9

FORGAVE
f their iniquity, and did not — Ps 78.38
released..and *f* him the debt. — Mt 18.27
wicked servant! I *f* you all — 18.32
When they could not pay, he *f* — Lk 7.42
as God in Christ *f* you. — Eph 4.32

FORGET — S — TING
he will not..*f* the covenant — Deut 4.31
take heed lest you *f* the LORD, — 6.12
lest you *f* the LORD your God, — 8.11
Why dost thou *f* our affliction — Ps 44.24
O daughter,..*f* your people — 45.10
do not *f* the life of thy poor — 74.19
and *f* not all his benefits, — 103.2
I will not *f* thy word. — 119.16
If I *f* you, O Jerusalem, let — 137.5

My son, do not *f* my teaching, — Prov 3.1
drink and *f* their poverty, — 31.7
who *f* my holy mountain, — Isa 65.11
to make my people *f* my name — Jer 23.27
Why dost thou *f* us for ever, — Lam 5.20
f the covenant of her God; — Prov 2.17
evil..*f* the LORD their God, — Judg 3.7
I do, *f* what lies behind — Phil 3.13

FORGIVE — S — N — ING
f the transgression of — Gen 50.17
if thou wilt *f* their sin— — Ex 32.32
and the LORD will *f* her. — Num 30.8
Pray *f* the trespass of — 1Sam 25.28
and when thou hearest, *f*. — 1Ki 8.30
and *f*, and act, and render — 8.39
and when thou hearest, *f*. — 2Chr 6.21
f their sin and heal their land. — 7.14
not *f* your transgressions — Josh 24.19
Consider..and *f* all my sins. — Ps 25.18
deliver us, and *f* our sins, — 79.9
f the iniquity of thy people; — 85.2
for I will *f* their iniquity, — Jer 31.34
I will *f* all the guilt of their sin — 33.8
f their iniquity and their sin." — 36.3
men..brought low—*f* them not! — Isa 2.9
And *f* us our debts, As we also — Mt 6.12
neither will your Father *f* — 6.15
if you do not *f* your brother — 18.35
blasphemy! Who can *f* sins but God — Mk 2.7
whenever you stand praying, *f*, — 11.25
f, and you will be forgiven; — Lk 6.37
and *f* us our sins, for we..*f* — 11.4
and if he repents, *f* him; — 17.3
Jesus said, "Father, *f* them; — 23.34
If you *f* the sins of any, — Jn 20.23
you should rather turn to *f* — 2Cor 2.7
he..will *f* our sins and cleanse — 1Jn 1.9
who *f* all your iniquity, who — Ps 103.3
who *f* an offense seeks love, — Prov 17.9
atonement..they shall be *f*. — Lev 4.20
the sin..shall be *f* him. — 19.22
they shall be *f*; because — Num 15.25
guilt of blood be *f* them.' — Deut 21.8
he whose transgression is *f*, — Ps 32.1
guilt is taken away,..sin *f*." — Isa 6.7
people..who dwell..will be *f* — 33.24
rebelled, and thou hast not *f*. — Lam 3.42
my son; your sins are *f*." — Mt 9.2
sin and blasphemy will be *f* — 12.31
paralytic,..your sins are *f*." — Mk 2.5
all sins will be *f*..men, — 3.28
"Man, your sins are *f* you." — Lk 5.20
word against the Son..be *f*; — 12.10
intent of your heart may be *f* — Acts 8.22
those whose iniquities are *f*, — Rom 4.7
having *f* us all our trespasses, — Col 2.13
your sins are *f* for his sake. — 1Jn 2.12
f iniquity and transgression — Ex 34.7
steadfast love, *f* iniquity — Num 14.18
thou wast a *f* God to them, but — Ps 99.8

FORGIVENESS
But there is *f* with thee, — Ps 130.4
To..our God belong mercy and *f*; — Dan 9.9
baptized..for the *f* of..sins; — Acts 2.38
believes in him receives *f* — 10.43
through this man *f* of sins — 13.38
they may receive *f* of sins — 26.18
redemption, the *f* of sins. — Col 1.14
without..shedding..blood..no *f* — Heb 9.22

FORGOT — TEN
chief butler..*f* him. — Gen 40.23

FORGOT — TEN (cont.)

they *f* the LORD their God;	1Sam 12.9
But they soon *f* his works;	Ps 106.13
in his heart, "God has *f*,	10.11
"Why hast thou *f* me? Why go I	42.9
though we have not *f* thee, or	44.17
Has God *f* to be gracious?	77.9
f the God of your salvation,	Isa 17.10
Israel, you will not be *f*	44.21
"The LORD has forsaken. .*f* me."	49.14
have *f* the LORD, your Maker,	51.13
Yet my people have *f* me days	Jer 2.32
you have *f* me and trusted. .lies.	13.25
But my people have *f* me, they	18.15
All your lovers have *f* you;	30.14
gone, they have *f* their fold.	50.6
you have *f* the law of your God,	Hos 4.6
they had *f* to bring bread;	Mk 8.14
not one of them. .*f* before God.	Lk 12.6

FORK

have winnowed them with. .*f*	Jer 15.7
winnowing *f* is in his hand,	Lk 3.17

FORM (n)

f of this world is passing	1Cor 7.31
though he was in the *f* of God,	Phil 2.6
holding the *f* of religion	2Tim 3.5

FORMED (v)

God *f* man of dust	Gen 2.7
out of the ground. .God *f*	2.19
was *f* from a piece of clay.	Job 33.6
LORD,. .who created. .who *f* you,	Isa 43.1
LORD. .who *f* you from the womb	44.2
"Before I *f* you in the womb	Jer 1.5
until Christ be *f* in you!	Gal 4.19

FORMER

Tell us the *f* things, what	Isa 41.22
f things I declared of old.	48.3

FORMS (v)

he who *f* the mountains,	Amos 4.13

FORSAKE — N — ING

he will not fail you or *f* you;	Deut 31.8
I will not fail you or *f* you.	Josh 1.5
if you *f* him, he will cast	1Chr 28.9
if you turn aside and *f* my	2Chr 7.19
Cast me not off, *f* me not, O	Ps 27.9
he will not *f* his saints.	37.28
LORD will not *f* his people;	94.14
statutes; O *f* me not utterly!	119.8
Let not. .faithfulness *f* you;	Prov 3.3
f not your mother's teaching.	6.20
those who *f*. .shall be consumed.	Isa 1.28
let the wicked *f* his way,	55.7
because he has *f* me, and	1Ki 11.33
because you have *f* the	18.18
Because they have *f* me and	2Ki 22.17
our God, and we have not *f*	2Chr 13.10
hast not *f* those who seek thee.	Ps 9.10
my God, why hast thou *f* me?	22.1
have not seen the righteous *f*	37.25
"God has *f* him; pursue and	71.11
They have *f* the LORD, they	Isa 1.4
f me and served foreign gods	Jer 5.19
'Because your fathers have *f*	16.11
the LORD has *f* the land.' "	Ezek 8.12
virgin Israel; *f* on her land,	Amos 5.2
my God, why hast thou *f* me?"	Mt 27.46
my God, why hast thou *f* me?"	Mk 15.34
persecuted, but not *f*; struck	2Cor 4.9
f me and serving other gods,	1Sam 8.8

all their wickedness in *f* me;	Jer 1.16
by *f* the LORD. .when he led you	2.17

FORSOOK

f the covenant of the LORD,	Deut 29.25
he *f* God who made him,	32.15
'Because they *f* the LORD	1Ki 9.9
Rehoboam. .*f* the law of. .LORD,	2Chr 12.1
For a brief moment I *f* you,	Isa 54.7
"Because they *f* the covenant	Jer 22.9
all the disciples *f* him and	Mt 26.56
they all *f* him, and fled.	Mk 14.50

FORTRESS

Be thou. .a strong *f* to save me!	Ps 31.2
thou art my rock and my *f*;	31.3
for thou, O God, art my *f*.	59.9
rock and my *f*, my stronghold	144.2
He shall honor the god of *f*	Dan 11.38

FORTUNES

God will restore your *f*,	Deut 30.3
LORD restored the *f* of Job,	Job 42.10
When the LORD restores the *f*	Ps 14.7
When God restores the *f* of his	53.6
thou didst restore the *f* of Jacob.	85.1
LORD restored the *f* of Zion,	126.1
when I restore their *f*: 'The	Jer 31.23
I will restore the *f* of Judah	33.7
restore the *f* of my people	Amos 9.14
mindful. .and restore their *f*.	Zeph 2.7
when I restore your *f* before	3.20

FORTY

rain upon the earth *f* days	Gen 7.4
on the mountain *f* days	Ex 24.18
in the wilderness *f* years,	Num 14.33
these *f* years the LORD	Deut 2.7
at the end of *f* days and	9.11
f stripes may be given him,	25.3
I have led you *f* years	29.5

FOUND — ED

"He *f* him in a desert land,	Deut 32.10
evil shall not be *f* in you	1Sam 25.28
have *f* the book of the law	2Chr 34.15
they *f* it written in the law	Neh 8.14
'Deliver him. .I. .*f* a ransom;	Job 33.24
I *f* him whom my soul loves.	Sol 3.4
Thy words were *f*, and I ate	Jer 15.16
I will be *f* by you, says the LORD	29.14
'Rejoice with me, for I have *f*	Lk 15.9
my son. .was lost, and is *f*.'	15.24
said. ."We have *f* the Messiah"	Jn 1.41
"We have *f* him of whom Moses	1.45
and having *f* him he said,	9.35
not *f* written in the book of	Rev 20.15
he has *f* it upon the seas, and	Ps 24.2
LORD by wisdom *f* the earth;	Prov 3.19

FOUNDATION — S

But the *f* of the temple was	Ezra 3.6
because the *f* of the house	3.11
were you when I laid the *f*	Job 38.4
didst lay the *f* of the earth,	Ps 102.25
laying in Zion for a *f* a stone,	Isa 28.16
the *f* of the. .temple was laid,	Hag 2.18
hidden since. .*f* of the world."	Mt 13.35
I build on another man's *f*,	Rom 15.20
no other *f* can any one lay	1Cor 3.11
But God's firm *f* stands,	2Tim 2.19
if the *f* are destroyed, what	Ps 11.3
f. .of the mountains trembled	18.7
the *f* of the earth tremble.	Isa 24.18
from the *f* of the earth?	40.21
lay your *f* with sapphires.	54.11

FOUNTAIN — S

with thee is the *f* of life;	Ps 36.9
fear of the LORD is a *f* of	Prov 14.27
Wisdom is a *f* of life to him	16.22
the *f* of wisdom is a gushing	18.4
muddied spring or a polluted *f*	25.26
pitcher is broken at the *f*,	Ecc 12.6
a garden locked, a *f* sealed.	Sol 4.12
they have forsaken me, the *f*	Jer 2.13
and my eyes a *f* of tears,	9.1
LORD, the *f* of living water.	17.13
a *f* shall come forth from	Joel 3.18
f opened for..house of David	Zech 13.1
f of the water of life	Rev 21.6
the *f* of the great deep burst	Gen 7.11

FOX — ES

if a *f* goes up on it he will	Neh 4.3
"Go and tell that *f*, 'Behold,	Lk 13.32
and caught three hundred *f*,	Judg 15.4
f, that spoil the vineyards,	Sol 2.15
prophets have been like *f*	Ezek 13.4
"F have holes, and birds of	Mt 8.20
"F have holes, and birds of	Lk 9.58

FRAGRANCE

The mandrakes give forth *f*,	Sol 7.13
the *f* of the knowledge of him	2Cor 2.14

FRANKINCENSE

They shall bring gold and *f*,	Isa 60.6
offered him gifts, gold and *f*	Mt 2.11

FREE — LY

I will not go out *f*,'	Ex 21.5
and be *f* of obligation to	Num 32.22
And when you let him go *f*	Deut 15.13
LORD sets the prisoners *f*;	Ps 146.7
the souls that you hunt go *f*	Ezek 13.20
the truth will make you *f*."	Jn 8.32
So if the Son makes you *f*,	8.36
But the *f* gift is not like	Rom 5.15
having been set *f* from sin,	6.18
the husband dies, she is *f*	1Cor 7.39
not *f*? Am I not an apostle?	9.1
there is neither slave nor *f*,	Gal 3.28
"You may *f* eat of every tree	Gen 2.16
will offer themselves *f* on	Ps 110.3
gives *f*, yet grows..richer;	Prov 11.24

FREED

he who has died is *f* from sin.	Rom 6.7
not be *f* by..law of Moses.	Acts 13.39
and has *f* us from our sins	Rev 1.5

FREEDOM

if you can gain your *f*,	1Cor 7.21
Spirit of the Lord is,..is *f*.	2Cor 3.17
to spy out our *f* which we have	Gal 2.4
For *f* Christ has set us free;	5.1
For you were called to *f*,	5.13
without using../ as a pretext	1Pet 2.16
They promise them *f*, but	2Pet 2.19

FREEWILL OFFERING — S

is a votive offering or a *f*..	Lev 7.16
with the tribute of a *f*..	Deut 16.10
f..for the house of God	Ezra 1.4
made *f*..for the house of God,	2.68

FRIEND — S

as a man speaks to his *f*.	Ex 33.11
descendants of Abraham thy *f*?	2Chr 20.7
withholds kindness from a *f*	Job 6.14
and bargain over your *f*.	6.27
as though I grieved for my *f*	Ps 35.14
Even my bosom *f* in whom I	41.9

But it is you,..my familiar *f*.	55.13
caused lover and *f* to shun me;	88.18
A *f* loves at all times, and	Prov 17.17
every one is a *f* to a man	19.6
Faithful are..wounds of a *f*;	27.6
'My father,..the *f* of my youth—	Jer 3.4
have no confidence in a *f*;	Mic 7.5
f of tax collectors..sinners!'	Mt 11.19
'F, I am doing you no wrong;	20.13
Jesus said.."F, why are you	26.50
a *f* of tax collectors and	Lk 7.34
'F, lend me three loaves;	11.5
say to you, 'F, go up higher';	14.10
f Lazarus has fallen asleep,	Jn 11.11
you are not Caesar's *f*;	19.12
he was called the *f* of God.	Jas 2.23
But thy *f* be like the sun	Judg 5.31
My *f* scorn me; my eye pours	Job 16.20
and my close *f* have failed	19.14
Job,..had prayed for his *f*;	42.10
whisperer separates close *f*.	Prov 16.28
There are *f* who pretend to be *f*,	18.24
Wealth brings many new *f*,	19.4
Make *f* quickly with..accuser,	Mt 5.25
when his *f* heard it, they went	Mk 3.21
"Go home to your *f*, and tell	5.19
my *f*, do not fear those who	Lk 12.4
I tell you, make *f*..by mammon,	16.9
lay down his life for his *f*.	Jn 15.13

FRIENDSHIP

the *f* of God was upon my tent;	Job 29.4
The *f* of the LORD is for those	Ps 25.14
f with a man given to anger,	Prov 22.24
f with the world is enmity	Jas 4.4

FRINGE

touched the *f* of his garment;	Mt 9.20
touch the *f* of his garment;	14.36

FROGS

plague..your country with *f*;	Ex 8.2
Their land swarmed with *f*,	Ps 105.30

FRUIT — S

showed..the *f* of the land	Num 13.26
in the *f* of your body, and	Deut 30.9
like a tree..yields its *f* in	Ps 1.3
shall eat the *f* of their way	Prov 1.31
My *f* is better than gold,	8.19
f of the righteous is..life,	11.30
punish..the *f* of your doings,	Jer 21.14
the *f* of my body for the sin	Mic 6.7
nor *f* be on the vines, the	Hab 3.17
to the tenants, to get his *f*;	Mt 21.34
word and accept it and bear *f*,	Mk 4.20
"May no one ever eat *f* from you	11.14
blessed is the *f* of your womb!	Lk 1.42
not bear good *f* is cut down	3.9
no good tree bears bad *f*,	6.43
bring forth *f* with patience.	8.15
if it dies, it bears much *f*,	Jn 12.24
he it is that bears much *f*,	15.5
the *f* of the Spirit is love,	Gal 5.22
bearing *f* in every good work	Col 1.10
peaceful *f* of righteousness	Heb 12.11
f for which thy soul longed	Rev 18.14
yielding its *f* each month;	22.2
the first *f* of your ground	Ex 34.26
"On the day of the first *f*,	Num 28.26
a cereal offering of first *f*	Lev 2.14
the sheaf of the first *f*	23.10
first *f* of all your produce.	Prov 3.9
orchard..with all choicest *f*,	Sol 4.13
You will know them by their *f*.	Mt 7.16

FRUIT — S (cont.)
kingdom of God. . *f* of it."   Mt 21.43
dough offered as first *f* is   Rom 11.16
from the dead, the first *f*   1Cor 15.20
with the *f* of righteousness   Phil 1.11
we should be a kind of first *f*   Jas 1.18

FRUSTRATE — S
counselors against them to *f*   Ezra 4.5
He *f* the devices of the crafty,   Job 5.12

FUGITIVE
you shall be a *f*. .on. .earth."   Gen 4.12
on that day a *f* will come   Ezek 24.26

FULFIL — S — LED — LING
I will *f* the oath. .I swore   Gen 26.3
to *f* the word of the LORD   2Chr 36.21
the LORD *f* all your petitions!   Ps 20.5
LORD will *f* his purpose for me;   138.8
I will *f* the promise I made   Jer 33.14
it is fitting for us to *f* all   Mt 3.15
not to abolish. .but to *f* them.   5.17
f what was spoken by. .Isaiah,   8.17
took place to *f* what was spoken   21.4
This was to *f* the scripture.   Jn 19.24
He *f*. .desire of all who fear   Ps 145.19
the LORD has *f* his promise   2Chr 6.10
the scriptures. .might be *f*."   Mt 26.56
"The time is *f*, and the kingdom   Mk 1.15
But let the scriptures be *f*."   14.49
scripture was *f* which says,   15.28*n*
"Today. .scripture has been *f*   Lk 4.21
I shall not eat. .until it is *f*,   22.16
and the psalms must be *f*."   24.44
that the scripture might be *f*.   Jn 17.12
they. .*f* all. .written of him,   Acts 13.29
who loves his neighbor has *f*   Rom 13.8
whole law is *f* in one word,   Gal 5.14
thus *f* the word of the LORD   1Ki 2.27
did not succeed in *f* that law.   Rom 9.31

FULL — Y
whole earth is *f* of his glory."   Isa 6.3
this joy of mine is now *f*.   Jn 3.29
until. .*f* number of. .Gentiles   Rom 11.25
let steadfastness have. .*f* effect,   Jas 1.4
every one when he is *f* taught   Lk 6.40
But when the time had *f* come,   Gal 4.4

FULLER — S'
white as no *f*. .could bleach   Mk 9.3
"For he is like. .*f* soap"   Mal 3.2

FULNESS
earth is the LORD's and the *f*   Ps 24.1
from his *f* have we all received,   Jn 1.16
come in the *f* of the blessing   Rom 15.29
filled with all the *f* of God.   Eph 3.19
in him the whole *f* of deity   Col 2.9
you have. .*f* of life in him,   2.10

FURNACE
forth out of the iron *f*,   Deut 4.20
silver refined in a *f* on the   Ps 12.6
the *f* is for gold, and a man   Prov 27.21
LORD. .whose *f* is in Jerusalem.   Isa 31.9
tried. .in. .*f* of affliction.   48.10
ordered. .*f* heated seven times   Dan 3.19
throw them into the *f* of fire;   Mt 13.42

FURY
Haman was filled with *f*.   Est 3.5
The LORD. .stirs up his *f*;   Isa 42.13
and I will satisfy my *f*;   Ezek 21.17
they were filled with *f* and   Lk 6.11

FUTILE
became *f* in their thinking   Rom 1.21
your faith is *f* and you   1Cor 15.17

FUTILITY
creation was subjected to *f*,   Rom 8.20
live. .in the *f* of their minds;   Eph 4.17

G

GABRIEL
"*G*, make this man understand   Dan 8.16
in prayer, the man *G*,. .came to me   9.21
"I am *G*, who stand in the   Lk 1.19
In the sixth month the angel *G*   1.26

GAD
Leah. .called his name *G*.   Gen 30.11
The sons of *G*: Ziphion,   46.16
the leader of the men of *G*:   Num 7.42
to the sons of *G* and. .Reuben   32.33

GAIN — S — ED (v)
What does man *g* by all the toil   Ecc 1.3
Whoever seeks to *g* his life   Lk 17.33
in order that I may *g* Christ   Phil 3.8
if he *g* the whole world and   Mt 16.26
g the whole world and loses   Lk 9.25
nothing to be *g* under the sun.   Ecc 2.11
What you. .*g*. .is given to God,   Mt 15.5
what they had *g* by trading.   Lk 19.15
nothing to be *g* by it, but I   2Cor 12.1

GAIN (n)
Incline my heart. .not to *g*!   Ps 119.36
for the *g* from it is better   Prov 3.14
what *g* has he that he toiled   Ecc 5.16
devote their *g* to the LORD,   Mic 4.13
Woe to him who gets evil *g*   Hab 2.9
is Christ, and to die is *g*.   Phil 1.21

GALATIA
the region of Phrygia and *G*,   Acts 16.6
region of *G* and Phrygia,   18.23
I directed the churches of *G*,   1Cor 16.1
with me, To the churches of *G*:   Gal 1.2
in Pontus, *G*, Cappadocia,   1Pet 1.1

GALILEAN
"You. .were with Jesus the *G*."   Mt 26.69
one of them; for you are a *G*."   Mk 14.70
whether the man was a *G*.   Lk 23.6

GALILEE
they set apart Kedesh in *G*   Josh 20.7
glorious. .*G* of the nations.   Isa 9.1
withdrew to the district of *G*.   Mt 2.22
arrested, he withdrew into *G*;   4.12
across the Jordan, *G* of the   4.15
great multitude from *G* followed;   Mk 3.7
he is going before you to *G*;   16.7
Joseph also went up from *G*,   Lk 2.4
was a marriage at Cana in *G*,   Jn 2.1
Judea and departed again to *G*.   4.3
"Are you from *G* too? Search   7.52
"Men of *G*, why do you stand   Acts 1.11

GALLIO
G was proconsul of Achaia,   Acts 18.12
But *G* paid no attention to this.   18.17

GALLOWS
"Let a *g* fifty cubits high   Est 5.14

GAMALIEL
a Pharisee in the council. .*G*,   Acts 5.34
brought up. .at the feet of *G*,   22.3

GAME
go out..and hunt g for me,   Gen 27.3

GARDEN — ER
God planted a g in Eden,   Gen 2.8
like the g of the LORD,   13.10
A g locked is my sister, my   Sol 4.12
and like a g without water.   Isa 1.30
you were in Eden,..g of God;   Ezek 28.13
The cedars in the g of God   31.8
become like the g of Eden;   36.35
The land is like the g of Eden   Joel 2.3
was crucified there was a g,   Jn 19.41
Supposing him to be the g,   20.15

GARLIC
the onions, and the g;   Num 11.5

GARMENT — S
he..left his g in her hand,   Gen 39.13
man put on a woman's g;   Deut 22.5
like a g that is moth-eaten.   Job 13.28
Take a man's g when he has   Prov 20.16
takes off a g on a cold day,   25.20
I had put off my g, how could   Sol 5.3
deeds are like a polluted g.   Isa 64.6
a man who had no wedding g;   Mt 22.11
unshrunk cloth on an old g;   Mk 2.21
the crowd and touched his g.   5.27
touch even the fringe of his g;   6.56
"No one tears..from a new g   Lk 5.36
touched the fringe of his g;   8.44
God made for Adam..g   Gen 3.21
make holy g for Aaron your   Ex 28.2
they divide my g among them,   Ps 22.18
Let your g be always white;   Ecc 9.8
his g became white as light.   Mt 17.2
spread their g on the road,   21.8
they divided his g among them   27.35
spread their g on the road,   Mk 11.8
and divided his g among them,   15.24
spread their g on the road.   Lk 19.36
cast lots to divide his g.   23.34
from supper, laid aside his g,   Jn 13.4
and g which Dorcas made   Acts 9.39
keeping the g of those who   22.20
awake, keeping his g that   Rev 16.15

GATE — S
Lot was sitting in the g   Gen 19.1
also suffered outside the g   Heb 13.12
its g which had been destroyed   Neh 2.13
the g of death been revealed   Job 38.17
Lift up your heads, O g! and   Ps 24.7
within your g, O Jerusalem!   122.2
Open the g, that..righteous   Isa 26.2
he is near, at the very g.   Mk 13.29

GATHER — S — ED — ING
let them g all the food   Gen 41.35
LORD has commanded: 'G of it,   Ex 16.16
LORD your God will g you,   Deut 30.4
g us from among the nations,   Ps 106.47
'The dead bodies..none shall g   Jer 9.22
I will g the remnant of my flock   23.3
g you from all the nations   29.14
who scattered Israel will g   31.10
g them from all the countries   32.37
I will g you into the midst   Ezek 22.19
nations round about. g..there.   Joel 3.11
save the lame..g the outcast,   Zeph 3.19
does not g with me scatters.   Mt 12.30
will g out of his kingdom   13.41
the angels, and g his elect   Mk 13.27
he who does not g with me   Lk 11.23

"G up the fragments left over,   Jn 6.12
to g into one the children   11.52
son who g in summer..prudent,   Prov 10.5
who g the outcasts of Israel,   Isa 56.8
"Let the waters..be g   Gen 1.9
Joseph g up all the money   47.14
and g in from the lands, from   Ps 107.3
I also g for myself silver   Ecc 2.8
that Israel might be g to him,   Isa 49.5
the summer fruit has been g,   Mic 7.1
two or three are g in my name,   Mt 18.20
How often would I have g your   Lk 13.34
man g sticks on the sabbath   Num 15.32

GAVE
our God g him over to us;   Deut 2.33
Solomon g to the queen of   2Chr 9.12
God g them into their hand.   13.16
the LORD g, and the LORD   Job 1.21
spirit returns to God who g it.   Ecc 12.7
who g himself for our sins   Gal 1.4
loved me and g himself for me.   2.20

GAZA
Canaanites..as far as G,   Gen 10.19
Judah also took G with its   Judg 1.18
Samson went to G, and..saw   16.1
see it, and be afraid; G too,   Zech 9.5
down from Jerusalem to G."   Acts 8.26

GAZINGSTOCK
contempt, and make you a g.   Nah 3.6

GENEALOGY — IES
The book of the g of Jesus   Mt 1.1
without father or mother or g,   Heb 7.3
and endless g which promote   1Tim 1.4

GENERATION — S
A g goes, and a g comes, but   Ecc 1.4
adulterous g seeks for a sign;   Mt 12.39
of my words in this..sinful g,   Mk 8.38
the g of the heavens..earth   Gen 2.4
book of the g of Adam.   5.1
the g of the sons of Noah,   10.1
and his faithfulness to all g.   Ps 100.5

GENEROUS — LY
food with glad and g hearts,   Acts 2.46
good deeds, liberal and g,   1Tim 6.18
the man who deals g and lends,   Ps 112.5

GENTILES
"Go nowhere among the G, and   Mt 10.5
'Why did the G rage, and the   Acts 4.25
the G also God has granted   11.18
would justify the G by faith,   Gal 3.8

GENTLE — NESS
I am g and lowly in heart,   Mt 11.29
we were g among you, like   1Thess 2.7
to avoid quarreling, to be g,   Tit 3.2
jewel of a g and quiet spirit,   1Pet 3.4
or with love in a spirit of g?   1Cor 4.21
by the meekness and g of   2Cor 10.1
restore him in a spirit of g.   Gal 6.1

GENUINENESS
the g of your faith, more   1Pet 1.7

GETHSEMANE
Jesus went with them to..G,   Mt 26.36
a place which was called G;   Mk 14.32

GHOST
terrified, saying, "It is a g!"   Mt 14.26
they thought it was a g, and   Mk 6.49

GIBEAH

but we will pass on to G."   Judg 19.12
went to his home at G,   1Sam 10.26
the watchmen of Saul in G   14.16
Ramah trembles, G..has fled.   Isa 10.29

GIDEON

son G was beating out wheat   Judg 6.11
(that is, G) and all the people   7.1
So G and the hundred men   7.19
And G came to the Jordan   8.4
G said.."I will not rule   8.23
G the son of Joash died   8.32
to tell of G, Barak, Samson,   Heb 11.32

GIFT — S

Accept, I pray you, my g   Gen 33.11
Levites as a g to Aaron   Num 8.19
A man's g makes room for him   Prov 18.16
A g in secret averts anger;   21.14
God's g to man..eat and drink   Ecc 3.13
receive the g of the..Spirit.   Acts 2.38
obtain..g of God with money!   8.20
If..God gave..same g to them   11.17
wages are not reckoned as a g   Rom 4.4
free g of God is eternal life   6.23
his own special g from God,   1Cor 7.7
to carry your g to Jerusalem.   16.3
God for his inexpressible g!   2Cor 9.15
the g of God's grace..given me   Eph 3.7
to the measure of Christ's g.   4.7
Not that I seek the g; but   Phil 4.17
Do not neglect the g you have,   1Tim 4.14
As each has received a g,   1Pet 4.10
people..sue your favor with g,   Ps 45.12
receiving g among men, even   68.18
Jerusalem kings bear g to thee.   68.29
of Sheba and Seba bring g!   72.10
loves a bribe..runs after g.   Isa 1.23
If you..know how to give good g   Mt 7.11
evil, know how to give good g   Lk 11.13
their g into the treasury;   21.1
Having g that differ according   Rom 12.6
there are varieties of g,   1Cor 12.4
earnestly desire..spiritual g,   14.1
and by g of the Holy Spirit   Heb 2.4

GILEAD

Jacob..fled..toward..G.   Gen 31.21
To Machir I gave G,   Deut 3.15
land, G as far as Dan,   34.1
boundary..is, half of G,   Josh 12.2
G is mine; Manasseh is mine;   Ps 60.7
Is there no balm in G? Is   Jer 8.22

GILGAL

encamped in G on the east   Josh 4.19
marched..all night from G.   10.9
by year to Bethel, G, and   1Sam 7.16
called out to join Saul at G.   13.4
to G,..multiply transgression;   Amos 4.4

GIRD — ED

and g him with the skilfully   Ex 29.5
For thou didst g me with   2Sam 22.40
G your sword upon your thigh,   Ps 45.3
thou hast..g me with gladness,   30.11

GIRDLE

Righteousness shall be the g   Isa 11.5
a leather g around his waist;   Mt 3.4
he took Paul's g and bound   Acts 21.11

GIRL — S — 'S

g is not dead but sleeping."   Mt 9.24
if a g marries..not sin.   1Cor 7.28

city..of boys and g playing   Zech 8.5
the g father made him stay,   Judg 19.4

GIVE — S — N — ING

land..I will g to you and   Gen 13.15
first-born..sons..g to me.   Ex 22.29
the poor shall not g less,   30.15
land which I swore to g   Deut 1.35
might g him into your hand,   2.30
and to Jacob, to g you,   6.10
LORD will g you there   28.65
"Pray, g loaves of bread   Judg 8.5
the LORD will g Israel also   1Sam 28.19
they would g the money that   2Ki 12.11
dost not g me up to Sheol,   Ps 16.10
"To you I will g..Canaan as   105.11
G me understanding, that I   119.34
My son, g me your heart,   Prov 23.26
How can I g you up, O Ephraim!   Hos 11.8
G us this day our daily bread;   Mt 6.11
you g them something to eat."   14.16
g you the keys of the kingdom   16.19
"You g them something to eat."   Mk 6.37
g, and it will be given to you;   Lk 6.38
said to her, "G me a drink."   Jn 4.7
"Lord, g us this bread always."   6.34
and I g them eternal life,   10.28
he will g you another Counselor,   14.16
more blessed to g than to   Acts 20.35
will he not..g us all things   Rom 8.32
husband should g to his wife   1Cor 7.3
may g you a spirit of wisdom   Eph 1.17
my Maker, who g songs in   Job 35.10
righteous is generous and g;   Ps 37.21
The Lord g the command; great   68.11
he who g food to all flesh,   136.25
For the LORD g wisdom; from   Prov 2.6
but the righteous g and   21.26
g to the poor will not want,   28.27
who pleases him God g wisdom   Ecc 2.26
"He scatters..g to the poor;   2Cor 9.9
I have g him into your hand,   Num 21.34
for I have g him and all   Deut 3.2
"Our god has g Samson..into   Judg 16.23
to him who has will more be g,   Mt 13.12
gained from me is g to God,   15.5
to him who has will more be g;   Mk 4.25
to him who has will more be g,   Lk 8.18
to whom much is g, of him   12.48
has g all judgment to the Son,   Jn 5.22
the Spirit had not been g,   7.39
the Spirit which he has g us.   1Jn 3.24
into partnership with me in g   Phil 5.15

GLAD — NESS

I will be g and exult in thee,   Ps 9.2
who seek thee rejoice and be g   40.16
a river whose streams make g   46.4
Egypt was g,..they departed,   105.38
I was g when they said to me,   122.1
A g heart makes a cheerful   Prov 15.13
let us be g and rejoice in   Isa 25.9
be g and rejoice for ever   65.18
I am g and rejoice with you   Phil 2.17
the day of your g also,   Num 10.10
ate and drank..with great g.   1Chr 29.22
a day for g and feasting   Est 9.19
Serve the LORD with g! Come   Ps 100.2
joy and g are taken away from   Isa 16.10
oil of g instead of mourning,   61.3
of mirth and the voice of g,   Jer 7.34

GLORIFY — IED

deliver you, and you shall g   Ps 50.15

GLORIFY — IED (cont.)
I will *g* my glorious house. Isa 60.7
Father, *g* thy name." Then Jn 12.28
the hour has come; *g* thy Son 17.1
So *g* God in your body. 1Cor 6.20
Who shall not fear and *g* thy Rev 15.4
LORD. .will be *g* in Israel. Isa 44.23
Israel, in whom I will be *g*." 49.3
Holy One. .for he has *g* you. 55.5
they *g* God and were filled Lk 5.26
they *g* God, saying, "A great 7.16
"Now is the Son of man *g*, Jn 13.31
Father may be *g* in the Son; 14.13
Father is *g*, that you bear 15.8
silenced. And they *g* God, Acts 11.18

GLORIOUS — LY
G things. .spoken of you, O city Ps 87.3
change. .to be like his *g* body, Phil 3.21
the LORD, for he has done *g*; Isa 12.5

GLORY (v)
that we may. .*g* in thy praise. Ps 106.47
g in this, that. .I am the LORD Jer 9.24
they shall *g* in his name," Zech 10.12
far be it from me to *g* except Gal 6.14

GLORY (n)
see the *g* of the LORD, Ex 16.7
The *g* of the LORD settled on 24.16
the *g* of the LORD filled the 40.34
filled with the *g* of the LORD, Num 14.21
the *g* of the LORD appeared 16.19
God has shown us his *g* Deut 5.24
"The *g* has departed from 1Sam 4.21
the *G* of Israel will not lie 15.29
the *g* of the LORD filled 1Ki 8.11
Declare his *g* among. .nations 1Chr 16.24
Thine, O LORD, is the. .*g*, 29.11
the *g* of the LORD filled 2Chr 5.14
Thou whose *g* above. .is chanted Ps 8.1
heavens are telling the *g* of God; 19.1
His *g* is great through thy help; 21.5
ascribe to the LORD *g* and 29.1
all the peoples behold his *g*. 97.6
but to thy name give *g*, for 115.1
in the east give *g* to. .LORD; Isa 24.15
g of Lebanon shall be given 35.2
They shall see the *g* of the LORD, 35.2
the *g* of the LORD. .revealed, 40.5
my *g* I give to no other, nor 42.8
this city. .a *g* before all Jer 33.9
likeness of the *g* of the LORD. Ezek 1.28
as the *g* of the LORD arose 3.12
lo, the *g* of the LORD stood there, 3.23
the *g* of the God. .had gone up 9.3
the *g* of the LORD went forth 10.18
manifest my *g* in the midst 28.22
set my *g* among the nations; 39.21
And behold, the *g* of the God 43.2
dominion and *g* and kingdom, Dan 7.14
knowledge of the *g* of the LORD, Hab 2.14
coming. .with power and great *g*; Mt 24.30
"*G* to God in the highest, and Lk 2.14
I do not receive *g* from men. Jn 5.41
own authority seeks his own *g*; 7.18
Yet I do not seek my own *g*; 8.50
"This illness is for the *g* of God, 11.4
with the *g* which I had with thee 17.5
my *g* which thou hast given me 17.24
exchanged the *g* of. .God for Rom 1.23
fall short of the *g* of God, 3.23
not worth comparing with the *g* 8.18
To him be *g* for ever. Amen. 11.36

in dishonor,. .raised in *g*. 1Cor 15.43
Christ in you, the hope of *g*. Col 1.27
from the *g* of his might, 2Thess 1.9
obtain the *g* of our Lord 2.14
him who called us to his own *g* 2Pet 1.3
saying, "Amen! Blessing and *g* Rev 7.12
"Fear God and give him *g*, 14.7

GNASH — ED — ING
they hiss, they *g* their teeth, Lam 2.16
men. .weep and *g* their teeth. Mt 24.51
he has *g* his teeth at me; Job 16.9
g at me with their teeth. Ps 35.16

GNAT — S
guides, straining out a *g* Mt 23.24
g throughout all. .Egypt.'" Ex 8.16

GO
"*G* into the ark, you and Gen 7.1
Rebekah. .said, "I will *g*." 24.58
'Let my people *g*, that they may Ex 5.1
"Let my people *g*, that they may 9.13
"Let us. .*g* back to Egypt." Num 14.4
"*G* and wash in the Jordan 2Ki 5.10
Teach me the way I should *g*, Ps 143.8
g again, naked as he came, Ecc 5.15
let us *g* up to the mountain Isa 2.3
"*G*, and say to this people: 6.9
G forth from Babylon, flee 48.20
show us the way we should *g*, Jer 42.3
They shall *g* after the LORD, Hos 11.10
LORD said to me, '*G*, prophesy Amos 7.15
let us *g* up to the mountain Mic 4.2
when you pray, *g* into your room Mt 6.6
Then *g*. .and tell his disciples 28.7
G. .and make disciples of all 28.19
"*G* home to your friends, and Mk 5.19
But *g*, tell his disciples 16.7
"*G* into all the world and 16.15n
g and proclaim the kingdom Lk 9.60
"Lord, to whom shall we *g*? Jn 6.68

GOADS
sayings of the wise are like *g*, Ecc 12.11
hurts. .to kick against. .*g*.' Acts 26.14

GOD
G created the heavens. .earth. Gen 1.1
you will be like *G*, knowing 3.5
But *G* remembered Noah 8.1
"*G* will visit you, and 50.25
And *G* heard their groaning, Ex 2.24
G did not lead them by way 13.17
The eternal *G* is your Deut 33.27
LORD *G*. .fought for Israel. Josh 10.42
Israel,. .*G* went to redeem 2Sam 7.23
my *G*, hearkening to the cry 1Ki 8.28
G also raised. .an adversary 11.23
G. .sent persistently to them 2Chr 36.15
mocking. .messengers of *G*, 36.16
made him little less than *G*, Ps 8.5
my *G*, why hast thou forsaken me? 22.1
the LORD *G* is my strength Isa 12.2
LORD *G* is an everlasting rock. 26.4
comfort my people, says your *G*. 40.1
worked on the house of. .*G*, Hag 1.14
Will man rob *G*? Yet you are Mal 3.8
"My *G*, my *G*, why hast thou Mk 15.34
answered. ."My Lord and my *G*!" Jn 20.28
This Jesus *G* raised up, and Acts 2.32
and said that he was a *g*. 28.6
G is not a *G* of confusion 1Cor 14.33
In their case the *g* of this 2Cor 4.4
But *G*, who is rich in mercy, Eph 2.4

GOD (cont.)

doing, it is the gift of *G*—	Eph 2.8
created after the likeness of *G*	4.24
be imitators of *G*, as beloved	5.1
the grace of *G* has appeared	Tit 2.11
the glory of our great *G*	2.13
its temple is the Lord *G*	Rev 21.22
flowing from the throne of *G*	22.1

GODLESS

hope of. . *g* man shall perish.	Job 8.13
a *g* man shall not come before	13.16
joy of the *g* but for a moment?	20.5
what is the hope of the *g* when	27.8
"The *g* in heart cherish anger;	36.13
G men utterly deride me, but	Ps 119.51
Let the *g* be put to shame,	119.78
With his mouth the *g* man	Prov 11.9
every one. . *g* and an evildoer,	Isa 9.17
Against a *g* nation I send him,	10.6
trembling has seized the *g*:	33.14

GODLINESS

teaching which accords with *g*,	1Tim 6.3
imagining. . *g* is a means of gain.	6.5
g with brotherly affection,	2Pet 1.7

GODLY

the Lord has set apart the *g*	Ps 4.3
there is no longer any that is *g*;	12.1
or let thy *g* one see the Pit.	16.10
who is *g* offer prayer to thee;	32.6
of mischief done against the *g*?	52.1
who desire to live a *g* life	2Tim 3.12

GODS

Rachel stole. . household *g*.	Gen 31.19
why did you steal my *g*?"	31.30
Rachel had taken. . household *g*	31.34
forsaken me. . served other *g*;	Judg 10.13
"Their *g* are *g* of the hills,	1Ki 20.23
"You are *g*, sons of the Most	Ps 82.6
the fire; for they were no *g*,	Isa 37.19
served foreign *g* in your land,	Jer 5.19
Can man make for himself *g*?	16.20
fourth is like a son of the *g*."	Dan 3.25
in whom. . spirit of the holy *g*—	4.8
to Aaron, 'Make for us *g* to	Acts 7.40
there may be so-called *g*	1Cor 8.5

GOLD

Havilah, where there is *g*;	Gen 2.11
and all *g* of the offering	Num 31.52
if the Almighty is your *g*,	Job 22.25
"If I have made *g* my trust,	31.24
More to be desired. . than *g*,	Ps 19.10
knowledge rather than. . *g*;	Prov 8.10
A word. . like apples of *g* in	25.11
bring *g* and frankincense,	Isa 60.6
How the *g* has grown dim, how	Lam 4.1
head of this image was of. . *g*,	Dan 2.32
"I have no silver and *g*, but	Acts 3.6
while the city was pure *g*,	Rev 21.18

GOLGOTHA

they came to a place called *G*	Mt 27.33
brought. . to the place called *G*	Mk 15.22
which is called in Hebrew *G*.	Jn 19.17

GOLIATH

a champion named *G*,	1Sam 17.4
Philistine of Gath, *G*	17.23
sword of *G* the Philistine,	21.9

GOMORRAH

before the Lord destroyed. . *G*.	Gen 13.11
kings of Sodom and *G* fled,	14.10

Lord rained on. . *G* brimstone	19.24
like that of Sodom and *G*,	Deut 29.23
like Sodom, and become like *G*.	Isa 1.9
and *G* than for that town.	Mt 10.15
just as Sodom and *G* and the	Jude 7

GOOD — LY

God saw. . light was *g*;	Gen 1.4
God saw that it was *g*.	1.10
The thing seemed *g* to me,	Deut 1.23
for he never prophesies *g*	1Ki 22.8
may the Lord do what seems *g*	1Chr 19.13
Hear, and know it for your *g*."	Job 5.27
there is none that does *g*,	Ps 14.3
I have no *g* apart from thee."	16.2
G and upright is the Lord;	25.8
Depart from evil, and do *g*; so	37.27
g to give thanks to the Lord,	92.1
g and pleasant. . when brothers	133.1
Let a *g* man strike or rebuke	141.5
A *g* wife who can find? She	Prov 31.10
She does. . *g*, and not harm,	31.12
g name is better than precious	Ecc 7.1
who call evil *g* and *g* evil,	Isa 5.20
accept that which is *g* and	Hos 14.2
Hate evil, and love *g*, and	Amos 5.15
you. . hate the *g* and love. . evil,	Mic 3.2
how *g* and. . fair it shall be!	Zech 9.17
Other seeds fell on *g* soil	Mt 13.8
sorted the *g* into vessels but	13.48
'Well done, *g* and faithful	25.21
other seeds fell into *g* soil	Mk 4.8
No one is *g* but God alone.	10.18
on the sabbath to do *g* or. . harm	Lk 6.9
some fell into *g* soil and	8.8
"Can. . *g* come out of Nazareth?"	Jn 1.46
it seemed *g* to the apostles	Acts 15.22
why not do evil that *g* may come?	Rom 3.8
no one does *g*, not even one."	3.12
nothing *g* dwells within me,	7.18
God works for *g* with those who	8.28
do not let what is *g* to you	14.16
wise as to what is *g* and	16.19
g child, she hid. . three months.	Ex 2.2

GOODNESS

Surely *g* and mercy shall follow	Ps 23.6
O how abundant is thy *g*, which	31.19

GOSPEL

this *g* of the kingdom will be	Mt 24.14
wherever this *g* is preached	26.13
the *g* of Jesus Christ, the Son	Mk 1.1
into Galilee, preaching the *g*	1.14
the *g* must first be preached	13.10
wherever the *g* is preached	14.9
preach the *g* to the whole	16.15*n*
there they preached the *g*.	Acts 14.7
testify to the *g* of. . grace	20.24
set apart for the *g* of God	Rom 1.1
I am not ashamed of the *g*:	1.16
according to my *g*, God judges	2.16
have not all heeded the *g*;	10.16
strengthen you according to my *g*	16.25
I preached to you the *g*,	1Cor 15.1
acknowledging the *g* of Christ,	2Cor 9.13
to you with the *g* of Christ.	10.14
turning to a different *g*—	Gal 1.6
the *g* which was preached by me	1.11
the *g* to the uncircumcised,	2.7
the *g* of your salvation, and	Eph 1.13
equipment of the *g* of peace;	6.15
be worthy of the *g* of Christ,	Phil 1.27
not shifting from. . hope of. . *g*	Col 1.23

GOSPEL (cont.)
our *g* came to you not only 1Thess 1.5
glorious *g* of the blessed God 1Tim 1.11
share of suffering for the *g* 2Tim 1.8
g was preached..to the dead, 1Pet 4.6
angel..with an eternal *g* to Rev 14.6

GOSSIPING (v)
who goes about *g* reveals Prov 20.19

GOSSIPS (n)
malignity, they are *g*, Rom 1.29
idlers but *g* and busybodies, 1Tim 5.13

GOVERN
who will *g* my people Israel.' " Mt 2.6

GOVERNMENT
g will be upon his shoulder, Isa 9.6

GOVERNOR — S
Joseph was *g* over the land; Gen 42.6
I was appointed to be their *g* Neh 5.14
appointed Gedaliah..*g* in the Jer 40.7
no evil? Present that to your *g*; Mal 1.8
made him *g* over Egypt and Acts 7.10
you will stand before *g* and Mk 13.9

GRACE — FUL
g is poured upon your lips; Ps 45.2
found *g* in the wilderness; Jer 31.2
amid shouts of '*G, g* to it!' " Zech 4.7
among us, full of *g* and truth; Jn 1.14
great *g* was upon them all. Acts 4.33
to continue in the *g* of God. 13.43
witness to..word of his *g*, 14.3
commended to the *g* of God 14.26
commended..to..*g* of the Lord. 15.40
through whom we..received *g* Rom 1.5
justified by his *g* as a gift, 3.24
that the promise may rest on *g* 4.16
access to..*g* in which we stand, 5.2
much more have the *g* of God 5.15
where sin increased, *g* abounded 5.20
continue in sin that *g* may abound? 6.1
because of the *g* given me by 15.15
by..*g* of God I am what I am, 1Cor 15.10
as *g* extends to more..people 2Cor 4.15
For you know the *g* of our Lord 8.9
"My *g* is sufficient for you, 12.9
The *g* of the Lord Jesus 13.14
him who called you in the *g* of Gal 1.6
you have fallen away from *g*. 5.4
according to..riches of his *g* Eph 1.7
immeasurable riches of his *g* 2.7
and good hope through *g*, 2Thess 2.16
the *g* of our Lord overflowed 1Tim 1.14
For the *g* of God has appeared Tit 2.11
we might be justified by his *g* 3.7
draw near the throne of *g*, Heb 4.16
heart be strengthened by *g*, 13.9
But he gives more *g*; therefore Jas 4.6
stewards of God's varied *g*; 1Pet 4.10
but gives *g* to the humble." 5.5
God of all *g*,..has called you 5.10
grow in the *g* and knowledge 2Pet 3.18
who pervert the *g* of our God Jude 4
How *g* are your feet in sandals, Sol 7.1

GRACIOUS
The LORD..be *g* to you: Num 6.25
the LORD was *g* to them and 2Ki 13.23
May God be *g* to us and bless Ps 67.1
The LORD is merciful and *g*, 103.8
The LORD is *g* and merciful, 145.8
praises to our God;..he is *g*, 147.1

and whose speech is *g*, will Prov 22.11
O LORD, be *g* to us; we wait Isa 33.2
for he is *g* and merciful, Joel 2.13
wondered at the *g* words which Lk 4.22
Let your speech always be *g*, Col 4.6

GRAIN
are no oxen, there is no *g*; Prov 14.4
then the full *g* in the ear. Mk 4.28
plucked and ate some ears of *g*, Lk 6.1
that there was *g* in Egypt, Acts 7.12
wheat or of some other *g*. 1Cor 15.37

GRAINFIELDS
through the *g* on the sabbath; Mt 12.1

GRANT — ED
God of Israel *g* your petition 1Sam 1.17
desire of..righteous..be *g*. Prov 10.24
all that the LORD has *g* us, Isa 63.7
God has *g* you all those Acts 27.24

GRAPES
with a single cluster of *g*, Num 13.23
he looked for it to yield *g*, Isa 5.2
fathers have eaten sour *g*, Jer 31.29
fathers have eaten sour *g*, Ezek 18.2
Like *g* in the wilderness, I Hos 9.10
reaper and the treader of *g* Amos 9.13

GRASS
they will soon fade like the *g*, Ps 37.2
man, his days are like *g*; 103.15
as dry *g* sinks..in the flame, Isa 5.24
All flesh is *g* and all its beauty 40.6
and ate *g* like an ox, and his Dan 4.33
if God so clothes the *g* which Lk 12.28
"All flesh is like *g* and all 1Pet 1.24
and all green *g* was burnt up. Rev 8.7

GRASSHOPPERS
seemed to ourselves like *g*, Num 13.33
its inhabitants are like *g*; Isa 40.22
Your princes are like *g*, Nah 3.17

GRAVE — S
straight to the *g*..descend, Ps 49.14
her company..about her *g*; Ezek 32.23
and raise you from your *g*, 37.12
like *g* which are not seen, Lk 11.44

GREAT — ER — EST
thou art *g*, O LORD God; 2Sam 7.22
he is *g* in power and justice, Job 37.23
say continually, "*G* is..LORD!" Ps 40.16
say evermore, "God is *g*!" 70.4
So I became *g* and surpassed Ecc 2.9
you seek *g* things for yourself? Jer 45.5
the LORD has done *g* things! Joel 2.21
you shall say, "*G* is the LORD, Mal 1.5
teaches them shall be called *g* Mt 5.19
"O woman, *g* is your faith! 15.28
he will be *g* before the Lord, Lk 1.15
alas, for the *g* city that Rev 18.16
And David became *g* and *g*, 2Sam 5.10
David became *g* and *g*, for 1Chr 11.9
something *g* than the temple Mt 12.6
something *g* than Solomon is 12.42
"Who is the *g* in the kingdom 18.1
discussed..who was the *g*. Mk 9.34
to be regarded as the *g*. Lk 22.24
but the *g* of these is love. 1Cor 13.13

GREATNESS
show thy servant thy *g* Deut 3.24
thou hast wrought all this *g*, 1Chr 17.19
and his *g* is unsearchable. Ps 145.3

GREATNESS (cont.)
praise him according to..g! Ps 150.2
"Whom are you like in your g? Ezek 31.2
I..show my g and my holiness 38.23

GREECE
the he-goat is the king of G; Dan 8.21
all against the kingdom of G. 11.2
O Zion, over your sons, O G, Zech 9.13
encouragement, he came to G. Acts 20.2

GREED — Y
His g is as wide as Sheol; Hab 2.5
guilty of immorality or g; 1Cor 5.11
never used..a cloak for g, 1Thess 2.5
in their g they will exploit 2Pet 2.3
They have hearts trained in g. 2.14
with g eye at my sacrifices 1Sam 2.29
every one is g for unjust gain; Jer 6.13
every one is g for unjust gain; 8.10
nor thieves, nor the g, nor 1Cor 6.10

GREEK — S
woman was a G, a Syrophoenician Mk 7.26
in letters of G and Latin Lk 23.38n
but his father was a G. Acts 16.1
at the feast were some G. Jn 12.20
believed, both..Jews and..G. Acts 14.1
heard..both Jews and G. 19.10
testifying..to Jews and to G 20.21
obligation both to G and to Rom 1.14
signs and G seek wisdom, 1Cor 1.22

GREET — ED (v)
G one another with a holy Rom 16.16
seen it and g it from afar, Heb 11.13

GREETING (n)
what sort of g this might be. Lk 1.29
Elizabeth heard the g of Mary, 1.41
I, Paul, write this g with 1Cor 16.21

GREW
Samuel g in the presence 1Sam 2.21
Samuel g, and the LORD was 3.19
g up before him like a..plant, Isa 53.2
the child g and became strong Lk 1.80
the child g and became strong, 2.40
But the word of God g and Acts 12.24
So the word of the Lord g 19.20

GRIEF
and the end of joy is g. Prov 14.13
foolish son is a g to his father 17.25
godly g produces a repentance 2Cor 7.10

GRIEVE — D
long will you g over Saul, 1Sam 16.1
do not g the Holy Spirit of Eph 4.30
you may not g as others 1Thess 4.13
it g him to his heart. Gen 6.6
and g him in the desert! Ps 78.40
rebelled and g his holy Spirit; Isa 63.10
not g over the ruin of Joseph! Amos 6.6
g at their hardness of heart, Mk 3.5

GROAN — S — ING
wicked rule, the people g. Prov 29.2
of Pharaoh, and he will g Ezek 30.24
How the beasts g! The herds Joel 1.18
the g of the prisoners come Ps 79.11
in Egypt and heard their g, Acts 7.34

GROPE
g at noonday as in the night. Job 5.14
g in the dark without light; 12.25
g for the wall like the blind, Isa 59.10

GROUND
and he g at the mill in Judg 16.21
g their teeth against him. Acts 7.54

GRUMBLE — ING
nor g, as some of them did 1Cor 10.10
Do all things without g or Phil 2.14

GUARANTEE
Spirit in our hearts as a g. 2Cor 1.22
given us the Spirit as a g. 5.5
the g of our inheritance Eph 1.14

GUARD — S — ED (v)
"He will g the feet of his 1Sam 2.9
angels..g..in all your ways. Ps 91.11
G me, O LORD, from..wicked; 140.4
understanding will g you; Prov 2.11
love her, and she will g you. 4.6
G your steps..to the house of Ecc 5.1
g what has been entrusted 1Tim 6.20
He who g his mouth preserves Prov 13.3
are g through faith for a 1Pet 1.5

GUARD (n)
and set a g as a protection Neh 4.9
thou settest a g over me? Job 7.12
Set a g over my mouth, O LORD, Ps 141.3
hand you over to..judge, and..g, Mt 5.25

GUARDIAN — S
Shepherd and G of your souls. 1Pet 2.25
Holy Spirit has made you g, Acts 20.28
he is under g and trustees Gal 4.2

GUEST — S
For I am thy passing g, a Ps 39.12
Where is the g room, where Lk 22.11
the LORD..consecrated his g. Zeph 1.7
wedding hall..filled with g. Mt 22.10

GUIDANCE
round and round by his g, Job 37.12
Where..no g, a people falls; Prov 11.14
by wise g you can wage..war, 24.6

GUIDE — D (v)
thy name's sake lead me and g Ps 31.3
with equity and g the nations 67.4
dost g me with thy counsel, 73.24
in paths..not known I will g Isa 42.16
LORD will g you continually, 58.11
Spirit of truth..will g you Jn 16.13
and g them in the wilderness Ps 78.52

GUIDE — S (n)
He will be our g for ever. Ps 48.14
Judas who was g to those Acts 1.16
you are a g to the blind, Rom 2.19
have countless g in Christ, 1Cor 4.15

GUILE
hatred be covered with g, Prov 26.26
Israelite..in whom is no g!" Jn 1.47
got the better of you by g. 2Cor 12.16

GUILT — Y
Why should he bring g upon 1Chr 21.3
pardon my g, for it is great. Ps 25.11
the g of your sister Sodom: Ezek 16.49
he incurred g through Baal Hos 13.1
remove the g of this land in Zech 3.9
"In truth we are g Gen 42.21
"When a ruler sins,..and is g, Lev 4.22
he shall in any of these be g. 5.4
who walks in his g ways. Ps 68.21
who acquit the g for a bribe, Isa 5.23
who will declare me g? Behold, 50.9

GUILT — Y (cont.)

All who ate of it became *g*;	Jer 2.3
become *g* by the blood. .shed,	Ezek 22.4
let not Judah become *g*.	Hos 4.15
I did not find this man *g* of	Lk 23.14
g of profaning the body and	1Cor 11.27

GUILTLESS

LORD will not hold him *g*	Deut 5.11
for ever *g* before the LORD	2Sam 3.28
sustain you to the end, *g*	1Cor 1.8
you have proved yourselves *g*	2Cor 7.11

GUILT OFFERING

bring his *g*. .to the LORD	Lev 5.6
"This is the law of the *g*...	7.1

H

HABAKKUK

oracle of God which *H*. .saw,	Hab 1.1
A prayer of *H* the prophet,	3.1

HADES

in *H*, being in torment, he	Lk 6.23
not abandon my soul to *H*,	Acts 2.27
name was Death, and *H* followed	Rev 6.8
Death and *H* were thrown into	20.14

HAGAR

maid whose name was *H*;	Gen 16.1
And *H* bore Abram a son;	16.15
Sarah saw the son of *H*	21.9
water, and gave it to *H*,	21.14
children for slavery;. .is *H*.	Gal 4.24

HAGGAI

prophets, *H* and Zechariah	Ezra 5.1
through the prophesying of *H*	6.14
word of the LORD came by *H*	Hag 1.1
word of the LORD came by *H*	2.1

HAIL — STONES

I will cause very heavy *h*	Ex 9.18
died because of the *h*	Josh 10.11

HAIR — S

instead of well-set *h*, baldness;	Isa 3.24
wiped them with the *h* of her	Lk 7.38
long *h*, it is her pride?	1Cor 11.15
more than the *h* of my head;	Ps 40.12
h of your head are numbered.	Mt 10.30
h of your head are. .numbered.	Lk 12.7

HALLOW — ED

and *h* my sabbaths that they	Ezek 20.20
blessed the seventh day. .*h* it,	Gen 2.3
I will be *h* among the people	Lev 22.32
art in heaven, *H* be thy name.	Mt 6.9
"Father, *h* be thy name. Thy	Lk 11.2

HAMATH

out to the entrance of *H*,	Num 34.8
from the entrance of *H* to	1Ki 8.65
Where are the gods of *H* and	Isa 36.19
thence go to *H* the great;	Amos 6.2

HAMMER

and took a *h* in her hand,	Judg 4.21
neither *h* nor axe. .was heard	1Ki 6.7
Is not my word like. .a *h*	Jer 23.29
the *h* of the whole earth is	50.23

HAND — S

into your *h* they are delivered.	Gen 9.2
father laid his right *h*	48.17
compelled by a mighty *h*,	Ex 3.19
"What is that in your *h*?"	4.2
stretch out thy right *h*,	15.12
lowered. .*h*, Amalek prevailed	17.11
lay his *h* upon the head of	Lev 4.24
"Is the LORD's *h* shortened?	Num 11.23
given him into your *h*,	21.34
h of the LORD was against	Deut 2.15
by war, by a mighty *h*	4.34
thence with a mighty *h*	5.15
out of Egypt with a mighty *h*	26.8
The *h* of the LORD was heavy	1Sam 5.6
then the *h* of the LORD will	12.15
"Let not my *h* be upon him,	18.17
strengthened his *h* in God.	23.16
the *h* of my servant David	2Sam 3.18
fall into the *h* of the LORD,	24.14
thy *h* might be with me,	1Chr 4.10
for the *h* of the LORD my	Ezra 7.28
nor take the *h* of evildoers.	Job 8.20
know that the *h* of the LORD	12.9
the *h* of God has touched me!	19.21
right *h* can give you victory.	40.14
My times are in thy *h*; deliver	Ps 31.15
day and night thy *h* was heavy	32.4
keep thy right *h* in thy bosom?	74.11
when thou openest thy *h*, they	104.28
right *h* of. .LORD is exalted,	118.16
their deeds are in. .*h* of God;	Ecc 9.1
Whatever your *h* finds to do,	9.10
his *h* is stretched out still.	Isa 5.25
spoke. .with his strong *h* upon me,	8.11
his *h* is stretched out still.	9.12
his *h* is stretched out still.	9.17
His *h* is stretched out, and	14.27
waters in the hollow of his *h*	40.12
the LORD's *h* is not shortened,	59.1
the *h* of the LORD. .upon me;	Ezek 3.14
h of the LORD was. .upon me;	3.22
My *h*. .against the prophets	13.9
mighty *h* and. .outstretched arm,	20.33
my *h* against the Philistines,	25.16
h of the LORD had been upon me	33.22
The *h* of the LORD was upon me,	37.1
fingers of a man's *h* appeared	Dan 5.5
His winnowing fork is in his *h*,	Mt 3.12
if your right *h* causes you to sin,	5.30
know what your right *h* is doing,	6.3
if your *h* or your.foot causes	18.8
the man, "Stretch out your *h*."	Mk 3.5
if your *h* causes you to sin,	9.43
whose right *h* was withered.	Lk 6.6
he did so, and. .*h* was restored.	6.10
and place my *h* in his side,	Jn 20.25
h of the Lord was with them,	Acts 11.21
the *h* of the Lord is upon you,	13.11
write. .greeting with. .own *h*.	2Thess 3.17
and he laid his *h* upon him,	Num 27.23
Thy *h* fashioned and made me;	Job 10.8
all the work of his *h*?	34.19
He who has clean *h* and a pure	Ps 24.4
They have *h*, but do not feel;	115.7
reaches out her *h* to. .needy.	Prov 31.20
into the *h* of the Chaldeans	Jer 32.28
unwashed *h* does not defile	Mt 15.20
disciples ate with *h* defiled,	Mk 7.2
See my *h* and my feet, that	Lk 24.39
but also my *h* and my head!"	Jn 13.9
showed them his *h* and. .side.	20.20
"Unless I see in his *h* the print	20.25
I have held out my *h* to a	Rom 10.21
a house not made with *h*,	2Cor 5.1
seen. .and touched with our *h*,	1Jn 1.1

HANDMAID
let..*h* speak in your ears, 1Sam 25.24
And your *h* had two sons, 2Sam 14.6
Mary said, "Behold, I am the *h* Lk 1.38

HANG — S — ED — ING
And the king said, "*H* him Est 7.10
and *h* the earth upon nothing. Job 26.7
a *h* man is accursed by God; Deut 21.23
his house in order, and *h* 2Sam 17.23
king about having Mordecai *h* Est 6.4
and he went and *h* himself. Mt 27.5
saw Absalom *h* in an oak." 2Sam 18.10
They put him to death by *h* Acts 10.39

HANNAH
the name of the one was *H*, 1Sam 1.2
H was speaking in her heart; 1.13
H also prayed and said, "My 2.1
visited *H*, and she conceived 2.21

HAPPY — IER
home one year, to be *h* with Deut 24.5
H are you, O Israel! Who is 33.29
H are your wives! *H* are 1Ki 10.8
H are your wives! *H* are 2Chr 9.7
h is the man..God reproves; Job 5.17
H is the man who takes refuge Ps 34.8
H is the man..his quiver full 127.5
H the people whose God is the 144.15
H is he whose help is..God 146.5
H is the man..finds wisdom, Prov 3.13
h..those who keep my ways. 8.32
those *h* who were steadfast. Jas 5.11
h if she remains as she is. 1Cor 7.40

HARD — ER
anything too *h* for the LORD? Gen 18.14
Nothing is too *h* for thee, Jer 32.17
way is *h*, that leads to life, Mt 7.14
I knew you to be a *h* man, 25.24
in them *h* to understand, 2Pet 3.16
I worked *h* than any of them, 1Cor 15.10

HARDEN — S — ED — ING
but I will *h* his heart, Ex 4.21
I will *h* Pharaoh's heart, 7.3
you shall not *h* your heart Deut 15.7
LORD's doing to *h* their Josh 11.20
Why should you *h* your hearts 1Sam 6.6
H not your hearts, as at Ps 95.8
why dost thou..*h* our heart, Isa 63.17
do not *h* your hearts as in Heb 3.8
he *h* the heart of whomever he Rom 9.18
But Pharaoh *h* his heart Ex 8.32
LORD your God *h* his spirit Deut 2.30
who has *h* himself against him, Job 9.4
spirit was *h* so that he dealt Dan 5.20
but their hearts were *h*. Mk 6.52
their eyes and *h* their heart, Jn 12.40
obtained it, but the rest were *h*, Rom 11.7
But their minds were *h*; for 2Cor 3.14
a *h*..upon part of Israel, Rom 11.25

HARDNESS
"For..*h* of heart Moses allowed Mt 19.8
grieved at their *h* of heart, Mk 3.5
"For your *h* of heart he wrote 10.5
unbelief and *h* of heart, 16.14*n*
due to their *h* of heart; Eph 4.18

HARLOT — S
Judah..thought her..a *h*, Gen 38.15
only Rahab the *h* and all Josh 6.17
Gaza, and there he saw a *h*, Judg 16.1
meets him, dressed as a *h*, Prov 7.10

For a *h* is a deep pit; an 23.27
You..played the *h* with many Jer 3.1
You played the *h* also with Ezek 16.28
"Oholah played the *h* while 23.5
their mother has played the *h*; Hos 2.5
By faith Rahab the *h* did not Heb 11.31
Rahab the *h* justified by works Jas 2.25
"Babylon..mother of *h* and of Rev 17.5

HARM
from me, and *h* befalls him, Gen 44.29
Then I will do you no *h*.' Jer 25.6
look after him well and do no *h*, 39.12
sabbath to do good or to do *h*, Lk 6.9
"Do not *h* yourself, for we Acts 16.28

HARMONY
grant you to live in such *h* Rom 15.5
love,..binds..in perfect *h*. Col 3.14

HARP — S
Awake, O *h* and lyre! I will Ps 108.2
instruments,..flute and..*h*, 1Cor 14.7
elders..each holding a *h*, Rev 5.8
harpers playing on their *h*, 14.2

HARVEST — S
earth remains,..*h*..not cease." Gen 8.22
reap its *h*, you shall bring Lev 23.10
snow in the time of *h* is a Prov 25.13
rejoice..as with joy at the *h*, Isa 9.3
for upon your fruit and your *h* 16.9
They shall eat up your *h* and Jer 5.17
"The *h* is past, the summer 8.20
sickle, for the *h* is ripe. Joel 3.13
"The *h* is plentiful, but the Mt 9.37
both grow together until the *h*; 13.30
sickle, because..*h* has come." Mk 4.29
send out laborers into his *h*. Lk 10.2
four months, then comes the *h*'? Jn 4.35
that I may reap..*h* among you Rom 1.13
the *h* of your righteousness. 2Cor 9.10
the *h* of the earth is..ripe." Rev 14.15
shall be ashamed of their *h* Jer 12.13

HASTE
Make *h*, escape there; Gen 19.22
Make *h* to help me, O Lord, Ps 38.22
O LORD, make *h* to help me! 70.1
O LORD; make *h* to me! Give 141.1
who makes *h* with his feet Prov 19.2
believes will not be in *h*.' Isa 28.16
went with *h*, and found Mary and Lk 2.16

HATE — S — D
I *h* the company of evildoers, Ps 26.5
let those who *h* him flee before 68.1
those who *h* me without cause; 69.4
I *h* the work of those who fall 101.3
I *h* doubled-minded men, but 119.113
poor man's brothers *h* him; Prov 19.7
this abominable thing..I *h*!' Jer 44.4
H evil, and love good, and Amos 5.15
"Blessed are you when men *h* Lk 6.22
and does not *h* his own father 14.26
but I do the very thing I *h*. Rom 7.15
h what is evil, hold fast to 12.9
if any man *h* his neighbor, Deut 19.11
six things which the LORD *h*, Prov 6.16
"If the world *h* you, know that Jn 15.18
no man ever *h* his own flesh, Eph 5.29
says, "I love God," and *h* his 1Jn 4.20
Now Esau *h* Jacob Gen 27.41
Amnon *h* her with very great 2Sam 13.15
those who *h* them ruled them. Ps 106.41

HATE — S — D (cont.)

I *h* all my toil in which I — Ecc 2.18
I have loved Jacob but..*h* Esau; Mal 1.3
you will be *h*..for my..sake. — Mt 10.22
h by all nations for my..sake. — 24.9
you will be *h* by all for my — Mk 13.13
you will be *h* by all for my — Lk 21.17
'They *h* me without a cause.' — Jn 15.25
and the world has *h* them — 17.14
"Jacob I loved, but Esau I *h*." — Rom 9.13
and *h* lawlessness; therefore — Heb 1.9

HATRED

if he stabbed him from *h*, — Num 35.20
with what violent *h* they hate — Ps 25.19
fear of..LORD is *h* of evil. — Prov 8.13

HAUGHTY

h eyes, a lying tongue, and — Prov 6.17
the daughters of Zion are *h* — Isa 3.16
eyes of the *h* are humbled. — 5.15
do not be *h*, but associate — Rom 12.16

HAWK

are an abomination:..the *h* — Lev 11.16
by your wisdom..the *h* soars, — Job 39.26

HEAD

put it under his *h* — Gen 28.11
and cut off his *h* with it. — 1Sam 17.51
to his father, "Oh, my *h*, — 2Ki 4.19
Your *h* crowns you like Carmel, — Sol 7.5
"Give me the *h* of John the — Mt 14.8
brought his *h* on a platter, — Mk 6.28
but also my hands and my *h*!" — Jn 13.9
the *h* of every man is Christ, — 1Cor 11.3
has made him the *h* over all — Eph 1.22
husband is the *h* of the wife — 5.23
He is the *h* of the body, — Col 1.18

HEAL — S — ED — ING (v)

"*H* her, O God, I beseech — Num 12.13
make alive; I wound and I *h*; — Deut 32.39
their sin and *h* their land. — 2Chr 7.14
h me, for I have sinned against — Ps 41.4
Peace,..and I will *h* him. — Isa 57.19
I will *h* your faithlessness." — Jer 3.22
H me, O LORD, and I shall be — 17.14
and your wounds I will *h*, — 30.17
I will *h* them and reveal to — 33.6
not able to..*h* your wound. — Hos 5.13
when I would *h* Israel, the — 7.1
I will *h* their faithlessness; — 14.4
H the sick, raise the dead, — Mt 10.8
and turn for me to *h* them.' — 13.15
disciples,..could not *h* him." — 17.16
'Physician, *h* yourself; — Lk 4.23
to preach the kingdom..and to *h*. — 9.2
"Is it lawful to *h* on the sabbath, — 14.3
to come down and *h* his son, — Jn 4.47
who *h* all your diseases, — Ps 103.3
He *h* the brokenhearted, and — 147.3
and *h* the wounds inflicted — Isa 30.26
and God *h* Abimelech, — Gen 20.17
for help, and thou hast *h* me. — Ps 30.2
he sent forth his word, and *h* — 107.20
with his stripes we are *h*. — Isa 53.5
h the wound of my people lightly, — Jer 6.14
We would have *h* Babylon, but — 51.9
they did not know that I *h* them. — Hos 11.3
and *h* all who were sick. — Mt 8.16
followed him, and he *h* them — 12.15
had compassion..and *h* their sick. — 14.14
every one of them and *h* them. — Lk 4.40
to be *h* of their diseases; — 6.17

women who had been *h* of evil — 8.2
she had been immediately *h*. — 8.47
come on those days and be *h*, — 13.14
touched his ear and *h* him. — 22.51
man who had been *h* did not know — Jn 5.13
putting his hands on him *h* — Acts 28.8
By his wounds you have been *h*. — 1Pet 2.24
h every disease and..infirmity — Mt 4.23

HEALER — S

I am the LORD, your *h*." — Ex 15.26
h, helpers, administrators, — 1Cor 12.28

HEALING (n)

It will be *h* to your flesh — Prov 3.8
he will be broken beyond *h*. — 6.15
suddenly be broken beyond *h*. — 29.1
We looked..for a time of *h*, — Jer 8.15
so that there is no *h* for us? — 14.19
medicines;..no *h* for you. — 46.11
and their leaves for *h*." — Ezek 47.12
rise, with *h* in its wings. — Mal 4.2
to another gifts of *h* by — 1Cor 12.9
leaves..for..*h* of the nations. — Rev 22.2

HEALTH

no *h* in my bones because..sin. — Ps 38.3
the soul and *h* to the body. — Prov 16.24
For I will restore *h* to you, — Jer 30.17
given the man this perfect *h* — Acts 3.16
and that you may be in *h*; — 3Jn 2

HEAP — S (v)

he *h* up silver like dust, — Job 27.16
h coals of fire on his head, — Prov 25.22
man *h* up, and knows not who — Ps 39.6

HEAP (n)

it shall be a *h* for ever, — Deut 13.16
waters..stand in one *h*." — Josh 3.13
make Jerusalem a *h* of ruins, — Jer 9.11

HEAR — S — D (v)

let them *h* my words, — Deut 4.10
"*H*, O Israel, the statutes — 5.1
"*H*, O Israel: The LORD our — 6.4
that they may *h* and learn — 31.12
when you *h* the sound of — 2Sam 5.24
then *h* thou in heaven thy — 1Ki 8.39
LORD, and *h*; open thy eyes, — 2Ki 19.16
then *h* thou in heaven, — 2Chr 6.27
'*H*, and I will speak'; I will — Job 42.4
H this, all peoples! Give ear, — Ps 49.1
H,..your father's instruction, — Prov 1.8
H, O heavens, and give ear, — Isa 1.2
'*H* and *h*, but do not understand; — 6.9
H, you who are far off, what — 33.13
I will let you *h* my words." — Jer 18.2
he that will *h*, let him *h*; — Ezek 3.27
who have ears to *h*, and *h* not: — 12.2
they *h*..but..will not do it; — 33.31
tell John what you *h* and see: — Mt 11.4
he said.."Take heed what you *h*; — Mk 4.24
came to *h* him and to be healed — Lk 6.17
sheep *h* his voice, and he calls — Jn 10.3
h, but never understand, — Acts 28.26
to *h* without a preacher? — Rom 10.14
Let every man be quick to *h*, — Jas 1.19
blessed are those who *h*, and — Rev 1.3
cry for help, the LORD *h*, and — Ps 34.17
"He who *h* you *h* me, and he — Lk 10.16
who *h* my word and believes — Jn 5.24
If any one *h* my sayings and — 12.47
God *h* the voice of the lad; — Gen 21.17
And God *h* their groaning, — Ex 2.24
From his temple he *h* my — 2Sam 22.7

HEAR — S — D (v) (cont.)

"I have *h* your prayer, and   2Chr 7.12
and *h* his supplication and   33.13
wept when they *h* the words of   Neh 8.9
The LORD has *h* my supplication;   Ps 6.9
words of the wise *h* in quiet   Ecc 9.17
Have you not known?..not *h*?   Isa 40.28
From of old no one has *h* or   64.4
Who has *h* such a thing? Who   66.8
I have *h* Ephraim bemoaning,   Jer 31.18
the LORD heeded and *h* them,   Mal 3.16
tell..what you have seen and *h*:   Lk 7.22
what we have seen and *h*."   Acts 4.20
Spirit fell on all who *h*   10.44
all the residents of Asia *h*   19.10
who have never *h* of him."   Rom 15.21
we have *h*, which we have seen   1Jn 1.1

HEARING (n)

in the *h* of the Hittites,   Gen 23.10
the book of Moses in the *h*   Neh 13.1
eye, where would be the *h*?   1Cor 12.17

HEARKEN — ED

Give heed to him and *h*   Ex 23.21
you *h* to these ordinances,   Deut 7.12
they did not *h* to the voice   Josh 5.6
if you will not *h* to the   1Sam 12.15
If they *h* and serve him,   Job 36.11
H to..father who begot you.   Prov 23.22
"*H* to me, you who pursue   Isa 51.1
h, O earth, and all that is   Mic 1.2
they *h* to the word of..LORD,   2Chr 11.4
he *h* to them in this matter,   Dan 1.14

HEART — S

imagination..man's *h* is evil   Gen 8.21
from every man whose *h*   Ex 25.2
upon his *h* before the LORD   28.30
whoever is of a generous *h*,   35.5
love..God with all your *h*,   Deut 6.5
then your *h* be lifted up,   8.14
"Do not say in your *h*, after   9.4
God with all your *h* and with   10.12
yet the LORD set his *h*   10.15
shall not harden your *h*   15.7
lest his *h* turn away;   17.17
his *h* may not be lifted   17.20
LORD will give..trembling *h*,   28.65
the *h* of your offspring,   30.6
mouth and in your *h*, so   30.14
crossed over, their *h* melted,   Josh 5.1
incline your *h* to the LORD,   24.23
direct your *h* to the LORD,   1Sam 7.3
God gave him another *h*;   10.9
a man after his own *h*;   13.14
the LORD looks on the *h*."   16.7
and his *h* died within him,   25.37
do all that is in your *h*;   2Sam 7.3
h is like the *h* of a lion,   17.10
David's *h* smote him after   24.10
uprightness of *h* toward thee;   1Ki 3.6
if they repent..with all their *h*   8.48
his *h* had turned away from   11.9
the *h* of Asa was wholly true   15.14
your *h* has lifted you up,   2Ki 14.10
because your *h* was penitent,   22.19
to the LORD with all his *h*   23.25
"Do all that is in your *h*,   1Chr 17.2
in my *h* to build a house   28.2
serve him with a whole *h*   28.9
that thou triest the *h*,   29.17
in the *h* of David..to build   2Chr 6.7

whose *h* is blameless toward   16.9
His *h* was courageous in the   17.6
your *h* has lifted you up in   25.19
his *h* was proud. Therefore   32.25
turned the *h* of the king   Ezra 6.22
Ezra had set his *h* to study   7.10
else but sadness of the *h*."   Neh 2.2
my *h* to do for Jerusalem.   2.12
"If you set your *h* aright,   Job 11.13
God has made my *h* faint;   23.16
"If my *h* has been enticed   31.9
godless in *h* cherish anger;   36.13
fool says in his *h*,..no God."   Ps 14.1
are right, rejoicing the *h*;   19.8
has clean hands and a pure *h*,   24.4
he knows the secrets of the *h*.   44.21
My *h* overflows with a goodly   45.1
Create in me a clean *h*, O God,   51.10
fool says in his *h*,..no God."   53.1
butter, yet war was in his *h*;   55.21
My *h* is steadfast, O God, my *h*   57.7
Insults have broken my *h*, so   69.20
commune with my *h* in the night;   77.6
They tested God in their *h*   78.18
will walk with integrity of *h*   101.2
My *h* is smitten like grass,   102.4
wine to gladden the *h* of man,   104.15
My *h* is steadfast, O God, my *h*   108.1
my *h* is stricken within me.   109.22
His *h* is steady, he will not   112.8
laid up thy word in my *h*,   119.11
my *h* within me is appalled.   143.4
wisdom will come into your *h*,   Prov 2.10
write them on..tablet of your *h*.   3.3
Keep your *h* with all vigilance;   4.23
a *h* that devises wicked plans,   6.18
Before destruction a man's *h*   18.12
Who can say,..my *h* clean;   20.9
king's *h* is a stream of water   21.1
My son, give me your *h*, and   23.26
smooth lips with an evil *h*.   26.23
nor let your *h* be hasty to   Ecc 5.2
wise man's *h* inclines..right,   10.2
Set me as a seal upon your *h*,   Sol 8.6
sick, and the whole *h* faint.   Isa 1.5
Make the *h* of this people fat,   6.10
faithfulness with a whole *h*,   38.3
but he did not take it to *h*.   42.25
people in whose *h* is my law;   51.7
why dost thou..harden our *h*,   63.17
Judah did not return..whole *h*,   Jer 3.10
shepherds after my own *h*, who   3.15
Jerusalem, wash your *h* from   4.14
My *h* is beating wildly; I writhe   4.19
whose *h* turns away from..LORD.   17.5
The *h* is deceitful above all   17.9
I will give them one *h* and   32.39
I will give them one *h*,   Ezek 11.19
"How lovesick is your *h*,   16.30
"Because your *h* is proud,   28.2
their *h* is set on their gain.   33.31
I will take out..*h* of stone   36.26
uncircumcised in *h* and flesh,   44.7
you..have not humbled your *h*,   Dan 5.22
Their *h* is false; now they   Hos 10.2
"return to me with all your *h*,   Joel 2.12
stout of *h* among the mighty   Amos 2.16
"Blessed are the pure in *h*,   Mt 5.8
adultery with her in his *h*.   5.28
treasure is, there will your *h*   6.21
said to the paralytic, "Take *h*,   9.2
this people's *h* has grown dull,   13.15
"Take *h*, it is I; have no fear."   14.27

HEART — S (cont.)

but their *h* is far from me;	Mt 15.8
out of the *h* come evil thoughts,	15.19
"Take *h*, it is I; have no fear."	Mk 6.50
but their *h* is far from me;	7.6
out of the *h* of man, come evil	7.21
"For your hardness of *h* he	10.5
love. . God with all your *h*,	12.30
unbelief and hardness of *h*,	16.14*n*
Mary. . pondering them in her *h*.	Lk 2.19
mother kept. . things in her *h*.	2.51
out of the good treasure of his *h*	6.45
'Out of his *h* shall flow	Jn 7.38
eyes and hardened their *h*,	12.40
therefore my *h* was glad,	Acts 2.26
were of one *h* and soul, and	4.32
into his *h* to visit his brother	7.23
uncircumcised in *h* and ears,	7.51
your *h* is not right before God.	8.21
David. . a man after my *h*,	13.22
God who knows the *h* bore witness	15.8
opened her *h* to give heed	16.14
weeping and breaking my *h*?	21.13
I now bid you take *h*; for	27.22
So take *h*, men, for I have	27.25
this people's *h* has grown dull,	28.27
and unceasing anguish in my *h*.	Rom 9.2
believe in your *h* that God	10.9
nor the *h* of man conceived,	1Cor 2.9
ministry. . we do not lose *h*.	2Cor 4.1
Corinthians; our *h* is wide.	6.11
his *h* goes out all the more	7.15
love that issues from a pure *h*	1Tim 1.5
discerning. . intentions of the *h*.	Heb 4.12
love one another. . from the *h*.	1Pet 1.22
yet closes his *h* against him,	1Jn 3.17
he who searches mind and *h*,	Rev 2.23
Absalom stole the *h* of the	2Sam 15.6
thou hast turned their *h*	1Ki 18.37
Harden not your *h*, as at	Ps 95.8
while their *h* are far from me,	Isa 29.13
I will write it upon their *h*;	Jer 31.33
made their *h* like adamant	Zech 7.12
he will turn the *h* of fathers	Mal 4.6
"Why. . question thus in your *h*?	Mk 2.8
but their *h* were hardened. ·	6.52
bread?. . Are your *h* hardened?	8.17
turn the *h* of the fathers to	Lk 1.17
"Did not our *h* burn within us	24.32
"Let not your *h* be troubled;	Jn 14.1
Let not your *h* be troubled,	14.27
"Lord, who knowest. . *h* of all	Acts 1.24
written on their *h*, while	Rom 2.15
he who searches the *h* of men	8.27
Lord direct your *h* to. . love	2Thess 3.5
do not harden your *h* as in	Heb 3.8
always go astray in their *h*;	3.10
voice, do not harden your *h*."	4.7
and write them on their *h*,	8.10
whenever our *h* condemn us;	1Jn 3.20

HEAVEN — S

God called the firmament *H*.	Gen 1.8
I will rain bread from *h*	Ex 16.4
I. . talked with you from *h*.	20.22
It is not in *h*, that you	Deut 30.12
Behold, *h*. . cannot contain thee	1Ki 8.27
should make windows in *h*,	2Ki 7.2
Behold, *h*. . cannot contain	2Chr 6.18
I ascend to *h*, thou art there!	Ps 139.8
"How you are fallen from *h*,	Isa 14.12
says the LORD: "*H* is my throne	66.1
till *h* and earth pass away,	Mt 5.18

Pray. . Our Father who art in *h*,	6.9
H and earth will pass away,	Mk 13.31
Jesus. . was taken up into *h*,	16.19*n*
H and earth will pass away,	Lk 21.33
a light from *h* flashed about	Acts 9.3
the image of the man of *h*.	1Cor 15.49
caught up to the third *h*—	2Cor 12.2
Christ, who has gone into *h*	1Pet 3.22
and lo, in *h* an open door!	Rev 4.1
great multitude in *h*, crying,	19.1
I saw a new *h* and a new earth;	21.1
The *h* are telling the glory of	Ps 19.1
h are high above the earth,	103.11
thy word is firmly fixed in. . *h*.	119.89
the *h* languish. . with the earth.	Isa 24.4
the *h* above. . withheld dew,	Hag 1.10
he saw the *h* opened and the	Mk 1.10
powers of the *h*. . be shaken.	Lk 21.26
by the word of God *h* existed	2Pet 3.5
we wait for new *h* and a new	3.13

HEAVENLY

believe if I tell you *h* things?	Jn 3.12
long to put on our *h* dwelling,	2Cor 5.2
spiritual blessing in *h* places,	Eph 1.3

HEAVY

charged with *h* tidings for	1Ki 14.6
day and night thy hand was *h*	Ps 32.4
evil which. . lies *h* upon men:	Ecc 6.1
all who labor and are *h* laden,	Mt 11.28
their ears are *h* of hearing,	13.15

HEBRON

Abram. . dwelt. . at *H*;	Gen 13.18
Canaanites who dwelt in *H*	Judg 1.10
David was king in *H* over	2Sam 2.11

HEED (v)

I should *h* his voice and let	Ex 5.2
to *h* all these words which	Deut 12.28
and thou dost not *h* me.	Job 30.20
Cursed. . man who does not *h*	Jer 11.3
to *h* the words of my. . prophets	26.5
and they will *h* my voice.	Jn 10.16

HEED (n)

you have not given *h* to	Judg 6.10
hast taken *h* of my adversities,	Ps 31.7
h. . the way that is blameless.	101.2
Give *h* to my reproof; behold,	Prov 1.23
Take *h* to. . path of your feet,	4.26
I have given *h* and listened,	Jer 8.6
O LORD, give *h* and act; delay	Dan 9.19
no *h* to the gods of his fathers,	11.37
stands take *h* lest he fall.	1Cor 10.12

HEEL

and you shall bruise his *h*."	Gen 3.15
taken hold of Esau's *h*;	25.26
has lifted his *h* against me.	Ps 41.9
took his brother by the *h*,	Hos 12.3

HEIFER •

"Bring me a *h* three years old,	Gen 15.9
bring you a red *h* without	Num 19.2
had not plowed with my *h*,	Judg 14.18

HEIGHT

nor *h*, nor depth, nor anything	Rom 8.39

HEIR — S

a slave. . will be my *h*."	Gen 15.3
in the end find him his *h*.	Prov 29.21
Israel no sons? Has he no *h*?	Jer 49.1
the *h*; come, let us kill him	Mt 21.38
"This is the *h*; come, let us	Mk 12.7

HEIR — S (cont.)

'This is the *h*; let us kill   Lk 20.14
I mean that the *h*, as long as   Gal 4.1
h of..righteousness..by faith.   Heb 11.7
if children, then *h*, *h* of God   Rom 8.17
how the Gentiles are fellow *h*,   Eph 3.6

HELL

says, 'You fool!'..liable to..*h*   Mt 5.22
your whole body..thrown into *h*.   5.29
be thrown into the *h* of fire.   18.9
has power to cast into *h*;   Lk 12.5

HELLENISTS

H murmured against..Hebrews Acts 6.1
and disputed against the *H*;   9.29

HELMET

h of salvation upon his head;   Isa 59.17
take the *h* of salvation, and   Eph 6.17
for a *h*..hope of salvation.   1Thess 5.8

HELP — S — ED (v)

shall be no one to *h* you.   Deut 28.31
there was none to *h* Israel.   2Ki 14.26
there is none like thee to *h*,   2Chr 14.11
h me when thou deliverest   Ps 106.4
fell down, with none to *h*.   107.12
H me, O LORD my God! Save me 109.26
O Israel; who can *h* you?   Hos 13.9
knelt..saying, "Lord, *h* me."   Mt 15.25
toiling one must *h* the weak,   Acts 20.35
the Lord GOD *h* me; therefore   Isa 50.7
Moses stood up and *h* them,   Ex 2.17
God *h* him against the   2Chr 26.7
have *h* him who has no power!   Job 26.2
brother *h* is like a strong   Prov 18.19
in a day of salvation I have *h*   Isa 49.8

HELP (n)

and thy *h* made me great.   2Sam 22.36
because I saw *h* in the gate;   Job 31.21
and thy *h* made me great.   Ps 18.35
I shall again praise him, my *h*   42.5
I shall again praise him, my *h*   42.11
Thou art my *h* and my deliverer;   70.5
My *h* comes from the LORD,   121.2
Egypt's *h* is worthless and   Isa 30.7
the *h* that comes from God,   Acts 26.22
in Thessalonica you sent me *h*   Phil 4.16

HELPER

I will make him a *h*   Gen 2.18
been the *h* of the fatherless.   Ps 10.14
Hear,..O LORD, be thou my *h*!'   30.10
"The Lord is my *h*, I will   Heb 13.6

HELPFUL

but not all things are *h*.   1Cor 6.12
but not all things are *h*.   10.23

HELPLESS

I suffer thy terrors; I am *h*.   Ps 88.15
our hands fall *h*; anguish   Jer 6.24
While we were..*h*,..Christ died   Rom 5.6

HERITAGE

to be thy *h*, as thou didst   1Ki 8.53
What..*h* from the Almighty   Job 31.2
I will make the nations your *h*,   Ps 2.8
yea, I have a goodly *h*.   16.6
whom he has chosen as his *h*!   33.12
LORD..will not abandon his *h*;   94.14
house, I have abandoned my *h*;   Jer 12.7
loosen your hand from your *h*   17.4
exult, O plunderers of my *h*,   50.11

HERMON

valley of..Arnon to Mount *H*   Deut 3.8
Mount Sirion (that is, *H*),   4.48
Lebanon below Mount *H*.   Josh 11.17
valley of..Arnon to Mount *H*,   12.1
Tabor and *H* joyously praise   Ps 89.12
It is like the dew of *H*, which   133.3
from the peak of Senir and *H*,   Sol 4.8

HEROD

born..in the days of *H* the king, Mt 2.1
for *H* is about to search for   2.13
Then *H*,..was in a furious rage,   2.16
when *H* died, behold, an angel   2.19
H the tetrarch heard about   14.1
King *H* heard of it; for Jesus'   Mk 6.14
Pharisees and..leaven of *H*."   8.15
and *H* being tetrarch of Galilee, Lk 3.1
for *H* wants to kill you."   13.31
he sent him over to *H*, who   23.7
both *H* and Pontius Pilate,   Acts 4.27
H the king laid violent hands   12.1
Now *H* was angry with..Tyre   12.20
H put on his royal robes,   12.21

HEZEKIAH

and *H* his son reigned in his   2Ki 16.20
H received the letter from   19.14
those days *H* became sick   20.1
H sent to all Israel and   2Chr 30.1
For *H* had prayed for them,   30.18
H closed the upper outlet   32.30
letters and a present to *H*,   Isa 39.1

HID — DEN

she *h* him three months.   Ex 2.2
man and his wife *h* themselves   3.8
killed the Egyptian and *h* him   Ex 2.12
And Moses *h* his face,   3.6
h him from Athaliah, so   2Chr 22.11
I have not *h* thy saving help   Ps 40.10
"My way is *h* from the LORD,   Isa 40.27
in..shadow of his hand he *h* me;   49.2
troubles..*h* from my eyes.   65.16
and *h* it by the Euphrates,   Jer 13.5
prophet, but the LORD *h* them.   36.26
city set on a hill cannot be *h*.   Mt 5.14
and *h* his master's money.   25.18
nothing *h*, except to be made   Mk 4.22
nothing is *h* that shall not   Lk 8.17
taken the two men and *h* them;   Josh 2.4
he had *h* himself among the   1Sam 10.22
Clear thou me from *h* faults.   Ps 19.12
trustworthy..keeps..thing *h*.   Prov 11.13
open rebuke than *h* love.   27.5
h these things from the wise   Lk 10.21
before him no creature is *h*,   Heb 4.13

HIDE — ST — ING

"Shall I *h* from Abraham   Gen 18.17
Do not *h* it from me. May   1Sam 3.17
h thyself in times of trouble?   Ps 10.1
How long wilt thou *h* thy face   13.1
h me in the shadow of thy wings,   17.8
he will *h* me in his shelter   27.5
H not thy face from me.   27.9
thou didst *h* thy face, I was   30.7
h not..from my supplication!   55.1
Wilt thou *h* thyself for ever?   89.46
I will *h* my eyes from you;   Isa 1.15
and *h* in the dust from before   2.10
I will not *h* my face any   Ezek 39.29
they *h* themselves on..Carmel,   Amos 9.3
When thou *h* thy face, they   Ps 104.29
thou art a God who *h* thyself,   Isa 45.15

HIDE — ST — ING (cont.)
Thou art my *h* place and my   Ps 119.114
like a *h* place from the wind,   Isa 32.2

HIGH — ER
folly is set in many *h* places,   Ecc 10.6
and make *h* the low tree,   Ezek 17.24
our iniquities have risen *h*   Ezra 9.6

HIGH PRIEST
when Abiathar was *h*..,and ate   Mk 2.26
they led Jesus to the *h*..;   14.53
h..then questioned Jesus   Jn 18.19
But the *h*..rose up and all   Acts 5.17
"Would you revile God's *h*..?"   23.4
faithful *h*..in the service   Heb 2.17
Jesus, the apostle and *h*..   3.1
then we have a great *h*..who   4.14
not exalt himself to be..a *h*..   5.5

HIGHWAY — S
will be a *h* from Assyria for   Isa 11.16
a *h* from Egypt to Assyria,   19.23
And a *h* shall be there, and   35.8
whose heart are the *h* to Zion.   Ps 84.5
my *h* shall be raised up.   Isa 49.11
'Go out to the *h* and hedges,   Lk 14.23

HILL — S
Who..ascend the *h* of the LORD?   Ps 24.3
gods of the *h*, and so they   1Ki 20.23
he went into the *h* to pray.   Mk 6.46
Jesus withdrew again to the *h*   Jn 6.15

HINDER
nothing can *h* the LORD from   1Sam 14.6
snatches away; who can *h* him?   Job 9.12

HINDRANCE
behind me, Satan! You are a *h*   Mt 16.23

HIRAM
And *H* king of Tyre sent   2Sam 5.11
Now *H* king of Tyre sent his   1Ki 5.1
Solomon sent and brought *H*   7.13
H also made the pots, the   7.40
when *H* came from Tyre to see   9.12
And *H* king of Tyre sent   1Chr 14.1

HIRE — D (n)
while no *h* was given to you;   Ezek 16.34
treat me as one of your *h*   Lk 15.19

HIRED (v)
they *h* against you Balaam   Deut 23.4
they *h* masons and carpenters   2Chr 24.12

HITTITE — S
Ephron the *H* answered   Gen 23.10
H, the Perizzites, the   15.20
Canaanites, the *H*, the Amorites, Ex 3.8
the Amorites, and the *H*,   23.23
nations before you, the *H*,   Deut 7.1
left of the Amorites, the *H*,   1Ki 9.20
hired against us..the *H* and   2Ki 7.6
from the Canaanites, the *H*,   Ezra 9.1

HOLD
I *h* fast my righteousness,   Job 27.6
I *h* back my feet from..evil   Ps 119.101
to them; do not *h* back a word.   Jer 26.2
"Do not *h* me, for I have not   Jn 20.17
we *h*..man..justified by faith   Rom 3.28
h fast to what is good; love   12.9

HOLE — S
there was a *h* in the wall.   Ezek 8.7
wages to put..into a bag with *h*. Hag 1.6

HOLINESS
O LORD,..majestic in *h*,   Ex 15.11
h befits thy house, O LORD,   Ps 93.5
manifest my *h* among you in   Ezek 20.41
vindicate the *h* of my..name,   36.23
O God, I vindicate my *h*   38.16
serve him..in *h*..righteousness   Lk 1.75
make *h* perfect in..fear of God. 2Cor 7.1
in true righteousness and *h*.   Eph 4.24
God has..called us..in *h*.   1Thess 4.7
for the *h* without which no   Heb 12.14

HOLLOW
touched the *h* of his thigh;   Gen 32.25
measured the waters in the *h*   Isa 40.12

HOLY
are standing is *h* ground."   Ex 3.5
priests and a *h* nation.   19.6
h place from the most *h*.   26.33
signet, '*H* to the LORD.'   28.36
inscription..."*H* to the LORD."   39.30
said, 'I will show myself *h*   Lev 10.3
to distinguish between the *h*   10.10
and be *h*, for I am *h*.   11.44
Israel, You shall be *h*;   19.2
You shall be *h* to me; for I   20.26
They shall be *h* to their God,   21.6
keep away from the *h* things   22.2
not..look upon the *h* things   Num 4.20
he separates himself to..be *h*;   6.5
all the congregation are *h*,   16.3
sabbath day, to keep it *h*,   Deut 5.12
"For you are a people *h*   7.6
a people *h* to the LORD   14.2
your camp must be *h*,   23.14
"There is none *h* like..LORD,   1Sam 2.2
"You are *h* to the LORD, and   Ezra 8.28
to keep the sabbath day *h*.   Neh 13.22
of the *h* ones will you turn?   Job 5.1
thou art *h*, enthroned on the   Ps 22.3
and give thanks to his *h* name.   30.4
His *h* mountain, beautiful in   48.2
Worship the LORD in *h* array;   96.9
and terrible one! *H* is he!   99.3
Lift up..hands to the *h* place,   134.2
the *H* God shows himself *h* in   Isa 5.16
"*H*, *h*, *h* is the LORD of hosts", 6.3
him you shall regard as *h*;   8.13
it shall be called the *H* way;   35.8
shall be called The *h* people,   62.12
Israel was *h* to the LORD,   Jer 2.3
but keep the sabbath day *h*,   17.22
aliens..come into..*h* places   51.51
between the *h* and..common.   Ezek 42.20
not kept charge of my *h* things;   44.8
Then I heard a *h* one speaking;   Dan 8.13
shattering of the power of the *h*   12.7
all the *h* ones with him.   Zech 14.5
"Do not give dogs what is *h*;   Mt 7.6
the..sacrilege..in the *h* place   24.15
John,..a righteous and *h* man,   Mk 6.20
male that opens the womb..*h*   Lk 2.23
where you are standing is *h*   Acts 7.33
So the law is *h*, and the   Rom 7.12
as a living sacrifice, *h* and   12.1
how to be *h* in body and   1Cor 7.34
we should be *h* and blameless   Eph 1.4
church..*h* and without blemish.   5.27
a high priest, *h*, blameless,   Heb 7.26
as he..is *h*, be *h* yourselves   1Pet 1.15
Lord came with his *h* myriads,   Jude 14
'The words of the *h* one,   Rev 3.7

HOLY (cont.)

"*H, h, h*, is the Lord God	Rev 4.8
the *h* city, new Jerusalem,	21.2

HOLY ONE

knowledge of..*H*..is insight.	Prov 9.10
Redeemer is the *H*..of Israel.	Isa 41.14
Redeemer, the *H*..of Israel:	43.14
from everlasting,..my *H*..?	Hab 1.12
that you are the *H*..of God."	Jn 6.69
'Thou wilt not let thy *H*..see	Acts 13.35

HOLY SPIRIT

and take not thy *h*..from me.	Ps 51.11
to be with child of the *H*..;	Mt 1.18
will baptize you with the *H*..."	Mk 1.8
men moved by the *H*..spoke	2Pet 1.21

HOME

God gives the desolate a *h*	Ps 68.6
"Go *h* to your friends, and tell	Mk 5.19
he sent him away to his *h*,	8.26
"Return to your *h*, and declare	Lk 8.39
and make our *h* with him.	Jn 14.23
disciple took her to his own *h:*	19.27
hungry, let him eat at *h*—	1Cor 11.34
ask their husbands at *h*.	14.35
while we are at *h* in the body	2Cor 5.6

HOMELAND

people who speak..seeking a *h*.	Heb 11.14

HONEST — Y

hold it fast in an *h* and good	Lk 8.15
So my *h* will answer for me	Gen 30.33

HONEY

land flowing with milk and *h*	Ex 3:8
like wafers made with *h*.	16.31
suck *h* out of the rock,	Deut 32.13
tasted a little of this *h*.	1Sam 14.29
gold; sweeter also than *h*	Ps 19.10
with *h* from the rock..satisfy	81.16
thy words..sweeter than *h*	119.103
son, eat *h*, for it is good,	Prov 24.13
h and milk..under your tongue;	Sol 4.11
He shall eat curds and *h* when	Isa 7.15
scroll..was..as sweet as *h*.	Ezek 3.3
was sweet as *h* in my mouth,	Rev 10.10

HONOR — S — ED (v)

"*H* your father..your mother,	Ex 20.12
h the face of an old man,	Lev 19.32
"'*H* your father and..mother,	Deut 5.16
those who *h* me I will *h*,	1Sam 2.30
"I have sinned; yet *h* me	15.30
H the LORD with your substance	Prov 3.9
h me with their lips, while	Isa 29.13
h it, not going your own ways,	58.13
shall *h* the god of fortresses	Dan 11.38
God commanded, '*H* your father	Mt 15.4
H your father and mother,	19.19
'*H* your father and..mother';	Mk 7.10
that all may *h* the Son, even	Jn 5.23
I *h* my Father, and you dishonor	8.49
"*H* your father and mother"	Eph 6.2
receive him..and *h* such men,	Phil 2.29
H widows who are real widows.	1Tim 5.3
thanksgiving..sacrifice *h* me;	Ps 50.23
"A son *h* his father, and a	Mal 1.6
people *h* me with their lips,	Mt 15.8
most *h* of all his family.	Gen 34.19
or *h* me with your sacrifices.	Isa 43.23
I will make them *h*, and they	Jer 30.19
h in the presence of all	Lk 14.10
Christ will be *h* in my body,	Phil 1.20

HONOR (n)

surely do you great *h*,	Num 22.17
them I shall be held in *h*."	2Sam 6.22
not asked..wealth, *h*, or the	2Chr 1.11
"What *h*..bestowed on Mordecai	Est 6.3
H and majesty are before him;	Ps 96.6
Thou art clothed with *h* and	104.1
and humility goes before *h*.	Prov 15.33
lowly in spirit..obtain *h*.	29.23
gifts and rewards and great *h*.	Dan 2.6
"A prophet is not without *h*	Mt 13.57
prophet is not without *h*, except	Mk 6.4
how they chose..places of *h*,	Lk 14.7
who..seek for glory and *h* and	Rom 2.7
outdo one another in..*h*	12.10
due, *h* to whom *h* is due.	13.7
You are held in *h*, but we	1Cor 4.10
in *h* and dishonor, in ill	2Cor 6.8
To him be *h* and eternal	1Tim 6.16

HONORABLE

Jabez was more *h* than his	1Chr 4.9
we aim at what is *h* not only	2Cor 8.21
whatever is *h*, whatever..just,	Phil 4.8
they who blaspheme that *h* name	Jas 2.7

HOPE — S — D (v)

upon us even as we *h* in thee.	Ps 33.22
H in God; for I shall again	42.5
H in God; for I shall again	43.5
But I will *h* continually, and	71.14
I *h* for thy salvation, O	119.166
in his name will..Gentiles *h*."	Mt 12.21
from whom you *h* to receive,	Lk 6.34
in him shall the Gentiles *h*."	Rom 15.12
For who *h* for what he sees?	8.24
who thus *h* in him purifies	1Jn 3.3
because I have *h* in thy word.	Ps 119.74
we had *h* that he was the one	Lk 24.21
we have *h* in Christ,	1Cor 15.19
we who first *h* in Christ	Eph 1.12

HOPE (n)

now there is *h* for Israel	Ezra 10.2
So the poor have *h*, and	Job 5.16
he will slay me; I have no *h*;	13.15
thou destroyest the *h* of man.	14.19
where then is my *h*? Who	17.15
my *h* has he pulled up like	19.10
what is the *h* of the godless	27.8
on those who *h* in his..love,	33.18
art the *h* of all the ends of	65.5
they should set their *h* in God,	78.7
whose *h* is in the LORD his	146.5
The *h* of the righteous ends	Prov 10.28
H deferred makes the heart sick,	13.12
your son while there is *h*;	19.18
There is more *h* for a fool	29.20
because of Ethiopia their *h*	Isa 20.5
We set our *h* on thee, for	Jer 14.22
There is *h* for your future,	31.17
bones..dried up..*h* is lost;	Ezek 37.11
Valley of Achor a door of *h*.	Hos 2.15
because of the *h* of Israel	Acts 28.20
In *h* he believed against *h*,	Rom 4.18
Rejoice in your *h*, be patient	12.12
you may know what is the *h*	Eph 1.18
h laid up for you in heaven.	Col 1.5
not shifting from the *h* of	1.23
Christ in you, the *h* of glory.	1.27
steadfastness of *h* in our Lord	1Thess 1.3
what is out *h*..joy or crown	2.19
awaiting our blessed *h*, the	Tit 2.13
to seize the *h* set before us.	Heb 6.18

HOPE (n) (cont.)

hold fast the confession of our *h* Heb 10.23
been born anew to a living *h* 1Pet 1.3

HORN — S

The *h* of Moab is cut off, Jer 48.25
cause a *h* to spring forth Ezek 29.21
hear the sound of the *h*, pipe, Dan 3.5
he. . raised up a *h* of salvation Lk 1.69
hold of the *h* of the altar. 1Ki 1.50
hold of the *h* of the altar. 2.28
a fourth beast,. . it had ten *h*. Dan 7.7
two *h*; and both *h* were high, 8.3
saw, and behold, four *h*! Zech 1.18
the ten *h* that you saw are Rev 17.12

HORSE — S

she laughs at the *h* and his Job 39.18
Be not like a *h* or a mule, Ps 32.9
The war *h* is a vain hope for 33.17
h is made ready for. . battle, Prov 21.31
A whip for the *h*, a bridle 26.3
a man riding upon a red *h*! Zech 1.8
multiply *h* for himself, Deut 17.16
hamstring their *h*, and burn Josh 11.6
Solomon's import of *h* was 1Ki 10.28
Solomon's import of *h* was 2Chr 1.16
four thousand stalls for *h* 9.25
Do *h* run upon rocks? Does Amos 6.12
The first chariot had red *h*, Zech 6.2
put bits into the mouths of *h* Jas 3.3

HOSANNAH

"*H* to the Son of David!" Mt 21.15
"*H*! Blessed is he who comes Mk 11.9

HOSEA

word of the LORD that came to *H* Hos 1.1
As indeed he says in *H*, Rom 9.25

HOSPITABLE

dignified, *h*, an apt teacher, 1Tim 3.2
but *h*, a lover of goodness, Tit 1.8

HOSPITALITY

needs of. . saints, practice *h*. Rom 12.13
Practice *h* ungrudgingly to 1Pet 4.9

HOST — S

finished,. . all the *h* of them. Gen 2.1
Though a *h* encamp against me, Ps 27.3
h under. . leadership of Moses Num 33.1
LORD of *h* is God over 2Sam 7.26
King of glory? The LORD of *h*, Ps 24.10
If the LORD of *h* had not left Isa 1.9

HOSTILE

eye be *h* to your. . brother, Deut 15.9
mind. . on the flesh is *h* to God; Rom 8.7
were estranged and *h* in mind, Col 1.21

HOUR

'These last worked only one *h*, Mt 20.12
know neither. . day nor the *h*. 25.13
that day or. . *h* no one knows, Mk 13.32
the *h* might pass from him. 14.35
the *h* has come; the Son of man 14.41
But this is your *h*, and the Lk 22.53
the *h* is coming when neither Jn 4.21
because his *h* had not yet come. 7.30
"The *h* has come for the Son 12.23
'Father, save me from this *h*'? 12.27
The *h* is coming, indeed it 16.32

HOUSE — S

h to be holy to the LORD, Lev 27.14
my *h*, we will serve. . LORD." Josh 24.15

LORD will make you a *h*. 2Sam 7.11
burned the *h* of the LORD, 2Ki 25.9
I have not dwelt in a *h* 1Chr 17.5
LORD will build you a *h*. 17.10
the *h* that is to be built 22.5
a *h* of rest for the ark 28.2
glory of the LORD filled. . *h* 2Chr 5.14
hid in the *h* of God, while 22.12
Joash. . restore the *h* of the LORD 24.4
cleansed all the *h* of the LORD, 29.18
foundation of the *h* of. . LORD Ezra 3.11
this *h* was finished on 6.15
is the *h* of God forsaken?" Neh 13.11
procession to the *h* of God, Ps 42.4
olive tree in the *h* of God. 52.8
zeal for thy *h* has consumed me, 69.9
doorkeeper in the *h* of my God 84.10
planted in the *h* of the LORD, 92.13
"Let us go to the *h* of. . LORD!" 122.1
h shared with a contentious Prov 25.24
better to go to. . *h* of mourning Ecc 7.2
to the *h* of the God of Jacob; Isa 2.3
the *h* was filled with smoke. 6.4
weight of his father's *h*, 22.24
Set your *h* in order; for you 38.1
not enter the *h* of mourning, Jer 16.5
'This *h* shall be like Shiloh, 26.9
he burned the *h* of the LORD, 52.13
h was filled with the cloud, Ezek 10:4
fountain. . from the *h* of. . LORD Joel 3.18
while this *h* lies in ruins? Hag 1.4
my *h* that lies in ruins, while 1.9
'My *h*. . called a *h* of prayer'; Mt 21.13
h of. . ruler of the synagogue, Mk 5.38
enter a *h*, stay there until 6.10
'My *h*. . called a *h* of prayer 11.17
I must be in my Father's *h*?" Lk 2.49
like a man building a *h*, who 6.48
whatever *h* you enter, stay there 9.4
wages; do not go from *h* to *h*. 10.7
laid waste, and *h* falls upon *h*. 11.17
Behold, your *h* is forsaken. 13.35
'My *h* shall be a *h* of prayer'; 19.46
my Father's *h* a *h* of trade." Jn 2.16
in public and from *h* to *h*, Acts 20.20
with the church in their *h*, 1Cor 16.19
built goodly *h* and live in Deut 8.12
Most High does not dwell in *h* Acts 7.48

HOUSEHOLD — ER

her *h*. . clothed in scarlet. Prov 31.21
looks well to. . ways of her *h*, 31.27
foes. . those of his own *h*. Mt 10.36
believed, and all his *h*. Jn 4.53
be saved, you and your *h*." Acts 16.31
who are of the *h* of faith. Gal 6.10
the saints. . of Caesar's *h*. Phil 4.22
must manage his own *h* well, 1Tim 3.4
to behave in the *h* of God, 3.15
like a *h* who brings out of his Mt 13.52

HOUSETOP — S

live in a corner of the *h* Prov 21.9
who is on the *h* not go down Mt 24.17
let him. . on the *h* not go down, Mk 13.15
Peter went up on the *h* to Acts 10.9
whispered, proclaim upon the *h*. Mt 10.27
be proclaimed upon the *h*. Lk 12.3

HUMAN

stone. . cut out by no *h* hand, Dan 2.34
no *h* being will be justified Rom 3.20
not taught by *h* wisdom 1Cor 2.13
no *h*. . can tame the tongue— Jas 3.8

HUMBLE — S — D (v)

will you refuse to *h* yourself	Ex 10.3
that he might *h* you, testing	Deut 8.2
if my people. .*h* themselves,	2Chr 7.14
that we might *h* ourselves	Ezra 8.21
God will give ear, and *h* them,	Ps 55.19
my God may *h* me before you,	2Cor 12.21
H yourselves before the Lord	Jas 4.10
H yourselves therefore under	1Pet 5.6
Whoever *h* himself like. .child,	Mt 18.4
whoever *h* himself will be	23.12
who *h* himself will be exalted."	Lk 18.14
lay with her and *h* her.	Gen 34.2
uncircumcised heart is *h*	Lev 26.41
seen how Ahab has *h* himself	1Ki 21.29
h yourself before the Lord,	2Ki 22.19
and the king *h* themselves	2Chr 12.6
few men of. .Zebulun *h*	30.11
But Hezekiah *h* himself for	32.26
you *h* yourself before God	34.27
eyes of the haughty are *h*.	Isa 5.15
They have not *h* themselves	Jer 44.10
you. .Belshazzar, have not *h*	Dan 5.22
h yourself before your God,	10.12
in human form he *h* himself	Phil 2.8

HUMBLE

Thou dost deliver a *h*	2Sam 22.28
thou dost deliver a *h* people;	Ps 18.27
leads the *h* in what is right,	25.9
he adorns the *h* with victory.	149.4
of a contrite and *h* spirit,	Isa 57.15
Seek the Lord, all your *h* of	Zeph 2.3
leave. .a people *h* and lowly.	3.12
victorious is he, *h* and riding	Zech 9.9
your king is coming to you, *h*,	Mt 21.5
a tender heart and a *h* mind.	1Pet 3.8

HUMILITY

and *h* goes before honor.	Prov 15.33
reward for *h* and fear of	22.4
but in *h* count others better	Phil 2.3

HUNG

On. .willows. .*h* up our lyres.	Ps 137.2

HUNGER (v)

they shall not *h* or thirst,	Isa 49.10
h and thirst for righteousness,	Mt 5.6
"Blessed are you that *h* now,	Lk 6.21
who comes to me shall not *h*,	Jn 6.35
To the present hour we *h* and	1Cor 4.11
They shall *h* no more, neither	Rev 7.16

HUNGER (n)

young lions suffer want and *h*;	Ps 34.10
cistern; and he will die. .of *h*,	Jer 38.9
your children, who faint for *h*	Lam 2.19
no more be consumed with *h*	Ezek 34.29
tumults, labors, watching, *h*;	2Cor 6.5
in *h* and thirst, often	11.27
of facing plenty and *h*,	Phil 4.12

HUNGRY

who were *h* have ceased to	1Sam 2.5
"If I were *h*,. .not tell you;	Ps 50.12
the *h* he fills with good	107.9
if he steals. .when he is *h*?	Prov 6.30
to one. .*h*. .bitter is sweet.	27.7
greatly distressed and *h* and	Isa 8.21
returning to. .city, he was *h*.	Mt 21.18
what David did, when he. .*h*,	Mk 2.25
came from Bethany, he was *h*.	11.12
filled the *h* with good things,	Lk 1.53
he became *h* and desired	Acts 10.10
is *h*, let him eat at home—	1Cor 11.34

HUNT — ED

thou dost *h* me like a lion,	Job 10.16
let evil *h* down the violent	Ps 140.11
you *h* down souls belonging	Ezek 13.18
"Israel is a *h* sheep driven	Jer 50.17

HUNTER

Nimrod..mighty *h* before..Lord;	Gen 10.9
Esau was a skilful *h*,	25.27

HURAM

Then *H* the king of Tyre	2Chr 2.11

HURT

that it might not *h* me!"	1Chr 4.10
man lords it over man to his *h*.	Ecc 8.9
They shall not *h* or destroy	Isa 11.9

HUSBAND — S — 'S

gave some to her *h*, and he ate.	Gen 3.6
and my *h* is old, shall I	18.12
Her *h* is known in the gates,	Prov 31.23
For your Maker is your *h*,	Isa 54.5
broke, though I was their *h*,	Jer 31.32
father of Joseph the *h* of Mary,	Mt 1.16
"Go, call your *h*, and come	Jn 4.16
woman. .bound by law to her *h*	Rom 7.2
and each woman her own *h*.	1Cor 7.2
is consecrated through her *h*.	7.14
affairs, how to please her *h*.	7.34
see that she respects her *h*.	Eph 5.33
bishop. .*h* of one wife,	1Tim 3.2
with contempt upon their *h*,	Est 1.17
H, love your wives, as Christ	Eph 5.25
H, love your wives, and do	Col 3.19
you *h*, live considerately	1Pet 3.7
h brother shall go in to her,	Deut 25.5

HYMN — S

And when they had sung a *h*,	Mt 26.30
And when they had sung a *h*,	Mk 14.26
each one has a *h*, a lesson,	1Cor 14.26
one another in psalms and *h*	Eph 5.19
as you sing psalms and *h*	Col 3.16

HYPOCRISY

leaven of the Pharisees. .is *h*.	Lk 12.1

HYPOCRITE — S

You *h*, first take the log out	Mt 7.5
no trumpet before you, as the *h*	6.2
you must not be like the *h*;	6.5
do not look dismal, like the *h*,	6.16
You *h*! Well did Isaiah prophesy	15.7
woe. .scribes and Pharisees, *h*!	23.13
"Woe. .scribes and Pharisees, *h*!	23.23
did Isaiah prophesy of you *h*,	Mk 7.6
"You *h*!. .on the sabbath untie	Lk 13.15

HYSSOP

Take a bunch of *h* and dip it	Ex 12.22
Purge me with *h*, and I shall	Ps 51.7
sponge full of. .vinegar on *h*	Jn 19.29

I

IDLE

But he said, "You are *i*,	Ex 5.17
he saw others standing *i* in	Mt 20.3

IDLENESS

brother who is living in *i*	2Thess 3.6

IDOL — S

The *i*! a workman casts it,	Isa 40.19
lest you. .say, 'My *i* did them,	48.5
or that an *i* is anything?	1Cor 10.19
shall make for yourselves no *i*	Lev 26.1

IDOL — S (cont.)

gods of the peoples are *i*;	1Chr 16.26
put away the abominable *i*	2Chr 15.8
those who pay regard to vain *i*;	Ps 31.6
sacrificed to the *i* of Canaan;	106.38
Their land is filled with *i*;	Isa 2.8
the *i* shall utterly pass away.	2.18
consult the *i* and . . sorcerers,	19.3
All who make *i* are nothing,	44.9
and they are mad over *i*.	Jer 50.38
takes his *i* into his heart	Ezek 14.4
nor defile . . with their *i*.	20.18
Ephraim is joined to *i*, let	Hos 4.17
made *i* for their own destruction.	8.4
all her *i* I will lay waste;	Mic 1.7
from the pollutions of *i*	Acts 15.20
the city was full of *i*.	17.16
sacrificed to *i* and from blood	21.25
concerning food offered to *i*:	1Cor 8.1
you turned to God from *i*,	1Thess 1.9
keep yourselves from *i*.	1Jn 5.21

IDOLATER — S

no . . *i*), has any inheritance	Eph 5.5
nor *i*, nor adulterers, nor	1Cor 6.9

IGNORANCE

times of *i* God overlooked,	Acts 17.30
alienated . . because of the *i*	Eph 4.18

IGNORANT

and *i*, I was like a beast	Ps 73.22
we do not want you to be *i*,	2Cor 1.8

ILL — NESS

"Lord, he whom you love is *i*."	Jn 11.3
why many . . are weak and *i*,	1Cor 11.30
you heard that he was *i*.	Phil 2.26
in his *i* thou healest all his	Ps 41.3
"This *i* is not unto death;	Jn 11.4

ILL — TREATMENT

choosing rather to share *i*	Heb 11.25

IMAGE — S

"Let us make man in our *i*,	Gen 1.26
not make . . yourself a graven *i*,	Ex 20.4
for yourself a graven *i*,	Deut 5.8
son, to make a graven *i* and	Judg 17.3
Danites set up the graven *i*	18.30
Michal took an *i* and laid	1Sam 19.13
O king, and behold, a great *i*.	Dan 2.31
since he is the *i* and glory	1Cor 11.7
the *i* of the invisible God,	Col 1.15
after the *i* of its creator.	3.10
destroy all their molten *i*,	Num 33.52
must make *i* of your tumors	1Sam 6.5
jealousy with their graven *i*.	Ps 78.58

IMAGINATION

every *i*. . was only evil	Gen 6.5
the *i* of man's heart is evil	8.21

IMITATE — ING

Beloved, do not *i* evil but	3Jn 11
Brethren, join in *i* me, and	Phil 3.17

IMITATORS

I urge you, then, be *i* of me.	1Cor 4.16
Be *i* of me, as I am of Christ.	11.1
i of God, as beloved children.	Eph 5.1
you became *i* of us and of	1Thess 1.6
not . . sluggish, but *i* of those	Heb 6.12

IMMANU-EL

and shall call his name *I*.	Isa 7.14
wings will fill . . land, O *I*."	8.8

IMMORAL — ITY

neither the *i*, nor idolaters,	1Cor 6.9
reported . . *i* among you,	5.1

IMMORTAL — ITY

exchanged the glory of. . *i* God	Rom 1.23
mortal nature must put on *i*.	1Cor 15.53

IMPERISHABLE

sown . . what is raised is *i*,	1Cor 15.42
to an inheritance which is *i*,	1Pet 1.4

IMPOSSIBLE

nothing . . will now be *i*	Gen 11.6
with God nothing will be *i*."	Lk 1.37
it is *i* that . . blood of bulls	Heb 10.4

IMPRISONED

enraged at Jeremiah, . . *i* him	Jer 37.15
I *i* . . those who believed	Acts 22.19

IMPRISONMENT — S

that *i* and afflictions await	Acts 20.23
that my *i* is for Christ;	Phil 1.13
Others suffered . . chains and *i*.	Heb 11.36
beatings, *i*, tumults, labors,	2Cor 6.5
greater labors, far more *i*,	11.23

IMPULSE

no prophecy . . by the *i* of man,	2Pet 1.21

IMPURITY

God gave them up . . to *i*, to	Rom 1.24
have not repented of the *i*,	2Cor 12.21

IMPUTE — S

Let not the king *i* anything	1Sam 22.15
to whom the LORD *i* no iniquity,	Ps 32.2

INCENSE

make an altar to burn *i* upon;	Ex 30.1
make an *i* blended as by the	30.35
altar of *i* of acacia wood;	37.25
censer, and put *i* upon it,	Num 16.17
still sacrificed and burned *i*	2Ki 14.4
who burned *i* to Baal, to	23.5
to burn *i* on the altar of	2Chr 26.16
Let my prayer be counted as *i*	Ps 141.2
gods to whom they burn *i*,	Jer 11.12
smoke of . . cloud of *i* went up.	Ezek 8.11
in every place *i* is offered	Mal 1.11
enter the temple . . and burn *i*.	Lk 1.9

INCITED

and *i* David to number Israel.	1Chr 21.1
the Jews *i* the devout women	Acts 13.50

INCLINE — ING

that he may *i* our hearts	1Ki 8.58
I my heart to thy testimonies,	Ps 119.36
O my God, *i* thy ear and hear;	Dan 9.18
i your heart to understanding;	Prov 2.2

INCREASE — S — D (v)

Thou wilt *i* my honor, and	Ps 71.21
righteous man . . *i* in learning.	Prov 9.9
When goods *i*, they *i* who eat	Ecc 5.11
He must *i*, . . I must decrease."	Jn 3.30
may the Lord make you *i*	1Thess 3.12
speech *i* persuasiveness.	Prov 16.21
were fruitful and *i* greatly;	Ex 1.7
But thou hast *i* the nation,	Isa 26.15
Jesus *i* in wisdom and . . stature,	Lk 2.52
they *i* in numbers daily.	Acts 16.5

INCREASE (n)

May the LORD give you *i*,	Ps 115.14
Of the *i* of his government	Isa 9.7
the earth shall yield its *i*,	Ezek 34.27

INCREDIBLE
Why is it thought *i* by any   Acts 26.8

INDICATE — S
not to *i* the charges against   Acts 25.27
By this the Holy Spirit *i*   Heb 9.8

INDICTMENT
Oh, that I had the *i* written   Job 31.35
Lord has an *i* against Judah,   Hos 12.2

INDIGNANT
disciples saw it, they were *i*,   Mt 26.8
when Jesus saw it he was *i*,   Mk 10.14
to be *i* at James and John.   10.41

INDISPENSABLE
seem to be weaker are *i*,   1Cor 12.22

INDULGE
who *i* in the lust of defiling   2Pet 2.10

INFANTS
i will be dashed in pieces   Isa 13.16
bringing even *i* to him that   Lk 18.15

INFERIOR
I am not *i* to you. Who does   Job 12.3
not..*i* to these..apostles,   2Cor 12.11

INFIRMITY — IES
you are freed from your *i*."   Lk 13.12
in..illness thou healest all his *i*.   Ps 41.3

INFORMED
things of which you have been *i*.   Lk 1.4
Jews *i* him against Paul;   Acts 25.2
you were once for all fully *i*,   Jude 5

INHABITED
city shall be *i* for ever.   Jer 17.25

INHABITS
lofty One who *i* eternity,   Isa 57.15

INHERIT
'You shall *i* their land,   Lev 20.24
You..*i* the land by lot   Num 33.54
land..you shall *i* by lot,   34.13
the Lord will *i* Judah as his   Zech 2.12
i the kingdom prepared for you   Mt 25.34
must I do to *i* eternal life?"   Mk 10.17
shall I do to *i* eternal life?"   Lk 10.25
shall I do to *i* eternal life?"   18.18
that they should *i* the world,   Rom 4.13

INHERITANCE
have no *i* in their land,   Num 18.20
i to pass to his daughter.   27.8
gives..for an *i* to possess),   Deut 15.4
Levi, shall have no..*i* with Israel;   18.1
cities..for an *i*, you shall save   20.16
possessions as an *i* to his sons,   21.16
are their *i*, as he said   Josh 13.14
forbid that I..give you the *i*   1Ki 21.3
as your portion for an *i*."   1Chr 16.18
Canaan as your portion..an *i*   Ps 105.11
A good man leaves an *i* to   Prov 13.22
An *i* gotten hastily in the   20.21
Our *i* has been turned over to   Lam 5.2
and this land..as your *i*.   Ezek 47.14
thy people..the flock of thy *i*;   Mic 7.14
and to give you the *i* among   Acts 20.32
For if the *i* is by the law,   Gal 3.18
the riches of his glorious *i*   Eph 1.18
receive the *i* as your reward;   Col 3.24
an *i* which is imperishable,   1Pet 1.4

INIQUITY — IES
visiting the *i* of the fathers   Ex 34.7

house with you shall bear *i*   Num 18.1
commits *i*, I will chasten   2Sam 7.14
if I have done *i*, I will do   Job 34.32
If I had cherished *i* in my   Ps 66.18
brought low through their *i*.   Ps 106.43
laid on him the *i* of us all.   Isa 53.6
into captivity for their *i*,   Ezek 39.23
to redeem us from all *i* and   Tit 2.14
for our *i* have risen higher   Ezra 9.6
sins, and blot out all my *i*.   Ps 51.9
The *i* of the wicked ensnare   Prov 5.22
cleanse you from all your *i*,   Ezek 36.33

INJUSTICE
do no *i* in judgment;   Lev 19.15
sows *i* will reap calamity,   Prov 22.8
and the city full of *i*; for   Ezek 9.9
Is there *i* on God's part?   Rom 9.14

INK
wrote..with *i* on the scroll."   Jer 36.18
written not with *i* but with   2Cor 3.3
rather not use paper and *i*,   2Jn 12

INN
no place for them in the *i*.   Lk 2.7
to an *i*, and took care of him.   10.34

INNOCENT — S
wilt thou slay an *i* people?   Gen 20.4
purge the guilt of *i* blood   Deut 19.13
acquitting the *i* and condemning   25.1
and lay not on us *i* blood;   Jonah 1.14
filled Jerusalem with *i* blood,   2Ki 24.4
who that was *i* ever perished?   Job 4.7
thou wilt not hold me *i*.   9.28
the *i* stirs himself up against   17.8
the *i* will divide the silver.   27.17
Job has said, 'I am *i*, and   34.5
I shall be blameless, and *i* of   Ps 19.13
'I am *i*; surely his anger   Jer 2.35
as serpents and *i* as doves.   Mt 10.16
from the blood of *i* Abel to   23.35
"I am *i* of this man's blood;   27.24
"Certainly this man was *i*!"   Lk 23.47
I am *i* of the blood of all   Acts 20.26
filled..with the blood of *i*,   Jer 19.4

INQUIRE — D
she went to *i* of the Lord.   Gen 25.22
come to me to *i* of God;   Ex 18.15
do not *i* about their gods,   Deut 12.30
"Go, *i* of the Lord for me,   2Ki 22.13
"Go, *i* of the Lord for me   2Chr 34.21
"*I* of the Lord for us, for   Jer 21.2
Is it to *i* of me that you come?   Ezek 20.3
My people *i* of a thing of wood,   Hos 4.12
and *i* of God, "Which of us   Judg 20.18
And Saul *i* of God, "Shall I   1Sam 14.37
David *i* of the Lord, "Shall I go   23.2
David *i* of the Lord, "Shall I   2Sam 2.1
David *i* of the Lord, "Shall I   5.19
David *i* of God, "Shall I   1Chr 14.10
should I let myself be *i* of   Ezek 14.3

INSCRIBED
Oh that they were *i* in a book!   Job 19.23
hand was sent,..writing was *i*.   Dan 5.24
is *i* in the book of truth: 10.21

INSCRIPTION
"Whose likeness and *i* is this?"   Mt 22.20
"Whose likeness and *i* is this?"   12.16
the *i* of the charge against him   15.26
There was also an *i* over him,   Lk 23.38

INSPIRED
All scripture is *i* by God 2Tim 3.16

INSPIRES
same God who *i* them all 1Cor 12.6

INSTRUCT — ED
Him will he *i* in the way that Ps 25.12
I will *i* you and teach you 32.8
writings which are able to *i* 2Tim 3.15
who *i* him in the fear of God; 2Chr 26.5
Moses was *i* in all the wisdom Acts 7.22
Moses..was *i* by God, Heb 8.5

INSTRUCTION
He opens their ears to *i*, Job 36.10
Take my *i* instead of silver, Prov 8.10
those who murmur..accept *i.*" Isa 29.24
True *i* was in his mouth, Mal 2.6

INSTRUMENT — S
he is a chosen *i* of mine to Acts 9.15
play loudly on musical *i*, 1Chr 15.16
sing..and invent..*i* of music; Amos 6.5

INSULT — S (v)
brought..a Hebrew to *i* us; Gen 39.14
mocks the poor *i* his Maker; Prov 17.5

INSULT — S (n)
the *i* of those who *i* thee have Ps 69.9
I have broken my heart, so 69.20
content with weaknesses, *i*, 2Cor 12.10

INTEGRITY
you still hold fast your *i*? Job 2.9
and in your teaching show *i*, Tit 2.7

INTERCEDE — S
man sins..who can *i* for him?" 1Sam 2.25
let them *i* with the LORD Jer 27.18
the Spirit himself *i* for us Rom 8.26

INTERCESSION
made *i* for the transgressors. Isa 53.12
he always lives to make *i* for Heb 7.25

INTEREST
Take no *i* from him..but fear Lev 25.36
Let us leave off this *i*. Neh 5.10
not put out his money at *i*, Ps 15.5

INTERMEDIARY
an *i* implies more than one; Gal 3.20

INTERPRET — ED
i..appearance of earth..sky: Lk 12.56
each in turn; and let one *i*. 1Cor 14.27
he *i*..concerning himself. Lk 24.27

INTERPRETATION
dream, and we will show the *i.*" Dan 2.4
we will tell the king its *i*. 2.36
O Belteshazzar, declare the *i* 4.18
Daniel..he will show the *i.*" 5.12
no prophecy..one's own *i*, 2Pet 1.20

INTERPRETER
there was an *i* between them. Gen 42.23

INVISIBLE
his *i* nature,..his eternal Rom 1.20
the image of the *i* God, Col 1.15
King..*i*, the only God, 1Tim 1.17

INVITED
Jesus also was *i* to..marriage, Jn 2.2
who are *i* to the marriage Rev 19.9

INVOKE — D
let the king *i* the LORD 2Sam 14.11
my name shall no more be *i* by Jer 44.26

IRON
Canaanites..chariots of *i*, Josh 17.16
a stick,..made the *i* float. 2Ki 6.6
labor with saws and *i* picks 1Chr 20.3
his neck..in a collar of *i*; Ps 105.18
I sharpens *i*, and one man Prov 27.17
in their place bars of *i*. Jer 28.13
the *i*, the clay, the bronze, Dan 2.35

IRONSMITH
The *i* fashions it and works Isa 44.12

ISAAC
*His birth foretold, Gen 18.1–15; born,
Gen 21.1–7; offered to God, Gen 22.1–19;
married Rebekah, Gen 24; father of twins,
Gen 25.19–26; dwelt in Gerar, Gen 26.1–
6; Isaac and Abimelech, Gen 26.7–33;
blessed Jacob, Gen 27.1–40; death and
burial, Gen 35.29.*
son..whom Sarah bore him, *I*. Gen 21.3
we,..like *I*, are children of Gal 4.28
By faith *I* invoked future Heb 11.20

ISAIAH
*Called, Isa 6; father of two sons, Isa 7.3;
8.3; prophesied during the reign of Uzziah,
Jotham, Ahaz and Hezekiah, Isa 1.1;
counselled Ahaz, Isa 7; counselled Hezekiah, 2Ki 19—20 (Isa 37—39).*
spoken of by the prophet *I* Mt 3.3
Well did *I* prophesy of you, 15.7
the book of the prophet *I*. Lk 4.17
he was reading the prophet *I*. Acts 8.28

ISHMAEL
you shall call his name *I*; Gen 16.11
"O that *I* might live 17.18
the descendants of *I*, 25.12

ISRAEL
name..no more..Jacob, but *I*, Gen 32.28
sons of *I* who came to Egypt Ex 1.1
I is my first-born son, 4.22
he pursued the people of *I* 14.8
after the people of *I* had gone 19.1
And the men of *I* did as Joshua Josh 4.8
Samuel judged the people of *I* 1Sam 7.6
Solomon was king over all *I*, 1Ki 4.1
So *I* has been in rebellion 12.19
"As the LORD..God of *I* lives, 17.1
anointed king over all *I*, 1Chr 14.8
passover to the..God of *I*. 2Chr 30.1
some of the people of *I*, Ezra 7.7
Redeem *I*, O God, out of all Ps 25.22
He made known..his acts to..*I*. 103.7
but *I* does not know, my people Isa 1.3
who will govern my people *I*.' " Mt 2.6
King of *I*; let him come down 27.42
for the consolation of *I*, and Lk 2.25
restore the kingdom to *I*?" Acts 1.6
so all *I* will be saved; as Rom 11.26
from the commonwealth of *I*, Eph 2.12
new covenant with..house of *I* Heb 8.8
tribes of the sons of *I* were Rev 21.12

ISSACHAR
Leah..called his name *I*. Gen 30.18
I is a strong ass, crouching 49.14
The sons of *I* according Num 26.23
thousand of the tribe of *I*, Rev 7.7

IVORY
also made a great *i* throne, 1Ki 10.18

IVORY (cont.)
the *i* house which he built,   1Ki 22.39
From *i* palaces. . instruments   Ps 45.8
the houses of *i* shall perish,   Amos 3.15
Woe to those. . upon beds of *i*,   6.4

J

JABBOK
crossed the ford of the *J*.   Gen 32.22
far over as the river *J*,   Deut 3.16
the river *J*, the boundary of   Josh 12.2

JACOB (ISRAEL)
*Born, Gen 25.19–26; obtained Esau's
birthright, Gen 25.27–34; received Isaac's
blessing, Gen 27.1–29; fled from Esau,
Gen 27.41—28.5; dream at Bethel and his
vow, Gen 28.10–22; served Laban for
Rachel and Leah, Gen 29.1–30; dealings
with Laban, Gen 30.25–43; departure
from Paddan-aram, Gen 31; wrestled at
Peniel, Gen 32.24–32; reconciled with
Esau, Gen 33.1–16; blessed by God at
Bethel, Gen 35.1–15; went down to Egypt,
Gen 46—47; blessed Ephraim and Manasseh, Gen 48; blessed his own sons, Gen
49.1–27; death and burial, Gen 49.28—
50.14.*

star. . come forth out of *J*,   Num 24.17
(*J* fled to the land of Aram,   Hos 12.12
and *J* in the kingdom of heaven,   Mt 8.11
written, "*J* I loved, but Esau   Rom 9.13
By faith *J*, when dying,   Heb 11.21
J well was there, and so Jesus   Jn 4.6

JAIRUS
one of. . rulers of. . synagogue, *J*   Mk 5.22
there came a man named *J*,   Lk 8.41

JAMES
he saw two other brothers, *J*   Mt 4.21
J the son of Alphaeus, and   10.3
Matthew, *J*. . son of Alphaeus   Acts 1.13
Then he appeared to *J*, then   1Cor 15.7

JAPHETH
God enlarge *J*, and let   Gen 9.27

JAR — S
"The *j* of meal shall not be   1Ki 17.14
a man carrying a *j* of water   Mk 14.13
a man carrying a *j* of water   Lk 22.10
So the woman left her water *j*,   Jn 4.28
empty *j*, with torches inside   Judg 7.16

JAWBONE
found a fresh *j* of an ass,   Judg 15.15

JEALOUS
his brothers were *j* of him,   Gen 37.11
"Are you *j* for my sake?   Num 11.29
he was *j* for his God,   25.13
devouring fire, a *j* God.   Deut 4.24
I. . your God am a *j* God,   5.9
LORD your God. . is a *j* God;   6.15
he is a *j* God; he will not   Josh 24.19
Will. . *j* wrath burn like fire?   Ps 79.5
When men. . were *j* of Moses   106.16
I will be *j* for my holy name.   Ezek 39.25
LORD became *j* for his land,   Joel 2.18
LORD is a *j* God and avenging   Nah 1.2
j for Zion with great jealousy,   Zech 8.2
the patriarchs, *j* of Joseph,   Acts 7.9
Gentiles,. . to make Israel *j*.   Rom 11.11
love is not *j* or boastful;   1Cor 13.4

JEALOUSY
if the spirit of *j* comes upon   Num 5.14
They have stirred me to *j*   Deut 32.21
provoked. . to *j* with their sins   1Ki 14.22
For *j* makes a man furious,   Prov 6.34
j is cruel as the grave. Its   Sol 8.6
j of Ephraim shall depart,   Isa 11.13
I, the LORD,. . spoken in my *j*,   Ezek 5.13
the seat of the image of *j*,   8.3
while there is *j* and strife   1Cor 3.3
I feel a divine *j* for you,   2Cor 11.2

JEHOSHAPHAT
and *J* his son reigned in his   1Ki 15.24
But *J* said, "Is there not   22.7
the Me-unites, came against *J*   2Chr 20.1
the realm of *J* was quiet,   20.30
J slept with his fathers,   21.1
down to the valley of *J*,   Joel 3.2

JEPHTHAH
J. . was a mighty warrior   Judg 11.1
J made a vow to the LORD,   11.30
to *J*, "Why did you cross   12.1
LORD sent. . *J*, and Samuel   1Sam 12.11
Samson, *J*, of David and   Heb 11.32

JEREMIAH
*Called, Jer 1.1–10; vision of almond rod
and boiling pot, Jer 1.11–19; sign of the
waistcloth, Jer 13.1–11; sign of the potter's
vessel, Jer 18; sign of the earthen flask,
Jer 19; put in stocks, Jer 20.1–6; sign
of the basket of figs, Jer 24; his life
threatened, Jer 26; sign of purchase of
field, Jer 32.6–44; prophesied to Rechab-
ites, Jer 35; wrote prophecies, Jer 36;
imprisoned, Jer 32.1–5; 37.11—38.28;
released, Jer 39.11–14; 40.1–6; taken into
Egypt, Jer 43.1–7.*

others say Elijah,. . others *J*   Mt 16.14

JERICHO
view the land, especially *J*."   Josh 2.1
I have given into your hand *J*,   6.2
Hiel of Bethel built *J*;   1Ki 16.34
leaving *J* with his disciples   Mk 10.46
By faith the walls of *J* fell   Heb 11.30

JEROBOAM
J. . also lifted up his hand   1Ki 11.26
when *J* the son of Nebat heard   12.2
Then *J* built Shechem in the   12.25
J was standing by the altar   13.1
Abijah. . son of *J* fell sick.   14.1
J reigned. . twenty-two years;   14.20
war between Rehoboam and *J*   14.30
Nadab the son of *J* began to   15.25
walked in. . way of *J* and in his sin   15.34
J the son of Joash, king of   2Ki 14.23
the rest of the acts of *J*,   14.28
J slept with his fathers,   14.29
in the days of *J* the son of   Hos 1.1
priest of Bethel sent to *J*   Amos 7.10

JERUSALEM
opposite Jebus (that is, *J*).   Judg 19.10
at *J* he reigned over all   2Sam 5.5
"In *J* will I put my name."   2Ki 21.4
to *J*, with harps and lyres   2Chr 20.28
broke down the wall of *J*,   36.19
build him a house at *J*,   36.23
in the second year. . at *J*,   Ezra 3.8
pleasure; rebuild. . walls of *J*,   Ps 51.18
Pray for the peace of *J*! "May   122.6

JERUSALEM (cont.)
If I forget you, O J, let my	Ps 137.5
LORD of hosts will protect J;	Isa 31.5
O J, herald of good tidings,	40.9
"O J, J, killing the prophets	Mt 23.37
witnesses in J and in..Judea	Acts 1.8
appointed to go up to J to	15.2
poor among the saints at J;	Rom 15.26
But the J above is free,	Gal 4.26
city of..God, the heavenly J,	Heb 12.22
new J, coming down out of	Rev 21.2

JESUS
His birth foretold, Lk 1.26–38; born, Mt 1.18–25; Lk 2.1–7; circumcised, Lk 2.21; presented in the temple, Lk 2. 22–38; visited by the wise men, Mt 2.1–12; fled to Egypt, Mt 2.13–18; brought to Nazareth, Mt 2.19–23 (Lk 2.39); boyhood visit to Jerusalem, Lk 2.41–50; his brothers and sisters, Mt 13.55–56 (Mk 6.3); baptized, Mt 3.13–17 (Mk 1.9–11; Lk 3.21–22; Jn 1.31–34); tempted by the devil, Mt 4.1–11 (Mk 1.12–13; Lk 4.1–13); called his disciples, Mt 4.18–22 (Mk 1.16–20; Lk 5.1–11); Mt 9.9 (Mk 2.13–14; Lk 5.27–28); Jn 1.35–51; commissioned the twelve, Mt 10.1–4 (Mk 3.13–19; Lk 6.12–16); Sermon on the Mount, Mt 5—7 (Lk 6.17–49); sent out disciples, Mt 9.35—11.1 (Mk 6.7–13; Lk 9.1–6; 10.1–24); foretold his death and resurrection, Mt 16.21–28 (Mk 8.31–38; Lk 9.22–27); Mt 17.22–23 (Mk 9.30–32; Lk 9.43–45); Mt 20.17–28 (Mk 10.32–45; Lk 18.31–34); transfigured, Mt 17.1–8 (Mk 9.2–8; Lk 9.28–36); triumphal entry into Jerusalem, Mt 21.1–11 (Mk 11.1–11; Lk 19.29–44; Jn 12.12–19); instituted the Lord's supper, Mt 26.26–29 (Mk 14.22–25; Lk 22.17–20; 1Cor 11.23–26); betrayed, arrested, and forsaken, Mt 26.47–57 (Mk 14.43–53; Lk 22.47–54; Jn 18.2–13); crucified, Mt 27.31–56 (Mk 15.20–41; Lk 23.26–49; Jn 19.16–30); appeared after his resurrection, Mt 28.9–20 (Mk 16.9–18n; Lk 24.13–49; Jn 20.11–31); Acts 1.3–8; 1Cor 15.5–7; ascended to heaven, Lk 24.50–53 (Mk 16.19n); Acts 1.9–11.

JETHRO
flock of his father-in-law, J	Ex 3.1
Moses went back to J	4.18
J, the priest of Midian,	18.1
J, Moses' father-in-law,	18.12

JEW — S
there was a J in Susa the	Est 2.5
the J who came up from you	Ezra 4.12
asked them concerning the J	Neh 1.2
in the presence of all the J	Jer 32.12
and maliciously accused the J.	Dan 3.8
"Where is he..born king of..J?	Mt 2.2
"Are you the King of the J?"	27.11
Jesus the King of the J."	27.37
J were..seeking to stone you,	Jn 11.8
officers of the J seized Jesus	18.12
testifying to the J that	Acts 18.5
heard..both J and Greeks.	19.10
both J and Greeks, are under	Rom 3.9
called, not from the J only	9.24
For J demand signs and Greeks	1Cor 1.22

To the J I became a J,	9.20
Give no offense to J or to	10.32

JEWEL — S
the..j of a gentle..spirit,	1Pet 3.4
for wisdom is better than j,	Prov 8.11

JEWELRY
servant brought forth j	Gen 24.53
j of silver and of gold,	Ex 3.22

JEZREEL
Its territory included J,	Josh 19.18
vineyard in J, beside the	1Ki 21.1
punish..Jehu for..blood of J,	Hos 1.4
oil, and they shall answer J;	2.22

JOAB
Murdered Abner, 2Sam 3.22–30; set Uriah in the forefront, 2Sam 11.6–21; reconciled David and Absalom, 2Sam 14.28–33; killed Absalom, 2Sam 18.9–17; pursued Sheba and slew Amasa, 2Sam 20.4–22; put to death by Solomon, 1Ki 2.28–34.

JOB
whose name was J; and that	Job 1.1
you considered my servant J,	2.3
go to my servant J, and offer	42.8
LORD restored..fortunes of J,	42.10
And J died, an old man,	42.17
even if..Noah, Daniel, and J	Ezek 14.14
heard of..steadfastness of J,	Jas 5.11

JOEL
word of the LORD..came to J,	Joel 1.1
was spoken by the prophet J:	Acts 2.16

JOHN (the Apostle)
Called, Mt 4.21 (Mk 1.19; Lk 5.10); sent out with the twelve, Mt 10.2 (Mk 3.17); desire for revenge rebuked, Lk 9.51–56; selfish request rejected, Mt 20.20–24 (Mk 10.35–41); healed and preached in the temple, Acts 3.1—4.22.

JOHN (the Baptist)
Birth foretold, Lk 1.5–25; born, Lk 1.57–66; preached and baptized, Mt 3.1–12 (Mk 1.4–11; Lk 3.1–17; Jn 1.6–8, 19–28); imprisoned, Mt 14.3–4 (Mk 6.17–18; Lk 3.19–20); sent messengers to Jesus, Mt 11.1–6 (Lk 7.18–23); commended by Jesus, Mt 11.7–15 (Lk 7.24–35); beheaded and buried, Mt 14.6–12 (Mk 6.17–29).

JOIN — ED
many shall j..with flattery;	Dan 11.34
nations shall j..to the LORD	Zech 2.11
people j in the covenant,	2Ki 23.3
leave..and be j to his wife,	Mt 19.5
What..God has j together,	19.6
mother and be j to his wife,	Mk 10.7
What..God has j together,	10.9

JONAH
he spoke by his servant J	2Ki 14.25
word of the LORD came to J	Jonah 1.1
Then J prayed to the LORD	2.1
word of the LORD came to J	3.1
it displeased J exceedingly,	4.1
as J was three days and three	Mt 12.40
no sign..except the sign of J."	16.4
J became a sign to..Ninevah,	Lk 11.30
repented at the preaching of J,	11.32

JONATHAN (Son of Saul)
Smote the Philistine garrison, 1Sam 13.2–

JONATHAN (Son of Saul) (cont.)
4; 14.1–15; unknowingly transgressed
Saul's oath, 1Sam 14.24–30; rescued by the
people, 1Sam 14.36–46; made a covenant
with David, 1Sam 18.1–5; friendship with
David, 1Sam 20; killed by the Philistines,
1Sam 31.2; mourned by David, 2Sam
1.17–27; covenant with him remembered by
David, 2Sam 9.

JOPPA
to you in rafts by sea to J,   2Chr 2.16
went. . to J and found a ship   Jonah 1.3
at J a disciple. . Tabitha,   Acts 9.36
send men to J, and bring   10.5

JORDAN
J valley was well watered   Gen 13.10
all Israel beyond the J   Deut 1.1
I should not cross the J,   4.21
finished passing over the J,   Josh 4.1
king came back to the J;   2Sam 19.15
wash in the J seven times,   2Ki 5.10
confident though J rushes   Job 40.23
from the land of J and of   Ps 42.6
Jesus came from Galilee to the J   Mt 3.1
they were baptized. . in the. . J, 3.6
region of Judea beyond the J;   19.1
who was with you beyond the J,   Jn 3.26
across the J to the place   10.40

JOSEPH (Husband of Mary, Jesus' mother)
Betrothed to Mary, Mk 1.18 (Lk 1.27);
instructed by an angel, Mt 1.19–21; went
to Bethlehem, Lk 2.4; fled into Egypt, Mt
2.13–15; returned to Nazareth, Mt 2.
19–23.

JOSEPH (of Arimathea)
man from Arimathea, named J, Mt 27.57
After this J of Arimathea,   Jn 19.38

JOSEPH (Son of Jacob)
Born, Gen 30.22–24; incurred jealousy by
his dreams, Gen 37.5–11; sold into Egypt,
Gen 37.12–28; refused Potiphar's wife,
Gen 39.1–18; imprisoned, Gen 39.19–23;
interpreted the prisoners' dreams, Gen 40;
interpreted Pharaoh's dreams, Gen 41.1–
36; made ruler over Egypt, Gen 41.37–49,
53–57; married, had two sons, Gen 41.50–
52; met his brothers, Gen 42–43; made
himself known to them, Gen 45; saw his
father again, Gen 46.28–34; died, Gen 50.
22–26; buried in Shechem, Josh 24.32.

And of J he said, "Blessed   Deut 33.13
sent a man ahead of them, J,   Ps 105.17
By faith J, at. . end of his life, Heb 11.22

JOSHUA (Priest, son of Jehozadak)
and to J the son of Jehozadak, Hag 1.1
and to J the son of Jehozadak, 2.2
he showed me J the high priest Zech 3.1
set it upon the head of J,   6.11

JOSHUA (Son of Nun)
Defeated the Amalekites, Ex 17.8–13;
in charge of the place of worship, Ex 33.11;
sent with the spies, Num 13.1–16; 14.6–9;
chosen to succeed Moses, Num 27.18–23;
Deut 3.28; commissioned by Moses, Deut
31.23; 34.9; encouraged by the LORD,
Josh 1.1–9; sent spies to Jericho, Josh 2;
passed over Jordan, Josh 3; captured
Jericho, Josh 6; captured Ai, Josh 7–8;
warred against the kings, Josh 10–12;

allotted the land, Josh 13.1–22.8; charged
the people, Josh 23.1–24.24; made a covenant, Josh 24.25–27; death and burial,
Josh 24.29–30.

JOSIAH
born to the house of David, J   1Ki 13.2
made J his son king in his   2Ki 21.24
J was eight years old when   22.1
year of King J this passover   23.23
J kept a passover to the   2Chr 35.1

JOY
to Jerusalem with j, for   2Chr 20.27
j of the LORD is. . strength."   Neh 8.10
Thou hast put more j in my   Ps 4.7
to God my exceeding j; . . praise 43.4
Shout to God with. . songs of j! 47.1
works of thy hands I sing for j. 92.4
let the hills sing for j   98.8
no stranger shares its j.   Prov 14.10
rejoice. . with j at the harvest, Isa 9.3
With j you will draw water   12.3
shall obtain j and gladness,   35.10
j and gladness. . found in her,   51.3
"For you shall go out in j,   55.12
majestic. . a j from age to age. 60.15
you will have j and gladness,   Lk 1.14
good news of a great j which   2.10
this j of mine is now full.   Jn 3.29
that my j may be in you, and   15.11
your sorrow will turn into j.   16.20
they may have my j fulfilled   17.13
there was much j in that city.   Acts 8.8
great j to all the brethren.   15.3
and j in the Holy Spirit;   Rom 14.17
j and peace in believing,   15.13
work with you for your j,   2Cor 1.24
rejoiced. . at the j of Titus,   7.13
I have derived much j and   Philem 7
writing this that our j may   1Jn 1.4

JUBILEE
it shall be a j for you,   Lev 25.10
when the j of. . Israel comes,   Num 36.4

JUDAH (Son of Jacob)
Born, Gen 29.35; saved Joseph's life, Gen
37.26–28; Judah and Tamar, Gen 38;
pleaded for Benjamin, Gen 44.14–34;
blessed by Jacob, Gen 49.8–12.
Tribe of Judah: blessed by Moses, Deut
33.7.

And the LORD was with J,   Judg 1.19
Israel and J loved David;   1Sam 18.16
Israel and J thirty-three years. 2Sam 5.5
but he chose the tribe of J,   Ps 78.68
men of J, judge, I pray you,   Isa 5.3
fear not; say to the cities of J, 40.9
and her false sister J saw it.   Jer 3.7
year of Zedekiah king of J,   39.1
J has gone into exile because   Lam 1.3
I restore the fortunes of J   Joel 3.1

JUDAISM
converts to J followed Paul   Acts 13.43
head of my former life in J,   Gal 1.13

JUDAS (Brother of James)
brother of James and Joses and J Mk 6.3

JUDAS ISCARIOT
and J, who betrayed him.   Mt 10.4
J. ., went to the chief priests   26.14
J, who betrayed him, said,   26.25
When J. . saw he was condemned,   27.3

JUDAS ISCARIOT (cont.)

and J.., who betrayed him.	Mk 3.19
Then Satan entered into J	Lk 22.3
"J, would you betray the Son	22.48
He spoke of J the son of Simon	Jn 6.71
But J.., one of his disciples	12.4
put it into the heart of J..,	13.2
concerning J who was guide	Acts 1.16

JUDE

J, a servant of Jesus Christ	Jude 1

JUDEA

Jesus was born in Bethlehem of J	Mt 2.1
preaching in the wilderness of J,	3.1
let those who are in J flee	Lk 21.21
"Men of J and all who dwell	Acts 2.14

JUDGE — S — ST — D (v)

God..j between us."	Gen 31.53
Moses sat to j the people,	Ex 18.13
congregation shall j between	Num 35.24
and j righteously between	Deut 1.16
The LORD will j the ends of	1Sam 2.10
May the LORD j between me	24.12
he comes to j the earth.	1Chr 16.33
for you j not for man but	2Chr 19.6
May he j..with righteousness,	Ps 72.2
set time..I will j with equity.	75.2
LORD..comes to j the earth.	96.13
He shall j between the nations,	Isa 2.4
with righteousness he shall j	11.4
j you according to your ways;	Ezek 7.3
"J not, that you be not j.	Mt 7.1
"J not, and you will not be j;	Lk 6.37
why..not j..what is right:	12.57
Do not j by appearances,	Jn 7.24
"Does our law j a man without	7.51
You j according to the flesh,	8.15
day on which he will j the	Acts 17.31
no excuse,..when you j another;	Rom 2.1
how could God j the world?	3.6
church whom you are to j?	1Cor 5.12
the saints will j the world?	6.2
know that we are to j angels?	6.3
ready to j..living and..dead.	1Pet 4.5
how long before thou wilt j	Rev 6.10
j the world with righteousness,	Ps 9.8
is a God who j on earth."	58.11
king j the people with equity	Prov 29.14
when..God j the secrets of men	Rom 2.16
in righteousness he j and	Rev 19.11
O LORD..who j righteously,	Jer 11.20
conduct and their deeds I j	Ezek 36.19
small thing..I..j by you	1Cor 4.3
But if we j ourselves truly,	11.31
be j under the law of liberty.	Jas 2.12
dead..j by what was written	Rev 20.12

JUDGE — S (n)

Shall not the J of all	Gen 18.25
he would play the j!	19.9
you a prince and a j over us?	Ex 2.14
LORD, the J, decide this day	Judg 11.27
lest he drag you to the j,	Lk 12.58
a j who neither feared God	18.2
'Who made you..a j over us?	Acts 7.27
LORD raised up j for them,	Judg 2.18

JUDGMENT — S

I will bring j on the nation	Gen 15.14
my God; thou hast appointed a j.	Ps 7.6
but it is God who executes j,	75.7
God will bring you into j.	Ecc 11.9
the rash will have good j,	Isa 32.4

he is entering into j with	Jer 25.31
Thus far is the j on Moab.	48.47
my four sore acts of j,	Ezek 14.21
I entered into j with your fathers	20.36
and j was given for the saints	Dan 7.22
my j goes forth as the light.	Hos 6.5
I will enter into j with them	Joel 3.2
kills shall be liable to j.'	Mt 5.21
Nineveh will arise at.the j	Lk 11.32
has given all j to the Son,	Jn 5.22
Now is the j of this world,	12.31
of righteousness and of j:	16.8
the j following one trespass	Rom 5.16
let not him who abstains pass j	14.3
all stand before the j seat	14.10
Why..pass j on your brother?	14.10
and drinks j upon himself.	1Cor 11.29
all appear before the j seat	2Cor 5.10
let no one pass j on you in	Col 2.16
to execute j on all, and to	Jude 15
God has given j for you	Rev 18.20
I will utter my j against them,	Jer 1.16
I execute j on you in anger	Ezek 5.15
Render true j, show kindness	Zech 7.9
How unsearchable are his j	Rom 11.33

JUST

You shall have j balances,	Lev 19.36
j weight you shall have,	Deut 25.15
j and right is he.	32.4
God of Israel, thou art j,	Ezra 9.15
Yet thou hast been j in all	Neh 9.33
can a man be j before God?	Job 9.2
A j balance and scales are	Prov 16.11
way of the Lord is not j.'	Ezek 18.25
"You shall have j balances,	45.10
husband Joseph, being a j man	Mt 1.19
rain on the j and on the unjust.	5.45
in order that the j requirement	Rom 8.4
law is not laid down for the j	1Tim 1.9
heard..angel..say, "J art thou	Rev 16.5

JUSTICE

Almighty will not pervert j.	Job 34.12
j to the weak and..fatherless;	Ps 82.3
receive instruction in..j,	Prov 1.3
in..place of j,..wickedness.	Ecc 3.16
Thus says the LORD: "Keep j,	Isa 56.1
look for j, but there is none;	59.11
let j roll down like waters,	Amos 5.24
and j never goes forth.	Hab 1.4
as he argued about j and	Acts 24.25
serves to show the j of God,	Rom 3.5

JUSTIFICATION

put to death..raised for our j.	Rom 4.25
if j were through the law,	Gal 2.21

JUSTIFY — IES — IED

desiring to j himself, said	Lk 10.29
He who j the wicked and he	Prov 17.15
he j him who has faith in	Rom 3.26
thou art j in thy sentence	Ps 51.4
by your words you will be j,	Mt 12.37
and the tax collectors j God,	Lk 7.29
this man..j rather than the other;	18.14
no human being will be j in	Rom 3.20
they are j by his grace as a gift,	3.24
For if Abraham was j by works,	4.2
you were j in the name of	1Cor 6.11
a man is not j by works of	Gal 2.16
that we might be j by faith.	3.24
that we might be j by his grace	Tit 3.7
Abraham our father j by works,	Jas 2.21

K

KADESH
Enmishpat (that is, *K*),   Gen 14.7
Moses sent messengers from *K* Num 20.14
LORD shakes..wilderness of *K*.   Ps 29.8

KADESH-BARNEA
sent..from *K* to see the land.   Num 32.8
time from..leaving *K* until   Deut 2.14
defeated them from *K* to   Josh 10.41

KEEP — S — ING
k alive for you many survivors.   Gen 45.7
you shall *k* this service   Ex 13.5
The LORD bless you and *k* you: Num 6.24
K them and do them; for that   Deut 4.6
and to *k* his commandments,   Josh 22.5
and *k* my commandments and   2Ki 17.13
"*K* the passover to the LORD   23.21
we *k* the charge of the LORD   2Chr 13.11
to *k* the passover to the LORD   30.1
for those who *k* his covenant   Ps 25.10
I remember..and *k* thy law.   119.55
LORD will *k* you from all evil;   121.7
If your sons *k* my covenant   132.12
K your heart with..vigilance;   Prov 4.23
eyes of the LORD *k* watch   22.12
For Zion's sake..not *k* silent,   Isa 62.1
enter life, *k*..commandments." Mt 19.17
Father, *k* them in thy name,   Jn 17.11
uncircumcised but *k* the law   Rom 2.27
will *k* your hearts and..minds Phil 4.7
k yourselves in the love of God; Jude 21
able to *k* you from falling   24
He who *k* his mouth and his Prov 21.23
who *k* the law is a wise son,   28.7
blessed is he who *k* the law.   29.18
who *k* my works until the end, Rev 2.26
k all the words of this law   Deut 17.19

KEEPER
am I my brother's *k*?"   Gen 4.9
I, the LORD, am its *k*; every   Isa 27.3

KEPT
And they *k* the passover   Num 9.5
the LORD has *k* me alive,   Josh 14.10
have you not *k* your oath   1Ki 2.43
our fathers have not *k* the   2Chr 34.21
precepts to be *k* diligently.   Ps 119.4
k..and given you as a covenant Isa 49.8
race, I have *k* the faith.   2Tim 4.7
and *k* for Jesus Christ: Jude 1
k by him in eternal chains   6
Because you have *k* my word   Rev 3.10

KEY — S
the *k* of the house of David;   Isa 22.22
taken away..*k* of knowledge;   Lk 11.52
one, who has the *k* of David,   Rev 3.7
the *k* of the bottomless pit   20.1
give you the *k* of the kingdom Mt 16.19
I have..*k* of Death and Hades. Rev 1.18

KILL — S — ED — ING
if..a son, you shall *k* him;   Ex 1.16
Do you mean to *k* me as you   2.14
"You shall not *k*.   20.13
deal thus with me, *k* me   Num 11.15
Now therefore, *k* every male   31.17
"'You shall not *k*.   Deut 5.17
k the body but cannot *k* the soul; Mt 10.28
Jesus said, "You shall not *k*,   19.18
the heir; come, let us *k* him   21.38

and scourge him, and *k* him;   Mk 10.34
do not fear those who *k* the   Lk 12.4
Jews sought all the more to *k* Jn 5.18
'Rise, Peter; *k* and eat.'   Acts 11.7
whoever *k* shall be liable to   Mt 5.21
Cain rose up..and *k* him.   Gen 4.8
he *k* the Egyptian and hid   Ex 2.12
"Have you *k*, and also taken 1Ki 21.19
and be rejected..and be *k*,   Mk 8.31
of the vineyard and *k* him.   Lk 20.15
k by the hands of lawless men. Acts 2.23
Antipas..was *k* among you,   Rev 2.13
"O..Jerusalem, *k* the prophets Mt 23.37

KIN
one of our nearest *k*."   Ruth 2.20
for you are next of *k*."   3.9
this day without next of *k*;   4.14

KIND — LY
who is *k* benefits himself,   Prov 11.17
happy..who is *k* to the poor.   14.21
who is *k* to the poor lends   19.17
and be *k* to one another,   Eph 4.32
as I have dealt *k* with you,   Josh 2.12
not be quarrelsome but *k*   2Tim 2.24

KINDNESS
great *k* in saving my life;   Gen 19.19
made this last *k* greater   Ruth 3.10
him *k* for Jonathan's sake?"   2Sam 9.1
who withholds *k* from a friend Job 6.4
show *k* and mercy each to his   Zech 7.9
God's *k* is meant to lead you   Rom 2.4
the *k* and..severity of God: 11.22
goodness and loving *k* of God Tit 3.4
tasted the *k* of the Lord.   1Pet 2.3

KING — S — 'S
the *k* of Egypt died.   Ex 2.23
'I will set a *k* over me,   Deut 17.14
there was no *k* in Israel.   Judg 18.1
there was no *k* in Israel;   21.25
will give strength to his *k*,   1Sam 2.10
appoint for us a *k* to govern   8.5
shouted, "Long live the *k*!"   10.24
they made Saul *k* before the LORD 11.15
LORD your God was your *k*.   12.12
you shall be *k* over Israel,   23.17
about bringing the *k* back?"   2Sam19.10
they proclaimed him *k*, and   2Ki 11.12
he is *k* over..sons of pride." Job 41.34
"I have set my *k* on Zion, my   Ps 2.6
Hearken..sound of my cry, my *K*   5.2
The LORD is *k* for ever and   10.16
the *K* of glory may come in.   24.7
Thou art my *K* and my God, who   44.4
Give the *k* thy justice, O God,   72.1
let..Zion rejoice in their *K*!   149.2
the word of the *k* is supreme, Ecc 8.4
Woe..when your *k* is a child,   10.16
k will reign in righteousness, Isa 32.1
Creator of Israel, your *K*."   43.15
Who would not fear thee, O *K*   Jer 10.7
k who sits on..throne of David,   29.16
David their *k*, I will raise up   30.9
sleep and not wake, says the *K*,   51.57
the Chaldeans said to the *k*,   Dan 2.4
You, O *k*, the *k* of *k*, to whom 2.37
their God, and David their *k*; Hos 3.5
Their *k* will pass on before   Mic 2.13
Lo, your *k* comes to you;   Zech 9.9
a *k* who gave a marriage feast Mt 22.2
the *k* will say to those at his   25.34
"Blessed is the *K* who comes   Lk 19.38

KING — S — 'S (cont.)

"Are you the K of the Jews?" Lk 23.3
You are the K of Israel!" Jn 1.49
to make him k, Jesus withdrew 6.15
Lord, even the K of Israel!" 12.13
"You say that I am a k. For 18.37
to the Jews, "Here is your K!" 19.14
k who had not known Joseph. Acts 7.18
there is another k, Jesus." 17.7
I am accused by Jews, O k! 26.7
To the K of ages, immortal, 1Tim 1.17
as k..the angel of the..pit; Rev 9.11
name inscribed, K of k and Lord 19.16
fear..k of..earth thy glory. Ps 102.15
By me k reign, and rulers Prov 8.15
It is not for k, O Lemuel, 31.4
four great beasts are four k Dan 7.17
Without us you have become k! 1Cor 4.8
for k and all who are in high 1Tim 2.2
way for the k from the east. Rev 16.12
he brought out the k son, 2Chr 23.11
The k heart is a stream of Prov 21.1

KINGDOM — S

you shall be to me a k of priests Ex 19.6
about the matter of the k, 1Sam 10.16
your k shall not continue; 13.14
I will establish his k. 2Sam 7.12
and I will establish his k. 1Chr 17.11
thine is the k, O Lord, 29.11
come to the k for such a time Est 4.14
glorious splendor of thy k. Ps 145.12
throne of David, and..his k, Isa 9.7
His k is an everlasting k, Dan 4.3
the Most High rules the k of 4.17
The k has departed from you, 4.31
the k and the dominion and 7.27
k shall be broken and divided 11.4
the k shall be the Lord's. Obad 1.21
the k of heaven is at hand." Mt 3.2
"Repent, for the k of heaven 4.17
preaching the gospel of the k 4.23
But seek first his k and his 6.33
and Jacob in the k of heaven, 8.11
'The k of heaven is at hand.' 10.7
never enter the k of heaven. 18.3
to such belongs the k of heaven." 19.14
k of God will be taken away 21.43
and k against k and there will 24.7
inherit the k prepared for you 25.34
with you in my Father's k." 26.29
k of God is at hand; repent, Mk 1.15
"The k of God is as if a man 4.26
before they see the k of God 9.1
Blessed is the k of our father 11.10
"You are not far from the k 12.34
nation, and k against k; 13.8
when I drink it new in the k 14.25
preach the good news of the k Lk 4.43
to know the secrets of the k 8.10
spoke to them of the k of God, 9.11
looks back is fit for the k 9.62
'The k of God has come near 10.9
"Every k divided against itself 11.17
seek his k, and these things 12.31
good news of the k of God 16.16
the k of God is in the midst 17.21
to such belongs the k of God. 18.16
for the sake of the k of God, 18.29
nation, and k against k; 21.10
know that the k of God is near. 21.31
as my Father appointed a k 22.29
he cannot enter the k of God. Jn 3.5

restore the k to Israel?" Acts 1.6
must enter the k of God. 14.22
pleading about the k of God; 19.8
testifying to the k of God 28.23
the k of God does not mean Rom 14.17
the k of God does not consist 1Cor 4.20
will inherit the k of God. 6.10
when he delivers the k to God 15.24
cannot inherit the k of God, 15.50
inheritance in the k of Christ Eph 5.5
worthy of the k of God, 2Thess 1.5
a k that cannot be shaken, Heb 12.28
entrance into the eternal k 2Pet 1.11
made us a k, priests to his God Rev 1.6
"The k of the world has become 11.15
four k..arise from his nation, Dan 8.22
overthrow the throne of k; Hag 2.22
showed him..the k of the world Mt 4.8
the devil..showed him all the k Lk 4.5

KINSMEN

no strife..for we are k. Gen 13.8
You are my k, you are my 2Sam 19.12
not go up..against your k 1Ki 12.24
and my k stand afar off. Ps 38.11

KISHON

The torrent K swept them Judg 5.21

KISS — ES — ED (v)

k.his feet, lest he be angry, Ps 2.12
righteousness and peace will k 85.10
O that you would k me with Sol 1.2
Sacrifice..Men k calves! Hos 13.2
"The one I shall k is the man; Mt 26.48
"The one I shall k is the man; Mk 14.44
drew near to Jesus to k him; Lk 22.47
She seizes him and k him, Prov 7.13
a right answer k the lips. 24.26
Jacob k Rachel, and wept Gen 29.11
Esau ran..and k him, 33.4
he k all his brothers 45.15
Joseph..k..and embraced them. 48.10
Orpah k her mother-in-law, Ruth 1.14
and they k one another, 1Sam 20.41
and the king k Absalom. 2Sam 14.33
and embraced him and k him. Lk 15.20
embraced Paul and k him, Acts 20.37

KISS (n)

You gave me no k, but from Lk 7.45
Greet..with a holy k. Rom 16.16
one another with a holy k. 1Cor 16.20
Greet one another with the k 1Pet 5.14

KNEE — S

"To me every k shall bow, Isa 45.23
every k shall bow to me, Rom 14.11
the k that have not bowed 1Ki 19.18
fell upon my k and spread Ezra 9.5
upon his k three times a day Dan 6.10
Peter..fell down at Jesus' k, Lk 5.8

KNEEL — LT

he made the camels k down Gen 24.11
let us k before the Lord, our Ps 95.6
had k with hands outstretched 1Ki 8.54

KNEW

Thus Joseph k his brothers, Gen 42.8
until he k that..God rules Dan 5.21
I who k you in the wilderness, Hos 13.5
k..the word of the Lord. Zech 11.11
he himself k what was in man. Jn 2.25
for although they k God they Rom 1.21

KNIFE

Abraham. .took. .the *k*.   Gen 22.6
took the *k* to slay his son.   22.10
put a *k* to your throat if   Prov 23.2

KNOCK — ING

k, and it will be opened to you.   Mt 7.7
k, and it will be opened to you.   Lk 11.9
k at the door, saying, 'Lord,   13.25
I stand at the door and *k*;   Rev 3.20
But Peter continued *k*: and   Acts 12.16

KNOW — S — EST — N

king. .who did not *k* Joseph.   Ex 1.8
Egyptians shall *k* that I am the LORD,   7.5
I *k* that the LORD is greater   18.11
k that I am the LORD their God,   29.46
you may *k* that I, the LORD   31.13
may *k* that I made the people   Lev 23.43
shown, that you might *k*   Deut 4.35
k therefore this day,   4.39
who did not *k* the LORD or the   Judg 2.10
all this assembly may *k*   1Sam 17.47
that all. .may *k* thy name and   1Ki 8.43
may *k* that the LORD is God;   8.60
shall *k* that I am the LORD.''   20.13
Solomon my son, *k* the God   1Chr 28.9
of yesterday, and *k* nothing,   Job 8.9
I *k* that my Redeemer lives,   19.25
they do not *k* the light.   24.16
I *k*. .thou wilt bring. .death,   30.23
Make me to *k* thy ways, O LORD;   Ps 25.4
still, and *k* that I am God.   46.10
This I *k*, that God is for me.   56.9
they say, "How can God *k*?   73.11
people who *k* the festal shout,   89.15
K that the LORD is God! It is   100.3
k that this is thy hand;   109.27
not *k* that want will come   Prov 28.22
I *k*. .whatever God does endures   Ecc 3.14
wise man will *k* the time and. .way.   8.5
Israel does not *k*, my people   Isa 1.3
kingdoms. .may *k*. .the LORD.''   37.20
that men may see and *k*, may   41.20
all flesh shall *k*. .your Savior,   49.26
my people shall *k* my name;   52.6
they shall *k* that. .I. .speak;   52.6
call nations that you *k* not,   55.5
my people *k* not the ordinance   Jer 8.7
a heart to *k* that I am the LORD.   24.7
no longer. .saying, '*K* the LORD,'   31.34
will *k* that I am the LORD.''   Ezek 6.14
you shall *k* that I, the LORD,   17.21
will *k* that I am the LORD.''   29.21
they will *k* that I am the LORD.   32.15
they shall *k*. .I am the LORD,   34.27
k that I the LORD sanctify   37.28
shall *k* that I am the LORD,   39.7
Let us *k*, let us press on to *k*   Hos 6.3
they did not *k*. .I healed them.   11.3
whoever is discerning, let him *k*   14.9
You shall *k* that I am in the   Joel 2.27
they do not *k* the thoughts   Mic 4.12
do not let your left hand *k*   Mt 6.3
that you may *k* that the Son of   9.6
and at an hour he does not *k*,   24.50
that you may *k* that the Son   Mk 2.10
you *k* neither the scriptures   12.24
you do not *k* when the master   13.35
I *k* who you are, the Holy One   Lk 4.34
that you may *k*. .the Son of man   5.24
I do not *k* where you come from   13.27
"Teacher, we *k* that you speak   20.21

I *k* my own and my own *k* me,   Jn 10.14
By this all men will *k* that   13.35
eternal life, that they *k* thee   17.3
may *k* that thou hast sent me   17.23
they did not *k* the scripture,   20.9
"Jesus I *k*, and Paul I *k*;   Acts 19.15
Do you not *k*. .you are God's   1Cor 3.16
I want you to *k*, brethren,   10.1
that you have come to *k* God,   Gal 4.9
you may *k* what is the hope   Eph 1.18
that I may *k* him and the   Phil 3.10
I *k* whom I have believed,   2Tim 1.12
shall not teach. .'*K* the Lord,'   Heb 8.11
By this we *k* the spirit of truth   1Jn 4.6
k that you have eternal life.   5.13
We *k* that we are of God, and   5.19
'' 'I *k* your works, your toil   Rev 2.2
he *k* the way that I take;   Job 23.10
LORD *k* the way of the righteous,   Ps 1.6
he *k* our frame; he remembers   103.14
the haughty he *k* from afar.   138.6
your Father *k* what you need   Mt 6.8
Father *k* that you need them   6.32
that day or. .hour no one *k*,   Mk 13.32
God who *k* the heart bore   Acts 15.8
thou *k* thy servant, O Lord   2Sam 7.20
my spirit is faint, thou *k* my   Ps 142.3
But thou, O LORD, *k* me; thou   Jer 12.3
God is *k*, his name is great   Ps 76.1
make himself *k* to. .Egyptians;   Isa 19.21
"You only have I *k* of all the   Amos 3.2
the tree is *k* by its fruit.   Mt 12.33
ordered them not to make him *k*.   Mk 3.12
the only Son,. .has made him *k*.   Jn 1.18
family became *k* to Pharaoh.   Acts 7.13
king who had not *k* Joseph.   7.18
make the word of God fully *k*,   Col 1.25
better. .never to have *k* the   2Pet 2.21
made it *k* by sending his angel   Rev 1.1

KNOWLEDGE

tree of the *k* of good and evil.   Gen 2.9
knows the *k* of the Most High,   Num 24.16
Such *k*. .too wonderful for me;   Ps 139.6
k and discretion to. .youth—   Prov 1.4
k of the Holy One is insight.   9.10
but *k* is easy for a man of   14.6
tongue of. .wise dispenses *k*,   15.2
nor have I *k* of the Holy One.   30.3
go into exile for want of *k*;   Isa 5.13
full of the *k* of the LORD   11.9
fro, and *k* shall increase.''   Dan 12.4
are destroyed for lack of *k*;   Hos 4.6
give *k* of salvation to his people   Lk 1.77
taken away the key of *k*;   11.52
with all speech and all *k*—   1Cor 1.5
"*K*" puffs up, but love builds   8.1
by your *k* this weak man is   8.11
by purity, *k*, forbearance,   2Cor 6.6
come to the *k* of the truth.   1Tim 2.4

KORAH — 'S

Now *K* the son of Izhar, son   Num 16.1
died in the affair of *K*.   16.49
and perish in *K* rebellion.   Jude 11

L

LABAN

brother whose name was *L*;   Gen 24.29
flee to *L* my brother   27.43
to *L*, the son of Bethuel   28.5
"Do you know *L* the son of   29.5

LABAN (cont.)
Jacob said to L, "Send me   Gen 30.25
L did not regard him   31.2
And Jacob outwitted L   31.20
L said, "This heap is a witness   31.48
L arose, and kissed   31.55

LABOR (v)
Six days you shall l,   Deut 5.13
those who build it l in vain.   Ps 127.1
for his hands refuse to l.   Prov 21.25
that peoples l only for fire,   Hab 2.13
Come to me, all who l and   Mt 11.28
Do not l for the food which   Jn 6.27

LABOR — S (n)
"Before she was in l she gave   Isa 66.7
your l is not in vain.   1Cor 15.58
you remember our l and toil,   1Thess 2.9
ceases from his l as God did   Heb 4.10

LABORER — S
Sweet is the sleep of a l,   Ecc 5.12
to hire l for his vineyard.   Mt 20.1
plentiful, but the l are few;   Lk 10.2
wages of the l who mowed your   Jas 5.4

LACK — S — ED
"You l one thing; go, sell   Mk 10.21
"One thing you still l. Sell   Lk 18.22
sandals, did you l anything?"   22.35
gathered little had no l."   2Cor 8.15
he l nothing..that he desires,   Ecc 6.2
you have l nothing.'   Deut 2.7

LAD — S
if the l is not with me?   Gen 44.34
I will send the l, saying,   1Sam 20.21
a l here who has five barley   Jn 6.9
bless the l; and in them   Gen 48.16

LAKE
into the l and were drowned.   Lk 8.33
thrown alive into the l of fire   Rev 19.20
thrown into the l of fire   20.10

LAMB — S
but where is the l   Gen 22.7
l shall be without blemish,   Ex 12.5
One l you shall offer in the   29.39
nothing but one little ewe l,   2Sam 12.3
like a l..to the slaughter.   Isa 53.7
The wolf and the l shall feed   65.25
But I was like a gentle l led   Jer 11.19
"Behold, the L of God, who   Jn 1.29
like that of a l without   1Pet 1.19
I saw a L standing, as though   Rev 5.6
"Worthy is the L who was slain,   5.12
and from the wrath of the L;   6.16
"Salvation belongs..to the L!"   7.10
on Mount Zion stood the L,   14.1
they will make war on the L,   17.14
marriage of the L has come,   19.7
the Bride, the wife of the L."   21.9
the twelve apostles of the L.   21.14
light, and its lamp is the L.   21.23
Go..as l in..midst of wolves.   Lk 10.3
He said to him, "Feed my l."   Jn 21.15

LAME
attack the l and the blind,   2Sam 5.8
then shall the l man leap   Isa 35.6
the l walking, and the blind   Mt 15.31
a man l from birth was being   Acts 3.2

LAMENT — ED
L like a virgin girded with   Joel 1.8

Israel l after the LORD.   1Sam 7.2
And David l..over Saul and   2Sam 1.17

LAMENTATION
most bitter l; for suddenly   Jer 6.26
man, raise a l over Tyre,   Ezek 27.2
Hear this..in l, O..Israel: Amos 5.1

LAMP — S
that a l may be set up   Ex 27.20
l of God had not..gone out,   1Sam 3.3
thou art my l, O LORD,   2Sam 22.29
always have a l before me   1Ki 11.36
God gave him a l in Jerusalem,   15.4
table, a chair, and a l, so   2Ki 4.10
since he promised to give a l   8.19
his l above him is put out.   Job 18.6
his l shone upon my head,   29.3
thou dost light my l; the LORD   Ps 18.28
Thy word is a l to my feet   119.105
For the commandment is a l   Prov 6.23
his l will be put out in   20.20
The spirit of man is the l   20.27
l of..wicked will be put out.   24.20
Her l does not go out at night.   31.18
Nor do men light a l and put   Mt 5.15
"The eye is the l of the body.   6.22
"Is a l..put under a bushel,   Mk 4.21
"No one after lighting a l   Lk 8.16
"No one after lighting a l   11.33
Your eye is the l of your body;   11.34
He was a burning and shining l,   Jn 5.35
and its l is the Lamb.   Rev 21.23
be girded and your l burning,   Lk 12.35

LAMPSTAND — S
make a l of pure gold.   Ex 25.31
also made the l of pure gold.   37.17
lamps in order upon the l   Lev 24.4
light in front of the l."   Num 8.2
behold, a l all of gold,   Zech 4.2
turning I saw seven golden l,   Rev 1.12

LAND — S
all the l which you see   Gen 13.15
l which I gave to Abraham   35.12
to the l which he swore   50.24
I will bring you into the l   Ex 6.8
and the l became defiled,   Lev 18.25
The l shall not be sold in   25.23
to the LORD part of the l   27.16
showed..the fruit of the l.   Num 13.26
let this l be given to your   32.5
this l shall be your possession   32.22
You..inherit the l by lot   33.54
You shall not defile the l   35.34
bringing you into a good l,   Deut 8.7
l..you are entering to take   11.10
the l..you are..to possess   11.11
LORD done thus to this l?   29.24
very much l to be possessed.   Josh 13.1
I gave you a l on which   24.13
went in and possessed the l,   Neh 9.24
LORD in the l of the living;   Isa 38.11
you defiled my l, and made   Jer 2.7
whole l shall be a desolation;   4.27
O l,..hear the word of the LORD!   22.29
these waste places in the l   Ezek 33.24
prophesy concerning the l of   36.6
the l as a holy district,   45.1
not remain in the l of the LORD;   Hos 9.3
go into the l which I will show   Acts 7.3
Paul..intending..to go by l.   20.13
but our bodies and our l.   Gen 47.18
the gospel in l beyond you,   2Cor 10.16

LANDMARK — S

not remove. .neighbor's *l*,	Deut 19.14
Remove not the ancient *l*	Prov 22.28
Do not remove an ancient *l*	23.10
Men remove *l*; they seize	Job 24.2

LANGUAGE

the whole earth had one *l*	Gen 11.1
not speak the *l* of Judah,	Neh 13.24
nation whose *l* you do not	Jer 5.15
foreign speech and a hard *l*,	Ezek 3.5
heard. .speaking in his own *l*.	Acts 2.6

LANGUISH — ES — ING

they will *l* who spread nets	Isa 19.8
My soul *l* for thy salvation;	Ps 119.81
I am *l*; O LORD, heal me, for my	6.2

LASHES

received. .the forty *l* less one.	2Cor 11.24

LAST

l state. .worse than the first.	Mt 12.45
many that are first will be *l*,	19.30
many that are first will be *l*,	Mk 10.31
loud cry, and breathed his *l*.	15.37
some are *l* who will be first,	Lk 13.30
in the *l* days there will come	2Tim 3.1
these *l* days he has spoken	Heb 1.2
I am the first and the *l*,	Rev 1.17

LAUGH — S — ED

and famine you shall *l*,	Job 5.22
The righteous. .shall *l* at him,	Ps 52.6
thou, O LORD, dost *l* at them;	59.8
I. .will *l* at your calamity;	Prov 1.26
that weep now, for you shall *l*.	Lk 6.21
he *l* at the rattle of javelins.	Job 41.29
He who sits in the heavens *l*;	Ps 2.4
the LORD *l* at the wicked, for	37.13
she *l* at the time to come.	Prov 31.25
fell on his face and *l*,	Gen 17.17
So Sarah *l* to herself,	18.12
but they *l* them to scorn,	2Chr 30.10
l at and held in derision,	Ezek 23.32
but sleeping." And they *l*	Mt 9.24
And they *l* at him. But he put	Mk 5.40
they *l* at him, knowing that	Lk 8.53

LAUGHTER

"God has made *l* for me;	Gen 21.6
Even in *l* the heart is sad,	Prov 14.13
I said of *l*, "It is mad,"	Ecc 2.2
Sorrow is better than *l*, for by	7.3

LAVER

also make a *l* of bronze,	Ex 30.17
And he made the *l* of bronze	38.8

LAW — S

the *l* of the burnt offering.	Lev 6.9
the *l* of the cereal offering.	6.14
the *l* of the sin offering.	6.25
the *l* of the guilt offering.	7.1
l of the sacrifice of peace	7.11
the *l* in cases of jealousy,	Num 5.29
the *l* for the Nazirite, when	6.13
explain this *l*, saying,	Deut 1.5
And Moses wrote this *l*,	31.9
read this *l* before all	31.11
"Take this book of the *l*,	31.26
This book of the *l* shall	Josh 1.8
read all the words of the *l*,	8.34
Rehoboam. .forsook the *l* of	2Chr 12.1
on his *l* he meditates day and	Ps 1.2
The *l* of the LORD is perfect,	19.7

I will keep thy *l* continually,	119.44
people in whose heart is my *l*;	Isa 51.7
my *l*, they have rejected it.	Jer 6.19
I will put my *l* within them,	31.33
unless. .with the *l* of his God."	Dan 6.5
out of Zion shall go. .the *l*,	Mic 4.2
not. .come to abolish the *l*	Mt 5.17
the *l* prophesied until John;	11.13
and teachers of the *l* sitting	Lk 5.17
one dot of the *l* to become void.	16.17
written about me in the *l* of	24.44
After the reading of the *l*	Acts 13.15
who have sinned under the *l*	Rom 2.12
For the *l* brings wrath, but	4.15
I delight in the *l* of God,	7.22
the *l* of the Spirit of life in Christ	8.2
Christ is the end of the *l*,	10.4
brother, does he dare go to *l*	1Cor 6.1
To those outside the *l* I became	9.21
book of the *l*, and do them."	Gal 3.10
Why then the *l*? It was added	3.19
we were confined under the *l*,	3.23
Tell me,. .do you not hear the *l*?	4.21
whole *l* is fulfilled in one word,	5.14
so fulfil the *l* of Christ.	6.2
we know that the *l* is good,	1Tim 1.8
the *l* made nothing perfect);	Heb 7.19
who looks into the perfect *l*,	Jas 1.25
convicted by. .*l* as transgressors.	2.9
if you judge the *l*, you are	4.11
true *l*, good statutes and	Neh 9.13

LAWFUL

not *l* to do on the sabbath."	Mt 12.2
l to do good on the sabbath."	12.12
not *l* for you to have her."	14.4
to Herod, "It is not *l* for you	Mk 6.18
Jews said. ."It is not *l* for us	Jn 18.31
"All things are *l* for me,"	1Cor 6.12

LAWLESS — NESS

the *l* one will be revealed,	2Thess 2.8
the man of *l* is revealed,	2.3
commits sin is guilty of *l*;	1Jn 3.4

LAWYER — S

a *l* stood up to put him to	Lk 10.25
he said, "Woe to you *l* also!	Lk 11.46

LAY — ING

I *l* prostrate before the LORD	Deut 9.18
Wise men *l* up knowledge,	Prov 10.14
"Do not *l* up for yourselves	Mt 6.19
Son of man has nowhere to *l* his	8.20
no other foundation can. .*l*	1Cor 3.11
thus *l* up for themselves	1Tim 6.19

LAZARUS

at his gate lay a poor man. .*L*,	Lk 16.20
a. .man was ill, *L* of Bethany,	Jn 11.1
a loud voice, "*L*, come out."	11.43
L. .whom Jesus had raised	12.1
priests planned to put *L*	12.10
with him when he called *L*	12.17

LEAD — S

I will *l* on slowly,	Gen 33.14
the LORD alone did *l* him,	Deut 32.12
Lead me,. .in thy righteousness	Ps 5.8
L me in thy truth, and teach	25.5
L thou me to the rock. .higher	61.2
a little child shall *l* them.	Isa 11.6
gently *l* those. .with young.	40.11
So thou didst *l* thy people,	63.14
And *l* us not into temptation,	Mt 6.13
"Can a blind man *l* a blind	Lk 6.39

LEAD — S (cont.)

let every one *l* the life	1Cor 7.17
I..beg you to *l* a life worthy	Eph 4.1
l a life worthy of the Lord,	Col 1.10
to *l* a life worthy of God,	1Thess 2.12
He *l* me beside still waters;	Ps 23.2
l..in the way you should go.	Isa 48.17
if a blind man *l* a blind man,	Mt 15.14

LEAF — VES

Wilt thou frighten a driven *l*	Job 13.25
they sewed fig *l* together	Gen 3.7
Their *l* will not wither	Ezek 47.12
he found nothing but *l*, for	Mk 11.13
its branch..puts forth its *l*,	13.28

LEAGUE

a *l* between me and you, as	1Ki 15.19
For you shall be in *l* with	Job 5.23
"Syria is in *l* with Ephraim,"	Isa 7.2

LEAH

name of the older was *L*,	Gen 29.16
loved Rachel more than *L*,	29.30
When *L* saw..she had ceased	30.9
called Rachel and *L* into the field	31.4
The sons of *L*: Reuben	35.23
and *L*, who together built	Ruth 4.11

LEAP — ED — ING

by my God I can *l* over a	2Sam 22.30
babe *l* in her womb;..Elizabeth	Lk 1.41
And *l* up he stood and walked	Acts 3.8

LEARN — ED (v)

l to fear the Lord your God,	Deut 31.12
I *l* thy righteous ordinances.	Ps 119.7
afflicted that I might *l* thy	119.71
O simple ones, *l* prudence;	Prov 8.5
l to do good; seek justice,	Isa 1.17
the world *l* righteousness.	26.9
"*L* not the way of the nations,	Jer 10.2
Go and *l* what this means,	Mt 9.13
yoke upon you, and *l* from me;	11.29
No one could *l* that song	Rev 14.3
I have *l* by divination	Gen 30.27
What you have *l* and received	Phil 4.9
I have *l*, in whatever state I am,	4.11
you *l* from us how..to live	1Thess 4.1
he *l* obedience through what	Heb 5.8

LEARNING (n)

wise man..may..increase in *l*,	Prov 1.5
understanding *l*, and competent	Dan 1.4
four youths, God gave them *l*	1.17
"How is it that this man has *l*,	Jn 7.15
great *l* is turning you mad."	Acts 26.24

LEAST

I am the *l* in my family."	Judg 6.15
from the *l* of the tribes	1Sam 9.21
by no means *l* among the rulers	Mt 2.6
be called *l* in the kingdom	5.19
who is *l* in..kingdom of heaven	11.11
who is *l* in the kingdom of God	Lk 7.28
who is *l* among you..is..great."	9.48
I am the *l* of the apostles,	1Cor 15.9
the very *l* of all the saints,	Eph 3.8

LEAVE

Elisha said,..I will not *l*	2Ki 2.2
as you..live, I will not *l*	4.30
L simpleness, and live, and	Prov 9.6
man shall *l*..father and mother	Mk 10.7

LEAVEN

you shall put away *l* out of	Ex 12.15

cereal offering..made with *l*;	Lev 2.11
kingdom of heaven is like *l*	Mt 13.33
beware of the *l* of..Pharisees	16.6
beware of..*l* of the Pharisees	Mk 8.15
"Beware of..*l* of the Pharisees,	Lk 12.1
like *l* which a woman took	13.21
a little *l* leavens the whole	1Cor 5.6
A little *l* leavens the whole	Gal 5.9

LEBANON

land of the Canaanites, and *L*,	Deut 1.7
devour the cedars of *L*.'	Judg 9.15
command that cedars of *L* be	1Ki 5.6
House of the Forest of *L*.	10.17
bring cedar trees from *L*	Ezra 3.7
Lord breaks the cedars of *L*.	Ps 29.5
His appearance is like *L*,	Sol 5.15
and *L* with its majestic trees	Isa 10.34
glory of *L* shall come to you,	60.13
Does the snow of *L* leave the	Jer 18.14

LED

the Lord has *l* me in the way	Gen 24.27
God *l* the people round by	Ex 13.18
and *l* him through..Canaan,	Josh 24.3
daytime he *l*..with a cloud,	Ps 78.14
he *l* them by a straight way,	107.7
to him who *l* his people	136.16
who *l* us in the wilderness,	Jer 2.6
I *l*..with cords of compassion,	Hos 11.4
Jesus was *l* up by the Spirit	Mt 4.1
l him to the brow of the hill	Lk 4.29
"As a sheep *l* to..slaughter	Acts 8.32
all who are *l* by the Spirit	Rom 8.14
if you are *l* by the Spirit	Gal 5.18

LEFT (v)

that the Lord had *l* him.	Judg 16.20
and I, even I only, am *l*;	1Ki 19.10
l alone, I fell upon my face,	Ezek 9.8
those who are *l* in Israel;	Zeph 3.13
l the boat and their father,	Mt 4.22
"Lo, we have *l* everything	19.27
they *l* their nets and followed	Mk 1.18
they *l* their father Zebedee	1.20
they *l* everything and followed	Lk 5.11

LEFT (n)

then I will go to the *l*."	Gen 13.9
do not let your *l* hand know	Mt 6.3
one at your right hand and..*l*,	20.21

LEGION — S

"My name is *L*; for we are many."	Mk 5.9
more than twelve *l* of angels?	Mt 26.53

LEGS

thighs..bronze, its *l*..iron,	Dan 2.33
they did not break his *l*.	Jn 19.33

LEHI

at *L*, and there came water	Judg 15.19
Philistines gathered..at *L*,	2Sam 23.11

LEND — S — ING

"If you *l* money to any	Ex 22.25
shall not *l* upon interest	Deut 23.19
shall *l* to many nations,	28.12
if you *l* to those from whom	Lk 6.34
who is kind..*l* to the Lord,	Prov 19.17
ever giving liberally and *l*,	Ps 37.26

LENGTH

l of..ark three hundred cubits,	Gen 6.15
the *l* of the measuring reed	Ezek 40.5
what is the breadth and *l*	Eph 3.18

LENT (v)
release what he has *l* to his	Deut 15.2
I have *l* him to the LORD;	1Sam 1.28
I have not *l*, nor..borrowed,	Jer 15.10

LEOPARD
l shall lie down with the kid,	Isa 11.6
his skin or the *l* his spots?	Jer 13.23
like a *l*, with four wings	Dan 7.6

LEPER — S
"This shall be..law of the *l*	Lev 14.2
put out of the camp every *l*,	Num 5.2
man of valor, but he was a *l*.	2Ki 5.1
king, so that he was a *l*	15.5
a *l* came..and knelt before him,	Mt 8.2
in the house of Simon the *l*,	26.6
a *l* came to him beseeching him,	Mk 1.40
in the house of Simon the *l*,	14.3
four men who were *l* at the	2Ki 7.3
the lame walk, *l* are cleansed	Mt 11.5
many *l* in Israel in the time	Lk 4.27
lame walk, *l* are cleansed,	7.22
he was met by ten *l*, who stood	17.12

LEPROUS — Y
behold, his hand was *l*,	Ex 4.6
and it turns into a *l* disease	Lev 13.2
I put a *l* disease in a house	14.34
behold, Miriam was *l*,	Num 12.10
the *l* of Naaman shall cleave	2Ki 5.27
became angry..*l* broke out	2Chr 26.19
there came a man full of *l*;	Lk 5.12

LETTER — S
David wrote a *l* to Joab,	2Sam 11.14
he brought the *l* to the king	2Ki 5.6
a *l* came to him from Elijah	2Chr 21.2
then answer be returned by *l*	Ezra 5.5
servant to me with an open *l*	Neh 6.5
Hezekiah received the *l* from	Isa 37.14
words of the *l* which Jeremiah	Jer 29.1
sent..with the following *l*:	Acts 15.23
together, they delivered the *l*.	15.30
he wrote a *l* to this effect:	23.25
delivered the *l* to the governor,	23.33
are our *l* of recommendation,	2Cor 3.2
when this *l* has been read	Col 4.16
l purporting to be from us,	1Thess 2.2
the mark in my *l* of mine;	2Thess 3.17
she wrote *l* in Ahab's name	1Ki 21.8
wrote *l* also to Ephraim	2Chr 30.1
l to..synagogues at Damascus,	Acts 9.2
I received *l* to the brethren,	22.5
need..*l* of recommendation	2Cor 3.1
not..frightening you with *l*.	10.9
with what large *l* I am writing	Gal 6.11
as he does in all his *l*.	2Pet 3.16

LEVI
his name was called L.	Gen 29.34
man from the house of L	Ex 2.1
L you shall not number, and	Num 1.49
set apart the tribe of L	Deut 10.8

LEVIATHAN
draw out L with a fishhook,	Job 41.1
strong sword will punish L	Isa 27.1

LEVITES
no portion..given to the L	Josh 14.4
service, the priests and..L,	2Chr 31.2
which the L,..had collected	34.9
And he said to the L who taught	35.3

LIAR — S
I should be a *l* like you;	Jn 8.55
not believe..made him a *l*,	1Jn 5.10
and all *l*, their lot shall be	Rev 21.8

LIBERTY
proclaim *l* throughout..land	Lev 25.10
and I shall walk at *l*, for	Ps 119.45
a proclamation of *l* to them,	Jer 34.8
gift..his to the year of *l*;	Ezek 46.21
glorious *l* of..children of God.	Rom 8.21
take care lest this *l* of yours	1Cor 8.9
why should my *l* be determined	10.29

LIE — S — D (v)
not man, that he should *l*,	Num 23.19
In peace I will both *l* down and	Ps 4.8
faithful witness does not *l*,	Prov 14.5
"Ananias, why..*l* to..Spirit	Acts 5.3
Do not *l* to one another,	Col 3.9
When he *l*, he speaks according	Jn 8.44
and drink water.' " But he *l*	1Ki 13.18

LIE — S (n)
l which they are prophesying	Jer 27.10
the truth about God for a *l*	Rom 1.25
in their mouth no *l* was found,	Rev 14.5
godless besmear me with *l*,	Ps 119.69
we have made *l* our refuge,	Isa 28.15
your lips have spoken *l*, your	59.3
bloody city, all full of *l*	Nah 3.1

LIFE — VES
everything that has..*l*,	Gen 1.30
tree of *l* also in the midst	2.9
l of the flesh is in blood;	Lev 17.11
set before you this day *l*	Deut 30.15
for that means *l* to you and	30.20
LORD kills and brings to *l*;	1Sam 2.6
the *l* of my lord shall be	25.29
whether for death or for *l*,	2Sam 15.21
your *l* shall go for his *l*,	1Ki 20.42
"Remember..my *l* is a breath;	Job 7.7
breath of..Almighty gives me *l*.	33.4
he may see the light of *l*.	33.30
dost show me the path of *l*;	Ps 16.11
What man is there who desires *l*,	34.12
with thee is the fountain of *l*;	36.9
steadfast love is better than *l*,	63.3
Remember,..the measure of *l*	89.47
against the *l* of the righteous,	94.21
they will be *l* for your soul	Prov 3.22
they are *l* to him who finds	4.22
he who finds me finds *l* and	8.35
path of righteousness is *l*,	12.28
fear of..LORD is a fountain of *l*,	14.27
I hated *l*, because what is	Ecc 2.17
Enjoy *l* with..wife..you love,	9.9
recorded for *l* in Jerusalem,	Isa 4.3
held back my *l* from the pit	38.17
Death shall be preferred to *l*	Jer 8.3
I set before you the way of *l*	21.8
let every man save his *l*!	51.6
you will have saved your *l*."	Ezek 3.21
LORD, take my *l* from me,	Jonah 4.3
way is hard, that leads to *l*,	Mt 7.14
he who loses his *l* for my sake	10.39
gains..world and forfeits his *l*?	16.26
the righteous into eternal *l*."	25.46
whoever would save his *l* will	Mk 8.35
whole world and forfeit his *l*?	8.36
in the age to come eternal *l*.	10.30
would save his *l* will lose it;	Lk 9.24
do not be anxious about your *l*,	12.22
I do to inherit eternal *l*?"	18.18
In him was *l*, and the *l* was	Jn 1.4
believes in the Son has eternal *l*;	3.36

LIFE — VES (cont.)

water welling up to eternal *l*."	4.14
and believes. .has eternal *l*;	5.24
you have the words of eternal *l*;	6.68
I came that they may have *l*,	10.10
lay down my *l* for the sheep.	10.15
and I give them eternal *l*,	10.28
"I am the resurrection and the *l*;	11.25
way and the truth, and the *l*;	14.6
eternal *l*, that they know thee	17.3
that believing you may have *l*	20.31
all the words of this *L*."	Acts 5.20
he himself gives to all men *l*	17.25
been brought from death to *l*,	Rom 6.13
free gift of God is eternal *l*	6.23
death, nor *l*, nor angels,	8.38
a fragrance from *l* to *l*.	2Cor 2.16
but the Spirit gives *l*.	3.6
so that the *l* of Jesus may	4.10
work in us, but *l* in you.	4.12
of my former *l* in Judaism,	Gal 1.13
the *l* I now live in the flesh	2.20
your *l*. .hid with Christ in God.	Col 3.3
lead a quiet and peaceable *l*,	1Tim 2.2
power of an indestructible *l*.	Heb 7.16
Keep your *l* free from love of	13.5
What is your *l*? For you are	Jas 4.14
"He that would love *l* and	1Pet 3.10
passed out of death into *l*,	1Jn 3.14
he laid down his *l* for us;	3.16
grant to eat of the tree of *l*,	Rev 2.7
blot. .name out of the book of *l*;	3.5
breath of *l* from God entered them,	11.11
in the book of *l* of the Lamb	13.8
They came to *l* again, and	20.4
fountain of the water of *l*.	21.6
in the Lamb's book of *l*.	21.27
the water of *l* without price.	22.17
lawlessness takes away *l*.	Prov 11.30
astray at the cost of your *l*.	Jer 42.20
endurance. .will gain your *l*.	Lk 21.19
men who have risked their *l*	Acts 15.26
l of holiness and godliness	2Pet 3.11
they loved not their *l* even	Rev 12.11

LIFT — ED — ING

L up your heads, O gates!	Ps 24.7
To thee, O LORD, I *l* up my soul.	25.1
to thee,. .do I *l* up my soul.	86.4
I *l* up my eyes to the hills.	121.1
L up your hands to the holy	134.2
LORD, my heart is not *l* up,	131.1
and *l* him out of the cistern.	Jer 38.13
must the Son of man be *l* up,	Jn 3.14
"When you have *l* up the Son	8.28
when I am *l* up from the earth,	12.32
not from the east. .comes *l* up;	Ps 75.6

LIGHT — S

God said, "Let there be *l*";	Gen 1.3
people of Israel had *l*	Ex 10.23
that a *l* may be burning	Lev 24.2
dawns on them like the. .*l*,	2Sam 23.4
they do not know the *l*.	Job 24.16
LORD is my *l* and my salvation;	Ps 27.1
your vindication as the *l*,	37.6
send out thy *l* and thy truth;	43.3
who will never more see the *l*.	49.19
L dawns for the righteous, and	97.11
Thy word. .a *l* to my path.	119.105
unfolding. .thy words gives *l*;	119.130
darkness is as *l* with thee.	139.12
path. .righteous is like the *l*	Prov 4.18

l of the righteous rejoices,	13.9
L is sweet, and it is pleasant	Ecc 11.7
walk in the *l* of the LORD.	Isa 2.5
darkness for *l* and *l* for darkness,	5.20
given you as. .a *l* to the nations,	42.6
I form *l* and create darkness,	45.7
give you as a *l* to the nations,	49.6
Then shall your *l* break forth	58.8
shine; for your *l* has come,	60.1
nations shall come to your *l*,	60.3
the LORD will be a *l* to me.	Mic 7.8
the people. .have seen a great *l*,	Mt 4.16
it gives *l* to all in the house.	5.15
his garments became white as *l*.	17.2
l to those who sit in darkness	Lk 1.79
a *l* for revelation to the Gentiles,	2.32
dark shall be heard in the *l*,	12.3
The *l* shines in the darkness,	Jn 1.5
the *l* has come into the world,	3.19
"I am the *l* of the world;	8.12
I am the *l* of the world."	9.5
Walk while you have the *l*,	12.35
a *l* from heaven flashed about	Acts 9.3
to be a *l* for the Gentiles,	13.47
great *l* from heaven suddenly	22.6
on the way a *l* from heaven,	26.13
may turn from darkness to *l*	26.18
and put on the armor of *l*;	Rom 13.12
comes, who will bring to *l*	1Cor 4.5
from seeing. .*l* of the gospel	2Cor 4.4
"Let *l* shine out of darkness,"	4.6
what fellowship has *l* with	6.14
now you are *l* in the Lord;	Eph 5.8
and Christ shall give you *l*."	5.14
darkness into his marvelous *l*.	1Pet 2.9
that God is *l* and in him is	1Jn 1.5
but if we walk in the *l*, as	1.7
the true *l* is already shining.	2.8
they need no *l* of lamp or sun,	Rev 22.5
let them be *l* in the firmament	Gen 1.15
coming. .from the Father of *l*	Jas 1.17

LIGHTNING — S

as the *l* comes from the east	Mt 24.27
as the *l* flashes and lights	Lk 17.24
loud noises, flashes of *l*,	Rev 8.5
he flashed forth *l*, and routed	Ps 18.14

LIKE — NESS

that I should be *l* him? says	Isa 40.25
change our lowly body to be *l*	Phil 3.21
created man. .in the *l* of God.	Gen 5.1
or what *l* compare with him?	Isa 40.18
"Whose *l* and inscription is	Mk 12.16
Whose *l* and inscription has	Lk 20.24
gods. .in the *l* of men!"	Acts 14.11
Son in the *l* of sinful flesh	Rom 8.3
being born in the *l* of men.	Phil 2.7

LILY — IES

rose of Sharon,. .*l* of. .valleys.	Sol 2.1
l of the field, how they grow;	Mt 6.28
Consider the *l*, how they grow;	Lk 12.27

LINEN

wrapped him in the *l* shroud,	Mk 15.46
her to be clothed with fine *l*,	Rev 19.8

LION — S — 'S

and when there came a *l*,	1Sam 17.34
slew a *l* in a pit on a day	2Sam 23.20
a *l* met him on the road	1Ki 13.24
slew a *l* in a pit. .when snow	1Chr 11.22
lest like a *l* they rend me,	Ps 7.2
Save me from the mouth of the *l*,	22.21

LION — S — 'S (cont.)

sluggard says, "There is a *l*   Prov 26.13
My heritage. .to me like a *l*   Jer 12.8
like a *l* and had eagle's wings.   Dan 7.4
young *l* to the house of Judah.   Hos 5.14
as if a man fled from a *l*,   Amos 5.19
devil. .like a roaring *l*,   1Pet 5.8
the *L* of the tribe of Judah,   Rev 5.5
young *l* roar for their prey,   Ps 104.21
Daniel. .cast into the den of *l*.   Dan 6.16
stopped the mouths of *l*,   Heb 11.33
I was rescued from. .*l* mouth.   2Tim 4.17

LIPS

our *l* are with us; who is our   Ps 12.4
Keep. .*l* from speaking deceit.   34.13
Truthful *l* endure for ever,   Prov 12.19
Righteous *l* are the delight   16.13
l of knowledge are. .precious   20.15
Your *l*. .like a scarlet thread,   Sol 4.3
honor me with their *l*, while   Isa 29.13
honors me with their *l*, but   Mt 15.8
people honors me with their *l*,   Mk 7.6
venom of asps. .under their *l*."   Rom 3.13
word is near you, on your *l*   10.8

LISTEN — S — ED — ING

shall not yield to him or *l*   Deut 13.8
to *l* to the voice of Samuel;   1Sam 8.19
not *l*, and Manasseh seduced   2Ki 21.9
to *l* is better than. .sacrifice   Ecc 5.1
But if any nation will not *l*,   Jer 12.17
if you *l* to me, says the LORD,   17.24
It may be they will *l*, and   26.3
my beloved Son; *l* to him."   Mk 9.7
my Son, my Chosen; *l* to him!"   Lk 9.35
who will *l* to anybody and   2Tim 3.7
a wise man *l* to advice.   Prov 12.15
God *l* to. .voice of Manoah,   Judg 13.9
does evil. .not *l* to my voice,   Jer 18.10

LITTLE

Better. .a *l*. .the righteous has   Ps 37.16
who gathers *l* by *l*. .increase   Prov 13.11
line, here a *l*, there a *l*."   Isa 28.10
Bethlehem Ephrathah, who are *l*   Mic 5.2
clothe you, O men of *l* faith?   Mt 6.30
you afraid, O men of *l* faith?"   8.26
gives to one of these *l* ones   10.42
"O man of *l* faith, why. .doubt?"   14.31
men of *l* faith, why do you discuss   16.8
whoever causes one of these *l*   18.6
who is forgiven *l*, loves *l*."   Lk 7.47
cause one of these *l* ones to sin.   17.2
who gathered *l* had no lack."   2Cor 8.15

LIVE — S — ING (v)

let the male children *l*.   Ex 1.17
let. .*l*, to show you my power,   9.16
man shall not see me and *l*."   33.20
by doing which a man shall *l*:   Lev 18.5
the bronze serpent and. *l*.   Num 21.9
that you may *l*, and go in   Deut 4.1
with man and man still *l*.   5.24
that you may *l*, and that   5.33
that you may *l* and multiply,   8.1
man does not *l* by bread alone,   8.3
that you may *l* and inherit   16.20
shouted, "Long *l* the king!"   1Sam 10.24
say, 'Long *l* King Solomon!'   1Ki 1.34
If a man die, shall he *l* again?   Job 14.14
I may *l* and observe thy word.   Ps 119.17
give. .understanding that I may *l*.   119.144
praise the LORD as long as I *l*;   146.2

keep my commandments, and *l*;   Prov 4.4
Leave simpleness, and *l*,   9.6
It is better to *l* in a corner   21.9
Thy dead shall *l*, their bodies   Isa 26.19
hear, that your soul may *l*;   55.3
serve him. .his people, and *l*.   Jer 27.12
If you. .enter Egypt and go to *l*   42.15
said to you in your blood, 'L,   Ezek 16.6
righteous, he shall surely *l*,   18.9
for. .righteousness. .he shall *l*.   18.22
by. .observance man shall *l*.   20.11
and right, he shall *l* by it.   33.19
"Son of man, can these bones *l*?"   37.3
that we may *l* before him.   Hos 6.2
and not evil, that you may *l*;   Amos 5.14
'Man shall not *l* by bread alone,   Mt 4.4
hand on her, and she will *l*."   9.18
not *l* according to the tradition   Mk 7.5
'Man shall not *l* by bread alone.'   Lk 4.4
do this, and you will *l*."   10.28
living; for all *l* to him."   20.38
who eats this bread will *l*   Jn 6.58
because I *l*, you will *l* also.   14.19
for 'In him we *l* and move   Acts 17.28
deeds of the body you will *l*.   Rom 8.13
on the law shall *l* by it.   10.5
to *l* according to scripture,   1Cor 4.6
faith is righteous shall *l*";   Gal 3.11
If we *l* by the Spirit, let   5.25
no longer *l* as the Gentiles   Eph 4.17
For to me to *l* is Christ,   Phil 1.21
Jesus the Lord, so *l* in him,   Col 2.6
we shall also *l* with him;   2Tim 2.11
to *l* sober, upright, and godly   Tit 2.12
know that my Redeemer *l*,   Job 19.25
None of us *l* to himself,   Rom 14.7
man became a *l* being.   Gen 2.7
the *l* God is among you,   Josh 3.10
the armies of the *l* God."   1Sam 17.36
has sent to mock the *l* God,   2Ki 19.4
My soul thirsts. .for the *l* God.   Ps 42.2
l God and. .everlasting King.   Jer 10.10
that day *l* waters shall flow   Zech 14.8
would have given you *l* water."   Jn 4.10
I am the *l* bread which came   6.51
As the *l* Father sent me,   6.57
Adam became a *l* being";   1Cor 15.45
to serve a *l* and true God,   1Thess 1.9
our hope set on the *l* God,   1Tim 4.10
fall away from the *l* God.   Heb 3.12
Gentiles. .*l* in licentiousness,   1Pet 4.3
the first. .last, and the *l* one;   Rev 1.18

LIVING (n)

between the dead and. .*l*;   Num 16.48
who has kept us among the *l*,   Ps 66.9
blotted out of the book of the *l*;   69.28
dead more fortunate than the *l*   Ecc 4.2
For the *l* know. .they will die,   9.5
the dead on behalf of the *l*?   Isa 8.19
The *l*, the *l*, he thanks thee,   38.19
not God of. .dead, but of. .*l*."   Mt 22.32
not God of the dead, but. .*l*;   Mk 12.27
everything she had, her whole *l*."   12.44
he squandered. .in loose *l*.   Lk 15.13
seek the *l* among the dead?   24.5

LIZARD

l according to its kind,   Lev 11.29
l you can take in. .hands,   Prov 30.28

LOAN

make your neighbor a *l*   Deut 24.10
by this woman for the *l*   1Sam 2.20

LOATHE — D

we *l* this worthless food." Num 21.5
"I *l* my life; I will give Job 10.1
do I not *l* them that rise up Ps 139.21
you will *l*. .your iniquities Ezek 36.31
forty years I *l* that generation Ps 95.10

LOAVES

"We have only five *l* here Mt 14.17
Jesus said. ."How many *l* have you?" 15.34
"How many *l* have you? Go and Mk 6.38
asked. ."How many *l* have you?" 8.5
no more than five *l* and two Lk 9.13
'Friend, lend me three *l*; 11.5
has five barley *l* and two fish; Jn 6.9
you ate your fill of the *l*. 6.26

LOCUST — S

of them you may eat: the *l* Lev 11.22
the swarming *l* has eaten. Joel 1.4
tomorrow I will bring *l* Ex 10.4
coming like *l* for number; Judg 6.5
He spoke, and the *l* came, Ps 105.34
the *l* have no king, yet Prov 30.27
behold, he was forming *l* in Amos 7.1
his food was *l* and wild honey. Mt 3.4
John. .ate *l* and wild honey. Mk 1.6
from. .smoke came *l* on. .earth, Rev 9.3

LODGE — D

father's house for us to *l* in?" Gen 24.23
and where you *l* I will *l*; Ruth 1.16
ark was *l* at Kiriath-jearim, 1Sam 7.2

LOFTY

stars, how *l* they are! Job 22.12
l One who inhabits eternity, Isa 57.15
not. .in *l* words or wisdom. 1Cor 2.1

LONELY

for I am *l* and afflicted. Ps 25.16
Jesus. .withdrew. .to a *l* place Mt 14.13
"Come away. .to a *l* place, and Mk 6.31

LONG — S — ED (v)

who *l* for death, but it comes not, Job 3.21
Behold, I *l* for thy precepts; Ps 119.40
As a hart *l* for flowing streams, 42.1
soul *l*, yea, faints for. .courts 84.2
king *l* to go. .to Absalom; 2Sam 13.39
righteous men *l* to see what Mt 13.17
fruit for which thy soul *l* Rev 18.14

LONGING (n)

My soul. .*l* for thy ordinances Ps 119.20
creation waits with eager *l* Rom 8.19

LOOK — S — ED — ING

l from the place where Gen 13.14
"*L* toward heaven, and number 15.5
do not *l* back or stop 19.17
l at the bronze serpent Num 21.9
L down from thy holy Deut 26.15
"Do not *l* on his appearance 1Sam 16.7
When I *l* at thy heavens, the Ps 8.3
God; *l* upon the face of thine 84.9
all *l* to thee, to give them 104.27
L on my affliction. .deliver 119.153
But you did not *l* to him who Isa 22.11
L upon Zion, the city of our 33.20
Hear, you deaf;. .*l*, you blind, 42.18
l to the rock from which you 51.1
and *l* at the earth beneath; 51.6

l for justice,. .there is none; 59.11
as for me, I will *l* to the Lord, Mic 7.7
and canst not *l* on wrong, Hab 1.13
when you fast, do not *l* dismal, Mt 6.16
I beg you to *l* upon my son, Lk 9.38
begin to take place, *l* up 21.28
L at what is before your eyes. 2Cor 10.7
The Lord *l* down from heaven, Ps 33.13
one who *l* at a woman lustfully Mt 5.28
who *l* into the perfect law, Jas 1.25
But Lot's wife. .*l* back, Gen 19.26
Abraham. .*l*, and. .was a ram, 22.13
because they *l* into the ark 1Sam 6.19
They *l*, but there was none 2Sam 22.42
All men have *l* on it; man Job 36.25
the Lord *l* at the earth, Ps 102.19
he *l* for justice, but behold, Isa 5.7
I *l*, . .there was no one to help. 63.5
I *l* for much,. .it came to little; Hag 1.9
he *l* forward to the city Heb 11.10
Joseph. .*l* for the kingdom Mk 15.43
l for. .consolation of Israel, Lk 2.25
he was *l* for the kingdom of God. 23.51
why. .stand *l* into heaven? Acts 1.11
l to Jesus the pioneer and Heb 12.2

LOOSE — S — D (v)

to *l* the bonds of wickedness, Isa 58.6
whatever you *l* on earth shall Mt 16.19
whatever you *l* on earth 18.18
and *l* the belt of the strong. Job 12.21
Lord,. .Thou hast *l* my bonds. Ps 116.16
his tongue *l*, and he spoke, Lk 1.64
Satan will be *l* from. .prison Rev 20.7

LOOSE

the people had broken *l* Ex 32.25
He let *l* on them his. .anger, Ps 78.49
lips of a *l* woman drip honey, Prov 5.3

LORD — S (n)

day that the *L* God made Gen 2.4
favor in the eyes of the *L*. 6.8
Now the *L* said to Abram, "Go 12.1
by my name the *L* I did not Ex 6.3
the *L* brought the people of 12.51
Israel sang this song to the *L*, 15.1
the *L* knew face to face, Deut 34.10
"May my *l* King David live 1Ki 1.31
delight is in the law of the *L*, Ps 1.2
thou alone, whose name is the *L*, 83.18
lovely. .thy dwelling place, O *L* 84.1
L has laid on him the iniquity Isa 53.6
Son of man is *l* of the sabbath." Mt 12.8
Prepare the way of the *L*, make Mk 1.3
"*L*, we do not know where you Jn 14.5
answered. ."My *L* and my God!" 20.28
made him both *L* and Christ, Acts 2.36
say "Jesus is *L*" except by 1Cor 12.3
confess that Jesus Christ is *L*, Phil 2.11
"Thou, *L*, didst found. .earth Heb 1.10
"Hallelujah! For the *L* our God Rev 19.6
many "gods" and many "*l*"— 1Cor 8.5

LORD JESUS

saved through. .grace of. .*L*.. Acts 15.11
"Believe in the *L*.., and 16.31

LORD JESUS CHRIST

when we believed in the *L*.., Acts 11.17
peace with God through our *L*. .Rom 5.1
the victory through our *L*... 1Cor 15.57
you know the grace of our *L*.., 2Cor 8.9
power and coming of our *L*.., 2Pet 1.16

LORD OF HOSTS
The *L*..is with us; the God	Ps 46.7
the *L*.., him you shall regard	Isa 8.13

LORDS (v)
man *l* it over man to his hurt.	Ecc 8.9

LOSE — S
would save his life will *l* it,	Mt 16.25
l nothing of all..he has given	Jn 6.39
he who *l* his life for my sake	Mt 10.39
whoever *l* his life for my sake	Mk 8.35
whoever *l* his life for my sake,	Lk 9.24
l one coin, does not light..lamp	15.8
whoever *l* his life will preserve it.	17.33

LOST (v)
gone astray like a *l* sheep;	Ps 119.176
riches..*l* in a bad venture;	Ecc 5.14
"Woe is me! For I am *l*; for	Isa 6.5
bones..dried up,..hope is *l*;	Ezek 37.11
go..to the *l* sheep of..Israel.	Mt 10.6
sent only to the *l* sheep of..Israel."	15.24
he was *l*, and is found.'	Lk 15.24
thou gavest me I *l* not one."	Jn 18.9

LOST (n)
seek the *l*, and..strayed,	Ezek 34.16
Son of man came to save the *l*	Mt 18.11*n*
to seek and to save the *l*."	Lk 19.10

LOT
Accompanied Abram to Canaan, Gen 11. 31; 12.5; separated from Abram to live at Sodom, Gen 13; rescued by Abram, Gen 14.1–16; sheltered angels, Gen 19.1–11; fled to Zoar, Gen 19.15–23; Lot and his daughters, Gen 19.30–38.

and *L* went with him. Abram	Gen 12.4
brought back his kinsman *L*	14.16
and *L* was sitting in the gate	19.1
in the days of *L*—they ate,	Lk 17.28
if he rescued righteous *L*,	2Pet 2.7

LOT — S
Then Saul said, "Cast the *l*	1Sam 14.42
throw in your *l* among us, we	Prov 1.14
The *l* is cast into the lap,	16.33
work, for that is his *l*;	Ecc 3.22
and the *l* fell upon Jonah.	Jonah 1.7
by *l* to enter the temple of	Lk 1.9
and the *l* fell on Matthias;	Acts 1.26
and Aaron shall cast *l* upon	Lev 16.8
for my raiment they cast *l*.	Ps 22.18
and cast *l* for Jerusalem,	Obad 1.11
among them by casting *l*;	Mt 27.35
cast *l* for it to see whose	Jn 19.24

LOVE — S — D (v)
those who *l* me and keep my	Ex 20.6
'I *l* my master, my wife,	21.5
l your neighbor as yourself:	Lev 19.18
thousands of those who *l*	Deut 5.10
you shall *l* the LORD your God	6.5
he will *l* you, bless you,	7.13
to *l* him, to serve the LORD	10.12
L the sojourner therefore;	10.19
to know whether you *l* the LORD	13.3
so that you will *l* the LORD	30.6
to *l* the LORD your God.	Josh 23.11
l those who hate the LORD?	2Chr 19.2
with those who *l* him and keep	Neh 1.5
I *l* thee, O LORD, my strength.	Ps 18.1
L the LORD, all you his saints;	31.23
you *l* righteousness and hate	45.7

those who *l* thy salvation say	70.4
I *l* the LORD, because he has heard	116.1
Oh, how I *l* thy law! It is my	119.97
l her, and she will guard you.	Prov 4.6
I *l* those who *l* me, and those	8.17
L not sleep, lest you come	20.13
time to *l*, and a time to hate;	Ecc 3.8
life with the wife whom you *l*,	9.9
For I the LORD *l* justice,	Isa 61.8
l a woman who is..adulteress;	Hos 3.1
I will *l* them no more; all	9.15
I will *l* them freely, for	14.4
Hate evil, and *l* good, and	Amos 5.15
hate the good and *l* the evil,	Mic 3.2
to *l* kindness,..to walk humbly	6.8
'You shall *l* your neighbor	Mt 5.43
l your neighbor as yourself."	19.19
"You shall *l* the Lord your God	22.37
they *l* the place of honor	23.6
you shall *l* the Lord your God	Mk 12.30
L your enemies, do good to	Lk 6.27
"If you *l* those who *l* you,	6.32
"You shall *l* the Lord your God	10.27
hate the one and *l* the other,	16.13
your Father, you would *l* me,	Jn 8.42
"Lord, he whom you *l* is ill."	11.3
that you also *l* one another.	13.34
"If you *l* me, you will keep	14.15
l one another as I have *l* you.	15.12
Lord; you know that I *l* you."	21.15
good with those who *l* him,	Rom 8.28
except to *l* one another;	13.8
prepared for those who *l* him,"	1Cor 2.9
If I *l* you the more, am I	2Cor 12.15
Husbands, *l* your wives, as	Eph 5.25
Husbands, *l* your wives, and	Col 3.19
train the young women to *l*	Tit 2.4
promised to those who *l* him?	Jas 2.5
Without having seen him you *l*	1Pet 1.8
L the brotherhood. Fear God.	2.17
Do not *l* the world or the	1Jn 2.15
we should *l* one another,	3.11
let us *l* one another; for *l*	4.7
We *l*, because he first *l* us.	4.19
l God and obey his commandments.	5.2
Those whom I *l*, I reprove	Rev 3.19
and his father *l* him."	Gen 44.20
because he *l* you and your	Deut 15.16
"Because the LORD *l* his	2Chr 2.11
Judah, Mount Zion, which he *l*.	Ps 78.68
LORD *l* those who hate evil;	97.10
LORD reproves him whom he *l*,	Prov 3.12
l discipline *l* knowledge,	12.1
l him who pursues righteousness	15.9
A friend *l* at all times,	17.17
He who *l* transgression *l* strife;	17.19
He who *l* pleasure will be a poor	21.17
He who *l* purity of heart,	22.11
who *l* money will not be satisfied	Ecc 5.10
I sought him whom my soul *l*;	Sol 3.1
LORD *l* him; he shall perform	Isa 48.14
who *l* father or mother more	Mt 10.37
he *l* our nation, and he built	Lk 7.5
For the Father *l* the Son,	Jn 5.20
For this reason the Father *l* me,	10.17
He who *l* his life loses it,	12.25
keeps them, he it is who *l* me;	14.21
for the Father himself *l* you,	16.27
one *l* God, one is known by him.	1Cor 8.3
for God *l* a cheerful giver.	2Cor 9.7
he who *l* his brother abides in	1Jn 2.10
To him who *l* us and has freed	Rev 1.5
he *l* her..Isaac was comforted	Gen 24.67

LOVE — S — D (v) (cont.)

but Rebekah *l* Jacob. 25.28
Now Israel *l* Joseph more 37.3
because he *l* your fathers Deut 4.37
the LORD your God *l* you. 23.5
he *l* his people; all those 33.3
and, although he *l* Hannah, 1Sam 1.5
And Saul *l* him greatly. 16.21
Jonathan *l* him as his own 18.1
Israel and Judah *l* David; 18.16
and that all Israel *l* him, 18.28
he *l* him as he *l* his own soul. 20.17
Solomon *l* the LORD, walking 1Ki 3.3
Because the LORD *l* Israel 10.9
Solomon *l* many foreign women: 11.1
l you with..everlasting love; Jer 31.3
Israel was a child, I *l* him, Hos 11.1
"I have *l* you," says the LORD. Mal 1.2
Jesus looking upon him *l* him, Mk 10.21
sins..forgiven, for she *l* much; Lk 7.47
For God so *l* the world that Jn 3.16
Jews said, "See how he *l* him!" 11.36
they *l* the praise of men more 12.43
world, he *l* them to the end. 13.1
As the Father has *l* me, so 15.9
thou hast sent me and..*l* them 17.23
disciple whom he *l* standing 19.26
"Jacob I *l*, but Esau I hated." Rom 9.13
Son of God, who *l* me and gave Gal 2.20
great love with which he *l* us, Eph 2.4
Thou hast *l* righteousness Heb 1.9
for they *l* not their lives Rev 12.11

LOVE (n)

LORD set his *l* upon you Deut 7.7
the loyal *l* of the LORD, 1Sam 20.14
not take my steadfast *l* 2Sam 7.15
Because he cleaves to me in *l*, Ps 91.14
let us take our fill of *l* Prov 7.18
but *l* covers all offenses. 10.12
dinner of herbs where *l* is 15.17
open rebuke than hidden *l*. 27.5
For your *l* is better than wine, Sol 1.2
you are beautiful, my *l*; 1.15
Behold, you are beautiful, my *l*, 4.1
better is your *l* than wine, 4.10
seal..for *l* is strong as death, 8.6
Many waters cannot quench *l*, 8.7
l song concerning his vineyard: Isa 5.1
in his *l* and..pity he redeemed 63.9
with..lips they show much *l*, Ezek 33.31
Your *l* is like a morning cloud, Hos 6.4
I led them with..bands of *l*, 11.4
most men's *l* will grow cold. Mt 24.12
you..neglect justice and..*l* Lk 11.42
Greater *l* has no man than this, Jn 15.13
that the *l* with which thou 17.26
God's *l* has been poured Rom 5.5
But God shows his *l* for us 5.8
separate us from the *l* of God 8.39
Let *l* be genuine; hate what 12.9
puffs up, but *l* builds up. 1Cor 8.1
but have not *l*, I am a noisy gong 13.1
the greatest of these is *l*. 13.13
the *l* of Christ controls us, 2Cor 5.14
by..the Holy Spirit, genuine *l*, 6.6
prove..that your *l*..is genuine. 8.8
of your *l* and of our boasting 8.24
Christ and the *l* of God and 13.14
but faith working through *l*. Gal 5.6
through *l* be servants of one 5.13
your *l* toward all the saints, Eph 1.15
to know the *l* of Christ 3.19

speaking the truth in *l*, 4.15
walk in *l*, as Christ loved us 5.2
prayer that your *l* may abound Phil 1.9
The latter do it out of *l*, 1.16
the *l* which you have for all Col 1.4
above all these put on *l*, 3.14
work of faith..labor of *l* 1Thess 1.3
concerning *l* of the brethren 4.9
Demas, in *l* with this present 2Tim 4.10
Let brotherly *l* continue. Heb 13.1
since *l* covers a multitude 1Pet 4.8
See what *l* the Father has given 1Jn 3.1
By this we know *l*, that he 3.16
blemishes on your *l* feasts, Jude 12
abandoned..*l* you had at first. Rev 2.4

LOVELY

How *l* is thy dwelling place, Ps 84.1
whatever is *l*, is gracious, Phil 4.8

LOVERS

and drink: drink deeply, O *l*! Sol 5.1
Your *l* despise you; they seek Jer 4.30
l shall go into captivity; 22.22
All your *l* have forgotten you; 30.14
gifts to all your *l*, bribing Ezek 16.33
rouse against you your *l* 23.22
alone; Ephraim has hired *l*. Hos 8.9
For men will be *l* of self, 2Tim 3.2

LOW — EST

haughty looks..be brought *l*, Isa 2.11
the lofty will be brought *l*. 10.33
He..lays it *l* to the ground, 26.5
with shame to take the *l* place. Lk 14.9

LOWLY

proud, but he saves the *l*. Job 22.29
better to be of a *l* spirit Prov 16.19
l in spirit will obtain honor. 29.23
leave..a people humble and *l*. Zeph 3.12

LOYAL — LY

"With the *l* thou dost show 2Sam 22.26
With the *l* thou dost show..*l*; Ps 18.25
"I will deal *l* with Hanun 1Chr 19.2

LOYALTY

you showed this *l* to Saul 2Sam 2.5
desired in a man is *l*, and Prov 19.22

LUKE

L the beloved physician and Col 4.14
L alone is with me. Get Mark 2Tim 4.11
and *L*, my fellow workers. Philem 24

LUKEWARM

So, because you are *l*, and Rev 3.16

LUST — FULLY

the *l* of the flesh and the *l* 1Jn 2.16
looks at a woman *l* has already Mt 5.28

LYING

Let the *l* lips be dumb, which Ps 31.18
against me with *l* tongues. 109.2
haughty eyes, a *l* tongue, and Prov 6.17

LYRE — S

father of all..who play the *l* Gen 4.21
Praise the LORD with the *l*, Ps 33.2
On the willows..we hung up our *l*. 137.2

LYSTRA

fled to *L* and Derbe, cities Acts 14.6
they returned to *L* and to 14.21
came also to Derbe and to *L*. 16.1
and at *L*, what persecutions 2Tim 3.11

M

MACEDONIA
a man of M..beseeching him　　Acts 16.9
and Timothy arrived from M,　　18.5
sent into M two of his helpers,　19.22
For M and Achaia have been　Rom 15.26
about you to the people of M,　2Cor 9.2
when I left M, no church　　Phil 4.15
word of Lord sounded..in M　1Thess 1.8

MAD — NESS
driven m by the sight　　Deut 28.34
feigned himself m in their　　1Sam 21.13
"I am not m,..Festus, but　Acts 26.25
consider wisdom..m and folly;　Ecc 2.12

MAGGOT
much less man, who is a m,　　Job 25.6

MAGNIFICENCE
Artemis..deposed from her m　Acts 19.27

MAGNIFICENT
house..must be exceedingly m　1Chr 22.5

MAGNIFY — IES — IED
O m the LORD with me, and let　Ps 34.3
and dishonor who m themselves　35.26
or the saw m itself against　Isa 10.15
m his law..make it glorious.　42.21
to..Gentiles, I m my ministry　Rom 11.13
Mary said, "My soul m the Lord,　Lk 1.46
thy name will be m for ever,　2Sam 7.26
thy name will be..m for ever,　1Chr 17.24
It m itself,..up to the Prince　Dan 8.11

MAGOG
Gog, of the land of M, the　Ezek 38.2
Gog and M, to gather them　Rev 20.8

MAID
Sarai said..go in to my m;　　Gen 16.2
little m from the land..Israel　2Ki 5.2
a m when she succeeds her　Prov 30.23
another m saw him, and..said　Mt 26.71

MAIDEN — S
"Let a young m be sought for　1Ki 1.2
the way of a man with a m.　Prov 30.19
between..m playing timbrels:　Ps 68.25
therefore the m love you.　　Sol 1.3
kingdom..compared to ten m　Mt 25.1

MAINTAIN
m the right of..man with God,　Job 16.21
m the rights of the poor　　Prov 31.9

MAINTENANCE
gifts for the m of the house　1Chr 26.27

MAJESTIC
our Lord, how m is thy name in　Ps 8.1
our Lord, how m is thy name in　8.9

MAJESTY
Will not his m terrify you,　Job 13.11
"Deck yourself with m and　40.10
there the LORD in m will be　Isa 33.21
Zion has departed all her m.　Lam 1.6
and for the glory of my m?"　Dan 4.30
my m and splendor returned　4.36
the m of the name of the LORD　Mic 5.4

MAKER
God..m of heaven and earth;　Gen 14.19
none says, 'Where is..my M,　Job 35.10
kneel before the LORD, our M!　Ps 95.6
men will regard their M, and　Isa 17.7

"Woe..who strives with his M,　45.9
For your M is your husband,　54.5

MALACHI
word of the LORD to Israel by M.　Mal 1.1

MALE
m and female he created　　Gen 1.27
Every m..shall be circumcised.　17.10
there is neither m nor female;　Gal 3.28

MALTA
the island was called M.　　Acts 28.1

MAMMON
You cannot serve God and m.　Mt 6.24
make friends..of unrighteous m,　Lk 16.9

MAN — 'S
make m in our image,　　Gen 1.26
God formed m of dust　　2.7
the m called every..creature,　2.19
m and his wife hid themselves　3.8
to David, "You are the m.　2Sam 12.7
a m be pure before his Maker?　Job 4.17
but m is born to trouble　　5.7
What is m, that thou dost　7.17
he is not a m, as I am,　　9.32
"M that is born of a woman　14.1
But m dies, and is laid low;　14.10
What is m, that he can be　15.14
what is m that thou dost regard　Ps 144.3
and one m sharpens another.　Prov 27.17
mind of m reflects the m.　27.19
way of m is not in himself,　Jer 10.23
declares to m..his thought;　Amos 4.13
what can a m give in return　Mk 8.37
no m to put me into the pool　Jn 5.7
"No m ever spoke like this m!"　7.46
as sin came..through one m　Rom 5.12
by your knowledge this weak m　1Cor 8.11
m was not made from woman,　11.8
create in himself one new m　Eph 2.15
"What is m that thou art　Heb 2.6
A m steps are ordered by　Prov 20.24

MANASSEH
Joseph called..first-born M,　Gen 41.51
two sons, M and Ephraim.　48.1
Of the people of M, their　Num 1.34
son of M, from the families　27.1
to the half-tribe of M.　　Deut 3.13
my clan is the weakest in M,　Judg 6.15
M. was twelve years old when　2Ki 21.1
M shed very much innocent　21.16
M slept with his fathers,　21.18
the altars which M had made　23.12
M was twelve years old when　2Chr 33.1
M knew that the LORD was　33.13
not..as M his father had　33.23

MANDRAKES
Reuben went and found m　Gen 30.14
The m give forth fragrance,　Sol 7.13

MANGER
and laid him in a m, because　Lk 2.7

MANIFEST — ED
Let thy work be m to thy　Ps 90.16
hid, except to be made m;　Mk 4.22
the life was made m, and we　1Jn 1.2
the love of God was made m　4.9
m thy might among the peoples.　Ps 77.14

MANIFESTATION
until..day of his m to Israel.　Lk 1.80
given the m of the Spirit　1Cor 12.7

MANNA
Israel called its name *m*; Ex 16.31
Israel ate the *m* forty years, 16.35
nothing at all but this *m* Num 11.6
the *m* ceased on the morrow, Josh 5.12
rained..upon them *m* to eat, Ps 78.24
Our fathers ate *m* in..wilderness; Jn 6.31
give some of the hidden *m*, Rev 2.17

MAN OF GOD
told her husband, "A *m*..came Judg 13.6
And there came a *m*..to Eli, 1Sam 2.27
there is a *m*..in this city, 9.6
a *m*..came out of Judah by 1Ki 13.1
m.., who disobeyed the word 13.26
I know that you are a *m*.., 17.24
a *m*..came near and said to 20.28
"If I am a *m*.., let fire come 2Ki 1.10
he died, as the *m*..had said 7.17
a *m*..came to him and said, 2Chr 25.7

MANTLE
he took up the *m* of Elijah 2Ki 2.13

MARK (JOHN MARK)
Cousin of Barnabas, Col 4.10; lived in Jerusalem, Acts 12.12; accompanied Barnabas and Paul to Antioch, Acts 12.25; began missionary work, Acts 13.5; deserted the group at Perga, Acts 13.13; subject of contention, Acts 15.37–38; went with Barnabas to Cyprus, Acts 15.39; ministered to Paul in Rome, Col 4.10; Philem 24; companion of Peter, 1Pet 5.13.

MARK — ED (v)
M the blameless man, and Ps 37.37
"*M* this,..you who forget God, 50.22
If thou,..*m* iniquities, Lord, 130.3
to be *m* on the right hand Rev 13.16

MARK — S (n)
LORD put a *m* on Cain, Gen 4.15
put a *m* upon the foreheads Ezek 9.4
receives a *m* on his forehead Rev 14.9
received the *m* of·the beast 19.20
on my body the *m* of Jesus. Gal 6.17

MARKET — S
like children sitting in the *m* Lk 7.32
love salutations in the *m* 20.46
and in the *m* place every day Acts 17.17
Eat whatever..in the meat *m* 1Cor 10.25
coastlands were..special *m*, Ezek 27.15

MARRIAGE — S
king who gave a *m* feast for Mt 22.2
in with him to the *m* feast; 25.10
come home from the *m* feast, Lk 12.36
forbid *m* and enjoin abstinence 1Tim 4.3
Let *m* be held in honor among Heb 13.4
Make *m*..give your daughters Gen 34.9
and make *m* with them, Josh 23.12

MARRY — IES — IED
when they rise..they neither *m* Mk 12.25
neither *m* nor are given in Lk 20.35
m her, if then she finds Deut 24.1
and whoever *m* a divorced woman Mt 5.32
m another, commits adultery." 19.9
divorces..wife and *m* another, Mk 10.11
who divorces his wife and *m* Lk 16.18
Cushite woman whom he had *m*, Num 12.1
m..daughter of a foreign god. Mal 2.11
To the *m* I give charge, 1Cor 7.10
the *m* man is anxious about 7.33

MARTHA
M received him into her house. Lk 10.38
village of Mary and..sister *M*. Jn 11.1
M said to him, "I know that 11.24
they made a supper; *M* served, 12.2

MARTYRS
the blood of the *m* of Jesus. Rev 17.6

MARVEL — ED
the angel said to me, "Why *m*? Rev 17.7
When Jesus heard him, he *m*, Mt 8.10
the men *m*,.."What sort of man 8.27
dumb man spoke;..the crowds *m*, 9.33
When they heard it, they *m*; 22.22
done for him; and all men *m*. Mk 5.20
he *m* because of their unbelief. 6.6
When Jesus heard this he *m* at Lk 7.9

MARVELOUS
m things without number: Job 5.9
and *m* things without number. 9.10
the LORD's doing; it is *m* Ps 118.23
do *m* things with this people, Isa 29.14

MARY (Magdalene)
Healed of demons, Lk 8.2; stood by the cross, Mt 27.56 (Mk 15.40; Jn 19.25); watched Jesus' burial, Mt 27.61 (Mk 15.47); came early to the sepulchre, Mt 28.1 (Mk 16.1; Lk 24.10; Jn 20.1); saw the risen Lord, Mt 28.9 (Mk 16.9n; Jn 20.11–18).

MARY (Mother of Jesus)
Betrothed to Joseph, Mt 1.18 (Lk 1.27); Jesus' birth foretold to her, Lk 1.26–38; visited Elizabeth, Lk 1.39–45; "The Magnificat," Lk 1.46–55; went to Bethlehem, Lk 2.4–5; birth of Jesus, Mt 1.25 (Lk 2.7); found Jesus in the temple, Lk 2.41–51; attended the marriage at Cana, Jn 2.1–5; concerned over Jesus' ministry, Mk 3.31–35; at the cross, Jn 19.25–27; in the upper room, Acts 1.14.

MARY (of Bethany)
Listened to the Lord's teaching, Lk 10.38–42; present at the raising of Lazarus, Jn 11.1–45; anointed Jesus' feet, Jn 12.1–8.

MASTER — S
m saw..the LORD was with him, Gen 39.3
'I love my *m*, my wife, Ex 21.5
who guards his *m*..honored. Prov 27.18
I am your *m*; I will take you, Jer 3.14
who is both their *M* and yours Eph 6.9
useful to the *m* of the house, 2Tim 2.21
"No one can serve two *m*; for Mt 6.24
Neither be called *m*, for you 23.10
Those who have believing *m* 1Tim 6.2
be submissive to your *m* with 1Pet 2.18

MATTHEW
he saw a man called *M* sitting Mt 9.9
Thomas and *M* the tax collector; 10.3
and *M*, and Thomas, and James Mk 3.18
and *M*, and Thomas, and James Lk 6.15
Thomas, Bartholomew and *M*, Acts 1.13

MATURE
among..*m* we do impart wisdom, 1Cor 2.6
to *m* manhood, to the measure Eph 4.13

MATURITY
go on to *m*, not laying again Heb 6.1

MEASURE — D — ING (v)
"Rise and *m* the temple of God   Rev 11.1
a measuring rod of gold to *m*   21.15
has *m* the waters in. .his hand   Isa 40.12
"If the heavens. .can be *m*,   Jer 31.37
He stood and *m* the earth;   Hab 3.6
man with a *m* line in his hand!   Zech 2.1

MEASURE (n)
what is the *m* of my days;   Ps 39.4
the *m* you give will be the *m*   Mk 4.24
the *m* you give will be the *m*   Lk 6.38

MEDE — S
by birth a *M*, who became king   Dan 9.1
and in the cities of the *M*.   2Ki 17.6
let it be written among. .*M*   Est 1.19
The LORD has stirred up. .*M*,   Jer 51.11
given to the *M* and Persians."   Dan 5.28
according to the law of the *M*   6.8

MEDIA
province of *M*, a scroll was   Ezra 6.2
of Persia and *M* and the nobles   Est 1.3
Chronicles of the kings of *M*   10.2
ram. .kings of *M* and Persia.   Dan 8.20

MEDIATOR
If there be for him. .a *m*,   Job 33.23
one *m* between God and men,   1Tim 2.5
is the *m* of a new covenant,   Heb 9.15
Jesus,. .*m* of a new covenant,   12.24

MEDITATE — S
Isaac went. .to *m* in the field   Gen 24.63
m on it day and night,   Josh 1.8
and *m* on thee in the watches   Ps 63.6
I will *m* on all thy work, and   77.12
I will *m* on thy precepts, and   119.15
I will *m* on thy precepts.   119.78
I *m* on all that thou hast done;   143.5
on his law he *m* day and night.   1.2

MEDITATION
and hindering *m* before God,   Job 15.4
Let the words. .and the *m* of my   Ps 19.14
wisdom; the *m* of my heart   49.3
May my *m* be pleasing to him,   104.34
thy law!. .is my *m* all the day.   119.97

MEEK — NESS
Moses was very *m*, more   Num 12.3
hear the desire of the *m*;   Ps 10.17
the *m* shall possess the land,   37.11
The *m* shall obtain fresh joy   Isa 29.19
"Blessed are the *m*, for they   Mt 5.5
by the *m* and gentleness of   2Cor 10.1
with all lowliness and *m*,   Eph 4.2
receive with *m* the implanted   Jas 1.21

MEET — ING
There I will *m* with you,   Ex 25.22
prepare to *m*. .God, O Israel!"   Amos 4.12
the city came out to *m* Jesus;   Mt 8.34
in. .clouds to *m* the Lord   1Thess 4.17
it did not *m* with faith in   Heb 4.2
not neglecting to *m* together,   10.25
burned all the *m* places of God   Ps 74.8

MEGIDDO
the king of *M*, one;   Josh 12.21
of *M* and its villages;   17.11
M, and all Bethshean which   1Ki 4.12
he fled to *M*, and died there.   2Ki 9.27
Pharaoh Neco slew him at *M*,   23.29
mourning. .in the plain of *M*.   Zech 12.11

MELCHIZEDEK
M king of Salem brought   Gen 14.18
priest. .after the order of *M*."   Ps 110.4
for ever, after the order of *M*."   Heb 5.6
for ever after the order of *M*.   6.20
this *M*, king of Salem, priest   7.1
his ancestor when *M* met him.   7.10
priest. .in the likeness of *M*,   7.15

MELT — S — ED
mountains *m* like wax before   Ps 97.5
sends forth his word, and *m*   147.18
inhabitants of Canaan. .*m*   Ex 15.15
heard it, our hearts *m*,   Josh 2.11
crossed over, their heart *m*,   5.1
the hearts of the people *m*,   7.5
my heart is like wax; it is *m*   Ps 22.14
so you shall be *m* in. .it;   Ezek 22.22

MEMBERS
Do not yield your *m* to sin   Rom 6.13
m do not have. .same function,   12.4
Shall I. .take the *m* of Christ   1Cor 6.15
because we are *m* of his body.   Eph 5.30

MEMORIAL
as a *m* between your eyes,   Ex 13.9
"Write this as a *m* in a book   17.14
these stones. .a *m* for ever."   Josh 4.7
thy *m* name is the desire of   Isa 26.8
alms have ascended as a *m*   Acts 10.4

MEMORY
His *m* perishes from. .earth   Job 18.17
his *m* be cut off from. .earth!   Ps 109.15
The *m* of the righteous is a   Prov 10.7
but the *m* of them is lost.   Ecc 9.5
will be told in *m* of her."   Mt 26.13

MEN
and acquit yourselves like *m*,   1Sam 4.9
my transgressions from *m*,   Job 31.33
know that they are but men!   Ps 9.20
and behaving like ordinary *m*?   1Cor 3.3
So let no one boast of *m*.   3.21
Paul an apostle—not from *m*   Gal 1.1

MENE
inscribed: *M*, *M*, TEKEL, and   Dan 5.25

MEPHIBOSHETH
Crippled by a fall, 2Sam 4.4; dined
continually at the royal table, 2Sam 9;
reported to David as a deserter, 2Sam
16.1–4; cleared himself before David,
2Sam 19.24–30.

MERCHANT — S
kingdom. .is like a *m* in search   Mt 13.45
You increased your *m* more   Nah 3.16
the *m* of the earth have grown   Rev 18.3

MERCIFUL
LORD being *m* to him,   Gen 19.16
house of Israel are *m* kings;   1Ki 20.31
art a God *m* and gracious, slow   Ps 86.15
thou art a gracious God and *m*,   Jonah 4.2
"Blessed are the *m*, for they   Mt 5.7
Be *m*, even as your Father is *m*.   Lk 6.36
m toward their iniquities,   Heb 8.12

MERCY — IES
God Almighty grant you *m*   Gen 43.14
show *m* on whom I will show *m*.   Ex 33.19
and show no *m* to them.   Deut 7.2
for his *m* is very great;   1Chr 21.13
grant him *m* in the sight of   Neh 1.11

MERCY — IES (cont.)

Have *m* on me, O God,..love;   Ps 51.1
crowns you with..love and *m*,   103.4
I will surely have *m* on him,   Jer 31.20
I will grant you *m*, that he   42.12
told them to seek *m* of the God Dan 2.18
known; in wrath remember *m*.   Hab 3.2
'I desire *m*, and not sacrifice.'   Mt 9.13
'I desire *m* and not sacrifice,'   12.7
"Have *m* on me, O Lord, Son of   15.22
"Have *m* on us, Son of David!"   20.30
law, justice and *m* and faith;   23.23
tell..how he has had *m* on you." Mk 5.19
his *m* is on those who fear   Lk 1.50
to perform the *m* promised to   1.72
one who showed *m* on him."   10.37
'Father Abraham, have *m* upon me, 16.24
"Jesus, Son of David, have *m*   18.38
have *m* on whom I have *m*,   Rom 9.15
he has *m* upon whomever he wills, 9.18
glory for the vessels of *m*,   9.23
now have received *m* because   11.30
ministry by the *m* of God,   2Cor 4.1
But God had *m* on him, and   Phil 2.27
his *m* never come to an end;   Lam 3.22

MERCY SEAT

and from above the *m*..,   Ex 25.22
within..veil, before the *m*..   Lev 16.2

MEROM

at the waters of *M*, to fight   Josh 11.5
by the waters of *M*, and fell   11.7

MESSAGE

"I have a *m* from God for   Judg 3.20
Haggai,..with the LORD's *m*,   Hag 1.13
confirmed the *m* by the signs Mk 16.20n
my *m*..not in plausible words 1Cor 2.4
This is the *m* we have heard   1Jn 1.5

MESSENGER — S

faithful *m* to those who send Prov 25.13
a *m*..sent among the nations: Jer 49.14
for he is the *m* of the LORD of Mal 2.7
send my *m* to prepare the way   3.1
I send my *m* before thy face,   Mt 11.10
I send my *m* before thy face,   Mk 1.2
I send my *m* before thy face,   Lk 7.27
a *m* of Satan, to harass me,   2Cor 12.7
Jacob sent *m*..to Esau   Gen 32.3
sent..to them by his *m*,   2Chr 36.15
"On that day swift *m* shall go Ezek 30.9
And he sent *m* ahead of him,   Lk 9.51

MESSIAH

said.."We have found the *M*"   Jn 1.41
"I know that *M* is coming   4.25

METHUSELAH

Thus all the days of *M*   Gen 5.27

MICAH

"*M* of Moresheth prophesied   Jer 26.18
word of the LORD that came to *M* Mic 1.1

MICHAL

*Married to David, 1Sam 18.20–30; helped
David escape, 1Sam 19.12–17; restored to
David, 2Sam 3.13–16; rebuked for despis-
ing David, 2Sam 6.12–23.*

the name of the younger *M*; 1Sam 14.49
bring *M*, Saul's daughter,   2Sam 3.13
M..saw King David dancing 1Chr 15.29

MICHMASH

thousand were with Saul in *M* 1Sam 13.2

on the north in front of *M*,   14.5
at *M* he stores his baggage;   Isa 10.28

MIDIAN — ITE

M, Ishbak, and Shuah.   Gen 25.2
Moses..stayed in..land of *M*;   Ex 2.15
LORD said to Moses in *M*,   4.19
Jethro, the priest of *M*,   18.1
Moab said to the elders of *M*, Num 22.4
into the hand of *M* seven years. Judg 6.1
the camp of *M* was below him   7.8
They set out from *M* and   1Ki 11.18
Do to them as thou didst to *M*, Ps 83.9
broken as on the day of *M*.   Isa 9.4
scourge, as when he smote *M*   10.26
Then *M* traders passed by;   Gen 37.28

MIDNIGHT

But Samson lay till *m*,   Judg 16.3
At *m* I rise to praise thee,   Ps 119.62
about *m* Paul and Silas were Acts 16.25
prolonged his speech until *m*.   20.7

MIDWIVES

king..said to the Hebrew *m*,   Ex 1.15

MIGHT

"Go in this *m*..and deliver   Judg 6.14
not by *m* shall a man prevail. 1Sam 2.9
"Do you give the horse his *m*? Job 39.19
But I will sing of thy *m*; I   Ps 59.16
to do, do it with your *m*; for   Ecc 9.10
men, whose own *m* is their god! Hab 1.11
Not by *m*, nor by power, but by Zech 4.6

MIGHTY — IER

"How are the *m* fallen   2Sam 1.25
the *m* men whom David had: 23.8
Why do the wicked..grow *m* in Job 21.7
God is *m*, and does not despise   36.5
With the *m* deeds of the Lord Ps 71.16
LORD..the *M* One of Israel: Isa 1.24
"Wonderful Counselor, *M* God,   9.6
vindication, *m* to save."   63.1
who does a *m* work in my name Mk 9.39
telling..the *m* works of God." Acts 2.11
A wise..*m* than a strong man, Prov 24.5
he who is *m* than I is coming,   Lk 3.16

MILE

if..one forces you to go one *m*, Mt 5.41

MILK

he took curds, and *m*,   Gen 18.8
a land flowing with *m* and honey, Ex 3.8
she opened a skin of *m*   Judg 4.19
thou not pour me out like *m*   Job 10.10
I fed you with *m*, not solid   1Cor 3.2
without getting some of the *m*?   9.7
You need *m*, not solid food;   Heb 5.12

MILLSTONE

woman threw an upper *m* upon Judg 9.53
a..*m* fastened round his neck Mt 18.6
better for him if a great *m*   Mk 9.42
better for him if a *m* were hung Lk 17.2

MIND — S

father kept the saying in *m*.   Gen 37.11
a *m* to understand, or eyes   Deut 29.4
an understanding *m* to govern 1Ki 3.9
m of the king..was..troubled 2Ki 6.11
repent with all their *m* and 2Chr 6.38
the people had a *m* to work.   Neh 4.6
call to *m* the deeds of..LORD; Ps 77.11
A tranquil *m* gives life to   Prov 14.30
A man's *m* plans his way,   16.9

MIND — S (cont.)

A man of crooked *m* does not | 17.20
m of man reflects the man. | 27.19
whose *m* is stayed on thee, | Isa 26.3
deluded *m* has led him astray, | 44.20
his *m* be changed from a man's, | Dan 4.16
clothed and in his right *m*, | Mk 5.15
m. .set on the flesh is hostile | Rom 8.7
who has known the *m* of the Lord, | 11.34
we have the *m* of Christ. | 1Cor 2.16
I will sing with the *m* also. | 14.15
speak five words with my *m*, | 14.19
do as he has made up his *m*, | 2Cor 9.7
Have this *m* among yourselves, | Phil 2.5
speak visions of their own *m*, | Jer 23.16
a veil lies over their *m*; | 2Cor 3.15
Set your *m* on things. .above, | Col 3.2

MINDFUL

Be *m* of thy mercy, O Lord, | Ps 25.6
The Lord has been *m* of us; | 115.12
their God will be *m* of them | Zeph 2.7
if, *m* of God, he endures pain | 1Pet 2.19

MINISTER — ED — ING (v)

as they *m* at the tabernacle; | Num 3.7
m in the name of the Lord | Deut 18.7
join. .the Lord, to *m* to him, | Isa 56.6
their kings shall *m* to you; | 60.10
And the boy *m* to the Lord, | 1Sam 2.11
went after Elijah, and *m* to | 1Ki 19.21
They *m* with song before | 1Chr 6.32
Samuel was *m* to the Lord | 1Sam 3.1
women. .followed. .*m* to him; | Mt 27.55

MINISTER — S (n)

to be a *m* of Christ Jesus | Rom 15.16
of which I, Paul, became a *m*. | Col 1.23
Tychicus. .faithful *m* and | 4.7
makest. .fire and flame thy *m*. | Ps 104.4
shall be *m* in my sanctuary, | Ezek 44.11

MINISTRY

and to the *m* of the word." | Acts 6.4
to. .Gentiles, I magnify my *m* | Rom 11.13
the work of *m*, for building | Eph 4.12

MIRACLE — S

'Prove. .by working a *m*,' | Ex 7.9
to another the working of *m*, | 1Cor 12.10
he who. .works *m* among you | Gal 3.5

MIRIAM

Song of Miriam, Ex 15.20–21; became
leprous for criticizing Moses, Num 12.1–
10; her leprosy healed, Num 12.11–16;
died in Kadesh, Num 20.1.

MIRROR — S

skies, hard as a molten *m*? | Job 37.18
now we see in a *m* dimly, | 1Cor 13.12
who observes his. .face in a *m*. | Jas 1.23
the *m* of the ministering women | Ex 38.8

MISCHIEF

Philistines. .I do them *m*." | Judg 15.3
wicked. .is pregnant with *m*, | Ps 7.14
He plots *m* while on his bed; | 36.4

MISCHIEF-MAKER

or a wrongdoer, or a *m*; | 1Pet 4.15

MISERABLE

m comforters are you all. | Job 16.2

MISFORTUNE

M pursues sinners, but | Prov 13.21

MISS — ES — ED

sling a stone. .and not *m*. | Judg 20.16
inspect. .fold and *m* nothing. | Job 5.24
who *m* me injures himself; | Prov 8.36
you will be *m*, because your | 1Sam 20.18

MIST

a *m* went up from the earth | Gen 2.6
You are a *m* that appears | Jas 4.14

MIZPAH

Laban. .named. .the pillar *M*, | Gen 31.49
words before the Lord at *M*. | Judg 11.11
"Gather all Israel at *M*, | 1Sam 7.5
together to the Lord at *M*; | 10.17
took captive. .people. .in *M*, | Jer 41.10

MOCK — S — ED — ING

sent to *m* the living God, | 2Ki 19.4
and after I have spoken, *m* on. | Job 21.3
All who see me *m* at me, they | Ps 22.7
Assyria has sent to *m*. .God, | Isa 37.4
those. .far from you. .*m* you, | Ezek 22.5
they will *m* him, and spit upon | Mk 10.34
who see it begin to *m* him, | Lk 14.29
m the poor insults his Maker; | Prov 17.5
all the day; every one *m* me. | Jer 20.7
you have *m* me, and told | Judg 16.10
at noon Elijah *m* them, | 1Ki 18.27
"Whom have you *m* and reviled | 2Ki 19.22
they *m* him, saying, "Hail, | Mt 27.29
also the chief priests *m* him | Mk 15.31
will be *m* and shamefully | Lk 18.32
The soldiers also *m* him, | 23.36
some *m*; but others said, | Acts 17.32
I shall seem to be *m* him, | Gen 27.12
kept *m* the messengers of | 2Chr 36.16

MOLECH

devote them by fire to *M*, | Lev 18.21
daughter. .an offering to *M*. | 2Ki 23.10

MONEY

refund. .*m* for his redemption. | Lev 25.52
redemption *m* from those who | Num 3.49
you shall turn it into *m*, | Deut 14.25
give the *m* that was weighed | 2Ki 12.11
who loves *m*. .not be satisfied | Ecc 5.10
wisdom is like the protection of *m*; | 7.12
and *m* answers everything. | 10.19
pieces of silver. .are blood *m*." | Mt 27.6
gave a sum of *m* to the soldiers | 28.12
Pharisees,. .were lovers of *m*, | Lk 16.14
brought the *m* and laid it at | Acts 4.37
Simon saw. .offered them *m*, | 8.18
love of *m* is the root of all | 1Tim 6.10
Keep. .life free from love of *m*, | Heb 13.5

MONEY-CHANGERS

overturned the tables of the *m* | Mt 21.12
overturned the tables of the *m* | Mk 11.15
and the *m* at their business. | Jn 2.14

MOON

fair as the *m*, bright as. .sun, | Sol 6.10
the *m* will not shed. .light. | Isa 13.10
light of the *m*. .as the sun, | 30.26
and the fixed order of the *m* | Jer 31.35
m shall not give its light. | Ezek 32.7
the *m* will not give its light, | Mt 24.29
and the *m* into blood, before | Acts 2.20
another glory of the *m*, | 1Cor 15.41

MORALS

"Bad company ruins good *m*." | 1Cor 15.33

MORDECAI
Counseled Esther, Est 2.5–20; informed Esther of a conspiracy, Est 2.21–23; refused to reverence Haman, Est 3.2–6; arrayed in royal apparel, Est 6.1–11; promoted next to the king, Est 8.1–2; 10.3; reversed Haman's decree, Est 8.3— 9.4; decreed feast of Purim, Est 9.20–31.

MORIAH
go to..M, and offer him there   Gen 22.2

MORNING
the *m* thou dost hear my voice;   Ps 5.3
but joy comes with the *m*.   30.5
The watchman says: "*M* comes, Isa 21.12
in the *m*,..he rose and went out Mk 1.35
I will give him the *m* star. Rev 2.28
I am..the bright *m* star."   22.16

MORSEL
Better is a dry *m* with quiet   Prov 17.1
he to whom I shall give this *m* Jn 13.26

MORTAL
m man..righteous before God? Job 4.17
sin..reign in your *m* bodies, Rom 6.12
this *m* nature must put on   1Cor 15.53
There is sin which is *m*;   1Jn 5.16

MOSES
Born, Ex 2.1–4; adopted by Pharaoh's daughter, Ex 2.5–10; trained at the Egyptian court, Acts 7.22; killed an Egyptian, Ex 2.11–12; fled to Midian, Ex 2.15–20; married Zipporah, Ex 2.21– 22; called by God, Ex 3.1—4.17; returned to Egypt, Ex 4.18–31; interceded with Pharaoh, Ex 5—11; led the Israelites across the Red Sea, Ex 14; sang for triumph, Ex 15.1–18; appointed rulers, Ex 18.13–26; met God on Sinai, Ex 19.3–13; 24—31; enraged by Israel's idolatry, Ex 32; talked with the LORD, Ex 33—34; built the taber- nacle, Ex 35—40; numbered the people, Num 1; vindicated before Aaron and Miriam, Num 12; sent twelve spies to Canaan, Num 13.1–20; consecrated Joshua as his successor, Num 27.18–23; Deut 31.23; recounted Israel's history, Deut 1– 3; exhorted Israel to obedience, Deut 4.1– 40; song of Moses, Deut 32.1–43; viewed Canaan, Deut 3.23–27; 32.48–52; 34.1–4; blessed the tribes, Deut 33; death and burial in Moab, Deut 34.5–7. (See also Acts 7.20–44.)

M, so I will be with you;   Josh 1.5
by the hand of *M* and Aaron. Ps 77.20
He made known his ways to *M*,   103.7
would destroy them—had not *M*, 106.23
to go at the right hand of *M*, Isa 63.12
M and Samuel stood before me, Jer 15.1
appeared to them *M* and Elijah, Mt 17.3
M allowed you to divorce..wives, 19.8
Abraham said, 'They have *M* Lk 16.29
beginning with *M*..he interpreted 24.27
the law was given through *M*; Jn 1.17
as *M* lifted up the serpent   3.14
If you believed *M*, you would   5.46
M said, 'The Lord God will   Acts 3.22
death reigned from Adam to *M*, Rom 5.14
fathers..were baptized into *M* 1Cor 10.2
whenever *M* is read a veil   2Cor 3.15
Jannes and Jambres opposed *M*, 2Tim 3.8

just as *M* also was faithful   Heb 3.2
By faith *M*, when..born, was   11.23
disputed about the body of *M*, Jude 9
they sing the song of *M*, the Rev 15.3
could not look at *M* face   2Cor 3.7

MOTH
consume like a *m* what is dear Ps 39.11
I am like a *m* to Ephraim,   Hos 5.12
treasures on earth, where *m*   Mt 6.19

MOTHER — S
she was the *m* of all living.   Gen 3.20
shall be a *m* of nations;   17.16
and called the child's *m*.   Ex 2.8
arose as a *m* in Israel.   Judg 5.7
his *m* used to make for him 1Sam 2.19
slay it; she is its *m*."   1Ki 3.27
his *m*, King Asa removed   2Chr 15.16
making her the joyous *m* of   Ps 113.9
only one in the sight of my *m*, Prov 4.3
As one whom his *m* comforts, Isa 66.13
"Who..my *m*, and..brothers?" Mt 12.48
my brother, and sister, and *m*." 12.50
a man shall leave..father and *m* 19.5
"Who are my *m* and brothers?" Mk 3.33
'Honor your father and your *m*'; 7.10
disciple, "Behold, your *m*!" Jn 19.27
is free, and she is our *m*.   Gal 4.26
Lois and your *m* Eunice and   2Tim 1.5
treat..older women like *m*,   1Tim 5.2

MOTHER-IN-LAW
Naomi her *m* said to her,   Ruth 3.1
Simon's *m* lay sick with..fever, Mk 1.30

MOUNTAIN — S
long enough at this *m*;   Deut 1.6
going about this *m* country   2.3
O mighty *m*, *m* of Bashan; O Ps 68.15
the *m* of the house of the LORD Isa 2.2
or destroy in all my holy *m*;   11.9
On this *m* the LORD of hosts   25.6
to go to the *m* of the LORD,   30.29
on my holy *m*, the *m* height Ezek 20.40
the stone..became a great *m* Dan 2.35
have drunk upon my holy *m*, Obad 1.16
the *m* of the LORD of hosts,   Zech 8.3
devil took him to a..high *m*,   Mt 4.8
he went up on the *m*, and when   5.1
led them up a high *m* apart.   17.1
says to this *m*, 'Be taken up Mk 11.23
went up on the *m* to pray.   Lk 9.28
Thy righteousness is like the *m* Ps 36.6
not fear..though the *m* shake   46.2
go before you and level the *m*, Isa 45.2
You *m* of Israel, hear the word Ezek 6.3
And the *m* will melt under him Mic 1.4
as the highest of the *m*,   4.1
Hear, you *m*, the controversy   6.2
on the *m* the feet of him   Nah 1.15
those..in Judea flee to the *m*; Mk 13.14
faith, so as to remove *m*,   1Cor 13.2

MOUNT OF OLIVES
feet shall stand on the *M*..   Zech 14.4
to the *M*.., then Jesus sent   Mt 21.1
on the *M*.., the disciples came 24.3
they went out to the *M*...   26.30
but Jesus went to the *M*...   Jn 8.1*n*

MOURN — ED — ING (v)
m for him, as..an only child, Zech 12.10
"Blessed are those who *m*, for Mt 5.4
who *m* as though they were not 1Cor 7.30
Jacob..*m*..his son many days. Gen 37.34

MOURN — ED — ING (v) (cont.)

they *m* and wept and fasted	2Sam 1.12
David *m* for his son day	13.37
Why go I *m*..the oppression of	Ps 43.2
Daniel, was *m* for three weeks.	Dan 10.2

MOURNING (n)

shall call the farmers to *m*	Amos 5.16
like the *m* for an only son,	8.10
neither shall there be *m*	Rev 21.4

MOUTH — S

out of the *m* of the LORD.	Deut 8.3
the child, putting his *m* upon	2Ki 4.34
I lay my hand on my *m*.	Job 40.4
praise..continually be in my *m*.	Ps 34.1
My *m* is filled with thy praise,	71.8
Set a guard over my *m*, O LORD,	141.3
put your hand on your *m*.	Prov 30.32
And he touched my *m*, and said:	Isa 6.7
True instruction was in his *m*,	Mal 2.6
"Their *m* is full of curses	Rom 3.14
that every *m* may be stopped,	3.19
deceitful *m* are..against me,	Ps 109.2
have *m*, but they speak not,	135.16

MOVE — D — ING

for 'In him we live and *m*	Acts 17.28
live in them and *m* among	2Cor 6.16
places where I have *m* with	1Chr 17.6
right hand, I shall not be *m*.	Ps 16.8
the Most High..shall not be *m*.	21.7
God is..she shall not be *m*;	46.5
He will not let your foot be *m*,	121.3
Jesus, deeply *m* again came to	Jn 11.38
men *m* by the Holy Spirit	2Pet 1.21
Spirit..was *m* over..the waters	Gen 1.2
I have been *m* about in a tent	2Sam 7.6

MULTIPLY — IED

let birds *m* on the earth."	Gen 1.22
God..bless you and..*m* you,	28.3
be fruitful and *m*; a nation	35.11
bless you, and *m* you;	Deut 7.13
Thou hast *m* the nation, thou	Isa 9.3

MULTITUDE — S

led them..a *m* keeping festival.	Ps 42.4
love covers a *m* of sins.	1Pet 4.8
behold, a great *m* which no man	Rev 7.9
m, in the valley of decision!	Joel 3.14

MURDER

evil thoughts, *m*, adultery,	Mt 15.19
who had committed *m* in the	Mk 15.7
thrown into prison..for *m*.	Lk 23.19

MURDERER

He was a *m* from the beginning,	Jn 8.44
asked for a *m* to be granted	Acts 3.14

MURMUR — ED

wicked congregation *m*	Num 14.27
what is Aaron that you *m*	16.11
people of Israel *m* against Moses	Ex 16.2
the people *m* against Moses,	17.3
m against Moses and Aaron;	Num 14.2
Israel *m* against Moses	16.41
and you *m* in your tents,	Deut 1.27
m against the leaders.	Josh 9.18
They *m* in their tents, and	Ps 106.25
The Jews then *m* at him,	Jn 6.41
Hellenists *m* against..Hebrews	Acts 6.1

MUSTARD

kingdom..is like a grain of *m*	Mt 13.31
faith as a grain of *m* seed,	17.20

It is like a grain of *m* seed,	Mk 4.31
It is like a grain of *m* seed	Lk 13.19
faith as a grain of *m* seed,	17.6

MYRRH

robes are all fragrant with *m*	Ps 45.8
gold and frankincense and *m*.	Mt 2.11
offered..wine mingled with *m*;	Mk 15.23

MYRTLE

instead of the brier..the *m*;	Isa 55.13
He was standing among the *m*	Zech 1.8

MYSTERY — IES

seek mercy..concerning this *m*,	Dan 2.18
you to understand this *m*,	Rom 11.25
to the revelation of the *m*	16.25
Lo! I tell you a *m*. We shall	1Cor 15.51
made known..the *m* of his will,	Eph 1.9
insight into the *m* of Christ,	3.4
This is a great *m*, and I take	5.32
proclaim the *m* of the gospel,	6.19
the *m* hidden for ages and	Col 1.26
the knowledge of God's *m*,	2.2
m of lawlessness is..at work;	2Thess 2.7
hold the *m* of the faith with	1Tim 3.9
Great..the *m* of our religion:	3.16
the *m* of God, as he announced	Rev 10.7
written a name of *m*: "Babylon	17.5
stewards of the *m* of God.	1Cor 4.1
and understand all *m* and	13.2

MYTHS

to occupy themselves with *m*	1Tim 1.4
giving heed to Jewish *m*	Tit 1.14
not follow cleverly devised *m*	2Pet 1.16

N

NAAMAN

N, commander of the army of	2Ki 5.1
cleansed,..only *N* the Syrian."	Lk 4.27

NAHUM

The book of the vision of *N*	Nah 1.1

NAILING (v)

set aside, *n* it to the cross.	Col 2.14

NAILS (n)

like *n* firmly fixed..sayings	Ecc 12.11
in..hands the print of the *n*,	Jn 20.25

NAKED — NESS

"*N* I came from my mother's	Job 1.21
They go about *n*, without	24.10
shall go again, *n* as he came,	Ecc 5.15
Isaiah..walked *n* and barefoot	Isa 20.3
when you see the *n*, to cover	58.7
and leave you *n* and bare.	Ezek 16.39
linen cloth and ran away *n*.	Mk 14.52
You shall not uncover the *n* of	Lev 18.7
Your *n* shall be uncovered,	Isa 47.3

NAME — S

Abram..called on the *n*..LORD.	Gen 12.8
"Tell me, I pray, your *n*."	32.29
ask..his *n*?' what shall I say	Ex 3.13
by my *n* the LORD I did not	6.3
my *n* may be declared throughout	9.16
the LORD is his *n*.	15.3
shall not take the *n* of the LORD	20.7
proclaimed the *n* of the LORD.	34.5
woman's son blasphemed the *N*,	Lev 24.11
not take the *n* of the LORD	Deut 5.11
by the *n* of the LORD:	28.10
this glorious and awful *n*	28.58

NAME — S (cont.)

I will proclaim the *n* of the LORD.	32.3
wilt..do for thy great *n*?"	Josh 7.9
"What is your *n*, so that	Judg 13.17
and it be called by my *n*."	2Sam 12.28
and put my *n* there for ever;	1Ki 9.3
blessed..in the *n* of the LORD,	1Chr 16.2
I will make for you a *n*,	17.8
and praise thy glorious *n*.	29.13
Lord, how majestic is thy *n* in	Ps 8.9
know thy *n* put their trust in	9.10
May his *n* endure for ever,	72.17
n endures to all generations;	102.12
enters in the *n* of the LORD!	118.26
exalted above everything thy *n*	138.2
n of the LORD is a strong	Prov 18.10
A good *n* is to be chosen	22.1
good *n* is better than precious	Ecc 7.1
n of..LORD comes from far,	Isa 30.27
brings out their host..by *n*;	40.26
surname..by the *n* of Israel."	44.5
all the day my *n* is despised.	52.5
give them an everlasting *n*	56.5
you shall be called by a new *n*	62.2
this house,..called by my *n*,	Jer 7.11
and thy *n* is great in might.	10.6
are prophesying lies in my *n*;	14.14
had concern for my holy *n*,	Ezek 36.21
be jealous for my holy *n*.	39.25
of hosts, the LORD is his *n*:	Hos 12.5
all who call upon the *n* of	Joel 2.32
not mention..*n* of the LORD."	Amos 6.10
the nations..called by my *n*,"	9.12
did we not prophesy in your *n*,	Mt 7.22
baptizing..in the *n* of the Father	28.19
casting out demons in your *n*,	Mk 9.38
Many will come in my *n*, saying,	13.6
you shall call his *n* Jesus.	Lk 1.31
casting out demons in your *n*,	9.49
"Father, hallowed be thy *n*.	11.2
I have come in my Father's *n*,	Jn 5.43
Father, glorify thy *n*." Then	12.28
will give it to you in my *n*.	16.23
his *n*, by faith in his *n*,	Acts 3.16
by the *n* of Jesus Christ of	4.10
no other *n* under heaven	4.12
performed through the *n* of	4.30
preached..about..the *n* of Jesus	8.12
carry my *n* before the Gentiles	9.15
the *n* of..Lord..was extolled.	19.17
to die..for the *n* of the Lord	21.13
"The *n* of God is blasphemed	Rom 2.24
that my *n* may be proclaimed	9.17
bestowed..the *n*..above every *n*,	Phil 2.9
in the *n* of the Lord Jesus,	Col 3.17
who names the *n* of the Lord	2Tim 2.19
n..more excellent than theirs.	Heb 1.4
blaspheme that honorable *n*	Jas 2.7
If..reproached for the *n*	1Pet 4.14
a white stone, with a new *n*	Rev 2.17
fear and glorify thy *n*, O Lord?	15.4
man gave *n* to all cattle,	Gen 2.20
engrave on them the *n*	Ex 28.9
The *n* of the twelve apostles	Mt 10.2
rejoice that your *n* are written	Lk 10.20
whose *n* are in the book of life.	Phil 4.3

NAPHTALI

Rachel..called his name *N*.	Gen 30.8
N is a hind let loose,	49.21
families of *N* according	Num 26.50
And of *N* he said,..possess	Deut 33.23
N did not drive out the	Judg 1.33

of Zebulun, the princes of *N*.	Ps 68.27
Zebulun and the land of *N*,	Isa 9.1
territory of Zebulun and *N*,	Mt 4.13

NARROW

"Enter by the *n* gate; for the	Mt 7.13
"Strive to enter by ..*n* door;	Lk 13.24

NATHAN

Counseled David about the people, 2Sam 7.2–17 (1Chr 17.1–15); rebuked David, 2Sam 12.1–23; anointed Solomon as king, 1Ki 1.8–45.

NATHANAEL

Philip found *N*, and said to him,	Jn 1.45

NATION — S

I will make of you a great *n*,	Gen 12.2
become a great and mighty *n*,	18.18
will make of you a great *n*.	46.3
For what great *n* is there	Deut 4.7
take a *n* for himself from	4.34
and there he became a *n*,	26.5
LORD will bring a *n* against you	28.49
What other *n* on earth is	2Sam 7.23
rejoice in..gladness of thy *n*,	Ps 106.5
Righteousness exalts a *n*,	Prov 14.34
n..not lift up sword against *n*,	Isa 2.4
Thou hast multiplied the *n*,	9.3
n that did not obey the voice	Jer 7.28
cease from being a *n* before me	31.36
make them one *n* in the land,	Ezek 37.22
to a *n* producing the fruits	Mt 21.43
in every *n*..who fears him	Acts 10.35
sons of Japheth..in their *n*.	Gen 10.5
father of a multitude of *n*.	17.5
all of the *n* of the earth bless	22.18
all the *n* of the earth shall bless	26.4
slaves from among the *n* that	Lev 25.44
govern us like all the *n*."	1Sam 8.5
his glory among the *n*, his	1Chr 16.24
save us from among the *n*,	16.35
make me the head of the *n*.	Ps 18.43
counsel of the *n* to nought;	33.10
Let the *n* be glad and sing	67.4
Pour out thy anger on the *n*	79.6
Declare his glory among the *n*,	96.3
execute judgment among the *n*,	110.6
then they said among the *n*,	126.2
all the *n* shall flow to it,	Isa 2.2
the *n* are like a drop from	40.15
give you as a light to the *n*,	49.6
n shall come to your light,	60.3
I am coming to gather all *n*	66.18
declare my glory among the *n*.	66.19
then *n* shall bless themselves	Jer 4.2
All the *n* shall serve him	27.7
worst..*n* to take possession	Ezek 7.24
removed them..among the *n*,	11.16
n will know..I am the LORD,	36.23
set my glory among the *n*;	39.21
a byword among the *n*. Why	Joel 2.17
I will gather all..*n* and bring	3.2
Let the *n* bestir themselves,	3.12
upon the *n* that did not obey.	Mic 5.15
Look among the *n*, and see;	Hab 1.5
all the *n* against Jerusalem	Zech 14.2
my name is great among the *n*,	Mal 1.11
all *n* will call you blessed,	3.12
hated by all *n* for my..sake.	Mt 24.9
house of prayer for all..*n*"?	Mk 11.17
preached in his name to all *n*,	Lk 24.47
The *n* raged, but thy wrath	Rev 11.18

NATION — S (cont.)
n..deceived by thy sorcery. 18.23
By its light shall the n walk. 21.24

NATURE
men, of like n with you, Acts 14.15
do by n what the law requires, Rom 2.14
by n a wild olive tree, and 11.24
Elijah was a man of like n Jas 5.17
for God's n abides in him, 1Jn 3.9

NAZARETH
he..dwelt in a city called N, Mt 2.23
leaving N he..dwelt in Capernaum 4.13
Jesus from N of Galilee." 21.11
"This man was with Jesus of N." 26.71
you seek Jesus of N, who was Mk 16.6
prophets wrote, Jesus of N, Jn 1.45
Jesus of N, a man attested Acts 2.22
how God anointed Jesus of N 10.38
'I am Jesus of N whom you 22.8

NAZIRITE
the vow of a N, to separate Num 6.2
the boy shall be a N to God Judg 13.5

NEBO
Moses went up..to Mount N, Deut 34.1

NEBUCHADNEZZAR
(NEBUCHADREZZAR)
*Won the battle of Carchemish, 2Ki 24.1–7;
Jer 46.2; conquered Judah, 2Ki 24.10–
25.10 (2Chr 36.6–19; Jer 39.1–8; 52.1–14);
deported the people, 2Ki 24.14–16; 25.11–
21 (2Chr 36.20–21; Jer 39.9–10; 52.15–
30); favored Jeremiah, Jer 39.11–14; his
dreams revealed, Dan 2.1–13; 4.4–18; set
up the golden image, Dan 3.1–7; punished
for boasting, Dan 4.31–33; his reason
returned, Dan 4.34–37.*

NECK — S
Your n is like..tower of David, Sol 4.4
break the yoke..off their n, Jer 30.8
put your feet upon the n of Josh 10.24
risked their n for my life, Rom 16.4

NEED — S (v)
Father knows that you n them Mt 6.32
and give him whatever he n. Lk 11.8

NEED — S (n)
we have no n to answer you Dan 3.16
say, 'The Lord has n of them,' Mt 21.3
'The Lord has n of it and will Mk 11.3
'The Lord has n of it.' " Lk 19.31
made to each as any had n. Acts 4.35
Contribute to..n of..saints, Rom 12.13

NEEDFUL
one thing is n. Mary has Lk 10.42

NEEDLE
through the eye of a n than Lk 18.25

NEEDY
to bring down the poor and n, Ps 37.14
I am poor and n; but the LORD 40.17
raises up the n out of affliction, 107.41
kind to the n honors him, Prov 14.31
reaches out her hands to the n. 31.20
the n lie down in safety; Isa 14.30
the n for a pair of shoes— Amos 2.6
not a n person among them, Acts 4.34

NEGLECT — ED — ING
not n the house of our God. Neh 10.39
how shall we escape if we n Heb 2.3

you..n the weightier matters Mt 23.23
done, without n the others. Lk 11.42

NEHEMIAH
The words of N the son of Neh 1.1
After him N the son of Azbuk, 3.16
in the days of N the governor 12.26

NEIGHBOR — S — 'S
love your n as yourself: Lev 19.18
kills his n unintentionally, Deut 4.42
kills his n unintentionally 19.4
if any man hates his n, 19.11
a reproach against his n; Ps 15.3
Him who slanders his n secretly 101.5
not plan evil against your n Prov 3.29
if..become surety for your n, 6.1
godless man would destroy..n, 11.9
despises his n is a sinner, 14.21
Better is a n who is near 27.10
each speaks peaceably to his n, Jer 9.8
proclaiming liberty,..to his n; 34.17
love your n and hate..enemy.' Mt 5.43
love your n as yourself. 22.39
love your n as yourself.' Mk 12.31
to Jesus, "And who is my n?" Lk 10.29
love your n as yourself." Rom 13.9
love your n as yourself." Gal 5.14
love your n as yourself," Jas 2.8
that they were their n, Josh 9.16
speak peace with their n, while Ps 28.3
I am..a horror to my n, an 31.11
n drink..the cup of his wrath, Hab 2.15
who goes in to his n wife; Prov 6.29
be seldom in your n house, 25.17

NEPHILIM
The N were on the earth Gen 6.4
And there we saw the N Num 13.33

NET — S
seizes the poor..into his n. Ps 10.9
take me out of the n which is 31.4
For in vain is a n spread Prov 1.17
I will spread my n over him, Ezek 17.20
kingdom of heaven is like a n Mt 13.47
brother of Simon casting a n Mk 1.16
who spread n upon the water. Isa 19.8
in their boat mending the n. Mk 1.19

NEW — NESS
LORD creates something n, Num 16.30
He put a n song in my mouth, Ps 40.3
O sing to the LORD a n song; 96.1
Sing to the LORD a n song, 149.1
"See, this is n"? It has been Ecc 1.10
and n things I now declare; Isa 42.9
Behold, I am doing a n thing; 43.19
I make you hear n things, 48.6
you shall be called by a n name 62.2
the n heavens and the n earth 66.22
when I will make a n covenant Jer 31.31
his mercies..n every morning Lam 3.23
A n heart I will give you, Ezek 36.26
in the n world, when the Son Mt 19.28
my blood of the n covenant, Mk 14.24n
tears a piece from a n garment Lk 5.36
A n commandment I give to you, Jn 13.34
or hearing something n. Acts 17.21
in the n life of the Spirit. Rom 7.6
"This cup is the n covenant 1Cor 11.25
ministers of a n covenant, 2Cor 3.6
in Christ, he is a n creation; 5.17
they sang a n song, saying, Rev 5.9
saw a n heaven and a n earth; 21.1

NEW — NESS (cont.)

"Behold, I make all things *n*." 21.5
we too might walk in *n* of life. Rom 6.4

NICODEMUS

named *N*, a ruler of the Jews. Jn 3.1
N, who had gone to him before, 7.50
N also, who had at first come 19.39

NIGHT

darkness he called *N*. Gen 1.5
that *n* God appeared to Solomon 2Chr 1.7
n to *n* declares knowledge. Ps 19.2
at *n* his song is with me, a 42.8
makest darkness, and it is *n*, 104.20
the time of *n* and darkness. Prov 7.9
toiled all *n* and took nothing! Lk 5.5
This *n* your soul is required 12.20
This man came to Jesus by *n* Jn 3.2
while it is day; *n* comes, 9.4
walks in the *n*, he stumbles, 11.10
he. . went out; and it was *n*. 13.30
there shall be no *n* there; Rev 21.25

NILE

the *N* shall become foul, Ex 7.18
'My *N* is my own; I made it.' Ezek 29.3

NIMROD

Cush became. . father of *N*; Gen 10.8

NINEVEH

into Assyria, and built *N*, Gen 10.11
"Arise, go to *N*, that great Jonah 1.2
And should not I pity *N*, 4.11
N is like a pool whose waters Nah 2.8
N will arise at the judgment Mt 12.41
Jonah. . a sign to the men of *N*, Lk 11.30
men of *N* will arise at. .judgment 11.32

NOAH

Born, Gen 5.29; walked with God, Gen 6.9;
built the ark, Gen 6.11–22; preserved
through the flood, Gen 7.1—8.19; built an
altar, Gen 8.20–22; covenant with God,
Gen 9.8–17; his drunkenness, Gen 9.20–21;
prophesied concerning his sons, Gen 9.22–
27; died, Gen 9.28–29.

NOBLE

Hear, for I will speak *n* things, Prov 8.6
these Jews were more *n* than Acts 17.11
not many were of *n* birth; 1Cor 1.26
for *n* use, some for ignoble, 2Tim 2.20

NOISE

Make a joyful *n* to God, all Ps 66.1
Make a joyful *n* to the LORD, 100.1

NORTH

He stretches out the *n* over Job 26.7
I stirred up one from the *n*, Isa 41.25
I will say to the *n*, Give up, 43.6

NOTHING

Is it not in your sight as *n*? Hag 2.3
have not love, I gain *n*. 1Cor 13.3

NOUGHT

"Does Job fear God for *n*? Job 1.9
every vision comes to *n*'? Ezek 12.22

NUMBER —ED (v)

stars, if you are able to *n* Gen 15.5
"Go, *n* Israel and Judah." 2Sam 24.1
"Go, *n* Israel, from Beer-sheba 1Chr 21.2
thou wouldest *n* my steps, Job 14.16
So teach us to *n* our days Ps 90.12
So he *n* them in the wilderness Num 1.19

the people of Israel as *n* by 2.32
was *n* with the transgressors; Isa 53.12

NUMBER (n)

I will let you go in by *n*. Ezek 20.37
the Lord added to their *n* Acts 2.47
beast, for it is a human *n*, Rev 13.18

O

OAK — S

like an *o*, whose leaf withers, Isa 1.30
or an *o*, whose stump remained 6.13
be called *o* of righteousness, 61.3

OATH

will be free from this *o* Gen 24.8
you will be free from my *o*.' 24.41
shall make her take an *o*, Num 5.19
an *o* to walk in God's law Neh 10.29
love no false *o*, for all Zech 8.17
o which he swore to our father Lk 1.73
o neither to eat nor drink Acts 23.21
And it was not without an *o*. Heb 7.20

OBADIAH

The vision of *O*. Thus says Obad 1.1

OBEDIENCE

to him shall be the *o* Gen 49.10
to bring about *o* of the faith Rom 1.5
while your *o* is known to all, 16.19
sanctified. .for *o* to Jesus 1Pet 1.2

OBEDIENT

If you are willing and *o*, Isa 1.19
came to Nazareth,. .was *o* to Lk 2.51
many of the priests were *o* Acts 6.7
and became *o* unto death, Phil 2.8

OBEY — ED — ING

son; only *o* my word, and go, Gen 27.13
my son, *o* my voice; 27.43
if you will *o* my voice Ex 19.5
your God and *o* his voice; Deut 4.30
commandments and *o* his voice, 13.4
son. .will not *o* our voice; 21.20
if you *o* the commandments 28.13
you did not *o* the voice 28.45
and *o* his voice in all that 30.2
shall again *o* the voice 30.8
obeyed Moses. .we will *o* you; Josh 1.17
not *o* the voice of the LORD? 1Sam 15.19
Behold, to *o* is better than 15.22
because they did not *o* the 2Ki 18.12
they refused to *o*, and were Neh 9.17
command I gave..,'O my voice, Jer 7.23
nation. .did not *o* the voice 7.28
and *o* the voice of the LORD 26.13
But they did not *o* thy voice 32.23
O now the voice of the LORD 38.20
will *o* the voice of the LORD 42.6
did not *o* the voice of the LORD, 43.4
dominions shall serve and *o* Dan 7.27
diligently *o* the voice of Zech 6.15
that even winds and sea *o* him?" Mt 8.27
even the unclean spirits,. .*o* Mk 1.27
even wind and sea *o* him?" 4.41
wind and water, and they *o* Lk 8.25
"We must *o* God rather than Acts 5.29
and do not *o* the truth, but Rom 2.8
every thought captive to *o* 2Cor 10.5
refuses to *o* what we say 2Thess 3.14
salvation to all who *o* him, Heb 5.9
O your leaders and submit 13.17

OBEY — ED — ING (cont.)

who do not o the gospel of	1Pet 4.17
because you have o my voice."	Gen 22.18
because Abraham o my voice	26.5
the people of Israel o him,	Deut 34.9
that you have not o my voice,	Jer 3.13
We have o the voice of Jonadab	35.8
o the voice of the LORD their	Hag 1.12
By faith Abraham o when he	Heb 11.8
as Sarah o Abraham, calling	1Pet 3.6
by not o the priest who	Deut 17.12
who hindered you from o the	Gal 5.7

OBSERVE — S — ING

o the feast of unleavened	Ex 12.17
his statutes, and o his laws.	Ps 105.45
Blessed are they who o justice,	106.3
and o it with my whole heart.	119.34
teaching them to o all that I	Mt 28.20
You o days, and months, and	Gal 4.10
all, and o all their deeds.	Ps 33.15
who o the wind will not sow;	Ecc 11.4
keep the sabbath, o	Ex 31.16

OCCUPATION

and says, 'What is your o?'	Gen 46.33
What is your o? And whence	Jonah 1.8
with the workmen of like o,	Acts 19.25

OFFENDED

baker o..the king of Egypt.	Gen 40.1
the Pharisees were o when they	Mt 15.12
nor against Caesar have I o	Acts 25.8

OFFENSE

who forgives an o seeks love,	Prov 17.9
a sanctuary, and a stone of o,	Isa 8.14
blessed is he who takes no o	Mt 11.6
the carpenter,..And they took o	Mk 6.3
blessed is he who takes no o	Lk 7.23
said.."Do you take o at this?	Jn 6.61
Give no o to Jews or..Greeks	1Cor 10.32

OFFER — ED (v)

go to..Moriah, and o him there	Gen 22.2
"You shall not o the blood	Ex 34.25
not o anything that has	Lev 22.20
the king take and o up	2Sam 24.22
O right sacrifices, and put	Ps 4.5
I will o in his tent sacrifices	27.6
O..sacrifice of thanksgiving,	50.14
reconciled..and then come and o	Mt 5.24
'Did you o to me slain beasts	Acts 7.42
o to God acceptable worship,	Heb 12.28
Israel..o sacrifices to..God	Gen 46.1
and o unholy fire before the	Lev 10.1
who o his offering the first	Num 7.12
who o themselves willingly	Judg 5.9
had o freely to the LORD;	1Chr 29.9
Solomon o up burnt offerings	2Chr 8.12
have freely o to the God of	Ezra 7.15
o to live in Jerusalem.	Neh 11.2
they o a sacrifice to..LORD	Jonah 1.16
eating of food o to idols,	1Cor 8.4
By faith Abel o to God a more	Heb 11.4
he was tested, o up Isaac,	11.17

OFFERING — S (n)

Take from among you an o	Ex 35.5
bring an o, and come before	1Chr 16.29
brethren..an o to the LORD,	Isa 66.20
o..shall belong to..priests;	Ezek 44.30
the o of Judah and Jerusalem	Mal 3.4
that the o of the Gentiles	Rom 15.16
May he remember all your o,	Ps 20.3

OFFICER — S

chief o in..house of the LORD,	Jer 20.1
o answered, "No man ever spoke	Jn 7.46

OFFSPRING

your o as the grass of the	Job 5.25
what does he desire? Godly o.	Mal 2.15
'For we are indeed his o.'	Acts 17.28

OIL

sacred anointing o blended	Ex 30.25
the house, except a jar of o."	2Ki 4.2
thou anointest my head with o,	Ps 23.5
anointed..with..o of gladness	45.7
they are not..softened with o.	Isa 1.6
but the wise took flasks of o	Mt 25.4
and anointed with o many..sick	Mk 6.13

OINTMENT — S

Dead flies make..perfumer's o	Ecc 10.1
expensive o, and she poured it	Mt 26.7
jar of o of pure nard, very	Mk 14.3
and prepared spices and o.	Lk 23.56

OLD

now o and well advanced	Josh 23.2
counsel which the o men gave	2Chr 10.8
unshrunk cloth on an o garment,	Mt 9.16
unshrunk cloth on an o garment;	Mk 2.21
things known from of o.'	Acts 15.18
when they read the o covenant,	2Cor 3.14

OLIVE

a freshly plucked o leaf;	Gen 8.11
your children..like o shoots	Ps 128.3
his beauty shall be like the o,	Hos 14.6
you, a wild o shoot,..grafted	Rom 11.17

OLIVET

lodged on the mount called O.	Lk 21.37
returned..from..mount..O,	Acts 1.12

OLIVE TREES

When you beat your o..,	Deut 24.20
And there are two o..by it,	Zech 4.3
These are the two o..and the	Rev 11.4

ONE

they become o flesh.	Gen 2.24
since o fate comes to all, to	Ecc 9.2
and the two shall become o.'	Mk 10.8
made from o every nation	Acts 17.26
and o Lord, Jesus Christ,	1Cor 8.6
and the two shall become o."	Eph 5.31

ONESIMUS

with him O, the faithful and	Col 4.9
I appeal..for my child, O,	Philem 10

OPEN — S — EST — ED

o thou my lips, and my mouth	Ps 51.15
O my eyes that I may behold	119.18
o your eyes, and you will	Prov 20.13
"O to me, my sister, my love,	Sol 5.2
he shall o, and none..shut;	Isa 22.22
O the gates, that the righteous	26.2
gates shall be o continually;	60.11
o thy eyes and behold our	Dan 9.18
upon..Judah I will o my eyes,	Zech 12.4
"I will o my mouth in parables,	Mt 13.35
to o their eyes, that they	Acts 26.18
have set before you an o door,	Rev 3.8
he o the ears of men, and	Job 33.16
She o her mouth with wisdom,	Prov 31.26
when thou o thy hand, they	Ps 104.28
your eyes will be o,	Gen 3.5
the eyes of both were o,	3.7
LORD o the mouth of the ass,	Num 22.28

OPEN — S — EST — ED (cont.)
I have *o* my mouth to the | Judg 11.35
LORD *o* the eyes of the young | 2Ki 6.17
I *o*..but my beloved had..gone. | Sol 5.6
The Lord GOD has *o* my ear, | Isa 50.5
So I *o* my mouth, and he gave | Ezek 3.2
the heavens were *o* and he saw | Mt 3.16
blind..And their eyes were *o*. | 9.30
the tombs also were *o*, and | 27.52
the heavens *o* and the Spirit | Mk 1.10
He *o* the book and found the | Lk 4.17
their eyes were *o* and they | 24.31
he *o* their minds to understand | 24.45
Jesus made..clay and *o* his eyes. | Jn 9.14
he had *o* a door of faith | Acts 14.27
The Lord *o* her heart to..heed | 16.14
effective work has *o* to me, | 1Cor 16.9
door was *o* for me in the Lord; | 2Cor 2.12
the Lamb *o* one of the..seals, | Rev 6.1

OPENLY
could no longer *o* enter..town, | Mk 1.45
Yet..no one spoke *o* of him. | Jn 7.13
teaching about the Lord..*o* | Acts 28.31

OPPORTUNITY
an *o* I will summon you." | Acts 24.25
concerned..but you had no *o*. | Phil 4.10

OPPOSE — S — D — ING
these men also *o* the truth, | 2Tim 3.8
son of perdition, who *o* | 2Thess 2.4
"God *o* the proud, but gives | 1Pet 5.5
Cephas..*I o* him to his face, | Gal 2.11
might even be found *o* God!" | Acts 5.39

OPPRESS — ES — ED (v)
"You shall not *o* a stranger; | Ex 23.9
not *o* your neighbor or rob | Lev 19.13
shall not *o* a hired servant | Deut 24.14
if you do not *o* the alien, | Jer 7.6
false balances, he loves to *o*. | Hos 12.7
o the poor,..crush the needy, | Amos 4.1
they *o* a man and his house, | Mic 2.2
o the widow, the fatherless, | Zech 7.10
who *o* the hireling in..wages, | Mal 3.5
who *o* a poor man insults his | Prov 14.31
who *o* the poor to increase | 22.16
A poor man who *o* the poor | 28.3
who..*o* the poor and needy, | Ezek 18.12
be *o* for four hundred years; | Gen 15.13
or if he has *o* his neighbor | Lev 6.2

OPPRESSED (n)
Let the *o* see it and be glad; | Ps 69.32
save all the *o* of the earth. | 76.9
by showing mercy to the *o*, | Dan 4.27

OPPRESSION — S
Why go I mourning..the *o* of | Ps 42.9
o and fraud do not depart | 55.11
o makes the wise man foolish, | Ecc 7.7
seek justice, correct *o*; | Isa 1.17
trust in *o* and perverseness, | 30.12
By *o* and judgment he was taken | 53.8
practicing *o* and violence." | Jer 22.17
the *o* that are practiced | Ecc 4.1

OPPRESSOR
to the needy, and crush the *o*! | Ps 72.4
"How the *o* has ceased, the | Isa 14.4
where is the fury of the *o*? | 51.13
no *o* shall again overrun them, | Zech 9.8

ORACLE — S
The *o* concerning Babylon | Isa 13.1
An *o* concerning Damascus. | 17.1

An *o* concerning Egypt. Behold, | 19.1
o concerning..wilderness of..sea. | 21.1
The *o* concerning Arabia. In | 21.13
The *o* concerning Tyre. Waii, | 23.1
An *o* concerning Nineveh. | Nah 1.1
o of God which Habakkuk..saw | Hab 1.1
An *O* The word of the LORD | Zech 9.1
An *O* The word of the LORD | 12.1
The *o* of the word of the LORD | Mal 1.1
Jews are entrusted with the *o* | Rom 3.2

ORDAIN — ED
anoint them and *o* them | Ex 28.41
O LORD, thou wilt *o* peace | Isa 26.12
"Today you have *o* yourselves | Ex 32.29
the LORD had *o* to defeat | 2Sam 17.14
unless the Lord has *o* it? | Lam 3.37
hast *o* them as a judgment; | Hab 1.12
the one *o* by God to be judge | Acts 10.42
as many as were *o* to eternal | 13.48
it was *o* by angels through | Gal 3.19

ORDER
priest for ever after the *o* of | Ps 110.4
empty, swept, and put in *o*. | Mt 12.44
be done decently and in *o*. | 1Cor 14.40

ORDINANCES
passover..its statutes and..*o* | Num 9.3
has..*o* so righteous as all | Deut 4.8
know the *o* of the heavens? | Job 38.33

ORGANIZED
David *o* them according to | 1Chr 24.3
Levites whom David had *o* | 2Chr 23.18

OVEN
will make them as a blazing *o* | Ps 21.9
tomorrow is thrown into the *o*, | Lk 12.28

OVERCOME — S
cheer, I have *o* the world." | Jn 16.33
evil, but *o* evil with good. | Rom 12.21
you are of God, and have *o* them; | 1Jn 4.4
one stronger..*o* him, he takes | Lk 11.22
the victory that *o* the world, | 1Jn 5.4

OVERFLOW — S — ED — ING
their hearts *o* with follies. | Ps 73.7
also *o* in many thanksgivings | 2Cor 9.12
grace of our Lord *o* for me | 1Tim 1.14
pour down..an *o* blessing. | Mal 3.10

OVERLOOK — ED
God is not so unjust as to *o* | Heb 6.10
times of ignorance God *o*, | Acts 17.30

OVERTHROW
to destroy and to *o*, to build | Jer 1.10
to *o* the throne of kingdoms; | Hag 2.22
Do we..*o* law by this faith? | Rom 3.31

OVERWHELM — S — ED
dost *o* me with all thy waves. | Ps 88.7
come upon me, and horror *o* me. | 55.5
I sat there *o* among them | Ezek 3.15
may be *o* by excessive sorrow. | 2Cor 2.7

OWE — D
O no one anything, except | Rom 13.8
who *o*..ten thousand talents, | Mt 18.24

OWN — ER
plant them on thy *o* mountain, | Ex 15.17
Jesus has made me his *o*. | Phil 3.12
The ox knows its *o*, | Isa 1.3

OX
"When an *o* gores a man | Ex 21.28

OX (cont.)

as the o licks up the grass	Num 22.4
not muzzle an o when it	Deut 25.4
he follows her, as an o goes	Prov 7.22
The o knows its owner, and	Isa 1.3
o that has fallen into a well,	Lk 14.5
shall not muzzle an o when	1Cor 9.9
shall not muzzle an o when	1Tim 5.18

P

PAIN

multiply. .p in childbearing;	Gen 3.16
feels only the p of his own	Job 14.22
all his days are full of p,	Ecc 2.23
put away p from your body;	11.10
Your p is incurable. Because	Jer 30.15
For if I cause you p, who	2Cor 2.2

PAINTED

Jezebel. .p her eyes, and	2Ki 9.30
you bathed. .p your eyes, and	Ezek 23.40

PALACE — S

enter the p of the king.	Ps 45.15
fully armed, guards his own p,	Lk 11.21
From ivory p. .instruments	Ps 45.8

PALM

righteous flourish like the p	Ps 92.12
I will climb the p tree and	Sol 7.8
they took branches of p trees	Jn 12.13

PANGS

Many. .the p of the wicked;	Ps 32.10
Will not p take hold of you,	Jer 13.21
The p of childbirth come from	Hos 13.13

PARABLE — S

I will open my mouth in a p;	Ps 78.2
kingdom. .what p shall we use	Mk 4.30
not speak to them without a p,	4.34
p. .The seed is the word of God.	Lk 8.11
he told them many things in p,	Mt 13.3

PARADISE

you will be with me in P."	Lk 23.43
man was caught up into P—	2Cor 12.3

PARALYTIC — S

they brought. .a p,. .on his bed.	Mt 9.2
they came, bringing to him a p	Mk 2.3
and p, and he healed them.	Mt 4.24

PARALYZED

"Lord, my servant is lying p	Mt 8.6
on a bed a man who was p,	Lk 5.18
Aeneas,. .bedridden. .and was p.	Acts 9.33

PARDON — ED — ING

p our iniquity and our sin,	Ex 34.9
P the iniquity of this	Num 14.19
LORD would not p him,	Deut 29.20
I pray, p my sin, and return	1Sam 15.25
may the LORD p your servant:	2Ki 5.18
and the LORD would not p.	24.4
"The good LORD p every one	2Chr 30.18
Why. .not p my transgression	Job 7.21
p my guilt, for it is great.	Ps 25.11
God, for he will abundantly p.	Isa 55.7
seeks truth; that I may p her.	Jer 5.1
"How can I p you? Your children	5.7
I will p those whom I leave	50.20
that her iniquity is p, that	Isa 40.2
Who is a God like thee, p	Mic 7.18

PARENTS

children will rise against p	Mt 10.21

his p went to Jerusalem every	Lk 2.41
who sinned, this man or his p,	Jn 9.2
they called the p of the man	9.18
but p for their children.	2Cor 12.14
obey your p in the Lord, for	Eph 6.1
disobedient to their p,	2Tim 3.2

PARTAKE

not to p of the. .holy food,	Ezra 2.63
not to p of the. .holy food,	Neh 7.65
we all p of the one bread.	1Cor 10.17

PARTED

the water was p to the. .side	2Ki 2.8
p my garments among them,	Jn 19.24

PARTIAL

you shall not be p to. .poor	Lev 19.15
shall not be p in judgment;	Deut 1.17
terrible God, who is not p	10.17
not good to be p to a wicked	Prov 18.5

PARTIALITY

you shall not show p;	Deut 16.19
perversion of justice. .or p,	2Chr 19.7
P in judging is not good.	Prov 24.23
To show p is not good; but	28.21
I perceive. .God shows no p,	Acts 10.34
For God shows no p.	Rom 2.11
God shows no p)—those, I say,	Gal 2.6
that there is no p with him.	Eph 5.9
favor, doing nothing from p.	1Tim 5.21
show no p as you hold the faith	Jas 2.1

PARTICIPATION

a p in the body of Christ?	1Cor 10.16
if. .any p in the Spirit, any	Phil 2.1

PARTNER — S

p of a thief hates. .life;	Prov 29.24
if you consider me your p,	Philem 17
to their p in the other boat	Lk 5.7
not want you. .p with demons.	1Cor 10.20

PARTNERSHIP

what p have righteousness	2Cor 6.14
thankful for your p in the	Phil 1.5
no church entered into p with me	4.15

PARTRIDGE

like one who hunts a p	1Sam 26.20
the p that gathers a brood	Jer 17.11

PASCHAL

For Christ, our p lamb, has	1Cor 5.7

PASS — ES — ED — ING

LORD will p over the door,	Ex 12.23
calling to those who p by,	Prov 9.15
When you p through the waters	Isa 43.2
nothing to you, all who p	Lam 1.12
Heaven and earth will p away,	Mt 24.35
Heaven and earth will p away,	Mk 13.31
knowledge, it will p away.	1Cor 13.8
life,. .he p like a shadow?	Ecc 6.12
have not p this way before.	Josh 3.4
I have p out of mind like one	Ps 31.12
he p by on the other side.	Lk 10.31
we. .p out of death into life,	1Jn 3.14
finished p over the Jordan.	Josh 3.17
p along by the Sea of Galilee,	Mk 1.16

PASSION — S

but p makes the bones rot.	Prov 14.30
men. .with p for one another,	Rom 1.27
if his p are strong, and	1Cor 7.36
we. .lived in the p of our flesh,	Eph 2.3
your p. .at war in your members?	Jas 4.1

PASSOVER

eat..in haste..the LORD's p.	Ex 12.11
evening, is the LORD's p.	Lev 23.5
kept the p in the first month,	Num 9.5
first month is the LORD's p,	28.16
and keep the p to the LORD	Deut 16.1
on the morrow after the p,	Josh 5.11
"Keep the p to the LORD	2Ki 23.21
to keep the p to the LORD	2Chr 30.1
who were present kept the p	35.17
returned exiles kept the p.	Ezra 6.19
after two days the P is coming,	Mt 26.2
It was..two days before the P	Mk 14.1
room, where I am to eat the p	14.14
on which the p lamb had to be	Lk 22.7
before the feast of the P,	Jn 13.1
release one man..at the P;	18.39
By faith he kept the P and	Heb 11.28

PASTORS

some evangelists, some p and	Eph 4.11

PASTURE — S

will restore Israel to his p,	Jer 50.19
makes me lie down in green p.	Ps 23.2

PATH — S

Lead me in the p of thy	Ps 119.35
Thy word..a light to my p.	119.105
p of the righteous is like	Prov 4.18
wise man's p leads upward	15.24
taught him the p of justice,	Isa 40.14
make them walk..a straight p	Jer 31.9
some seeds fell along the p,	Mt 13.4
some seed fell along the p,	Mk 4.4
the p of all who forget God;	Job 8.13
passes along the p of the sea.	Ps 8.8
held fast to thy p, my feet	17.5
in p that they have not known	Isa 42.16

PATIENCE

'Have p with me,..I will pay	Mt 18.29
and bring forth fruit with p.	Lk 8.15
we wait for it with p.	Rom 8.25
God,..has endured with much p	9.22
lowliness, meekness, and p,	Col 3.12
example of suffering and p,	Jas 5.10

PATIENT — LY

p in tribulation, be constant	Rom 12.12
Love is p and kind; love	1Cor 13.4
be p. Establish your hearts,	Jas 5.8
your toil and your p endurance,	Rev 2.2
faith..service and p endurance,	2.19
suffer for it you take it p,	1Pet 2.20

PATMOS

was on the island called P	Rev 1.9

PAUL

Born in Tarsus, Acts 22.3; educated under Gamaliel, Acts 22.3; consented to Stephen's death, Acts 7.58; 8.1 (22.20); persecuted the church, Acts 8.3; 9.1–2 (22.4–5; 26.10–11; 1Cor 15.9; Gal 1.13; Phil 3.6); went into Arabia, Gal 1.17; preached in Damascus, Gal 1.17; went up to Jerusalem, Acts 9.26–28; Gal 1.18– 19; name changed to Paul, Acts 13.9; missionary work, Acts 13—14; 15.36—18. 22; 18.23—21.17; attended the Council of Jerusalem, Acts 15.1–29; Gal. 2.1–10; arrested in Jerusalem, Acts 21.27–40; imprisoned in Caesarea, Acts 23.23–35; defended himself before Felix, Acts 24; appealed to Caesar, Acts 25.10–12;

defended himself before Agrippa, Acts 26; journeyed to Rome, Acts 27.1—28.16; preached during imprisonment, Acts 28.17– 31.

divided? Was P crucified for	1Cor 1.13
one says, "I belong to P,"	3.4
our beloved brother P wrote	2Pet 3.15

PAY — ING

Joseph will hate us and p	Gen 50.15
then I will p for it;	Num 20.19
I will p thee my vows,	Ps 66.13
I will p my vows to the LORD	116.18
You received without p, give	Mt 10.8
P all of them their dues,	Rom 13.7
you p me back for something?	Joel 3.4

PEACE

I will give p in the land,	Lev 26.6
The LORD..give you p.	Num 6.26
offer terms of p to it.	Deut 20.10
"P be to you; do not fear,	Judg 6.23
present. But he held his p.	1Sam 10.27
shall be p from the LORD	1Ki 2.33
"Why not, if there will be p	2Ki 20.19
son of Jesse! P, p to you,	1Chr 12.18
they made p with David,	19.19
give p and quiet to Israel	22.9
for the LORD gave him p.	2Chr 14.6
beasts..be at p with you.	Job 5.23
For they do not speak p, but	Ps 35.20
righteousness and p will kiss	85.10
Great p..who love thy law;	119.165
I am for p; but when I speak,	120.7
Pray for the p of Jerusalem!	122.6
and all her paths are p.	Prov 3.17
in his eyes..one who brings p.	Sol 8.10
of p there will be no end,	Isa 9.7
dost keep him in perfect p,	26.3
O LORD, thou wilt ordain p	26.12
let them make p with me, let	27.5
effect of righteousness..p,	32.17
king of Assyria: Make your p	36.16
be p and security in my days."	39.8
Then your p..like a river,	48.18
no p,".."for the wicked."	48.22
publishes p,..brings good tidings	52.7
my covenant of p shall not	54.10
joy, and be led forth in p;	55.12
P, p, to the far and..near,	57.19
I will make your overseers p	60.17
'P, p,' when there is no p.	Jer 6.14
'P, p,' when there is no p.	8.11
We looked for p,..no good came;	14.19
seek p,..there shall be none.	Ezek 7.25
misled my people, saying, 'P,'	13.10
the prophets saw..visions of p	13.16
"I will make..a covenant of p	34.25
I will make a covenant of p	37.26
cry "P" when they have..to eat,	Mic 3.5
And..p, when the Assyrian comes	5.5
tidings, who proclaims p!	Nah 1.15
shall command p to..nations;	Zech 9.10
I have not come to bring p,	Mt 10.34
to the sea, "P! Be still!"	Mk 4.39
be at p with one another."	9.50
our feet into the way of p."	Lk 1.79
on earth p among men with whom	2.14
faith has saved you; go in p."	7.50
faith..made you well; go in p."	8.48
say, 'P be to this house!'	10.5
come to give p on earth? No,	12.51
said to them, "P to you!"	24.36n

PEACE (cont.)
P I leave with you; my *p* I | Jn 14.27
that in me you may have *p*. | 16.33
said to them, "*P* be with you." | 20.19
said..again, "*P* be with you. | 20.21
preaching good news of *p* | Acts 10.36
we have *p* with God through our | Rom 5.1
pursue what makes for *p* and | 14.19
God of *p* will soon crush | 16.20
Grace to you and *p* from God | 2Cor 1.2
For he is our *p*, who has made | Eph 2.14
place of the two, so making *p*, | 2.15
he came and preached *p* to you | 2.17
the *p* of God, which passes all | Phil 4.7
God of *p* will be with you. | 4.9
p by the blood of his cross. | Col 1.20
let the *p* of Christ rule in | 3.15
may the God of *p* who brought | Heb 13.20
let him seek *p* and pursue it. | 1Pet 3.11
rider was permitted to take *p* | Rev 6.4

PEACEABLY
could not speak *p* to him. | Gen 37.4
she said, "Do you come *p*?" | 1Ki 2.13
If possible,..live *p* with all. | Rom 12.18

PEACEMAKERS
"Blessed are the *p*, for they | Mt 5.9

PEACE OFFERING — S
offering is a sacrifice of *p*.., | Lev 3.1
people..Israel from their *p*..; | Ex 29.28
law of the sacrifice of *p*.. | Lev 7.11

PEARLS
do not throw your *p* before swine, | Mt 7.6
merchant in search of fine *p*, | 13.45

PEN
Oh that with an iron *p* and | Job 19.24
my tongue is like the *p* of a | Ps 45.1
the false *p* of the scribes | Jer 8.8
written with a *p* of iron; | 17.1
rather not write with *p* and | 3Jn 13

PENNY
two sparrows sold for a *p*? | Mt 10.29
put in two copper coins,..a *p*. | Mk 12.42

PENTECOST
When the day of *P* had come, | Acts 2.1
stay in Ephesus until *P*, | 1Cor 16.8

PEOPLE — S
beating a Hebrew, one of his *p*. | Ex 2.11
I will take you for my *p*, | 6.7
"Let my *p* go, that they may serve | 7.16
till the *p* pass by whom | 15.16
burn hot against thy *p*," | 32.11
that this nation is thy *p*." | 33.13
your God,..you shall be my *p*. | Lev 26.12
art in the midst of this *p*; | Num 14.14
stubbornness of this *p*, | Deut 9.27
chosen you to be a *p* for his | 14.2
p for his own possession, | 26.18
establish you..as his *p*, | 29.13
LORD's portion is his *p*, | 32.9
the *p* served the LORD all the | Judg 2.7
visited his *p* and given them | Ruth 1.6
your *p* shall be my *p*, and | 1.16
abhorred by his *p* Israel; | 1Sam 27.12
I will save my *p* Israel | 2Sam 3.18
Israel to be thy *p* for ever; | 7.24
'Since..I brought my *p* Israel | 1Ki 8.16
my *p* as your *p*, my horses | 22.4
I am as you are, my *p* as your | 2Ki 3.7

they should be the LORD's *p*; | 11.17
a place for my *p* Israel, | 1Chr 17.9
What..nation..is like thy *p* | 17.21
make thy *p* Israel to be thy *p* | 17.22
if my *p* who are called by | 2Chr 7.14
had compassion on his *p* | 36.15
he led forth his *p* like sheep, | Ps 78.52
we are his *p*, and the sheep | 100.3
anger..kindled against his *p*, | 106.40
Your *p* will offer themselves | 110.3
LORD is round about his *p*, | 125.2
Happy the *p* whose God is the | 144.15
raised up a horn for his *p*, | 148.14
LORD takes pleasure in his *p*; | 149.4
For thou hast rejected thy *p*, | Isa 2.6
My *p*—children are..oppressors, | 3.12
my *p* go into exile for want | 5.13
The *p* who walked in darkness | 9.2
angry with my *p*, I profaned my | 47.6
declare to..*p* their transgression, | 58.1
he said, Surely they are my *p*, | 63.8
rejoice..and be glad in my *p*; | 65.19
my *p* have committed two evils: | Jer 2.13
God, and you shall be my *p*; | 7.23
for me a *p*, a name, a praise, | 13.11
But my *p* have forgotten me, | 18.15
they shall be my *p* and I will | 24.7
And you shall be my *p*, and | 30.22
And they shall be my *p*, and | 32.38
they..my *p*, and I..their God. | Ezek 11.20
that they may be my *p* and | 14.11
you..my *p*, and I..your God. | 36.28
to them, "You are not my *p*," | Hos 1.10
say to Not my *p*, 'You are my *p*'; | 2.23
the LORD had pity on his *p*. | Joel 2.18
like the Ethiopians..O *p* of | Amos 9.7
LORD has a controversy with his *p*, | Mic 6.2
have many *p* in this city." | Acts 18.10
not my *p* I will call 'my *p*,' | Rom 9.25
Once..no *p* but now..God's *p*; | 1Pet 2.10
that all the *p* of the earth | 1Ki 8.60
Let the *p* praise thee, O God; | Ps 67.5
hills; and *p* shall flow to it, | Mic 4.1

PERCEIVE — D
shall indeed see but never *p*. | Mt 13.14
may indeed see but not *p*, | Mk 4.12
no bread? Do you not yet *p* | 8.17
I *p*..God shows no partiality, | Acts 10.34
Gideon *p*..he was the angel | Judg 6.22
sanctuary..then I *p* their end. | Ps 73.17
no one has heard or *p* by..ear, | Isa 64.4
he *p* that it was out of envy | Mk 15.10
they *p* that he had told this | Lk 20.19
and deity, has been clearly *p* | Rom 1.20

PERFECT — ED
which cannot *p* the conscience | Heb 9.9
in him truly love for God is *p*. | 1Jn 2.5

PERFECT — LY
This God—his way is *p*; | 2Sam 22.31
one who is *p* in knowledge | Job 36.4
This God—his way is *p*; | Ps 18.30
My dove, my *p* one, is only one, | Sol 6.9
Thou dost keep him in *p* peace, | Isa 26.3
You, therefore must be *p*, as | Mt 5.48
"If you would be *p*, go, sell | 19.21
thou hast brought *p* praise'?" | 21.16
but when the *p* comes, the | 1Cor 13.10
Not that I..am already *p*; | Phil 3.12
make the pioneer..salvation *p* | Heb 2.10
being made *p* he became the | 5.9
Son who has been made *p* for ever. | 7.28

PERFECT — LY (cont.)
every *p* gift is from above, Jas 1.17
that they may become *p* one, Jn 17.23

PERFECTION
Out of Zion, the *p* of beauty, Ps 50.2
have seen a limit to all *p*, 119.96
Now if *p* had been attainable Heb 7.11

PERFORM — ED
to *p* the words of..covenant 2Ki 23.3
your vows to..God, and *p* them; Ps 76.11
I will speak the word and *p* Ezek 12.25
to *p* the mercy promised to our Lk 1.72
Who has *p* and done this, Isa 41.4

PERIL
bread at the *p* of our lives, Lam 5.9
Why am I in *p* every hour? 1Cor 15.30

PERISH — ES — ED — ING
shall *p* among the nations, Lev 26.38
you will soon utterly *p* Deut 4.26
that you shall surely *p*. 8.19
you shall *p* quickly from Josh 23.16
"So *p* all thine enemies, Judg 5.31
go to the king,..if I *p*, I *p*." Est 4.16
he will *p* for ever like his Job 20.7
But the wicked *p*; the enemies Ps 37.20
who are far from thee shall *p*; 73.27
They will *p*, but thou..endure; 102.26
they *p*,..righteous increase. Prov 28.28
our God has doomed us to *p*, Jer 8.14
repent..so that we *p* not?" Jonah 3.9
one of..little ones should *p*. Mt 18.14
who take the sword will *p* by 26.52
unless you repent you will..*p*. Lk 13.3
they will *p*,..thou remainest; Heb 1.11
the wicked dies, his hope *p*, Prov 11.7
they stumbled and *p* before thee. Ps 9.3
veiled..to those who are *p*. 2Cor 4.3

PERISHABLE
do it to receive a *p* wreath, 1Cor 9.25
What is sown is *p*, what is 15.42
ransomed..not with *p* things 1Pet 1.18

PERMITS
with you, if the Lord p. 1Cor 16.7
this we will do if God p. Heb 6.3

PERPLEXED
but the city of Susa was *p*. Est 3.15
Herod..was *p*, because it was Lk 9.7
While they were *p*.about this, 24.4
p, but not driven to despair; 2Cor 4.8

PERSECUTE — D
those..put to shame who *p* me, Jer 17.18
When they *p* you in one town, Mt 10.23
whom they will kill and *p*,' Lk 11.49
and *p* you, delivering you up 21.12
If they *p* me, they will *p* you; Jn 15.20
did not your fathers *p*? And Acts 7.52
Saul, why do you *p* me?" 9.4
Saul, why do you *p* me?' 22.7
Bless those who *p* you; bless Rom 12.14
who are *p* for righteousness' Mt 5.10
this was why the Jews *p* Jesus, Jn 5.16
I *p* this Way to the death, Acts 22.4
I *p* them even to foreign cities. 26.11
bless; when *p*, we endure; 1Cor 4.12
because I *p* the church of God. 15.9
p, but not forsaken; struck 2Cor 4.9
how I *p* the church of God Gal 1.13
p him..born according to..Spirit, 4.29

not..*p* for the cross of Christ. 6.12
in Christ Jesus will be *p*, 2Tim 3.12

PERSECUTION — S
when tribulation or *p* arises Mt 13.21
p arose against the church Acts 8.1
scattered because of the *p* 11.19
children and lands, with *p*, Mk 10.30
and faith in all your *p* and 2Thess 1.4
at Lystra, what *p* I endured; 2Tim 3.11

PERSIA
first year of Cyrus king of *P*, Ezra 1.1
wrote to Artaxerxes king of *P*; 4.7
reign of Darius king of *P*. 4.24
banquet for..army chiefs of *P* Est 1.3
prince of the kingdom of *P* Dan 10.13

PERSUADE — D — ING
fear of the Lord, we *p* men; 2Cor 5.11
some..were *p*, and joined Paul Acts 17.4
and *p* Jews and Greeks. 18.4
Paul has *p* and turned away 19.26
man is *p* men to worship God 18.13

PERVERT — ED — ING
does the Almighty *p* the right? Job 8.3
Almighty will not *p* justice. 34.12
you *p* the words of..God, Jer 23.36
abhor justice and *p* all equity, Mic 3.9
because they have *p* their way, Jer 3.21
found this man *p* our nation, Lk 23.2

PESTILENCE
The LORD will make the *p* Deut 28.21
three days' *p* in your land? 2Sam 24.13
p that stalks in darkness, Ps 91.6
on them sword, famine, and *p*, Jer 29.17

PETER (CEPHAS, SIMON, SYMEON)
*Called to be a fisher of men, Mt 4.18–20
(Mk 1.16–18; Lk 5.1–11); also named
Cephas, which means "rock", Jn 1.42n;
sent out with the twelve, Mt 10.2 (Mk
3.16); walked on the sea, Mt 14.28–33;
confessed Jesus as the Christ, Mt 16.13–20
(Mk 8.27–30; Lk 9.18–22); interceded for
by the Lord, Lk 22.31–32; cut off the
servant's ear, Jn 18.10–11; denied Jesus
three times, Mt 26.69–75 (Mk 14.66–72;
Lk 22.54–62; Jn 18.15–18, 25–27); "Feed
my sheep," Jn 21.15–19; addressed the
disciples, Acts 1.15–26; preached at
Pentecost, Acts 2.14–42; healed the lame
man, Acts 3.1–10; witnessed in Solomon's
portico, Acts 3.11–26; preached to the
Council, Acts 4.1–12; imprisoned and
released, Acts 5.17–42; denounced Simon
Magus, Acts 8.14–24; visited Cornelius
after the vision, Acts 10; reported to the
Jerusalem Church, Acts 11.1–18; imprisoned and delivered, Acts 12.1–19; at
the Council of Jerusalem, Acts 15.6–12;
visited by Paul, Gal 1.18; blamed by Paul,
Gal 2.11–14; Peter's wife's mother, Mt
8.14 (Mk 1.30; Lk 4.38); his wife, 1Cor
9.5.*

PETITION — S
whoever makes *p* to..god or man Dan 6.7
the LORD fulfil all your *p*! Ps 20.5

PHARISEES
when he saw many of the *P* and Mt 3.7
exceeds..the scribes and *P*, 5.20
when the *P* saw this, they said, 9.11
But when the *P* saw it, they 12.2

PHARISEES (cont.)
P went out and took counsel Mt 12.14
beware of the leaven of the *P* 16.6
And *P* came up..and tested him 19.3
the *P* went and took counsel 22.15
and the *P* sit on Moses' seat; 23.2
priests and the *P* gathered 27.62
man of the *P*, named Nicodemus, Jn 3.1
and the *P* brought a woman 8.3*n*
the *P* rose up, and said, Acts 15.5
Sadducees and the other *P*, 23.6

PHILEMON
To *P* our beloved fellow Philem 1

PHILIP
P and Bartholomew; Thomas Mt 10.3
Jesus..found *P* and said to him, Jn 1.43
Jesus said to *P*, "How are we 6.5
Greeks..came to *P*, who was 12.21
P said to him, "Lord, show us 14.8
and Andrew, *P* and Thomas, Acts 1.13
P went..to a city of Samaria, 8.5
But *P* was found at Azotus, 8.40
we entered the house of *P* 21.8

PHILIPPI
voyage..from there to *P*, Acts 16.12
we sailed away from *P* after 20.6
in Christ Jesus who are at *P*, Phil 1.1
shamefully treated at *P*, 1Thess 2.2

PHILISTIA
on the inhabitants of *P*. Ex 15.14
"Rejoice not, O *P*, all of Isa 14.29
"What are you to me, O..*P*? Joel 3.4
make an end of the pride of *P*. Zech 9.6

PHILISTINES
Abimelech king of the *P*. Gen 26.1
the *P* seized him and gouged Judg 16.21
out to battle against the *P*; 1Sam 4.1
When the *P* captured the ark of God, 5.1
out of the hand of the *P*." 7.3
the *P* fought against Israel; 31.1
David defeated the *P* and 2Sam 8.1
and of soothsayers like the *P*, Isa 2.6
P from Caphtor and the Syrians Amos 9.7

PHILOSOPHERS
Epicurean and Stoic *p* met Acts 17.18

PHILOSOPHY
makes a prey of you by *p* and Col 2.8

PHYSICAL
If there is a *p* body, there 1Cor 15.44

PHYSICIAN — S
Gilead? Is there no *p* there? Jer 8.22
well have no need of a *p*, Mt 9.12
well have no need of a *p*, Mk 2.17
proverb, '*P*, heal yourself; Lk 4.23
well have no need of a *p*, 5.31
Luke the beloved *p* and Demas Col 4.14
p to embalm his father. Gen 50.2
worthless *p* are you all. Job 13.4
suffered much under many *p*, Mk 5.26
spent all her living upon *p* Lk 8.43*n*

PIECES
twelve baskets full of broken *p* Mk 6.43
broken *p* did you take up?" 8.19
twelve baskets of broken *p*. Lk 9.17

PIERCE — D
sword will *p* through your..soul Lk 2.35
they have *p* my hands and Ps 22.16
look on him whom they..*p*, Zech 12.10

one of..soldiers *p* his side Jn 19.34
see him, every one who *p* him; Rev 1.7

PIETY
"Beware of practicing your *p* Mt 6.1
by our own power or *p* we Acts 3.12

PIGEON — S
"Bring me..a young *p*." Gen 15.9
bring his offering..of young *p*. Lev 1.14

PILATE (PONTIUS)
Governor of Judea, Lk 3.1; killed some Galileans, Lk 13.1; sentenced Jesus to be crucified, Mt 27.1–25 (Mk 15.1–15; Lk 23.1–26; Jn 18.28—19.22); Jesus "suffered under Pontius Pilate," Acts 3.13; 13.28; 1Tim 6.13.

PILLAR — S
she became a *p* of salt. Gen 19.26
stone..set it up for a *p* 28.18
in a *p* of cloud to lead them Ex 13.21
set up for himself the *p* 2Sam 18.18
p..of Baal, and burned it. 2Ki 10.26
by a *p* of fire in the night Neh 9.12
"Let me feel the *p* on which Judg 16.26
who were reputed to be *p*, Gal 2.9

PIONEER
make the *p* of their salvation Heb 2.10
Jesus the *p* and perfecter 12.2

PIT
or let thy godly..see the *P*. Ps 16.10
thrust you down into the *P*, Ezek 28.8
bring up my life from the *P*, Jonah 2.6

PITY — IES — IED (v)
your eye shall not *p* them; Deut 7.16
LORD said, "You *p* the plant, Jonah 4.10
As a father *p* his children, Ps 103.13
No eye *p*..out of compassion Ezek 16.5
of all men most to be *p*. 1Cor 15.19

PITY (n)
She took *p* on him and said, Ex 2.6
have *p* on me, O..my friends, Job 19.21
It hurls at him without *p*; 27.22
He has *p* on the weak and Ps 72.13
he who has *p*..will lead them, Isa 49.10
will not spare..nor..have *p*; Ezek 7.4
not spare, nor will I have *p*; 8.18
have *p* on the house of Judah, Hos 1.7
LORD..had *p* on his people. Joel 2.18
For I will no longer have *p* Zech 11.6
out of *p*..the lord..released Mt 18.27
Jesus out..touched their eyes, 20.34
with *p*, he stretched out his Mk 1.41
have *p* on us and help us." 9.22

PLACE
the dove found no *p* to set Gen 8.9
till all these things take *p*. Mt 24.34
was no *p* for them in the inn. Lk 2.7

PLAGUE — S
severe *p* upon your cattle Ex 9.3
"Yet one *p* more I will bring 11.1
smote..with a very great *p*. Num 11.33
died by *p* before the LORD 14.37
p had already begun among 16.47
those that died by the *p* 25.9
that the *p* may be averted 1Chr 21.22
Phinehas..the *p* was stayed. Ps 106.30
p..will smite..the peoples Zech 14.12
great *p* because of Sarai, Gen 12.17

PLAN — S
God had frustrated their *p*,	Neh 4.15
carry out a *p*, but not mine;	Isa 30.1
and devising a *p* against you.	Jer 18.11
according to the definite *p*	Acts 2.23
if this *p*..is of men, it will	5.38
a *p* for the fulness of time,	Eph 1.10
the *p* of the mystery hidden	3.9
past, my *p* are broken off,	Job 17.11
crafty *p* against thy people;	Ps 83.3
Many are the *p* in the mind	Prov 19.21
P are established by counsel;	20.18
I know the *p* I have for you,	Jer 29.11

PLANT — S — ED (v)
bring them in, and *p* them	Ex 15.17
Israel, and will *p* them,	1Chr 17.9
nations; but them thou didst *p*;	Ps 44.2
I will *p* them in this land	Jer 32.41
I will *p* them upon their land,	Amos 9.15
Who *p*..vineyard without eating	1Cor 9.7
stock which thy right hand *p*.	Ps 80.15
Yet I *p* you a choice vine,	Jer 2.21
plant..my..Father has not *p*	Mt 15.13
I *p*, Apollos watered, but God	1Cor 3.6

PLANT — S (n)
when no *p*..yet in the earth	Gen 2.5
God appointed a *p*, and made	Jonah 4.6
"Let the earth put forth..*p*	Gen 1.11
the *p*..they will teach you;	Job 12.8

PLATTER
head of John..Baptist on a *p*."	Mk 6.25

PLAY — ING
and drink, and rose up to *p*.	Ex 32.6
child shall *p* over the hole	Isa 11.8
son of Hagar..*p* with..Isaac.	Gen 21.9

PLEAD — S
stand still, that I may *p*	1Sam 12.7
P my cause and redeem me;	Ps 119.154
the LORD will *p* their cause	Prov 22.23
"*P* with your mother, *p*—	Hos 2.2
God..*p*..cause of his people:	Isa 51.22

PLEASANT — NESS
made to grow every tree..*p*	Gen 2.9
lines have fallen..in *p* places;	Ps 16.6
they despised the *p* land,	106.24
p it is when brothers dwell	133.1
knowledge will be *p* to your	Prov 2.10
bread eaten in secret is *p*."	9.17
Her ways are ways of *p*, and	3.17

PLEASE — S — D — ING
may it *p* thee to bless	2Sam 7.29
may it *p* thee to bless the	1Chr 17.27
that it would *p* God to crush	Job 6.9
When a man's ways *p* the LORD,	Prov 16.7
nor awaken love until it *p*.	Sol 2.7
nor awaken love until it *p*.	3.5
nor awaken love until it *p*.	8.4
in the flesh cannot *p* God.	Rom 8.8
weak, and not to *p* ourselves;	15.1
unmarried..how to *p* the Lord;	1Cor 7.32
just as I try to *p* all men	10.33
make it our aim to *p* him.	2Cor 5.9
Or am I trying to *p* men? If	Gal 1.10
not to *p* men, but to *p* God	1Thess 2.4
"Get her..for she *p* me well."	Judg 14.3
maiden who *p* the king be queen	Est 2.4
Whatever the LORD *p* he does,	Ps 135.6
he who *p* God escapes her, but	Ecc 7.26
for he does whatever he *p*.	8.3

because we..do what *p* him.	1Jn 3.22
Manassites spoke, it *p* them	Josh 22.30
it has *p* the LORD to make	1Sam 12.22
it *p* David well to be the king's	18.26
that the king did *p* all	2Sam 3.36
And the advice *p* Absalom	17.4
It *p* the Lord that Solomon	1Ki 3.10
it *p* the king to send me;	Neh 2.6
p, for..righteousness' sake,	Isa 42.21
Will the LORD be *p* with..rams,	Mic 6.7
p with you or show you favor?	Mal 1.8
Son, with whom I am well *p*."	Mt 3.17
Son, with whom I am well *p*;	17.5
Son; with thee I am well *p*."	Mk 1.11
Son; with thee I am well *p*."	Lk 3.22
with most..God was not *p*;	1Cor 10.5
was *p* to reveal his Son to me,	Gal 1.16
fulness of God was *p* to dwell,	Col 1.19
attested as having *p* God.	Heb 11.5
words of the pure are *p* to	Prov 15.26
Preacher sought..*p* words,	Ecc 12.10
I always do what is *p* to him."	Jn 8.29
learn what is *p* to the Lord.	Eph 5.10
sacrifice acceptable and *p*	Phil 4.18
worthy of the Lord, fully *p*	Col 1.10
such sacrifices are *p* to God.	Heb 13.16

PLEASURE — S
any *p* to the Almighty if you	Job 22.3
takes *p* in those who fear	Ps 147.11
LORD takes *p* in his people;	149.4
who loves *p* will be a poor	Prov 21.17
I will make a test of *p*; enjoy	Ecc 2.1
I kept my heart from no *p*,	2.10
for he has no *p* in fools. Pay	5.4
Have I any *p* in the death	Ezek 18.23
no *p* in the death of the wicked,	33.11
the house, that I may take *p* in	Hag 1.8
I have no *p* in you, says..LORD	Mal 1.10
your Father's good *p* to give	Lk 12.32
you might have a double *p*;	2Cor 1.15
and to work for his good *p*.	Phil 2.13
had *p* in unrighteousness.	2Thess 2.12
in..offerings thou hast..no *p*.	Heb 10.6
You..lived..in luxury and..*p*;	Jas 5.5
in thy right hand are *p* for	Ps 16.11
choked by..riches and *p* of life,	Lk 8.11
than to enjoy the fleeting *p*	Heb 11.25

PLEDGE
garment in *p*,..restore it	Ex 22.26
or an upper millstone in *p*;	Deut 24.6
shall not sleep in his *p*;	24.12
hold him in *p* when he gives	Prov 20.16
hold him in *p* when he gives	27.13
the wicked restores the *p*,	Ezek 33.15
lay..upon garments taken in *p*;	Amos 2.8

PLENTY
seven years of great *p*	Gen 41.29
tills his land will have *p*	Prov 12.11
the secret of facing *p* and	Phil 4.12

PLOT — S
do you *p* against the LORD?	Nah 1.9
A worthless man *p* evil, and	Prov 16.27

PLOW — S — ED (v)
not *p* with an ox and an ass	Deut 22.10
those who *p* iniquity..reap	Job 4.8
The sluggard does not *p* in	Prov 20.4
the plowman should *p* in hope	1Cor 9.10
Does he who *p* for sowing plow	Isa 28.24
The plowers *p* upon my back;	Ps 129.3
Zion shall be *p* as a field;	Jer 26.18

PLOW — S — ED (v) (cont.)
You have *p* iniquity, you   Hos 10.13
Zion shall be *p* as a field;   Mic 3.12

PLOW (n)
hand to the *p* and looks back   Lk 9.62

PLOWSHARES
Beat your *p* into swords,   Joel 3.10
shall beat their swords into *p*,   Mic 4.3

PLUCK — ED
will *p* up the house of Judah   Jer 12.14
eye causes you to sin, *p* it out, Mt 5.29
you would have *p* out your eyes   Gal 4.15

PLUMB LINE
beside..wall built with a *p*..,   Amos 7.7

PLUNDER — ED — ING
the lot of those who *p* us.   Isa 17.14
enter..house and *p* his goods,   Mt 12.29
p the city, because their sister Gen 34.27
and *p* the camp of the Syrians,   2Ki 7.16
Because you have *p* many nations, Hab 2.8
accepted..*p* of your property,   Heb 10.34

POMP
Man cannot abide in his *p*,   Ps 49.12
Your *p* is brought..to Sheol,   Isa 14.11

PONDERING
Mary kept all these things, *p*   Lk 2.19
Peter was *p* the vision,   Acts 10.19

POOL — S
Jerusalem by the Sheep Gate a *p*, Jn 5.2
"Go, wash in the *p* of Siloam"   9.7
islands, and dry up the *p*.   Isa 42.15

POOR — EST
the *p* of your people may eat;   Ex 23.11
the *p* shall not give less,   30.15
leave them for the *p* and for   Lev 19.10
gleanings..leave..for the *p*   23.22
"If your brother becomes *p*,   25.25
"If..is among you a *p* man,   Deut 15.7
For the *p* will never cease   15.11
raises up the *p* from..dust;   1Sam 2.8
the *p* man had nothing but   2Sam 12.3
So the *p* have hope, and   Job 5.16
crushed and abandoned the *p*,   20.19
thrust the *p* off the road;   24.4
because I delivered the *p*   29.12
withheld anything that the *p*   31.16
hope of the *p* shall not perish   Ps 9.18
the wicked hotly pursue the *p*;   10.2
This *p* man cried,..LORD heard   34.6
I am *p* and needy; but the LORD   40.17
Blessed..who considers the *p*!   41.1
May he defend..cause of the *p*   72.4
answer me, for I am *p* and needy.   86.1
For I am *p* and needy, and   109.22
raises the *p* from the dust,   113.7
poverty of..*p* is their ruin.   Prov 10.15
p man who walks in..integrity   19.1
a *p* man's brothers hate him;   19.7
The rich and the *p* meet   22.2
king judges..*p* with equity   29.14
spoil of..*p* is in your houses.   Isa 3.14
with righteousness..judge the *p*,   11.4
thou..a stronghold to the *p*,   25.4
who oppress the *p*, who crush   Amos 4.1
because you trample upon the *p*   5.11
we may buy the *p* for silver   8.6
"Blessed are the *p* in spirit,   Mt 5.3
the *p* have good news preached   11.5

give to the *p*, and you will   19.21
you always have the *p* with you,   26.11
go, sell..and give to the *p*,   Mk 10.21
sold..and given to the *p*."   14.5
to preach good news to the *p*.   Lk 4.18
"Blessed are you *p*, for yours   6.20
give a feast, invite the *p*,   14.13
at..gate lay a *p* man..Lazarus,   16.20
Sell..and distribute to the *p*,   18.22
half of my goods I give to the *p*;   19.8
not sold..and given to the *p*?"   Jn 12.5
The *p* you always have with you,   12.8
as *p*, yet making many rich;   2Cor 6.10
for your sake he became *p*,   8.9
"He scatters..gives to the *p*;   9.9
have us remember the *p*,   Gal 2.10
God chosen those who are *p*   Jas 2.5
you are wretched, pitiable, *p*,   Rev 3.17
p of..land to be vinedressers   2Ki 25.12

PORTENT — S
I have been as a *p* to many;   Ps 71.7
a great *p* appeared in heaven,   Rev 12.1
I saw another *p* in heaven,   15.1
I will give *p* in the heavens   Joel 2.30

PORTION — S
LORD's *p* is his people,   Deut 32.9
would give Hannah only one *p*, 1Sam 1.5
"We have no *p* in David,   2Sam 20.1
"What *p* have we in David?   1Ki 12.16
the wicked man's *p* from God,   Job 20.29
The LORD is my chosen *p* and   Ps 16.5
The LORD is my *p*; I promise   119.57
Thou art my refuge, my *p* in   142.5
he who is the *p* of Jacob,   Jer 10.16
LORD is my *p*," says my soul.   Lam 3.24
send *p* to him for whom nothing   Neh 8.10

POSSESS — ED — ING
his descendants shall *p* it.   Num 14.24
p the inheritance of his fathers.   36.8
give it, and they shall *p* it.   Deut 1.39
given you this land to *p*;   3.18
p the lake and the south."   33.23
Will you not *p* what Chemosh   Judg 11.24
enter in and *p* the land.   18.9
tell them to go in to *p* the   Neh 9.15
his children shall *p* the land.   Ps 25.13
who wait for the LORD shall *p*   37.9
house of Israel will *p* them   Isa 14.2
they shall *p* it for ever,   34.17
descendants will *p* the nations   54.3
they shall *p* the land for ever,   60.21
shall you then *p* the land?   Ezek 33.26
and they shall *p* you, and   36.12
and *p* the kingdom for ever,   Dan 7.18
Jacob shall *p* their own   Obad 1.17
remnant of this people to *p*   Zech 8.12
my daughter is..*p* by a demon."   Mt 15.22
nothing,..yet *p* everything.   2Cor 6.10

POSSESSION — S
Canaan, for an everlasting *p*;   Gen 17.8
this land for an everlasting *p*.'   48.4
you shall be my own *p*   Ex 19.5
that is their perpetual *p*.   Lev 25.34
this land shall be your *p*   Num 32.22
go in and take *p* of the land   Deut 1.8
to be a people of his own *p*,   4.20
take *p* of the good land   6.18
a people for his own,   14.2
a people for his own *p*,   26.18
take *p* of the land which   Josh 1.11
go in..take *p* of the land,   18.3

POSSESSION — S (cont.)

to drive us out of thy *p*,	2Chr 20.11
he apportioned them for a *p*	Ps 78.55
himself, Israel as his own *p*.	135.4
they entered and took *p* of it.	Jer 32.23
no *p* in Israel; I am their *p*.	Ezek 44.28
my special *p* on the day when	Mal 3.17
until we acquire *p* of it,	Eph 1.14
I had also great *p* of herds	Ecc 2.7
sorrowful; for he had great *p*.	Mt 19.22
will set him over all his *p*.	24.47
not..abundance of his *p*."	Lk 12.15

POSSIBLE

with God all things are *p*."	Mt 19.26
All..*p* to him who believes."	Mk 9.23
all things are *p* with God."	10.27
if it were *p*, the hour might	14.35
with men is *p* with God."	Lk 18.27

POSTERITY

P shall serve him; men shall	Ps 22.30
May his *p* be cut off; may	109.13

POT — S

there is death in the *p*!"	2Ki 4.40
"I see a boiling *p*,	Jer 1.13
as when earthen *p* are broken	Rev 2.27

POTTER — 'S

trample..as the *p* treads clay.	Isa 41.25
an earthen vessel with the *p*!	45.9
Has the *p* no right over the	Rom 9.21
dash..in pieces like a *p* vessel."	Ps 2.9
breaking is like..a *p* vessel	Isa 30.14
go down to the *p* house, and	Jer 18.2
like the clay in the *p* hand,	18.6
"Go, buy a *p* earthen flask,	19.1
earthen pots, the work of a *p*	Lam 4.2
bought with them the *p* field,	Mt 27.7

POUR — ED — ING

remember, as I *p* out my soul:	Ps 42.4
p water on the thirsty land,	Isa 44.3
wrath of the LORD;.."*P* it out	Jer 6.11
P out..wrath upon the nations	10.25
soon *p* out my wrath upon you,	Ezek 7.8
I..*p* out my wrath like water.	Hos 5.10
p out my spirit on all flesh;	Joel 2.28
p out..spirit of compassion	Zech 12.10
I will *p* out my Spirit upon	Acts 2.17
drew water and *p* it out	1Sam 7.6
he *p* it out to the LORD,	2Sam 23.16
he *p* it out to the LORD,	1Chr 11.18
until the Spirit is *p* upon us	Isa 32.15
and my wrath will be *p* out	Jer 7.20
ointment,..she *p*..on his head,	Mt 26.7
she broke the jar and *p* it	Mk 14.3
God's love..*p* into our hearts	Rom 5.5
I have been *p* out my soul	1Sam 1.15

POVERTY

p will come..like a vagabond,	Prov 6.11
P and disgrace come to him	13.18
and *p* will come upon you	24.34
worthless..have plenty of *p*.	28.19
but she out of her *p* has put	Mk 12.44
joy and..*p* have overflowed	2Cor 8.2
and your *p* (but you are rich)	Rev 2.9

POWER

no *p* to stand before..enemies.	Lev 26.37
and the *p*, and the glory,	1Chr 29.11
God has *p* to help or to	2Chr 25.8
contend with me in..his *p*?	Job 23.6
his *p* who can understand?"	26.14

We will sing and praise thy *p*.	Ps 21.13
my soul from the *p* of Sheol,	49.15
So great is thy *p* that thy	66.3
thy saving *p* among all nations.	67.2
Ascribe *p* to God, whose	68.34
delivered them from the *p* of	106.10
kingdom, and tell of thy *p*,	145.11
when it is in your *p* to do it.	Prov 3.27
not give him *p* to enjoy them,	Ecc 6.2
No man has *p* to retain..spirit,	8.8
because he is strong in *p* not	Isa 40.26
He gives *p* to the faint, and	40.29
I will make them know my *p*	Jer 16.21
and the earth by thy great *p*	32.17
His *p* shall be great, and	Dan 8.24
as for me, I am filled with *p*,	Mic 3.8
nor by *p*, but by my Spirit,	Zech 4.6
the *p* and the glory, forever.	Mt 6.13*n*
scriptures nor the *p* of God.	22.29
perceiving in himself that *p*	Mk 5.30
kingdom of God come with *p*."	9.1
scriptures nor the *p* of God?	12.24
Son..at the right hand of *P*,	14.62
the *p* of the Most High will	Lk 1.35
the *p* of the Lord was with him	5.17
touch him, for *p* came forth	6.19
that *p* has gone forth from me."	8.46
far country to receive kingly *p*	19.12
coming in a cloud with *p*	21.27
hour, and the *p* of darkness."	22.53
right hand of the *p* of God."	22.69
until you are clothed with *p*	24.49
I have *p* to lay it down,	Jn 10.18
I have *p* to release you,	19.10
receive *p* when the Holy Spirit	Acts 1.8
as though by our own *p* or	3.12
with great *p* the apostles	4.33
Stephen, full of grace and *p*,	6.8
that *p* of God..called Great."	8.10
from the *p* of Satan to God,	26.18
the *p* of God for salvation	Rom 1.16
by the *p* of the Holy Spirit	15.13
by the *p* of the Holy Spirit,	15.19
saved it is the *p* of God.	1Cor 1.18
demonstration of..Spirit and *p*,	2.4
not..in..men but in the *p* of God.	2.5
assembled..with the *p* of our Lord	5.4
and every authority and *p*.	15.24
weakness, it is raised in *p*.	15.43
speech, and the *p* of God;	2Cor 6.7
p of Christ may rest upon me.	12.9
my *p*..made perfect in weakness."	12.9
but lives by the *p* of God.	13.4
greatness of his *p* in us who	Eph 1.19
by the *p* at work within us	3.20
the *p* of his resurrection,	Phil 3.10
not only in word, but..in *p*	1Thess 1.5
him who has the *p* of death,	Heb 2.14
who by God's *p* are guarded	1Pet 1.5
His divine *p* has granted to us	2Pet 1.3
give him *p* over the nations,	Rev 2.26
thou hast taken thy great *p*	11.17
give over their *p*..to the beast;	17.13

PRAISE — D (v)

thank thee, our God, and *p*	1Chr 29.13
P the LORD with the lyre,	Ps 33.2
also *p* thee with the harp for	71.22
wrath of men shall *p* thee;	76.10
servants of the LORD, *p* the name	113.1
At midnight I rise to *p* thee,	119.62
P the LORD, O Jerusalem!	147.12
P him, all his angels, *p* him,	148.2

PRAISE — D (v) (cont.)

Let everything that breathes p	Ps 150.6
Let another p you, and not	Prov 27.2
death cannot p thee; those	Isa 38.18
I will p thee among..Gentiles,	Rom 15.9
"P the Lord, all Gentiles;	15.11
LORD, and greatly to be p,	1Chr 16.25
I blessed the Most High, and p	Dan 4.34

PRAISE — S (n)

He is your p; he is your God	Deut 10.21
render p to him; and tell	Josh 7.19
thy p reaches to the ends of	Ps 48.10
P is due to thee, O God, in	65.1
My mouth is filled with thy p,	71.8
Accept my offerings of p, O	119.108
Jerusalem..a p in the earth.	Isa 62.7
loved the p of men more than	Jn 12.43
every tongue shall give p	Rom 14.11
any cheerful? Let him sing p	Jas 5.13
Sing p to God, sing p! Sing	Ps 47.6
So will I ever sing p to thy name,	61.8

PRAY — S — ED — ING

Let me go over, I p, and see	Deut 3.25
"P for your servants to	1Sam 12.19
by ceasing to p for you;	12.23
has found courage to p	2Sam 7.27
David said, "O LORD, I p	15.31
hand, I p thee, be against me	24.17
acknowledge thy name, and p	1Ki 8.33
found courage to p before	1Chr 17.25
Job shall p for you, for I	Job 42.8
P for the peace of Jerusalem!	Ps 122.6
comes to his sanctuary to p,	Isa 16.12
do not p for this people,	Jer 7.16
do not p for this people, or	11.14
Then you will..p to me, and	29.12
"P for us to the LORD our God."	37.3
Love your enemies and p for	Mt 5.44
they love to stand and p in	6.5
P then like this: Our Father	6.9
p..the Lord of the harvest	9.38
into the hills by himself to p.	14.23
lay his hands on them and p	19.13
P that your flight may not be	24.20
"Sit here, while I go..and p."	26.36
Watch and p that you may not	26.41
he went into the hills to p.	Mk 6.46
P that it..not happen in winter.	13.18
Take heed, watch and p;	13.33n
he said.."Sit here, while I p."	14.32
Watch and p that you may not	14.38
he went out into the hills to p;	Lk 6.12
p for those who abuse you.	6.28
went up on the mountain to p.	9.28
laborers are few; p therefore	10.2
"Lord, teach us to p, as John	11.1
that they ought always to p	18.1
And I will p the Father,	Jn 14.16
I do not p that thou..take them	17.15
"I do not p for these only,	17.20
Simon answered, "P for me	Acts 8.24
we do not know how to p as	Rom 8.26
p..with her head uncovered?	1Cor 11.13
I will p with the mind also;	14.15
we p God that you may not	2Cor 13.7
P at all times in the Spirit,	Eph 6.18
have not ceased to p for you,	Col 1.9
p constantly, give thanks	1Thess 5.17
we always p for you, that	2Thess 1.11
every place the men should p,	1Tim 2.8
P for us, for we are sure	Heb 13.18

Is any..suffering? Let him p.	Jas 5.13
beloved,..p in the Holy Spirit;	Jude 20
man p to God, and he accepts	Job 33.26
Then Abraham p to God;	Gen 20.17
and Moses p to the LORD,	Num 11.2
and I p for Aaron also at	Deut 9.20
And I p to the LORD, 'O Lord	9.26
deeply distressed and p	1Sam 1.10
For this child I p; and the	1.27
And Samuel p to the LORD.	8.6
two of them,..p to the LORD.	2Ki 4.33
Elisha p, and said, "O LORD,	6.17
Hezekiah p before the LORD,	19.15
his face to the wall, and p	20.2
Hezekiah..p because of this	2Chr 32.20
He p to him, and God	33.13
we p to our God, and set a	Neh 4.9
Job,..had p for his friends;	Job 42.10
when they were sick—..I p	Ps 35.13
And Hezekiah p to the LORD:	Isa 37.15
turned..face to the wall, and p	38.2
p and gave thanks before..God,	Dan 6.10
Jonah p to the LORD his God	Jonah 2.1
he..p for the third time,	Mt 26.44
lonely place, and there he p.	Mk 1.35
to the wilderness and p.	Lk 5.16
The Pharisee stood and p thus	18.11
he..knelt down and p,	22.41
they p and said, "Lord,..show	Acts 1.24
when they had p, the place	4.31
who came down and p for them	8.15
But Peter..knelt down and p;	9.40
on the beach we p and bade	21.5
and Paul visited him and p,	28.8
I continued fasting and p	Neh 1.4
p to a god that cannot save.	Isa 45.20
people..p outside at the hour	Lk 1.10
when Jesus..was p, the heaven	3.21
as he was p alone the disciples	9.18
I am p for them; I am not p	Jn 17.9
Saul; for behold, he is p,	Acts 9.11
gathered together and were p.	12.12
after fasting and p they laid	13.3
Paul and Silas were p and	16.25
p earnestly night and day	1Thess 3.10

PRAYER — S

granted his p, and Rebekah	Gen 25.21
have regard to the p of thy	2Chr 6.19
their p came to his holy	30.27
heard..the LORD accepts my p.	Ps 6.9
Give ear to my p from lips free	17.1
godly offer p to thee;	32.6
night his song is with me, a p	42.8
O thou who hearest p! To thee	65.2
May p be made for him..and	72.15
regard the p of the destitute,	102.17
accuse me, even as I make p	109.4
Let my p be counted as incense	141.2
p of..upright is his delight.	Prov 15.8
hears..p of the righteous.	15.29
a p when thy chastening was	Isa 26.16
your p for the remnant that	37.4
a house of p for all peoples.	56.7
I call and..he shuts out my p;	Lam 3.8
so that no p can pass through.	3.44
Lord God, seeking him by p	Dan 9.3
never comes out except by p	Mt 17.21n
shall be called a house of p';	21.13
And whatever you ask in p, you	21.22
driven out by anything but p."	Mk 9.29
called a house of p for all	11.17
whatever you ask in p, believe	11.24

PRAYER — S (cont.)

Zechariah, for your *p* is heard,	Lk 1.13
house shall be a house of *p*';	19.46
devoted themselves to *p*,	Acts 1.14
the hour of *p*, the ninth hour.	3.1
we will devote ourselves to *p*	6.4
ninth hour of *p* in my house;	10.30
Peter. .in prison; but earnest *p*	12.5
appointed. .with *p* and fasting,	14.23
there was a place of *p*;	16.13
tribulation, be constant in *p*.	Rom 12.12
may devote yourselves to *p*;	1Cor 7.5
You also must help us by *p*,	2Cor 1.11
in every *p* of mine for you	Phil 1.4
by *p* and supplication with	4.6
Continue steadfastly in *p*,	Col 4.2
The *p* of a righteous man	Jas 5.16
a pretense you make long *p*;	Mt 23.14*n*
for a pretense make long *p*.	Mk 12.40
disciples. .fast. .and offer *p*,	Lk 5.33
for a pretense make long *p*.	20.47
"Your *p* and your alms have	Acts 10.4
mention you always in my *p*,	Rom 1.9
together with me in your *p*	15.30
remembering you. .in his *p*,	Col 4.12
I urge that supplications, *p*,	1Tim 2.1
continues in. .*p* night and day;	5.5
when I remember you. .in my *p*.	2Tim 1.3
Jesus offered up *p* and	Heb 5.7
your *p* may not be hindered.	1Pet 3.7
sane and sober for your *p*.	4.7
which are the *p* of the saints;	Rev 5.8

PREACH — ED — ING

"Do not *p*"—thus they *p*—	Mic 2.6
twelve,. .to be sent out to *p*	Mk 3.14
p. .gospel to. .whole creation.	16.15*n*
to *p* good news to the poor.	Lk 4.18
p the good news of the kingdom	4.43
he sent them out to *p* the kingdom	9.2
God had called us to *p* the	Acts 16.10
While you *p* against stealing,	Rom 2.21
men *p* unless they are sent?	10.15
my ambition to *p* the gospel,	15.20
not. .to baptize but to *p* the	1Cor 1.17
what we *p* is not ourselves,	2Cor 4.5
Some. .*p* Christ from envy and	Phil 1.15
p the word,. .urgent in season	2Tim 4.2
wherever this gospel is *p*	Mt 26.13
he *p*,. ."After me comes he who	Mk 1.7
and *p* that men should repent.	6.12
the gospel must first be *p*	13.10
forgiveness of sins. .be *p*	Lk 24.47
that I *p* the gospel to you	Gal 4.13
while we *p* to you the gospel	1Thess 2.9
p to the spirits in prison,	1Pet 3.19
came John. .*p* in the wilderness	Mt 3.1
p the gospel of the kingdom,	9.35
and he was *p* the word to them.	Mk 2.2
about the Jordan, *p* a baptism	Lk 3.3
those. .scattered went about *p*	Acts 8.4
Paul was occupied with *p*,	18.5
p the kingdom of God and	28.31
what is heard comes by the *p*	Rom 10.17
once persecuted us is now *p*	Gal 1.23
who labor in *p* and teaching;	1Tim 5.17

PREACHER

The words of the *P*, the son	Ecc 1.1
be the *p* for this people!	Mic 2.11
they to hear without a *p*?	Rom 10.14
For this I was appointed a *p*	1Tim 2.7

PRECEPT — S

For it is *p* upon *p*, *p* upon *p*,	Isa 28.10
the *p* of the LORD are right,	Ps 19.8
all his *p* are trustworthy,	111.7
companion of all. .keep thy *p*.	119.63
I will never forget thy *p*;	119.93
for I give you good *p*; do not	Prov 4.2

PRECIOUS

his eye sees every *p* thing.	Job 28.10
How *p* is thy steadfast love,	Ps 36.7
p is their blood in his sight.	72.14
P in the sight of the LORD is	116.15
like the *p* oil upon the head,	133.2
How *p* to me are thy thoughts,	139.17
She is more *p* than jewels,	Prov 3.15
lips of knowledge. .a *p* jewel.	20.15
wife. .more *p* than jewels.	31.10
Because you are *p* in my eyes,	Isa 43.4
nor as *p* to myself, if only	Acts 20.24
your faith, more *p* than gold	1Pet 1.7
a cornerstone chosen and *p*,	2.6

PREDESTINED

thy plan had *p* to take place.	Acts 4.28
those whom he *p* he also called;	Rom 8.30

PREDICTED

man of God. .*p* these things	2Ki 23.17
as Isaiah *p*, "If the Lord	Rom 9.29

PREDICTING

p the sufferings of Christ	1Pet 1.11

PREPARATION

since it was the day of *P*,	Mk 15.42
It was the day of *P*, and	Lk 23.54

PREPARE — S — D

P yourselves according to	2Chr 35.4
"In the wilderness *p* the way	Isa 40.3
go through the gates, *p* the way	62.10
p to meet your God, O Israel"	Amos 4.12
"Where will you have us *p*	Mt 26.17
P the way of the Lord, make	Mk 1.3
p for you to eat the passover?"	14.12
before the Lord to *p* his ways,	Lk 1.76
P the way of the Lord, make	3.4
who shall *p* thy way before thee."	7.27
when I go and *p* a place for you,	Jn 14.3
p a guest room for me, for I	Philem 22
he *p* rain for the earth, he	Ps 147.8
to him for whom nothing is *p*;	Neh 8.10
I. .*p* a lamp for my anointed.	Ps 132.17
a burning place has. .been *p*;	Isa 30.33
the LORD has *p* a sacrifice	Zeph 1.7
it has been *p* by my Father."	Mt 20.23
those for whom it has been *p*."	Mk 10.40
ready for the Lord a people *p*."	Lk 1.17
thou hast *p* in the presence	2.31
he has *p* beforehand for glory,	Rom 9.23
God has *p* for those who love	1Cor 2.9
a body hast thou *p* for me; ·	Heb 10.5

PRESENCE

Cain went away from the *p*	Gen 4.16
"If thy *p* will not go with me,	Ex 33.15
in thy *p* there is fulness of joy,	Ps 16.11
Tremble,. .at the *p* of the LORD,	114.7
fleeing. .the *p* of the LORD,	Jonah 1.10
Gabriel, who stand. .*p* of God;	Lk 1.19
to appear in the *p* of God	Heb 9.24
without blemish before the *p*	Jude 24

PRESENT — ED

to Jerusalem to *p* him to the	Lk 2.22
here *p* in the sight of God,	Acts 10.33

PRESENT — ED (cont.)

to *p* your bodies as a living | Rom 12.1
p you as a pure bride to her | 2Cor 11.2
he might *p*..church to himself | Eph 5.27
to *p* you holy and blameless | Col 1.22
that we may *p* every man mature | 1.28
to *p* you without blemish | Jude 1.24
and *p* them to Pharaoh. | Gen 47.2
They *p* many gifts to us; | Acts 28.10

PRESENT (n)

a *p* for his brother Esau, | Gen 32.13
"Give me a *p*; since you | Josh 15.19
a *p* to the king of Assyria. | 2Ki 16.8
allowance of food and a *p*, | Jer 40.5

PRESERVE — S — ST — D — ING

sent me before you to *p* life. | Gen 45.5
P me, O God, for in thee I | Ps 16.1
integrity and uprightness *p* me, | 25.21
thy faithfulness ever *p* me! | 40.11
p my life from dread of..enemy, | 64.1
in thy justice *p* my life. | 119.149
trouble, thou dost *p* my life; | 138.7
and faithfulness *p* the king, | Prov 20.28
he *p* the lives of his saints; | Ps 97.10
The LORD *p* the simple; when | 116.6
The LORD *p* all who love him; | 145.20
guards his way *p* his life. | Prov 16.17
thou *p* me from trouble; thou | Ps 32.7
and *p* us in all the way | Josh 24.17
he has *p* us and given into | 1Sam 30.23
and *p* the way of his saints. | Prov 2.8

PRESS — ED

let us *p* on to know the LORD; | Hos 6.3
I *p* on toward the goal for | Phil 3.14
she *p* him hard with..words | Judg 16.16
I am hard *p* between the two. | Phil 1.23

PRESUMPTUOUS

thy servant also from *p* sins; | Ps 19.13

PRETENSE

for a *p* you make long prayers; | Mt 23.14*n*
for a *p* make long prayers. | Mk 12.40
whether in *p* or in truth, | Phil 1.18

PREVAIL — ED

When our transgressions *p* over | Ps 65.3
striven with God and..*p*." | Gen 32.28
held up his hand, Israel *p*; | Ex 17.11
strove with the angel and *p*, | Hos 12.4

PREVENT — ED

What..*p* my being baptized?" | Acts 8.37
John would have *p* him, saying, | Mt 3.14

PRICE

give the *p* of the field; | Gen 23.13
without money and without *p*. | Isa 55.1
you were bought with a *p*. | 1Cor 6.20
You were bought with a *p*; | 7.23

PRIDE

Reuben..pre-eminent in *p* | Gen 49.3
and cut off *p* from man; | Job 33.17
king over all the sons of *p*." | 41.34
P and arrogance and the way | Prov 8.13
When *p* comes, then..disgrace; | 11.2
P goes before destruction, | 16.18
the inhabitants..who say in *p* | Isa 9.9
We..heard of the *p* of Moab— | Jer 48.29
has blossomed, *p* has budded. | Ezek 7.10
The *p* of Israel testifies to | Hos 5.5
p of your heart has deceived | Obad 1.3

lot in return for their *p*, | Zeph 2.10
envy, slander, *p*, foolishness. | Mk 7.22

PRIEST — S

Melchizedek..was *p* of God | Gen 14.18
for myself a faithful *p*, | 1Sam 2.35
"You are a *p* for ever after | Ps 110.4
the people, so with the *p*; | Isa 24.2
shall be a *p* by his throne, | Zech 6.13
while..serving as *p* before God | Lk 1.8
"Go and show yourself to the *p*, | 5.14
since we have a great *p* over | Heb 10.21
land of the *p* alone did not | Gen 47.26
to me a kingdom of *p* | Ex 19.6
let the *p* who come near | 19.22
kill the *p* of the LORD; | 1Sam 22.17
he deposed the idolatrous *p* | 2Ki 23.5
his own *p* for..high places, | 2Chr 11.15
not driven out the *p* of the LORD, | 13.9
called the *p* of the LORD, | Isa 61.6
and the iniquities of her *p*, | Lam 4.13
Levitical *p*,..sons of Zadok, | Ezek 44.15
sackcloth and lament, O *p*, | Joel 1.13
you, O *p*, who despise my name. | Mal 1.6
for any but the *p* to eat, | Lk 6.4
many of the *p* were obedient | Acts 6.7
made us a kingdom, *p* to his God | Rev 1.6
made them a kingdom and *p* | 5.10

PRIESTHOOD

would you seek the *p* also? | Num 16.10
you shall attend to your *p* | 18.7
through the Levitical *p* | Heb 7.11
he holds his *p* permanently, | 7.24
a holy *p*, to offer spiritual | 1Pet 2.5

PRINCE — S

is *p* among his brothers. | Deut 33.16
appointed you *p* over Israel, | 1Sam 25.30
that you should be *p* over | 2Sam 7.8
Everlasting Father, *P* of Peace." | Isa 9.6
say to the *p* of Tyre, Thus | Ezek 28.2
rise up against the *P* of *p*; | Dan 8.25
p and..judge ask for a bribe, | Mic 7.3
Your *p* are rebels..companions | Isa 1.23
When the *p* of Judah heard | Jer 26.10

PRISON

master..put him into the *p*, | Gen 39.20
while you remain in *p*, | 42.16
freed..king of Judah from *p*; | 2Ki 25.27
Bring me out of *p*, that I may | Ps 142.7
had gone from *p* to the throne | Ecc 4.14
Zedekiah,..in *p* till..death. | Jer 52.11
guard, and you be put in *p*; | Mt 5.25
seized John and..put him in *p*, | 14.3
in *p* till he..pay the debt. | 18.30
I was in *p* and you came to me.' | 25.36
seized John, and bound him in *p* | Mk 6.17
Herod..shut up John in *p*. | Lk 3.20
So Peter was kept in *p*; but | Acts 12.5
they threw them into *p*, | 16.23
out of the *p*, and visited Lydia; | 16.40
many of the saints in *p*, | 26.10
preached to the spirits in *p*, | 1Pet 3.19
throw some of you into *p*, | Rev 2.10

PRISONER — S

notorious *p*, called Barabbas. | Mt 27.16
release for them one *p* whom | Mk 15.6
I, Paul, a *p* for Christ Jesus | Eph 3.1
I..a *p* for the Lord, beg you | 4.1
Paul, a *p* for Christ Jesus, | Philem 1
Let the groans of the *p* come | Ps 79.11
to hear the groans of the *p*, | 102.20

PRISONER — S (cont.)

p in affliction and in irons,	107.10
The LORD sets the p free;	146.7
to bring. .p from the dungeon,	Isa 42.7
your stronghold, O p of hope;	Zech 9.12
The. .plan was to kill the p,	Acts 27.42
you had compassion on the p,	Heb 10.34

PROCLAIM — S — ED — ING

p liberty throughout the land	Lev 25.10
p the name of the LORD.	Deut 32.3
and p his deliverance to a	Ps 22.31
Go, and p these words toward	Jer 3.12
"Stand. .and p there this word,	7.2
"Sing. .p, give praise,. .say,	31.7
P this among the nations:	Joel 3.9
go to Nineveh,. .and p to it	Jonah 3.2
what you hear whispered, p	Mt 10.27
he. .began to p in the Decapolis	Mk 5.20
worship as unknown, this I p	Acts 17.23
who p the gospel should get	1Cor 9.14
you p the Lord's death until	11.26
p Christ out of partisanship,	Phil 1.17
Many a man p his own loyalty,	Prov 20.6
p to the end of the earth:	Isa 62.11
immediately he p Jesus,	Acts 9.20
at Salamis, they p the word	13.5
p. .how much Jesus had done	Lk 8.39
p in Jesus the resurrection	Acts 4.2

PROCLAMATION

Cyrus. .made a p throughout	2Chr 36.22
Cyrus. .made a p throughout	Ezra 1.1

PROFANE — S — D

Molech, and so p the name	Lev 18.21
"Do not p your daughter by	19.29
appear and p the temple and	Dan 11.31
every one who p it shall	Ex 31.14
so that I am p among them.	Ezek 22.26
in. .trade. .p your sanctuaries;	28.18
I will not let my. .name be p	39.7

PROFIT — S (v)

people that cannot p them,	Isa 30.5
God, who teaches you to p,	48.17
what will it p a man, if he	Mt 16.26
what does it p a man, to gain	Mk 8.36
What does it p, my brethren,	Jas 2.14
'It p a man nothing that he	Job 34.9

PROFIT (n)

"What p is. .in my death, if	Ps 30.9
In all toil there is p, but	Prov 14.23
What p is an idol when its	Hab 2.18

PROMISE — D (v)

I will bring. .good that I p	Jer 32.42
They p them freedom, but	2Pet 2.19
bless you, as he has p you!	Deut 1.11
territory, as he has p	12.20
the land which he p to give	19.8
as the LORD your God p	Josh 23.5
thou hast p this good thing	2Sam 7.28
gave Solomon wisdom, as he p	1Ki 5.12
according to all that he p;	8.56
throne of Israel, as. .LORD p,	2Chr 6.10
but p to give it to him in	Acts 7.5
what God p to the fathers,	13.32
which he p beforehand through	Rom 1.2
God. .able to do what he. .p.	4.21
God, who never lies, p ages ago	Tit 1.2
the p eternal inheritance,	Heb 9.15
of God and receive what is p.	10.36
did not receive what was p,	11.39
God has p to those who love	Jas 1.12

PROMISE — S (n)

God, let thy p to David	2Chr 1.9
having no faith in his p.	Ps 106.24
eyes fail. .watching for thy p;	119.82
I send the p of my Father	Lk 24.49
wait for the p of the Father,	Acts 1.4
p is to you and. .your children	2.39
the time of the p drew near,	7.17
on trial for hope in the p	26.6
The p to Abraham and his	Rom 4.13
that the p may rest on grace	4.16
children of the p are reckoned	9.8
son of. .free woman through p.	Gal 4.23
like Isaac, are children of p.	4.28
partakers of the p in Christ	Eph 3.6
the p of entering his rest	Heb 4.1
"Where is the p of his coming?	2Pet 3.4
Lord is not slow about his p	3.9
his p at an end for all time?	Ps 77.8
the p given to the patriarchs,	Rom 15.8
all the p of God find their	2Cor 1.20
Since we have these p, beloved,	7.1
the p were made to Abraham	Gal 3.16
law then against the p of God?	3.21
and patience inherit the p.	Heb 6.12
it is enacted on better p.	8.6
his precious and very great p,	2Pet 1.4

PROOF — S

put the LORD to the p	Ex 17.7
put me to the p. .ten times	Num 14.22
your fathers. .put me to the p,	Ps 95.9
gift. .for a p to the people."	Mt 8.4
what Moses commanded, for a p	Mk 1.44
as Moses commanded, for a p	Lk 5.14
give p, before the churches,	2Cor 8.24
p that Christ is speaking in me.	13.3
presented. .alive. .by many p,	Acts 1.3

PROPHECY

Where there is no p the	Prov 29.18
miracles, to another p,	1Cor 12.10
and our p is imperfect;	13.9
words of the p of this book.	Rev 22.7

PROPHESY — ING — IES — IED

who should p with lyres,	1Chr 25.1
smooth things, p illusions,	Isa 30.10
the prophets p falsely, and	Jer 5.31
"Do not p. .or you will die	11.21
the LORD had sent him to p,	19.14
against those who p lying	23.32
"You,. .p against them all	25.30
"Why do you p and say, 'Thus	32.3
you shall p against the city.	Ezek 4.7
Therefore p against them, p,	11.4
p against. .prophets of Israel,	13.2
p against the land of Israel	21.2
p to the mountains of Israel,	36.1
"P to these bones, and say	37.4
son of man, p, and say to Gog,	38.14
saying, 'You shall not p.'	Amos 2.12
eat bread there, and p there;	7.12
did we not p in your name,	Mt 7.22
saying, "P to us, you Christ!	26.68
strike him, saying. .,"P!"	Mk 14.65
"P! Who is it that struck you?"	Lk 22.64
sons and. .daughters shall p,	Acts 2.17
p, in proportion to our faith;	Rom 12.6
I want you. .even more to p.	1Cor 14.5
I was told, "You must again p	Rev 10.11
prophets are p lies in my name;	Jer 14.14
a lie which they are p to you	29.9
never p good concerning me,	1Ki 22.8

PROPHESY — ING — IES — IED (cont.)

never *p* good concerning me,	2Chr 18.7
spirit. .upon them, they *p*.	Num 11.25
they *p* by Baal and led. .astray.	Jer 23.13
I did not speak. .yet they *p*.	23.21
"Micah of Moresheth *p* in the	26.18
And his father Zechariah. .*p*,	Lk 1.67
spoke with tongues and *p*.	Acts 19.6
Enoch. .*p*, saying, "Behold,	Jude 14

PROPHET — S

restore. .wife; for he is a *p*,	Gen 20.7
your brother shall be your *p*.	Ex 7.1
If there is a *p* among you,	Num 12.6
"If a *p* arises among you,	Deut 13.1
will raise up for you a *p*	18.15
not arisen a *p* since in Israel	34.10
a *p* to the people of Israel;	Judg 6.8
Samuel. .as a *p* of the LORD.	1Sam 3.20
dwelt an old *p* in Bethel.	1Ki 13.11
"Is there not here another *p*	22.7
he may know that there is a *p*	2Ki 5.8
not here another *p*. .of whom	2Chr 18.6
a *p* of the LORD was there,	28.9
before Jeremiah the *p*,	36.12
there is no longer any *p*,	Ps 74.9
and the *p* who teaches lies is	Isa 9.15
p to priest. .deals falsely.	Jer 8.10
know that there has been a *p*	Ezek 2.5
I, the LORD, have deceived that *p*,	14.9
know. .a *p* has been among them."	33.33
The *p* is a fool, the man of	Hos 9.7
By a *p* the LORD brought Israel	12.13
Amos answered…,"I am no *p*,	Amos 7.14
receives a *p* because he is a *p*	Mt 10.41
"A *p* is not without honor except	13.57
fulfil what was spoken by the *p*,	21.4
"This is the *p* Jesus from	21.11
"A *p* is not without honor,	Mk 6.4
all held that John was a. .*p*.	11.32
no *p* is acceptable in his	Lk 4.24
"A great *p* has arisen among us:"	7.16
convinced that John was a *p*."	20.6
they asked. ."Are you the *p*?"	Jn 1.21
I perceive that you are a *p*.	4.19
said, "This is really the *p*."	7.40
will raise up for you a *p*	Acts 7.37
a *p* of their own, said,	Tit 1.12
and with it the false *p* who	Rev 19.20
all the LORD's people. .*p*,	Num 11.29
you will meet a band of *p*	1Sam 10.5
Is Saul also among the *p*?"	10.11
"Is Saul also among the *p*?"	19.24
spoke by his servants the *p*.	2Ki 24.2
believe his *p*, and you will	2Chr 20.20
warn. .by thy Spirit through. .*p*;	Neh 9.30
appalled and the *p* astounded."	Jer 4.9
The *p* will become wind; the	5.13
sent all my servants the *p*	7.25
So do not listen to your *p*,	27.9
I sent. .my servants the *p*,	44.4
p have seen. .false. .visions;	Lam 2.14
This was for the sins of her *p*	4.13
Her *p* are wanton, faithless	Zeph 3.4
"O. .Jerusalem, killing the *p*	Mt 23.37
Christs and false *p* will arise	24.24
and others one of the *p*."	Mk 8.28
fathers did to the false *p*.	Lk 6.26
one of the old *p* has risen."	9.19
p and kings desired to see	10.24
Jerusalem, killing the *p* and	13.34
the *p* and the psalms must be	24.44
reading of. .law and the *p*,	Acts 13.15

"Lord, they have killed thy *p*,	Rom 11.3
first apostles, second *p*,	1Cor 12.28
the spirits of *p* are subject	14.32
should be apostles, some *p*,	Eph 4.11
p who prophesied of. .grace	1Pet 1.10
false *p*. .arose among. .people,	2Pet 2.1
announced to. .servants the *p*,	Rev 10.7

PROPHETESS

Deborah, a *p*, the wife of	Josh 4.4
p,. .conceived and bore a son.	Isa 8.3

PROPHETIC

And if I have *p* powers, and	1Cor 13.2
the *p* word made more sure	2Pet 1.19

PROSELYTE

and land to make a single *p*,	Mt 23.15

PROSPER — S — ED

send. .angel. .and *p* your way;	Gen 24.40
the LORD made it *p*.	39.23
that you may *p* in all that	1Ki 2.3
he sought. .God made him *p*.	2Chr 26.5
"May they *p* who love you!	Ps 122.6
He who conceals. .will not *p*,	Prov 28.13
and he will *p* in his way.	Isa 48.15
will of. .LORD shall *p* in his hand;	53.10
no weapon. .against you shall *p*,	54.10
p in. .things for which I sent it.	55.11
and you will not *p* by them.	Jer 2.37
does the way of the wicked *p*?	12.1
store it up, as he may *p*,	1Cor 16.2
and *p* in their hands.	Ezra 5.8
In all that he does, he *p*.	Ps 1.3
fret not. .over him who *p* in	37.7
wherever he turns he *p*.	Prov 17.8
whether the LORD had *p*	Gen 24.21
wherever he went forth, he *p*.	2Ki 18.7
with all his heart, and *p*.	2Chr 31.21
Daniel *p* during the reign of	Dan 6.28

PROSPERITY

One who dies in full *p*, being	Job 21.23
He himself shall abide in *p*,	Ps 25.13
I said in my *p*, "I shall never	30.6
the meek. .in abundant *p*.	37.11
In the day of *p* be joyful	Ecc 7.14
extend *p* to her like a river,	Isa 66.12
in this place I will give *p*,	Hag 2.9

PROSPEROUS

you shall make your way *p*,	Josh 1.8

PROTECT — S

name of the God of Jacob *p* you!	Ps 20.1
God, *p* me from those who rise	59.1
so the LORD. .will *p* Jerusalem;	Isa 31.5
LORD of hosts will *p* them,	Zech 9.15
the LORD *p* him and keeps him	Ps 41.2
new thing. .a woman *p* a man."	Jer 31.22

PROUD

he was strong, he grew *p*,	2Chr 26.16
one that is *p*, and abase him.	Job 40.11
ease, the contempt of the *p*.	Ps 123.4
Haughty eyes and a *p* heart,	Prov 21.4
Hear and give ear; be not *p*,	Jer 13.15
he has scattered the *p* in	Lk 1.51
"God opposes the *p*, but gives	Jas 4.6

PROVE — D — ING

P me, O LORD, and try me; test	Ps 26.2
Neither can they *p* to you	Acts 24.13
which they could not *p*.	25.7
p what is the will of God,	Rom 12.2
p. .that your love. .is genuine.	2Cor 8.8

PROVE — D — ING (cont.)

and there he *p* them,	Ex 15.25
Saul. .*p* that Jesus was the	Acts 9.22
explaining and *p* that it was	17.3

PROVERB — S

shall become a horror, a *p*,	Deut 28.37
became a *p*, "Is Saul also	1Sam 10.12
Israel will become a *p* and	1Ki 9.7
I will incline my ear to a *p*;	Ps 49.4
to understand a *p*. .a figure,	Prov 1.6
a *p* in the mouth of fools	26.9
"Son of man, what is this *p*	Ezek 12.22
p about you, 'Like mother,	16.44
p, 'Physician, heal yourself;	Lk 4.23
uttered three thousand *p*;	1Ki 4.32

PROVIDE — S — D

"God will *p*. .the lamb	Gen 22.8
there I will *p* for you,	45.11
Who *p* for the raven its prey,	Job 38.41
and *p* food for her household	Prov 31.15
And Joseph *p* his father,	Gen 47.12
I have *p* for the house of	1Chr 22.14
I have *p* for the house of my God.	29.2

PROVISION — S

p for. .father on. .journey.	Gen 45.23
Solomon's *p* for one day was	1Ki 4.22
make no *p* for the flesh,	Rom 13.14
and went and made ready *p*,	Josh 9.4

PROVOKE — D — ING

And her rival used to *p* her	1Sam 1.6
why should you *p* trouble	2Ki 14.10
why should you *p* trouble	2Chr 25.19
people who *p* me to my face	Isa 65.3
I whom they *p*? says the LORD.	Jer 7.19
Why do you *p* me to anger with	44.8
p him to speak of many things,	Lk 11.53
we *p* the Lord to jealousy?	1Cor 10.22
Fathers, do not *p* your children	Eph 6.4
you *p* the LORD to wrath.	Deut 9.22
p me with their idols.	32.21
they *p* the LORD to anger.	Judg 2.12
they *p* him to jealousy with	1Ki 14.22
and *p* the LORD, the God of	22.53
and *p* the Holy One of Israel.	Ps 78.41
p him. .with their high places;	78.58
I was *p* with that generation,	Heb 3.10
the Lord, *p* him to anger.	2Ki 17.17
to other gods, *p* to anger	2Chr 28.25

PRUDENT

a *p* wife is from the LORD.	Prov 19.14
he who is *p* will keep silent	Amos 5.13

PSALMIST

David,. .the sweet *p* of	2Sam 23.1

PSALMS

prophets and the *p* must be	Lk 24.44
addressing one another in *p*	Eph 5.19
as you sing *p* and hymns	Col 3.16

PUBLISH — ED

p it not in the streets	2Sam 1.20
he made a proclamation and *p*	Jonah 3.7

PUFFED

that none of you may be *p* up	1Cor 4.6

PUFFS

"Knowledge" *p* up, but love	1Cor 8.1

PULPIT

Ezra the scribe stood on a. .*p*	Neh 8.4

PUNISH — ED

Awake to *p* all the nations;	Ps 59.5
then I will *p*. .with the rod	89.32
he will *p*. .arrogant boasting	Isa 10.12
p the world for its evil,	13.11
On that day the LORD will *p*	24.21
Shall I not *p* them for these	Jer 5.9
Shall I not *p* them for these	9.9
p. .those who are circumcised	9.25
p. .according to your. .doings,	21.14
will *p* the images of Babylon;	51.47
I will *p* her for the feast days	Hos 2.13
iniquity, and *p* their sins;	8.13
iniquity, he will *p* their sins.	9.9
p Jacob according to his ways,	12.2
on the day I *p* Israel for	Amos 3.14
as *p*, and yet not killed;	2Cor 6.9

PUNISHMENT

p is greater than I can bear.	Gen 4.13
will you do on the day of *p*,	Isa 10.3
greater than the *p* of Sodom,	Lam 4.6
so long shall you bear the *p*	Ezek 4.5
they shall bear their *p*—	14.10
The days of *p* have come, the	Hos 9.7
p by the majority is enough	2Cor 2.6
p of eternal destruction	2Thess 1.9

PURCHASE — ED

gave the deed of *p* to Baruch	Jer 32.12
the field which Abraham *p*	Gen 25.10
pass by whom thou hast *p*.	Ex 15.16

PURE — R

with the *p* thou dost show	2Sam 22.27
a man be *p* before his Maker?	Job 4.17
if you are *p* and upright,	8.6
you say, 'My doctrine is *p*,	11.4
promises of the LORD. .are *p*,	Ps 12.6
with the *p* thou dost show. .*p*;	18.26
commandment of the LORD is *p*,	19.8
clean hands and a *p* heart,	24.4
good. .to those who are *p* in	73.1
can a young man keep. .way *p*?	119.9
words of the *p* are pleasing	Prov 15.26
ways of a man are *p* in his	16.2
who are *p* in their own eyes	30.12
"Blessed are the *p* in heart,	Mt 5.8
led astray from. .*p* devotion	2Cor 11.3
man's sins; keep yourself *p*.	1Tim 5.22
To the *p* all things are *p*,	Tit 1.15
of *p* eyes than to behold evil	Hab 1.13

PURGE — D

P me with hyssop, and I shall	Ps 51.7
I will *p* out the rebels from	Ezek 20.38
and *p* Judah and Jerusalem.	2Chr 34.5

PURIFICATION

when the time came for their *p*	Lk 2.22
When he had made *p* for sins,	Heb 1.3

PURIFY — ING — IES — IED

You shall *p* every garment,	Num 31.20
p yourselves, you who bear	Isa 52.11
Many shall *p* themselves,	Dan 12.10
he will *p* the sons of Levi	Mal 3.3
p your conscience from dead	Heb 9.14
disciples and a Jew over *p*.	Jn 3.25
hopes in him *p* himself as	1Jn 3.3
and the Levites *p* themselves;	Neh 12.30
Paul. .*p* himself with them	Acts 21.26
everything is *p* with blood,	Heb 9.22
Having *p*. .souls by. .obedience	1Pet 1.22

PURPOSE — D (v)
I *p* to build a house for	1Ki 5.5
Solomon *p* to build a temple	2Chr 2.1

PURPOSE — S (n)
to frustrate their *p*, all the	Ezra 4.5
p in a man's mind is like	Prov 20.5
let the *p* of the Holy One	Isa 5.19
p..concerning the whole earth;	14.26
will fear because of the *p*	19.17
I will accomplish all my *p*,	46.10
lawyers rejected the *p* of God	Lk 7.30
the Lord with steadfast *p*;	Acts 11.23
p which he set forth in Christ	Eph 1.9
p of him who accomplishes all	1.11
according to the eternal *p*	3.11
but in virtue of his own *p*	2Tim 1.9
unchangeable character of..*p*,	Heb 6.17
carry out his *p* by being of	Rev 17.17
the Lord's *p* against Babylon	Jer 51.29

PURSUE — S — D
Why do you, like God, *p* me?	Job 19.22
thou *p* them with thy tempest	Ps 83.15
I will *p* them with sword,	Jer 29.18
p..in anger and destroy them	Lam 3.66
then *p* what makes for peace	Rom 14.19
p righteousness and kindness	Prov 21.21
he *p* the people of Israel	Ex 14.8
but *p* the poor and needy	Ps 109.16
p his brother with the sword,	Amos 1.11

PUT
But *p* on the Lord Jesus	Rom 13.14
to *p* on our heavenly dwelling,	2Cor 5.2
P off your old nature which	Eph 4.22
and *p* on the new nature,	4.24
P on then, as God's chosen	Col 3.12

Q

QUARREL — ING
quit before the *q* breaks	Prov 17.14
a wife's *q* is a continual	19.13
that there is a *q* among you,	1Cor 1.11
perhaps there may be *q*,	2Cor 12.20
holy hands without anger or *q*;	1Tim 2.8

QUEEN
made her *q* instead of Vashti.	Est 2.17
at your right hand stands the *q*	Ps 45.9
The *q* of the South will arise	Mt 12.42
The *q* of the South will arise	Lk 11.31

QUENCH — ED
Many waters cannot *q* love,	Sol 8.7
burn together, with none to *q*	Isa 1.31
burning wick he will not *q*;	42.3
or *q* a smoldering wick, till	Mt 12.20
Do not *q* the Spirit,	1Thess 5.19
die, and the fire is not *q*.	Mk 9.48

QUESTION — ED (v)
you *q* me about my children,	Isa 45.11
"Why..*q* thus in your heart?	Mk 2.8
men *q*..concerning John,	Lk 3.15

QUESTIONS (n)
to test him with hard *q*.	1Ki 10.1
to test him with hard *q*,	2Chr 9.1

QUIET — LY
he is *q*, who can condemn?	Job 34.29
resolved to divorce her *q*.	Mt 1.19
to aspire to live *q*,	1Thess 4.11

QUIETNESS
Better is a handful of *q* than	Ecc 4.6
result of righteousness, *q*	Isa 32.17

QUIVER
Happy is the man..his *q* full	Ps 127.5

R

RACE
the *r* is not to the swift,	Ecc 9.11
in a *r* all the runners	1Cor 9.24
the *r* that is set before us,	Heb 12.1

RACHEL
and see, *R* his daughter	Gen 29.6
name of the younger was *R*.	29.16
Jacob loved *R*; and he said,	29.18
loved *R* more than Leah,	29.30
Then God remembered *R*,	30.22
R had taken..household gods	31.34
R died, and she was buried	35.19
like *R* and Leah, who..built	Ruth 4.11
R weeping for her children;	Mt 2.18

RADIANT
Look to him, and be *r*;	Ps 34.5
Then you shall see and be *r*,	Isa 60.5
r over..goodness of..Lord,	Jer 31.12

RAFTS
make it into *r* to go by sea	1Ki 5.9
bring it to you in *r* by sea	2Chr 2.16

RAGE — S — D — ING
nations *r*, the kingdoms totter;	Ps 46.6
his heart *r* against the Lord.	Prov 19.3
The nations *r*, but thy wrath	Rev 11.18
'I know..your *r* against me.	Isa 37.28

RAIN (v)
God had not caused it to *r*	Gen 2.5
R in abundance, O God, thou	Ps 68.9
skies *r* down righteousness;	Isa 45.8

RAIN — S (n)
seven days I will send *r*	Gen 7.4
give the *r* for your land	Deut 11.14
give the *r* of your land	28.12
there is no *r* because they	1Ki 8.35
nor *r* these years, except by	17.1
sound of the rushing of *r*."	18.41
he gives *r* upon the earth	Job 5.10
"Has the *r* a father, or	38.28
plants a cedar..*r* nourishes	Isa 44.14
"For as the *r* and the snow	55.10
God,..gives..*r* in its season,	Jer 5.24
the early and the latter *r*,	Joel 2.23
I also withheld the *r* from you	Amos 4.7
Ask *r* from the Lord in the	Zech 10.1
there will be no *r* upon them.	14.17
sends *r* on..just and..unjust.	Mt 5.45
r fell, and the floods came,	7.25
that no *r* may fall during	Rev 11.6
give..your *r* in their season,	Lev 26.4
gave you from heaven *r* and	Acts 14.17

RAINBOW
and round the throne was a *r*	Rev 4.3

RAISE — S — D
r me up, that I may requite	Ps 41.10
look up and *r* your heads,	Lk 21.28
but *r* it up at the last day.	Jn 6.39
and the Lord will *r* him up;	Jas 5.15
as the Father *r* the dead	Jn 5.21
thought incredible..God *r*	Acts 26.8

RAISE — S — D (cont.)
He has r up a horn for his | Ps 148.14
the Baptist,..r from the dead; | Mt 14.2
and on the third day be r. | 16.21
until the Son of man is r | 17.9
he will be r on the third day." | 20.19
But after I am r up, I will go | 26.32
"John the baptizer has been r | Mk 6.14
after I am r up, I will go | 14.28
that John had been r from..dead Lk 9.7
God r the Lord and will..r us 1Cor 6.14
he was r on the third day | 15.4
then Christ has not been r; | 15.13
he who r the Lord..will r us 2Cor 4.14
Author of life, whom God r | Acts 3.15
God r him on the third day | 10.40
God r him from the dead; | 13.30
to Pharaoh, "I have r you up Rom 9.17
when he r him from the dead Eph 1.20
r us up with him, and made us | 2.6
If..you have been r with Christ, Col 3.1
confidence in God, who r him 1Pet 1.21

RAM
Bring..a r three years old, | Gen 15.9
a r, caught in a thicket | 22.13

RAMAH
at R. And Elkanah knew | 1Sam 1.19
Then Elkanah went home to R. | 2.11
elders..came to Samuel at R, | 8.4
and he came to Samuel at R, | 19.18
Israel..buried him in R, | 28.3
against Judah, and built R, | 2Chr 16.1
R trembles, Gibeah..has fled. | Isa 10.29
"A voice is heard in R, | Jer 31.15
voice was heard in R, wailing | Mt 2.18

RAMOTH-GILEAD
go to battle against R, or | 1Ki 22.6
oil in your hand, and go to R. | 2Ki 9.1

RAN
they..r to tell his disciples. | Mt 28.8
both r, but the other disciple | Jn 20.4

RANSOM — ED (v)
Or, 'R me from the hand of | Job 6.23
Truly no man can r himself, | Ps 49.7
Shall I r them from..Sheol? | Hos 13.14
thy blood didst r men for God | Rev 5.9
So the people r Jonathan, | 1Sam 14.45
You know that you were r | 1Pet 1.18

RANSOM (n)
each..give a r for himself | Ex 30.12
'Deliver him..I..found a r; | Job 33.24
greatness of the r turn you | 36.18
the r of his life is costly, | Ps 49.8
The wicked is a r for the | Prov 21.18
I give Egypt as your r, | Isa 43.3
his life as a r for many." | Mt 20.28
give his life..a r for many." | Mk 10.45
who gave himself as a r for | 1Tim 2.6

RARE
word..was r in those days; | 1Sam 3.1
make men more r than..gold, | Isa 13.12

RASH
therefore my words have been r. Job 6.3
Be not r with your mouth, nor Ecc 5.2

RAVEN — S
Noah..sent forth a r; | Gen 8.7
Who provides for the r its | Job 38.41

commanded the r to feed you | 1Ki 17.4
the r:..neither sow nor reap, | Lk 12.24

RAVISH — ED
R them and do..what seems Judg 19.24
You have r my heart, my sister, Sol 4.9

RAZOR
no r shall come upon his head; Num 6.5
Your tongue is like a sharp r, Ps 52.2
the Lord will shave with a r Isa 7.20
sword; use it as a barber's r Ezek 5.1

READ — S — ING
he shall r in it all the days Deut 17.19
r this law before all | 31.11
he r in their hearing all | 2Ki 23.2
he r from it facing the square Neh 8.3
they r from the book of Moses | 13.1
"R this," he says, "I cannot, Isa 29.11
r from the book of the LORD: | 34.16
you shall r the words of..LORD Jer 36.6
and Jehudi r it to the king | 36.21
I will r the writing to the king Dan 5.17
"Have you..r in..scriptures: Mt 21.42
Have you not r this scripture: Mk 12.10
not r in the book of Moses, | 12.26
"Have you not r what David did Lk 6.3
to be known and r by all 2Cor 3.2
"Whoever r this writing, and Dan 5.7
so he may run who r it. Hab 2.2
Blessed is he who r aloud Rev 1.3
he was r the prophet Isaiah. Acts 8.28

READY
I have made r my dinner, | Mt 22.4
Then he said.."The wedding is r, | 22.8
Therefore you also must be r; | 24.44
who were r went in with him | 25.10
but did not make r or act Lk 12.47
who will get r for battle? 1Cor 14.8
saying that Achaia has been r 2Cor 9.2

REAP — S
you shall not r your field Lev 19.9
"And when you r the harvest | 23.22
and sow trouble r the same. Job 4.8
who sow in tears r with..joy! Ps 126.5
sows injustice..r calamity Prov 22.8
regards the clouds will not r. Ecc 11.4
You shall sow, but not r; Mic 6.15
the birds..neither sow nor r Mt 6.26
we r your material benefits? 1Cor 9.11
man sows, that he will also r. Gal 6.7
r, for..hour to r has come, Rev 14.15
He who r receives wages, Jn 4.36

REBEKAH (REBECCA)
became the father of R. Gen 22.23
behold, R, who was born | 24.15
So they sent away R | 24.59
Then Isaac..took R, | 24.67
but R loved Jacob. | 25.28
R was listening when | 27.5
they buried Isaac and R | 49.31
when R had conceived children Rom 9.10

REBEL — LED — LING (v)
do not r against the LORD; Num 14.9
who r against the light, Job 24.13
But if you refuse and r, you Isa 1.20
you r against my command Num 20.24
you r against my word | 27.14
but r against the command Deut 1.26
you r against the command | 1.43
Moab r against the king of 2Ki 3.5

REBEL — LED — LING (v) (cont.)

for they have r against thee. Ps 5.10
How often they r against him 78.40
r against the words of God, 107.11
but they have r against me. Isa 1.2
now. .that you have r against me? 36.5
r and grieved his holy Spirit; 63.10
because she has r against me, Jer 4.17
rebels, who have r against me; Ezek 2.3
Israel r against me in the 20.13
she has r against her God; Hos 13.16
Are you r against the king?" Neh 2.19
r against the Most High in the Ps 78.17

REBEL — S (n)

from birth you were called a r. Isa 48.8
"Hear now, you r; Num 20.10
Your princes are r. .companions Isa 1.23
r. .sinners. .destroyed together, 1.28

REBELLION

an altar this day in r Josh 22.16
r is as. .sin of divination, 1Sam 15.23
Israel has been in r against 1Ki 12.19
So Israel has been in r 2Chr 10.19
For he adds r to his sin; Job 34.37
talked r against the LORD.' " Jer 29.32

REBELLIOUS

and r son, who will not obey Deut 21.18
a r city, hurtful to kings Ezra 4.15
"Woe to the r children," says Isa 30.1
"Say now to the r house, Ezek 17.12

REBUILD

r the house of the LORD, Ezra 1.3
If he tears down, none can r; Job 12.14
r the walls of Jerusalem, Ps 51.18

REBUKE — D (v)

surely r you if in secret Job 13.10
O LORD, r me not in thy anger, Ps 6.1
LORD, r me not in thy anger, 38.1
Thou dost r the insolent, 119.21
those who r the wicked will Prov 24.25
"The LORD r you, O Satan!" Zech 3.2
Peter took him and began to r Mt 16.22
Peter took him, and began to r Mk 8.32
Do not r an older man but 1Tim 5.1
but said, "The Lord r you." Jude 9
God saw my. .labor. .and r Gen 31.42
his father r him, and said 37.10
he r kings on their account, 1Chr 16.21
he r kings on their account, Ps 105.14
r the Red Sea,. .it became dry; 106.9
why have you not r Jeremiah Jer 29.27
Jesus r him,. .demon came out Mt 17.18
Jesus. .r the unclean spirit, Mk 9.25
Jesus r him,. ."Be silent, and Lk 4.35
Jesus r the unclean spirit, 9.42
But he turned and r them. 9.55

REBUKE (n)

and are astounded at his r. Job 26.11
At thy r, O God of Jacob, both Ps 76.6
At thy r they fled; at the sound 104.7
A r goes deeper into a man Prov 17.10
Better is open r than hidden love. 27.5

RECEIVE — S — D — ING

and shall we not r evil?" Job 2.10
R instruction from his mouth, 22.22
heritage which oppressors r 27.13
what does he r from your hand? 35.7
will r blessing from the LORD, Ps 24.5

from. .Sheol, for he will r me. 49.15
thou wilt r me to glory. 73.24
r instruction in wise dealing, Prov 1.3
if you r my words and treasure 2.1
He who is able to r this, Mt 19.12
they thought they would r more; 20.10
you will r, if you have faith." 21.22
immediately r it with joy; Mk 4.16
if any place will not r you 6.11
r the kingdom. .like a child 10.15
who will not r a hundredfold 10.30
"Master, let me r my sight." 10.51
sinners lend to sinners, to r Lk 6.34
wherever they do not r you, 9.5
the people would not r him, 9.53
town and they do not r you, 10.10
who will not r manifold more 18.30
"R your sight; your faith 18.42
"No one can r anything except Jn 3.27
his own name, him you will r. 5.43
to them, "R the Holy Spirit. 20.22
"Did you r the Holy Spirit Acts 19.2
that you may r her in the Lord Rom 16.2
unspiritual man does not r 1Cor 2.14
Did you r the Spirit by works Gal 3.2
r the promise of the Spirit 3.14
we might r adoption as sons. 4.5
For every one who asks r, Mt 7.8
"He who r you r me, and he 10.40
"Whoever r one such child in my 18.5
"Whoever r one such child Mk 9.37
"Whoever r this child in my name Lk 9.48
every one who asks r, and he 11.10
he who r any one whom I send Jn 13.20
he has r him safe and sound.' Lk 15.27
came down, and r him joyfully. 19.6
But to all who r him, who Jn 1.12
who r his word were baptized, Acts 2.41
For I r from the Lord what 1Cor 11.23
what I also r, that Christ 15.3
but r me as an angel of God, Gal 4.14
As. .you r Christ. .the Lord, Col 2.6
r the word in. .affliction, 1Thess 1.6
we are r the due reward of Lk 23.41

RECKON — ED — ING

r with him who bought him Lev 25.50
God r righteousness apart Rom 4.6
he r it. .as righteousness. Gen 15.6
r to him as righteousness Ps 106.31
r with the transgressors" Mk 15.28n
he was r with transgressors'; Lk 22.37
believed God, and it was r Rom 4.3
We say. .faith was r to Abraham 4.9
faith was "r. .as righteousness." 4.22
comes a r for his blood." Gen 42.22
like one who is inwardly r. Prov 23.7
When he began the r, one was Mt 18.24

RECOMPENSE — D (v)

Let him r it to themselves, Job 21.19
will doubly r their iniquity Jer 16.18
r. .according to their deeds 25.14
LORD has r me according to 2Sam 22.25
Therefore the LORD has r me Ps 18.24

RECONCILE — D

might r us both to God in one Eph 2.16
through him to r. .all things, Col 1.20
first be r to your brother, Mt 5.24
much more, now that we are r, Rom 5.10
else be r to her husband)— 1Cor 7.11
who through Christ r us to 2Cor 5.18

RECONCILIATION
we have now received our *r*. Rom 5.11
if their rejection means. .*r* 11.15

RECOUNT — S
I shall live, and *r* the deeds Ps 118.17
I will *r* the steadfast love Isa 63.7
He *r* to men his salvation, Job 33.26

RECOVER
'Shall I *r* from this sickness?' 2Ki 8.8
second time to *r* the remnant Isa 11.11

REDEEM — S — ED (v)
r you with an outstretched arm Ex 6.6
the first-born. .you shall *r* 34.20
But if he wishes to *r* it, Lev 27.13
the first-born. .you shall *r*, Num 18.15
If you will *r* it, *r* it; Ruth 4.4
to *r* to be his people, 2Sam 7.23
God went to *r* to be his 1Chr 17.21
In famine he will *r* you Job 5.20
R Israel, O God, out of all Ps 25.22
r me, and be gracious to me. 26.11
Draw near to me, *r* me, set me 69.18
with thy arm *r* thy people, 77.15
and *r* you from the grasp of Jer 15.21
I would *r* them, but they speak Hos 7.13
he was the one to *r* Israel. Lk 24.21
to *r* those. .under the law, Gal 4.5
gave himself for us to *r* us Tit 2.14
the LORD *r* the life of his Ps 34.22
who *r* your life from the Pit, 103.4
the angel who has *r* me from Gen 48.16
the people whom thou hast *r*, Ex 15.13
then he shall let her be *r*; 21.8
and *r* you from the house of Deut 7.8
r through thy greatness, 9.26
LORD lives, who has *r* my life 2Sam 4.9
LORD lives, who has *r* my soul 1Ki 1.29
thy people, whom thou hast *r* Neh 1.10
He has *r* my soul from Job 33.28
hast *r* me, O LORD, faithful Ps 31.5
Zion shall be *r* by justice, Isa 1.27
"Fear not, for I have *r* you; 43.1
LORD has *r* his servant Jacob!" 48.20
you shall be *r* without money. 52.3
r you from. .house of bondage; Mic 6.4
for I have *r* them, and they Zech 10.8
Lord. .visited and *r* his people, Lk 1.68
Christ *r* us from the curse Gal 3.13

REDEEMED (n)
Let the *r* of the LORD say so, Ps 107.2
but the *r* shall walk there. Isa 35.9
a way for the *r* to pass over? 51.10
holy people, The *r* of the LORD; 62.12

REDEEMER
For I know that my *R* lives, Job 19.25
O LORD, my rock and my *r*. Ps 19.14
the Most High God their *r*. 78.35
For their *R* is strong; he Prov 23.11
your *R* is the Holy One of Isa 41.14
King of Israel and his *R*, 44.6
Our *R*—the LORD of hosts is 47.4
compassion on you, says. .your *R*. 54.8
he will come to Zion as *R*, 59.20
Their *R* is strong; the LORD Jer 50.34

REDEMPTION
give for the *r* of his life Ex 21.30
shall grant a *r* of the land. Lev 25.24
exercise his right of *r*, 25.33
refund the money for his *r*. 25.52

So Moses took the *r* money Num 3.49
Take my right of *r* yourself, Ruth 4.6
He sent *r* to his people; he Ps 111.9
and with him is plenteous *r*. 130.7
a poor man has no means of *r*. Prov 13.8
for the right of *r*. .is yours.' Jer 32.7
looking for the *r* of Jerusalem. Lk 2.38
your *r* is drawing near." 21.28
r which is in Christ Jesus. Rom 3.24
Jesus, whom God made our. .*r*; 1Cor 1.30
we have *r* through his blood, Eph 1.7
were sealed for the day of *r*. 4.30
thus securing an eternal *r*. Heb 9.12

RED SEA
and drove them into the *R*. .; Ex 10.19
officers are sunk in the *R*... 15.4
led Israel onward from the *R*. ., 15.22
LORD your God did to the *R*. ., Josh 4.23
the *R*. .,and it became dry; Ps 106.9
in Egypt and at the *R*. ., Acts 7.36
By faith. .crossed the *R*. . Heb 11.29

REED
Egypt, that broken *r* of a 2Ki 18.21
a bruised *r* he will not break, Isa 42.3
a measuring *r* in his hand; Ezek 40.3
A *r* shaken by the wind? Mt 11.7
he will not break a bruised *r* 12.20
A *r* shaken by the wind? Lk 7.24

REFINE — D
I will *r* them and test them, Jer 9.7
r them as one refines silver, Zech 13.9
r you, but not like silver; Isa 48.10
buy from me gold *r* by fire, Rev 3.18

REFLECTS
the mind of man *r* the man. Prov 27.19
He *r* the glory of God and bears Heb 1.3

REFRESH — ES — ED
that you may *r* yourselves, Gen 18.5
r me with apples; for I am sick Sol 2.5
r the spirit of his masters. Prov 25.13
and the alien, may be *r*. Ex 23.12
and be *r* in your company. Rom 15.32
they *r* my spirit as well as 1Cor 16.18
Onesiphorus,. .often *r* me; 2Tim 1.16
the saints. .*r* through you. Philem 7

REFUGE
six cities of *r*, where Num 35.6
be cities of *r* for you, 35.11
rock in which they took *r*, Deut 32.37
'Appoint the cities of *r*, Josh 20.2
you have come to take *r*!" Ruth 2.12
Blessed. .all who take *r* in him. Ps 2.12
my God, in thee do I take *r*; 7.1
poor, but the LORD is his *r*. 14.6
O God, for in thee I take *r*. 16.1
In thee, O LORD, do I seek *r*; 31.1
God is our *r* and strength, 46.1
of thy wings I will take *r*, 57.1
thou art my *r*, a strong tower 61.3
In thee, O LORD, do I take *r*; 71.1
but thou art my strong *r*. 71.7
GOD my *r*, that I may tell of 73.28
say to the LORD, "My *r* and my 91.2
better to take *r* in the LORD 118.8
no *r* remains. .,no man cares 142.4
finds *r* through. .integrity. Prov 14.32
shield to those who take *r* 30.5
r and a shelter from the storm Isa 4.6
for we have made lies our *r*, 28.15

REFUGE (cont.)

he who takes r..shall possess	Isa 57.13
my r in the day of trouble,	Jer 16.19
my r in the day of evil.	17.17
LORD is a r to his people,	Joel 3.16
he knows those who take r	Nah 1.7
seek r in..name of the LORD,	Zeph 3.12

REFUSE — D

r the evil and choose..good.	Isa 7.15
they r to know me, says..LORD.	Jer 9.6
evil people, who r to hear my	13.10
Do not r one another except	1Cor 7.5
See that you do not r him	Heb 12.25
he r..his master's wife,	Gen 39.8
Thus Edom r to give Israel	Num 20.21
the people r to listen to	1Sam 8.19
they r to obey, and were not	Neh 9.17
But Queen Vashti r to come	Est 1.12
r to walk according to..law.	Ps 78.10
called and you r to listen,	Prov 1.24
they r to take correction.	Jer 5.3
they have r to return to me.	Hos 11.5
But they r to hearken, and	Zech 7.11
they r to love the truth	2Thess 2.10
r to be called the son of	Heb 11.24

REGARD — S — ED (v)

not r any..wise in..conceit."	Job 37.24
men will r their Maker, and	Isa 17.7
I will r as good the exiles	Jer 24.5
you do not r..position of men,	Mk 12.14
nor r the rich more than	Job 34.19
he r their distress, when	Ps 106.44
for he has r the low estate	Lk 1.48

REGARD (n)

the LORD had r for Abel	Gen 4.4
And I will have r for you	Lev 26.9
Yet have r to the prayer	1Ki 8.28
and see; have r for this vine,	Ps 80.14

REHOBOAM

and R his son reigned in his	1Ki 11.43
R went to Shechem, for all	12.1
Now R the son of Solomon	14.21
war between R and Jeroboam	15.6
and Solomon the father of R,	Mt 1.7

REIGN — S — ED

"Are you indeed to r over us?	Gen 37.8
The LORD will r for ever	Ex 15.18
'Shall Saul r over us?'	1Sam 11.12
a godless man should not r,	Job 34.30
The LORD will r for ever,	Ps 146.10
By me kings r, and rulers	Prov 8.15
LORD..will r on Mount Zion	Isa 24.23
king will r in righteousness,	32.1
r as king and deal wisely,	Jer 23.5
thou, O LORD, dost r for ever;	Lam 5.19
will r over them in Mount Zion	Mic 4.7
will r over the house of Jacob	Lk 1.33
"We do not want this man to r	19.14
grace also might r through	Rom 5.21
Let not sin..r in your..bodies,	6.12
must r until he has put all	1Cor 15.25
he shall r for ever and ever."	Rev 11.15
let them say.."The LORD r!"	1Chr 16.31
God r over the nations; God	Ps 47.8
The LORD r;..robed in majesty;	93.1
LORD r; let the earth rejoice;	97.1
Lord our God the Almighty r.	Rev 19.6
time that David r over Israel	1Ki 2.11
r with Christ a thousand years.	Rev 20.4

REJECT — S — ED — ING

I r you from being a priest	Hos 4.6
who r reproof goes astray.	Prov 10.17
who r me r him who sent me."	Lk 10.16
who r me and does not receive	Jn 12.48
you have r the LORD who	Num 11.20
have r me from being king	1Sam 8.7
this day r your God, who	10.19
stone which the builders r	Ps 118.22
For thou has r thy people,	Isa 2.6
LORD..r those..whom you trust,	Jer 2.37
as for my law, they have r it.	6.19
for the LORD has r them."	6.30
the LORD has r and forsaken	7.29
Or hast thou utterly r us?	Lam 5.22
because they have r the law	Amos 2.4
stone which the builders r	Mt 21.42
stone which the builders r	Mk 12.10
r by..elders and chief priests	Lk 9.22
and be r by this generation.	17.25
stone which the builders r	20.17
then, has God r his people?	Rom 11.1
r my ordinances and..statutes.	Ezek 5.6
fine way of r the commandment	Mk 7.9

REJOICE — S — D — ING

you shall r before the LORD	Lev 23.40
shall r before the LORD	Deut 16.11
those who seek the LORD r!	1Chr 16.10
all who take refuge in thee r,	Ps 5.11
R in the LORD, O you righteous!	33.1
my soul shall r in the LORD,	35.9
righteous will r when he sees	58.10
that thy people may r in thee?	85.6
let us r and be glad in it.	118.24
sons of Zion r in their King!	149.2
r in the wife of your youth,	Prov 5.18
in authority, the people r;	29.2
desert shall r and blossom;	Isa 35.1
you shall r in the LORD; in	41.16
I will greatly r in the LORD,	61.10
so shall your God r over you.	62.5
"R with Jerusalem, and be glad	66.10
the maidens r in the dance,	Jer 31.13
made the enemy r over you,	Lam 2.17
Let not the buyer r, nor	Ezek 7.12
sons of Zion,..r in the LORD,	Joel 2.23
yet I will r in the LORD,	Hab 3.18
R greatly, O daughter of Zion!	Zech 9.9
R and be glad, for your reward	Mt 5.12
R in that day,..leap for joy,	Lk 6.23
do not r..that the spirits are	10.20
began to r and praise God	19.37
we r in our hope of sharing	Rom 5.2
we..r in God through..Christ,	5.11
R with those who r, weep with	12.15
"R, O Gentiles, with his people";	15.10
who r as though they were not	1Cor 7.30
Love..does not r at wrong,	13.6
proclaimed; and in that I r.	Phil 1.18
brethren, r in the Lord.	3.1
R in the Lord always; again	4.4
R always, pray constantly,	1Thess 5.16
you believe in him and r	1Pet 1.8
But r in so far as you share	4.13
the righteous, the city r;	Prov 11.10
The light of the eyes r the heart,	15.30
he r over it more than over	Mt 18.13
my spirit r in God my Savior,	Lk 1.47
the ark, they r to see it.	1Sam 6.13
people r because these had	1Chr 29.9
city of Susa shouted and r.	Est 8.15
When they saw the star, they r	Mt 2.10

REJOICE — S — D — ING (cont.)

people r at all the..things..	Lk 13.17
Abraham r that he was to see	Jn 8.56
loved me, you would have r,	14.28
he r with all his household	Acts 16.34
precepts..right, r the heart;	Ps 19.8
lays it on his shoulders, r.	Lk 15.5

REKINDLE

to r the gift of God..within you	2Tim 1.6

RELEASE — D (v)

to r for them one prisoner	Mk 15.6
chastise him and r him."	Lk 23.16
have me r..King of the Jews?"	Jn 18.39
Pilate..r for them Barabbas;	Mk 15.15

RELEASE (n)

years you shall grant a r.	Deut 15.1
time of the year of r,	31.10
I would wait, till my r	Job 14.14

RELIEF

Noah..shall bring us r	Gen 5.29
speak, that I may find r;	Job 32.20
to send r to the brethren	Acts 11.29

RELIGION

strictest party of our r I	Acts 26.5
Great..the mystery of our r:	1Tim 3.16
form of r..denying the power	2Tim 3.5
R that is pure and undefiled	Jas 1.27

RELIGIOUS

in every way you are very r.	Acts 17.22
If any one thinks he is r,	Jas 1.26

RELY — ING

make you to r on the Lord	2Ki 18.30
God, for we r on thee, and	2Chr 14.11
not r on the Lord your God,	16.7
they r on empty pleas, they	Isa 59.4
to make us r not on ourselves	2Cor 1.9
you are r now on Egypt,	2Ki 18.21

REMAIN — S — ED

r every man of you in his	Ex 16.29
ark..must not r with us;	1Sam 5.7
If you will r in this land,	Jer 42.10
to death; r here, and watch."	Mk 14.34
And r in the same house,	Lk 10.7
my will that he r until I come,	Jn 21.22
in whatever state..let him r	1Cor 7.24
there r yet very much land	Josh 13.1
but the earth r for ever.	Ecc 1.4
yet his bow r unmoved,	Gen 49.24

REMEMBER — S — ED — ING

I will r my covenant	Gen 9.15
butler said to Pharaoh, "I r	41.9
"R this day, in which	Ex 13.3
R Abraham, Isaac, and	32.13
r my covenant with Jacob,	Lev 26.42
We r the fish we ate in Egypt	Num 11.5
tassel to look upon and r	15.39
r what the Lord your God did	Deut 7.18
R..how you provoked the Lord	9.7
r that you were a slave	15.15
r that you were a slave	16.12
r that you were a slave	24.18
R the days of old, consider	32.7
Israel did not r the Lord	Judg 8.34
"O Lord God, r me, I pray	16.28
thy maidservant, and r me,	1Sam 1.11
"R now, O Lord,..how I have	2Ki 20.3
R the wonderful works that	1Chr 16.12
R thy steadfast love for	2Chr 6.42

Joash..did not r the kindness	24.22
R the word which thou didst	Neh 1.8
R the Lord, who is great and	4.14
R for my good, O my God, all	5.19
R Tobiah and Sanballat, O my	6.14
R me, O my God, concerning	13.14
therefore I r thee from the	Ps 42.6
R thy congregation, which thou	74.2
Do not r against us..iniquities	79.8
R, O Lord,..the measure of life	89.47
R the wonderful works that	105.5
R, O Lord, against the Edomites	137.7
and r their misery no more.	Prov 31.7
r that the days of darkness	Ecc 11.8
R..your Creator in the days	12.1
"R now, O Lord, I beseech	Isa 38.3
"R not the former things,	43.18
and I will not r your sins.	43.25
"R this and consider, recall it	46.8
I r the devotion of your youth,	Jer 2.2
R how I stood before thee	18.20
not r..days of your youth,	Ezek 16.22
there you shall r your ways	20.43
Then you will r your evil ways,	36.31
that I r all their evil works.	Hos 7.2
Tyre..did not r the covenant	Amos 1.9
people, r what Balak..devised,	Mic 6.5
known; in wrath r mercy.	Hab 3.2
far countries..shall r me,	Zech 10.9
"R the law of my servant Moses,	Mal 4.4
there r..something against you,	Mt 5.23
Abraham said, 'Son, r that	Lk 16.25
R Lot's wife.	17.32
"Jesus, r me when you come	23.42
R the word that I said to you,	Jn 15.20
they would have us r the poor,	Gal 2.10
Therefore r that at one time	Eph 2.11
R Jesus Christ, risen from	2Tim 2.8
I will r their sins no more."	Heb 8.12
R those who are in prison,	13.3
r, beloved, the predictions	Jude 17
R then what you received and	Rev 3.3
Jerusalem r in..her affliction	Lam 1.7
God r Noah and all the beasts	Gen 8.1
God r Abraham, and sent Lot	19.29
Then God r Rachel,	30.22
And Joseph r the dreams	42.9
God r his covenant with	Ex 2.24
thus I am to be r throughout	3.15
I have r my covenant.	6.5
cause my name to be r	20.24
may be r before the Lord	Num 10.9
these days should be r and	Est 9.28
They r..God was their rock,	Ps 78.35
He has r his steadfast love	98.3
righteous..will be r for ever.	112.6
who r us in our low estate,	136.23
former things shall not be r	Isa 65.17
I r the Lord; and my prayer	Jonah 2.7
Peter r the saying of Jesus,	Mt 26.75
And they r his words,	Lk 24.8
God has r her iniquities.	Rev 18.5
increased her harlotry, r	Ezek 23.19
r you earnestly in his prayers,	Col 4.12

REMEMBRANCE

bear their names..for r.	Ex 28.12
to be stones of r for the sons	39.7
bring the people of Israel to r	30.16
they shall serve you for r	Num 10.10
make the r of them cease	Deut 32.26
my sin to r, and to cause	1Ki 17.18
in death there is no r of thee;	Ps 6.5

REMEMBRANCE (cont.)
is no r of former things,	Ecc 1.11
You who put the LORD in r,	Isa 62.6
a book of r was written before	Mal 3.16
for you. Do this in r of me."	Lk 22.19n
Do this in r of me."	1Cor 11.24

REMNANT
surviving r..of Judah shall	2Ki 19.30
cast off..r of my heritage,	21.14
may turn again to the r of	2Chr 30.6
our God, to leave us a r,	Ezra 9.8
that day the r of Israel and	Isa 10.20
your prayer for the r that	37.4
surviving r of..house of Judah	37.31
the r of the house of Israel,	46.3
I will gather..r of my flock	Jer 23.3
LORD..saved his people, the r	31.7
king..had left a r in Judah	40.11
gracious to the r of Joseph.	Amos 5.15
they may possess the r of Edom	9.12
I will gather the r of Israel;	Mic 2.12
the lame I will make the r;	4.7
r of Jacob..among the nations,	5.8
for the r of his inheritance?	7.18
marvelous in..sight of the r	Zech 8.6
r of this people to possess	8.12
only a r of them will be saved;	Rom 9.27
there is a r, chosen by grace.	11.5

REMOVE — D
shall not r your neighbor's	Deut 19.14
LORD said, "I will r Judah	2Ki 23.27
so far..r our transgressions	Ps 103.12
R not the ancient landmark	Prov 22.28
R vexation from your mind,	Ecc 11.10
I will r the guilt of this land	Zech 3.9
hills..r, but..love shall not	Isa 54.10

RENDER — ED
r them their due reward.	Ps 28.4
What shall I r to the LORD	116.12
to..coastlands..r requital.	Isa 59.18
"R therefore to Caesar the	Mt 22.21
Jesus said.."R to Caesar the	Mk 12.17
"Then r to Caesar the things	Lk 20.25
r to..man according to..works:	Rom 2.6
to her as she herself has r,	Rev 18.6

RENEW — ED
and there r the kingdom."	1Sam 11.14
LORD shall r their strength,	Isa 40.31
O LORD,..R our days as of old!	Lam 5.21
the midst of the years r it;	Hab 3.2
he will r you in his love;	Zeph 3.17
youth is r like the eagle's.	Ps 103.5
being r in knowledge after	Col 3.10

RENOUNCE — S
whoever of you does not r all	Lk 14.33
the man greedy..r the LORD.	Ps 10.3

RENOWN
These were..mighty men..of r.	Gen 6.4
thy r, O LORD, throughout all	Ps 135.13

REPAIR — ED — ING
let the priests..r the house	2Ki 12.5
he r the altar of the LORD	1Ki 18.30
And next to them Meremoth..r.	Neh 3.4
to the workmen who were r	2Ki 12.14
at the house of the LORD, r	22.5

REPENT — S — ED
"Lest the people r when	Ex 13.17
r of this evil against thy people.	32.12

not man,..that he should r.	Num 23.19
"I r that I have made Saul	1Sam 15.11
been carried captive, and r,	1Ki 8.47
if they r with all their mind	2Chr 6.38
despise myself, and r in dust	Job 42.6
who r, by righteousness.	Isa 1.27
turns from its evil, I will r	Jer 18.8
the LORD will r of the evil	26.13
did not the LORD r of the evil	26.19
Thus says the Lord GOD: R	Ezek 14.6
R and turn away from all	18.30
God may yet r and turn from	Jonah 3.9
"R, for the kingdom of heaven	Mt 3.2
"R, for the kingdom of heaven	4.17
done, because they did not r.	11.20
they..preached..men should r.	Mk 6.12
unless you r you will..perish."	Lk 13.3
from the dead they will r.'	16.30
Peter said to them, "R, and	Acts 2.38
R therefore, and turn again,	3.19
he commands all men..to r,	17.30
grant that they will r and	2Tim 2.25
for he found no chance to r,	Heb 12.17
r and do the works you did	Rev 2.5
R then. If not, I will come	2.16
I gave her time to r, but	2.21
mankind..did not r of the works	9.20
they did not r and give him	16.9
no man r of his wickedness,	Jer 8.6
LORD r that he had made	1Sam 15.35
the LORD r of the evil,	2Sam 24.16
the LORD saw, and he r of	1Chr 21.15
The LORD r concerning this;	Amos 7.3
r at the preaching of Jonah,	Mt 12.41
but afterward he r and went.	21.29
he r and brought back..silver	27.3
they would have r long ago,	Lk 10.13
they r at the preaching of Jonah,	11.32

REPENTANCE
Bear fruit that befits r,	Mt 3.8
preaching a baptism of r for	Mk 1.4
preaching a baptism of r for	Lk 3.3
Bear fruits that befit r,	3.8
come to call..sinners to r."	5.32
than..persons who need no r.	15.7
that r and forgiveness of sins	24.47
to give r to Israel and	Acts 5.31
Gentiles also God has granted r	11.18
to Jews and to Greeks of r	20.21
perform deeds worthy of their r.	26.20
is meant to lead you to r?	Rom 2.4
godly grief produces a r	2Cor 7.10
to restore again to r those	Heb 6.4
but that all should reach r.	2Pet 3.9

REPORT
r was heard in Pharaoh's	Gen 45.16
an evil r of the land	Num 13.32
we have heard a r of him,	Josh 9.9
be not fearful at the r heard	Jer 51.46
a r concerning him went out	Lk 4.14
r went abroad concerning him;	5.15

REPROACH — ES — ED (v)
sheaves, and do not r her.	Ruth 2.15
in saying this you r us also."	Lk 11.45
I may answer him who r me.	Prov 27.11
ointment..And they r her.	Mk 14.5
If you are r for the name of	1Pet 4.14

REPROACH — ES (n)
"God has taken away my r";	Gen 30.23
I have rolled away..r of Egypt	Josh 5.9
word of the LORD..for me a r	Jer 20.8

REPROACH — ES (n) (cont.)

You shall be a r and a taunt,	Ezek 5.15
made you a r to the nations,	22.4
no more..a r among..nations.	Joel 2.19
to take away my r among men."	Lk 1.25
a bishop must be above r,	1Tim 3.2
turn back upon him his r.	Hos 12.14
"The r of..thee fell on me."	Rom 15.3

REPROOF

Give heed to my r; behold,	Prov 1.23
and my heart despised r!	5.12
he who heeds r is honored.	13.18
The rod and r give wisdom,	29.15

REPROVE — D

not r you for your sacrifices;	Ps 50.8
r a man of understanding,	Prov 19.25
and your apostasy will r you.	Jer 2.19
who is often r, yet stiffens	Prov 29.1

REPUTE

a poor man and of no r?"	1Sam 18.23
LORD gave Solomon great r	1Chr 29.25

REQUEST

Queen Esther? What is your r?	Est 5.3
and my people at my r.	7.3
"O that I might have my r,	Job 6.8
not withheld the r of his lips.	Ps 21.2
Daniel made r of the king,	Dan 2.49

REQUIRE — S — D

God r of you, but to fear	Deut 10.12
his blood..r at your hand.	Ezek 3.18
blood I..r at..watchman's hand.	33.6
what does the LORD r of you	Mic 6.8
who r of you this trampling	Isa 1.12
whatever else is r for..house	Ezra 7.20
the blood..may be r of this	Lk 11.50
This night your soul is r of you;	12.20
given, of him will much be r;	12.48

REQUITE — S — D

work of a man he will r him,	Job 34.11
They r me evil for good; my	Ps 35.12
dost r a man according to his	62.12
nor r us according to our	103.10
R her according to her deeds,	Jer 50.29
"Thou wilt r them, O LORD,	Lam 3.64
but I will r their deeds	Ezek 9.10
and r them for their deeds.	Hos 4.9
Lord will r him for his deeds.	2Tim 4.14
Happy shall he be who r you	Ps 137.8
your lewdness shall be r	Ezek 23.49

RESCUE — D

congregation shall r the	Num 35.25
LORD, wilt thou look on? R me	Ps 35.17
r me from sinking in the mire;	69.14
In thy righteousness..r me;	71.2
R those who are being taken	Prov 24.11
r my sheep from their mouths,	Ezek 34.10
no one..could r from his power;	Dan 8.4
Lord..r me from every evil	2Tim 4.18
David r his two wives.	1Sam 30.18
my soul also,..thou hast r.	Ps 71.23
and r us from our foes, for	136.24
sent his angel and r me	Acts 12.11
and if he r righteous Lot,	2Pet 2.7

RESIST

R the devil and he will flee	Jas 4.7
R him, firm in your faith,	1Pet 5.9

RESOLVED

Daniel r that he would not	Dan 1.8

RESPECT — S

saying, 'They will r my son.'	Mt 21.37
saying, 'They will r my son.'	Mk 12.6
it may be they will r him.'	Lk 20.13
see that she r her husband.	Eph 5.33

REST — S — ED (v)

r yourselves under the tree,	Gen 18.4
seventh day you shall r;	Ex 23.12
land shall r, and enjoy its	Lev 26.34
the man will not r, but will	Ruth 3.18
the night his mind does not r.	Ecc 2.23
Spirit of..LORD..r upon him,	Isa 11.2
you shall r, and shall stand	Dan 12.13
they may r from their labors,	Rev 14.13
spirit of Elijah r on Elisha."	2Ki 2.15
he r on the seventh day	Gen 2.2
God r on the seventh day from	Heb 4.4

REST (n)

a sabbath of solemn r to you,	Lev 16.31
sabbath of solemn r for the land,	25.4
until the LORD gives r	Deut 3.20
r from all your enemies	12.10
God has given you r from	25.19
until the LORD gives r to	Josh 1.15
the land had r from war.	11.23
LORD had given r to Israel	23.1
the land had r forty years.	Judg 3.11
land had r for forty years.	5.31
LORD had given him r from	2Sam 7.1
with the r of the multitude,	2Ki 25.11
to build a house of r for	1Chr 28.2
after they had r they did evil	Neh 9.28
there the weary are at r.	Job 3.17
and take your r in safety.	11.18
they should not enter my r.	Ps 95.11
Return, O my soul, to your r;	116.7
"In returning and r you	Isa 30.15
what is the place of my r?	66.1
the r of his brethren..return	Mic 5.3
Come..and I will give you r.	Mt 11.28
still sleeping and taking..r?	Mk 14.41
waterless places seeking r;	Lk 11.24
Macedonia, our bodies had no r	2Cor 7.5
'They shall never enter my r.' "	Heb 3.11
there remains a sabbath r	4.9
and the r were terrified	Rev 11.13

RESTORE — S — D

then r the man's wife;	Gen 20.7
you shall r it to him.	Deut 22.2
Joash..r the house of the	2Chr 24.4
R us, O LORD God of hosts! let	Ps 80.19
R us.., O God of our salvation,	85.4
r your judges as at the first,	Isa 1.26
For I will r their fortunes,	Jer 33.26
R us to thyself, O LORD, that	Lam 5.21
word to r and build Jerusalem	Dan 9.25
I will r to you the years	Joel 2.25
"Elijah does come,..he is to r	Mt 17.11
at this time r the kingdom to	Acts 1.6
spiritual should r him in a	Gal 6.1
it is impossible to r again	Heb 6.4
still waters; he r my soul.	Ps 23.3
to the woman whose son he had r	2Ki 8.1
He also r the altar of the	2Chr 33.16
health of..people not been r?	Jer 8.22
the sanctuary shall be r to	Dan 8.14
was r, whole like the other.	Mt 12.13
he did so, and his hand was r.	Lk 6.10

RESTRAIN — S — ED — ING

and he did not r them.	1Sam 3.13
I will not r my mouth; I will	Job 7.11

RESTRAIN — S — ED — ING (cont.)

r thyself at these things,	Isa 64.12
r his words has knowledge,	Prov 17.27
people were r from bringing;	Ex 36.6
you know what is r him now	2Thess 2.6

RESTRAINT

but a fool throws off r and	Prov 14.16
no prophecy..people cast off r,	29.18
not to lay any r upon you,	1Cor 7.35

RESURRECTION

who say that there is no r;	Mt 22.23
who say that there is no r;	Mk 12.18
repaid at the r of the just."	Lk 14.14
who say that there is no r,	20.27
done good, to the r of life,	Jn 5.29
"I am the r and the life;	11.25
became..a witness to his r."	Acts 1.22
foresaw and spoke of the r	2.31
he preached Jesus and the r.	17.18
respect to..hope and the r	23.6
that there will be a r of	24.15
united with him in a r like his.	Rom 6.5
there is no r of the dead?	1Cor 15.12
holding that the r is past	2Tim 2.18
received their dead by r.	Heb 11.35
living hope through the r of	1Pet 1.3
This is the first r.	Rev 20.5

RETURN — S — ED — ING

"R to your mistress,	Gen 16.9
the LORD said to Jacob, "R	31.3
LORD who didst say to me, 'R	32.9
"R, O LORD, to the ten	Num 10.36
you will r to the LORD	Deut 4.30
and r to the LORD your God,	30.2
I go whence I shall not r,	Job 10.21
If you r to the Almighty	22.23
and sinners will r to thee.	Ps 51.13
R, O my soul, to your rest;	116.7
R, r, O Shulammite, r, r, that	Sol 6.13
ransomed of the LORD shall r,	Isa 35.10
r to me, for I have redeemed	44.22
ransomed of the LORD shall r,	51.11
it shall not r to me empty,	55.11
lovers; and would you r to me?	Jer 3.1
'R, faithless Israel, says	3.12
"If you r, O Israel, says the	4.1
"If you r, I will restore	15.19
r to me with their whole heart.	24.7
Jacob shall r and have quiet	30.10
'I will..r to my first husband,	Hos 2.7
"Come, let us r to the LORD;	6.1
R, O Israel, to the LORD	14.1
yet you did not r to me,"	Amos 4.8
R to me, says..LORD of hosts,	Zech 1.3
R to me, and I will r to you,	Mal 3.7
"R to your home, and declare	Lk 8.39
'I will r to my house from	11.24
Was no one found to r and give	17.18
'After this I will r, and	Acts 15.16
spirit r to God who gave it.	Ecc 12.7
'Why have you r evil for good?	Gen 44.4
Joseph r to Egypt with his	50.14
half-tribe of Manasseh r	Josh 22.9
"If you are r to the LORD	1Sam 7.3

REUBEN (Son of Jacob)

Born, Gen 29.32; found mandrakes for Leah, Gen 30.14; rescued Joseph, Gen 37.21–22; blessed by Jacob, Gen 49.3–4. Tribe of Reuben: blessed by Moses, Deut 33.6

REVEAL — S — ED — ING

the Son chooses to r him.	Mt 11.27
the Son chooses to r him."	Lk 10.22
pleased to r his Son to me,	Gal·1.16
who goes about gossiping r	Prov 20.19
God in heaven who r mysteries,	Dan 2.28
things that are r belong	Deut 29.29
had not yet been r to him.	1Sam 3.7
LORD r himself to Samuel	3.21
the LORD had r to Samuel:	9.15
he has r his vindication in	Ps 98.2
LORD of hosts has r himself	Isa 22.14
the arm of the LORD been r?	53.1
come, and my deliverance be r.	56.1
the mystery was r to Daniel	Dan 2.19
covered that will not be r,	Mt 10.26
hidden..and r them to babes;	11.25
flesh and blood has not r this	16.17
r to him by the Holy Spirit	Lk 2.26
thoughts of many hearts..r."	2.35
hidden..and r them to babes;	10.21
covered up that will not be r,	12.2
when the Son of man is r.	17.30
that he might be r to Israel."	Jn 1.31
the arm of the Lord been r?"	12.38
the righteousness of God is r	Rom 1.17
God has r to us through the	1Cor 2.10
it will be r with fire,	3.13
when the Lord Jesus is r	2Thess 1.7
It was r to them that they	1Pet 1.12
be glad when his glory is r.	4.13
nothing, without r his secret	Amos 3.7
the r of the sons of God;	Rom 8.19
you wait for the r of our Lord	1Cor 1.7

REVELATION

according to the r of the	Rom 16.25
through a r of Jesus Christ.	Gal 1.12
I went up by r; and I laid	2.2
was made known to me by r,	Eph 3.3
at the r of Jesus Christ.	1Pet 1.13

REVENGE

not spare when he takes r.	Prov 6.34
and take our r on him."	Jer 20.10

REVENUE

royal r will be impaired.	Ezra 4.13
your r was..grain of Shihor,	Isa 23.3
Pay..r to whom r is due,	Rom 13.7

REVERENCE

and r my sanctuary: I am	Lev 19.30
sabbaths and r my sanctuary:	26.2
in your hearts r Christ as	1Pet 3.15

REVERENT

older women likewise to be r	Tit 2.3
they see your r..behavior.	1Pet 3.2

REVILE — D

"You shall not r God,	Ex 22.28
Is the enemy to r thy name	Ps 74.10
"Blessed are you when men r you	Mt 5.11
you r God's high priest?"	Acts 23.4
not afraid to r the glorious	2Pet 2.10
have you mocked and r?	2Ki 19.22
and r me upon the hills, I	Isa 65.7
When r, we bless; when	1Cor 4.12

REVIVE — D — ING

Will they r the stones out	Neh 4.2
Wilt thou not r us again, that	Ps 85.6
r me according to thy word!	119.25
to r..spirit of the humble,	Isa 57.15
for food to r their strength.	Lam 1.11

REVIVE — D — ING (cont.)

After two days he will r us;	Hos 6.2
their father Jacob r;	Gen 45.27
spirit returned, and he r.	Judg 15.19
into him again, and he r.	1Ki 17.22
the bones of Elisha, he r,	2Ki 13.21
have r your concern for me;	Phil 4.10
law of the LORD..r the soul;	Ps 19.7

REWARD (v)

may..LORD r you with good	1Sam 24.19
So they r me evil for good,	Ps 109.5
who sees in secret will r you.	Mt 6.6

REWARD (n)

your r shall be very great."	Gen 15.1
in keeping them there is..r.	Ps 19.11
there is a r for the righteous;	58.11
behold, his r is with him,	Isa 40.10
for your r is great in heaven,	Mt 5.12
who love you, what r have you?	5.46
shall receive a prophet's r,	10.41
will by no means lose his r.	Mk 9.41
expecting nothing..r..great,	Lk 6.35
What then is my r? Just this:	1Cor 9.18

RIBS

God..took one of his r	Gen 2.21

RICH — ER

Now Abram was very r	Gen 13.2
'I have made Abram r.'	14.23
The r shall not give more,	Ex 30.15
The r man had..many flocks	2Sam 12.2
he will not be r, and his	Job 15.29
blessing of..LORD makes r,	Prov 10.22
but the r has many friends.	14.20
The r and the poor meet	22.2
hard for a r man to enter	Mt 19.23
came a r man from Arimathea,	27.57
than for a r man to enter the	Mk 10.25
the r he has sent empty away.	Lk 1.53
"But woe to you that are r,	6.24
land of a r man brought forth	12.16
a r man who had a steward,	16.1
r man,..was clothed in purple	16.19
became sad, for he was very r.	18.23
Already you have become r!	1Cor 4.8
who desire to be r fall into	1Tim 6.9
for the r in this world,	6.17
the r in his humiliation,	Jas 1.10
you r, weep and howl for the	5.1
your poverty (but you are r)	Rev 2.9
For you say, I am r, I have	3.17
grown r with..her wantonness."	18.3
gives freely, yet grows..r;	Prov 11.24

RICHES

Solomon excelled..in r and	1Ki 10.23
swallows down r and vomits	Job 20.15
I delight as much as in..r.	Ps 119.14
R do not profit in the day	Prov 11.4
and violent men get r.	11.16
He who trusts in his r will	11.28
for r do not last for ever;	27.24
who gets r but not by right;	Jer 17.11
r they gained have perished.	48.36
delight in r choke the word,	Mt 13.22
cares..and the delight in r,	Mk 4.19
hard..for those who have r	10.23
presume upon the r of his	Rom 2.4
if their trespass means r for	11.12
O the depth of the r and	11.33
the unsearchable r of Christ,	Eph 3.8

according to..r of his glory	3.16
according to his r in glory	Phil 4.19

RIDDLE

"Let me now put a r to you;	Judg 14.12
those who had told the r.	14.19

RIGHT — S

then I will go to the r;	Gen 13.9
man doing whatever is r	Deut 12.8
what was r in his own eyes.	Judg 17.6
what was r in his own eyes.	21.25
Joash did what was r in	2Chr 24.2
you are not r. I will answer	Job 33.12
Do you say, 'It is my r before	35.2
gives the afflicted their r.	36.6
not spoken of me what is r,	42.7
Let thy eyes see the r!	Ps 17.2
decree what is r, you gods? Do	58.1
that you may be proved r.	Isa 43.26
"The LORD is in the r, for I	Lam 1.18
for all his works are r and	Dan 4.37
one at your r hand..one at	Mt 20.21
sat down at..r hand of God.	Mk 16.19n
exalted at the r hand of God,	Acts 2.33
Jesus standing at the r hand	7.55
does what is r is acceptable	10.35
use of my r in the gospel.	1Cor 9.18
Love..rejoices in the r.	13.6
if we are in our r mind,	2Cor 5.13
made him sit at his r hand	Eph 1.20
Whoever knows what is r to do	Jas 4.17
who does r is born of him.	1Jn 2.29
righteous man knows the r of	Prov 29.7
maintain the r of the poor	31.9
not defend the r of the needy.	Jer 5.28

RIGHTEOUS

Noah was a r man,	Gen 6.9
spare it for the fifty r	18.24
"She is more r than I,	38.26
die the death of the r,	Num 23.10
so r as all this law	Deut 4.8
"You are more r than I;	1Sam 24.17
and vindicating the r by	1Ki 8.32
mortal man be r before God?	Job 4.17
Yet the r holds to his way,	17.9
can a man be r before God?	25.4
Job..was r in his own eyes.	32.1
the LORD knows the way of the r,	Ps 1.6
God is a r judge, and a God who	7.11
destroyed, what can the r do"?	11.3
with the generation of the r.	14.5
The r shall possess the land,	37.29
Let the r rejoice in the LORD,	64.10
But let the r be joyful; let	68.3
My mouth will tell of thy r acts,	71.15
The r flourish like..palm tree,	92.12
Light dawns for the r, and joy	97.11
R art thou, O LORD, and	119.137
no man living is r before thee.	143.2
path of the r is like..light	Prov 4.18
memory of the r..a blessing,	10.7
wage of the r leads to life,	10.16
hope of the r ends in gladness,	10.28
the r escapes from trouble.	12.13
r man turns away from evil,	12.26
In the house of the r there	15.6
tower; the r man runs into it	18.10
r man who walks in..integrity—	20.7
justice..is a joy to the r,	21.15
a r man..before the wicked.	25.26
the r are bold as a lion.	28.1
they perish, the r increase.	28.28

RIGHTEOUS (cont.)

God will judge the r and the	Ecc 3.17
not a r man on earth who does	7.20
r men to whom it happens	8.14
one fate comes to all, to the r	9.2
Tell the r..it shall be well	Isa 3.10
that the r nation..may enter	26.2
make many to be accounted r;	53.11
The r man perishes, and no one	57.1
r deeds..like a polluted garment.	64.6
cause a r Branch to spring	Jer 33.15
if you warn the r..not to sin,	Ezek 3.21
"If a man is r and does	18.5
But when a r man turns away	18.24
When a r man turns away	18.26
the r shall live by his faith.	Hab 2.4
The LORD within her is r,	Zeph 3.5
the r will shine like the sun	Mt 13.43
separate the evil from the r,	13.49
Then the r will answer him,	25.37
nothing to do with that r man,	27.19
feared John,..a r and holy man,	Mk 6.20
they were both r before God,	Lk 1.6
Simeon, and this man was r	2.25
were r and despised others:	18.9
who through faith is r shall	Rom 1.17
"None is r, no, not one;	3.10
to prove..that he himself is r	3.26
one will hardly die for a r	5.7
by one..many will be made r.	5.19
"He who through faith is r	Gal 3.11
my r one shall live by faith,	Heb 10.38
you have killed the r man;	Jas 5.6
the r for the unrighteous,	1Pet 3.18
the r man is scarcely saved,	4.18
if he rescued r Lot, greatly	2Pet 2.7
by what that r man saw and heard	2.8
fine linen is the r deeds of	Rev 19.8

RIGHTEOUSNESS

reckoned to him as r.	Gen 15.6
by doing r and justice;	18.19
in r..judge your neighbor.	Lev 19.15
it will be r for us, if we	Deut 6.25
"It is because of my r that the	9.4
r to you before the LORD	24.13
rewards every man for his r	1Sam 26.23
I hold fast my r, and will	Job 27.6
I put on r, and it clothed me;	29.14
and ascribe r to my Maker.	36.3
r he will not violate.	37.23
He loves r and justice; the	Ps 33.5
Thy r is like the mountains	36.6
you love r and hate wickedness.	45.7
The heavens declare his r,	50.6
thy power and thy r, O God,	71.19
R and justice are the foundation	89.14
who exult..and extol thy r.	89.16
will judge the world with r,	96.13
been reckoned to him as r	106.31
and his r endures for ever.	112.3
Thy r is righteous for ever,	119.142
Then you will understand r	Prov 2.9
but r delivers from death.	10.2
steadfast in r will live,	11.19
In the path of r is life,	12.28
R exalts a nation, but sin	14.34
throne is established by r.	16.12
who pursues r and kindness	21.21
man who perishes in his r,	Ecc 7.15
for r, but behold, a cry!	Isa 5.7
with r he shall judge the poor,	11.4
r abide in the fruitful field.	32.16

fill Zion with justice and r;	33.5
in..LORD,..are r and strength;	45.24
In r you shall be established;	54.14
tell of your r and..doings,	57.12
as if..a nation that did r	58.2
put on r as a breastplate,	59.17
they may be called oaks of r,	61.3
covered me with the robe of r,	61.10
Do justice and r, and deliver	Jer 22.3
called: 'The LORD is our r.'	23.6
their own lives by their r,	Ezek 14.14
for the r which he has done	18.22
r..shall not deliver him when	33.12
break off your sins by..r,	Dan 4.27
To thee, O Lord, belongs r	9.7
not..on the ground of our r,	9.18
Sow for yourselves r, reap	Hos 10.12
r like an everflowing stream.	Amos 5.24
fitting for us to fulfil all r."	Mt 3.15
unless your r exceeds..scribes	5.20
John came..in the way of r,	21.32
in holiness and r before him	Lk 1.75
of sin..of r and of judgment:	Jn 16.8
he will judge the world in r	Acts 17.31
the r of God is revealed	Rom 1.17
the r of God has been manifested	3.21
was reckoned to him as r."	4.3
God reckons r apart from works:	4.6
one man's act of r leads to	5.18
yield your members to r for	6.19
Gentiles who did not pursue r	9.30
ignorant of the r that comes	10.3
Jesus, whom God made our..r	1Cor 1.30
dispensation of r must..exceed	2Cor 3.9
we might become the r of God.	5.21
it was reckoned to him as r."	Gal 3.6
r would indeed be by the law.	3.21
in true r and holiness.	Eph 4.24
the r..that depends on faith;	Phil 3.9
aim at r, godliness, faith,	1Tim 6.11
and for training in r,	2Tim 3.16
an heir of the r which comes	Heb 11.7
anger..not work the r of God.	Jas 1.20
harvest of r is sown in peace	3.18

RING — S

the king took his signet r	Est 3.10
and put a r on his hand,	Lk 15.22
r that were in their ears;	Gen 35.4
"Take off the r of gold	Ex 32.2

RISE — S — N — ING

R up, take your journey,	Deut 2.24
R up, come to our help!	Ps 44.26
your light r in the darkness	Isa 58.10
to the paralytic—"R, take up	Mt 9.6
r, take up your pallet and go	Mk 2.11
and after three days r again.	8.31
after three days he will r."	9.31
r, take up your bed and go	Lk 5.24
and on the third day r."	24.7
"R, take up your pallet, and	Jn 5.8
"Your brother will r again."	11.23
to Philip, "R and go toward	Acts 8.26
but r and enter the city,	9.6
"R, Peter; kill and eat."	10.13
by being the first to r	26.23
dead in Christ will r first;	1Thess 4.16
falls seven times, and r	Prov 24.16
tell the people, 'He has r	Mt 27.64
He is not here; for he has r,	28.6
until the Son of man..r from	Mk 9.9
He has r, he is not here;	16.6

RISE — S — N — ING (cont.)

He is not here, but has r	Lk 24.5n
"The Lord has r indeed, and	24.34
Remember Jesus Christ, r	2Tim 2.8
From the r of the sun to its	Ps 113.3
fall and r of many in Israel,	Lk 2.34

RIVER — S

A r flowed out of Eden	Gen 2.10
a r whose streams make glad	Ps 46.4
razor..hired beyond the R—	Isa 7.20
peace would have been like a r,	48.18
prosperity to her like a r,	66.12
the r of the water of life,	Rev 22.1
He turns r into a desert,	Ps 107.33
place of broad r and streams,	Isa 33.21
open r on the bare heights,	41.18
my eyes flow with r of tears	Lam 3.48

ROADSIDE

blind beggar,..by the r.	Mk 10.46

ROAR — S

Let the sea r, and all	1Chr 16.32
let the sea r, and all that	Ps 96.11
LORD, he will r like a lion;	Hos 11.10
Does a lion r in the forest,	Amos 3.4
"The LORD r from Zion, and	1.2

ROB — S — BED

Do not r the poor, because	Prov 22.22
Will man r God? Yet you are	Mal 3.8
r his father or his mother	28.24
r other churches by accepting	2Cor 11.8

ROBBER — S

you come out as against a r,	Mk 14.48
Now Barabbas was a r.	Jn 18.40
this house,..become a den of r	Jer 7.11
you have made it a den of r."	Mk 11.17
with him they crucified two r,	15.27
he fell among r, who stripped	Lk 10.30
from rivers, danger from r,	2Cor 11.26

ROBE — S

a long r with sleeves.	Gen 37.3
stripped him of his r,	37.23
took Joseph's r, and killed	37.31
also made the r of the ephod	Ex 39.22
will clothe him with your r,	Isa 22.21
with the r of righteousness,	61.10
'Bring quickly the best r,	Lk 15.22
crown of thorns and..purple r,	Jn 19.5
they were each given a white r	Rev 6.11
your r are all fragrant with	Ps 45.8
princess..with gold-woven r;	45.13
of gold, and wearing of r,	1Pet 3.3

ROCK

strike the r, and water shall	Ex 17.6
tell the r..to yield..water	Num 20.8
R, his work is perfect;	Deut 32.4
their r is not as our R,	32.31
there is no r like our God.	1Sam 2.2
"The LORD is my r, and my	2Sam 22.2
The LORD is my r, and my	Ps 18.2
who is a r, except our God?—	18.31
he will set me high upon a r.	27.5
To thee, O LORD, I call; my r,	28.1
bog, and set my feet upon a r,	40.2
the r that is higher than I;	61.2
He only is my r and..salvation,	62.6
Thou art my r and my fortress.	71.3
made streams come out of..r,	78.16
and the R of my salvation.'	89.26
LORD is upright; he is my r,	92.15

He opened the r, and water	' 105.41
who turns the r into a pool	114.8
not remembered..R of..refuge;	Isa 17.10
shade of a great r in a weary land.	32.2
the r from which you were hewn,	51.1
like a hammer..breaks the r	Jer 23.29
built his house upon the r;	Mt 7.24
Peter, and on this r I will build	16.18
laid the foundation upon r;	Lk 6.48
supernatural R..was Christ.	1Cor 10.4

ROD

in your hand?" He said, "A r."	Ex 4.2
Moses took the r of God.	4.20
Aaron's name upon..r of Levi.	Num 17.3
break them with a r of iron,	Ps 2.9
spares the r hates his son,	Prov 13.24
the r of discipline drives it far	22.15
If you beat him with a r,	23.14
a r for the back of fools.	26.3
Assyria, the r of my anger,	Isa 10.5
Shall I come to you with a r,	1Cor 4.21

ROLL (v)

"Who will r away the stone	Mk 16.3
like a mantle..r them up,	Heb 1.12

ROLL (n)

in the r of the book..written	Ps 40.7
of me in the r of the book."	Heb 10.7

ROMAN — S

scourge a man who is a R	Acts 22.25
the R will come and destroy	Jn 11.48
not lawful for..R to accept	Acts 16.21
not the custom of the R to	25.16

ROME

Cyrene, and visitors from R,	Acts 2.10
commanded..Jews to leave R.	18.2
bear witness also at R."	23.11
when we came into R, Paul	28.16
To all God's beloved in R,	Rom 1.7
preach to you..who are in R.	1.15
he arrived in R he searched	2Tim 1.17

ROOF

Make a r for the ark,	Gen 6.16
they removed the r above him;	Mk 2.4

ROOM — S

Thou hast given me r when I was	Ps 4.1
A man's gift makes r for him	Prov 18.16
when you pray, go into your r	Mt 6.6
done, and still there is r.'	Lk 14.22
will show you a large upper r	22.12
they went up to the upper r,	Acts 1.13
prepare a guest r for me,	Philem 22
whispered in private r shall	Lk 12.3
In my Father's house are many r;	Jn 14.2

ROOT — ED (v)

and r up Israel out of this	1Ki 14.15
gathering the weeds you r up	Mt 13.29
the treacherous will be r out	Prov 2.22
"Every plant..will be r up.	Mt 15.13
being r and grounded in love,	Eph 3.17
r and built up in him and	Col 2.7

ROOT (n)

but the r of the righteous	Prov 12.3
the r of Jesse shall stand as	Isa 11.10
Judah shall again take r	37.31
scarcely has their stem taken r	40.24
axe is laid to..r of the trees;	Mt 3.10
"The r of Jesse shall come,	Rom 15.12
love of money is the r of	1Tim 6.10
I am the r and the offspring	Rev 22.16

ROPE — S
she let them down by a *r*   Josh 2.15
they drew Jeremiah up with *r*   Jer 38.12

ROSE
I am a *r* of Sharon, a lily of   Sol 2.1

ROUTED
the LORD *r* the Egyptians   Ex 14.27
And the LORD *r* Sisera and all   Judg 4.15

RUDE
love..is not arrogant or *r*.   1Cor 13.5

RUIN — S
Let *r* come upon them unawares! Ps 35.8
folly brings his way to *r*,   Prov 19.3
the fortified city a *r*; the   Isa 25.2
This whole land..become a *r*   Jer 25.11
Memphis shall become a..*r*,   46.19
A *r*, *r*, *r* I will make it;   Ezek 21.27
not grieved over..*r* of Joseph!   Amos 6.6
laid his strongholds in *r*.   Ps 89.40

RULE — S — D (v)
lesser light to *r* the night;   Gen 1.16
husband..shall *r* over you."   3.16
shall *r* over many nations,   Deut 15.6
the LORD will *r* over you."   Judg 8.23
who can *r* this thy people,   2Chr 1.10
dost *r* the raging of the sea;   Ps 89.9
R in the midst of your foes!   110.2
much less for a slave to *r*   Prov 19.10
and babes shall *r* over them.   Isa 3.4
who shall *r* with great dominion Dan 11.3
supposed to *r* over..Gentiles   Mk 10.42
he shall *r* them with a rod   Rev 2.27
male child, one who is to *r*   12.5
he will *r* them with a rod   19.15
and he *r* over the nations.   Ps 22.28
who *r* his spirit than he who   Prov 16.32
and his arm *r* for him;   Isa 40.10
the Most High *r* the kingdom   Dan 4.17
the Most High *r* the kingdom   4.25
learned that the Most High *r*   4.32
Solomon *r* over all..kingdoms   1Ki 4.21
he *r* over all the kings   2Chr 9.26
who hated them *r* over them.   Ps 106.41
lords besides thee have *r*   Isa 26.13
with..harshness you..*r* them.   Ezek 34.4

RULE (n)
my *r* in all the churches.   1Cor 7.17
after destroying every *r*   15.24
upon all who walk by this *r*,   Gal 6.16
far above all *r* and authority   Eph 1.21

RULER — S
r over all the land of Egypt.   Gen 45.8
Joseph is..*r* over..Egypt."   45.26
"When a *r* sins,..unwittingly   Lev 4.22
Without having any..*r*, she   Prov 6.7
When you..eat with a *r*,   23.1
If a *r* listens to falsehood,   29.12
our judge, the LORD is our *r*,   Isa 33.22
one who is to be *r* in Israel,   Mic 5.2
r came in and knelt before him, Mt 9.18
Jairus,..*r* of the synagogue;   Lk 8.41
r of the synagogue, indignant   13.14
now shall the *r* of this world   Jn 12.31
the *r* of this world is judged.   16.11
seized Sosthenes, the *r* of   Acts 18.17
and the *r* of kings on earth.   Rev 1.5
be warned, O *r* of the earth.   Ps 2.10
makes the *r*..as nothing.   Isa 40.23
the *r* transgressed against me;   Jer 2.8

Peter..said.."*R* of the people   Acts 4.8
For *r* are not a terror to good   Rom 13.3
None of the *r* of this age   1Cor 2.8

RUMOR — S
he shall hear a *r* and return   2Ki 19.7
so that he shall hear a *r*,   Isa 37.7
a *r*! Behold, it comes!—   Jer 10.22
hear of wars and *r* of wars;   Mt 24.6

RUN — S — NING
I will *r* in the way of thy   Ps 119.32
R to and fro through the streets Jer 5.1
Many shall *r* to and fro, and   Dan 12.4
so he may *r* who reads it.   Hab 2.2
let us *r* with perseverance   Heb 12.1
to the earth; his word *r*   Ps 147.15
be *r* or had run in vain.   Gal 2.2
You were *r* well; who hindered you 5.7

RUNNER — S
"My days are swifter than a *r*; Job 9.25
all the *r* compete, but only   1Cor 9.24

RUTH
and the name of the other *R*.   Ruth 1.4
R the Moabitess said to Naomi,   2.2
"I am *R*, your maidservant;   3.9
Boaz took *R* and she became   4.13
Boaz the father of Obed by *R*,   Mt 1.5

S

SABBATH — S
a *s*, there will be none."   Ex 16.26
"Remember the *s* day, to keep   20.8
observing the *s* throughout   31.16
a *s* of solemn rest to you,   Lev 16.31
s of solemn rest for the land,   25.4
gathering sticks on the *s*   Num 15.32
" 'Observe the *s* day, to keep   Deut 5.12
doing, profaning the *s* day?   Neh 13.17
Blessed..who keeps the *s*,   Isa 56.2
"If you turn back..from the *s*,   58.13
s to *s*, all flesh shall..worship 66.23
not bear a burden on the *s*   Jer 17.21
went through..grainfields on..*s*; Mt 12.1
flight may not be..on a *s*.   24.20
after the *s*, toward the dawn   28.1
One *s*..through the grainfields; Mk 2.23
he would heal him on the *s*,   3.2
And when the *s* was past, Mary   16.1
on the *s*..he stood up to read;   Lk 4.16
a *s*,..through the grainfields,   6.1
Jesus had healed on the *s*,   13.14
One *s* when he went to dine   14.1
"It is the *s*, it is not lawful   Jn 5.10
If on the *s* a man receives   7.23
s day when Jesus made the clay 9.14
the *s* day we went outside   Acts 16.13
keep my *s* and reverence my   Lev 19.30
keep my *s* and reverence my   26.2
my *s*, as a sign between me   Ezek 20.12
they shall keep my *s* holy.   44.24

SACKCLOTH
they girded *s* on their loins,   1Ki 20.32
and put *s* upon his flesh,   21.27
covered himself with *s*, and   2Ki 19.1
Mordecai..put on *s* and ashes,   Est 4.1
when they were sick—I wore *s*,   Ps 35.13
When I made *s* my clothing, I   69.11
loose the *s* from your loins,   Isa 20.2
covered himself with *s*, and   37.1

SACKCLOTH (cont.)
proclaimed a fast,..put on s,   Jonah 3.5
ago, sitting in s and ashes.   Lk 10.13

SACRED
Artemis, and of the s stone   Acts 19.35
acquainted with..s writings   2Tim 3.15

SACRIFICE — S — D (v)
wilderness, that we may s   Ex 3.18
you shall not s it to the   Deut 15.21
he shall s upon you..priests   1Ki 13.2
S and offering thou dost not   Ps 40.6
a freewill offering I will s   54.6
they s flesh and eat it;   Hos 8.13
I with..thanksgiving will s   Jonah 2.9
what pagans s they offer to   1Cor 10.20
one fate..to him who s and   Ecc 9.2
our paschal lamb, has been s.   1Cor 5.7

SACRIFICE — S (n)
to obey is better than s,   1Sam 15.22
in the morning I prepare a s   Ps 5.3
thou hast no delight in s;   51.16
s of the wicked..abomination   Prov 15.8
is more acceptable..than s.   21.3
The s of the wicked is an   21.27
to offer the s of fools;   Ecc 5.1
cause s and offering to cease;   Dan 9.27
steadfast love and not s.   Hos 6.6
you offer blind animals in s,   Mal 1.8
'I desire mercy, and not s.'   Mt 9.13
'I desire mercy, and not s,'   12.7
to offer a s according to..law   Lk 2.24
your bodies as a living s,   Rom 12.1
fragrant offering and s to God. Eph 5.2
a s acceptable and pleasing   Phil 4.18
to put away sin by the s of   Heb 9.26
for all time a single s for sins, 10.12
performed s to the LORD,   1Chr 29.21
is the multitude of your s?   Isa 1.11
nor your s pleasing to me.   Jer 6.20
bring your s every morning,   Amos 4.4
love..is much more than..s."   Mk 12.33

SACRILEGE
when you see the desolating s   Mt 24.15
when you see the desolating s   Mk 13.14

SACRILEGIOUS
men here who are neither s   Acts 19.37

SADDUCEES
and S coming for baptism, he   Mt 3.7
And the Pharisees and S came,   16.1
leaven of..Pharisees and S."   16.6
The same day S came to him,   22.23
and the S came upon them,   Acts 4.1
the S,..filled with jealousy   5.17
one part were S and the other   23.6

SAFE — LY
strength, and made my way s.   Ps 18.32
Oh to be s under the shelter of 61.4
Hold me up, that I may be s   119.117
bring him s to Felix the   Acts 23.24

SAFETY
O LORD, makest me dwell in s.   Ps 4.8
"I will place him in the s   12.5
the needy lie down in s;   Isa 14.30

SAIL — ED
that we should s for Italy,   Acts 27.1
from there they s to Cyprus.   13.4
Paul..s for Syria, and with   18.18

SAINTS
the s in the land, they are   Ps 16.3
you his s, and give thanks   30.4
O fear the LORD, you his s,   34.9
he will not forsake his s.   37.28
flesh of thy s to the beasts   79.2
Precious..is the death of his s. 116.15
preserving the way of his s.   Prov 2.8
But the s of the Most High   Dan 7.18
given to the people of the s   7.27
destroy..the people of the s.   8.24
bodies of the s..were raised,   Mt 27.52
evil he has done to thy s   Acts 9.13
I..shut up many of the s in   26.10
contribute to..needs of..s,   Rom 12.13
Jerusalem with aid for the s.   15.25
called to be s together with   1Cor 1.2
the s will judge the world?   6.2
about the offering for the s,   2Cor 9.1
you, as is fitting among s.   Eph 5.3
now made manifest to his s.   Col 1.26
washed the feet of the s,   1Tim 5.10
the s have been refreshed   Philem 7
with the prayers of all the s   Rev 8.3
allowed to make war on the s   13.7
for the endurance of the s,   14.12
men have shed the blood of s   16.6
surrounded the camp of the s   20.9

SALT — ED
she became a pillar of s.   Gen 19.26
"You are the s of the earth;   Mt 5.13
"S is good; but if s has lost   Lk 14.34
every one will be s with fire.   Mk 9.49

SALUTATIONS
and s in the market places,   Mt 23.7
have s in the market places   Mk 12.38
you love..s in the market   Lk 11.43

SALVATION
I wait for thy s, O LORD.   Gen 49.18
see the s of the LORD,   Ex 14.13
and he has become my s;   15.2
because I rejoice in thy s.   1Sam 2.1
my shield..the horn of my s,   2Sam 22.3
Tell of his s from day to   1Chr 16.23
given me the shield of thy s,   22.36
my heart shall rejoice in thy s. Ps 13.5
The LORD is my light and my s;   27.1
The s..is from the LORD; he is   37.39
him..I will show the s of God!" 50.23
Restore to me the joy of thy s, 51.12
silence; from him comes my s.   62.1
May those who love thy s say   70.4
With long life..show him my s.   91.16
I will lift up the cup of s   116.13
my song; he has become my s.   118.14
eyes fail..watching for..s,   119.123
our s in the time of trouble.   33.2
God is my s; I will trust, and   Isa 12.2
earth open, that s may sprout   45.8
saved..with everlasting s;   45.17
but my s will be for ever,   51.6
publishes s, who says to Zion,   52.7
for soon my s will come,   56.1
you shall call your walls S,   60.18
in..God is the s of Israel.   Jer 3.23
wait quietly for..s of..LORD.   Lam 3.26
I will wait for the God of my s; Mic 7.7
Thou wentest forth for the s   Hab 3.13
I will joy in the God of my s.   3.18
raised up a horn of s for us   Lk 1.69
give knowledge of s to his people 1.77

SALVATION (cont.)

mine eyes have seen thy *s*	Lk 2.30
all flesh shall see the *s* of God."	3.6
"Today *s* has come to this house,	19.9
know, for *s* is from the Jews.	Jn 4.22
there is *s* in no one else,	Acts 4.12
bring *s* to the uttermost parts	13.47
this *s* of God has been sent	28.28
it is the power of God for *s*	Rom 1.16
For *s* is nearer to us now	13.11
behold, now is the day of *s*.	2Cor 6.2
heard..the gospel of your *s*,	Eph 1.13
their destruction,..your *s*,	Phil 1.28
work out your own *s* with fear	2.12
to obtain *s* through our Lord	1Thess 5.9
those who are to obtain *s*?	Heb 1.14
obtain the *s* of your souls.	1Pet 1.9
forbearance of our Lord as *s*.	2Pet 3.15
write to you of our common *s*,	Jude 3
"*S* belongs to our God who	Rev 7.10
"Now the *s* and the power and	12.10
"Hallelujah! *S* and glory	19.1

SAMARIA

He bought the hill of *S*	1Ki 16.24
Ahab..reigned over Israel in *S*	16.29
king of Assyria captured *S*,	2Ki 17.6
the head of *S* is the son of	Isa 7.9
And your elder sister is *S*,	Ezek 16.46
I have spurned your calf, O *S*.	Hos 8.5
make *S* a heap in the..country,	Mic 1.6
along between *S* and Galilee.	Lk 17.11
He had to pass through *S*.	Jn 4.4
a woman of *S* to draw water.	4.7
my witnesses in..Judea and *S*	Acts 1.8
Philip went..to a city of *S*,	8.5

SAMARITANS

and enter no town of the *S*,	Mt 10.5
to many villages of the *S*.	Acts 8.25

SAMSON

and called his name *S*;	Judg 13.24
S went down to Timnah,	14.1
S went to visit his wife	15.1
S went to Gaza, and there	16.1
S said, "Let me die with	16.30
to tell of Gideon, Barak, *S*,	Heb 11.32

SAMUEL

Born, 1Sam 1.19–20; dedicated to God, 1Sam 1.21–28; ministered before God, 1Sam 2.11, 18–21; called, 1Sam 3.1–18; judged Israel, 1Sam 7.3–17; warned Israel for requesting a· king, 1Sam 8. 10–18; anointed Saul king, 1Sam 10.1–8; reasoned with Israel, 1Sam 12; reproved Saul, 1Sam 13.8–15; 15.10–23; hewed Agag in pieces, 1Sam 15.33; anointed David, 1Sam 16.1–13; died, 1Sam 25.1; 28.3.

Moses and *S* stood before me,	Jer 15.1
prophets who have spoken,..*S*	Acts 3.24
he gave them judges until *S*	13.20

SANCTIFICATION

Jesus, whom God made our..*s*	1Cor 1.30
this is..will of God, your *s*:	1Thess 4.3

SANCTIFY — IES — IED

"*S* yourselves; for tomorrow	Josh 3.5
Up, *s* the people, and say,	7.13
Levites! Now *s* yourselves,	2Chr 29.5
they will *s* the Holy One of	Isa 29.23
that I the LORD *s* them.	Ezek 20.12

S a fast, call a solemn	Joel 1.14
S them in the truth; thy word	Jn 17.17
s her, having cleansed her by	Eph 5.26
God of peace himself *s* you	1Thess 5.23
to *s* the people through his	Heb 13.12
he who *s* and those who are *s*	2.11
with the ashes of a heifer *s*	9.13
shall be *s* by my glory;	Ex 29.43
and the Levites *s* themselves	1Chr 15.14
place among those who are *s*	Acts 26.18
to those *s* in Christ Jesus,	1Cor 1.2
you were washed, you were *s*,	6.11
we have been *s* through the	Heb 10.10
for all time those who are *s*.	10.14

SANCTUARY

let them make me a *s*,	Ex 25.8
in the construction of the *s*	36.1
nor come into the *s*, until	Lev 12.4
nor profane the *s* of his God;	21.12
build the *s* of the LORD God,	1Chr 22.19
build a house for the *s*;	28.10
Go out of the *s*; for you	2Chr 26.18
May he send..help from the *s*,	Ps 20.2
have looked upon thee in the *s*,	63.2
until I went into the *s* of God;	73.17
They set thy *s* on fire; to the	74.7
Judah became his *s*, Israel his	114.2
And he will become a *s*, and	Isa 8.14
comes to his *s* to pray,	16.12
drink it in..courts of my *s*."	62.9
throne..the place of our *s*.	Jer 17.12
seen the nations invade her *s*,	Lam 1.10
scorned..altar, disowned his *s*;	2.7
you have defiled my *s* with	Ezek 5.11
yet I have been a *s* to them	11.16
they have defiled my *s* on	23.38
Behold, I will profane my *s*,	24.21
the *s* in the midst of it.	48.8
then the *s* shall be restored	Dan 8.14
thy face to shine upon thy *s*,	9.17
Bethel,..is the king's *s*,	Amos 7.13
Judah has profaned the *s* of	Mal 2.11
for worship and an earthly *s*.	Heb 9.1
way into the *s* is not..opened	9.8
to enter the *s* by the blood	10.19

SAND

multiply..descendants as..*s*	Gen 22.17
your descendants as the *s*	32.12
stone is heavy;..*s* is weighty,	Prov 27.3
Israel..as the *s* of the sea,	Isa 10.22
of Israel shall be like the *s*	Hos 1.10
who built his house upon the *s*;	Mt 7.26
sons of Israel be as the *s*	Rom 9.27
innumerable grains of *s* by	Heb 11.12

SANDAL — S

pull his *s* off his foot,	Deut 25.9
drew off his *s* and gave it to	Ruth 4.7
whose *s* I am not worthy to	Mk 1.7
wear *s* and not put on two tunics.	6.9
thong of whose *s* I am not	Lk 3.16
s..I am not worthy to untie.'	Acts 13.25

SARAH (SARAI)

Wife of Abraham, Gen 11.29; barren, Gen 11.30; Sarai and Hagar, Gen 16.1–6; represented as Abraham's sister, Gen 12.10–20; 20.1–18; name changed to Sarah, Gen 17.15; laughed at the LORD's promise, Gen 18.9–15; bore Isaac, Gen 21.1–8; jealous of Ishmael, Gen 21.9–11; died at Hebron, Gen 23.2; buried in Machpelah, Gen 23.19.

SARAH (SARAI) (cont.)
S..barren; she had no child. Gen 11.30
S, Abram's wife, bore..no children. 16.1
"Where is S your wife?" 18.9
LORD did to S as he had promised. 21.1
By faith S herself received Heb 11.11
as S obeyed Abraham, calling 1Pet 3.6
the barrenness of S womb. Rom 4.19

SAT
Bethel, and s there till evening Judg 21.2
river Chebar. And I s there Ezek 3.15
colt..on which no one..ever s; Mk 11.2
and s down at the right hand 16.19n
he s down at the right hand Heb 1.3
he s down at the right hand 10.12

SATAN
S stood up against Israel, 1Chr 21.1
and S also came among them. Job 1.6
and S also came among them 2.1
S standing at his right hand Zech 3.1
Jesus said to him, "Begone, S! Mt 4.10
if S casts out S, he is divided 12.26
to Peter, "Get behind me, S! 16.23
"I saw S fall like lightning Lk 10.18
"Ananias, why has S filled Acts 5.3
to keep S from gaining the 2Cor 2.11
S disguises..as an angel of light. 11.14
but are a synagogue of S. Rev 2.9
serpent..called the Devil and S, 12.9
dragon,..who is the Devil and S, 20.2

SATISFY — IES — IED
S us..with thy steadfast love, Ps 90.14
I will s her poor with bread. 132.15
labor for that which does not s? Isa 55.2
and s your desire with good 58.11
For I will s the weary soul, Jer 31.25
they cannot s their hunger Ezek 7.19
governor's ears, we will s him Mt 28.14
to s the one who enlisted him. 2Tim 2.4
For he s him who is thirsty, Ps 107.9
afflicted shall eat and be s; 22.26
s with the goodness of thy house, 65.4
earth is s with..fruit of thy work. 104.13
never s are the eyes of man. Prov 27.20
Three things are never s; 30.15
the eye is not s with seeing, Ecc 1.8
who loves money will not be s 5.10
travail of his soul and be s; Isa 53.11
people..s with my goodness, Jer 31.14
You shall eat, but not be s, Mic 6.14
the Father, and we shall be s." Jn 14.8

SATYR — S
s shall cry to his fellow; Isa 34.14
slay their sacrifices for s Lev 17.7
for..high places, and..s, 2Chr 11.15

SAUL (King of Israel)
Son of Kish, 1Sam 9.1–2; met Samuel,
1Sam 9.5–24; anointed by Samuel, 1Sam
10.1–8; prophesied with the prophets,
1Sam 10.9–13; chosen king at Mizpah,
1Sam 10.20–24; defeated the Ammonites,
1Sam 11.5–11; made king in Gilgal, 1Sam
11.12–15; reproved for his burnt offering,
1Sam 13.8–15; built an altar, 1Sam 14.35;
rejected as king, 1Sam 15.11–30; refreshed
by David's harp playing, 1Sam 16.14–23;
became jealous of David, 1Sam 18.6–30;
sought to kill David, 1Sam 19.1–17; killed
the priests of Nob, 1Sam 22.11–19; spared
by David, 1Sam 24.1–7; 26.1–12; con-

sulted the woman of Endor, 1Sam 28.3–25;
died and buried, 1Sam 31.

king; and God gave them S Acts 13.21

SAUL (PAUL)
S, who is also called Paul, Acts 13.9

SAVE — S — D — ING
God walks in the midst..to s Deut 23.14
may come among us and s us 1Sam 4.3
our God, s us, I beseech 2Ki 19.19
I will defend this city to s it, 19.34
gather and s us from among 1Chr 16.35
and thou wilt hear and s.' 2Chr 20.9
O s thy people, and bless thy Ps 28.9
God will s Zion and rebuild 69.35
judgment to s all the oppressed 76.9
s thy servant who trusts in thee. 86.2
I beseech thee, s my life!" 116.4
s yourself like a gazelle Prov 6.5
s his life from Sheol. 23.14
waited..that he might s us. Isa 25.9
our God, s us from his hand, 37.20
there is no one to s you. 47.15
vindication, mighty to s." 63.1
for I am with you to s you Jer 15.20
s me, and I shall be saved; 17.14
I will s you from afar, and 30.10
I will s you from afar, and 46.27
let every man s his life! 51.6
speak to warn..to s his life, Ezek 3.18
I will s my flock, they 34.22
Where now is your king, to s Hos 13.10
Assyria shall not s us, we 14.3
nor..the mighty s his life; Amos 2.14
s the lame and..the outcast, Zeph 3.19
his name Jesus, for he will s Mt 1.21
"S, Lord; we are perishing." 8.25
Peter..cried out, "Lord, s me." 14.30
whoever would s his life will 16.25
Son of man came to s the lost 18.11n
it in three days, s yourself! 27.40
whoever would s his life will Mk 8.35
s yourself, and come down 15.30
whoever would s his life will Lk 9.24
men's lives but to s them" 9.55n
you will s your husband? 1Cor 7.16
might by all means s some. 9.22
into the world to s sinners. 1Tim 1.15
s..yourself and your hearers. 4.16
able..to s those who draw near Heb 7.25
but to s those who are eagerly 9.28
will s his soul from death Jas 5.20
s some, by snatching them Jude 23
the LORD s not with sword 1Sam 17.47
But he s the fatherless Job 5.15
Thus the LORD s Israel Ex 14.30
be s from your enemies. Num 10.9
a people s by the LORD, Deut 33.29
Rahab..Joshua s alive; Josh 6.25
he s them from the hand of Judg 2.18
I am s from my enemies. 2Sam 22.4
warn him, so that he s himself 2Ki 6.10
So the LORD s Hezekiah and 2Chr 32.22
and I am s from my enemies. Ps 18.3
LORD heard him, and s him out 34.6
face shine, that we may be s! 80.3
he s them for his name's sake, 106.8
and rest you shall be s; Isa 30.15
long time, and shall we be s? 64.5
summer..ended,..we are not s." Jer 8.20
In his days Judah will be s, 23.6
yet he shall be s out of it. 30.7

SAVE — S — D — ING (cont.)

In those days Judah will be s — Jer 33.16
you will have s your life. — Ezek 3.19
saying, "Who then can be s?" — Mt 19.25
endures to the end will be s. — 24.13
to him, "Then who can be s?" — Mk 10.26
the woman, "Your faith has s — Lk 7.50
will those who are s be few?" — 13.23
said, "Then who can be s?" — 18.26
"He s others; let him save — 23.35
say this that you may be s. — Jn 5.34
calls on..Lord shall be s.' — Acts 2.21
by which you will be s, — 11.14
of Moses, you cannot be s." — 15.1
we shall be s through..grace — 15.11
what must I do to be s?" — 16.30
the ship, you cannot be s." — 27.31
be s by him from the wrath of — Rom 5.9
For in this hope we were s. — 8.24
prayer..that they may be s. — 10.1
and believe..you will be s. — 10.9
and so all Israel will be s; — 11.26
but to us who are being s — 1Cor 1.18
though he himself will be s, — 3.15
that his spirit may be s in the day — 5.5
of many, that they may be s. — 10.33
gospel,..by which you are s, — 15.2
Gentiles that they..be s— — 1Thess 2.16
God chose you..to be s, — 2Thess 2.13
who desires all men to be s — 1Tim 2.4
who s us and called us with — 2Tim 1.9
he s us, not because of deeds — Tit 3.5
eight persons, were s through — 1Pet 3.20
righteous man is scarcely s, — 4.18
he who s a people out of the land — Jude 5
can hinder the LORD from s — 1Sam 14.6
know the s acts of the LORD." — Mic 6.5

SAVIOR — S

a s, so that they escaped — 2Ki 13.5
They forgot God, their S, — Ps 106.21
he will send them a s, and — Isa 19.20
Holy One of Israel, your S. — 43.3
and besides me there is no s. — 43.11
a righteous God and a S; — 45.21
that I, the LORD, am your S — 60.16
thou hope of Israel, its s — Jer 14.8
besides me there is no s. — Hos 13.4
my spirit rejoices in God my S, — Lk 1.47
born in the city of David a S, — 2.11
has brought to Israel a S, — Acts 13.23
in the sight of God our S, — 1Tim 2.3
who is the S of all men, — 4.10
Son as the S of the world. — 1Jn 4.14
only God, our S through Jesus — Jude 25
S shall go up to Mount Zion — Obad 1.21

SAYING — S

The s is sure and worthy of — 1Tim 1.15
The s is sure and worthy of — 4.9
hears my s and does not keep — Jn 12.37

SCALES

A just balance and s are — Prov 16.11
and false s are not good. — 20.23
acquit the man with wicked s — Mic 6.11

SCARLET

bind..s cord in the window — Josh 2.18
though your sins are like s, — Isa 1.18
and put a s robe upon him, — Mt 27.28

SCATTER — S — ED

and s them in Israel. — Gen 49.7
I will s you among..nations, — Lev 26.33

And the LORD will s you — Deut 4.27
the LORD will s you among — 28.64
I will s them among the nations — Jer 9.16
I will s you like chaff driven — 13.24
Like the east wind I will s — 18.17
I swore..that I would s them — Ezek 20.23
the wolf snatches them and s — Jn 10.12
and all their flock is s. — Jer 10.21
s them among the countries, — Ezek 11.16
the horns which s Judah, — Zech 1.21
I s them with a whirlwind — 7.14
I s them among the nations, — 10.9
hour..come, when you will be s, — Jn 16.32
who were s went..preaching — Acts 8.4

SCEPTER

The s shall not depart — Gen 49.10
s and with their staves." — Num 21.18
s shall rise out of Israel; — 24.17
Your royal s is a s of equity; — Ps 45.6
Ephraim..my helmet; Judah is my s. — 60.7

SCOFFED

s at..Rock of his salvation. — Deut 32.15
heard..this, and..s at him. — Lk 16.14

SCOFFER — S

s does not listen to rebuke. — Prov 13.1
A s seeks wisdom in vain, — 14.6
A s does not like to be reproved; — 15.12
Strike a s, and the simple — 19.25
the s cease, and all who — Isa 29.20
nor sits in the seat of s; — Ps 1.1
How long will s delight in — Prov 1.22
'Behold, you s, and wonder, — Acts 13.41

SCORCH — ED

allowed to s men with fire; — Rev 16.8
inhabitants of..earth are s, — Isa 24.6
when the sun rose they were s; — Mt 13.6

SCORN — S — ED (v)

you did not s or despise me, — Gal 4.14
God s the wicked, but the — Prov 14.9
have utterly s the LORD, — 2Sam 12.14

SCORN (n)

they laughed them to s, — 2Chr 30.10
I am the s of..my adversaries, — Ps 31.11
become the s of his neighbors. — 89.41
word of the LORD..object of s, — Jer 6.10
bear the s of the peoples." — Mic 6.16

SCOURGE — D (v)

they will s him and kill him, — Lk 18.33
mocked and s and crucified, — Mt 20.19
having s Jesus, delivered him — 27.26
Pilate took Jesus and s him. — Jn 19.1

SCOURGE — ING (n)

hid from the s of the tongue, — Job 5.21
will wield against them a s, — Isa 10.26
him to be examined by s, — Acts 22.24

SCRIBE — S

the s of the law of the God — Ezra 7.12
a s came up and said to him, — Mt 8.19
every s who has been trained — 13.52
Where is the s? Where is — 1Cor 1.20
"The s and the Pharisees sit — Mt 23.2
s who came down from Jerusalem — Mk 3.22
crowd..and s arguing with them. — 9.14
"Beware of the s, who like — 12.38

SCRIPTURE — S

Have you not read this s: — Mk 12.10
the s was fulfilled which says, — 15.28n
"Today..s has been fulfilled — Lk 4.21

SCRIPTURE — S (cont.)
they believed the *s* and the Jn 2.22
(and *s* cannot be broken), 10.35
that the *s* may be fulfilled, 13.18
that the *s* might be fulfilled. 17.12
This was to fulfil the *s*. 19.24
(to fulfil the *s*), "I thirst." 19.28
s says, "They shall look on him 19.37
Philip..beginning with this *s* Acts 8.35
man, well versed in the *s*. 18.24
For the *s* says to Pharaoh, Rom 9.17
the *s*, foreseeing that God Gal 3.8
the *s* consigned all things 3.22
the *s* say? "Cast out the slave 4.30
royal law, according to the *s*, Jas 2.8
the *s* was fulfilled which says, 2.23
that the *s* says, "He yearns 4.5
no prophecy of *s*..one's own 2Pet 1.20
"Have you never read in the *s*: Mt 21.42
know neither the *s* nor..power 22.29
how..should the *s* be fulfilled, 26.54
you know neither the *s* nor Mk 12.24
But let the *s* be fulfilled." 14.49
while he opened to us the *s*?" Lk 24.32
minds to understand the *s*, 24.45
You search the *s*, because Jn 5.39
argued with them from the *s*, Acts 17.2
examining the *s* daily to see 17.11
the *s* we might have hope. Rom 15.4
died..in accordance with..*s*, 1Cor 15.3
twist as they do the other *s*. 2Pet 3.16

SCROLL
the skies roll up like a *s*. Isa 34.4
"Take a *s* and write on it Jer 36.2
wrote them with ink on the *s*." 36.18
s was consumed in the fire 36.23
Then Jeremiah took another *s* 36.32
lo, a written *s* was in it; Ezek 2.9
saw, and behold, a flying *s*! Zech 5.1
s written within and on..back, Rev 5.1
the sky vanished like a *s* 6.14
He had a little *s* open in his hand. 10.2
told him to give me the little *s*; 10.9

SEA — S
LORD drove the *s* back Ex 14.21
in rafts by *s* to Joppa, 2Chr 2.16
thou didst divide the *s* Neh 9.11
but the *s* is not full; to the Ecc 1.7
arose a great storm on the *s*, Mt 8.24
came to them, walking on the *s*. Mk 6.48
they saw Jesus walking on the *s* Jn 6.19
in the cloud and in the *s*, 1Cor 10.2
standing beside the *s* of glass Rev 15.2
waters..he called *S*. Gen 1.10

SEAL — ED (v)
and *s* it with the king's ring; Est 8.8
to *s* both vision and prophet, Dan 9.24
s the book, until..the end. 12.4
"*S* up what the seven thunders Rev 10.4
"Do not *s* up the words of 22.10
my transgression would be *s* Job 14.17
words of a book that is *s*. Isa 29.11
the words are shut up and *s* Dan 12.9
s with the promised..Spirit, Eph 1.13
God, in whom you were *s* for 4.30
a scroll..*s* with seven seals; Rev 5.1
till we have *s* the servants 7.3

SEAL — S — ING (n)
his testimony sets his *s* to Jn 3.33
on him God the Father set his *s*." 6.27
circumcision as a sign or *s* Rom 4.11

the *s* of my apostleship in 1Cor 9.2
he has put his *s* upon us 2Cor 1.22
the Lamb opened the seventh *s*, Rev 8.1
those..who have not the *s* of God 9.4
Lamb opened one of the seven *s*, 6.1
sepulchre secure by *s* the stone Mt 27.66

SEA OF GALILEE
by the *S*..he saw two brothers, Mt 4.18
Jesus..passed along the *S*.. 15.29
to the other side of the *S*.., Jn 6.1

SEARCH — ES — ED — ING (v)
S me, O God, and know my Ps 139.23
"I the LORD *s* the mind and Jer 17.10
I will *s* out and take them; Amos 9.3
I will *s* Jerusalem with lamps, Zeph 1.12
"Go..*s* diligently for the child, Mt 2.8
You *s* the scriptures, because Jn 5.39
S and you will see..no prophet 7.52
who *s* the hearts of men knows Rom 8.27
For the Spirit *s* everything, 1Cor 2.10
I am he who *s* mind and heart, Rev 2.23
this we have *s* out; it is Job 5.27
thou hast *s* me and known me! Ps 139.1
"Every one is *s* for you." Mk 1.37

SEARCH (n)
go in *s* of the one..astray? Mt 18.12

SEASON (v)
lost..saltness, how will you *s* Mk 9.50

SEASON — S (n)
For everything there is a *s*, Ecc 3.1
lights..for signs and for *s* Gen 1.14

SEAT
gave him a *s* above the seats 2Ki 25.28
I might come even to his *s*! Job 23.3
prepared my *s* in the square, 29.7
for you love the best *s* in Lk 11.43

SECRET — S
"The *s* things belong to Deut 29.29
Absalom sent *s* messengers 2Sam 15.10
our *s* sins in the light of thy Ps 90.8
into judgment, with every *s* Ecc 12.14
I did not speak in *s*, in a Isa 45.19
I have not spoken in *s*, from 48.16
Can a man hide himself in *s* Jer 23.24
nothing, without revealing..*s* Amos 3.7
so that your alms may be *s*; Mt 6.4
given the *s* of the kingdom Mk 4.11
s, except to come to light. 4.22
we impart..*s* and hidden wisdom 1Cor 2.7
he knows the *s* of the heart. Ps 44.21
a talebearer reveals *s*, but Prov 11.13
to know the *s* of the kingdom Mt 13.11
when..God judges the *s* of men Rom 2.16
s of his heart are disclosed; 1Cor 14.25

SECRETLY
Why..flee *s*, and cheat me, Gen 31.27
Israel did *s* against the LORD 2Ki 17.9
The king questioned him *s* Jer 37.17
Herod summoned the wise men *s* Mt 2.7

SECT
of the *s* of the Nazarenes. Acts 24.5
with regard to this *s* we know 28.22

SECURITY
in a matter of deposit or *s*, Lev 6.2
saw..how they dwelt in *s*, Judg 18.7
He gives them *s*, and they Job 24.23
I am oppressed; be thou my *s*! Isa 38.14

SEE — S — N — ING
go and *s* him before I die." Gen 45.28

SEE — S — N — ING (cont.)

I have let you *s* it with your — Deut 34.4
without my flesh. . *s* God, — Job 19.26
or *s* the work of his hands. — Isa 5.12
eyes, so that they cannot *s*, — 44.18
earth shall *s* the salvation — 52.10
he shall *s* his offspring, — 53.10
pure in heart, . . shall *s* God. — Mt 5.8
tell John what you hear and *s*: — 11.4
indeed *s* but never perceive. — 13.14
risen, . . Come, *s* . . where he lay. — 28.6
may indeed *s* but not perceive, — Mk 4.12
all flesh shall *s* the salvation — Lk 3.6
s how the fields are. . white — Jn 4.35
keeps my word, . . will never *s* death." — 8.51
though I was blind, now I *s*." — 9.25
that those who do not *s* may *s*, — 9.39
"Sir, we wish to *s* Jesus." — 12.21
a little while, and you will *s* me." — 16.16
"Unless I *s* in his hands the — 20.25
indeed *s* but never perceive. — Acts 28.26
now we *s* in a mirror dimly, — 1Cor 13.12
But we *s* Jesus, who for a — Heb 2.9
for we shall *s* him, as he is. — 1Jn 3.2
and every eye will *s* him, — Rev 1.7
for the LORD *s* not as man *s*; — 1Sam 16.7
prudent man *s* danger and — Prov 27.12
who say, "Who *s* us? Who — Isa 29.15
I have *s* the affliction of — 1Sam 9.16
people. . have *s* a great light, — Mt 4.16
practicing. . piety. . to be *s* by them; — 6.1
"Go. . tell John what you have *s* — Lk 7.22
light, that it may be clearly *s* — Jn 3.21
what we have *s* and heard." — Acts 4.20
on the road he had *s* the Lord, — 9.27
have heard, which we have *s* — 1Jn 1.1
"Thou art a God of *s*"; — Gen 16.13
keep them from *s* the light — 2Cor 4.4

SEED

every plant yielding *s* — Gen 1.29
enmity. . between your *s* — 3.15
goes. . weeping, bearing the *s* — Ps 126.6
In the morning sow your *s*, — Ecc 11.6
who sowed good *s* in his field; — Mt 13.24
good *s* means. . sons of. . kingdom; — 13.38
as if a man should scatter *s* — Mk 4.26

SEEK — S — ING

to *s* out a resting place for — Num 10.33
there you will *s* the LORD — Deut 4.29
S the LORD and his strength, — 1Chr 16.11
If you *s* him, he will be found — 28.9
and pray and *s* my face, — 2Chr 7.14
commanded Judah to *s* the LORD, — 14.4
in his disease he did not *s* — 16.12
set your heart to *s* God." — 19.3
not forsaken those who *s* thee. — Ps 9.10
if there are any. . that *s* after God. — 14.2
who *s* the face of the God of — 24.6
Thou hast said, "*S* ye my face." — 27.8
may all who *s* thee rejoice — 40.16
are wise, that *s* after God. — 53.2
ruthless men *s* my life; they — 54.3
God, I *s* thee, my soul thirsts — 63.1
who *s* God, let. . hearts revive, — 69.3
those who *s* the LORD rejoice! — 105.3
s him with their whole heart, — 119.2
For. . God, I will *s* your good. — 122.9
They will *s* me diligently but — Prov 1.28
he will *s* at harvest and — 20.4
I applied my mind to *s* and — Ecc 1.13
people did not. . *s* the LORD of — Isa 9.13

S and read from the book of — 34.16
I did not say. . '*S* me in chaos.' — 45.19
"*S*. . LORD while he may be found, — 55.6
You will *s* me and find me; — Jer 29.13
you *s* great things for yourself? — 45.5
s peace, . . there shall be none. — Ezek 7.25
so will I *s* out my sheep; — 34.12
shall return and *s* the LORD — Hos 3.5
their guilt and *s* my face, — 5.15
Israel: "*S* me and live; — Amos 5.4
S good, and not evil, that — 5.14
S the LORD, all you humble — Zeph 2.3
nations. . come to *s* the LORD — Zech 8.22
But *s* first his kingdom and — Mt 6.33
s, and you will find; knock, — 7.7
s, and you will find; knock, — Lk 11.9
Instead, *s* his kingdom, and — 12.31
Son of man came to *s* and to — 19.10
"Why do you *s* the living among — 24.5
I *s* not my own will but the — Jn 5.30
you *s* me, not because you saw — 6.26
you will *s* me and. . not find me; — 7.34
you will *s* me and die in your sin; — 8.21
Yet I do not *s* my own glory; — 8.50
said to them, "Whom do you *s*?" — 18.4
you weeping? Whom do you *s*?" — 20.15
rest of men may *s* the Lord, — Acts 15.17
that they should *s* God, in — 17.27
am left, and they *s* my life." — Rom 11.3
I *s* not what is yours but — 2Cor 12.14
s the things that are above, — Col 3.1
he that *s* my life *s* your — 1Sam 22.23
God *s* what has been driven away. — Ecc 3.15
spirit within me earnestly *s* — Isa 26.9
good. . to the soul that *s* him. — Lam 3.25
evil generation; it *s* a sign, — Lk 11.29
such the Father *s* to worship — Jn 4.23
understands, no one *s* for God. — Rom 3.11
s his God, he did with all — 2Chr 31.21
Lord God, *s* him by prayer and — Dan 9.3
come *s* fruit on this fig tree, — Lk 13.7

SEER — S

prophet was. . called a *s*.) — 1Sam 9.9
who say to me, "See not"; — Isa 30.10
the *s* shall be disgraced, — Mic 3.7

SELF-CONTROL

man without *s* is like a city — Prov 25.28
argued about justice and *s* — Acts 24.25
if they cannot exercise *s*, — 1Cor 7.9
Every athlete exercises *s* — 9.25

SELFISHNESS

anger, *s*, slander, gossip, — 2Cor 12.20
Do nothing from *s* or conceit, — Phil 2.3

SELL — S

"First *s* me your birthright." — Gen 25.31
because they *s* the righteous — Amos 2.6
S your possessions, and give — Lk 12.33
in his joy he goes and *s* all — Mt 13.44

SEND — S

Come, I will *s* you to Pharaoh — Ex 3.10
Oh *s* out thy light and. . truth; — Ps 43.3
He will *s* from heaven and save — 57.3
I said, "Here am I! *S* me." — Isa 6.8
I *s* my messenger to prepare — Mal 3.1
s. . laborers into his harvest." — Mt 9.38
Son of man will *s* his angels, — 13.41
I *s* my messenger before thy face, — Mk 1.2
begged him, "*S* us to the swine, — 5.12
believed that thou didst *s* me. — Jn 17.8
thou didst *s* me into the world, — 17.18

SEND — S (cont.)

sent me, even so I s you."	Jn 20.21
did not s me to baptize but	1Cor 1.17
He s forth his command to	Ps 147.15

SENNACHERIB

S king of Assyria came up	2Ki 18.13
hear the words of S, which	19.16
S king of Assyria departed,	19.36
S..came and invaded Judah	2Chr 32.1
hear all the words of S,	Isa 37.17
S king of Assyria departed,	37.37

SENT

God s me before you	Gen 45.5
"The LORD s me to prophesy	Jer 26.12
These twelve Jesus s out,	Mt 10.5
me receives him who s me.	10.40
John..s word by his disciples	11.2
he s two of his disciples,	Mk 11.1
he s two of the disciples,	Lk 19.29
As the living Father s me,	Jn 6.57
God s forth his Son, born of	Gal 4.4
God has s the Spirit of his Son	4.6
God s his only Son into the	1Jn 4.9

SEPARATE — D

lights to s..day from..night;	Gen 1.14
brow of him who was s	49.26
s for you the holy place	Ex 26.33
Israel s from..uncleanness	Lev 15.31
For thou didst s them from	1Ki 8.53
do his will; s yourselves	Ezra 10.11
he will s..one from another	Mt 25.32
Who shall s us from the love	Rom 8.35
able to s us from the love	8.39
unbelieving partner..to s,	1Cor 7.15
be s from them, says the Lord,	2Cor 6.17
God s the light from..darkness	Gen 1.4
they s from each other.	13.11
have s you from the peoples.	Lev 20.24
have not s themselves from	Ezra 9.1
they s from Israel all those	Neh 13.3
Cephas..s himself, fearing the	Gal 2.12

SEPARATION

his s to God is upon his head.	Num 6.7
your iniquities have made a s	Isa 59.2
make a s between the holy	Ezek 42.20

SERAPHIM

Above him stood the s; each	Isa 6.2

SERPENT — S

the s was more subtle	Gen 3.1
became a s; and Moses fled	Ex 4.3
his rod..became a s.	7.10
"Make a fiery s, and set	Num 21.8
broke in pieces the bronze s	2Ki 18.4
At..last it bites like a s,	Prov 23.32
punish Leviathan the fleeing s,	Isa 27.1
as Moses lifted up the s in	Jn 3.14
s deceived Eve by..cunning,	2Cor 11.3
the dragon, that ancient s,	Rev 20.2
LORD sent fiery s among	Num 21.6
I am sending among you s,	Jer 8.17
You s, you brood of vipers,	Mt 23.33
they will pick up s, and	Mk 16.18n
tread upon s and scorpions,	Lk 10.19

SERVANT — S

Not so with my s Moses;	Num 12.7
you were a s in the land	Deut 5.15
"If you will be a s to this people	1Ki 12.7
"Have you considered my s Job,	Job 2.3
my s Job shall pray for you,	42.8
Keep back thy s..from..sins;	Ps 19.13

He chose David his s, and	78.70
give thy strength to thy s,	86.16
shame; may thy s be glad!	109.28
adversaries, for I am thy s.	143.12
Do not slander a s to his	Prov 30.10
But you, Israel, my s, Jacob,	Isa 41.8
Behold my s, whom I uphold,	42.1
Who is blind but my s, or	42.19
"and my s whom I have chosen,	43.10
"But now hear, O Jacob my s,	44.1
my s shall prosper, he shall	52.13
the king of Babylon, my s,	Jer 25.9
fear not, O Jacob my s, says	30.10
one shepherd, my s David,	Ezek 34.23
Daniel, s of the living God,	Dan 6.20
I will bring my s the Branch.	Zech 3.8
greatest among you..be your s;	Mt 23.11
'Well done, good and faithful s;	25.23
he must be last..and s of all."	Mk 9.35
would be great..be your s,	10.43
he sent a s to the tenants,	12.2
He has helped his s Israel,	Lk 1.54
now lettest thou thy s depart	2.29
Does he thank the s because	17.9
'Well done, good s! Because	19.17
he sent a s to the tenants,	20.10
s..not greater than his master;	Jn 13.16
God, having raised up his s,	Acts 3.26
David, thy s, didst say by	4.25
against thy holy s Jesus,	4.27
Paul, a s of Jesus Christ,	Rom 1.1
he is God's s for your good.	13.4
the Lord's s must not be	2Tim 2.24
a s to testify to the things	Heb 3.5
For they are my s, whom I	Lev 25.42
my s whom I brought forth	25.55
spoke by his s the prophets.	2Ki 24.2
hand of..LORD is with his s,	Isa 66.14
sent all my s the prophets	Jer 7.25
to you all his s the prophets,	25.4
he sent his s to the tenants,	Mt 21.34
called his s and entrusted	25.14
treat me as one of your..s." '	Lk 15.19
No longer do I call you s,	Jn 15.15
with ourselves as your s	2Cor 4.5
Are they s of Christ? I am	11.23
S, be submissive to..masters	1Pet 2.18
sealed the s of our God upon	Rev 7.3
and his s shall worship him;	22.3

SERVE — S — D — ING

elder shall s the younger."	Gen 25.23
s God upon this mountain."	Ex 3.12
let us s the Egyptians'?	14.12
not bow down to..or s them;	20.5
to s me as priests—Aaron	28.1
fear..God; you shall s him,	Deut 6.13
all the people..shall s you.	20.11
you shall s other gods,	28.36
to s him with all your heart	Josh 22.5
my house, we will s the LORD."	24.15
yoke upon us, and we will s	1Ki 12.4
and s the king of Babylon,	2Ki 25.24
and s him with a whole heart	1Chr 28.9
Almighty,..we should s him?	Job 21.15
S the LORD with fear, with	Ps 2.11
will not s you shall perish;	Isa 60.12
shall s the king of Babylon	Jer 25.11
All the nations shall s him	27.7
But they shall s the LORD	30.9
we will not s your gods or	Dan 3.18
said, 'It is vain to s God.	Mal 3.14
the Son of man came..to s,	Mt 20.28

SERVE — S — D — ING (cont.)

No servant can s two masters;	Lk 16.13
appoint you to s and bear	Acts 26.16
we s not under the old written	Rom 7.6
do not s our Lord Christ,	16.18
ministering spirits sent. .to s,	Heb 1.14
God, and s him day and night	Rev 7.15
the leader as one who s.	Lk 22.26
If any. .s me, he must follow	Jn 12.26
and they s other gods.	Josh 24.2
the people s the LORD all the	Judg 2.7
and they s their gods.	3.6
forsaken me. .s other gods;	10.13
and they s the LORD only.	1Sam 7.4
whom I had not known s me	2Sam 22.44
and they s idols, of which	2Ki 17.12
They s their idols,. .a snare	Ps 106.36
a thousand thousands s him,	Dan 7.10
fever left. .she rose and s him.	Mt 8.15
fever left her; and she s them.	Mk 1.31
immediately she rose and s	Lk 4.39
has s with me in the gospel.	Phil 2.22
Martha was distracted with. .s;	Lk 10.40
for his sake in s the saints,	Heb 6.10

SERVICE

lives bitter with hard s,	Ex 1.14
all who can enter the s, to do	Num 4.3
"Has not man a hard s upon	Job 7.1
think he is offering s to God.	Jn 16.2
if s, in our serving; he who	Rom 12.7
those. .employed in. .temple s	1Cor 9.13
devoted. .to the s of the saints;	16.15

SETH

and called his name S,	Gen 4.25
his image, and named him S.	5.3
son of S, the son of Adam,	Lk 3.38

SEVEN

march around the city s times,	Josh 6.4
S times a day I praise thee	Ps 119.164
s loaves of the four thousand,	Mt 16.10
forgive. .As many as s times?"	18.21
there were s brothers among us;	22.25
Now there were s brothers;	Lk 20.29
who has the s spirits of God	Rev 3.1

SEVENFOLD

If Cain is avenged s,	Gen 4.24
chastise. .s for your sins,	Lev 26.18
if. .caught, he will pay s;	Prov 6.31

SEVENTH

s day God finished his work	Gen 2.2
the s day is a sabbath	Ex 20.10
God rested on the s day from	Heb 4.4

SEVENTY

shall serve. .Babylon s years.	Jer 25.11
When s years are completed	29.10
of Jerusalem, namely, s years.	Dan 9.2
"S weeks of years are decreed	9.24
the Lord appointed s others,	Lk 10.1

SEVERE

famine was s in the land.	Gen 12.10
I may not have to be s in	2Cor 13.10

SEX

the woman as the weaker s,	1Pet 3.7

SHADOW

let the s go back ten steps."	2Ki 20.10
our days. .are like a s,	1Chr 29.15
he flees like a s, and	Job 14.2
My days. .like an evening s;	Ps 102.11

life,. .he passes like a s?	Ecc 6.12
With. .delight I sat in his s,	Sol 2.3
at least his s. .fall on some	Acts 5.15
only a s of what is to come;	Col 2.17
since the law has but a s of	Heb 10.1

SHADRACH

Hananiah he called S, Mishael	Dan 1.7
and he appointed S, Meshach,	2.49
you. .appointed. .S, Meshach, and	3.12
S, Meshach, and Abednego, fell	3.23
Then the king promoted S,	3.30

SHAKE — S — N

go out. .and s myself free."	Judg 16.20
and s the house of Israel	Amos 9.9
I will s the heavens and. .earth	Hag 2.6
s off the dust from your feet	Mt 10.14
I will s not only the earth	Heb 12.26
voice of. .LORD s. .wilderness,	Ps 29.8
at. .hand that I may not be s;	Acts 2.25
the place. .was s; and they	4.31

SHAME

covered with s the faces	2Sam 19.5
he returned with s of face	2Chr 32.21
how long. .my honor suffer s?	Ps 4.2
let me never be put to s;	31.1
Let me not be put to s, O LORD,	31.17
to s, for God has rejected them.	53.5
be wrapped in their own s as	109.29
Then I shall not be put to s,	119.6
when. .neighbor puts you to s?	Prov 25.8
protection of Pharaoh. .your s	Isa 30.3
you shall not be put to s	45.17
shall not be put to s."	49.23
I hid not my face from s and	50.6
forget the s of your youth,	54.4
Instead of. .s. .a double portion,	61.7
Bel is put to s, Merodach is	Jer 50.2
s is upon all faces, and	Ezek 7.18
will change their glory into s.	Hos 4.7
Ephraim shall be put to s,	10.6
never again be put to s.	Joel 2.26
and unwilling to put her to s,	Mt 1.19
his adversaries were put to s;	Lk 13.17
I say this to your s. Can it	1Cor 6.5
I say this to your s.	15.34
not shrink from him in s at	1Jn 2.28

SHARE

Gentiles have come to s in	Rom 15.27
who serve at the altar s in	1Cor 9.13
as you s in our sufferings,	2Cor 1.7
who is taught the word s all	Gal 6.6
and may s his sufferings,	Phil 3.10
s in. .inheritance of. .saints	Col 1.12
children s in flesh and blood,	Heb 2.14
do good and. .s what you have,	13.16
as you s Christ's sufferings,	1Pet 4.13

SHARP

Your arrows are s in the heart	Ps 45.5
their tongue s as a serpent's,	140.3

SHATTER — S — ED — ING

God will s the heads. .enemies	Ps 68.21
iron breaks to pieces and s	Dan 2.40
"We are s but we will rebuild	Mal 1.4
the s of the power of the holy	Dan 12.7

SHAVE — D

the Lord will s with a razor	Isa 7.20
They shall not s their heads	Ezek 44.20
that they may s their heads.	Acts 21.24
and s off half the beard	2Sam 10.4

SHEAVES
joy, bringing his s with him.   Ps 126.6

SHEBA
queen of S heard of the fame   1Ki 10.1
the kings of S..bring gifts!   Ps 72.10
frankincense..to me from S,   Jer 6.20

SHECHEM
their father's flock near S.   Gen 37.12
they could not live on at S.   Judg 9.41
they were carried back to S   Acts 7.16

SHED
hands did not s this blood,   Deut 21.7
Manasseh s..much innocent   2Ki 21.16

SHEEP
s which have no shepherd."   Num 27.17
David..who is with the s."   1Sam 16.19
took..from following the s,   2Sam 7.8
these s, what have they done?   24.17
as s that have no shepherd;   1Ki 22.17
s, what have they done?   1Chr 21.17
as s that have no shepherd;   2Chr 18.16
made us like s for slaughter,   Ps 44.11
accounted as s for..slaughter.   44.22
Like s..appointed for Sheol;   49.14
Why..anger smoke against the s   74.1
led forth his people like s,   78.52
pasture, and the s of his hand.   95.7
we are his people, and the s   100.3
gone astray like a lost s;   119.176
we like s have gone astray;   Isa 53.6
Pull them out like s for the   Jer 12.3
scatter the s of my pasture!"   23.1
"My people have been lost s;   50.6
my s, the s of my pasture,   Ezek 34.31
like s without a shepherd.   Mt 9.36
lost s of the house of Israel.   10.6
one s and it falls into a pit   12.11
as a shepherd separates the s   25.32
the s..will be scattered.'   26.31
and the s will be scattered.'   Mk 14.27
hundred s, if he has lost one   Lk 15.4
I lay down my life for the s.   Jn 10.15
My s hear my voice, and I know   10.27
He said to him, "Tend my s."   21.16
"As a s led to the slaughter   Acts 8.32
we are regarded as s to be   Rom 8.36
you were straying like s,   1Pet 2.25

SHEEPFOLD — S
who does not enter the s by   Jn 10.1
He chose David..from the s;   Ps 78.70

SHEET
descending, like a great s,   Acts 10.11

SHEKEL
according to the s of the   Ex 30.13
its mouth you will find a s;   Mt 17.27

SHELTER
For he will hide me in his s   Ps 27.5
who dwells in..s of..Most High,   91.1
s from the storm and a shade   Isa 25.4

SHEM
"Blessed by..God be S;   Gen 9.26

SHEOL
S is naked before God, and   Job 26.6
The wicked shall depart to S,   Ps 9.17
thou dost not give me up to S,   16.10
If I make my bed in S, thou   139.8
her steps follow..path to S;   Prov 5.5
Her house is the way to S,   7.27

S and Abaddon lie open   15.11
S has enlarged its appetite   Isa 5.14
S..is stirred up to meet you   14.9
with S we have an agreement;   28.15
and sent down even to S.   57.9
speak..out of..midst of S;   Ezek 32.21
S, where is your destruction?   Hos 13.14

SHEPHERD — S
as sheep which have no s."   Num 27.17
be s of my people Israel,   2Sam 5.2
LORD is my s, I shall not want;   Ps 23.1
Give ear, O S of Israel, thou   80.1
He will feed his flock like a s,   Isa 40.11
says of Cyrus, 'He is my s,·   44.28
break..the s and his flock;   Jer 51.23
I will set up over them one s,   Ezek 34.23
S thy people with thy staff,   Mic 7.14
afflicted for want of a s.   Zech 10.2
I became the s..doomed to be slain   11.7
a s who does not care for   11.16
"Strike the s, that the sheep   13.7
helpless,..sheep without a s.   Mt 9.36
'I will strike the s, and   26.31
were like sheep without a s;   Mk 6.34
written, 'I will strike the s,   14.27
who enters by the door is the s   Jn 10.2
I am the good s. The good s   10.11
Jesus, the great s of the   Heb 13.20
the chief S is manifested   1Pet 5.4
the Lamb..will be their s,   Rev 7.17
and the men are s,   Gen 46.23
your children shall be s   Num 14.33
s also have no understanding;   Isa 56.11
brought..out of the sea the s   63.11
For the s are stupid, and do   Jer 10.21
Woe to the s who destroy and   23.1
"Wail, you s, and cry, and   25.34
prophesy against the s of   Ezek 34.2
s, hear the word of the LORD: 34.7
Amos, who was among the s of   Amos 1.1
Your s are asleep, O king   Nah 3.18
there were s out in the field,   Lk 2.8
the s returned, glorifying..God   2.20

SHIBBOLETH
"Then say S," and he said   Judg 12.6

SHIELD
my s and the horn of my   2Sam 22.3
thou, O LORD, art a s about me,   Ps 3.3
cover..with favor as with a s.   5.12
My s is with God, who saves   7.10
my s, and the horn of my   18.2
a s for all..who take refuge   18.30
given me the s of..salvation,   18.35
LORD is my strength and my s;   28.7
Take hold of s and buckler,   35.2
the LORD God is a sun and s;   84.11
For our s belongs to the LORD,   89.18
his faithfulness is a s and   91.4
He is their help and their s.   115.9
he is a s to those who walk   Prov 2.7
put a s about..Jerusalem   Zech 12.8
taking the s of faith, with   Eph 6.16

SHILOH
before the LORD in S."   Josh 18.8
to the LORD of hosts at S,   1Sam 1.3
in S, wearing an ephod.   14.3
He forsook his dwelling at S,   Ps 78.60
I will make this house like S,   Jer 26.6

SHINE — D
make his face to s upon you,   Num 6.25

SHINE — D (cont.)

light will s on your ways.	Job 22.28
man's wisdom makes his face s,	Ecc 8.1
those who are wise shall s	Dan 12.3
they shall s on his land.	Zech 9.16
Let your light so s before men,	Mt 5.16
righteous will s like the sun	13.43
you s as lights in the world,	Phil 2.15
darkness, on them has light s.	Isa 9.2

SHIP — S

way of a s on the high seas,	Prov 30.19
Jehoshaphat made s of	1Ki 22.48
There go the s, and Leviathan	Ps 104.26
went down to the sea in s,	107.23
shall go forth in s	Ezek 30.9n

SHIPWRECK — ED

have made s of their faith,	1Tim 1.19
Three times I have been s;	2Cor 11.25

SHOES

put off your s from your feet,	Ex 3.5
"Put off your s from your	Josh 5.15
his hand, and s on his feet;	Lk 15.22
'Take off the s from your	Acts 7.33

SHORTENED

hand s, that it cannot redeem?	Isa 50.2
if those days had not been s,	Mt 24.22
if the Lord had not s the days,	Mk 13.20

SHOUT — S

"S; for the LORD has given	Josh 6.16
S, and sing for joy, O..Zion,	Isa 12.6
The LORD..cries out, he s	42.13

SHOW — S — ED — N

"I pray thee, s me thy glory."	Ex 33.18
I will s them marvelous things.	Mic 7.15
go, s yourself to the priest,	Mt 8.4
"Lord, s us the Father, and	Jn 14.8
to s by what death he was to	21.19
to s God's righteousness,	Rom 3.25
But God s his love for us	5.8
God s no partiality)—those,	Gal 2.6
LORD s him all the land,	Deut 34.1
He..s you, O man, what is good;	Mic 6.8
he s them his hands and his	Lk 24.40n
but God has s me that I	Acts 10.28

SHOWERS

the s have been withheld, and	Jer 3.3
they shall be s of blessing.	Ezek 34.26
he will come to us as the s,	Hos 6.3
dew from the LORD, like s	Mic 5.7

SHUN

S immorality. Every other sin	1Cor 6.18
s the worship of idols.	10.14
you, man of God, s all this;	1Tim 6.11

SHUT

the LORD s him in.	Gen 7.16
he shall open, and none..s;	Isa 22.22
s the kingdom..against men;	Mt 23.13

SICK

Hezekiah became s and was	2Ki 20.1
were s through their sinful	Ps 107.17
Hope deferred..heart s,	Prov 13.12
tell him I am s with love.	Sol 5.8
The whole head is s, and the	Isa 1.5
my heart is s within me.	Jer 8.18
his mother-in-law lying s	Mt 8.14
physician, but those who are s.	9.12
any..s with various diseases	Lk 4.40
physician, but those who are s;	5.31

slave..s..at the point of death.	7.2
they even carried out the s	Acts 5.15
Is any among you s? Let him	Jas 5.14

SICKLE

shall not put a s to your	Deut 23.25
Put in the s, for the harvest	Joel 3.13
"Put in your s, and reap,	Rev 14.15

SICKNESS

take away from you all s;	Deut 7.15
'Shall I recover from this s?'	2Ki 8.8
vexation and s and resentment?	Ecc 5.17
wasting s among..warriors,	Isa 10.16
When Ephraim saw his s, and	Hos 5.13

SIDE

the LORD who was on our s,	Ps 124.1
one of..soldiers pierced his s	Jn 19.34

SIDON

father of S, his first-born,	Gen 10.15
had been done in Tyre and S,	Mt 11.21
to the district of Tyre and S.	15.21
Tyre and S a great multitude,	Mk 3.8
Elijah..sent to..the land of S,	Lk 4.26
The next day we put in at S;	Acts 27.3

SIDONIANS

the S call Hermon Sirion,	Deut 3.9
how they were far from the S	Judg 18.7
how to cut timber like the S."	1Ki 5.6
the abomination of the S,	2Ki 23.13

SIGH — ING

years come to an end like a s.	Ps 90.9
sorrow, and my years with s;	31.10

SIGHT

good in the s of all..people	1Sam 18.5
Better is the s of the eyes	Ecc 6.9
not only in the Lord's s but	2Cor 8.21

SIGN — S

"This is the s of the covenant	Gen 9.12
"or heed the first s,	Ex 4.8
a s between me and you	31.13
shall be a s to the people	Num 16.38
this may be a s among you,	Josh 4.6
show me a sign..who speakest	Judg 6.17
shall be the sign to you:	1Sam 2.34
the s that the LORD has	1Ki 13.3
"Ask a s of the LORD your God,	Isa 7.11
Lord himself will give you a s.	7.14
this shall be the s for you:	37.30
the s to you from the LORD,	38.7
a memorial,..an everlasting s	55.13
This shall be the s to you,	Jer 44.29
a s for the house of Israel.	Ezek 4.3
for I have made you a s for	12.6
make him a s and a byword	14.8
shall Ezekiel be to you a s;	24.24
no s shall be given..except	Mt 12.39
show them a s from heaven.	16.1
what will be the s of your coming	24.3
betrayer had given them a s,	26.48
Pharisees..seeking from him a s	Mk 8.11
what will be the s when these	13.4
betrayer had given them a s,	14.44
this will be a s for you:	Lk 2.12
for a s that is spoken against	2.34
sought..a s from heaven.	11.16
it seeks a s, but no s shall	11.29
the s when this is about to	21.7
to see some s done by him.	23.8
"What s have you to show us	Jn 2.18
"John did no s, but everything	10.41

SIGN — S (cont.)

notable *s* has been performed	Acts 4.16
circumcision as a *s* or seal	Rom 4.11
tongues. . a *s* . . for unbelievers,	1Cor 14.22
lights. . for *s* and for seasons	Gen 1.14
I and the children. . are *s* and	Isa 8.18
dismayed at. . *s* of the heavens	Jer 10.2
How great are his *s*, how mighty	Dan 4.3
interpret the *s* of the times.	Mt 16.3
false prophets will. . show *s*	Mk 13.22
these *s* will accompany those	16.17n
first of his *s*, Jesus did	Jn 2.11
believed. . when they saw the *s*	2.23
"Unless you see *s* and wonders	4.48
because they saw the *s* which	6.2
Now Jesus did many other *s*	20.30
many *s* and wonders were done	Acts 5.12
s and wonders God had done	15.12
Jews demand *s* and Greeks	1Cor 1.22
great *s*, . making fire come	Rev 13.13
by the *s*. . it deceives those	13.14
demonic spirits, performing *s*,	16.14

SIGNAL

He will raise a *s* for a nation	Isa 5.26
On a bare hill raise a *s*,	13.2
a *s* is raised on the mountains,	18.3
"I will *s*. . and gather them in,	Zech 10.8

SIGNET

the *s* ring on my right hand,	Jer 22.24
king sealed it with his own *s*	Dan 6.17

SILAS

They sent Judas. . and *S*,	Acts 15.22
Paul chose *S* and departed,	15.40
they seized Paul and *S* and	16.19
persuaded, . . joined Paul and *S*;	17.4
When *S* and Timothy arrived	18.5

SILENCE

if you keep *s* at such a time	Est 4.14
O God, do not keep *s*; do not	Ps 83.1
all the earth keep *s* before him.	Hab 2.20
no one to interpret, . . keep *s*	1Cor 14.28
women. . keep *s* in the churches.	14.34
Let a woman learn in *s* with	1Tim 2.11
there was a *s* in heaven for about	Rev 8.1

SILENT

But the people were *s* and	2Ki 18.36
commune. . on your beds, and be *s*.	Ps 4.4
I was dumb and *s*, . . to no avail;	39.2
a fool who keeps *s* is. . wise;	Prov 17.28
Be *s* before the Lord God!	Zeph 1.7
Be *s*, all flesh, before the	Zech 2.13
But Jesus was *s*. And the high	Mt 26.63
"Be *s*, and come out of him!"	Mk 1.25
you will be *s* and unable to	Lk 1.20

SILOAM

upon whom the tower in *S* fell	Lk 13.4
"Go, wash in the pool of *S*"	Jn 9.7

SILVANUS

preached among you, *S* and	2Cor 1.19
Paul, *S* and Timothy, To the	1Thess 1.1
By *S*, a faithful brother as	1Pet 5.12

SILVER

promises. . pure, *s* refined in	Ps 12.6
and my yield than choice *s*.	Prov 8.19
Your *s* has become dross, your	Isa 1.22
Refuse *s* they are called, for	Jer 6.30
The *s* is mine, and the gold	Hag 2.8
paid him thirty pieces of *s*.	Mt 26.15
brought back the. . pieces of *s*	27.3

ten *s* coins, if she loses one	Lk 15.8
Peter said, "I have no *s* and	Acts 3.6

SILVERSMITH

s, . . made it. . a graven image	Judg 17.4
Demetrius, a *s*, who made	Acts 19.24

SIMEON (Son of Jacob)

Born, Gen 29.33; detained as a hostage, Gen 42.24; his future predicted, Gen 49.5–7.

SIMEON (the Prophet)

name was *S*, and this man was	Lk 2.25
and *S* blessed them and said	2.34

SIMON

S the Cananaean, and Judas	Mt 10.4
Thaddaeus, and *S* the Cananaean,	Mk 3.18
and *S* the Zealot and Judas	Acts 1.13

SIMPLE

testimony. . making wise the *s*;	Ps 19.7
The Lord preserves the *s*;	116.6
imparts understanding to the *s*.	119.130
"How long, O *s* ones, will you	Prov 1.22
"Whoever is *s*, . . turn in here!"	9.4

SIN — S — NED — NING (v)

and so to *s* against the Lord	Deut 20.18
should *s* against the Lord	1Sam 12.23
"Let not the king *s* against	19.4
no man who does not *s*—	1Ki 8.46
"If they *s* against thee—	2Chr 6.36
If I *s*, what do I do to thee,	Job 7.20
If I *s*, thou dost mark me,	10.14
I might not *s* against thee.	Ps 119.11
If. . right eye causes you to *s*,	Mt 5.29
or your foot causes you to *s*,	18.8
causes. . who believe in me to *s*,	Mk 9.42
if your hand causes you to *s*,	9.43
cause one of. . little ones to *s*.	Lk 17.2
"See, you are well! *S* no more,	Jn 5.14
weak, you *s* against Christ.	1Cor 8.12
if we *s* deliberately after	Heb 10.26
writing. . that you may not *s*;	1Jn 2.1
If any one *s* unwittingly in	Lev 4.2
if a man *s* against the Lord,	1Sam 2.25
a righteous man. . who. . never *s*.	Ecc 7.20
"If your brother *s* against you,	Mt 18.15
if your brother *s*, rebuke him,	Lk 17.3
immoral man *s* against his own	1Cor 6.18
no one who *s* has either seen	1Jn 3.6
Pharaoh. . said. . "I have *s* this	Ex 9.27
"You have *s* a great sin.	32.30
done foolishly and have *s*."	Num 12.11
promised; for we have *s*."	14.40
"I have *s*, for I did not know	22.34
'We have *s* against the Lord;	Deut 1.41
you had *s* against the Lord	9.16
Israel has *s*; they have	Josh 7.11
"We have *s* against thee,	Judg 10.10
"We have *s* against the Lord."	1Sam 7.6
said to Samuel, "I have *s*;	15.24
I have not *s* against you,	24.11
"I have *s* against the Lord."	2Sam 12.13
David said. . "I have *s* greatly	24.10
Jeroboam. . *s* and. . made Israel	1Ki 14.16
Israel had *s* against the Lord	2Ki 17.7
David said to God, "I have *s*	1Chr 21.8
which we have *s* against thee.	Neh 1.6
'I *s*, and perverted what	Job 33.27
If you have *s*, what do you	35.6
they still *s*; despite . . wonders	Ps 78.32
Lord, against whom we have *s*,	Isa 42.24

SIN — S — NED — NING (v) (cont.)

because we. .s against the LORD. Jer 8.14
many, we have s against thee.   14.7
Jerusalem s grievously,   Lam 1.8
Our fathers s, and are no more;   5.7
we have s and done wrong and Dan 9.5
you have s, O Israel; there   Hos 10.9
because I have s against him,   Mic 7.9
"I have s in betraying innocent Mt 27.4
"Father, I have s against. .you; Lk 15.18
who s, this man or his parents,   Jn 9.2
All who have s without the law Rom 2.12
all have s and fall short   3.23
are s against the LORD,   1Sam 14.33

SIN — S — NING (n)

s is couching at the door;   Gen 4.7
What is my s, that you   31.36
wickedness,. .s against God?"   39.9
Whoever curses his God. .s.   Lev 24.15
your s will find you out.   Num 32.23
put to death for his own s.   Deut 24.16
the s of the young men was   1Sam 2.17
forgive the s of. .Israel,   1Ki 8.36
bring my s to remembrance,   17.18
besides the s. .he made Judah 2Ki 21.16
forgive the s of thy people   2Chr 6.25
shall die for his own s."   25.4
iniquity and search for my s,   Job 10.6
Make me know. .and my s,   13.23
I acknowledged my s to thee,   Ps 32.5
I confess. .I am sorry for my s.   38.18
caught in the toils of his s. Prov 5.22
say,. .I am pure from my s"?   20.9
The devising of folly is s,   24.9
Let not. .mouth lead you into s, Ecc 5.6
who draw s as with cart ropes, Isa 5.18
that they may add s to s;   30.1
"The s of Judah is written   Jer 17.1
fruit of my body for the s of   Mic 6.7
every s and blasphemy will be Mt 12.31
gather out. .all causes of s   13.41
takes away the s of the world! Jn 1.29
"Let him who is without s   8.7n
will seek me and die in your s;   8.21
Which of you convicts me of s?   8.46
they have no excuse for their s. 15.22
he will convince the world of s   16.8
do not hold this s against   Acts 7.60
are under the power of s,   Rom 3.9
as s came into the world   5.12
s will have no dominion over you, 6.14
the wages of s is death,   6.23
law, I should not have known s.   7.7
It was s, working death in me   7.13
not proceed from faith is s.   14.23
he made him. .s who knew no s, 2Cor 5.21
consigned all things to s,   Gal 3.22
As for those who persist in s, 1Tim 5.20
by the deceitfulness of s.   Heb 3.13
In your struggle against s   12.4
He committed no s; no guile   1Pet 2.22
If we say we have no s, we   1Jn 1.8
and in him there is no s.   3.5
No one born of God commits s;   3.9
not a mortal, he will ask,   5.16
plagues. .as many as your s.   Lev 26.21
or woman commits any of. .s   Num 5.6
they did not depart from the s 2Ki 13.6
Have you not s of your own   2Chr 28.10
Remember not. .s of my youth,   Ps 25.7
deliver us, and forgive our s,   79.9
not deal. .according to our s,   103.10

cast. .my s behind thy back.   Isa 38.17
you. .burdened me with your s,   43.24
to the house of Jacob their s.   58.1
was for the s of her prophets Lam 4.13
break off your s by practicing Dan 4.27
and how great are your s—   Amos 5.12
save his people from their s." Mt 1.21
paralytic,. .your s are forgiven." Mk 2.5
all s will be forgiven. .men,   3.28
"Man, your s are forgiven   Lk 5.20
If you forgive the s of any,   Jn 20.23
wash away your s, calling   Acts 22.16
you are still in your s.   1Cor 15.17
who gave himself for our s   Gal 1.4
dead through. .trespasses and s Eph 2.1
remember their s. .no more."   Heb 10.17
bore our s in his body on   1Pet 2.24
Christ also died for s once   3.18
tempted as we. .yet without s. Heb 4.15

SINAI

into the wilderness of S.   Ex 19.1
LORD came down upon Mount S,   19.20
Moses came down from Mount S,   34.29
"The LORD came from S, and Deut 33.2
S quaked at. .presence of God, Ps 68.8
from Mount S, bearing children Gal 4.24

SINFUL

Ah, s nation, a people laden   Isa 1.4
for I am a s man, O Lord."   Lk 5.8

SING — S — ING

"Spring up, O well!—S   Num 21.17
S to him, s praises to him,   1Chr 16.9
appointed those. .to s to   2Chr 20.21
caused the widow's heart to s Job 29.13
But I will s of thy might;   Ps 59.16
s praises to the God of Jacob.   75.9
S aloud to God our strength;   81.1
I will s of thy steadfast love,   89.1
O come, let us s to the LORD;   95.1
S to the LORD, bless his name;   96.2
I will s and make melody!   108.1
"S praises to the LORD, for   Isa 12.5
in the dust, awake and s for joy! 26.19
tongue of the dumb s for joy.   35.6
s to stringed instruments   38.20
S to the LORD a new song,   42.10
S, O heavens, for the LORD   44.23
together they s for joy; for   52.8
"S, O barren one, who did not   54.1
my servants. .s for gladness   65.14
S to the LORD; praise the   Jer 20.13
S and rejoice, O daughter of   Zech 2.10
Gentiles, and s to thy name"; Rom 15.9
I will s with the mind also.   1Cor 14.15
they s a new song before the   Rev 14.3
righteous man s and rejoices. Prov 29.6
the time of s has come, and   Sol 2.12
they break forth into s.   Isa 14.7
exult over you with loud s   Zeph 3.17
praying and s hymns to God,   Acts 16.25

SINNER — S

to the s he gives the work   Ecc 2.26
woman of the city, who was a s, Lk 7.37
more joy in heaven over one s   15.7
guest of a man who is a s."   19.7
can a man who is a s do such   Jn 9.16
we know that this man is a s."   9.24
still being condemned as a s?   Rom 3.7
whoever brings back a s from   Jas 5.20
he instructs s in the way.   Ps 25.8

SINNER — S (cont.)

s be consumed from the earth, Ps 104.35
Misfortune pursues s, but Prov 13.21
and to destroy its s from it. Isa 13.9
many tax collectors and s came Mt 9.10
not to call. .righteous, but s." 9.13
collectors and s were sitting Mk 2.15
not to call. .righteous, but s." 2.17
betrayed into the hands of s. 14.41
For even s love those who love Lk 6.32
Even s lend to s, to receive 6.34
these Galileans were worse s 13.2
"This man receives s and eats 15.2
by one. .many were made s, Rom 5.19
ourselves were found to be s, Gal 2.17
but for the ungodly and s, 1Tim 1.9

SIN OFFERING

fire outside the camp;. .a s. . Ex 29.14
bull without blemish. .for a s. . Lev 4.3
This is the law of the s... 6.25

SISTER — S

Say you are my s, Gen 12.13
said of. .his wife, "She is my s." 20.2
about his wife. ."She is my s"; 26.7
And his s stood at a distance, Ex 2.4
Say to wisdom, "You are my s," Prov 7.4
You. .ravished my heart, my s, Sol 4.9
a little s,. .has no breasts. 8.8
your s Sodom and. .daughters Ezek 16.48
my brother, and s, and mother." Mk 3.35
the son of Paul's s heard Acts 23.16
accompanied by a s as wife, 1Cor 9.5n
children of your elect s greet 2Jn 13
treat. .younger women like s, 1Tim 5.2

SIT — TING

"S at my right hand, till I Ps 110.1
s in. .company of merrymakers, Jer 15.17
s every man under his vine Mic 4.4
"Grant us to s, one at your Mk 10.37
said to my Lord, S at my right 12.36
said to my Lord, S at my right Lk 20.42
my Lord, S at my right hand, Acts 2.34
I saw the Lord s upon a throne, Isa 6.1
Son of man s at the right hand Mk 14.62
like children s in the market Lk 7.32

SIXTH

from the s hour. .was darkness Mt 27.45
In. .s month the angel Gabriel Lk 1.26
to pray, about the s hour. Acts 10.9

SKILFUL

s in playing the lyre; 1Sam 16.16
guided them with a s hand. Ps 78.72
see a man s in his work? Prov 22.29

SKIN — S

took bread and a s of water, Gen 21.14
"S for s! all. .he will give for Job 2.4
my s hardens, then breaks out 7.5
escaped by the s of my teeth. 19.20
Can. .Ethiopian change his s Jer 13.23
God made. .garments of s, Gen 3.21
the wine will burst the s, Mk 2.22

SKIRT

spread your s over your Ruth 3.9
Saul laid hold upon the s 1Sam 15.27
cut off the s of Saul's robe. 24.4
and I spread my s over you, Ezek 16.8

SKULL

(. .means the place of a s), Mt 27.33
(which means the place of a s). Mk 15.22

The S, there they crucified Lk 23.33
called the place of a s, Jn 19.17

SKY — IES

righteousness. .from the s. Ps 85.11
interpret the. .earth and s; Lk 12.56
the s vanished like a scroll Rev 6.14
the s roll up like a scroll. Isa 34.4

SLAIN

Nay, for thy sake we are s Ps 44.22
who had been s for the word Rev 6.9
book. .of the Lamb that was s. 13.8

SLANDER — S — ED

who does not s with his tongue, Ps 15.3
you s your own mother's son. 50.20
Do not s a servant to his Prov 30.10
who s his neighbor secretly Ps 101.5
when s, we try to conciliate; 1Cor 4.13

SLANDERER

not go up and down as a s Lev 19.16
s, haters of God, insolent, Rom 1.30

SLAUGHTER — ED

accounted as sheep for the s. Ps 44.22
gentle lamb led to the s. Jer 11.19
regarded as sheep to be s." Rom 8.36

SLAVE — S

"Cursed be Canaan; a s Gen 9.25
son of this s woman shall 21.10
shall not treat her as a s, Deut 21.14
much less for a s to rule Prov 19.10
"Is Israel a s?. .a homeborn Jer 2.14
first among you must be your s; Mt 20.27
first among you must be s Mk 10.44
struck the s of the high priest 14.47
struck the s of the high priest Lk 22.50
who commits sin is a s to sin. Jn 8.34
Were you a s when called? 1Cor 7.21
there is neither s nor free, Gal 3.28
child, is no better than a s, 4.1
no longer as a s but more Philem 16
'We were Pharaoh's s in Deut 6.21
some of you shall always be s, Josh 9.23
I have seen s on horses, and Ecc 10.7
took back. .s they had set free, Jer 34.11
S rule over us; there is none Lam 5.8
to any one as obedient s, Rom 6.16
we were s to the elemental spirits Gal 4.3
S, be obedient to. .masters, Eph 6.5
S, obey. .your earthly masters, Col 3.22
Bid s. .be submissive to. .masters Tit 2.9
they. .are s of corruption; 2Pet 2.19

SLAVERY

not receive. .spirit of s to Rom 8.15
submit again to a yoke of s. Gal 5.1

SLAY

thou s an innocent people? Gen 20.4
"My father, shall I s them? 2Ki 6.21
he will s me; I have no hope; Job 13.15
the Lord Jesus will s him 2Thess 2.8

SLEEP — ING (v)

I lie down and s;. .Lord sustains Ps 3.5
lighten my eyes, lest I s the s 13.3
he. .will neither slumber nor s. 121.4
who s in the dust of the earth Dan 12.2
let us not s, as others do, 1Thess 5.6
the girl is not dead but s." Mt 9.24
disciples and found them s; 26.40
The child is not dead but s." Mk 5.39
And he came and found them s, 14.37

SLEEP — ING (v) (cont.)

again he came and found them s, Mk 14.40
he..found them s for sorrow, Lk 22.45

SLEEP (n)

God caused a deep s Gen 2.21
deep s from the LORD had 1Sam 26.12
he gives to his beloved in s. Ps 127.2
I will not give s to my eyes 132.4
lie down,..s will be sweet. Prov 3.24
Give your eyes no s and your 6.4
little s, a little slumber, 24.33
Sweet is the s of a laborer, Ecc 5.12
upon you a spirit of deep s, Isa 29.10
swoon..and s a perpetual s Jer 51.39
I fell on my face in a deep s Dan 10.9
I go to awake him out of s." Jn 11.11

SLEPT

I s, but my heart was awake. Sol 5.2

SLIP — S — PED

when their foot shall s; Deut 32.35
Thou..and my feet did not s. Ps 18.36
his heart; his steps do not s. 37.31
who boast..when my foot s!" 38.16
thy paths, my feet have not s. 17.5

SLIPPERY

Let their way be dark and s, Ps 35.6
dost set them in s places; 73.18

SLOW

who is s to anger is better Prov 16.32
sense makes a man s to anger, 19.11

SLUGGARD

Go to the ant, O s; consider Prov 6.6
s craves, and gets nothing, 13.4
desire of the s kills him 21.25
The s says, "There is a lion 22.13
s buries his hand in the dish; 26.15
s is wiser in his own eyes 26.16

SLUMBER — S

he who keeps you will not s. Ps 121.3
A little sleep, a little s, Prov 6.10
none stumbles,..s or sleeps, Isa 5.27

SMALL — EST

I am of s account; what shall Job 40.4
mustard..is the s of all seeds, Mt 13.32

SMELLED

he s..his garments, Gen 27.27

SMELT

and will s away your dross Isa 1.25

SMITE

I will s all the first-born Ex 12.12
LORD..s you with the boils Deut 28.27
sun shall not s you by day, Ps 121.6

SMITH

no s to be found throughout 1Sam 13.19
I..created the s who blows Isa 54.16

SMITTEN

You have s Uriah the Hittite 2Sam 12.9
My heart is s like grass, and Ps 102.4
Why will you still be s, Isa 1.5
yet we esteemed him..s by God, 53.4
Thou hast s them, but they felt Jer 5.3

SMOKE

the s of the land went up Gen 19.28
As s is driven away, so drive Ps 68.2
teeth, and s to the eyes, Prov 10.26
filled with s from the glory Rev 15.8

SMOOTH

adventuress with her s words, Prov 2.16
speak to us s things, prophesy Isa 30.10
rough ways shall be made s; Lk 3.5

SMOTE

LORD s all the first-born Ex 12.29
David's heart s him, because 1Sam 24.5
David's heart s him after 2Sam 24.10
as he s those who s them? Isa 27.7
I s you and all the products Hag 2.17

SNARE — S

will surely be a s to you." Ex 23.33
that would be a s to you. Deut 7.16
and their gods shall be a s Judg 2.3
and it became a s to Gideon 8.27
she may be a s for him, 1Sam 18.21
table before them become a s; Ps 69.22
his lips are a s to himself. Prov 18.7
entangle yourself in a s. 22.25
The fear of man lays a s, 29.25
I set a s for you..O Babylon, Jer 50.24
he shall be taken in my s; Ezek 12.13
upon you suddenly like a s; Lk 21.34
fall into..the s of the devil. 1Tim 3.7
Therefore s are round..you, Job 22.10
who seek my life lay their s, Ps 38.12
they talk of laying s secretly, 64.5
they..laid s for my feet. Jer 18.22

SNATCH — ING

those who s the fatherless Job 24.9
no one shall s them out of Jn 10.28
save some, by s them out of Jude 23

SNOW

slew a lion..when s had fallen. 2Sam 23.20
If I wash myself with s, Job 9.30
the storehouses of the s, 38.22
wash me,..I..be whiter than s. Ps 51.7
He gives s like wool; he 147.16
cold of s in the..harvest Prov 25.13
Like s in summer or rain in 26.1
She is not afraid of s for 31.21
they shall be as white as s; Isa 1.18
Does the s of Lebanon leave Jer 18.14
Her princes were purer than s, Lam 4.7
and his raiment white as s. Mt 28.3

SOBER

let us keep awake and be s. 1Thess 5.6
be s, set your hope fully 1Pet 1.13

SODOM

in the direction of S, Gen 10.19
men of S were wicked, 13.13
Lot..who dwelt in S, 14.12
LORD rained on S..brimstone 19.24
overthrew S and Gomorrah Jer 50.40
the land of S and Gomorrah Mt 10.15
the mighty works..done in S, 11.23
when Lot went out from S Lk 17.29
city..allegorically called S Rev 11.8

SOFT

A s answer turns away wrath, Prov 15.1
To see a man clothed in s Mt 11.8

SOILED

who have not s their garments; Rev 3.4

SOJOURN — S — ED

Abram went..to Egypt to s Gen 12.10
"This fellow came to s, 19.9
LORD, who shall s in thy tent? Ps 15.1
"When a stranger s with you Lev 19.33

SOJOURN — S — ED (cont.)
And if a stranger *s* among you,	Num 9.14
Jacob *s* in the land of Ham.	Ps 105.23
By faith he *s* in the land	Heb 11.9

SOJOURNER — S
for the poor and for the *s*:	Lev 19.10
law for the *s* and for the native;	24.22
loves the *s*, giving him	Deut 10.18
Love the *s* therefore;	10.19
the justice due to the *s*	24.17
s has not lodged in the street;	Job 31.32
I am thy passing guest, a *s*,	Ps 39.12
I am a *s* on earth; hide not	119.19
oppress. .the *s*, or the poor;	Zech 7.10
The LORD watches over the *s*,	Ps 146.9

SOLD
For he has *s* us,	Gen 31.15
and *s* him to the Ishmaelites	37.28
Joseph. .*s* to the Egyptians,	41.56
Joseph, whom you *s* into Egypt.	45.4
not be *s* in perpetuity,	Lev 25.23
shall be *s* or redeemed;	27.28
he *s* them into the power of	Judg 2.14
none who *s* himself to do	1Ki 21.25
and *s* themselves to do evil	2Ki 17.17
For we are *s*, I and my people,	Est 7.4
s thy people for a trifle,	Ps 44.12
Joseph, who was *s* as a slave	105.17
of lands or houses *s* them,	Acts 4.34
jealous of Joseph, *s* him into	7.9
I am carnal, *s* under sin.	Rom 7.14

SOLDIER — S
as a *s* at his own expense?	1Cor 9.7
gave a sum of money to the *s*	Mt 28.12
S. .asked. .what shall we do?"	Lk 3.14
with *s* under me: and I say to	7.8
When the *s* had crucified Jesus	Jn 19.23

SOLE
Every place on which the *s*	Deut 11.24
place that the *s* of your foot	Josh 1.3

SOLID
fed. .with milk, not *s* food;	1Cor 3.2
You need milk, not *s* food;	Heb 5.12

SOLOMON — 'S
Born, 2Sam 12.24; anointed king, 1Ki 1.32–40; established his kingdom, 1Ki 2.12–46; married Pharaoh's daughter, 1Ki 3.1; asked for wisdom, 1Ki 3.5–15; judged wisely, 1Ki 3.16–28; conferred with Hiram, 1Ki 5; 7.13–14; built the temple, 1Ki 6; 7.15–51; built his own house, 1Ki 7.1–12; dedicated the temple, 1Ki 8; the LORD's covenant with Solomon, 1Ki 9.1–9; visited by the queen of Sheba, 1Ki 10.1–13; turned from the LORD, 1Ki 11.1–40; died, 1Ki 11.41–43. (See also 2Chr 1—9.)

proverbs of *S*, son of David,	Prov 1.1
even *S* in all his glory was not	Mt 6.29
came. .to hear the wisdom of *S*,	Lk 11.31
something greater than *S* is here.	11.31
temple, in the portico of *S*.	Jn 10.23
The Song of Songs, which is *S*.	Sol 1.1
in the portico called *S*,	Acts 3.11

SON — S
your wife shall have a *s*."	Gen 18.10
"Take your *s*, your only *s*	22.2

stubborn and rebellious *s*,	Deut 21.18
and he shall be my *s*.	2Sam 7.14
of you, O Absalom, my *s*,	18.33
no *s*, and her husband is old."	2Ki 4.14
when. .you shall embrace a *s*."	4.16
woman whose *s* he had restored	8.1
and he shall be my *s*;	1Chr 17.13
He said to me, "You are my *s*,	Ps 2.7
My *s*, if you receive my words	Prov 2.1
LORD reproves. .as a father the *s*	3.12
A wise *s* makes a glad father,	10.1
spares the rod hates his *s*,	13.24
A foolish *s* is a grief to his father	17.25
He. .is a *s* who causes shame	19.26
Hear, my *s*, and be wise,	23.19
My *s*, give me your heart,	23.26
Be wise, my *s*, and make my	27.11
Discipline your *s*, and he	29.17
and bear a *s*,. .Immanu-el.	Isa 7.14
to us a child is born,. .a *s* is given;	9.6
Is Ephraim my dear *s*? Is he	Jer 31.20
The *s* shall not suffer for	Ezek 18.20
no prophet, nor a prophet's *s*;	Amos 7.14
s treats. .father with contempt,	Mic 7.6
if his *s* asks him for bread,	Mt 7.9
"Have mercy on us, *S* of David."	9.27
"Can this be the *S* of David?"	12.23
Is not this the carpenter's *s*?	13.55
'They will respect my *s*.'	21.37
gave a marriage feast for his *s*,	22.2
said to him, "The *s* of David."	22.42
"Thou art my beloved *S*; with	Mk 1.11
my beloved *S*; listen to him."	9.7
"Teacher, I brought my *s* to you,	9.17
a beloved *s*;. .he sent him to them,	12.6
Christ, the *S* of the Blessed?"	14.61
bear a *s*, and you shall call	Lk 1.31
Elizabeth. .gave birth to a *s*.	1.57
his mother said to him, "*S*, why	2.48
being carried out, the only *s*	7.12
I beg you to look upon my *s*,	9.38
if his *s* asks for a fish, will	11.11
be divided, father against *s*	12.53
the *s* said to him, 'Father,	15.21
he also is a *s* of Abraham.	19.9
I will send my beloved *s*;	20.13
Lord; so how is he his *s*?"	20.44
glory as of the only *S* from	Jn 1.14
that he gave his only *S*,	3.16
to come down and heal his *s*,	4.47
So if the *S* makes you free,	8.36
this. .our *s*. .was born blind;	9.20
lost but the *s* of perdition,	17.12
"Woman, behold, your *s*!"	19.26
"You *s* of the devil, you	Acts 13.10
'Thou art my *S*, today I	13.33
pleased to reveal his *S* to me,	Gal 1.16
God sent forth his *S*, born of	4.4
a *s*, and if a *s* then an heir.	4.7
the kingdom of his beloved *S*,	Col 1.13
he has spoken to us by a *S*,	Heb 1.2
faithful over God's house as a *s*.	3.6
"Thou art my *S*, today I have	5.5
ready to offer up his only *s*,	11.17
"My *s*, do not regard lightly	12.5
and with his *S* Jesus Christ.	1Jn 1.3
No one who denies the *S* has	2.23
God sent his only *S* into the world,	4.9
sent his *S* as the Savior of	4.14
He who has the *S* has life;	5.12
the *s* of God saw. .daughters	Gen 6.2
if only your *s* take heed	2Chr 6.16
s are a heritage from the LORD,	Ps 127.3

SON — S (cont.)

If your s keep my covenant	Ps 132.12
May our s in their youth be	144.12
Hear, O s,..instruction, and	Prov 4.1
delighting in the s of men.	8.31
"S..I reared and brought up,	Isa 1.2
a rebellious people, lying s,	30.9
your s..taught by the Lord,	54.13
Zion..brought forth her s.	66.8
wife, nor shall you have s or	Jer 16.2
s shall eat their fathers;	Ezek 5.10
them, "S of the living God."	Hos 1.10
peacemakers,..called s of God.	Mt 5.9
Jesus said..the s are free.	17.26
A man had two s; and he went	21.28
you will be s of the Most High;	Lk 6.35
wiser..than the s of light.	16.8
you may become s of light."	Jn 12.36
led by the Spirit..s of God.	Rom 8.14
men of faith..s of Abraham.	Gal 3.7
to be his s through Jesus	Eph 1.5
upon the s of disobedience.	Col 3.6n
you are all s of light and	1Thess 5.5

SONG — S

Lord is my strength and my s,	Ex 15.2
therefore write this s,	Deut 31.19
now I have become their s,	Job 30.9
with my s I give thanks to him.	Ps 28.7
Sing to him a new s, play	33.3
He put a new s in my mouth,	40.3
Raise a s, sound the timbrel,	81.2
Lord is my strength and my s;	118.14
sing a new s to thee, O God;	144.9
Sing to the Lord a new s, his	149.1
love s concerning his vineyard:	Isa 5.1
God is my strength and my s,	12.2
In that day this s will be sung	26.1
You shall have a s as in..night	30.29
they shall take up a taunt s	Mic 2.4
a new s, saying, "Worthy art	Rev 5.9
they sing the s of Moses,	15.3
my Maker, who gives s in	Job 35.10
the drunkards make s about me.	Ps 69.12
noise to him with s of praise!	95.2
Thy statutes have been my s	119.54
our captors required of us s,	137.3
who sings s to a heavy heart	Prov 25.20
I am the burden of their s.	Lam 3.63
like one who sings love s	Ezek 33.32

SON OF GOD

"If you are the S.., command	Mt 4.3
have you to do with us, O S..?	8.29
"Truly you are the S..."	14.33
tell us if you are..the S..."	26.63
If you are the S.., come down	27.40
said, "Truly this was the S...!	27.54
"Truly this man was the S..!"	Mk 15.39
will be called holy, the S...	Lk 1.35
witness that this is the S..."	Jn 1.34
not believed in..the only S...	3.18
because I said, 'I am the S..'?	10.36
he has made himself the S..."	19.7
saying, "He is the S..."	Acts 9.20
and designated S..in power	Rom 1.4
attain..knowledge of the S..,	Eph 4.13
high priest..Jesus, the S..,	Heb 4.14
since they crucify the S..on their	6.6
man who has spurned the S..,	10.29
confesses..Jesus is the S..,	1Jn 4.15
words of the S.., who has eyes	Rev 2.18

SON OF MAN

s..that thou dost care for him?	Ps 8.4
"S.., stand upon your feet,	Ezek 2.1
"S.., I have made you a watchman	3.17
"S.., speak to..elders of Israel,	20.3
"S.., I have broken the arm	30.21
there came one like a s..,	Dan 7.13
but the S..has nowhere to lay	Mt 8.20
the S..has authority on earth	9.6
Israel, before the S..comes.	10.23
the S..is lord of the sabbath."	12.8
word against the S..forgiven;	12.32
sows the good seed is the S..	13.37
S..is to come with his angels	16.27
"The S..is to be delivered	17.22
so will be the coming of the S...	24.27
the sign of the S..in heaven,	24.30
"When the S..comes in his glory,	25.31
and the S..will be delivered up	26.2
The S..goes as it is written	26.24
hereafter you will see the S..	26.64
S..has authority..to forgive	Mk 2.10
"The S..will be delivered into	9.31
the S..goes as it is written	14.21
you will see the S..sitting	14.62
"The S..is lord of the sabbath."	Lk 6.5
"The S..must suffer many things,	9.22
S..delivered into the hands of	9.44
the S..seated at the right hand	22.69
descended from heaven, the S...	Jn 3.13
so must the S..be lifted up,	3.14
heavens opened, and the S..	Acts 7.56
..midst of..lampstands..a s..	Rev 1.13
on the cloud one like a s..,	14.14

SONSHIP

received the spirit of s.	Rom 8.15
Israelites,..to them belong the s,	9.4

SONS OF GOD

when the s..came to present	Job 1.6
all the s..shouted for joy?	38.7
you are all s..,through faith.	Gal 3.26

SORCERESS

not permit a s to live.	Ex 22.18

SORROW — S

How long must I..have s in my	Ps 13.2
For my life is spent with s,	31.10
My soul melts away for s;	119.28
knowledge increases s	Ecc 1.18
S is better than laughter,	7.3
and s and sighing shall flee	Isa 35.10
and s and sighing shall flee	51.11
from..womb to see toil and s,	Jer 20.18
Lord has added s to my pain;	45.3
if there is any s like my s	Lam 1.12
with drunkenness and s.	Ezek 23.33
you, s has filled your hearts.	Jn 16.6
your s will turn into joy.	16.20
I have great s and unceasing	Rom 9.2
overwhelmed by excessive s.	2Cor 2.7
another god multiply their s;	Ps 16.4
man of s,..acquainted with grief;	Isa 53.3

SORROWFUL

s; for he had great possessions.	Mk 10.22
"My soul is very s, even to death;	14.34
as s, yet always rejoicing;	2Cor 6.10

SORRY

Lord was s..he had made man	Gen 6.6
I confess..I am s for my sin.	Ps 38.18
And the king was s; but because	Mt 14.9

SOSTHENES
S,..ruler of the synagogue, Acts 18.17
Paul,..and our brother S, 1Cor 1.1

SOUGHT
Preacher s..pleasing words, Ecc 12.10
I s him whom my soul loves; Sol 3.1
they have s and worshiped; Jer 8.2
I s for a man among them Ezek 22.30

SOUL — S
idols;..my s will abhor you. Lev 26.30
keep your s diligently, Deut 4.9
the s of Jonathan was knit 1Sam 18.1
in the bitterness of my s. Job 7.11
my s is poured out within me; 30.16
still waters; he restores my s. Ps 23.3
Why are you cast down, O my s, 42.11
delivered my s from death, 56.13
Bless the LORD, O my s; and 103.1
The s of the wicked desires Prov 21.10
the s is torn by trouble. 27.9
Tell me, you whom my s loves, Sol 1.7
appointed feasts my s hates; Isa 1.14
my s will weep in secret for Jer 13.17
I will satisfy the weary s, 31.25
the s that sins shall die. Ezek 18.4
body for the sin of my s?" Mic 6.7
he whose s is not upright in Hab 2.4
body but cannot kill the s; Mt 10.28
heart, and with all your s, 22.37
heart, and with all your s, Mk 12.30
"My s is very sorrowful, even 14.34
Mary said, "My s magnifies Lk 1.46
S, you have ample goods laid up 12.19
thou wilt not abandon my s Acts 2.27
that it is well with your s. 3Jn 2
fruit for which thy s longed Rev 18.14
you hunt down s belonging Ezek 13.18
Having purified your s by 1Pet 1.22
slaves, that is, human s. Rev 18.13
I saw the s of those..beheaded 20.4

SOUND — NESS
they heard the s of the LORD Gen 3.8
wings like the s of..waters, Ezek 1.24
the s of the day of the LORD Zeph 1.14
when your eye is s, your..body Lk 11.34
Follow..pattern of..s words 2Tim 1.13
sensible, s in faith, in love, Tit 2.2
s speech that cannot be censured, 2.8
There is no s in my flesh Ps 38.3
to the head, there is no s Isa 1.6

SOW — S — ED — N
you shall s the land. Gen 47.23
s fields,..plant vineyards, Ps 107.37
who s in tears reap with..joy! 126.5
observes the wind will not s; Ecc 11.4
you who s beside all waters, Isa 32.20
ground, and s not among thorns. Jer 4.3
I will s the house of Israel 31.27
For they s the wind, and..reap Hos 8.7
S for yourselves righteousness, 10.12
You shall s, but not reap; Mic 6.15
birds..neither s nor reap nor Mt 6.26
'Sir, did you not s good seed 13.27
"Listen! A sower went out to s. Mk 4.3
ravens: they neither s nor reap, Lk 12.24
What you s does not come to 1Cor 15.36
who s discord among brothers. Prov 6.19
He who s injustice..reap calamity 22.8
true, 'One s and another reaps." Jn 4.37
he who s sparingly will..reap 2Cor 9.6

whatever a man s,..also reap. Gal 6.7
Isaac s in that land, Gen 26.12
I reap where I have not s, Mt 25.26
have s wheat..reaped thorns, Jer 12.13
if we have s spiritual good 1Cor 9.11

SOWER
saying: "A s went out to sow. Mt 13.3
"Hear..the parable of the s. 13.18
The s sows the word. Mk 4.14
"A s went out to sow his seed; Lk 8.5

SPAIN
as I go to S, and to be sped Rom 15.24
go on by way of you to S; 15.28

SPAN
add one cubit to his s of life? Mt 6.27
can add..to his s of life? Lk 12.25

SPARE — S — D
your power; only s his life." Job 2.6
thy steadfast love s my life, Ps 119.88
not s when he takes revenge. Prov 6.34
He who did not s his own Son Rom 8.32
who s the rod hates his son, Prov 13.24
Saul and the people s Agag, 1Sam 15.9
some bade me kill you, but I s 24.10
king s Mephibosheth, the son 2Sam 21.7
that the wicked man is s in Job 21.30

SPARROW — S
Even the s finds a home, and Ps 84.3
Are not two s for a penny? Mt 10.29
five s sold for two pennies? Lk 12.6

SPAT
they s in his face and struck Mt 26.67
he s and touched his tongue; Mk 7.33
they struck..and s upon him, 15.19

SPEAK — S — ING
let not God s to us, lest we die." Ex 20.19
I will s with you of all that 25.22
the LORD would s with Moses. 33.9
went into..to s with the LORD, Num 7.89
With him I s mouth to mouth, 12.8
we have this day seen God s Deut 5.24
'S, LORD, for thy servant 1Sam 3.9
says to me, that I will s." 1Ki 22.14
God says, that I will s." 2Chr 18.13
he will s peace to his people, Ps 85.8
keep silence, and a time to s; Ecc 3.7
S tenderly to Jerusalem, and Isa 40.2
I do not know how to s, for Jer 1.6
wilderness,..s tenderly to her. Hos 2.14
he..would not allow them to s, Lk 4.41
began to s in other tongues, Acts 2.4
not to s in the name of Jesus, 5.40
For God s in one way, and Job 33.14
LORD, s and summons the earth Ps 50.1
who s a word against the Son Lk 12.10
that s evil against a brother Jas 4.11
through his faith he is still s. Heb 11.4

SPEAR — S
with one stroke of the s, 1Sam 26.8
pierced his side with a s, Jn 19.34
their s into pruning hooks; Isa 2.4

SPECK
see the s..in your brother's eye, Mt 7.3
s that is in your brother's eye, Lk 6.41

SPEECH
but I am slow of s and Ex 4.10
Day to day pours forth s, and Ps 19.2
Fine s..not becoming to a fool; Prov 17.7

SPEECH (cont.)

not. .to a people of foreign s   Ezek 3.5
change the s. .to a pure s,   Zeph 3.9
enriched in him with all s   1Cor 1.5
and his s of no account."   2Cor 10.10
Let your s always be gracious,   Col 4.6

SPEECHLESS

wedding garment?'. .he was s.   Mt 22.12
The men. .with him stood s,   Acts 9.7

SPEND — T

we will s. .night in. .street."   Gen 19.2
our money is all s;   47.18
I am utterly s and crushed; I   Ps 38.8

SPEW

I will s you out of my mouth.   Rev 3.16

SPICE — S

fragrance of. .oils than. .s!   Sol 4.10
in linen cloths with the s,   Jn 19.40

SPIES (n)

took us to be s of the land.   Gen 42.30
secretly from Shittim as s,   Josh 2.1
men who had been s went in,   6.23
And the s saw a man coming   Judg 1.24

SPIRIT — S

"My s shall not abide. .for ever,   Gen 6.3
some of the s which is upon   Num 11.17
put his s upon them!"   11.29
a man in whom is the s,   27.18
God sent an evil s between   Judg 9.23
an evil s from the LORD came   1Sam 19.9
"Divine for me by a s, and   28.8
a s came forward and stood   1Ki 22.21
"The s of Elijah rests on   2Ki 2.15
with you in s when the man   5.26
gavest thy good S to instruct   Neh 9.20
you turn your s against God,   Job 15.13
But it is the s in a man,   32.8
and saves the crushed in s.   Ps 34.18
I meditate, and my s faints.   77.3
s was not faithful to God.   78.8
When thou sendest forth thy S,   104.30
for they made his s bitter,   106.33
.Whither shall I go from thy S?   139.7
my s is faint, thou knowest   142.3
thy good s lead me on a level   143.10
but the LORD weighs the s.   Prov 16.2
downcast s dries up the bones.   17.22
A man's s will endure. .but   18.14
The s of man is the lamp   20.27
Who knows whether the s of man   Ecc 3.21
No man has power to retain. .s,   8.8
do not know how the s comes   11.5
and the s returns to God who   12.7
a s of judgment and. .burning.   Isa 4.4
until the S is poured upon us   32.15
I have put my S upon him,   42.1
my S upon your descendants,   44.3
wherever the s would go, they   Ezek 1.12
the s. .was in the wheels.   1.20
S lifted me up between earth   8.3
the s of the living creatures   10.17
I will put my s within you,   36.27
I will put my S within you,   37.14
in whom is the s of. .holy gods –   Dan 4.8
in whom is the s of the holy gods.   5.11
pour out my s on all flesh;   Joel 2.28
S abides among you; fear not.   Hag 2.5
nor by power, but by my S,   Zech 4.6
formed the s of man within him: 12.1

Jesus was led up by the S into   Mt 4.1
"Blessed are the poor in s,   5.3
the S of your Father speaking   10.20
I will put my S upon him,   12.18
s. .is willing,. .flesh is weak."   26.41
voice and yielded up his s.   27.50
a man with an unclean s;   Mk 1.23
the s indeed is willing, but   14.38
my s rejoices in God my Savior,   Lk 1.47
And Jesus. .was led by the S   4.1
supposed that they saw a s.   24.37
which is born of the S is s.   Jn 3.6
not by measure. .he gives the S;   3.34
words. .I have spoken. .are s   6.63
I will pour out my S upon all   Acts 2.17
to Jerusalem, bound in the S,   20.22
according to the S of holiness   Rom 1.4
law of the S of life in Christ   8.2
not. .flesh but according to the S.   8.4
who live according to the S   8.5
to set the mind on S is life   8.6
by the power of the Holy S,   15.19
revealed to us through the S.   1Cor 2.10
that God's S dwells in you?   3.16
by one S we were all baptized   12.13
given us his S in our hearts   2Cor 1.22
God has sent the S of his Son   Gal 4.6
who sows to the S will from   6.8
sealed with the promised. .S,   Eph 1.13
but be filled with the S,   5.18
who worship God in s, and   Phil 3.3
Do not quench the S,   1Thess 5.19
did not give us a s of timidity   2Tim 1.7
through the eternal S offered   Heb 9.14
body apart from the s is dead,   Jas 2.26
yearns jealously over the s   4.5
by the S which he has given us.   1Jn 3.24
the S, the water, and the blood;   5.8
let him hear what the S says   Rev 2.7
The S and the Bride say,   22.17
he commands the unclean s,   Lk 4.36
Are they not all ministering s   Heb 1.14
him who has the seven s of God   Rev 3.1
fire, which are the seven s of God;   4.5

SPIRIT OF GOD

S. .was moving over. .the waters   Gen 1.2
man. .in whom is the S. :?"   41.38
filled him with the S. .,   Ex 31.3
And the S. .came upon him,   Num 24.2
s. .came mightily upon Saul   1Sam 11.6
S. .came upon the messengers   19.20
The S. .came upon Azariah   2Chr 15.1
the S. .took possession of   24.20
the s. .is in my nostrils;   Job 27.3
The s. .has made me, and   33.4
all. .led by the S. .are sons   Rom 8.14
By this you know the S. .   1Jn 4.2

SPIRIT OF THE LORD

The S. .came upon him, and he   Judg 3.10
the S. .took possession of Gideon;   6.34
the S. .came upon Jephthah,   11.29
the S. .began to stir him   13.25
the S. .came mightily upon him   15.14
the S. .came mightily upon   1Sam 16.13
the S. .will carry you whither   1Ki 18.12
"How did the S. .go from me   22.24
the S. .came upon Jahaziel   2Chr 20.14
the S. .shall rest upon him,   Isa 11.2
Who has directed the S. .,   40.13
And the S. .fell upon me, and   Ezek 11.5
Is the S. .impatient? Are these   Mic 2.7

SPIRIT OF THE LORD (cont.)
"The *S*..is upon me, because he Lk 4.18
together to tempt the *S*..? Acts 5.9
where the *S*..is,..is freedom. 2Cor 3.17

SPIRITUAL
circumcison is..*s*..not literal. Rom 2.29
We know that the law is *s*; 7.14
Spirit, interpreting *s* truths 1Cor 2.13
I..could not address you as *s* 3.1
concerning *s* gifts, brethren, 12.1
there is also a *s* body. 15.44
who are *s* should restore him Gal 6.1

SPIT
and *s* in his face;..and say Deut 25.9
some began to *s* on him, and Mk 14.65

SPLENDOR
your beauty..through the *s* Ezek 16.14
The latter *s* of this house Hag 2.9
permanent must have..more *s*. 2Cor 3.11

SPOIL — S
and our enemies have gotten *s*. Ps 44.10
like one who finds great *s*. 119.162
they got no *s* of silver. Judg 5.19

SPOKE — N
God *s* all these words, Ex 20.1
in the cloud and *s* to him, Num 11.25
LORD *s* with you face to face Deut 5.4
Jesus *s* to him first, saying, Mt 17.25
"No man ever *s* like this man!" Jn 7.46
Glorious things are *s* of..city Ps 87.3

SPOKESMAN
elders and a *s*,..Tertullus. Acts 24.1

SPREAD — S
Philistines had come and *s* 2Sam 5.18
letter..*s* it before the LORD. 2Ki 19.14
I *s* out my hands to thee. Ps 88.9
I *s* out my hands all the day Isa 65.2
and I *s* my skirt over you, Ezek 16.8
crowd *s*..garments on the road. Mt 21.8
many *s*..garments on the road, Mk 11.8
they *s*..garments on the road. Lk 19.36
flatters his neighbor *s* a net Prov 29.5

SPRING — S
his *s* shall be parched; it Hos 13.15
Does a *s* pour forth..fresh Jas 3.11
give me also *s* of water." Josh 15.19
Thou makest *s* gush forth in Ps 104.10
These are waterless *s* and 2Pet 2.17

SPROUT
the rod of the man..shall *s*; Num 17.5
the wicked *s* like grass Ps 92.7

SPURN — S — ED
if you *s* my statutes, and if Lev 26.15
is not good; he *s* not evil. Ps 36.4
who has *s* the Son of God, Heb 10.29

SPY — IED (v)
"Send men to *s* out the land Num 13.2
to *s* out the land of Canaan, 13.17
to overthrow and to *s* out 1Chr 19.3
s out our freedom which we have Gal 2.4
and *s* out the land from..Zin Num 13.21

SQUANDERED
he *s* his property in loose Lk 15.13

SQUANDERS
with harlots *s* his substance. Prov 29.3

STABILITY
a king gives *s* to the land, Prov 29.4
he will be..*s* of your times, Isa 33.6

STAFF
who bear the marshal's *s*; Judg 5.14
lay my *s* upon the face of 2Ki 4.29
nothing for..journey except a *s*; Mk 6.8

STAGGER — ED
makes them *s* like a drunken Job 12.25
and *s* like drunken men, and Ps 107.27

STALLS
four thousand *s* for horses 2Chr 9.25

STAMMERING
s in a tongue..you cannot Isa 33.19

STAND — S — ING
able to *s* against you, Deut 7.24
s before the LORD to minister 10.8
"You *s* this day all of you 29.10
made all..present..*s* to it. 2Chr 34.32
none can *s* before thee Ezra 9.15
boastful may not *s* before thy Ps 5.5
mark iniquities,..who could *s*? 130.3
you that *s* in..house of..LORD, 135.2
I..purposed, so shall it *s*, Isa 14.24
"*S* by the roads, and look, Jer 6.16
"Son of man, *s* upon your feet, Ezek 2.1
to *s* before the Son of man." Lk 21.36
Be watchful, *s* firm in your 1Cor 16.13
set us free; *s* fast therefore, Gal 5.1
S therefore, having girded Eph 6.14
s firm thus in the Lord, Phil 4.1
if you *s* fast in the Lord. 1Thess 3.8
grace of God; *s* fast in it. 1Pet 5.12
who thinks that he *s*..heed 1Cor 10.12
But God's firm foundation *s*, 2Tim 2.19
Son of man *s* at the right Acts 7.56

STANDARD
shall encamp each by his own *s*, Num 2.2
The *s* of the camp of the men 10.14
his officers desert the *s* Isa 31.9
Raise a *s* toward Zion, flee Jer 4.6

STAR — S
a *s* shall come forth out of Num 24.17
fallen from heaven, O Day *S*, Isa 14.12
we have seen his *s* in the East, Mt 2.2
the morning *s* rises in your 2Pet 1.19
a great *s* fell from heaven, Rev 8.10
I am..the bright morning *s*." 22.16
he made the *s* also. Gen 1.16
Look..and number the *s*, 15.5
multiply..descendants as the *s* 22.17
s of heaven for multitude. Deut 1.10
has made you as the *s* 10.22
Whereas you were as the *s* 28.62
From heaven fought the *s*, Judg 5.20
Israel as many as the *s* of 1Chr 27.23
we labored..till the *s* came Neh 4.21
the morning *s* sang together, Job 38.7
He determines..number of..*s*, Ps 147.4
host of the *s* it cast down Dan 8.10
shine..like the *s* for ever 12.3
descendants as many as the *s* Heb 11.12
right hand he held seven *s*, Rev 1.16

STATE
last *s*..worse than the first. Mt 12.45
last *s* of..man becomes worse Lk 11.26
should remain in the *s* in 1Cor 7.20

STATURE
increased in wisdom and in *s*, Lk 2.52

STATUTE — S

for a *s* and ordinance to you	Num 35.29
therefore keep my *s* and my	Lev 18.5
I will meditate on thy *s*.	Ps 119.48
and not walking in my *s*.	Ezek 5.6

STAY — ING

and *s* themselves on the God	Isa 48.2
s with him until you depart."	Mt 10.11
I must *s* at your house today."	Lk 19.5
Teacher), where are you *s*?"	Jn 1.38
while *s* with them he charged	Acts 1.4

STEADFAST — NESS

My heart is *s*, O God, my heart	Ps 57.7
brethren, be *s*, immovable,	1Cor 15.58
for our instruction, that by *s*	Rom 15.4
love of God and. .*s* of Christ.	2Thess 3.5
testing of. .faith produces *s*.	Jas 1.3
and self-control with *s*, and	2Pet 1.6

STEADFAST LOVE

show *s*. .to my master Abraham	Gen 24.12
I am not worthy of. .all the *s*. .	32.10
the LORD. .showed him *s*. .,	39.21
LORD. .keeping *s*. .for thousands,	Ex 34.7
for his *s*. .endures for ever!	1Chr 16.34
for his *s*. .endures for ever."	2Chr 7.3
who extended to me his *s*. .	Ezra 7.28
Wondrously show thy *s*. .,	Ps 17.7
mercy, O LORD, and of thy *s*. .,	25.6
according to thy *s*. .remember me,	25.7
For thy *s*. .is before my eyes,	26.3
How precious is thy *s*. ., O God!	36.7
I have not concealed thy *s*. .	40.10
thy *s*. .is better than life,	63.3
Answer me. .for thy *s*. .is good;	69.16
Has his *s*. .for ever ceased?	77.8
S. .and faithfulness will meet;	85.10
thy *s*. .was established for ever,	89.2
declare thy *s*. .in the morning,	92.2
his *s*. .endures for ever.	100.5
s. .of the LORD is. .everlasting	103.17
thank the LORD for his *s*. .,	107.8
consider the *s*. .of the LORD.	107.43
his *s*. .endures for ever.	118.1
in thy *s*. .spare my life,	119.88
for his *s*. .endures for ever.	136.1
recount the *s*. .of the LORD,	Isa 63.7
taken away. .my *s*. .and mercy.	Jer 16.5
s. .of the LORD never ceases,	Lam 3.22
I desire *s*. .and not sacrifice,	Hos 6.6

STEAL — S

why did you *s* my gods?"	Gen 31.30
"You shall not *s*.	Ex 20.15
" 'Neither shall you *s*.	Deut 5.19
Will you *s*, murder, commit	Jer 7.9
thieves do not break in and *s*.	Mt 6.20
You shall not *s*, You shall not	19.18
Let the thief no longer *s*,	Eph 4.28
"If a man *s* an ox or a sheep,	Ex 22.1
he *s* to satisfy his appetite	Prov 6.30

STEEP

herd rushed down the *s* bank	Mt 8.32

STEP — S

a *s* between me and death."	1Sam 20.3
shadow. .or go back ten *s*?"	2Ki 20.9
thou wouldest number my *s*,	Job 14.16
His strong *s* are shortened	18.7
ways and number all my *s*?	31.4
wide place for my *s* under me,	Ps 18.36
The *s* of a man. .from the LORD,	37.23
nor have our *s* departed from	44.18

my *s* had well nigh slipped.	. 73.2
Keep steady my *s* according	119.133
but the LORD directs his *s*.	Prov 16.9
man's *s* are ordered by the LORD;	20.24
dial of Ahaz turn back ten *s*."	Isa 38.7
not in man. .to direct his *s*.	Jer 10.23
Men dogged our *s* so that we	Lam 4.18
Did we not take the same *s*?	2Cor 12.18

STEPHEN

they chose *S*, a man full of	Acts 6.5
arose and disputed with *S*.	6.9
as they were stoning *S*, he	7.59
Devout men buried *S*, and made	8.2
persecution. .arose over *S*	11.19
the blood of *S* thy witness	22.20

STEWARD — S

of the vineyard said to his *s*,	Mt 20.8
is the faithful and wise *s*,	Lk 12.42
a rich man who had a *s*,	16.1
and *s* of the mysteries of God.	1Cor 4.1

STEWARDSHIP

Turn in the account of your *s*,	Lk 16.2
s of God's grace that was given	Eph 3.2

STICK — S

take a *s* and write on it,	Ezek 37.16
gathering *s* on the sabbath	Num 15.32
there is a friend who *s* closer	Prov 18.24

STIFF-NECKED

for you are a *s* people."	Ex 33.3
Do not now be *s* as your	2Chr 30.8
"You *s* people, uncircumcised	Acts 7.51

STILL

And the sun stood *s*, and	Josh 10.13
after the fire a *s* small voice.	1Ki 19.12
Be *s* before the LORD, and wait	Ps 37.7
"Be *s*, and know that I am God.	46.10
he made the storm be *s*, and	107.29

STING — S

O death, where is thy *s*?"	1Cor 15.55
tails like scorpions, and *s*,	Rev 9.10

STIR — S — RED

s up one another to love and	Heb 10.24
A greedy man *s* up strife,	Prov 28.25
"He *s* up the people, teaching	Lk 23.5
every one whose heart *s* him,	Ex 35.21
LORD *s* up. .spirit of Cyrus	2Chr 36.22
the LORD *s* up the spirit of	Hag 1.14
they *s* up the people and the	Acts 6.12
your zeal. .*s* up most of them.	2Cor 9.2

STOCKS

puttest my feet in the *s*,	Job 13.27
prophet, and put him in the *s*	Jer 20.2
fastened their feet in the *s*.	Acts 16.24

STOLE — N

Absalom *s* the hearts of the	2Sam 15.6
have men of Judah *s* you away,	19.41

STOMACH

into. .mouth passes into. .*s*,	Mt 15.17
enters, not his heart but. .*s*,	Mk 7.19
for the *s* and the *s* for food"	1Cor 6.13
wine for the sake of your *s*	1Tim 5.23

STONE — D — ING (v)

let all the congregation *s*	Lev 24.14
congregation said to *s* them	Num 14.10
You shall *s* him to death	Deut 13.10
city shall *s* him to death,	21.21
Moses commanded us to *s* such.	Jn 8.5*n*

STONE — D — ING (v) (cont.)

Jews took up stones again to s	Jn 10.31
congregation..s him to death	Num 15.36
And all Israel s him with	Josh 7.25
out of the city and s him;	Acts 7.58
with rods; once I was s.	2Cor 11.25
killing the prophets and s	Mt 23.37

STONE — S — ING (n)

wrote..upon two tables of s,	Deut 5.22
'Hew two tables of s like the first,	10.1
he took a great s, and set	Josh 24.26
The great s, beside which	1Sam 6.18
Samuel took a s and set it up	7.12
him, and he became as a s.	25.37
The s..the builders rejected	Ps 118.22
s is heavy,..sand is weighty,	Prov 27.3
a foundation a s, a tested s,	Isa 28.16
to a s, 'You gave me birth.'	Jer 2.27
the s that struck the image	Dan 2.35
s will cry out from the well,	Hab 2.11
for bread, will give him a s?	Mt 7.9
s which the builders rejected	21.42
who falls on this s will be	21.44n
not be left here one s upon	24.2
sealing the s and setting a guard.	27.66
s which the builders rejected	Mk 12.10
will not be left here one s	13.2
saw that the s was rolled back;	16.4
command this s to become bread."	Lk 4.3
a loaf, will give him a s;	11.11n
s which the builders rejected	20.17
shall not be left here one s	21.6
they found the s rolled away	24.2
Jesus said, "Take away the s."	Jn 11.39
saw that the s had been taken	20.1
is the s which was rejected	Acts 4.11
not on tablets of s but on	2Cor 3.3
Behold, I am laying in Zion a s,	1Pet 2.6
you engrave the two s with	Ex 28.11
'What do those s mean to you?'	Josh 4.6
and chose five smooth s	1Sam 17.40
able from these s to raise up	Lk 3.8
the very s would cry out."	19.40
So they took up s to throw	Jn 8.59
the people spoke of s him,	1Sam 30.6

STONY

I will take the s heart out	Ezek 11.19

STOOD

still s before the LORD.	Gen 18.22
And he s between the dead	Num 16.48
And the sun s still, and	Josh 10.13
he opened it all the people s.	Neh 8.5

STOOL

till I make thy enemies a s	Lk 20.43
make thy enemies a s for thy	Acts 2.35
enemies should be made a s	Heb 10.13

STOPPED

the mouths of liars will be s.	Ps 63.11
that every mouth may be s,	Rom 3.19

STORED

And Joseph s up grain	Gen 41.49
heavens..earth..s up for fire,	2Pet 3.7

STOREHOUSE — S

Bring..tithes into the s,	Mal 3.10
Joseph opened all the s,	Gen 41.56
entered the s of the snow,	Job 38.22
bottle; he put the deeps in s.	Ps 33.7
all that was found in his s.	Isa 39.2
brings..the wind from his s.	Jer 10.13

STORK

are an abomination:..the s	Lev 11.19
the s in the heavens knows	Jer 8.7

STORM

he made the s be still, and	Ps 107.29
the s of the LORD! Wrath has	Jer 23.19
arose a great s on the sea,	Mt 8.24
And a great s of wind arose,	Mk 4.37

STRAIGHT

and he will make s your paths.	Prov 3.6
blameless keeps his way s,	11.5
make s what he..made crooked	Ecc 7.13
I will make s all his ways;	Isa 45.13
go to the street called S,	Acts 9.11

STRAIGHTFORWARD

not s about the truth of the	Gal 2.14

STRAINING

blind guides, s out a gnat	Mt 23.34
s forward to what lies ahead,	Phil 3.13

STRANGE

forth our hands to a s god,	Ps 44.20
s lips..with an alien tongue	Isa 28.11

STRANGER — S

"I am a s and a sojourner	Gen 23.4
"You shall not oppress a s;	Ex 23.9
The s who sojourns with you	Lev 19.34
gleanings..leave..for the s:	23.22
one law..for you and..the s	Num 15.16
become a s to my brethren,	Ps 69.8
why shouldst thou be like a s	Jer 14.8
I was a s and you welcomed me,	Mt 25.35
we are s before thee, and	1Chr 29.15
inheritance..turned over to s,	Lam 5.2
s..never again pass through	Joel 3.17
s to the covenants of promise,	Eph 2.12

STRAW

no longer give the people s	Ex 5.7
That they are like s before	Job 21.18
has s in common with wheat?	Jer 23.28

STREAMS

like a tree planted by s of water,	Ps 1.3
As a hart longs for flowing s,	42.1
My eyes shed s of tears,	119.136
s of water in a dry place,	Isa 32.2
break forth..s in the desert;	35.6

STREET — S

go to the s called Straight,	Acts 9.11
cast..out like..mire of the s.	Ps 18.42

STRENGTH

The LORD is my s and my song,	Ex 15.2
but now our s is dried up,	Num 11.6
days, so shall your s be.	Deut 33.25
wherein your great s lies,	Judg 16.6
thou didst gird me with s	2Sam 22.40
What is my s, that I should	Job 6.11
contest of s, behold him!	9.19
His s is hunger-bitten,	18.12
God who girded me with s,	Ps 18.32
In thy s the king rejoices, O	21.1
ascribe to the LORD glory and s.	29.1
May the LORD give s to his	29.11
show thy s, O God, thou who	68.28
God is the s of my heart and	73.26
Sing aloud to God our s; shout	81.1
Blessed..whose s is in thee,	84.5
s and beauty..in his sanctuary.	96.6
broken my s in mid-course;	102.23
Seek the LORD and his s,	105.4

STRENGTH (cont.)

LORD is my s and my song;	Ps 118.14
Wisdom gives s to the wise	Ecc 7.19
feast at the proper time, for s,	10.17
"By the s of my hand I have	Isa 10.13
in trust shall be your s."	30.15
lift up your voice with s,	40.9
my God has become my s—	49.5
put on s, O arm of the LORD;	51.9
awake, put on your s, O Zion;	52.1
LORD, my s and my stronghold,	Jer 16.19
GOD, the Lord, is my s;	Hab 3.19
He has shown s with his arm,	Lk 1.51
praying that you may have s	21.36
not..tempted beyond your s,	1Cor 10.13
and in the s of his might.	Eph 5.10
by the s which God supplies;	1Pet 4.11

STRENGTHEN — S — ED — ING

I could s you with my mouth,	Job 16.5
my arm also shall s him.	Ps 89.21
S the weak hands,..make firm	Isa 35.3
I will s you, I will help you,	41.10
lengthen..cords and s..stakes.	54.2
and I will s the weak, and	Ezek 34.16
"I will s the house of Judah,	Zech 10.6
to him who is able to s you	Rom 16.25
restore, establish, and s you.	1Pet 5.10
Awake, and s what remains	Rev 3.2
all things in him who s me.	Phil 4.13
and s his hand in God.	1Sam 23.16
David s himself in the LORD	30.6
they s their hands for the	Neh 2.18
you have s the weak hands.	Job 4.3
a man touched me and s me.	Dan 10.18
that..he may grant you to be s	Eph 3.16
May you be s with all power,	Col 1.11
Cilicia, s the churches.	Acts 15.41
s all the disciples.	18.23

STRETCH — ES — ED

let Ethiopia..s out her hands	Ps 68.31
to the man, "S out your hand."	Mt 12.13
Zion s out her hands, but	Lam 1.17
he s himself upon the child	1Ki 17.21
who alone s out the heavens,	Job 9.8
s out the heavens like a tent,	Ps 104.2

STRIFE

s between the herdsmen	Gen 13.7
see violence and s in the city.	Ps 55.9
the heedless make s, but	Prov 13.10
house full of feasting with s.	17.1
The beginning of s is like	17.14
A fool's lips bring s, and	18.6
A greedy man stirs up s,	28.25
A man of wrath stirs up s,	29.22
pressing anger produces s.	30.33
jealousy and s among you,	1Cor 3.3

STRIKE — S

Let a good man s or rebuke me	Ps 141.5
'I will s the shepherd, and	Mk 14.27
or puts on airs, or s you	2Cor 11.20

STRIP — PED

not s your vineyard bare,	Lev 19.10
Moses s Aaron of..garments,	Num 20.28
He has s from me my glory,	Job 19.9
for plunderers have s them	Nah 2.2

STRIVE — N — ING

who keep the law s against	Prov 28.4
those who s..shall perish.	Isa 41.11
"S to enter by..narrow door;	Lk 13.24

s to excel in building up	1Cor 14.12
how greatly I s for you,	Col 2.1
S for peace with all men,	Heb 12.14
name..Israel, for you have s	Gen 32.28
with one mind s side by side	Phil 1.27

STRONG — ER

Out of the s came..sweet."	Judg 14.14
though Judah became s among	1Chr 5.2
"Be s and of good courage,	28.20
he was s, he grew proud,	2Chr 26.16
Wait for the LORD; be s,	Ps 27.14
my s deliverer,..covered my	140.7
nor the battle to the s, nor	Ecc 9.11
can one enter a s man's house	Mt 12.29
When a s man,..guards his	Lk 11.21
s ought to bear with..weak,	Rom 15.1
God chose..to shame the s,	1Cor 1.27
Finally, be s in the Lord	Eph 5.10
my son, be s in the grace	2Tim 2.1
young men, because you are s,	1Jn 2.14
and David grew s and s,	2Sam 3.1
not able to dispute with one s	Ecc 6.10
weakness of God is s than men.	1Cor 1.25

STRONGHOLD

LORD is a s for the oppressed,	Ps 9.9
horn of my salvation, my s.	18.2
The LORD is the s of my life;	27.1
the LORD has become my s,	94.22
thou hast been a s to..poor,	Isa 25.4
a s to the people of Israel.	Joel 3.16
a s in the day of trouble;	Nah 1.7

STRUCK

and s the rock with his rod	Num 20.11
And the LORD s the child	2Sam 12.15
"They s me," you will say,	Prov 23.35
s the slave of the high priest	Lk 22.50
officers standing by s Jesus	Jn 18.22

STRUGGLE

In your s against sin you	Heb 12.4

STUBBLE

Egypt, to gather s for straw.	Ex 5.12
like s, the fire consumes	Isa 47.14
and all evildoers will be s;	Mal 4.1
stones, wood, hay, s—	1Cor 3.12

STUBBORN — NESS

for you are a s people.	Deut 9.6
practices or their s ways.	Judg 2.19
would not listen, but were s,	2Ki 17.14
gave them over to..s hearts,	Ps 81.12
Israel are..of a s heart.	Ezek 3.7
I walk in the s of my heart.'	Deut 29.19
s..as iniquity and idolatry.	1Sam 15.23

STUDY

s is a weariness of the flesh.	Ecc 12.12

STUMBLE — D

and your foot will not s.	Prov 3.23
not know over what they s.	4.19
feet s on..twilight mountains,	Jer 13.16
my persecutors will s, they	20.11
The proud one shall s and fall,	50.32
walks in the day, he does not s,	Jn 11.9
that makes your brother s.	Rom 14.21
For Jerusalem has s, and Judah	Isa 3.8
s over the stumbling stone,	Rom 9.32
have they s so as to fall?	11.11

STUMBLING BLOCK — S

decide never to put a s..or	Rom 14.13
Christ crucified, a s..to Jews	1Cor 1.23

STUMBLING BLOCK — S (cont.)
become a s..to the weak.   1Cor 8.9
the s..of the cross has been   Gal 5.11
who taught Balak to put a s..   Rev 2.14
lay before this people s..   Jer 6.21

SUBDUE — D
fill the earth and s it;   Gen 1.28
I would soon s their enemies,   Ps 81.14
no one had..strength to s him.   Mk 5.4
He s peoples under us, and   Ps 47.3

SUBJECT — ED
Israel, and became s to   2Sam 10.19
David, and became s to him.   1Chr 19.19
demons..s to us in your name!"   Lk 10.17
s to..governing authorities.   Rom 13.1
spirits of prophets are s   1Cor 14.32
Wives, be s to your husbands,   Eph 5.22
Wives, be s to your husbands,   Col 3.18
Be s for the Lord's sake to   1Pet 2.13
Son himself will also be s   1Cor 15.28

SUBMISSIVE
Bid slaves to be s to..masters   Tit 2.9
Remind them to be s to rulers   3.1
wives, be s to your husbands,   1Pet 3.1

SUBORDINATE
women..should be s, as even   1Cor 14.34

SUBSTANCE
Honor the LORD with your s   Prov 3.9

SUCCEED — ED
do many things and will s   1Sam 26.25
you may s in building the   1Chr 22.11
none of his offspring shall s   Jer 22.30
fight..you shall not s'?"   32.5
a large army. Will he s?   Ezek 17.15
himself against him, and s?—   Job 9.4

SUCCESS — FUL
then you shall have good s.   Josh 1.8
David had more s than all   1Sam 18.30
Joseph,..became a s man;   Gen 39.2

SUFFER — S — ED — ING (v)
I s from those who hate me,   Ps 9.13
simple go on, and s for it.   Prov 27.12
So also the Son of man will s   Mt 17.12
that the Son of man must s   Mk 8.31
Son of man must s many things,   Lk 9.22
first he must s many things   17.25
necessary that the Christ..s   24.26
written, that..Christ should s   24.46
that his Christ should s,   Acts 3.18
counted worthy to s dishonor   5.41
that the Christ must s, and   26.23
heirs..provided we s with him   Rom 8.17
one member suffers, all s   1Cor 12.26
but also s for his sake,   Phil 1.29
none of you s as a murderer,   1Pet 4.15
epileptic and he s terribly;   Mt 17.15
I have s much over him today   27.19
For his sake I have s the loss   Phil 3.8
but though we had already s   1Thess 2.2
he..has s and been tempted,   Heb 2.18
because Christ also s for you,   1Pet 2.21
he s, he did not threaten;   2.23
Christ s in the flesh, arm   4.1
over what I am s for you,   Eph 3.13

SUFFERING — S (n)
knowing..s produces endurance   Rom 5.3

s as a good soldier of Christ   2Tim 2.3
taskmasters; I know their s,   Ex 3.7
I rejoice in my s for your sake,   Col 1.24

SUFFICIENT
Let the day's own trouble be s   Mt 6.34
Not..s of ourselves to claim   2Cor 3.5
"My grace is s for you, for   12.9

SUMMER
earth remains,..s..not cease."   Gen 8.22
Like snow in s or rain in   Prov 26.1
s is ended, and we are not   Jer 8.20

SUN
"S, stand thou still at   Josh 10.12
he has set a tent for the s,   Ps 19.4
LORD God is a s and shield;   84.11
From the rising of the s to   113.3
is nothing new under the s.   Ecc 1.9
the s will be dark at..rising   Isa 13.10
LORD,..gives the s for light   Jer 31.35
cover the s with a cloud,   Ezek 32.7
s shall be turned to darkness,   Joel 2.31
make the s go down at noon,   Amos 8.9
The s and moon stood still   Hab 3.11
s of righteousness shall rise,   Mal 4.2
his s rise on..evil and..good   Mt 5.45
the s will be darkened, and   24.29
the s..turned into darkness   Acts 2.20
There is one glory of the s,   1Cor 15.41
do not let the s go down on   Eph 4.26

SUPERNATURAL
all ate the same s food   1Cor 10.3

SUPPER
likewise the cup after s,   Lk 22.20n
during the s, when the devil   Jn 13.2
it is not the Lord's s that   1Cor 11.20

SUPPLICATION — S
If you will seek God and make s   Job 8.5
Hear the voice of my s, as I   Ps 28.2
They will make s to you,   Isa 45.14
"Let our s come before you,   Jer 42.2
LORD heeded s for the land,   2Sam 24.25
he has heard the voice of my s.   Ps 28.6

SUPPLY
their abundance..s your want,   2Cor 8.14
my God will s every need of   Phil 4.19

SUPPORT
land could not s both of them   Gen 13.6
Those who s Egypt shall fall,   Ezek 30.6
by accepting s from them   2Cor 11.8
So we ought to s such men,   3Jn 8

SURE
I am s that neither death,   Rom 8.38
I am s that he who began   Phil 1.6
we feel s of better things   Heb 6.9
we may be s that we know him,   1Jn 2.3

SURROUND — ED
"Master, the multitudes s you   Lk 8.45
all the people..s the house;   Gen 19.4
They s me, s me on every   Ps 118.11
since we are s by so great   Heb 12.1

SURVIVORS
"The s..who escaped exile   Neh 1.3
among the s shall be those   Joel 2.32

SUSA
I was in S the capital,   Neh 1.1
royal throne in S the capital,   Est 1.2

SUSA (cont.)
a Jew in *S* the capital whose	Est 2.5
the city of *S* shouted and	8.15
the Jews who were in *S*	9.18

SUSPENSE
"How long will you keep us in *s*?	Jn 10.24

SUSTAIN
s them in the wilderness,	Neh 9.21
the LORD, and he will *s* you;	Ps 55.22
Christ; . . will *s* you to the end,	1Cor 1.8

SWADDLING
wrapped him in *s* cloths, and	Lk 2.7

SWALLOW — S — ED (v)
He will *s* up death for ever,	Isa 25.8
a great fish to *s* up Jonah;	Jonah 1.17
and *s* them up, with all	Num 16.30
not say, "We have *s* him up."	Ps 35.25
"Death is *s* up in victory."	1Cor 15.54
what is mortal may be *s* up	2Cor 5.4

SWALLOW (n)
Like a *s* or a crane I clamor,	Isa 38.14
the turtledove, *s*, and crane	Jer 8.7

SWARMING (adj)
"Every *s* thing. . abomination;	Lev 11.41

SWARMS (n)
"Let the waters bring forth *s*	Gen 1.20
I will send *s* of flies on you	Ex 8.21

SWEAR — S
make you *s* by the LORD,	Gen 24.3
any. . rash oath that men *s*,	Lev 5.4
not *s* by my name falsely,	19.12
who *s* by the name of the LORD,	Isa 48.1
if you *s*, 'As the LORD lives,'	Jer 4.2
I *s* by myself, says the LORD,	22.5
Do not *s* at all, either by	Mt 5.34
do not *s*, either by heaven	Jas 5.12
who *s* to his own hurt and	Ps 15.4
every one who *s* falsely shall	Zech 5.3
s by the gold of the temple,	Mt 23.16

SWEAT
in the *s* of your face	Gen 3.19
his *s* became like great drops	Lk 22.44

SWEET
strong came something *s*."	Judg 14.14
David, . . the *s* psalmist of	2Sam 23.1
How *s* are thy words to my	Ps 119.103

SWEPT
I have *s* away your. . sins like	Isa 44.22
empty, *s*, and put in order.	Mt 12.44

SWIFT
the race is not to the *s*, nor	Ecc 9.11

SWINE — 'S
s, because it parts the hoof	Lev 11.7
send us. . into the herd of *s*."	Mt 8.31
"Send us to the *s*, let us enter	Mk 5.12
herd of *s* was feeding there	Lk 8.32
into his fields to feed *s*.	15.15
a gold ring in a *s* snout	Prov 11.22

SWORD — S
flaming *s* which turned	Gen 3.24
the *s* of Gideon the son of	Judg 7.14
"A *s* for the LORD and for	7.20
king said, "Bring me a *s*."	1Ki 3.24
He made my mouth like a. . *s*,	Isa 49.2
I will send the *s* after them,	Jer 9.16

because of. . *s* of the oppressor,	25.38
a *s* is sharpened and. . polished,	Ezek 21.9
O *s*, against my shepherd,	Zech 13.7
not. . to bring peace, but a *s*.	Mt 10.34
drew his *s*, and struck the slave	26.51
his *s*, and struck the slave	Mk 14.47
a *s* will pierce through your	Lk 2.35
and the *s* of the Spirit,	Eph 6.17
sharper than any two-edged *s*,	Heb 4.12
issued a sharp two-edged *s*,	Rev 1.16
his mouth issues a sharp *s*	19.15
beat their *s* into plowshares,	Isa 2.4
Beat your plowshares into *s*,	Joel 3.10
beat their *s* into plowshares,	Mic 4.3

SWORE — N
which he *s* to your fathers,	Deut 6.10
LORD has *s* and will not change	Ps 110.4
LORD has *s* by his right hand	Isa 62.8
I have *s* by my great name,	Jer 44.26
GOD has *s* by his holiness	Amos 4.2
to the Lord what you have *s*.'	Mt 5.33

SYCAMORE
and a dresser of *s* trees,	Amos 7.14
climbed up into a *s* tree to see	Lk 19.4

SYCHAR
a city of Samaria, called *S*,	Jn 4.5

SYMPATHY
showed. . *s* and comforted him	Job 42.11
all of you have unity of spirit, *s*,	1Pet 3.8

SYNAGOGUE
house of the ruler of the *s*,	Mk 5.38
he began to teach in the *s*;	6.2
nation, and he built us our *s*."	Lk 7.5
Jairus. . a ruler of the *s*;	8.41
he argued in the *s* every	Acts 18.4
And he entered the *s* and	19.8

SYRIA
commander of the army of. . *S*,	2Ki 5.1
For the head of *S* is Damascus,	Isa 7.8
fame spread throughout all *S*,	Mt 4.24
Quirinius was governor of *S*.	Lk 2.2
went through *S* and Cilicia,	Acts 15.41

SYRIANS
the *S* came no more on raids	2Ki 6.23
Caphtor and the *S* from Kir?	Amos 9.7

T

TABERNACLE — S
pattern of. . *t*, and. . furniture,	Ex 25.9
erect the *t* according to the plan	26.30
erect the *t* of the tent of meeting	40.2
Jews' feast of *T* was at hand.	Jn 7.2

TABLE — S
make a *t* of acacia wood;	Ex 25.23
made the *t* of acacia wood;	37.10
put there for him a bed, a *t*,	2Ki 4.10
Thou preparest a *t* before me	Ps 23.5
their own *t*. . become a snare;	69.22
"Can God spread a *t* in the	78.19
that the LORD's *t* is polluted,	Mal 1.12
partake of the *t* of the Lord	1Cor 10.21
two *t* of the testimony,	Ex 31.18
"Cut two *t* of stone like	34.1
two *t* of stone written	Deut 9.10
give up preaching. . to serve *t*.	Acts 6.2

TABLET — S

"Take a large *t* and write upon	Isa 8.1
he asked for a writing *t*, and	Lk 1.63
but on *t* of human hearts.	2Cor 3.3

TAKE — S — N

that they *t* for me an offering;	Ex 25.2
T my instruction instead of	Prov 8.10
"*T*, eat; this is my body."	Mt 26.26
said, "*T*; this is my body."	Mk 14.22
glad to *t* him into the boat,	Jn 6.21
I will come again and will *t* you	14.3
lawlessness *t* away lives.	Prov 11.30
any one *t* away from the words	Rev 22.19
"Thou hast *t* up my cause, O	Lam 3.58
found, because God had *t* him.	Heb 11.5

TALE

seemed to them an idle *t*,	Lk 24.11

TALEBEARER

a *t* reveals secrets, but	Prov 11.13

TALENTS

who owed him ten thousand *t*,	Mt 18.24
to one he gave five *t*,	25.15

TALK — ED — ING (v)

my tongue will *t* of thy..help	Ps 71.24
began to *t* freely about it,	Mk 1.45
the angel who *t* with me said	Zech 1.14
Paul *t* with them, intending	Acts 20.7
While they were *t*..Jesus	Lk 24.15

TALK (n)

man full of *t* be vindicated?	Job 11.2
"Should he argue in unprofitable *t*,	15.3
put devious *t* far from you.	Prov 4.24

TAME

no human being can *t* the tongue	Jas 3.8

TAMPER

or to *t* with God's word,	2Cor 4.2

TARSHISH

The sons of Javan:..*T*,	Gen 10.4
the king's ships went to *T*	2Chr 9.21
building ships to go to *T*,	20.36
didst shatter the ships of *T*.	Ps 48.7
kings of *T*..render him tribute,	72.10
Wail, O ships of *T*, for your	Isa 23.14
Jonah rose to flee to *T*	Jonah 1.3

TARSUS

for a man of *T* named Saul;	Acts 9.11
went to *T* to look for Saul;	11.25
"I am a Jew, from *T* in Cilicia,	21.39

TASKMASTERS

t over them to afflict them	Ex 1.11
Pharaoh commanded the *t*	5.6

TASTE — D (v)

O *t* and see..the LORD is good!	Ps 34.8
not *t* death before they see	Mt 16.28
not *t* death before they see	Mk 9.1
some..who will not *t* death	Lk 9.27
to *t* no food till we have	Acts 23.14
Do not *t*, Do not touch"	Col 2.21
he might *t* death for every one.	Heb 2.9
who have *t* the heavenly gift,	6.4
t the kindness of the Lord	1Pet 2.3

TASTE (n)

is there any *t* in the slime	Job 6.6
but if salt has lost its *t*,	Mt 5.13

TAUGHT

Behold, I have *t* you statutes	Deut 4.5
they *t* in Judah, having	2Chr 17.9
I have *t* you..of wisdom;	Prov 4.11
tongue of those who are *t*,	Isa 50.4
I have *t* them persistently	Jer 32.33
he *t*..as one who had authority,	Mt 7.29
he *t* them in their synagogue,	13.54
he *t*..as one who had authority,	Mk 1.22
t them many things in parables,	4.2
he *t* in their synagogues,	Lk 4.15
they shall all be *t* by God.'	Jn 6.45
he spoke and *t* accurately	Acts 18.25
Let him who is *t* the word share	Gal 6.6
about him and were *t* in him,	Eph 4.21

TAUNT (v)

my adversaries *t* me,.."Where	Ps 42.10
All the day my enemies *t* me,	102.8

TAUNT (n)

Thou hast made us the *t* of	Ps 44.13
t against the king of Babylon:	Isa 14.4
take up their *t* against him,	Hab 2.6

TAX — ES

Matthew sitting at the *t* office;	Mt 9.9
"Does..your teacher pay the *t*?"	17.24
Levi..sitting at the *t* office,	Mk 2.14
Levi, sitting at the *t* office;	Lk 5.27
Is it lawful to pay *t* to Caesar,	Mt 22.17
lawful to pay *t* to Caesar,	Mk 12.14
same reason you also pay *t*,	Rom 13.6

TEACH — ES — ING (v)

t you what you shall speak."	Ex 4.12
you shall *t* them the statutes	18.20
you..*t* the people of Israel	Lev 10.11
ordinances which I *t* you,	Deut 4.1
may *t* their children so.'	4.10
which you shall *t* them,	5.31
you shall *t* them diligently	6.7
t them to your children,	11.19
that they may not *t* you	20.18
write this song, and *t* it	31.19
t Jacob thy ordinances,	33.10
come again to us, and *t* us	Judg 13.8
and to *t* his statutes and	Ezra 7.10
ask the beasts,..they will *t*	Job 12.7
Will any *t* God knowledge,	21.22
ways. O LORD; *t* me thy paths.	Ps 25.4
T me thy way, O LORD; and lead	27.11
I will *t* you the fear of the LORD.	34.11
T me thy way, O LORD, that I	86.11
So *t* us to number our days	90.12
O LORD; *t* me thy statutes!	119.12
T me,..the way of thy statutes;	119.33
T me to do thy will, for thou	143.10
t a righteous man and he will	Prov 9.9
that he may *t* us his ways	Isa 2.3
"Whom will he *t* knowledge,	28.9
no longer shall each man *t*	Jer 31.34
t my people the difference	Ezek 44.23
t them the letters and language	Dan 1.4
its priests *t* for hire,	Mic 3.11
that he may *t* us his ways	4.2
on the sabbath he began to *t*	Mk 6.2
to *t* them that the Son of man	8.31
"Lord, *t* us to pray, as John	Lk 11.1
the Holy Spirit will *t* you	12.12
Holy Spirit,..will *t* you all	Jn 14.26
that Jesus began to do and *t*,	Acts 1.1
not to speak or *t* at all in	4.18
will you not *t* yourself?	Rom 2.21
as you *t* and admonish one	Col 3.16

TEACH — ES — ING (v) (cont.)

I permit no woman to *t* or   1Tim 2.12
they shall not *t* every one   Heb 8.11
He who *t* men knowledge, the   Ps 94.10
If any one *t* otherwise and   1Tim 6.3
as his anointing *t* you about   1Jn 2.27
and without a *t* priest,   2Chr 15.3
he went about all Galilee, *t*   Mt 4.23
he was *t* his disciples, saying   Mk 9.31
I was with you in the temple *t*,   14.49
he was *t* them on the sabbath;   Lk 4.31
men. .you put in prison are. .*t*   Acts 5.25
in Antioch, *t* and preaching   15.35
This is the man who is *t*   21.28

TEACHER — S

God. .who is a *t* like him?   Job 36.22
your eyes shall see your *T*.   Isa 30.20
disciple is not above his *t*,   Mt 10.24
"Does not your *t* pay the tax?"   17.24
not. .rabbi, for you have one *t*,   23.8
'The *T* says, My time is at hand;   26.18
Why trouble the *T* any further?"   Mk 5.35
A disciple is not above his *t*,   Lk 6.40
"The *T* is here and is calling   Jn 11.28
"Rabboni!" (which means *T*).   20.16
more understanding than. .*t*,   Ps 119.99
Pharisees and *t* of the law   Lk 5.17
some pastors and *t*,   Eph 4.11
desiring to be *t* of the law,   1Tim 1.7

TEACHING (n)

May my *t* drop as the rain,   Deut 32.2
reject not your mother's *t*;   Prov 1.8
The *t* of the wise is a fountain   13.14
beware of. .*t* of the Pharisees   Mt 16.12
they were astonished at his *t*,   Lk 4.32
"My *t* is not mine, but his   Jn 7.16
about his disciples and his *t*.   18.19
devoted. .to the apostles' *t*   Acts 2.42
filled Jerusalem with your *t*   5.28
they did not cease *t* and   5.42
"May we know what this new *t* is   17.19
obedient. .to the standard of *t*   Rom 6.17
attend. .to preaching, to *t*.   1Tim 4.13
who labor in preaching and *t*,   5.17
t which accords with godliness,   6.3
Now you have observed my *t*,   2Tim 3.10
profitable for *t*, for reproof,   3.16

TEAR — S

God will wipe away every *t*   Rev 7.17
he will wipe away every *t*   21.4
My *t* have been my food day   Ps 42.3
put thou my *t* in thy bottle!   56.8
Lord GOD will wipe away *t*   Isa 25.8
heard your prayer,. .seen your *t*; 38.5
I wrote you. .with many *t*,   2Cor 2.4

TEETH

escaped by the skin of my *t*.   Job 19.20
Your *t*. .like a flock of ewes   Sol 4.2
children's *t* are set on edge'?   Ezek 18.2

TEKOA

Joab sent to *T*, and fetched   2Sam 14.2
into the wilderness of *T*;   2Chr 20.20
Blow the trumpet in *T*, and   Jer 6.1
among the shepherds of *T*,   Amos 1.1

TELL

t the rock. .to yield. .water   Num 20.8
T it not in Gath, publish it   2Sam 1.20
t of all his wonderful works!   Ps 105.2

T us the former things, what   Isa 41.22
will *t* you great and hidden   Jer 33.3
Jeremiah said. ."If I *t* you,   38.15
go quickly and *t* his disciples   Mt 28.7
go, *t* his disciples and Peter   Mk 16.7

TEMPER

quick *t* acts foolishly,   Prov 14.17

TEMPEST

the *t* passes, the wicked is   Prov 10.25
great *t* has come upon you."   Jonah 1.12

TEMPESTUOUS

For the sea grew more. .*t*.   Jonah 1.11
soon a *t* wind, called the   Acts 27.14

TEMPLE

The LORD is in his holy *t*,   Ps 11.4
in his *t* all cry, "Glory!"   29.9
God, in the midst of thy *t*.   48.9
be satisfied with. .thy holy *t*!   65.4
they have defiled thy holy *t*;   79.1
of the *t*, 'Your foundation   Isa 44.28
deceptive words:. .*t* of the LORD, Jer 7.4
glory of the LORD filled. .*t*.   Ezek 43.5
portray the *t*,. .arrangement,   43.11
appear and profane the *t* and   Dan 11.31
the LORD is in his holy *t*;   Hab 2.20
build the *t* of the LORD.   Zech 6.12
set him on. .pinnacle of the *t*,   Mt 4.5
Jesus entered the *t* of God   21.12
point out. .buildings of the *t*.   24.1
able to destroy the *t* of God,   26.61
"You who would destroy the *t*   27.40
he entered the *t* and began to   Mk 11.15
carry anything through the *t*.   11.16
say, 'I will destroy this *t*   14.58
You who would destroy the *t*   15.29
they found him in the *t*,   Lk 2.46
set him on. .pinnacle of the *t*,   4.9
"Two men went up into the *t*   18.10
entered. .*t* and began to drive   19.45
In the *t* he found those who   Jn 2.14
"Destroy this *t*, and in three   2.19
even tried to profane the *t*,   Acts 24.6
know that you are God's *t*   1Cor 3.16
your body is a *t* of the Holy   6.19
we are the *t* of. .living God;   2Cor 6.16
grows into a holy *t* in. .Lord;   Eph 2.21
"Rise and measure the *t* of God   Rev 11.1
God's *t* in heaven was opened,   11.19
the *t* was filled with smoke   15.8
its *t* is the Lord God the   21.22

TEMPT — ED

'You shall not *t* the Lord   Mt 4.7
'You shall not *t* the Lord   Lk 4.12
to *t* the Spirit of the Lord?   Acts 5.9
lest Satan *t* you through lack   1Cor 7.5
forty days, *t* by Satan; and   Mk 1.13
in the wilderness, *t* by. .devil.   Lk 4.2
able to help those who are *t*.   Heb 2.18
t as we are, yet without sinning. 4.15
Let no one say when he is *t*,   Jas 1.13

TEMPTATION — S

And lead us not into *t*, but   Mt 6.13
that you may not enter into *t*;   26.41
that you may not enter into *t*;   Mk 14.38
and in time of *t* fall away.   Lk 8.13
and lead us not into *t*."   11.4
No *t* has overtaken you that   1Cor 10.13
"*T* to sin are sure to come;   Lk 17.1

TEMPTER
And the *t* came and said to him,   Mt 4.3
fear that..the *t* had tempted   1Thess 3.5

TEN
Suppose *t* are found there."   Gen 18.32
that is, the *t* commandments   Deut 4.13
he was met by *t* lepers,   Lk 17.12

TENANTS
vineyard,..let it out to *t*,   Mt 21.33
tower, and let it out to *t*,   Mk 12.1
come and destroy those *t*,   Lk 20.16

TEND — ED
T the flock of God that is   1Pet 5.2
With upright heart he *t* them,   Ps 78.72

TENT — S
Bethel, and pitched his *t*,   Gen 12.8
place where his *t* had been   13.3
consecrate the *t* of meeting   Ex 29.44
called it the *t* of meeting.   33.7
spoke..from the *t* of meeting,   Lev 1.1
the *t* of meeting there;   Josh 18.1
ark of God dwells in a *t*."   2Sam 7.2
but the ark..is under a *t*."   1Chr 17.1
friendship of God..upon my *t*;   Job 29.4
who shall sojourn in thy *t*?   Ps 15.1
he has set a *t* for the sun,   19.4
t of the upright..flourish.   Prov 14.11
Jerusalem,..an immovable *t*,   Isa 33.20
spreads..like a *t* to dwell in;   40.22
My *t* is destroyed, and all   Jer 10.20
fathers had the *t* of witness   Acts 7.44
if the earthly *t* we live in   2Cor 5.1
Moses was about to erect the *t*,   Heb 8.5
temple of the *t* of witness   Rev 15.5
father of those who dwell in *t*   Gen 4.20

TENTH
And Abram gave him a *t*   Gen 14.20
I will give the *t* to thee."   28.22
every *t* animal..holy to..Lord   Lev 27.32
And though a *t* remain in it,   Isa 6.13
to him Abraham apportioned a *t*   Heb 7.2

TENT-MAKERS
for by trade they were *t*.   Acts 18.3

TERRIFY — IED
distress and anguish *t* him;   Job 15.24
and *t* them in his fury, saying,   Ps 2.5
the Almighty has *t* me;   Job 23.16
t, saying, "It is a ghost!"   Mt 14.26

TERROR
appoint over you sudden *t*,   Lev 26.16
not fear the *t* of the night,   Ps 91.5
from before the *t* of the Lord,   Isa 2.19
At evening time, behold, *t*!   17.14
for..healing, but behold, *t*,   Jer 8.15
will make you a *t* to yourself   20.4
He who flees..the *t* shall fall   48.44

TEST — S — ED — ING (v)
by them I may *t* Israel,   Judg 2.22
she came to *t* him with hard   1Ki 10.1
Let us *t* and examine our ways,   Lam 3.40
"*T* your servants for ten days;   Dan 1.12
sign from heaven, to *t* him.   Mk 8.11
to *t* him, sought from him a   Lk 11.16
This he said to *t* him, for   Jn 6.6
This they said to *t* him,   8.6n
T yourselves. Do you not   2Cor 13.5
let each one *t* his own work,   Gal 6.4

t everything; hold fast   1Thess 5.21
but *t* the spirits to see   1Jn 4.1
The Lord *t* the righteous and   Ps 11.5
God *t* Abraham, and said   Gen 22.1
By this you shall be *t*:   42.15
For thou, O God, hast *t* us;   Ps 66.10
They *t* God in their heart   78.18
t and rebelled against..God,   78.56
I *t* you at the waters of Meribah.   81.7
when your fathers *t* me, and   95.9
the word of the Lord *t* him   105.19
Pharisees came up..and *t* him   Mt 19.3
humble you, *t* you..to know   Deut 8.2
Lord your God is *t* you, to know   13.3

TEST — ING (n)
not put the Lord..to the *t*,   Deut 6.16
put God to *t* in the desert;   Ps 106.14
not put the Lord to the *t*."   Isa 7.12
put me to the *t*, says the Lord   Mal 3.10
but when they put God to the *t*   3.15
"Why put me to the *t*, you   Mt 22.18
"Why put me to the *t*? Bring   Mk 12.15
not put the Lord to the *t*,   1Cor 10.9
in a severe of affliction,   2Cor 8.2
the *t* of your faith produces   Jas 1.3

TESTIFY — ING — IES — IED
Here I am; *t* against me   1Sam 12.3
you own lips *t* against you.   Job 15.6
O Israel, I will *t* against you.   Ps 50.7
and our sins *t* against us;   Isa 59.12
our iniquities *t* against us,   Jer 14.7
things they *t* against you?"   Mt 27.13
I *t*..that its works are evil.   Jn 7.7
I affirm and *t* in the Lord,   Eph 4.17
we have seen and *t* that the   1Jn 4.14
Demetrius..I *t* to him too,   3Jn 12
t both to Jews and to Greeks   Acts 20.21
pride of Israel *t* to his face;   Hos 5.5
who *t* to these things says,   Rev 22.20
when they had *t* and spoken   Acts 8.25
and *t* to the truth of your life.   3Jn 3

TESTIMONY — IES
put into the ark the *t*   Ex 25.16
the *t* of the Lord is sure,   Ps 19.7
He established a *t* in Jacob,   78.5
Bind..the *t*, seal the teaching   Isa 8.16
preached..as..*t* to all nations;   Mt 24.14
whole council sought false *t*   26.59
shake off the dust..for a *t*   Mk 6.11
for my sake, to bear *t* before them.   13.9
council sought *t* against Jesus   14.55
dust from your feet as a *t*   Lk 9.5
a time for you to bear *t*.   21.13
"What further *t* do we need?   22.71
He came for *t*, to bear witness   Jn 1.7
believed..because of..woman's *t*,   4.39
said..your *t* is not true."   8.13
the *t* of two men is true;   8.17
the *t* to Christ was confirmed   1Cor 1.6
not..*t* of God in lofty words   2.1
the *t* of our conscience   2Cor 1.12
If we receive the *t* of men,   1Jn 5.9
on those who..bear *t* to Jesus.   Rev 12.17
the *t* of Jesus is the spirit   19.10
with this *t* for the churches.   22.16
they kept his *t*, and..statutes   Ps 99.7

THADDAEUS
the son of Alphaeus, and *T*;   Mt 10.3
T, and Simon the Cananaean,   Mk 3.18

THANK — ED (v)

Let them *t* the LORD for his	Ps 107.21
For Sheol cannot *t* thee,	Isa 38.18
Jesus declared, "I *t* thee,	Mt 11.25
"I *t* thee, Father, Lord of	Lk 10.21
Does he *t* the servant because	17.9
"Father, I *t* thee that thou	Jn 11.41
First, I *t* my God through Jesus	Rom 1.8
I *t*..God in all my remembrance	Phil 1.3
we also *t* God constantly	1Thess 2.13
seeing them Paul *t* God and	Acts 28.15

THANK OFFERING — S

offer with the *t*..unleavened	Lev 7.12
bring sacrifices and *t*..to	2Chr 29.31
I will render *t*..to thee.	Ps 56.12
bringing *t*..to the house of	Jer 17.26

THANKS (n)

and gave *t* to the LORD,	2Chr 7.3
who gave *t* stood in the house	Neh 12.40
give to the LORD the *t* due	Ps 7.17
I will give *t* to thee for ever.	30.12
We give *t* to thee, O God; we	75.1
It is good to give *t* to the LORD,	92.1
Give *t* to him, bless his name!	100.4
O give *t* to the LORD, for he	107.1
I give thee *t*, O LORD, with	138.1
"I will give *t* to thee, O	Isa 12.1
I give *t* and praise, for thou	Dan 2.23
having given *t* he broke them	Mt 15.36
at Jesus' feet, giving him *t*.	Lk 17.16
giving *t* to God in the	Acts 27.35
honor..God or give *t* to him,	Rom 1.21
But *t* be to God, that you	6.17
T be to God through Jesus	7.25
abstains..and gives *t* to God.	14.6
you may give *t* well enough,	1Cor 14.17
But *t* be to God, who gives	15.57
t be to God, who in Christ	2Cor 2.14
But *t* be to God who puts	8.16
not cease to give *t* for you,	Eph 1.16
giving *t* in the name of our LORD	5.20
giving *t* to God the Father	Col 3.17
give *t* in all circumstances;	1Thess 5.18
to give *t* to God always for	2Thess 1.3

THANKSGIVING

sacrifice of *t* to the LORD,	Lev 22.29
appointed that *t* be sung	1Chr 16.7
singing aloud a song of *t*,	Ps 26.7
Offer to God a sacrifice of *t*,	50.14
He who brings *t* as his sacrifice	50.23
I will magnify him with *t*.	69.30
to thee the sacrifice of *t*	116.17
t and the voice of song.	Isa 51.3
out of them..come songs of *t*,	Jer 30.19
offer a sacrifice of *t* of	Amos 4.5
what *t* can we render to God	1Thess 3.9
if it is received with *t*;	1Tim 4.4
glory and wisdom and *t* and	Rev 7.12

THESSALONICA

they came to *T*, where there	Acts 17.1
more noble than those in *T*,	17.11
Aristarchus..Macedonian from *T*.	27.2
even in *T* you sent me help	Phil 4.16
deserted me and gone to *T*;	2Tim 4.10

THICKET

a ram, caught in a *t*	Gen 22.13

THIEF — VES

then that *t* shall die;	Deut 24.7

see a *t*, you are a friend	Ps 50.18
Do not despise a *t* if he	Prov 6.30
partner of a *t* hates..life;	29.24
"As a *t* is shamed when caught,	Jer 2.26
the night the *t* was coming,	Mt 24.43
known at what hour the *t* was	Lk 12.39
but because he was a *t*,	Jn 12.6
the day..will come like a *t*,	2Pet 3.10
I will come like a *t*, and	Rev 3.3
where *t* break in and steal,	Mt 6.19

THIGH

"Put your hand under my *t*,	Gen 24.2
touched the hollow of his *t*;	32.25

THINK — S

when I *t* of thee upon my bed,	Ps 63.6
and his mind does not so *t*;	Isa 10.7
"*T* not that I have come to	Mt 5.17
"What do you *t* of the Christ?	22.42
not to *t* of himself more	Rom 12.3
that no one may *t* more of me	2Cor 12.6
than all that we ask or *t*,	Eph 3.20
T over what I say, for the	2Tim 2.7
one *t* that he is a prophet,	1Cor 14.37
if any one *t* he is something,	Gal 6.3

THIRD

he will be raised on..*t* day."	Mt 17.23
he..prayed for the *t* time,	26.44
only the *t* hour of the day;	Acts 2.15

THIRST — S — ED (v)

hunger and *t* for righteousness,	Mt 5.6
"If any one *t*, let him come	Jn 7.37
fulfil the scripture), "I *t*."	19.28
hunger no more, neither *t*	Rev 7.16
My soul *t* for God, for the	Ps 42.2
my soul *t* for thee; my flesh	63.1
my soul *t* for thee like a	143.6
"Ho, every one who *t*, come	Isa 55.1
They *t* not when he led them	48.21

THIRST (n)

for my *t* they gave me vinegar	Ps 69.21
tongue is parched with *t*,	Isa 41.17
young men shall faint for *t*.	Amos 8.13
in hunger and *t*, often	2Cor 11.27

THIRSTY

cold water to a *t* soul, so	Prov 25.25
a *t* man dreams he is drinking	Isa 29.8
to deprive the *t* of drink.	32.6
the *t* ground springs of water;	35.7
drink, but you shall be *t*;	65.13
I was *t* and you gave me drink,	Mt 25.35
if he is *t*, give him drink;	Rom 12.20
let him who is *t* come, let	Rev 22.17

THIRTY

wages *t* shekels of silver.	Zech 11.12
paid him *t* pieces of silver.	Mt 26.15
brought back the *t* pieces of silver	27.3

THOMAS

Bartholomew; *T* and Matthew	Mt 10.3
Matthew, and *T*, and James	Mk 3.18
T, called the Twin, said	Jn 11.16
T said to him, "Lord, we do	14.5
to *T*, "Put your finger here,	20.27
Simon Peter, *T* called the Twin,	21.2

THONG

the *t* of whose sandals I am not	Mk 1.7

THORN — S

t was given me in the flesh,	2Cor 12.7

THORN — S (cont.)

t and thistles..bring forth	Gen 3.18
and t in your sides,	Num 33.55
briers and t shall grow up;	Isa 5.6
Other seeds fell upon t, and	Mt 13.7
a crown of t..on his head,	27.29
Other seed fell among t and	Mk 4.7
a crown of t they put it on	15.17
figs are not gathered from t,	Lk 6.44
And some fell among t; and	8.7
wearing the crown of t and	Jn 19.5
if it bears t and thistles,	Heb 6.8

THOUGHT — S

but the LORD takes t for me.	Ps 40.17
We have t on they steadfast love,	48.9
and declares to man..his t;	Amos 4.13
take every t captive to obey	2Cor 10.5
"Behold, I know your t, and	Job 21.27
his t are, "There is no God."	Ps 10.4
multiplied,..thy t toward us;	40.5
their t are against me for evil.	56.5
O LORD! Thy t are very deep!	92.5
the LORD, knows the t of man,	94.11
precious to me are thy t, O	139.17
I will pour out my t to you;	Prov 1.23
t of the righteous are just;	12.5
The t of the wicked are an	15.26
For my t are not your t,	Isa 55.8
their t are t of iniquity,	59.7
know their works and their t,	66.18
may know the t of your mind.	Dan 2.30
they do not know the t of	Mic 4.12
Jesus, knowing their t, said	Mt 9.4
out of the heart come evil t,	15.19
But he knew their t, and he said	Lk 6.8
But he, knowing their t, said	11.17
no one comprehends the t of	1Cor 2.11
t of the wise are futile."	3.20
discerning..t and intentions	Heb 4.12

THOUSAND — S

mine, the cattle on a t hills.	Ps 50.10
day in thy courts..better than a t	84.10
One man among a t I found,	Ecc 7.28
distinguished among ten t.	Sol 5.10
and a t years as one day.	2Pet 3.8
bound him for a t years,	Rev 20.2
"Saul has slain his t, And	1Sam 18.7
With..t upon t, the LORD came	Ps 68.17

THREE

his petition t times a day."	Dan 6.13
I will make t booths here,	Mt 17.4
There are t witnesses, the Spirit,	1Jn 5.8

THRESH — ED — ING

you shall t the mountains	Isa 41.15
heifer that loved to t,	Hos 10.11
because they have t Gilead	Amos 1.3
tonight at the t floor.	Ruth 3.2
Babylon is like a t floor	Jer 51.33

THRESHER

t thresh in hope of a share	1Cor 9.10

THROAT

seizing him by the t he said,	Mt 18.28
"Their t is an open grave,	Rom 3.13

THRONE — S

he shall sit upon my t"?	1Ki 1.13
Solomon, and make his t	1.37
your royal t over Israel for	9.5
also made a great ivory t,	10.18

I will establish his t for	1Chr 17.12
thou hast sat on the t giving	Ps 9.4
Your divine t endures for ever	45.6
thy t..established from of old;	93.2
LORD has..t in the heavens,	103.19
"One of the sons..on your t.	132.11
for the t is established by	Prov 16.12
and his t will be established	25.5
had gone from prison to the t	Ecc 4.14
I saw the Lord sitting upon a t,	Isa 6.1
t..established in steadfast love	16.5
"Heaven is my t and the earth	66.1
Jerusalem..the t of the LORD,	Jer 3.17
A glorious t set on high from	17.12
set his t above these stones	43.10
thy t endures to..generations.	Lam 5.19
the t of his father David,	Lk 1.32
'Heaven is my t, and earth	Acts 7.49
took his seat upon the t,	12.21
"Thy t, O God, is for ever	Heb 1.8
draw near the t of grace,	4.16
at the right hand of the t of	8.1
and lo, a t stood in heaven,	Rev 4.2
I saw a great white t and	20.11
flowing from the t of God	22.1
As I looked, t were placed	Dan 7.9
you..will also sit on twelve t,	Mt 19.28
twenty-four t, and seated on	Rev 4.4
I saw t, and seated on them	20.4

THRONG

praise him in..midst of..t.	Ps 109.30
the great t heard him gladly.	Mk 12.37

THROW — N

and t you like a ball into	Isa 22.18
Son of God, t yourself down;	Mt 4.6
and t them into the furnace	13.42
sons of the kingdom will be t	8.12

THUMMIN

put the Urim and the T,	Ex 28.30
he put the Urim and the T.	Lev 8.8

THUNDER — S — ED

LORD, that he may send t	1Sam 12.17
Boanerges, that is, sons of t;	Mk 3.17
God of glory t,..upon..waters.	Ps 29.3
The LORD t from heaven,	2Sam 22.14
LORD also t in the heavens,	Ps 18.13

TIDINGS

charged with heavy t for you.	1Ki 14.6
host of those who bore the t:	Ps 68.11
O Zion, herald of good t;	Isa 40.9
Jerusalem a herald of good t.	41.27
t from the east..alarm him,	Dan 11.44

TIGLATH-PILESER (PUL)

*Received tribute from Menahem, 2Ki 15.
19–20; carried the people captive to
Assyria, 2Ki 15.29; paid homage by Ahaz,
2Ki 16.7–10 (2Chr 28.20–21); deported
some of the tribes of Israel, 1Chr 5.26.*

TIGRIS

name of the third river is T,	Gen 2.14
great river, that is, the T,	Dan 10.4

TILL

there was no man to t	Gen 2.5
God sent him..to t the ground	3.23

TILLER

Noah was the first t	Gen 9.20
I am a t of the soil;	Zech 13.5

TIME — S

t of which God had spoken	Gen 21.2
t that the people of Israel	Ex 12.40
Was it a *t* to accept money	2Ki 5.26
to the kingdom for such a *t*	Est 4.14
It is *t* for the LORD to act,	Ps 119.126
and a *t* for every matter under	Ecc 3.1
every matter has its *t* and way,	8.6
t and chance happen to. .all.	9.11
a day of clouds, a *t* of doom	Ezek 30.3
still the vision awaits its *t*;	Hab 2.3
people say. .*t* has not yet come	Hag 1.2
to torment us before the *t*?"	Mt 8.29
Teacher says, My *t* is at hand;	26.18
"My *t* has not yet come, but	Jn 7.6
appointed *t* has grown. .short;	1Cor 7.29
making the most of the *t*,	Eph 5.16
making the most of the *t*.	Col 4.5
therein; for the *t* is near.	Rev 1.3
she is to be nourished for a *t*,	12.14
My *t* are in thy hand; deliver	Ps 31.15
I will bless the LORD at all *t*;	34.1
he prophesies of *t* far off.'	Ezek 12.27

TIMOTHY

Paul's son in the Lord, 1Cor 4.17; 1Tim 1.2, 18; 2Tim 1.2; son of a Greek father and a Jewish mother, Acts 16.1; brought up in a devout home, 2Tim 1.5; 3.14–15; lived in Lystra (or Derbe), Acts 16.1; circumcised, Acts 16.3; accompanied Paul in the second missionary journey, Acts 16.1–4; 17.14–15; 18.5; 1Thess 3.2–6; ordained, 1Tim 4.14; 2Tim 1.6; sent to the church in Corinth, 1Cor 4.17; 16.10; accompanied Paul in the third missionary journey, Acts 20.4; in charge of the church in Ephesus, 1Tim 1.3; 4.12; urged by Paul to visit him in prison, 2Tim 4.9, 13; imprisoned and released, Heb 13.23.

Therefore I sent to you *T*,	1Cor 4.17
When *T* comes, see that you	16.10

TITHE (v)

t all the yield of your seed,	Deut 14.22
you *t* mint. .dill and cummin,	Mt 23.23
Pharisees! for you *t* mint	Lk 11.42

TITHE — S (n)

redeem any of his *t*, he shall	Lev 27.31
Levites I have given. .*t*	Num 18.21
t of the people of Israel	18.24
finished paying all the *t*	Deut 26.12
to bring to the Levites the *t*	Neh 10.37
robbing thee?' In your *t* and	Mal 3.8
t, paid *t* through Abraham,	Heb 7.9

TITLE

Pilate also wrote a *t* and put	Jn 19.19

TITUS

not find my brother *T* there.	2Cor 2.13
comforted us by. .coming of *T*,	7.6
Accordingly we have urged *T*	8.6
As for *T*, he is my partner	8.23
Did *T* take advantage of you?	12.18
with Barnabas, taking *T* along	Gal 2.1
to Galatia, *T* to Dalmatia.	2Tim 4.10
To *T*, my true child in. .faith:	Tit 1.4

TODAY

O that *t* you would hearken to	Ps 95.7
t you will be with me in	Lk 23.43
"*T*, when you hear his voice,	Heb 3.15

TOGETHER

went both of them *t*.	Gen 22.8
they were all *t* in one place.	Acts 2.1
attending the temple *t* and	2.46
in him all things hold *t*:	Col 1.17

TOIL — ED (v)

Do not *t* to acquire wealth;	Prov 23.4
they neither *t* nor spin;	Lk 12.27
For this I *t*, striving with	Col 1.29
"Master, we *t* all night and took	Lk 5.5

TOIL (n)

In all *t* there is profit,	Prov 14.23
What does a man gain by.. *t*	Ecc 1.3
take pleasure in all his *t*.	3.13
all *t* and all skill in work	41.4
quietness than two hands. .of *t*	4.6
yet there is no end to. .his *t*,	4.8
and find enjoyment in his *t*—	5.19
the *t* of man is for his mouth,	6.7
The *t* of a fool wearies him,	10.15
in *t* and hardship, through	2Cor 11.27
"'I know your works, your *t*	Rev 2.2

TOLD

land which thou hadst *t* their	Neh 9.23
t the glad news of deliverance	Ps 40.9
The herdsmen fled, and *t* it	Mk 5.14
Philip. .*t* him the good news	Acts 8.35
things that cannot be *t*,	2Cor 12.4

TOLL

they will not pay. .*t*,	Ezra 4.13
not lawful to impose. .*t* upon	7.24
From whom do kings. .take *t*	Mt 17.25

TOMB — S

a *t*. .hewn out of the rock;	Mt 15.46
stone to the door of the *t*,	27.60
his body, and laid it in a *t*.	Mk 6.29
went to the *t*, taking. .spices	Lk 24.1
going to the *t* to weep there.	Jn 11.31
in the garden a new *t* where	19.41
went into the *t*; he saw the linen	20.6
you are like whitewashed *t*,	Mt 23.27
and he lived. .among the *t*.	Lk 8.27
build the *t* of the prophets	11.47
all. .in the *t* will hear his voice	Jn 5.28

TOMORROW

Do not boast about *t*, for	Prov 27.1
eat and drink, for *t* we die."	Isa 22.13
today is alive and *t* is thrown	Mt 6.30
and drink, for *t* we die."	1Cor 15.32
you do not know about *t*.	Jas 4.14

TONGUE — S

hid from the scourge of the *t*,	Job 5.21
they flatter with their *t*.	Ps 5.9
Keep your *t* from evil, and	34.13
Then my *t* shall tell of thy	35.28
that I may not sin with my *t*;	39.1
my *t* is like the pen of a. .scribe.	45.1
Your *t* is like a sharp razor,	52.2
t of. .righteous is. .silver;	Prov 10.20
perverse *t* will be cut off.	10.31
t of the wise brings healing.	12.18
are in the power of the *t*,	18.21
soft *t* will break a bone.	25.15
bow, every *t* shall swear.'	Isa 45.23
you shall confute every *t*	54.17
taught their *t* to speak lies;	Jer 9.5
Their *t* is a deadly arrow; it	9.8
t was released, and he spoke	Mk 7.35

TONGUE — S (cont.)

one who speaks in a *t* speaks	1Cor 14.2
and does not bridle his *t*	Jas 1.26
So the *t* is a little member	3.5
shelter from the strife of *t*.	Ps 31.20
who whet their *t* like swords,	64.3
they will speak in new *t*;	Mk 16.17*n*
appeared to them *t* as of fire,	Acts 2.3
spoke with *t* and prophesied.	19.6
to another various..*t*,	1Cor 12.10
If I speak in the *t* of men	13.1
written, "By men of strange *t*	14.21
t are a sign..for unbelievers,	14.22

TOOTH

eye for eye, *t* for *t*,	Ex 21.24
eye for eye, *t* for *t*,	Deut 19.21
bad *t* or a foot that slips.	Prov 25.19

TORCH — ES

t passed between..pieces.	Gen 15.17
empty jars, with *t* inside	Judg 7.16
before the throne burn seven *t*	Rev 4.5

TORMENT — ED (v)

"How long will you *t* me,	Job 19.2
Have you come here to *t* us	Mt 8.29
adjure you by God, do not *t* me."	Mk 5.7
I beseech you, do not *t* me."	Lk 8.28
they will be *t* day and night	Rev 20.10

TORMENT (n)

you shall lie down in *t*.	Isa 50.11
in Hades,..in *t*, he lifted up	Lk 16.23

TORN

The LORD has *t* the kingdom	1Sam 15.28
curtain of the temple was *t*	Mk 15.38

TOSSING

I am full of *t* till the dawn.	Job 7.4
wicked are like the *t* sea;	Isa 57.20

TOUCH — ES — ED

fruit..neither shall you *t* it,	Gen 3.3
there shall no evil *t* you.	Job 5.19
saying, "*T* not my anointed	Ps 105.15
"If I only *t* his garment, I	Mt 9.21
only *t*..fringe of his garment	14.36
"If I *t* even his garments, I	Mk 5.28
they might *t* even the fringe	6.56
for a man not to *t* a woman.	1Cor 7.1
and *t* nothing unclean; then	2Cor 6.17
the evil one does not *t* him.	1Jn 5.18
it *t* you, and you are dismayed.	Job 4.5
who *t*..the apple of his eye:	Zech 2.8
whose hearts God had *t*.	1Sam 10.26
forth his hand and *t* my mouth;	Jer 1.9
stretched out his hand and *t* him,	Mt 8.3
he *t* her hand, and the fever	8.15
Then he *t* their eyes, saying,	9.29
Jesus in pity *t* their eyes,	20.34
said, "Who was it that *t* me?"	Lk 8.45

TOWEL

and girded himself with a *t*.	Jn 13.4

TOWER — S

let us build..a city, and a *t*	Gen 11.4
and station myself on the *t*,	Hab 2.1
upon whom the *t* in Siloam fell	Lk 13.4
build a *t*,..count the cost,	14.28

TRADED

land of Israel *t* with you;	Ezek 27.17
five talents..and *t* with them;	Mt 25.16

TRADITION — S

transgress the *t* of the elders?	Mt 15.2
not live according to the *t*	Mk 7.5
and hold fast the *t* of men."	7.8
stand firm..hold to the *t*	2Thess 2.15

TRAIN — S — ED — ING

T up a child in the way he	Prov 22.6
so *t* the young women to love	Tit 2.4
who *t* my hands for war, and	Ps 144.1
Abram..led forth his *t* men,	Gen 14.14
divine *t* that is in faith;	1Tim 1.4
bodily *t* is of some value,	4.8
t us to renounce irreligion	Tit 2.12

TRAITOR

Judas Iscariot, who became a *t*.	Lk 6.16

TRAMPLE — D

Be gracious..men *t* upon me;	Ps 56.1
didst *t* the sea with..horses,	Hab 3.15
and *t* the waves of the sea;	Job 9.8

TRANSFER — RED

to *t* the kingdom from..Saul,	2Sam 3.10
and *t* us to the kingdom of	Col 1.13

TRANSFIGURED

t before them,..his face shone	Mt 17.2
and he was *t* before them,	Mk 9.2

TRANSFORMED

t by the renewal of your mind,	Rom 12.2

TRANSGRESS — ES — ED

if you *t* the covenant	Josh 23.16
my mouth does not *t*.	Ps 17.3
"Come to Bethel, and *t*; to	Amos 4.4
When a land *t* it has many	Prov 28.2
I have not *t* any of thy	Deut 26.13
people have *t* my covenant	Judg 2.20
but *t* his covenant, even	2Ki 18.12
But they *t* against the God	1Chr 5.25
the men who *t* my covenant	Jer 34.18
"We have *t* and rebelled, and	Lam 3.42
at Adam they *t* the covenant;	Hos 6.7

TRANSGRESSION — S

Forgive, I pray you, the *t*	Gen 50.17
Blessed is he..*t* is forgiven,	Ps 32.1
punish their *t* with the rod	89.32
When words are many, *t* is	Prov 10.19
Are you not children of *t*,	Isa 57.4
All this is for the *t* of Jacob	Mic 1.5
sins..not like the *t* of Adam,	Rom 5.14
and because of their *t*,	Lev 16.16
if I have concealed my *t*	Job 31.33
Deliver me from all my *t*.	Ps 39.8
For I know my *t*, and my sin	51.3
who conceals his *t* will not	Prov 28.13
t are multiplied before thee,	Isa 59.12
t are many,..apostasies..great.	Jer 5.6
None of the *t* which he has	Ezek 18.22
their uncleanness and their *t*,	39.24
"For three *t* of Damascus,	Amos 1.3
on the day I punish Israel for his *t*,	3.14

TRANSGRESSOR — S

then I prove myself a *t*.	Gal 2.18
"He was reckoned with the *t*"	Mk 15.28*n*
he was reckoned with *t*';	Lk 22.37

TRANSIENT

things that are seen are *t*,	2Cor 4.18

TRAVAIL (n)

anguish as of a woman in *t*.	Ps 48.6

TRAVAIL (n) (cont.)

like. .pangs of a woman in t;	Isa 21.3
fruit of the t of his soul	53.11
pain as of a woman in t.	Jer 6.24
When a woman is in t she	Jn 16.21
whole creation groaning in t	Rom 8.22
with whom I am again in t	Gal 4.19
as t comes upon a woman	1Thess 5.3

TRAVEL — ED

appointed by. .churches to t	2Cor 8.19
ships of Tarshish t for you	Ezek 27.25

TREACHEROUS

My brethren are t as a	Job 6.15
crookedness of the t destroys	Prov 11.3
the t deal. .treacherously,	Isa 24.16
men will be. .t, reckless	2Tim 3.4

TREACHERY

confess their. .t. .against me,	Lev 26.40
'What is this t which you	Josh 22.16
fled, saying to Ahaziah, "T,	2Ki 9.23
their houses are full of t;	Jer 5.27

TREAD — S — ING

through thy name we t down	Ps 44.5
t on the lion and the adder,	91.13
t our iniquities under foot.	Mic 7.19
makes me t upon. .high places.	Hab 3.19
you shall t down the wicked,	Mal 4.3
the sole of your foot t	Deut 11.24
ox when it is t out the grain."	1Cor 9.9

TREASON

Athaliah. .and cried, "T! t!"	2Ki 11.14
Athaliah. .and cried, "T!	2Chr 23.13

TREASURE — D (v)

receive my words and t up my	Prov 2.1
have t in my bosom the words	Job 23.12

TREASURE — S (n)

put t in your sacks for you;	Gen 43.23
showed them all his t house,	2Ki 20.13
In the. .righteous. .is much t,	Prov 15.6
great t and trouble with it.	15.16
Precious t remains in a wise	21.20
silver and gold and the t of	Ecc 2.8
the fear of the Lord is his t.	Isa 33.6
out of his good t brings. .good,	Mt 12.35
kingdom. .is like t hidden in	13.44
out of his t what is new and	13.52
out of the good t of his heart	Lk 6.45
who lays up t for himself,	12.21
where your t is, there will	12.34
we have this t in earthen	2Cor 4.7
he took away the t of the	1Ki 14.26
search for it as. .hidden t;	Prov 2.4
give you the t of darkness	Isa 45.3
your t I will give as spoil,	Jer 15.13
the t of the kings of Judah	20.5
Can I forget. .t of wickedness	Mic 6.10
t of all nations shall come in,	Hag 2.7
opening their t, they offered	Mt 2.11
"Do not lay up for yourselves t	6.19
in whom are hid all the t of	Col 2.3

TREASURY

go into the t of the Lord."	Josh 6.19
"Cast it into the t"—	Zech 11.13
putting money into the t.	Mk 12.41
These words he spoke in the t,	Jn 8.20

TREE — S

the t of life also in the midst	Gen 2.9

Lord showed him a t, and he	Ex 15.25
shall not plant any t as an	Deut 16.21
and you hang him on a t,	21.22
sat down under a broom t;	1Ki 19.4
hope for a t, if it be cut	Job 14.7
I am like a green olive t in	Ps 52.8
gentle tongue is a t of life,	Prov 15.4
like a t planted by water,	Jer 17.8
no t in the garden of God	Ezek 31.8
a t in the midst of the earth;	Dan 4.10
sit every man. .under his fig t,	Mic 4.4
every sound t bears good fruit,	Mt 7.17
the t is known by its fruit;	12.33
no good t bears bad fruit,	Lk 6.43
into a sycamore t to see him,	19.4
took him down from the t,	Acts 13.29
every one who hangs on a t"—	Gal 3.13
He. .bore our sins. .on the t,	1Pet 2.24
grant to eat of the t of life,	Rev 2.7
the t of life with its twelve	22.2
have. .right to the t of life	22.14
shall not destroy its t	Deut 20.19
The t. .watered abundantly,	Ps 104.16
I saw upon the bank. .many t	Ezek 47.7

TREMBLE (v)

Lord reigns; let the peoples t!	Ps 99.1
I will make the heavens t,	Isa 13.13
the man who made the earth t,	14.16
foundations of the earth t.	24.18
T, you women who are at ease,	32.11
nations. .t at thy presence!	64.2
Lord, you who t at his word:	66.5
Shall not the land t on this	Amos 8.8

TREMBLING (n)

woman,. .came in fear and t	Mk 5.33
for t and astonishment had come	16.8

TRESPASS — ES

the t of your handmaid;	1Sam 25.28
man is overtaken in any t,	Gal 6.1
For if you forgive men their t,	Mt 6.14
Father. .may forgive. .your t."	Mk 11.26
put to death for our t and	Rom 4.25
not counting. .t against them,	2Cor 5.19
having forgiven us all our t,	Col 2.13

TRIAL — S

let me make t only this once	Judg 6.39
why do you make t of God	Acts 15.10
to rescue the godly from t,	2Pet 2.9
keep you from the hour of t	Rev 3.10
continued with me in my t;	Lk 22.28
and with tears and with t	Acts 20.19

TRIBE — S

"One t is cut off from Israel	Judg 21.6
and Israel is the t of his	Jer 51.19
sealed, out of every t of the	Rev 7.4
t go up, the t of the Lord,	Ps 122.4

TRIBULATION — S

When you are in t and	Deut 4.30
besieged. .with bitterness and t;	Lam 3.5
when t or persecution arises	Mt 13.21
then there will be great t,	24.21
after the t of those days	24.29
such t as has not been from	Mk 13.19
after that t, the sun will	13.24
In the world you have t; but	Jn 16.33
There will be t and distress	Rom 2.9
Shall t, or distress, or persecution,	8.35
be patient in t, be constant	12.12

TRIBULATION — S (cont.)
share with you in Jesus the *t* Rev 1.9
" 'I know your *t* and..poverty 2.9
I will throw into great *t*, 2.22
have come out of the great *t*; 7.14
through many *t* we must enter Acts 14.22

TRIBUTE
the LORD's *t* of sheep was Num 31.37
Israel sent *t*..to Eglon Judg 3.15
Is it lawful for us to give *t* Lk 20.22

TRIUMPH — ED — ING (v)
When the righteous *t*, there Prov 28.12
offspring of Israel shall *t* Isa 45.25
"Sing to the LORD,..he has *t* Ex 15.21
in that my enemy has not *t* Ps 41.11
t over them in him. Col 2.15

TRIUMPH — S (n)
God,..always leads us in *t*, 2Cor 2.14
repeat the *t* of the LORD, Judg 5.11
Great *t* he gives to his 2Sam 22.51
Great *t* he gives to his king, Ps 18.50

TROAS
Mysia, they went down to *T*. Acts 16.8
were waiting for us at *T*, 20.5
When I came to *T* to preach 2Cor 2.12
that I left with Carpus at *T*, 2Tim 4.13

TROUBLE — D (v)
shall *t* you in the land Num 33.55
t the hearts of many peoples, Ezek 32.9
"Why do you *t* the woman? Mt 26.10
why do you *t* her? She has done Mk 14.6
dead; do not *t* the Teacher Lk 8.49
but there are some who *t* you Gal 1.7
let no man *t* me; for I bear 6.17
the king heard this, he was *t*, Mt 2.3
greatly distressed and *t*. Mk 14.33
Martha, you are anxious and *t* Lk 10.41
"Why are you *t*, and why do 24.38
the pool, and *t* the water: Jn 5.4*n*
the pool when the water is *t*, 5.7
"Now is my soul *t*. And what 12.27
Jesus..was *t* in spirit, and 13.21
"Let not your hearts be *t*; 14.1

TROUBLE — S (n)
"Why do you bring *t* on us? Josh 7.25
now when you are in *t*?" Judg 11.7
see how this man is seeking *t*; 1Ki 20.7
have no rest; but *t* comes." Job 3.26
man is born to *t* as the sparks 5.7
of few days, and full of *t*. 14.1
his shelter in the day of *t*; Ps 27.5
refuge in the time of *t*. 37.39
a very present help in *t*. 46.1
call upon me in the day of *t*; 50.15
promised when I was in *t*. 66.14
not in *t* as other men are; 73.5
their span is but toil and *t*; 90.10
great treasure and *t* with it. Prov 15.16
but the soul is torn by *t*. 27.9
there shall be a time of *t*, Dan 12.1
stronghold in the day of *t*; Nah 1.7
will deliver you from six *t*; Job 5.19
saved him out of all his *t*. Ps 34.6
who marry..have worldly *t*, 1Cor 7.28

TRUE
his heart was not wholly *t* 1Ki 11.4
the words..prophesied come *t*, Jer 28.6
"I am the *t* vine, and my Father Jn 15.1

Let God be *t* though every man Rom 3.4
brethren, whatever is *t*, Phil 4.8
This testimony is *t*. Tit 1.13

TRUMPET — S
and a very loud *t* blast, Ex 19.16
blew the *t*, and proclaimed, 2Ki 9.13
that day a great *t* will be Isa 27.13
heard the sound of the *t*, Ezek 33.5
Blow the *t* in Zion; sound Joel 2.1
Is a *t* blown in a city, and Amos 3.6
Lord GOD will sound the *t*, Zech 9.14
give alms, sound no *t* before you, Mt 6.2
t will sound, and the dead 1Cor 15.52
the sound of the *t* of God. 1Thess 4.16
proclaimed with blast of *t*, Lev 23.24
"Make two silver *t*; Num 10.2
three companies, and put *t* Judg 7.16
With *t*..make a joyful noise Ps 98.6

TRUST — S — ED — ING (v)
O my God, in thee I *t*, let me Ps 25.2
But I *t* in thee, O LORD, I 31.14
because we *t* in his holy name. 33.21
T in the LORD, and do good; 37.3
men who *t* in their wealth 49.6
days. But I will *t* in thee. 55.23
T in him at all times, O people; 62.8
fortress; my God, in whom I *t*." 91.2
like them;..all who *t* in them. 115.8
Those who *t*..are like Mount Zion, 125.1
T in the LORD with all your Prov 3.5
T in a faithless man in time 25.19
T in the LORD for ever, for Isa 26.4
Woe to those..who *t* in chariots 31.1
to shame, who *t* in..images, 42.17
not *t* in these deceptive words: Jer 7.4
Shemaiah..made you *t* in a lie, 29.31
for those who *t* in riches Mk 10.24*n*
Jesus did not *t* himself to them, Jn 2.24
For the king *t* in the LORD; Ps 21.7
blessed is..man who *t* in thee! 84.12
He who *t* in his riches will Prov 11.28
happy is he who *t* in the LORD. 16.20
he who *t*..will be enriched. 28.25
t in the name of the LORD Isa 50.10
"Cursed is..man who *t* in man Jer 17.5
t him who justifies the ungodly, Rom 4.5
walls, in which you *t*, Deut 28.52
He *t* in the LORD the God 2Ki 18.5
from the tent in which he *t*, Job 18.14
have *t* in thy steadfast love; Ps 13.5
but *t* in the abundance of his 52.7
forgotten me and *t* in lies. Jer 13.25
because you *t* in..strongholds 48.7
because he had *t* in his God. Dan 6.23
you have *t* in your chariots Hos 10.13
heart is firm, *t* in the LORD. Ps 112.7

TRUST (n)
his *t* is a spider's web. Job 8.14
"If I have made gold my *t*, 31.24
Blessed..who makes..LORD his *t*, Ps 40.4
Put not your *t* in princes, 146.3
your *t* may be in the LORD, Prov 22.19
quietness and *t* for ever. Isa 32.17
the man..whose *t* is in the LORD. Jer 17.7
Put no *t* in a neighbor, have Mic 7.5
"I will put my *t* in him." Heb 2.13

TRUSTWORTHY
all his precepts are *t*, Ps 111.7
required of stewards..*t*. 1Cor 4.2
these words are *t* and true." Rev 21.5

TRUTH

and speaks *t* from his heart;   Ps 15.2
speaks the *t* gives honest   Prov 12.17
Buy *t*, and do not sell it;   23.23
I the LORD speak the *t*, I   Isa 45.19
confess. .not in *t* or right.   48.1
t was cast down to the ground,   Dan 8.12
that you may know the *t*   Lk 1.4
and you will know the *t*,   Jn 8.32
"I am the way, and the *t*,   14.6
Pilate said. . "What is *t*?"   18.38
exchanged the *t* about God for   Rom 1.25
unleavened bread of. .and *t*.   1Cor 5.8
the *t*, but only for the *t*.   2Cor 13.8
in him, as the *t* is in Jesus.   Eph 4.21
whether in pretense or in *t*,   Phil 1.18
and the *t* is not in him;   1Jn 2.4

TRUTHFUL

T lips endure for ever.   Prov 12.19
A *t* witness saves lives,   14.25

TRY — IES — IEST — IED

Does not the ear *t* words   Job 12.11
Prove me, O LORD, and *t* me;   Ps 26.2
T me and know my thoughts!   139.23
"I the LORD. .*t* the heart,   Jer 17.10
gold, and the LORD *t* hearts.   Prov 17.3
thou who *t* the minds and hearts, Ps 7.9
If thou *t* my heart, if thou   17.3
and *t* my mind toward thee.   Jer 12.3
O LORD. .who *t* the righteous,   20.12
when he has *t* me, I. .as gold.   Job 23.10
Would that Job were *t* to the end, 34.36
Thy promise is well *t*, and   Ps 119.140

TUMULT

a day of *t* and trampling and   Isa 22.5
the *t* of war shall arise   Hos 10.14
lest. .a *t* among the people."   Mt 26.5
lest there be a *t* of. .people."   Mk 14.2

TUNICS

sandals and not put on two *t*.   Mk 6.9
money; and do not have two *t*.   Lk 9.3

TURMOIL

My heart is in *t*, and is   Job 30.27
for nought are they in *t*; man   Ps 39.6

TURN — S — ED

every seer, saying, "*T* from   2Ki 17.13
T, O LORD, save my life;   Ps 6.4
who does not *t* to the proud,   40.4
"*T* back, O children of men!"   90.3
I do not *t* away from thy law.   119.51
t your foot away from evil.   Prov 4.27
T away from man. .for of what   Isa 2.22
understand. .*t* and be healed."   6.10
"*T* to me and be saved, all   45.22
they did not *t* from their ways.   Jer 15.7
'*T* now, every one. .from. .evil   25.5
I will *t*. .mourning into joy,   31.13
saying, '*T*. .from his evil way,   35.15
and *t* away from your idols;   Ezek 14.6
t back from your evil ways;   33.11
right cheek, *t* to him the other   Mt 5.39
and *t* for me to heal them.'   13.15
t and become like children,   18.3
lest they should *t* again,   Mk 4.12
he will *t* many of the sons   Lk 1.16
t from these vain things   Acts 14.15
and *t* for me to heal them.'   28.27
righteous man *t*. .from evil,   Prov 12.26
that nation,. .*t* from its evil,   Jer 18.8

your God *t* the curse into   Deut 23.5
no king like him,. .*t* to. .LORD   2Ki 23.25
had *t* the heart of the king   Ezra 6.22
I *t* my mind to know and to   Ecc 7.25
we. .*t* every one to his own way; Isa 53.6
abundance. .shall be *t* to you,   60.5
they have *t* aside and gone   Jer 5.23
and when you have *t* again,   Lk 22.32
who have *t* the world upside   Acts 17.6
how you *t* to God from idols,   1Thess 1.9

TURTLEDOVE — S

"Bring me. .a *t* and a young   Gen 15.9
the voice of the *t* is heard   Sol 2.12
bring his offering of *t* or of   Lev 1.14
law of the Lord, "a pair of *t*,   Lk 2.24

TWELVE

and tore it into *t* pieces.   1Ki 11.30
names of the *t* apostles are   Mt 10.2
appointed *t*, to be with him,   Mk 3.14
And he called to him the *t*,   6.7
evening he came with the *t*.   14.17
when he was *t* years old,   Lk 2.42
and chose from them *t*, whom   6.13
an only daughter, about *t* years   8.42
Jesus said to the *t*, "Will you   Jn 6.67

TWINKLING

in the *t* of an eye, at the   1Cor 15.52

TWINS

there were *t* in her womb.   Gen 25.24
there were *t* in her womb.   38.27

TWO

bring *t* of every sort   Gen 6.19
T are better than one, because   Ecc 4.9
and with *t* he covered his feet,   Isa 6.2
"No one can serve *t* masters;   Mt 6.24
where *t* or three are gathered   18.20
A man had *t* sons; and he went   21.28
t men will be in the field;   24.40
"Which of the *t* do you want   27.21
That very day *t* of them were   Lk 24.13
"The *t* shall become one."   1Cor 6.16

TYPE

a *t* of. .one who was to come.   Rom 5.14

TYRE

the fortified city of *T*;   Josh 19.29
king of *T* sent his servants   1Ki 5.1
Hiram king of *T* had supplied   9.11
his father was a man of *T*.   2Chr 2.14
people of *T* will sue. .favor   Ps 45.12
The oracle concerning *T*. Wail,   Isa 23.1
T and Sidon a great multitude,   Mk 3.8
if the mighty works. .done in *T*   Lk 10.13
to Syria, and landed at *T*;   Acts 21.3

U

UNBELIEF

did not. .because of their *u*.   Mt 13.58
he marveled because of their *u*.   Mk 6.6
said, "I believe; help my *u*!"   9.24
broken off because of. .*u*,   Rom 11.20

UNBELIEVERS

against brother,. .before *u*?   1Cor 6.6
and outsiders or *u* enter,   14.23
Do not be mismated with *u*.   2Cor 6.14

UNBELIEVING

the *u* husband is consecrated   1Cor 7.14
To the. .*u* nothing is pure;   Tit 1.15

UNCHASTITY
except on the ground of *u*, Mt 5.32
write..to abstain from..*u* Acts 15.20

UNCIRCUMCISED
no *u* person shall eat of it. Ex 12.48
wife from the *u* Philistines?" Judg 14.3
the *u* because of their faith. Rom 3.30
at the time of his call *u*? 1Cor 7.18

UNCLEAN
he shall pronounce him *u*. Lev 13.3
cover..lip and cry, '*U*, *u*.! 13.45
shall be *u* seven days; Num 19.11
for I am a man of *u* lips, and Isa 6.5
no more..uncircumcised and..*u*. 52.1
become like one who is *u*, 64.6
what they offer there is *u*. Hag 2.14
"When the *u* spirit has gone Mt 12.43
met him. man with an *u* spirit, Mk 5.2
was possessed by an *u* spirit, 7.25
had the spirit of an *u* demon; Lk 4.33
Jesus rebuked the *u* spirit, 9.42
"When the *u* spirit has gone 11.24
never eaten..common or *u*." Acts 10.14
should not call any man..*u*. 10.28
your children would be *u*, 1Cor 7.14

UNCLEANNESS
Or if he touches human *u*, Lev 5.3
end to end with their *u*. Ezra 9.11
cleanse them from sin and *u*. Zech 13.1
to practice every kind of *u*. Eph 4.19
appeal..not..from error or *u*, 1Thess 2.3

UNCONDEMNED
beaten us publicly, *u*, men Acts 16.37
is a Roman citizen, and *u*?" 22.25

UNDERSTAND (v)
not *u* one another's speech." Gen 11.7
Aramaic language, for we *u* 2Ki 18.26
of his power who can *u*?" Job 26.14
uttered what I did not *u*, 42.3
I *u* more than the aged, for Ps 119.100
Evil men do not *u* justice, Prov 28.5
speak..in Aramaic,..we *u* it; Isa 36.11
have not heard they shall *u*. 52.15
so wise that he can *u* this? Jer 9.12
In the latter days you will *u* 23.20
"*U*, O son of man,..the vision Dan 8.17
shall indeed hear but never *u*, Mt 13.14
they did not *u* about the loaves, Mk 6.52
you *u* what you are reading?" Acts 8.30
and *u* with their heart, 28.27
I want you to *u* this mystery, Rom 11.25

UNDERSTANDING (n)
there is no *u* in them. Deut 32.28
hast closed their minds to *u*, Job 17.4
who by *u* made the heavens, Ps 136.5
his *u* is beyond measure. 147.5
discretion..*u* will guard you. Prov 2.11
who heeds admonition gains *u*. 15.32
fool takes no pleasure in *u*, 18.2
who formed it, "He has no *u*?" Isa 29.16
showed him the way of *u*? 40.14
by his *u* stretched out the Jer 10.12
people without *u*..come to ruin. Hos 4.14
"Are you also still without *u*? Mt 15.16
"Then are you also without *u*? Mk 7.18
to love him..with all the *u*, 12.33
all..amazed at his *u* and answers. Lk 2.47

UNDERSTOOD
that the people *u* the reading. Neh 8.8

"Have you *u* all this?" They Mt 13.51
as you have *u* in part, that 2Cor 1.14

UNDYING
love our Lord..with love *u*. Eph 6.24

UNFAITHFUL — NESS
punish..put him with the *u*. Lk 12.46
U creatures! Do you not know Jas 4.4
So Saul died for his *u*; 1Chr 10.13

UNFRUITFUL
choke the word,..it proves *u*. Mt 13.22
spirit prays but..mind is *u*. 1Cor 14.14
to help..and not to be *u*. Tit 3.14

UNGODLY
God gives me up to the *u*, Job 16.11
are the dwellings of the *u*, 18.21
my cause against *u* people; Ps 43.1
time Christ died for the *u*. Rom 5.6

UNINTENTIONALLY
any one kills his neighbor *u* Deut 19.4

UNITE — D
to *u* all things in him, Eph 1.10
against the city, *u* as one Judg 20.11
who is *u* to the Lord becomes 1Cor 6.17

UNITY
good..when brothers dwell in *u*! Ps 133.1
maintain the *u* of the Spirit Eph 4.3
attain to the *u* of the faith 4.13

UNJUST — LY
from the grasp of the *u* and Ps 71.4
hates *u* gain will prolong Prov 28.16
An *u* man is an abomination 29.27
but the *u* knows no shame. Zeph 3.5
rain on the just and on the *u*. Mt 5.45
"How long will you judge *u* and Ps 82.2

UNKNOWN
inscription, 'To an *u* god.' Acts 17.23
as *u*, and yet well known; 2Cor 6.9

UNLEAVENED
feast of *u* bread to the LORD; Lev 23.6
you shall eat *u* bread; Deut 16.8
kept the feast of *u* bread 2Chr 30.21

UNMARRIED
To the *u* and the widows I say 1Cor 7.8

UNRIGHTEOUS — NESS
not..faithful in the *u* mammon, Lk 16.11
who builds his house by *u*, Jer 22.13

UNSEARCHABLE
who does great things and *u*, Job 5.9
the LORD,..his greatness is *u*. Ps 145.3
so the mind of kings is *u*. Prov 25.3
How *u* are his judgments and Rom 11.33
to the Gentiles the *u* riches Eph 3.8

UNSKILLED
Even if I am *u* in speaking, 2Cor 11.6
u in..word of righteousness, Heb 5.13

UNSTAINED
u and free from reproach 1Tim 6.14
u, separated from sinners, Heb 7.26
keep oneself *u* from the world. Jas 1.27

UNTIE
not worthy to stoop down and *u*. Mk 1.7
u it and bring it here. Lk 19.30

UNVEILED
prophesies with her head *u* 1Cor 11.5
u face, beholding the glory 2Cor 3.18

UNWASHED
hands defiled, that is, *u*. Mk 7.2

UNWITTINGLY
If any one sins *u* in any Lev 4.2
done *u* without the knowledge Num 15.24

UNWORTHY
you..say, 'We are *u* servants; Lk 17.10
the cup of the Lord in an *u* 1Cor 11.27

UPBUILDING
speaks to men for their *u* 1Cor 14.3
and all for your *u*, beloved. 2Cor 12.19

UPHOLD — S
There is none to *u* your cause, Jer 30.13
but the LORD *u* the righteous. Ps 37.17
thy right hand *u* me. 63.8

UPPER
will show you a large *u* room Lk 22.12
they went up to the *u* room, Acts 1.13

UPRIGHT — NESS
for the Levites were more *u* 2Chr 29.34
where were the *u* cut off? Job 4.7
God, who saves the *u* in heart. Ps 7.10
the *u* shall behold his face. 11.7
shout for joy, all you *u* in heart! 32.11
The *u* see it and are glad; 107.42
the *u* will inhabit the land, Prov 2.21
the *u* are in his confidence. 3.32
God made man *u*, but they have Ecc 7.29
he whose soul is not *u* in him Hab 2.4
who walks in *u* fears..LORD, Prov 14.2

UR
Haran died..in the land..*U* Gen 11.28
went forth together from *U* 11.31
LORD who brought you from *U* 15.7
Abram and bring him..out of *U* Neh 9.7

URGE — D
I *u* you, then, be imitators 1Cor 4.16
necessary to *u* the brethren 2Cor 9.5
woman lived, who *u* him to eat 2Ki 4.8
accept two talents." And he *u* 5.23

URIM
put the *U* and the Thummim, Ex 28.30
in..breastpiece he put the *U* Lev 8.8
dreams..*U*, or by prophets. 1Sam 28.6

USEFUL
he is very *u* in serving me. 2Tim 4.11
now he is indeed *u* to you Philem 11

UZ
The sons of Aram: *U*, Gen 10.23
a man in the land of *U*, Job 1.1
the kings of the land of *U* Jer 25.20
dweller in the land of *U*; Lam 4.21

UZZIAH
people of Judah took *U*, 2Chr 26.1
Moreover *U* had an army 26.11
not for you, *U*, to burn 26.18
King *U* was a leper to the 26.21
all that..*U* had done—only 27.2
Jerusalem in the days of *U*, Isa 1.1
In the year that King *U* died 6.1
and Joram the father of *U*, Mt 1.8

V

VAIN
for *v* is the help of man! Ps 60.11
"Men are all a *v* hope." 116.11
those who build it labor in *v*. 127.1
beauty is *v*, but a woman who Prov 31.30
Bring no more *v* offerings; Isa 1.13
"But they say, 'That is in *v*! Jer 18.12
turn from these *v* things Acts 14.15
then our preaching is in *v* 1Cor 15.14

VALLEY — S
the *v* of the shadow of death, Ps 23.4
concerning the *v* of vision. Isa 22.1
Every *v* shall be lifted up, 40.4
called..the *V* of Slaughter, Jer 19.6
the *v*; it was full of bones. Ezek 37.1
in the *v* of decision! For Joel 3.14
Every *v* shall be filled, and Lk 3.5
he is not a god of the *v*," 1Ki 20.28

VALUE
finding one pearl of great *v*, Mt 13.46
you are of more *v* than many Lk 12.7
bodily training is of some *v*, 1Tim 4.8

VANISH — ED
their days *v* like a breath Ps 78.33
the angel..*v* from his sight. Judg 6.21
you have *v* from the seas, Ezek 26.17
and he *v* out of their sight. Lk 24.31
the sky *v* like a scroll Rev 6.14

VANITY
V of vanities, says the Preacher, Ecc 1.2
also is *v* and a great evil. 2.21
V of vanities, says the Preacher; 12.8

VARIETIES
there are *v* of gifts, but 1Cor 12.4
there are *v* of service, but 12.5

VEIL — ED
took her *v* and covered Gen 24.65
the *v* shall separate for you Ex 26.33
he put a *v* on his face; 34.33
made the *v* of blue and purple 36.35
holy place within the *v*, Lev 16.2
same *v* remains unlifted, 2Cor 3.14
gospel is *v*, it is *v* only to 4.3

VENGEANCE
If any one slays Cain, *v* Gen 4.15
not take *v* or bear any grudge Lev 19.18
V is mine, and recompense, Deut 32.35
rejoice when he sees the *v*; Ps 58.10
O LORD, thou God of *v*,..shine 94.1
day of *v* was in my heart, Isa 63.4
visit me, and take *v* for me Jer 15.15
this is the *v* of the LORD: 50.15
LORD takes *v* on..adversaries Nah 1.2
"*V* is mine, I will repay, Rom 12.19
"*V* is mine, I will repay." Heb 10.30

VERSED
were *v* in law and judgment, Est 1.13
well *v* in the scriptures. Acts 18.24

VESSEL — S
I have become like a broken *v*. Ps 31.12
glaze covering an earthen *v* Prov 26.23
the *v* he was making of clay Jer 18.4
as one breaks a potter's *v*, 19.11
Coniah..a *v* no one cares for? 22.28
among the nations..a useless *v*. Hos 8.8

VESSEL — S (cont.)
one *v* for beauty and another   Rom 9.21
empty *v* and not too few.   2Ki 4.3
who bear the *v* of the LORD.   Isa 52.11
sorted the good into *v* but   Mt 13.48
this treasure in earthen *v*,   2Cor 4.7
there are not only *v* of gold   2Tim 2.20

VICTORIOUS
uphold you with my *v*..hand.   Isa 41.10
v is he, humble and riding   Zech 9.9

VICTORY
the LORD..to give you the *v*.'   Deut 20.4
has wrought this great *v*   1Sam 14.45
the LORD gave *v* to David   2Sam 8.6
v..was turned into mourning   19.2
the arrow of *v* over Syria!   2Ki 13.17
the LORD gave *v* to David   1Chr 18.6
stand still, and see the *v*   2Chr 20.17
right hand can give you *v*.   Job 40.14
we shout for joy over your *v*,   Ps 20.5
nor did..own arm give them *v*;   44.3
who givest *v* to kings, who   144.10
the *v* belongs to the LORD.   Prov 21.31
whom *v* meets at every step?   Isa 41.2
so my own arm brought me *v*,   63.5
midst, a warrior who gives *v*;   Zeph 3.17
LORD will give *v* to..Judah   Zech 12.7
till he brings justice to *v*;   Mt 12.20
"Death..swallowed up in *v*."   1Cor 15.54
the *v* that overcomes the world,   1Jn 5.4

VIGILANCE
Keep your heart with all *v*;   Prov 4.23

VINDICATE — S — ING
LORD will *v* his people   Deut 32.36
V me, O God, and defend my   Ps 43.1
the LORD will *v* his people,   135.14
'*V* me against my adversary.'   Lk 18.3
he who *v* me is near. Who will   Isa 50.8
v the righteous by rewarding   1Ki 8.32
v the righteous by rewarding   2Chr 6.23

VINDICATION
v from..God of his salvation.   Ps 24.5
revealed his *v* in the sight of   98.2
The LORD works *v* and justice   103.6

VINE — S
every man under his *v*   1Ki 4.25
didst bring a *v* out of Egypt;   Ps 80.8
see; have regard for this *v*,   80.14
Your mother was like a *v*   Ezek 19.10
Israel is a luxuriant *v* that   Hos 10.1
sit every man under his *v*   Mic 4.4
not drink..this fruit of the *v*   Mt 26.29
fruit of the *v* until that day   Mk 14.25
"I am the true *v*, and my Father   Jn 15.1
and planted it with choice *v*;   Isa 5.2
It has laid waste my *v*, and   Joel 1.7

VINEGAR
for my thirst they gave me *v*   Ps 69.21
Like *v* to the teeth, and   Prov 10.26

VINEYARD — S
Noah..planted a *v*;   Gen 9.20
planted a *v* and..not enjoyed   Deut 20.6
sow your *v* with two kinds of seed,   22.9
Naboth..had a *v* in Jezreel,   1Ki 21.1
but, my own *v* I have not kept!   Sol 1.6
My beloved had a *v* on a very   Isa 5.1
"A pleasant *v*, sing of it!   27.2

to hire laborers for his *v*.   Mt 20.1
'Son, go and work in the *v*   21.28
a *v*, and set a hedge around it,   21.33
parables. "A man planted a *v*,   Mk 12.1
"A man planted a *v*, and let   Lk 20.9
for our *v* are in blossom."   Sol 2.15

VINTAGE
the *v* will fail, the fruit   Isa 32.10
upon your..*v* the destroyer   Jer 48.32
gathered the *v* of the earth,   Rev 14.19

VIOLATE — D
righteousness he will not *v*.   Job 37.23
A man who has *v* the law of   Heb 10.28

VIOLENCE
deliver me from men of *v*.   2Sam 22.49
although there is no *v* in my   Job 16.17
cry out, '*V*!' but I am not   19.7
on his own pate his *v* descends.   Ps 7.16
v covers them as a garment.   73.6
gain by *v*;..takes away..life   Prov 1.19
do no wrong or *v* to the alien,   Jer 22.3
destruction and *v*..before me;   Hab 1.3
covering one's garment with *v*,   Mal 2.16
kingdom of heaven..suffered *v*,   Mt 11.12
"Rob no one by *v* or by false   Lk 3.14

VIPER — S
tongue of a *v* will kill him.   Job 20.16
a *v* came out because of   Acts 28.3
"You brood of *v*! Who warned you   Mt 3.7
brood of *v*! how can you speak   12.34

VIRGIN — S
fair to look upon, a *v*,   Gen 24.16
shall take to wife a *v* of his   Lev 21.14
king, with her *v* companions,   Ps 45.14
as a young man marries a *v*,   Isa 62.5
the *v* daughter of my people   Jer 14.17
may comfort you, O *v* daughter   Lam 2.13
Lament like a *v* girded with   Joel 1.8
"Fallen,..is the *v* Israel;   Amos 5.2
v shall conceive and bear a son,   Mt 1.23
to a *v* betrothed to a man   Lk 1.27
four hundred young *v* who   Judg 21.12

VIRGINITY
in her the tokens of *v*,'   Deut 22.14
broken out..tokens of her *v*   22.15
bewailed her *v* upon the   Judg 11.38

VIRTUE
supplement your faith with *v*,   2Pet 1.5

VISION — S
in a *v*, "Fear not, Abram,   Gen 15.1
known to him in a *v*,   Num 12.6
there was no frequent *v*.   1Sam 3.1
v of Isaiah the son of Amoz,   Isa 1.1
concerning the valley of *v*.   22.1
v of..this has become..sealed.   29.11
prophesying to you a lying *v*,   Jer 14.14
her prophets obtain no *v*   Lam 2.9
seek a *v* from the prophet,   Ezek 7.26
the Spirit..brought me in the *v*   11.24
and every *v* comes to nought'?   12.22
seen a delusive *v*, and uttered   13.7
Daniel said, "I saw in my *v*   Dan 7.2
Daniel, alone saw the *v*, for   10.7
The *v* of Obadiah. Thus says   Obad 1.1
LORD answered.."Write the *v*;   Hab 2.2
prophet..ashamed of his *v*   Zech 13.4
had even seen a *v* of angels,   Lk 24.23
and in a trance I saw a *v*,   Acts 11.5

VISION — S (cont.)

a v appeared to Paul in..night:	Acts 16.9
Lord said to Paul one night in a v,	18.9
not disobedient to the..v,	26.19
Amid thoughts..v of the night,	Job 4.13
and terrify me with v,	7.14
they speak v of their own	Jer 23.16
opened, and I saw v of God.	Ezek 1.1
brought me in the v of God	40.2
Daniel..understanding in all v	Dan 1.17
it was I who multiplied v,	Hos 12.10
your young men shall see v,	Acts 2.17
but I will go on to v and	2Cor 12.1

VISIT — EST — ED

"God will v you; then you	Ex 13.19
I will v their sin upon them."	32.34
dost v him every morning,	Job 7.18
seventy years..I will v you,	Jer 29.10
Thou v the earth and waterest it	Ps 65.9
The Lord v Sarah as he	Gen 21.1
the Lord had v his people	Ruth 1.6
God first v the Gentiles,	Acts 15.14

VOICE — S

"The v is Jacob's voice,	Gen 27.22
v speaking to him from above	Num 7.89
saw no form;..only a v.	Deut 4.12
ever hear the v of a god	4.33
would not obey the v of..Lord	8.20
you did not obey the v	28.45
lips moved,..v was not heard;	1Sam 1.13
after the fire a still small v.	1Ki 19.12
v of the Lord..upon the waters.	Ps 29.3
sends forth his v,..mighty v.	68.33
I hear a v I had not known:	81.5
you would hearken to his v!	95.7
The v of my beloved! Behold,	Sol 2.8
I heard the v of the Lord	Isa 6.8
his majestic v to be heard	30.30
A v says, "Cry!" And I said,	40.6
The v of the Lord, rendering	66.6
mirth and the v of gladness,	Jer 7.34
make to cease..v of mirth and	16.9
will obey the v of the Lord	42.6
The Lord utters his v before	Joel 2.11
v of..Lord cries to the city—	Mic 6.9
"The v..crying in the wilderness:	Mt 3.3
lo, a v from heaven, saying,	3.17
and a v from the cloud said,	17.5
and a v came from heaven,	Mk 1.11
a v came out of the cloud,	9.7
"The v of one crying in the	Lk 3.4
a v came out of the cloud,	9.35
"I am the v of one crying in	Jn 1.23
dead will hear the v of the Son	5.25
His v you have never heard,	5.37
and they will heed my v.	10.16
the v of the Lord came,	Acts 7.31
"The v of a god,..not of man!"	12.22
I heard a v saying to me	26.14
"Their v has gone out to all	Rom 10.18
this v borne from heaven,	2Pet 1.18
I heard a v from heaven like	Rev 14.2
lifted their v together to God	Acts 4.24

VOID

earth..without form and v,	Gen 1.2
earth,..it was waste and v;	Jer 4.23
I will make v the plans of Judah	19.7

VOMIT — S — ED (v)

be sated with it and v it.	Prov 25.16
swallows down riches and v	Job 20.15

land v out its inhabitants.	Lev 18.25
the fish, and it v out Jonah	Jonah 2.10

VOMIT (n)

dog that returns to his v	Prov 26.11
dog turns back to his own v,	2Pet 2.22

VOW — S — ED (v)

you v a v to God, do not delay	Ecc 5.4
When a man v..to the Lord,	Num 30.2
Israel v a vow to the Lord,	21.2

VOW — S (n)

Then Jacob made a v,	Gen 28.20
Bethel, where you..made a v	31.13
offering,..in payment of a v	Lev 22.18
makes a special v of persons	27.2
special v,..of a Nazirite,	Num 6.2
"When you make a v to	Deut 23.21
Jephthah made a v to the	Judg 11.30
vowed a v and said, "O Lord	1Sam 1.11
cut his hair,..he had a v.	Acts 18.18
my v I will pay before those	Ps 22.25
My v to thee I must perform,	56.12
to thee shall v be performed,	65.1
I will pay my v to the Lord	116.18

VOYAGE

the v will be with injury	Acts 27.10

W

WAGES

name your w, and I will	Gen 30.28
changed my w ten times,	31.7
I will give you your w."	Ex 2.9
and does not give him his w;	Jer 22.13
earns w to put them into a bag	Hag 1.6
and be content with your w."	Lk 3.14
the w of sin is death, but	Rom 6.23
his w according to his labor.	1Cor 3.8

WAIT — S — ING

none that w for thee..to shame;	Ps 25.3
for thee I w all the day long.	25.5
W for the Lord; be strong,	27.14
Be still before the Lord, and w	37.7
W for the Lord, and keep to	37.34
I w for the Lord, my soul	130.5
repay evil"; w for the Lord,	Prov 20.22
I will w for the Lord, who	Isa 8.17
O Lord, we w for thee; thy	26.8
who w for the Lord shall renew	40.31
the coastlands w for his law.	42.4
those who w..not..put to shame."	49.23
the coastlands shall w for me,	60.9
God..who works for those who w	64.4
good that one should w quietly	Lam 3.26
w continually for your God."	Hos 12.6
w for the God of my salvation;	Mic 7.7
w for me," says the Lord,	Zeph 3.8
as we w for adoption as sons,	Rom 8.23
as you w for the revealing	1Cor 1.7
to eat, w for one another—	11.33
by faith, we w for the hope	Gal 5.5
w for his Son from heaven,	1Thess 1.10
For God..my soul w in silence;	Ps 62.1
Lord w to be gracious to you,	Isa 30.18
Blessed is he who w and comes	Dan 12.12
I w patiently for the Lord;	Ps 40.1
As they have w for my life,	56.6
My eyes grow dim..w for my God.	69.3
they were all w for him.	Lk 8.40

WAIT — S — ING (cont.)
men who are *w* for their master   Lk 12.36
w for and hastening the   2Pet 3.12

WAKE — NS
for you to *w* from sleep.   Rom 13.11
Morning by morning he *w*, he   Isa 50.4

WALK — S — ED — ING
Arise, *w* through the..land,   Gen 13.17
"I am God Almighty; *w* before me,   17.1
LORD, before whom I *w*,   24.40
shall not *w* in the customs   Lev 20.23
"If you *w* in my statutes and   26.3
And I will *w* among you, and   26.12
"Then if you *w* contrary   26.21
not hearken..but *w* contrary   26.27
w in all the way which   Deut 5.33
to *w* in all his ways,   10.12
You shall *w* after the LORD   13.4
and to *w* in all his ways,   Josh 22.5
sons did not *w* in his ways,   1Sam 8.3
if you will *w* in my ways,   1Ki 3.14
if you..*w* before me, as David   9.4
Jehu was not careful to *w* in   2Ki 10.31
did not *w* in the way of the LORD.   21.22
love to thy servants who *w*   2Chr 6.14
if you *w* before me, as David   7.17
Ought you not to *w* in..fear   Neh 5.9
an oath to *w* in God's law   10.29
W about Zion, go round about   Ps 48.12
may *w* before God in the light   56.13
refused to *w* according to..law.   78.10
that Israel would *w* in my ways!   81.13
they *w* about in darkness; all   82.5
who *w*, O LORD, in the light of   89.15
will *w* with integrity of heart   101.2
I *w* before the LORD   116.9
who *w* in the law of the LORD!   119.1
Though I *w* in..trouble, thou   138.7
my son, do not *w* in the way   Prov 1.15
you will *w* in the way of good   2.20
I *w* in the way of righteousness,   8.20
w in the ways of your heart   Ecc 11.9
that we may *w* in his paths."   Isa 2.3
warned me not to *w* in the way   8.11
"This is the way, *w* in it,"   30.21
they shall *w* and not faint.   40.31
spirit to those who *w* in it: 42.5
in whose ways they would not *w*,   42.24
who *w* in their uprightness.   57.2
rebellious people,..*w* in a way   65.2
the good way is; and *w* in it,   Jer 6.16
I will make them *w* by brooks   31.9
they may *w* in my statutes   Ezek 11.20
your God; *w* in my statutes,   20.19
"Do two *w* together, unless   Amos 3.3
w each in the name of its god,   Mic 4.5
to *w* humbly with your God?   6.8
If you will *w* in my ways   Zech 3.7
or to say, 'Rise and *w*'?   Mt 9.5
take up your pallet, and *w*."   Jn 5.8
W while you have the light,   12.35
in the name of Jesus..*w*."   Acts 3.6
we..might *w* in newness of life.   Rom 6.4
who *w* not according to..flesh   8.4
But I say, *w* by the Spirit,   Gal 5.16
let us also *w* by the Spirit.   5.25
that we should *w* in them.   Eph 2.10
w in love, as Christ loved us-   5.2
Lord; *w* as children of light   5.8
ought to *w* in the same way   1Jn 2.6
they shall *w* with me in white,   Rev 3.4
God *w* in the midst of..camp   Deut 23.14

he *w* on the vault of heaven.'   Job 22.14
Blessed..who *w* in his ways!   Ps 128.1
who *w* in integrity *w* securely,   Prov 10.9
poor who *w* in his integrity   28.6
He who *w* in integrity will   28.18
but the fool *w* in darkness;   Ecc 2.14
He who *w* righteously and   Isa 33.15
not in man who *w* to direct   Jer 10.23
If any one *w* in the day,   Jn 11.9
Enoch *w* with God after   Gen 5.22
Noah *w* with God.   6.9
I have *w* before you from my   1Sam 12.2
because he *w* before thee in   1Ki 3.6
he *w* in all the sins which   15.3
he *w* in..way of Jeroboam   16.26
to sin, but *w* in them;   2Ki 13.6
he *w* in the way of the kings   16.3
and *w* in the customs of the   17.8
but *w* in the customs which   17.19
with Jehoshaphat,..he *w* in   2Chr 17.3
you have not *w* in the ways   21.12
for I have *w* in my integrity,   Ps 26.1
God's house we *w* in fellowship.   55.14
The people who *w* in darkness   Isa 9.2
have not *w* in my statutes,   Ezek 11.12
you have in their counsels;   Mic 6.16
Peter..*w* on the water and came   Mt 14.29
and sins in which you once *w*,   Eph 2.2
heard..God *w* in the garden   Gen 3.8
by *w* in his ways, and   Deut 30.16
I see four men..*w* in..fire,   Dan 3.25
w..in mourning before the LORD   Mal 3.14
came to them, *w* on the sea.   Mt 14.25
he came to them, *w* on the sea.   Mk 6.48
but they look like trees, *w*."   8.24
w in all the commandments   Lk 1.6
they saw Jesus *w* on the sea and   Jn 6.19
and *w* in the fear of the Lord   Acts 9.31
you are no longer *w* in love.   Rom 14.15

WALL — S
waters being a *w* to them   Ex 14.22
they were a *w*..both by night   1Sam 25.16
inspected the *w*; and I turned   Neh 2.15
So the *w* was finished on   6.15
at the dedication of the *w*   12.27
by my God I can leap over a *w*.   Ps 18.29
like..high *w* protecting him.   Prov 18.11
man's hand..wrote on..the *w*   Dan 5.5
I will build a *w* against her,   Hos 2.6
I will be to her a *w* of fire   Zech 2.5
let him down over the *w*,   Acts 9.25
strike you, you white-washed *w*!   23.3
broken down the dividing *w*   Eph 2.14
cities fortified with..*w*,   Deut 3.5
salvation as *w* and bulwarks.   Isa 26.1
an iron pillar, and bronze *w*,   Jer 1.18
By faith the *w* of Jericho   Heb 11.30

WANDER — S — ED — ING
w in the wilderness forty   Num 32.13
May his children *w* about and   Ps 109.10
"They have loved to *w* thus,   Jer 14.10
w from..way of understanding   Prov 21.16
if any..*w* from the truth   Jas 5.19
Some *w* in desert wastes,   Ps 107.4
w, blind, through the streets,   Lam 4.14
Better..than the *w* of desire;   Ecc 6.9
'A *w* Aramean was my father;   Deut 26.5

WANDERER — S
shall be a fugitive and a *w*   Gen 4.12
shall be *w* among the nations.   Hos 9.17

WANT

my shepherd, I shall not w;	Ps 23.1
those who fear him have no w!	34.9
Not that I complain of w;	Phil 4.11

WAR — RED (v)

those who w..shall be..nothing	Isa 41.12
They w against Midian,	Num 31.7

WAR — S (n)

w with Bera king of Sodom,	Gen 14.2
He trains my hands for w, so	Ps 18.34
though w arise against me, yet	27.3
who trains my hands for w,	144.1
neither shall they learn w	Isa 2.4
to Jerusalem to wage w against it,	7.1
in w, will not sit down first	Lk 14.31
not carrying on a worldly w,	2Cor 10.4
Now w arose in heaven, Michael	Rev 12.7
dragon..went off to make w	12.17
He makes w cease to the end	Ps 46.9
you will hear of w and rumors	Mt 24.6
when you hear of w and rumors	Mk 13.7
when you hear of w and tumults,	Lk 21.9
What causes w, and what causes	Jas 4.1

WARFARE

cry to her'that..w is ended,	Isa 40.2
weapons of..w..not worldly	2Cor 10.4
you may wage the good w.	1Tim 1.19

WARMING

with the guards, and w himself	Mk 14.54
Peter..standing and w himself.	Jn 18.18

WARN — ED (v)

I solemnly w you this day	Deut 8.19
Thus he used to w him, so	2Ki 6.10
w them, lest they..come into	Lk 16.28
w them to speak no more	Acts 4.17
"The man solemnly w us,	Gen 43.3
the LORD w Israel and Judah	2Ki 17.13
I w them on the day when	Neh 13.15
by them is thy servant w;	Ps 19.11
I solemnly w your fathers	Jer 11.7
w in a dream not to return	Mt 2.12
vipers! Who w you to flee	3.7
By faith Noah, being w by God	Heb 11.7

WARNING — S (n)

and they became a w.	Num 26.10
you shall give them w from me	Ezek 3.17
trumpet, and did not take w;	33.5
happened to them as a w,	1Cor 10.11
these things are w for us,	10.6

WARRIOR

Jephthah..was a mighty w,	Judg 11.1
he runs upon me like a w.	Job 16.14
midst, a w who gives victory;	Zeph 3.17

WASH — ED

and w them with water.	Ex 29.4
w them off into the water	Num 5.23
elders..shall w their hands	Deut 21.6
w in the Jordan seven times,	2Ki 5.10
If I w myself with snow,	Job 9.30
I w my hands in innocence, and	Ps 26.6
W me..from my iniquity, and	51.2
W..make yourselves clean;	Isa 1.16
Though you w yourself with lye	Jer 2.22
Jerusalem, w your heart from	4.14
fast, anoint your head and w	Mt 6.17
did not first w before dinner.	Lk 11.38
"Go, w in the pool of Siloam"	Jn 9.7

began to w the disciples' feet,	13.5
w away your sins, calling	Acts 22.16
and w my hands in innocence,	Ps 73.13
the Lord..w away the filth	Isa 4.4
took water and w his hands	Mt 27.24
But you were w,..sanctified,	1Cor 6.11

WASTE

the LORD will lay w the earth	Isa 24.1
to generation it shall lie w;	34.10
land a w; your cities..ruins	Jer 4.7
indignant, saying, "Why this w?	Mt 26.8
But Saul laid w the church,	Acts 8.3

WATCH — ES — ED — ING (v)

"The LORD w between you	Gen 31.49
I will take my stand to w,	Hab 2.1
W..for you do not know on	Mt 24.42
W..for you know neither the day	25.13
remain here, and w with me."	26.38
W and pray that you may not	26.41
heed, w; for you do not know	Mk 13.33
death; remain here, and w."	14.34
But w at all times, praying	Lk 21.36
the LORD,..w all his paths.	Prov 5.21
days when God w over me;	Job 29.2
w over my word to perform it."	Jer 1.12
friends, w for my fall.	20.10
traffickers..who were w me,	Zech 11.11

WATCH (n)

keeping w on the evil and	Prov 15.3
they..kept w over him there.	Mt 27.36

WATCHFUL

Be w, stand firm in..faith,	1Cor 16.13
in prayer, being w in it with	Col 4.2

WATCHMAN — MEN

the w called out and told	2Sam 18.25
"W, what of the night? W,	Isa 21.11
have made you..w for..Israel	Ezek 3.17
But if the w sees the sword	33.6
prophet is the w of Ephraim,	Hos 9.8
my soul waits..more than w	Ps 130.6
O Jerusalem, I have set w;	Isa 62.6
I set w over you, saying,	Jer 6.17
when w will call in..Ephraim:	31.6

WATER — S — ED (v)

keeper; every moment I w it.	Isa 27.3
one who w will himself be w.	Prov 11.25
mist went up..and w..ground—	Gen 2.6
Jordan valley was well w	13.10
Jacob..w the flock of Laban	29.10
I planted, Apollos w, but God	1Cor 3.6

WATER — S (n)

there was no w for the people	Ex 17.1
shall have..w of bitterness	Num 5.18
no w for the congregation	20.2
w out of the flinty rock,	Deut 8.15
"Fill four jars with w, and	1Ki 18.33
struck the w, saying, "Where	2Ki 2.14
cold w to a thirsty soul,	Prov 25.25
w from the wells of salvation.	Isa 12.3
his bread..his w will be sure.	33.16
pour w on the thirsty land,	44.3
they find no w, they return	Jer 14.3
He is like a tree planted by w,	17.8
LORD,..fountain of living w.	17.13
sprinkle clean w upon you,	Ezek 36.25
w was issuing from below	47.1
baptize..with w for repentance,	Mt 3.11
w because he is a disciple,	10.42

WATER — S (n) (cont.)

took *w* and washed his hands	Mt 27.24
w to drink because you bear	Mk 9.41
"I baptize you with *w*; but he	Lk 3.16
his finger in *w* and cool my	16.24
"I baptize with *w*; but among	Jn 1.26
said. ."Fill the jars with *w*."	2.7
born of *w* and the Spirit,	3.5
the *w* that I shall give him	4.14
waiting for. .moving of the *w*;	5.3*n*
flow rivers of living *w*.' "	7.38
eunuch said, "See, here is *w*!	Acts 8.36
"Can any one forbid *w* for	10.47
Christ, not with the *w* only	1Jn 5.6
who desires take. .*w* of life	Rev 22.17
the *w* of Gihon and directed	2Chr 32.30
he drew me out of many *w*,	Ps 18.16
the *w* have come up to my neck.	69.1
By the *w* of Babylon,. .wept,	137.1
Many *w* cannot quench love,	Sol 8.7
When you pass through the *w* I	Isa 43.2
a spring. .whose *w* fail not.	58.11
O that my head were *w*, and	Jer 9.1
let justice roll down like *w*,	Amos 5.24
as the *w* cover the sea.	Hab 2.14
living *w* shall flow out from	Zech 14.8

WAVE — S

he who doubts is like a *w* of	Jas 1.6
all thy *w*. .have gone over me.	Ps 42.7
overwhelm me with all thy *w*.	88.7
all thy *w* and thy billows	Jonah 2.3
boat. .was. .beaten by the *w*;	Mt 14.24
and the *w* beat into the boat,	Mk 4.37

WAVE OFFERING

for a *w*. .before the LORD.	Ex 29.24
brought the sheaf of the *w*. .;	Lev 23.15
Levites. .a *w*. .from the people	Num 8.11

WAVERING

trusted in the LORD without *w*.	Ps 26.1
of our hope without *w*, for	Heb 10.23

WAY — S

guard the *w* to the tree	Gen 3.24
LORD has prospered my *w*;	24.56
became impatient on the *w*.	Num 21.4
to walk in the *w* of the LORD	Judg 2.22
of God, to tell us our *w*."	1Sam 9.8
This God—his is perfect;	2Sam 22.31
walked in. .*w* of Jeroboam	1Ki 16.26
the *w*. .I shall not return.	Job 16.22
He has walled up my *w*, so	19.8
he knows the *w* that I take;	23.10
Man does not know the *w* to	28.13
"God understands the *w* to it,	28.23
w to the dwelling of light,	38.19
LORD knows. .*w* of the righteous,	Ps 1.6
make thy *w* straight before me.	5.8
This God—his *w* is perfect;	18.30
and teaches the humble his *w*.	25.9
Commit your *w* to the LORD;	37.5
him in whose *w* he delights;	37.23
Wait. .and keep to his *w*, and	37.34
that thy *w* may be known upon	67.2
Thy *w*, O God, is holy. What	77.13
walks in the *w* that is blameless	101.6
can a young man keep. .*w* pure?	119.9
lead me in the *w* everlasting!	139.24
preserving. .*w* of his saints.	Prov 2.8
Her house is the *w* to Sheol,	7.27
walk in. .*w* of righteousness,	8.20

to him whose *w* is upright,	10.29
but the *w* of the faithless	13.15
w which seems right to a man,	14.12
The *w* of the wicked is an	15.9
w of a sluggard is overgrown	15.19
w which seems right to a man,	16.25
can man understand his *w*?	20.24
Train up a child in the *w* he	22.6
"This is the *w*, walk in it,"	Isa 30.21
prepare the *w* of the LORD,	40.3
"My *w* is hid from the LORD,	40.27
who makes a *w* in the sea,	43.16
turned every one to his own *w*;	53.6
Remove. .from my people's *w*."	57.14
The *w* of peace they know not,	59.8
do not know the *w* of the LORD,	Jer 5.4
w of man is not in himself,	10.23
I set before you the *w* of life	21.8
their *w* shall be. .slippery	23.12
w of the Lord is not just.'	Ezek 18.25
the wicked turn from his *w*	33.11
w of the Lord is not just';	33.17
His *w* is in whirlwind and	Nah 1.3
their own country by another *w*.	Mt 2.12
Prepare the *w* of the Lord,	3.3
who shall prepare thy *w* before	11.10
teach the *w* of God truthfully,	22.16
messenger. .shall prepare thy *w*;	Mk 1.2
but truly teach the *w* of God.	12.14
Prepare the *w* of the Lord,	Lk 3.4
who shall prepare thy *w* before	7.27
"I am the *w*, and the truth,	Jn 14.6
found any belonging to the *W*,	Acts 9.2
to you the *w* of salvation."	16.17
expounded to him the *w* of God	18.26
no little stir concerning the *W*.	19.23
I persecuted this *W* to the death,	22.4
the *W*. .they call a sect,	24.14
w of peace they do not know."	Rom 3.17
the *w* into the sanctuary	Heb 9.8
by the new and living *w*	10.20
known the *w* of righteousness	2Pet 2.21
prepare the *w* for the kings	Rev 16.12
kept the *w* of the LORD,	2Sam 22.22
your God, walking in his *w*	1Ki 2.3
if you will walk in my *w*.	3.14
walked in the *w* of the kings	2Chr 28.2
the knowledge of thy *w*.	Job 21.14
his eyes are upon their *w*.	24.23
Does not he see my *w*, and	31.4
I have kept the *w* of the LORD,	Ps 18.21
and they do not regard my *w*."	95.10
He made known his *w* to Moses,	103.7
man's *w* are before. .the LORD,	Prov 5.21
All the *w* of a man are pure	16.2
She looks well to the *w* of	31.27
that he may teach us his *w*	Isa 2.3
will make straight all his *w*;	45.13
so are my *w* higher than your *w*	55.9
Your *w* and your doings have	Jer 4.18
my eyes are upon all their *w*;	16.17
every man according to his *w*,	17.10
judge you according to your *w*;	Ezek 7.3
works are right. .*w* are just;	Dan 4.37
that he may teach us his *w*	Mic 4.2
sank low. His *w* were as of old.	Hab 3.6
and how inscrutable his *w*!	Rom 11.33
Just and true are thy *w*, O	Rev 15.3

WAYFARER

saw the *w* in the open square	Judg 19.17
opened my doors to the *w*);	Job 31.32
a *w* who turns aside to tarry	Jer 14.8

WEAK

and all knees *w* as water.   Ezek 7.17
The *w*..have not strengthened,   34.4
help the *w*, remembering   Acts 20.35
the man who is *w* in faith,   Rom 14.1
bear with..failings of the *w*,   15.1
God chose what is *w* in the   1Cor 1.27
We are *w*, but you are strong.   4.10
conscience, being *w*, is defiled.   8.7
To the *w* I became *w*, that   9.22
Who is *w*, and I am not *w*?   2Cor 11.29
when I am *w*, then I am strong.   12.10
help the *w*, be patient with   1Thess 5.14
w women, burdened with sins   2Tim 3.6

WEAKNESS — ES

the *w* of God is stronger   1Cor 1.25
I was with you in *w* and in   2.3
For he was crucified in *w*,   2Cor 13.4
to sympathize with our *w*,   Heb 4.15

WEALTH

have gotten me this *w*.'   Deut 8.17
if I..rejoiced because my *w*   Job 31.25
men who trust in their *w*   Ps 49.6
W and riches are in his house;   112.3
diligent man will get..*w*.   Prov 12.27
pretends to be poor, yet has..*w*.   13.7
W hastily gotten will dwindle,   13.11
the sinner's *w* is laid up   13.22
Do not toil to acquire *w*; be   23.4
to whom God has given *w* and   Ecc 5.19
offered for love all the *w* of   Sol 8.7
eat the *w* of the nations,   Isa 61.6
become proud in your *w*—   Ezek 28.5
w of liberality on their part.   2Cor 8.2
abuse..for..Christ great *w*   Heb 11.26
this *w* has been laid waste."   Rev 18.17

WEAPON — S

"You are my hammer and *w* of Jer 51.20
Wisdom..better than *w* of war, Ecc 9.18
with the *w* of righteousness   2Cor 6.7
for the *w* of our warfare   10.4

WEAR

"A woman shall not *w*   Deut 22.5
or she will *w* me out by her   Lk 18.5

WEARINESS

All things are full of *w*;   Ecc 1.8
much study is a *w* of the flesh.   12.12

WEARY — IES — IED (v)

w men, that you *w* my God also? Isa 7.13
The toil of a fool *w* him, so   Ecc 10.15
w me with your iniquities.   Isa 43.24
w with your many counsels;   47.13
w with the length of your way,   57.10
In what have I *w* you? Answer   Mic 6.3
w the LORD with your words.   Mal 2.17

WEARY

there the *w* are at rest.   Job 3.17
fought..and David grew *w*.   2Sam 21.15
feasts.I am *w* of bearing them.   Isa 1.14
None is *w*, none stumbles,   5.27
have been *w* of me, O Israel!   43.22
you;—I am *w* of relenting.   Jer 15.6
let us not grow *w* in well-doing   Gal 6.9
do not be *w* in well-doing.   2Thess 3.13

WEATHER

you say, 'It will be fair *w*;   Mt 16.2

WEAVER — 'S

like a *w*..rolled up my life;   Isa 38.12
swifter than a *w* shuttle,   Job 7.6

WEB

his trust is a spider's *w*.   Job 8.14

WEDDING

Then he said..'The *w* is ready,   Mt 22.8

WEEDS

his enemy came and sowed *w*   Mt 13.25

WEEKS

keep the feast of *w*   Deut 16.10
"Seventy *w* of years..decreed   Dan 9.24

WEEP — ING

had no more strength to *w*.   1Sam 30.4
time to *w*,..a time to laugh;   Ecc 3.4
gone..to the high places to *w*;   Isa 15.2
my soul will *w* in secret for   Jer 13.17
W not for him who is dead,   22.10
"For these things I *w*; my eyes Lam 1.16
they *w* over you in bitterness Ezek 27.31
the ministers of the LORD, *w*   Joel 2.17
Tell it not in Gath, *w* not   Mic 1.10
there men will *w* and gnash   Mt 8.12
men..*w* and gnash their teeth.   24.51
"Blessed are you that *w* now,   Lk 6.21
"Do not *w*; for she is not dead   8.52
do not *w* for me, but *w* for   23.28
going to the tomb to *w* there.   Jn 11.31
rejoice, *w* with those who *w*.   Rom 12.15
will *w* and wail over her   Rev 18.9
My face is red with *w*, and   Job 16.16
I drench my couch with my *w*.   Ps 6.6
for the LORD has heard..my *w*.   6.8
W may tarry for the night, but   30.5
Rachel is *w* for her children;   Jer 31.15
My eyes are spent with *w*;   Lam 2.11
there sat women *w* for Tammuz. Ezek 8.14
Rachel *w* for her children;   Mt 2.18
Mary stood *w* outside the tomb, Jn 20.11
"Woman, why are you *w*? Whom   20.15
"What are you doing, *w* and   Acts 21.13

WEIGH — S — ED

let..others *w* what is said.   1Cor 14.29
but the LORD *w* the spirit.   Prov 16.2
but the LORD *w* the heart.   21.2
who *w* the heart perceive it?   24.12
and by him actions are *w*.   1Sam 2.3
"O that my vexation were *w*,   Job 6.2
(Let me be *w* in a just balance,   31.6
and *w* the mountains in scales   Isa 40.12
and *w* the money on scales.   Jer 32.10
TEKEL, you have been *w* in   Dan 5.27
And they *w* out as my wages   Zech 11.12

WEIGHTS

in your bag two kinds of *w*,   Deut 25.13
Diverse *w*..an abomination   Prov 20.10

WELCOME — D

W one another, therefore,   Rom 15.7
Jesus returned, the crowd *w*   Lk 8.40
he *w* them and spoke to them   9.11
and *w* all who came to him,   Acts 28.30

WELFARE

inquired about their *w*,   Gen 43.27
come to seek the *w* of..Israel. Neh 2.10
who delights in the *w* of his   Ps 35.27
abundant *w* will they give you.   Prov 3.2
in its *w* you will find your *w*.   Jer 29.7
not seeking the *w* of his people,   38.4

WELL — S (n)
she saw a *w* of water;	Gen 21.19
Abimelech about a *w* of water	21.25
outside the city by the *w*	24.11
moved. .and dug another *w*,	26.22
"Spring up, O *w*!—Sing	Num 21.17
from the *w* of Bethlehem	2Sam 23.15
a *w* of living water,	Sol 4.15
As a *w* keeps its water fresh,	Jer 6.7
ox that has fallen into a *w*,	Lk 14.5
Jacob's *w* was there, and so	Jn 4.6
from the *w* of salvation.	Isa 12.3

WELL (adv)
"Is it *w* with the young	2Sam 18.29
your faith has made you *w*."	Mt 9.22
she may be made *w*, and live."	Mk 5.23
many as touched it were made *w*.	6.56
it is *w* that we are here;	Lk 9.33
he had faith to be made *w*,	Acts 14.9

WEPT
Esau lifted. .his voice and *w*.	Gen 27.38
turned away from them and *w*;	42.24
Joseph. .entered. .and *w* there	43.30
he *w* aloud, so. .the Egyptians	45.2
Joseph. .*w* on his neck	46.29
and *w* before the LORD until	Judg 20.23
had seen the first house, *w*	Ezra 3.12
and *w*, and mourned for days;	Neh 1.4
the people *w* when they heard	8.9
w, when we remembered Zion.	Ps 137.1
he went out and *w* bitterly.	Mt 26.75
Peter. .broke down and *w*.	Mk 14.72
saw the city he *w* over it,	Lk 19.41
he went out and *w* bitterly.	22.62
Jesus *w*.	Jn 11.35
I *w* much that no one was found	Rev 5.4

WEST
far as the east is from the *w*,	Ps 103.12
many will come from east and *w*	Mt 8.11
men will come from east and *w*,	Lk 13.29

WHALE
in the belly of the *w*, so will	Mt 12.40

WHEAT
Gideon was beating out *w*	Judg 6.11
has straw in common with *w*?	Jer 23.28
sowed weeds among the *w*,	Mt 13.25
the weeds you root up the *w*	13.29
gather the *w* into his granary,	Lk 3.17
unless a grain of *w* falls	Jn 12.24

WHEEL
there he was working at his *w*.	Jer 18.3
as it were a *w* within a *w*.	Ezek 1.16
as if a *w* were within a *w*.	10.10

WHIP
A *w* for the horse, a bridle	Prov 26.3
making a *w* of cords, he drove	Jn 2.15

WHIRLWIND
Elijah went up by a *w* into	2Ki 2.11
and their wheels like the *w*.	Isa 5.28
sow. .and they shall reap the *w*.	Hos 8.7

WHISPER
All who hate me *w* together	Ps 41.7
speech shall *w* out of. .dust.	Isa 29.4

WHISPERER
a *w* separates close friends.	Prov 16.28
words of a *w* are like delicious	17.8
words of a *w* are like delicious	26.22

WHITE
Let your garments be always *w*;	Ecc 9.8
garments became. .intensely *w*,	Mk 9.3
two men stood. .in *w* robes,	Acts 1.10
his head and his hair were *w*	Rev 1.14

WHITEWASH — ED
As for you, you *w* with lies;	Job 13.4
for you are like *w* tombs,	Mt 23.27
shall strike you, you *w* wall!	Acts 23.3

WHOLESOME
I have made this water *w*;	2Ki 2.21
ear heeds *w* admonition	Prov 15.31

WICK
burning *w* he will not quench;	Isa 42.3
or quench a smoldering *w*, till	Mt 12.20

WICKED — LY
men of Sodom were *w*,	Gen 13.13
"Should you help the *w* and	2Chr 19.2
given into the hand of the *w*;	Job 9.24
the eyes of the *w* will fail;	11.20
The *w* man writhes in pain	15.20
that the *w* man is spared in	21.30
portion of a *w* man with God,	27.13
Break thou the arm of the *w*	Ps 10.15
and the *w* will be no more;	37.10
seen a *w* man overbearing,	37.35
how long shall the *w* exult?	94.3
The *w* man sees it and is angry;	112.10
indignation. .because of the *w*,	119.53
that thou wouldst slay the *w*,	139.19
my prayer. .against their *w*	141.5
the *w*. .cut off from the land,	Prov 2.22
the mouth of the *w* conceals	10.6
w will not dwell in the land.	10.30
but sin overthrows the *w*.	13.6
God scorns the *w*, but the	14.9
the *w* for the day of trouble.	16.4
w flee when no one pursues,	28.1
If favor is shown to the *w*,	Isa 26.10
they made his grave with the *w*	53.9
does the way of the *w* prosper?	Jer 12.1
when a *w* man turns away	Ezek 18.27
if the *w* restores the pledge,	33.15
but the *w* shall do wickedly;	Dan 12.10
'You *w* servant! I forgave you	Mt 18.32
'You *w* and slothful servant!	25.26
"Drive out the *w* person from	1Cor 5.13
brethren, do not act so *w*;	Judg 19.23
have sinned and done very *w*.	1Chr 21.17
and we have acted *w*;	Neh 9.33

WICKEDNESS
LORD saw. .*w* of man was great	Gen 6.5
was this *w* brought to pass?"	Judg 20.3
wicked comes forth *w*';	1Sam 24.13
"Though *w* is sweet in his	Job 20.12
w is. .abomination to my lips.	Prov 8.7
For *w* burns like a fire, it	Isa 9.18
fast. .to loose the bonds of *w*,	58.6
so she keeps fresh her *w*;	Jer 6.7
before your *w* was uncovered?	Ezek 16.57
in turning. .you from your *w*."	Acts 3.26
by their *w* suppress the truth.	Rom 1.18
filled with all manner of *w*,	1.29

WIDOW — S
fatherless, and the *w*,	Deut 14.29
fatherless, and his wife a *w*!	Ps 109.9
fatherless, plead for the *w*.	Isa 1.17
How like a *w* has she become,	Lam 1.1
poor *w*. .put in two. .coins,	Mk 12.42

WIDOW — S (cont.)

the only son..she was a w;	Lk 7.12
poor w put in two copper coins.	21.2
You have sent w away empty,	Job 22.9
that w may be their spoil,	Isa 10.2
and let your w trust in me."	Jer 49.11
many w in Israel in the days	Lk 4.25
their w were neglected in	Acts 6.1
Honor w who are real w.	1Tim 5.3
take a w garment in pledge;	Deut 24.17
I caused the w heart to sing	Job 29.13
maintains the w boundaries.	Prov 15.25
for you devour w houses and	Mt 23.14n
scribes..who devour w houses	Mk 12.40

WIFE — 'S

his w'; then they will kill	Gen 12.12
If any man's w goes astray	Num 5.12
Ruth and she became his w;	Ruth 4.13
Abigail, to make her his w.	1Sam 25.39
then let my w grind for	Job 31.10
Your w will be..fruitful vine	Ps 128.3
rejoice in..w of your youth,	Prov 5.18
goes in to his neighbor's w;	6.29
who finds a w finds a good	18.22
prudent w is from the LORD.	19.14
A good w who can find? She	31.10
Enjoy life with..w..you love,	Ecc 9.9
"If a man divorces his w and	Jer 3.1
as a faithless w leaves her	3.20
and at evening my w died.	Ezek 24.18
"Go, take..a w of harlotry	Hos 1.2
Israel did service for a w,	12.12
she is your..w by covenant.	Mal 2.14
took his w, but knew her not	Mt 1.24
'Whoever divorces his w, let	5.31
leave..and be joined to his w,	19.5
his w sent word to him,	27.19
lawful..man to divorce his w?"	Mk 10.2
take the w, and raise up children	12.19
'I have married a w, and	Lk 14.20
Remember Lot's w.	17.32
his w came in, not knowing	Acts 5.7
the w does not rule over her	1Cor 7.4
Are you bound to a w? Do not	7.27
A w is bound to her husband	7.39
right to be accompanied by a w,	9.5
man shall..be joined to his w,	Eph 5.31
you know how to take a w	1Thess 4.4
w quarreling is a continual	Prov 19.13

WILDERNESS

"They shall die in the w."	Num 26.65
the great and terrible w,	Deut 8.15
the strongholds in the w,	1Sam 23.14
What is..coming up from the w,	Sol 3.6
w and..dry land shall be glad,	Isa 35.1
make the w a pool of water,	41.18
holy cities have become a w,	64.10
brought them into the w.	Ezek 20.10
he was in the w forty days,	Mk 1.13
for forty days in the w, tempted	Lk 4.2
go out into the w to behold?	7.24

WILL — S (v)

touched him, saying, 'I w; be	Mt 8.3
"If you w,..make me clean."	Mk 1.40
not what I w, but what thou w."	14.36
to w and to work for his good	Phil 2.13
ought to say, "If the Lord w,	Jas 4.15

WILL (n)

according to the w of your	Ezra 7.18
I delight to do thy w, O my	Ps 40.8

w of the LORD to bruise him;	Isa 53.10
Thy w be done, On earth as it	Mt 6.10
whoever does..w of my Father	12.50
it is not the w of my Father	18.14
unless I drink it, thy w be done."	26.42
does..w of God is my brother,	Mk 3.35
"My food is to do the w of him	Jn 4.34
but the w of him who sent me.	5.30
but the w of him who sent me;	6.38
if any man's w is to do his w,	7.17
"The w of the Lord be done."	Acts 21.14
by God's w I may..succeed	Rom 1.10
know his w and approve what	2.18
it depends not upon man's w	9.16
prove what is the w of God,	12.2
if I do this of my own w,	1Cor 9.17
and to us by the w of God.	2Cor 8.5
according to the w of our God	Gal 1.4
what the w of the Lord is.	Eph 5.17
assured in all the w of God.	Col 4.12
For this is the w of God,	1Thess 4.3
I have come to do thy w, O	Heb 10.7
God's w that by doing right	1Pet 2.15
if that should be God's w,	3.17
passions but by the w of God.	4.2
who does the w of God abides	1Jn 2.17
by thy w they existed and	Rev 4.11

WILLING — LY

"Father, if thou art w, remove	Lk 22.42
Who then will offer w,	1Chr 29.5

WILLOWS

boughs..and w of the brook;	Lev 23.40
On the w..we hung..our lyres.	Ps 137.2

WIN

slave to all, that I might w	1Cor 9.19
not lose..but..w a full reward.	2Jn 8

WIND

strong w rent the mountains,	1Ki 19.11
By his w..heavens..made fair;	Job 26.13
from the raging w and tempest."	Ps 55.8
a stormy w came out of..north,	Ezek 1.4
For they sow the w, and..reap	Hos 8.7
Ephraim..pursues the east w	12.1
east w, the w of the LORD,	13.15
like the rush of a mighty w,	Acts 2.2
he awoke and rebuked the w	Lk 8.24
The w blows where it wills,	Jn 3.8

WINDOW — S

in a basket through a w in	2Cor 11.33
w of the heavens..opened	Gen 7.11
"If the LORD..make w in	2Ki 7.2
he had w in his upper chamber	Dan 6.10

WINE

Noah awoke from his w	Gen 9.24
made their father drink w	19.35
"Drink no w nor strong drink	Lev 10.8
shall separate himself from w	Num 6.3
drink no w or strong drink,	Judg 13.4
heart is merry with w,	2Sam 13.28
the king was merry with w,	Est 1.10
W is a mocker, strong drink	Prov 20.1
Those who tarry long over w,	23.30
how to cheer my body with w—	Ecc 2.3
For your love is better than w,	Sol 1.2
tarry..till w inflames them!	Isa 5.11
who are heroes at drinking w,	5.22
an outcry..for lack of w;	24.11
they say, "let us get w,	56.12
answered, "We will.drink no w,	Jer 35.6
No priest shall drink w,	Ezek 44.21

WINE (cont.)
drank *w*, and praised the gods Dan 5.4
W and new *w* take away the Hos 4.11
who drink *w* in bowls, and Amos 6.6
Moreover, *w* is treacherous; Hab 2.5
they offered him *w* to drink, Mt 27.34
puts new *w* into old wineskins; Mk 2.22
offered..*w* mingled with myrrh; 15.23
no one puts new *w* into old Lk 5.37
tasted the water now become *w*, Jn 2.9
"They are filled with new *w*." Acts 2.13
And do not get drunk with *w*, Eph 5.18
use a little *w* for the sake 1Tim 5.23

WINE PRESS
beating out wheat in the *w*.., Judg 6.11
"I have trodden the *w*..alone, Isa 63.3
threw it into the great *w*.. Rev 14.19

WINESKINS
new wine put into old *w*; if Mt 9.17
no one puts new wine into old *w*; Lk 5.37

WINGS
I bore you on eagles' *w* Ex 19.4
under those *w* you have come Ruth 2.12
hide me in..shadow of thy *w*, Ps 17.8
came..upon the *w* of the wind. 18.10
refuge in the shadow of thy *w*. 36.7
"O that I had *w* like a dove! 55.6
safe under the shelter of thy *w*! 61.4
takes..*w*, flying like..eagle Prov 23.5
the seraphim; each had six *w*: Isa 6.2

WINKS
w with his eyes, scrapes with Prov 6.13
He who *w*..eye causes trouble, 10.10

WINNOW
You shall *w* them and the wind Isa 41.16
Babylon..and they shall *w* her, Jer 51.2

WINTER
earth remains,..*w*..not cease." Gen 8.22
w is past, the rain is over Sol 2.11
harbor was not suitable to *w* Acts 27.12
or even spend the *w*, so that 1Cor 16.6
Do your best..come before *w*. 2Tim 4.21
decided to spend the *w* there. Tit 3.12

WISDOM
that will be your *w* and your Deut 4.6
my lord has *w* like the *w* 2Sam 14.20
And God gave Solomon *w* and 1Ki 4.29
he was full of *w*, understanding, 7.14
seen all the *w* of Solomon, 10.4
Solomon excelled..and in *w*. 10.23
Give me now *w* and knowledge 2Chr 1.10
greatness of your *w* was not told 9.6
and *w* will die with you. Job 12.2
"But where shall *w* be found? 28.12
Who has put *w* in the clouds, 38.36
mouth of..righteous utters *w*, Ps 37.30
My mouth shall speak *w*; the 49.2
fear of..LORD..beginning of *w*; 111.10
That men may know *w* and Prov 1.2
W cries aloud in the street; 1.20
w will come into your heart, 2.10
for *w* is better than jewels, 8.11
W builds her house, but folly 14.1
To get *w* is better than gold; 16.16
He who gets *w* loves himself; 19.8
No *w*, no understanding, no 21.30
By a house is built, and 24.3
She opens her mouth with *w*, 31.26
search..by *w* all that is done Ecc 1.13

protection of *w* is like.the 7.12
the poor man's *w* is despised, 9.16
spirit of *w* and understanding, Isa 11.2
prudent? Has their *w* vanished? Jer 49.7
established the world by his *w*, 51.1
And in every matter of *w* and Dan 1.20
and *w*, like the *w* of the gods, 5.11
I have..come out to give you *w* 9.22
w is justified by her deeds." Mt 11.19
to hear the *w* of Solomon, 12.42
"Where did this man get this *w* 13.54
Jesus increased in *w* and in Lk 2.52
w is justified by..her children." 7.35
to hear the *w* of Solomon, 11.31
will give you a mouth and *w*, 21.15
Moses was instructed in..*w* Acts 7.22
w and knowledge of God! Rom 11.33
and not with eloquent *w*, 1Cor 1.17
the power..and the *w* of God. 1.24
Jesus, whom God made our *w*, 1.30
among the mature we do impart *w*, 2.6
the *w* of this world is folly 3.19
To one..the utterance of *w*, 12.8
may give you a spirit of *w* Eph 1.17
w of God might..be made known 3.10
If any of you lacks *w*, let him Jas 1.5
w from above is first pure, 3.17
according to the *w* given him, 2Pet 3.15

WISE
If they were *w*, they would Deut 32.29
I give you a *w* and..mind, 1Ki 3.12
the *w* in their own craftiness; Job 5.13
see that even the *w* die, Ps 49.10
The *w* of heart will heed Prov 10.8
A *w* son hears his father's 13.1
and a *w* man will appease it. 16.14
hear the words of the *w*, and 22.17
who are *w* in their own eyes, Isa 5.21
Where then are your *w* men? 19.12
"How can you say, 'We are *w*, Jer 8.8
commanded that all the *w* men Dan 2.12
those who are *w* shall shine 12.3
is *w*, let him understand Hos 14.9
w men from the East came to Mt 2.1
does them will be like a *w* man 7.24
be *w* as serpents and innocent 10.16
hidden these things from the *w* 11.25
the faithful and *w* servant, 24.45
Where is the *w* man? Where 1Cor 1.20
bear with fools, being *w* 2Cor 11.19
not as unwise men but as *w*, Eph 5.15
Who is *w* and understanding Jas 3.13

WISER
thy commandment makes me *w* Ps 119.98
you are indeed *w* than Daniel; Ezek 28.3
are *w* in their own generation Lk 16.8

WITHER — S — ED
and *w* like the green herb. Ps 37.2
Their leaves will not *w* nor Ezek 47.12
The grass *w*, the flower fades, Isa 40.7
the trees of the field are *w*; Joel 1.12
there was a man with a *w* hand. Mt 12.10
And the fig tree *w* at once. 21.19
man was there who had a *w* hand. Mk 3.1
since it had no root it *w* away. 4.6
tree which you cursed has *w*." 11.21
man..whose right hand was *w*. Lk 6.6

WITHHELD
you have not *w* your son, Gen 22.12
"If I have *w*..that the poor Job 31.16

WITHHELD (cont.)

not *w* the request of his lips.	Ps 21.2
I also *w* the rain from you	Amos 4.7

WITHHOLD

No good thing does the LORD *w*	Ps 84.11
Do not *w* good from those to	Prov 3.27
do not *w* your coat as well.	Lk 6.29

WITNESS — ES (v)

call heaven and earth to *w*	Deut 4.26
call heaven and earth to *w*	30.19
Thus you *w* against yourselves,	Mt 23.31
w that this is the Son of God."	Jn 1.34
The pride of Israel *w* against	Hos 7.10

WITNESS — ES (n)

you may be a *w* for me	Gen 21.30
God is *w* between you and me."	31.50
"You shall not bear false *w*	Ex 20.16
the testimony of one *w*.	Num 35.30
" 'Neither..bear false *w*	Deut 5.20
that this song may be a *w* for me	31.19
be a *w* between us and you,	Josh 22.27
LORD will be *w* between us;	Judg 11.10
behold, my *w* is in heaven,	Job 16.19
A faithful *w* does not lie,	Prov 14.5
A truthful *w* saves lives,	14.25
false *w* will not go unpunished,	19.5
Be not a *w* against..neighbor	24.28
A man who bears false *w*	25.18
made him a *w* to the peoples,	Isa 55.4
and I am *w*, says the LORD.' "	Jer 29.23
true and faithful *w* against us	42.5
let the Lord GOD be a *w* against	Mic 1.2
the LORD was *w* to the covenant	Mal 2.14
swift *w* against the sorcerers,	3.5
bear *w* to what we have seen;	Jn 3.11
to whom you bore *w*, here he is,	3.26
bears *w* to what he has seen	3.32
If I bear *w* to myself, my	5.31
Father..himself borne *w* to me.	5.37
it is they that bear *w* to me;	5.39
Spirit..will bear *w* to me;	15.26
bear *w* to the wrong; but if	18.23
bearing *w* to these things,	21.24
Lord, who bore *w* to the word	Acts 14.3
not leave himself without *w*,	14.17
you will be a *w* for him to all	22.15
blood of Stephen thy *w* was	22.20
you must bear *w* also at Rome."	23.11
and bear *w* to the things	26.16
For God is my *w*, whom I serve	Rom 1.9
the prophets bear *w* to it,	3.21
Spirit..bearing *w* with our spirit	8.16
who bore *w* to the word of God	Rev 1.2
Jesus Christ the faithful *w*,	1.5
the faithful and true *w*, the	3.14
slain..for the *w* they had borne;	6.9
On the evidence of two *w*	Deut 17.6
And they said, "We are *w*."	Josh 24.22
"We are *w*. May the LORD make	Ruth 4.11
"You are my *w*," says..LORD,	Isa 43.10
declared it? And you are my *w*!	44.8
I signed the deed,..got *w*,	Jer 32.10
evidence of two or three *w*.	Mt 18.16
"Why do we still need *w*?	Mk 14.63
You are *w* of these things.	Lk 24.48
you also are *w*, because	Jn 15.27
shall be my *w* in Jerusalem	Acts 1.8
and of that we all are *w*.	2.32
we are *w* to these things,	5.32
we are *w* to all that he did	10.39
evidence of two or three *w*.	2Cor 13.1

You are *w*, and God also,	1Thess 2.10
by so great a cloud of *w*,	Heb 12.1
three *w*, the Spirit, the water,	1Jn 5.8
I will grant my two *w* power	Rev 11.3

WIVES

W, be subject to..husbands,	Eph 5.22
W, be subject to..husbands,	Col 3.18
w, be submissive to..husbands,	1Pet 3.1

WOE

If I am wicked, *w* to me!	Job 10.15
W to those who join house to	Isa 5.8
W to those who rise early in	5.11
"*W* is me! For I am lost; for	6.5
I make weal and create *w*, I	45.7
w to that man by whom the Son	Mk 14.21
W to me if I do not preach	1Cor 9.16
as it flew in midheaven, "*W*,	Rev 8.13

WOLF — VES

w shall dwell with the lamb,	Isa 11.6
The *w* and the lamb shall feed	65.25
after my departure fierce *w*	Acts 20.29

WOMAN

she shall be called *W*,	Gen 2.23
"The *w* whom thou gavest	3.12
A foolish *w* is noisy; she is	Prov 9.13
a *w* who fears the LORD is	31.30
the *w* whose heart is snares	Ecc 7.26
a young *w* shall conceive and	Isa 7.14
a *w* who had..a hemorrhage	Mt 9.20
w of the city, who was a sinner,	Lk 7.37
w..had a spirit of infirmity	13.11
"O *w*, what have you to do with	Jn 2.4
a *w*..caught in adultery,	8.3n
When a *w* is in travail she	16.21
for a man not to touch a *w*.	1Cor 7.1
created for *w*, but *w* for man.)	11.9
sent forth his Son, born of *w*,	Gal 4.4
a *w* clothed with the sun,	Rev 12.1
the *w* fled into the wilderness,	12.6
a *w* sitting on a scarlet beast	17.3

WOMB

how the spirit comes..in the *w*	Ecc 11.5
"Blessed is the *w* that bore	Lk 11.27
second time into his mother's *w*	Jn 3.4

WOMEN

Solomon loved many foreign *w*:	1Ki 11.1
seven *w*..take hold of one man	Isa 4.1
you *w* who are at ease, hear	32.9
also *w* looking on from afar,	Mk 15.40
be two *w* grinding together;	Lk 17.35
and the *w* who had followed	23.49
natural relations with *w*	Rom 1.27
the *w* should keep silence	1Cor 14.34
that *w* should adorn..modestly	1Tim 2.9
W received their dead by	Heb 11.35

WONDER — ED (v)

why do you *w* at this, or why	Acts 3.12
no..answer, so that Pilate *w*.	Mk 15.5
all who heard it *w* at what	Lk 2.18
they *w*; and they recognized	Acts 4.13

WONDERFUL

my name, seeing it is *w*?"	Judg 13.18
your love to me was *w*,	2Sam 1.26
not understand, things too *w*	Job 42.3
Thy testimonies are *w*;	Ps 119.129
Such knowledge..too *w* for me;	139.6
W are thy works! Thou knowest	139.14
Three things are too *w* for	Prov 30.18
will be called "*W* Counselor,	Isa 9.6

WONDERFUL (cont.)
for thou hast done w things, | Isa 25.1
"Great and w are thy deeds, | Rev 15.3

WONDERS (n)
smite Egypt with all the w | Ex 3.20
glorious deeds, doing w? | 15.11
has done, the w he wrought | 1Chr 16.12
Dost thou work w for the dead? | Ps 88.10
him who alone does great w, | 136.4
I will show w in the heaven | Acts 2.19

WONDROUS
and telling all thy w deeds. | Ps 26.7
who alone does w things. | 72.18
behold w things out of thy law. | 119.18

WOOL
mingled stuff, w and linen | Deut 22.11
She seeks w and flax, and | Prov 31.13
they shall become like w. | Isa 1.18

WORD — S
whether my w will come true | Num 11.23
But the w is very near you; | Deut 30.14
"If one ventures a w with you, | Job 4.2
and my w dropped upon them. | 29.22
In God, whose w I praise, | Ps 56.10
he sent forth his w, and healed | 107.20
guarding it according to thy w. | 119.9
laid up thy w in my heart, | 119.11
thy w is firmly fixed in the | 119.89
to the earth; his w runs swiftly. | 147.15
a good w makes him glad. | Prov 12.25
w in season, how good it is! | 15.23
w fitly spoken is like apples | 25.11
w of. . God will stand for ever. | Isa 40.8
a w that shall not return: | 45.23
so shall my w be that goes | 55.11
let him. . speak my w faithfully. | Jer 23.28
shall know whose w will stand, | 44.28
not. . bread alone, but by every w | Mt 4.4
say the w, and my servant will | 8.8
account for every careless w | 12.36
he was preaching the w to them. | Mk 2.2
The sower sows the w. | 4.14
and ministers of the w, | Lk 1.2
in peace, according to thy w; | 2.29
for his w was with authority. | 4.32
at your w I will let down the nets." | 5.5
say the w, and let my servant | 7.7
with God, and the W was God. | Jn 1.1
who hears my w and believes | 5.24
do not have his w abiding in you, | 5.38
"If you continue in my w, you | 8.31
because my w finds no place | 8.37
already made clean by the w | 15.3
and they have kept thy w. | 17.6
Sanctify them. . thy w is truth. | 17.17
fell on all who heard the w. | Acts 10.44
Gentiles should hear the w | 15.7
received the w with. . eagerness, | 17.11
and to the w of his grace, | 20.32
not as though the w. . failed. | Rom 9.6
w is near you, on your lips | 10.8
from the Gentiles, by w and | 15.18
not, . . peddlers of God's w; | 2Cor 2.17
Let him who is taught the w | Gal 6.6
washing of water with the w, | Eph 5.26
holding fast the w of life, | Phil 2.16
Let. . w of Christ dwell in you | Col 3.16
received. . w in. . affliction, | 1Thess 1.6
rightly handling. . w of truth. | 2Tim 2.15
preach the w, be urgent in | 4.2

must hold firm to the sure w | Tit 1.9
first principles of God's w. | Heb 5.12
but the w of the oath, which | 7.28
with meekness the implanted w, | Jas 1.21
may be won without a w by | 1Pet 3.1
the prophetic w made sure | 2Pet 1.19
concerning the w of life— | 1Jn 1.1
liar, and his w is not in us. | 1.10
whoever keeps his w, in him | 2.5
and yet you have kept my w | Rev 3.8
earth had one language. . few w. | Gen 11.1
let them hear my w, | Deut 4.10
lay up these w of mine | 11.18
put my w in his mouth, | 18.18
tells the king of Israel the w | 2Ki 6.12
not denied the w of the Holy | Job 6.10
think that you can reprove w, | 6.26
or in w. . can do no good? | 15.3
"How long will you hunt for w? | 18.2
lay up his w in your heart. | 22.22
treasured in my bosom the w | 23.12
is no speech, nor are there w; | Ps 19.3
Let the w of my mouth and | 19.14
see a man. . hasty in his w? | Prov 29.20
The w of Agur son of Jakeh | 30.1
therefore let your w be few. | Ecc 5.2
The w of a wise man's mouth | 10.12
Thy w were found, and I ate | Jer 15.16
let us not heed any of his w." | 18.18
but my w will not pass away. | Mt 24.35
but my w will not pass away. | Mk 13.31
but my w will not pass away. | Lk 21.33
You have the w of eternal life; | Jn 6.68
The w that I say to you I | 14.10
speak to the people all the w | Acts 5.20
speak five w with my mind, | 1Cor 14.19

WORD OF GOD
make known to you the w. . ." | 1Sam 9.27
the w. . came to Shemaiah the | 1Ki 12.22
Every w. . proves true; he | Prov 30.5
you have made void the w. . | Mt 15.6
making void the w. . through | Mk 7.13
the w. . came to John the son | Lk 3.2
people pressed. . to hear the w. ., | 5.1
parable. . The seed is the w. . . | 8.11
who hear the w. . and do it." | 8.21
who hear the w. . and keep it!" | 11.28
give up. . preaching the w. . | Acts 6.2
And the w. . increased; | 6.7
Samaria had received the w. ., | 8.14
Gentiles also. . received the w. . | 11.1
the w. . grew and multiplied. | 12.24
It was necessary that the w. . | 13.46
sword of the Spirit. . is the w. . . | Eph 6.17
much more bold to speak the w. . | Phil 1.14
accepted it. . as. . the w. ., | 1Thess 2.13
consecrated by. . w. . and prayer. | 1Tim 4.5
But the w. . is not fettered. | 2Tim 2.9
that the w. . not be discredited. | Tit 2.5
the w. . is living and active, | Heb 4.12
tasted the goodness of the w. . | 6.5
the living and abiding w. .; | 1Pet 1.23
by the w. . heavens existed | 2Pet 3.5
and the w. . abides in you, | 1Jn 2.14
who bore witness to the w. . | Rev 1.2
those. . slain for the w. . | 6.9
name. . is called. . The W. . . | 19.13
had been beheaded for. . the w. . | 20.4

WORD — S OF THE LORD
w. . came to Abram in a vision, | Gen 15.1
Then he who feared the w. . | Ex 9.20

WORD — S OF THE LORD (cont.)

go beyond..w.., to do..good	Num 24.13
to declare to you the w..;	Deut 5.5
the w..was rare in those days;	1Sam 3.1
the w..came to Nathan,	2Sam 7.4
according to the w.., which	1Ki 14.18
"This is the w.., which he	2Ki 9.36
Hezekiah to Isaiah, "The w..	20.19
defiled it, according to the w..	23.16
the w..came to Nathan,	1Chr 17.3
For the w..is upright; and all	Ps 33.4
By the w..heavens were made,	33.6
came to pass the w..tested him	105.19
law, and the w..from Jerusalem.	Isa 2.3
Then the w..came to Isaiah:	38.4
w..you have spoken is good."	39.8
Hear the w.., you who tremble	66.5
w..came in the days of Josiah	Jer 1.2
the w..is..an object of scorn,	6.10
they have rejected the w..,	8.9
w..has become..a reproach	20.8
The w..that came to Hosea the	Hos 1.1
The w..that came to Joel,	Joel 1.1
the w..came to Jonah the son	Jonah 1.1
the w..which came to Zephaniah	Zeph 1.1
w..grew and prevailed mightily	Acts 12.20
they spoke the w..to him	16.32
that the w..may speed on	2Thess 3.1
therefore hearken to the w...	1Sam 15.1
read the w..from the scroll	Jer 36.6
famine..of hearing the w..,	Amos 8.11

WORK — S — ED — ING (v)

the people had a mind to w.	Neh 4.6
w, for I am with you, says	Hag 2.4
We must w the works of him	Jn 9.4
one who' does not w but trusts	Rom 4.5
w out your own salvation	Phil 2.12
If any one will not w, let	2Thess 3.10
and w with willing hands.	Prov 31.13
God w for good with those who	Rom 8.28
'These last w only one hour,	Mt 20.12
while the Lord w with them	Mk 16.20n
w through me..for..Gentiles),	Gal 2.8
there he was w at his wheel.	Jer 18.3
working still, and I am w."	Jn 5.17
W together with him, then,	2Cor 6.1

WORK — S (n)

rested..from all his w	Gen 2.2
your w, but on the seventh	Ex 23.12
seen all the great w of the	Deut 11.7
necks to the w of their Lord.	Neh 3.5
to despise the w of thy hands	Job 10.3
according to the w of a man	34.11
do not regard..w of his hands,	Ps 28.5
heavens are the w of thy hands.	102.25
Man goes forth to his w and	104.23
the w..comes back to him.	Prov 12.14
Commit your w to the LORD,	16.3
I saw all the w of God, that	Ecc 8.17
I am doing a w in your days	Hab 1.5
thy w, O LORD, do I fear.	3.2
having accomplished the w	Jn 17.4
each man's w will become	1Cor 3.13
nearly died for..w of Christ,	Phil 2.30
esteem..because of their w.	1Thess 5.13
establish..in every good w	2Thess 2.17
equipped for every good w.	2Tim 3.17
heavens are the w of thy hands;	Heb 1.10
tell of all his wonderful w!	1Chr 16.9
consider the wondrous w of	Job 37.14
LORD, how manifold are thy w!	Ps 104.24

All thy w shall give thanks	145.10
w praise her in the gates.	Prov 31.31
I know their w and..thoughts,	Isa 66.18
w which the Father..granted me	Jn 5.36
the w of God..manifest in him.	9.3
The w that I do in my Father's	10.25
Dorcas..was full of good w	Acts 9.36
justified in his sight by w	Rom 3.20
not because of w but..of..call,	9.11
no longer on the basis of w;	11.6
receive..Spirit by w of the law,	Gal 3.2
the w of the flesh are plain:	5.19
not because of w, lest any man	Eph 2.9
faith..if it has no w, is dead.	Jas 2.17
Abraham..justified by w,	2.21

WORKERS

A w appetite works for him;	Prov 16.26
depart..you w of iniquity!'	Lk 13.27
we are fellow w for God;	1Cor 3.9
may be fellow w in the truth.	3Jn 8

WORKMAN — SHIP

as one approved, a w who	2Tim 2.15
Are not you my w in the Lord?	1Cor 9.1
For we are his w, created	Eph 2.10

WORLD — LY

their words to the end of..w.	Ps 19.4
the field is the w, and the	Mt 13.38
"Go into all the w and preach	Mk 16.15n
gains the whole w and loses	Lk 9.25
you are of this w, I am not	Jn 8.23
"For judgment I came into..w,	9.39
the w has gone after him."	12.19
In the w you have tribulation;	16.33
even as I am not of the w.	17.14
the w may believe that thou	17.21
turned the w upside down	Acts 17.6
as sin came into the w through	Rom 5.12
spectacle to the w, to angels,	1Cor 4.9
For though we live in the w	2Cor 10.3
the w was created by the word	Heb 11.3
of whom the w was not worthy—	11.38
Do not love the w or the	1Jn 2.15
Do not wonder..w hates you.	3.13
They are of the w, therefore	4.5
weapons..not w but have divine	2Cor 10.4

WORM — S

But I am a w, and no man;	Ps 22.6
Fear not, you w Jacob, you	Isa 41.14
where their w does not die,	Mk 9.48
he was eaten by w and died.	Acts 12.23

WORSE

no avail; my distress grew w,	Ps 39.2
last state..w than the first.	Mt 12.45
from bad to w, deceivers	2Tim 3.13

WORSHIP — S — ED — ING

lad will go yonder and w,	Gen 22.5
elders of Israel, and w afar	Ex 24.1
(for you shall w no other god,	34.14
w before the LORD your God;	Deut 26.10
by year from his city to w	1Sam 1.3
W the LORD in holy array;	1Chr 16.29
I will w toward thy holy temple	Ps 5.7
nations shall w before him.	22.27
w the LORD in holy array.	29.2
come, let us w and bow down,	95.6
W the LORD in holy array;	96.9
let us w at his footstool!"	132.7
their idols..they made..to w,	Isa 2.20
will come and w the LORD	27.13

WORSHIP — S — ED — ING (cont.)

"You shall *w* before this altar"?	Isa 36.7
who enter these gates to *w*	Jer 7.2
and *w* any god except their own	Dan 3.28
year after year to *w*..King,	Zech 14.16
East, and have come to *w* him."	Mt 2.2
if you will fall down and *w* me."	4.9
'You shall *w* the Lord your God	4.10
If you, then, will *w* me, it	Lk 4.7
nor in Jerusalem will you *w*	Jn 4.21
must *w* in spirit and truth."	4.24
among those who went up to *w*	12.20
over to *w* the host of heaven,"	Acts 7.42
to *w* God contrary to the law."	18.13
she whom..Asia and..world *w*."	19.27
he will *w* God and declare	1Cor 14.25
true circumcision, who *w* God	Phil 3.3
"Let all God's angels *w* him."	Heb 1.6
who dwell on earth will *w* it,	Rev 13.8
and *w* him who made heaven	14.7
I fell down at his feet to *w*	19.10
I fell down to *w* at the feet	22.8
All the earth *w* thee; they sing	Ps 66.4
also he makes a god and *w* it,	Isa 44.15
man bowed his head and *w*	Gen 24.26
bowed their heads and *w*.	Ex 4.31
bowed their heads and *w*.	12.27
served other gods and *w*	Deut 17.3
rose..and *w* before the Lord;	1Sam 1.19
house of the Lord, and *w*;	2Sam 12.20
summit, where God was *w*,	15.32
bowed their heads, and *w*	1Chr 29.20
fell upon the ground, and *w*.	Job 1.20
they fell down and *w* him.	Mt 2.11
And those in the boat *w* him,	14.33
hold of his feet and *w* him.	28.9
they *w* him, and returned	Lk 24.52n
I believe"; and he *w* him.	Jn 9.38
Cornelius met him..and *w*	Acts 10.25
the elders fell down and *w*.	Rev 5.14
Men *w* the dragon, for he had	13.4
Jerusalem fell down..*w* the	2Chr 20.18
w with fasting and prayer	Lk 2.37

WORSHIPER — S

if any one is a *w* of God	Jn 9.31
all the *w* of Baal came, so	2Ki 10.21

WORTH

that you are a woman of *w*.	Ruth 3.11
you are *w* ten thousand of	2Sam 18.3
sufferings..not *w* comparing	Rom 8.18
But Timothy's *w* you know,	Phil 2.22

WORTHY

not *w* of the least of all	Gen 32.10
sandals I am not *w* to carry;	Mt 3.11
"Lord, I am not *w* to have you	8.8
mother more than me is not *w*	10.37
sandals I am not *w* to..untie.	Mk 1.7
"He is *w* to have you do this	Lk 7.4
I am not *w* to have you come	7.6
I am no longer *w* to be called	15.21
sandal I am not *w* to untie."	Jn 1.27
counted *w* to suffer dishonor	Acts 5.41
sandals..I am not *w* to untie.'	13.25
that our God may make you *w*	2Thess 1.11
Jesus..*w* of as much more glory	Heb 3.3
of whom the world was not *w*—	11.38
in white, for they are *w*.	Rev 3.4
"*W* art thou, our Lord and God,	4.11
"Who is *w* to open the scroll	5.2
"*W* art thou to take the scroll	5.9

WOUND — ED — ING (v)

make alive; I *w* and I heal;	Deut 32.39
"Turn about,..for I am *w*."	1Ki 22.34
"Turn about,..for I am *w*."	2Chr 18.33
was *w* for our transgressions,	Isa 53.5
For the wound..is my heart *w*,	Jer 8.21
another servant, and they *w* him	Mk 12.4
this one they *w* and cast out.	Lk 20.12
and *w* their conscience when	1Cor 8.12

WOUND — S (n)

my hurt! My *w* is grievous.	Jer 10.19
Why is..my *w* incurable,	15.18
and your *w* is grievous.	30.12
For her *w* is incurable; and	Mic 1.9
hurt, your *w* is grievous.	Nah 3.19
but its mortal *w* was healed,	Rev 13.3
My *w* grow foul and fester	Ps 38.5
Who has *w* without cause?	Prov 23.29
Faithful are..*w* of a friend;	27.6
and sores and bleeding *w*;	Isa 1.6
are these *w* on your back?'	Zech 13.6
bound up his *w*, pouring on oil	Lk 10.34

WRAPPED

hast *w* thyself with a cloud	Lam 3.44
w him in the linen shroud,	Mk 15.46
and *w* him in swaddling cloths,	Lk 2.7

WRATH

great is the *w* of the Lord	2Ki 22.13
till the fierce *w* of our God	Ezra 10.14
He has torn me in his *w*,	Job 16.9
the *w* of men shall praise	Ps 76.10
king's *w* is like..growling	Prov 19.12
dread *w* of a king is like	20.2
I..pour out my *w* like water.	Hos 5.10
known; in *w* remember mercy.	Hab 3.2
Was thy *w* against the rivers,	3.8
the day of the *w* of the Lord.	Zeph 2.2
to flee from the *w* to come?	Mt 3.7
not see life,.but the *w* of God	Jn 3.36
w for yourself on the day of *w*	Rom 2.5
God..unjust to inflict *w* on us?	3.5
For the law brings *w*, but	4.15
account of these the *w* of God	Col 3.6
who delivers us from the *w*	1Thess 1.10
and from the *w* of the Lamb;	Rev 6.16
wine press of the *w* of God;	14.19

WREATH — S

to receive a perishable *w*,	1Cor 9.25
nets..with *w* of chain work	1Ki 7.17

WRESTLED

I have *w* with my sister,	Gen 30.8
a man *w* with him until	32.24

WRETCHED — NESS

W man that I am! Who will	Rom 7.24
that I may not see my *w*."	Num 11.15

WRITE — ING (v)

"*W* this as a memorial in a	Ex 17.14
I will *w* upon the tables	34.1
w them on the doorposts	Deut 6.9
w them upon the doorposts	11.20
w for himself in a book	17.18
w upon them all the words	27.3
w them on..tablet of..heart.	Prov 7.3
W in a book all the words	Jer 30.2
"Take a scroll and *w* on it	36.2
Were I to *w* for him my laws	Hos 8.12
Lord answered.."*W* the vision;	Hab 2.2
and *w* them on their hearts,	Heb 8.10
and *w* them on their minds,"	10.16

ZEAL (cont.)

z for thy house..consumed me,	Ps 69.9
My z consumes me, because	119.139
z of the LORD..will do this.	Isa 9.7
see thy z for thy people, and	26.11
z of the LORD will accomplish	37.32
Where are thy z and..might?	63.15
"Z for thy house will consume	Jn 2.17
they have a z for God, but	Rom 10.2
he told us of..your z for me,	2Cor 7.7
that your z for us might be	7.12
your z has stirred up most	9.2
as to z a persecutor of the	Phil 3.6

ZEALOUS

they are all z for the law,	Acts 21.20
being z for God as you all are	22.3
so extremely z was I for the	Gal 1.14
be z to be found by him	2Pet 3.14

ZEBULUN

Leah..called his name Z.	Gen 30.20
Z shall dwell at the shore	49.13
The sons of Z, according	Num 26.26
And of Z he said, "Rejoice,	Deut 33.18
the princes of Z, the princes	Ps 68.27
the land of Z and..Naphtali,	Isa 9.1

territory of Z and Naphtali,	Mt 4.13
thousand of the tribe of Z,	Rev 7.8

ZECHARIAH

the prophets, Haggai and Z	Ezra 5.1
Haggai the prophet and Z	6.14
word of the LORD came to Z	Zech 1.1
the word of the LORD came to Z	7.1

ZEPHANIAH

word of the LORD..came to Z	Zeph 1.1

ZERUBBABEL

They came with Z, Jeshua,	Ezra 2.2
they approached Z and the	4.2
Then Z the son of Shealtiel	5.2
They came with Z, Jeshua,	Neh 7.7
the word..came by Haggai..to Z	Hag 1.1
"Speak now to Z the son of	2.2
word..to Z: Not by might,	Zech 4.6

ZION

set my king on Z, my holy hill."	Ps 2.6
Mount Z, in the far north,	48.2
Out of Z, the perfection of	50.2
daughter of Z is..like a booth	Isa 1.8
out of Z shall go forth the law,	2.3
you have come to Mount Z	Heb 12.22